CLYMER®
HONDA
SHADOW 1100 AMERICAN CLASSIC EDITION • 1995-1999

The world's finest publisher of mechanical how-to manuals

PRIMEDIA
Business Directories & Books

P.O. Box 12901, Overland Park, Kansas 66282-2901

Copyright ©2002 PRIMEDIA Business Magazines & Media Inc.

FIRST EDITION
First Printing March, 1998

SECOND EDITION
Updated by James Grooms to include 1998-1999 models
First Printing October, 2002

Printed in U.S.A.

CLYMER and colophon are registered trademarks of PRIMEDIA Business Magazines & Media Inc.

ISBN: 0-89287-844-4

Library of Congress: 2002113363

MEMBER MOTORCYCLE INDUSTRY COUNCIL, INC.

TECHNICAL PHOTOGRAPHY: Ron Wright, with assistance by Clawson Motorsports in Fresno, California and Mike Biggs.

TECHNICAL ILLUSTRATIONS: Steve Amos.

WIRING DIAGRAM: Robert Caldwell.

COVER: Mark Clifford Photography, Los Angeles, California. Honda ACE courtesy of Rice Honda of LaPuente, La Puente, California.

TOOLS AND EQUIPMENT: K & L Supply Co. at www.klsupply.com.

All rights reserved. Reproduction or use, without express permission, of editorial or pictorial content, in any manner, is prohibited. No patent liability is assumed with respect to the use of the information contained herein. While every precaution has been taken in the preparation of this book, the publisher assumes no responsibility for errors or omissions. Neither is any liability assumed for damages resulting from use of the information contained herein. Publication of the servicing information in this manual does not imply approval of the manufacturers of the products covered.

All instructions and diagrams have been checked for accuracy and ease of application; however, success and safety in working with tools depend to a great extent upon individual accuracy, skill and caution. For this reason, the publishers are not able to guarantee the result of any procedure contained herein. Nor can they assume responsibility for any damage to property or injury to persons occasioned from the procedures. Persons engaging in the procedure do so entirely at their own risk.

Chapter One
General Information

Chapter Two
Troubleshooting

Chapter Three
Lubrication, Maintenance and Tune-up

Chapter Four
Engine Top End

Chapter Five
Engine Bottom End

Chapter Six
Clutch and External Shift Mechanism

Chapter Seven
Transmission

Chapter Eight
Fuel and Emission Control Systems

Chapter Nine
Electrical System

Chapter Ten
Cooling System

Chapter Eleven
Front Suspension and Steering

Chapter Twelve
Rear Suspension

Chapter Thirteen
Brakes

Chapter Fourteen
Body and Exhaust System

Index

Wiring Diagrams

CLYMER PUBLICATIONS
PRIMEDIA Business Magazines & Media
Chief Executive Officer Timothy M. Andrews
President Ron Wall

EDITORIAL

Editor
James Grooms

Associate Editor
Jason Beaver

Technical Writers
Ron Wright
Ed Scott
George Parise
Mark Rolling
Michael Morlan
Jay Bogart

Production Supervisor
Dylan Goodwin

Lead Editorial Production Coordinator
Shirley Renicker

Editorial Production Coordinators
Greg Araujo
Shara Pierceall

Editorial Production Assistants
Susan Hartington
Holly Messinger
Darin Watson

Technical Illustrators
Steve Amos
Robert Caldwell
Mitzi McCarthy
Bob Meyer
Mike Rose

MARKETING/SALES AND ADMINISTRATION

Vice President,
PRIMEDIA Business Directories & Books
Rich Hathaway

Marketing Manager
Elda Starke

Advertising & Promotions Coordinator
Melissa Abbott

Associate Art Directors
Chris Paxton
Tony Barmann

Sales Manager/Marine
Dutch Sadler

Sales Manager/Motorcycles
Matt Tusken

Operations Manager
Patricia Kowalczewski

Sales Manager/Manuals
Ted Metzger

Customer Service Manager
Terri Cannon

Customer Service Supervisor
Ed McCarty

Customer Service Representatives
Susan Kohlmeyer
April LeBlond
Courtney Hollars
Jennifer Lassiter
Ernesto Suarez

Warehouse & Inventory Manager
Leah Hicks

The following books and guides are published by PRIMEDIA Business Directories & Books.

CLYMER®   I&T SHOP SERVICE™   AC-U-KWIK   EC&M Books

CLYMER® PROSERIES   The Electronics Source Book   PRIMEDIA PRICE DIGESTS — Your Valuation & Specification Authority   EQUIPMENT WATCH™ www.equipmentwatch.com

More information available at *primediabooks.com*

CONTENTS

QUICK REFERENCE DATA IX

CHAPTER ONE
GENERAL INFORMATION 1

- Manual organization
- Notes, cautions and warnings
- Safety first
- Service hints
- Serial numbers
- Torque specifications
- Fasteners
- Lubricants
- Sealant, cements and cleaners
- Expendable supplies
- Basic hand tools
- Precision measuring tools
- Test equipment
- Special tools
- Mechanic's tips
- Ball bearing replacement
- Seals

CHAPTER TWO
TROUBLESHOOTING 40

- Operating requirements
- Starting the engine
- Starting difficulties
- Engine performance
- Engine noises
- Engine lubrication
- Hydraulic tappets
- Engine leakdown test
- Clutch
- Gearshift linkage
- Transmission
- Electrical troubleshooting
- Test equipment
- Basic test procedures
- Electrical problems
- Charging system
- Ignition system troubleshooting
- Starter system troubleshooting
- Carburetor troubleshooting
- Excessive vibration
- Front suspension and steering
- Brake problems

CHAPTER THREE
LUBRICATION, MAINTENANCE AND TUNE-UP 66

- Routine inspection
- Service intervals
- Tires and wheels
- Battery
- New battery installation
- Lubricants
- Periodic lubrication
- Periodic maintenance
- Engine tune-up

CHAPTER FOUR
ENGINE TOP END 104

Engine principles
Service notes
Cylinder head cover and rocker arms
Hydraulic tappets
Camshafts
Cylinder head
Valves and valve components
Cylinders
Piston and piston rings
Oil jet
Cylinder stud replacement

CHAPTER FIVE
ENGINE BOTTOM END 157

Servicing engine in frame
Subframe
Engine removal
Engine installation
Left crankcase rear cover
Clutch lifter arm
Starter drive gear and torque limiter
Left crankcase cover and stator coil
Flywheel (rotor)
Starter driven gear and starter clutch
Crankcase and crankshaft
Crankshaft
Connecting rods
Output gear assembly
Engine break-in

CHAPTER SIX
CLUTCH AND EXTERNAL SHIFT MECHANISM 204

Clutch
Right crankcase cover
Clutch outer
Primary drive gear
External shift mechanism
Oil pump
Clutch cable replacement

CHAPTER SEVEN
TRANSMISSION AND INTERNAL SHIFT MECHANISM 227

Transmission identification
Transmission troubleshooting
Transmission overhaul
Transmission inspection
Internal shift mechanism

CHAPTER EIGHT
FUEL AND EMISSION CONTROL SYSTEMS 242

Fuel system identification
Air filter housing
Carburetor operation
Carburetor service
Carburetor adjustment
Throttle cable replacement
Choke cable replacement
Fuel filter
Fuel pump
Fuel tank
Crankcase breather system, U.S. only
Evaporative emission control system
    California only

CHAPTER NINE
ELECTRICAL SYSTEM 274

Charging system
Alternator
Ignition system
Ignition pulse generator
ICM unit
Ignition coil
Electric starting system
Starter relay switch
Clutch diode
Lighting system
Headlight housing
Speedometer
Switches
Electrical components
Fuses
Wiring diagrams

CHAPTER TEN
COOLING SYSTEM 317

Cooling system check
Radiator
Cooling fan
Coolant reserve tank
Thermostat
Water pump
Hoses

CHAPTER ELEVEN
FRONT SUSPENSION AND STEERING 328

Front wheel
Front hub
Rim and spoke service
Tire changing
Wheel balance
Handlebar
Front forks
Steering head
Steering bearing preload check

CHAPTER TWELVE
REAR SUSPENSION 365

Rear wheel
Rear hub
Tire changing and tire repairs
Rim and spoke service
Shock absorber
Final gearcase and drive shaft
Rear swing arm

CHAPTER THIRTEEN
BRAKES 388

Brake fluid selection
Preventing brake fluid damage
Disc brake
Front caliper
Front master cylinder
Rear caliper
Rear master cylinder
Rear master cylinder reservoir
Brake hose replacement
Brake disc
Rear brake pedal
Brake fluid draining
Brake bleeding

CHAPTER FOURTEEN
BODY AND EXHAUST SYSTEM 426

Seat
Side covers
Front fender
Rear fender

Rear fender stay
Steering side covers
Exhaust system

INDEX 438

WIRING DIAGRAMS 442

QUICK REFERENCE DATA

MOTORCYCLE INFORMATION

MODEL: _____ YEAR: _____
VIN NUMBER: _____
ENGINE SERIAL NUMBER: _____
CARBURETOR SERIAL NUMBER OR I.D. MARK: _____

GENERAL TORQUE SPECIFICATIONS

Fastener size or type	N•m	in.-lb.	ft.-lb.
5 mm screw	4	35	–
5 mm bolt and nut	5	44	–
6 mm screw	9	80	–
6 mm bolt and nut	10	88	–
6 mm flange bolt (8 mm head, small flange)	9	80	–
6 mm flange bolt (10 mm head) and nut	12	106	–
8 mm bolt and nut	22	–	16
8 mm flange bolt and nut	27	–	20
10 mm bolt and nut	35	–	25
10 mm flange bolt and nut	40	–	29
12 mm bolt and nut	55	–	40

TECHNICAL ABBREVIATIONS

ABDC	After bottom dead center
ATDC	After top dead center
BBDC	Before bottom dead center
BDC	Bottom dead center
BTDC	Before top dead center
C	Celsius (Centigrade)
cc	Cubic centimeters
CDI	Capacitor discharge ignition
cu. in.	Cubic inches
F	Fahrenheit
ft.-lb.	Foot-pounds
gal.	Gallons
H/A	High altitude
hp	Horsepower
in.	Inches
kg	Kilogram
kg/cm2	Kilograms per square centimeter
kgm	Kilogram meters
km	Kilometer

TECHNICAL ABBREVIATIONS (continued)

ml	Milliliter
mm	Millimeter
N•m	Newton-meters
oz.	Ounce
psi	Pounds per square inch
PTO	Power take off
pt.	Pint
qt.	Quart
rpm	Revolutions per minute
l	Liter
m	Meter
MAG	Magneto

TIRE INFLATION PRESSURE*

	psi	kPa
Up to 200 lbs. (90 kg) load		
Front		
1995-1996	33	225
1997-1999	29	200
Rear	33	225
Up to maximum weight capacity		
Front	33	225
Rear	41	280

*The tire inflation pressures listed here are for original equipment tires. Aftermarket tires may require different inflation pressure; refer to tire manufacturer's specifications.

BATTERY SPECIFICATIONS

Capacity	12 volts, 16 amp hours

RECOMMENDED LUBRICANTS AND FUEL

Battery refilling	Distilled water
Brake fluid	DOT4
Control cables	Cable lubricant
Cooling system	Ethylene glycol
Engine oil	
Grade	API SF or SG
Viscosity	SAE 10W-40
Final drive gear oil	Hypoid gear oil, SAE 80
Fork oil	SAE 10W fork oil
Fuel	See text
Speedometer cable	Cable lubricant

ENGINE OIL CAPACITY

	Liters	U.S. qt.	Imp. qt.
Drain engine oil only	3.3	3.5	2.9
Engine oil and filter	3.5	3.7	3.1
After engine disassembly	4.2	4.4	3.7

FINAL DRIVE OIL CAPACITY

	cc	U.S. oz.	Imp. oz.
At oil change	130	4.4	4.6
After disassembly	150	5.1	5.3

FORK OIL CAPACITY

	cc	U.S. oz.	Impl oz.
1995-1998	482	16.3	16.9
1999	495	16.7	17.4

ENGINE COOLANT CAPACITY

	Liters	U.S. qt.	Imp. qt.
Radiator and engine capacity	2.0	2.1	1.8
Reserve tank capacity	0.39	0.41	0.34

TUNE-UP SPECIFICATIONS

Carburetor vacuum difference	Within 40 mm HG (1.6 in. HG)
Engine compression	1,275 ± 196 kPa (185 ± 28 psi)
Engine idle speed	1,000 ± 100 rpm
Spark plug type	
Standard heat range	NGK DPR7EA-9 or Denso X22EPR-U0
Cold (below 5° C [41° F])	NGK DPR6EA-9 or Denso X20EPR-U9
Hot (extended high speed riding)	NGK DPR8EA-9 or Denso X24EPR-U9
Spark plug gap	0.8-0.9 mm (0.031-0.035 in.)

GENERAL ENGINE SPECIFICATIONS

Engine	
Type and number of cylinders	V-2 cylinder 45° V transferse, DOHC, liquid cooled
Bore × stroke	87.5 × 91.4 mm 3.44 × 3.60 in.)
Displacement	1099 cc (67.1 cu. in.)
Compression ratio	8.0:1
Valve timing	
Intake valve opens @ 1 mm lift	
Front	5° BTDC
Rear	2° BTDC
Intake valve closes @ 1 mm lift	
Front	30° ABDC
Rear	33° ABDC
Exhaust valve closes at 1 mm lift	
Front	30° BBDC
Rear	37° BBDC
Exhaust valve opens at 1 mm lift	
Front	5° ATDC
Rear	-2° ATDC
Oil pump type	Trochoid
Cylinder number	
Front	No. 2
Rear	No. 1
Cylinder firing position	
Rear	405°
Front	315°
Engine weight	96.0 kg (212 lb.)

CHAPTER ONE

GENERAL INFORMATION

This detailed, comprehensive manual covers the 1995-1999 Honda VT1100C2 Shadow ACE (American Classic Edition).

Troubleshooting, tune-up, maintenance and repair are not difficult, if you know what tools and equipment to use and what to do. Step-by-step instructions guide you through jobs ranging from simple maintenance to complete engine and suspension overhaul.

This manual can be used by anyone from a first time do-it-yourselfer to a professional mechanic. Detailed drawings and clear photographs give you all the information you need to do the work right.

Some of the procedures in this manual require the use of special tools. The resourceful mechanic can, in many cases, think of acceptable substitutes for special tools—there is always another way. This can be as simple as using a few pieces of threaded rod, washers and nuts to remove or install a bearing. If you find that a tool can be designed and safely made, but will require some type of machine work, you may want to search out a local community college or high school that has a machine shop curriculum. Some shop teachers welcome this type of outside work for advanced students.

Table 1 lists model coverage with engine serial numbers.
Table 2 lists general vehicle dimensions.
Table 3 lists weight specifications.
Table 4 lists decimal and metric equivalents.
Table 5 lists conversion tables.
Table 6 lists general torque specifications.
Table 7 lists technical abbreviations.
Table 8 lists metric tap drill sizes.
Table 9 lists windchill factors.
Tables 1-9 are at the end of the chapter.

MANUAL ORGANIZATION

This chapter provides general information and discusses equipment and tools useful both for preventive maintenance and troubleshooting.

Chapter Two provides methods and suggestions for quick and accurate diagnosis and repair of problems. Troubleshooting procedures discuss typical symptoms and logical methods to pinpoint the trouble.

Chapter Three explains all periodic lubrication and routine maintenance necessary to keep your Honda operating well. Chapter Three also includes recommended tune-up procedures, eliminating the need to consult other chapters constantly on the various assemblies.

Subsequent chapters describe specific systems such as the engine top end, engine bottom end, clutch, transmission, fuel, electrical, suspension, drive train, steering, brakes, body and exhaust. Each chapter provides disassembly, repair, and assembly procedures in simple step-by-step form. If a repair is impractical for a home mechanic, it is so indicated. It is usually faster and less expensive to take such repairs to a Honda dealer or competent repair shop. Specifications concerning a particular system are included at the end of the appropriate chapter.

NOTES, CAUTIONS AND WARNINGS

The terms NOTE, CAUTION and WARNING have specific meanings in this manual. A NOTE provides additional information to make a step or procedure easier or clearer. Disregarding a NOTE could cause inconvenience, but would not cause damage or personal injury.

A CAUTION emphasizes areas where equipment damage could occur. Disregarding a CAUTION could cause permanent mechanical damage; however, personal injury is unlikely.

A WARNING emphasizes areas where personal injury or even death could result from negligence. Mechanical damage may also occur. WARNINGS *are to be taken seriously*. In some cases, serious injury and death have resulted from disregarding similar warnings.

SAFETY FIRST

Professional mechanics can work for years and never sustain a serious injury. If you observe a few rules of common sense and safety, you can enjoy many safe hours servicing your own machine. If you ignore these rules you can hurt yourself or damage the equipment.

1. *Never* use gasoline as a cleaning solvent.
2. *Never* smoke or use a torch in the vicinity of flammable liquids, such as cleaning solvent stored in an open container.
3. If welding or brazing is required on the machine, remove the fuel tank and rear shock to a safe distance, at least 50 feet (15 m) away.
4. Use the proper sized wrenches to avoid damage to fasteners and injury to yourself.
5. When loosening a tight or stuck nut, be guided by what would happen if the wrench should slip.
6. When replacing a fastener, make sure to use one with the same measurements and strength as the old one. Incorrect or mismatched fasteners can result in damage to the vehicle and possible personal injury. Beware of fastener kits that are filled with cheap and poorly made nuts, bolts, washers and cotter pins. Refer to *Fasteners* in this chapter for additional information.
7. Keep all hand and power tools in good condition. Wipe greasy and oily tools after using them. They are difficult to hold and can cause injury. Replace or repair worn or damaged tools.
8. Keep your work area clean and uncluttered.
9. Wear safety goggles (**Figure 1**) during all operations involving drilling, grinding, the use of a cold chisel or *anytime* you feel unsure about the safety of your eyes. Safety goggles must be worn when using solvent and compressed air to clean parts.

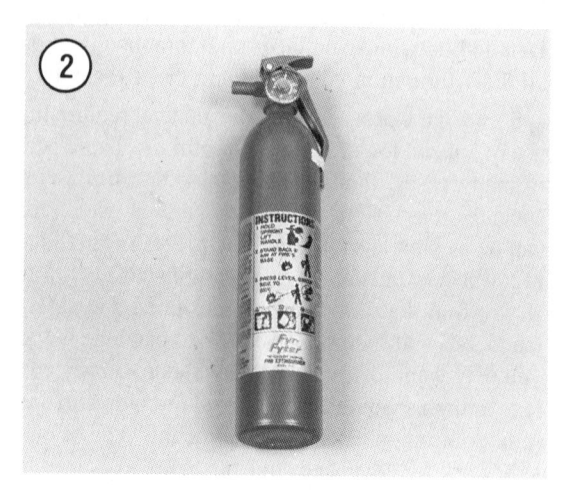

GENERAL INFORMATION

10. Keep an approved fire extinguisher (**Figure 2**) nearby. Be sure it is rated for gasoline (Class B) and electrical (Class C) fires.

11. When drying bearings or other rotating parts with compressed air, never allow the air jet to rotate the bearing or part. The air jet is capable of rotating them at speeds far in excess of those for which they were designed. The bearing or rotating part is very likely to disintegrate and cause serious injury. To prevent bearing damage when using compressed air, hold the inner bearing race from turning (**Figure 3**).

SERVICE HINTS

Most of the service procedures covered are straightforward and can be performed by anyone reasonably handy with tools. It is suggested, however, that you consider your own capabilities carefully before attempting any operation involving major disassembly of the engine assembly.

Take your time and do the job right. Do not forget that a newly rebuilt engine must be broken in the same way as a new one.

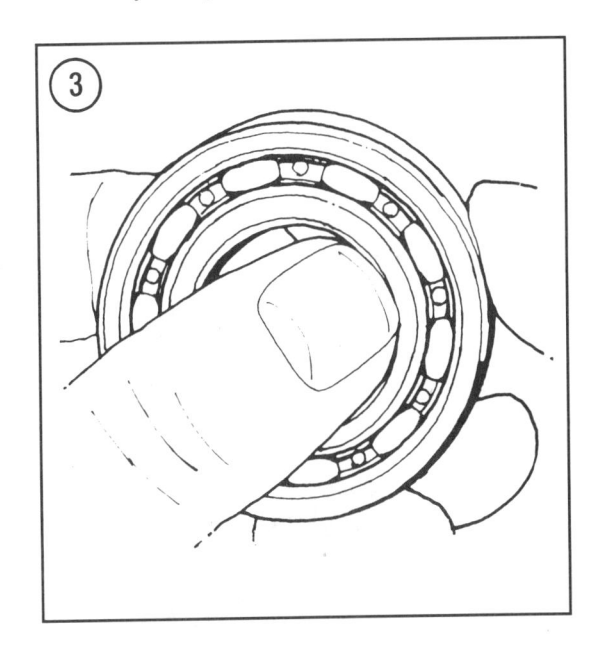

1. *Front,* as used in this manual, refers to the front of the vehicle; the front of any component is the end closest to the front of the vehicle. The *left-* and *right-hand* sides refer to the position of the parts as viewed by a rider sitting on the seat facing forward. For example, the throttle control is on the right-hand side. These rules are simple, but confusion can cause a major inconvenience during service.

2. Whenever servicing the engine or clutch, or when removing a suspension component, secure the vehicle in a safe manner using the proper equipment.

> *WARNING*
> *Never disconnect the positive (+) battery cable unless the negative (−) cable has first been disconnected. Disconnecting the positive cable while the negative cable is still connected may cause a spark. This could ignite hydrogen gas given off by the battery, causing an explosion.*

3. Disconnect the negative battery cable (**Figure 4**) when working on or near the electrical, clutch, or starter systems and before disconnecting any electrical wires. On most batteries, the negative terminal is marked with a minus (−) sign and the positive terminal with a plus (+) sign.

4. Tag all similar internal parts for location and mark all mating parts for position (**Figure 5**). Record the number and thickness of any shims or washers as they are removed. Identify and store small parts

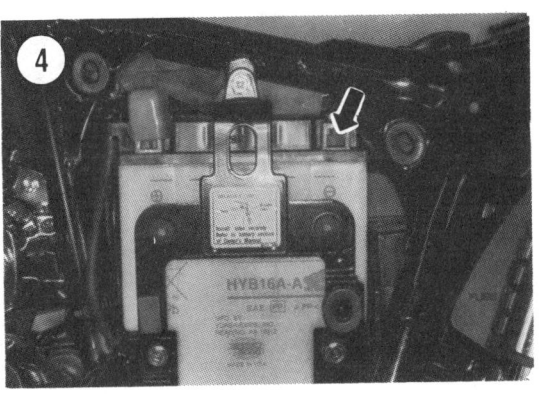

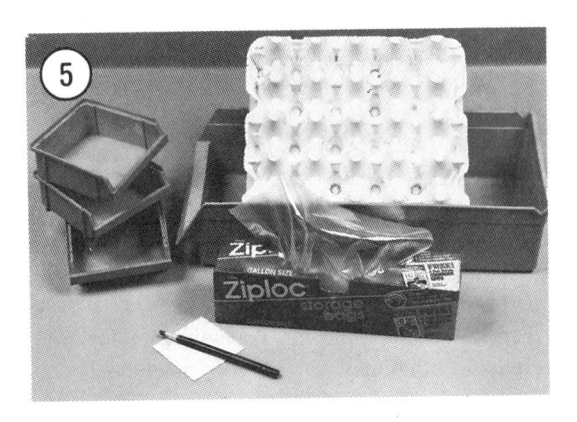

in plastic bags (**Figure 5**). Seal and label them with masking tape.

5. Place parts from a specific area of the engine (such as the cylinder head, cylinder, clutch and shift mechanism) into plastic boxes (**Figure 5**) to keep them separated.

6. When disassembling transmission shaft assemblies, use an egg flat (the type that restaurants get their eggs in) and set the parts from the shaft in one of the depressions in the same order in which it is removed.

7. Tag disconnected wires and connectors with masking tape and a marking pen. Again, do not rely on memory alone.

8. Protect finished surfaces from physical damage or corrosion. Keep gasoline and brake fluid off painted surfaces.

9. Use penetrating oil on frozen or tight bolts, then strike the bolt head a few times with a hammer and punch (use a screwdriver on screws). Avoid the use of heat where possible, as it can warp, melt or affect the temper of parts. Heat also ruins finishes, especially paint and plastics.

10. No parts removed or installed (other than bushings, bearings and crankshaft) in the procedures given in this manual require unusual force during disassembly or assembly. If a part is difficult to remove or install, find out why before proceeding.

11. Cover all openings after removing parts or components to prevent dirt, small tools or other contamination from falling in.

12. Read each procedure *completely* while looking at the actual parts before starting a job. Make sure you *thoroughly* understand what is to be done, then carefully follow the procedure, step by step.

13. The recommendation is occasionally made to refer service or maintenance to a Honda dealership or a specialist in a particular field. In these cases, the work will be done more quickly and economically than if you performed the job yourself.

14. In procedural steps, the term *replace* means to discard a defective part and replace it with a new or exchange unit. *Overhaul* means to remove, disassemble, inspect, measure, repair or replace defective parts, reassemble and install major systems or parts.

15. Some operations require the use of an arbor or hydraulic press. It is wiser to have these operations performed by a shop equipped for such work, rather than to try to do the job yourself with makeshift equipment that may damage your machine.

16. Repairs go much faster and easier if your machine is clean before you begin work. There are many special cleaners on the market, like Bel-Ray Degreaser, for washing the engine and related parts. Follow the manufacturer's directions on the container for the best results. Clean all oily or greasy parts with cleaning solvent as you remove them.

WARNING
Never *use gasoline to clean parts or tools as it presents an extreme fire hazard. Be sure to work in a well-ventilated area when using cleaning solvent. Keep a fire extinguisher, rated for gasoline fires, handy in any case.*

CAUTION
If you use a car wash to clean your vehicle, do not direct the high pressure water hose at steering bearings, carburetor hoses, suspension linkage components, wheel bearings, electrical components or the O-ring drive chain. The water will flush grease out of the bearings or damage the seals.

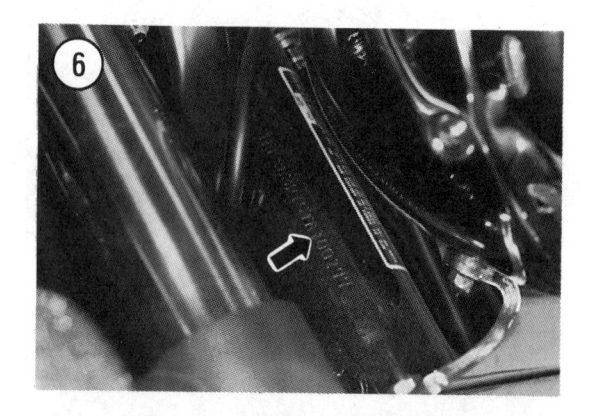

GENERAL INFORMATION

17. Much of the labor charge for a repair made at a dealership is for the time involved in the removal, disassembly, assembly, and reinstallation of other parts in order to reach the defective part. It is frequently possible to perform the preliminary operations yourself then take the defective unit to the dealer for repair at considerable savings.

18. If special tools are required, make arrangements to get them before you start. It is frustrating and time-consuming to get partly into a job then be unable to complete it.

19. Make diagrams (or take a Polaroid picture) wherever similar-appearing parts are found. You may think you can remember where everything came from—but mistakes are costly. There is also the possibility that you may be sidetracked and not return to work for days or even weeks—in which time the carefully laid out parts may become disturbed.

20. When assembling parts, be sure all shims and washers are replaced exactly as they came out.

21. Whenever a rotating part butts against a stationary part, look for a shim or washer. Use new gaskets if there is any doubt about the condition of the old ones. A thin coat of oil on non-pressure type gaskets may help them seal more effectively.

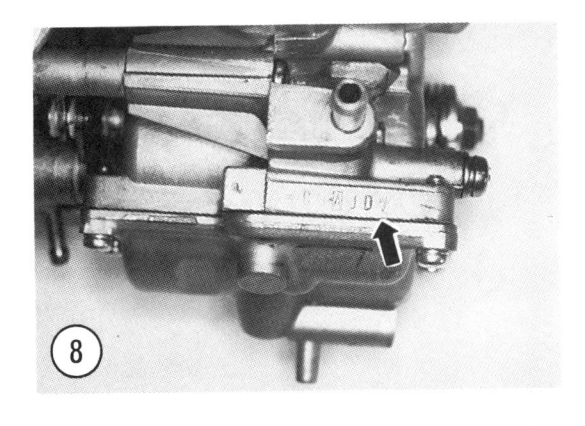

22. Heavy grease can be used to hold small parts in place if they tend to fall out during assembly. However, keep grease and oil away from electrical and brake components.

SERIAL NUMBERS

Honda makes frequent changes during a model year, some minor, some relatively major. When you order parts, always order by frame and engine numbers.

The frame number serial number is stamped on the right side of the steering head (**Figure 6**).

The engine number is stamped on a raised pad on the right crankcase (**Figure 7**).

The vehicle identification number (VIN) decal is placed on the left side of the steering head.

The carburetor identification number is stamped on the intake side of the carburetor (**Figure 8**).

The color label is attached to the tool bag holder behind the right side cover (**Figure 9**).

Write the numbers down and carry them with you. Compare new parts to old before purchasing them. If they are not alike, have the parts manager explain the difference to you. **Table 1** lists engine and frame serial numbers for the models covered in this manual.

TORQUE SPECIFICATIONS

The proper tightening procedure and the correct torque is very important when installing many of the fasteners on your Honda. Cylinder head warpage, leakage, premature bearing failure and suspension failure can result from improperly tightened fasteners (overtightened or undertightened). Use an accurate torque wrench along with the torque specifications in this manual to ensure properly tightened fasteners.

Torque specifications throughout this manual are given in Newton-meters (N·m) and foot-pounds (ft.-lb.).

Existing torque wrenches calibrated in meter kilograms can be used by performing a simple conversion. All you have to do is move the decimal point one place to the right; for example, 3.5 mkg = 35 N·m. This conversion is accurate enough for mechanical work even though the exact mathematical conversion is 3.5 mkg = 34.3 N•m.

Refer to **Table 6** for standard torque specifications for various size screws, bolts and nuts that may not be listed in the respective chapters.

FASTENERS

Fasteners (screws, bolts, nuts, studs, pins, clips, etc.) are used to secure various pieces of the engine, frame and suspension together. Proper selection and installation of fasteners are important to ensure that the vehicle operates satisfactorily; otherwise, a breakdown is possible.

Threaded Fasteners

Most of the components on your motorcycle are held together by threaded fasteners (screws, bolts, nuts, and studs). Most fasteners are tightened by turning clockwise (right-hand threads), although some fasteners may have left-hand threads if rotating parts can cause loosening.

Two dimensions are needed to match thread size: the number of threads in a given distance and the outside diameter of the threads. Two standards are currently used in the United States to specify the dimensions of threaded fasteners, the U.S. standard system and the metric system (**Figure 10**) Pay particular attention when working with unidentified fasteners; mismatching thread types can damage threads.

NOTE
Threaded fasteners must be hand tightened during initial assembly to be sure mismatched fasteners are not being used and cross-threading is not occurring. If fasteners are hard to turn, determine the cause before applying a tool for final tightening.

Metric screws and bolts are classified by length (L, **Figure 11**), diameter (D) and distance between thread crests (T). A typical bolt might be identified by the numbers 8 × 1.25—130, which would indicate that the bolt has a diameter of 8 mm, the distance between threads crests is 1.25 mm and bolt length is 130 mm.

The strength of metric screws and bolts is indicated by numbers located on top of the screw or bolt as shown in **Figure 11**. The higher the number the stronger the screw or bolt. Unnumbered screws and bolts are the weakest.

CAUTION
Do not *install screws or bolts with a lower grade classification than installed originally by the manufacturer. Doing so may cause vehicle failure and possible injury.*

Tightening a screw or bolt increases the clamping force it exerts. The stronger the screw or bolt, the greater the potential clamping force. Critical torque specifications are listed in a table at the end of appropriate chapter. If not, use the torque specifications listed in **Table 6**.

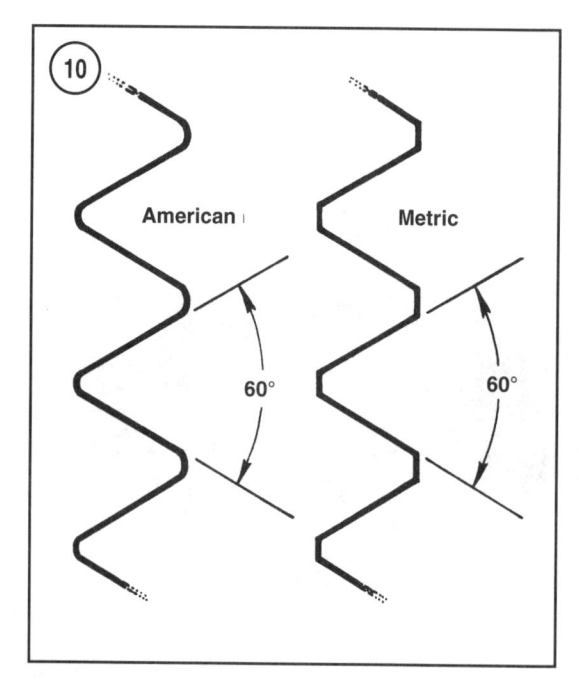

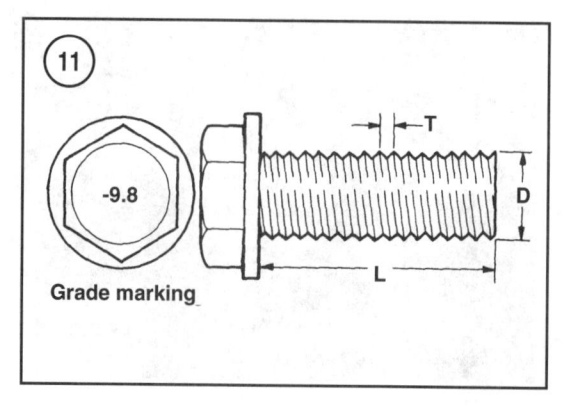

Grade marking

GENERAL INFORMATION

Screws and bolts are manufactured with a variety of head shapes to fit specific design requirements. Your motorcycle is equipped with the common hex and slotted head types, but other types, like those shown in **Figure 12** and **Figure 13** will also be encountered.

The most common nut used is the hex nut (**Figure 14**), often used with a lockwasher. Self-locking nuts have a nylon insert that prevents loosening; no lockwasher is required. Wing nuts, designed for fast removal by hand, are used for convenience in non critical locations. Nuts are sized using the same system as screws and bolts. On hex-type nuts, the distance between two opposing flats indicates the proper wrench size to use.

Self-locking screws, bolts and nuts may use a locking mechanism that uses an interference fit between mating threads. Manufacturers achieve interference in various ways: by distorting threads, coating threads with dry adhesive or nylon, distorting the top of an all-metal nut or using a nylon insert in the center or at the top of a nut. Self-locking fasteners offer greater holding strength and better vibration resistance than standard fasteners. For greatest safety, install new self-locking fasteners during reassembly.

Washers

There are 2 basic types of washers: flat washers and lockwashers. Flat washers are simple discs with a hole to fit a screw or bolt. Manufacturers design lockwashers to prevent a fastener from working loose due to vibration, expansion and contraction. Install lockwashers between a bolt head or nut and a flat washer. **Figure 15** shows several types of washers. Washers are also used in the following functions:

a. As spacers.
b. To prevent galling or damage of the equipment by the fastener.
c. To help distribute fastener load when tightening fasteners.
d. As fluid seals (copper or laminated washers).

Note that flat washers are often used between a lockwasher and a fastener to provide a smooth bearing surface.

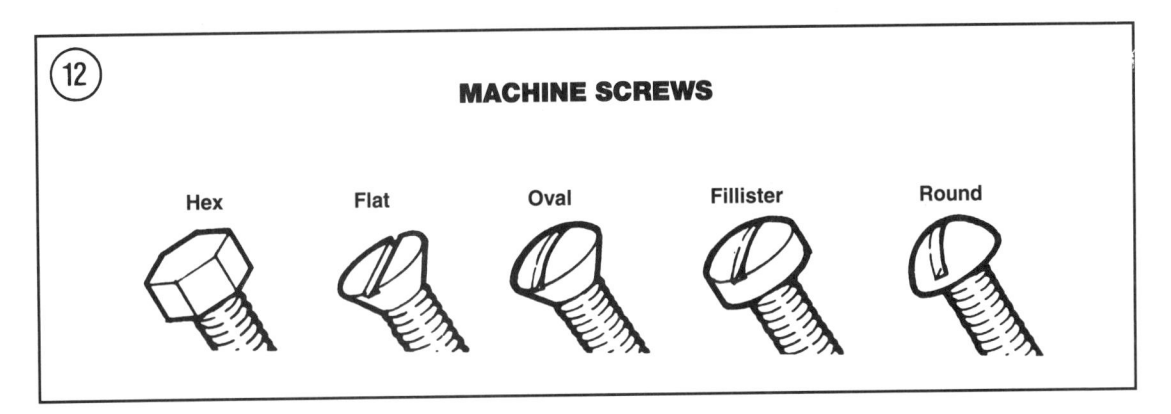

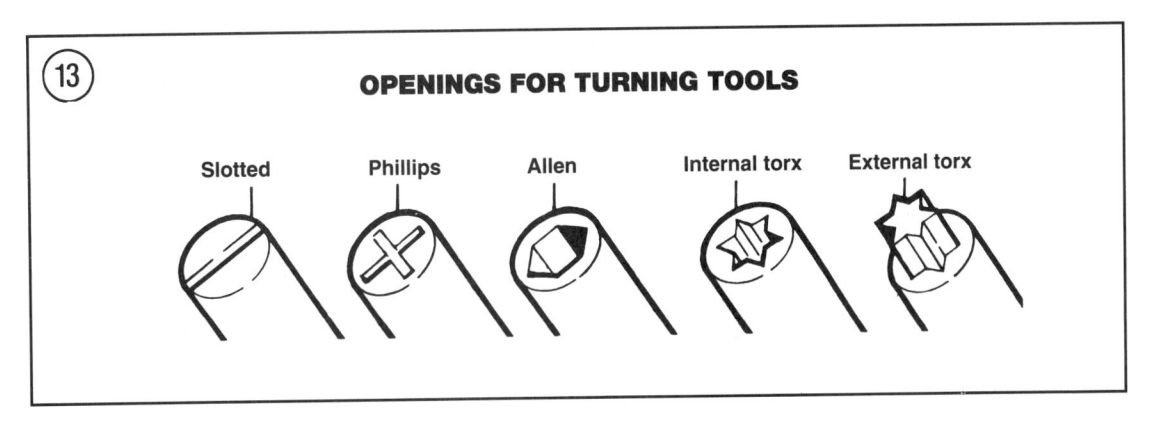

⑫ **MACHINE SCREWS**

Hex   Flat   Oval   Fillister   Round

⑬ **OPENINGS FOR TURNING TOOLS**

Slotted   Phillips   Allen   Internal torx   External torx

NOTE
The same care must be given to the selection and purchase of washers as that given to bolts, nuts and other fasteners. Beware of washers made of thin and weak materials. These will deform and crush the first time they are used in a high torque application.

Cotter Pins

In certain applications, a fastener must be secured so it cannot possibly loosen. The rear axle nut on a motorcycle is one such application. For this purpose, a cotter pin (**Figure 16**) and slotted or castellated nut is often used. To use a cotter pin, first make sure the pin fits snugly, but not too tight. Then, align a slot in the fastener with the hole in the bolt or axle. Insert the cotter pin through the nut and bolt or axle and bend the ends over to secure the cotter pin tightly. If the holes do not align, tighten the nut just enough to obtain the proper alignment. Unless specifically instructed to do so, never loosen the fastener to align the slot and hole. Because the cotter pin is weakened after installation and removal, never reuse a cotter pin. Cotter pins are available in several styles, lengths and diameters. Measure cotter pin length from the bottom of its head to the tip of its shortest prong.

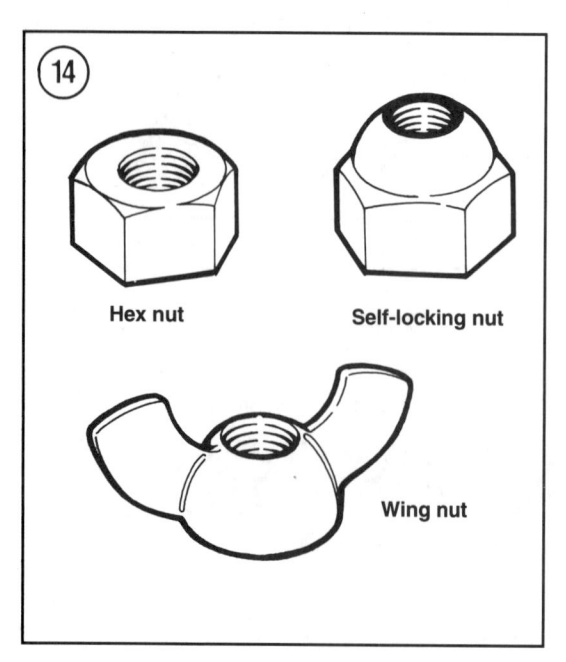

Circlips

Circlips can be of internal or external design. Circlips retain items on shafts (external type) or within tubes (internal type). In some applications, circlips of varying thicknesses are used to control the end play of assembled parts. These are often called selective circlips. You must replace circlips during reassembly and installation, as removal weakens and deforms them.

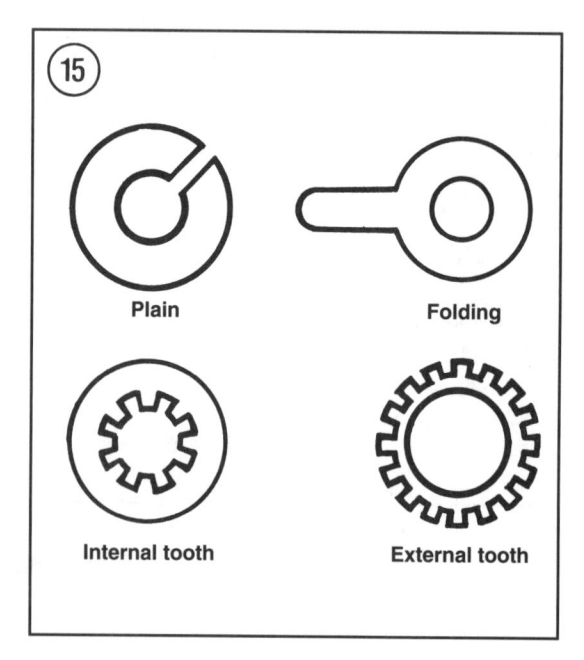

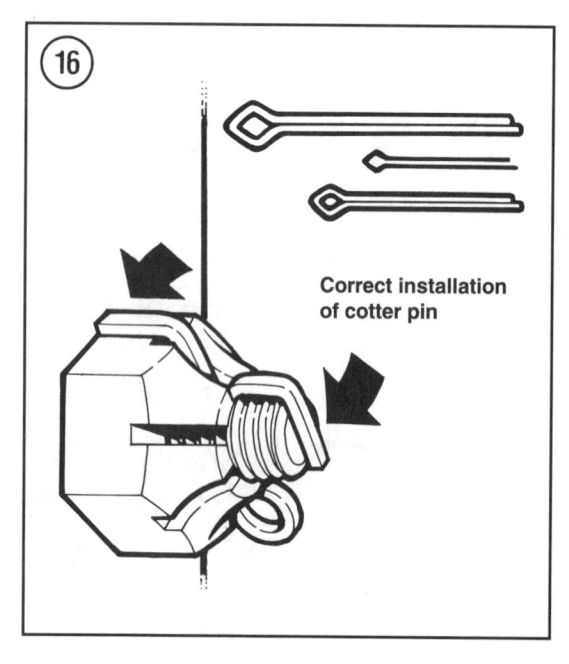

GENERAL INFORMATION

Two basic styles of circlips are available: machined and stamped circlips. Machined circlips (**Figure 17**) can be installed in either direction (shaft or housing) because both faces are machined, thus creating two sharp edges. Stamped circlips (**Figure 18**) are manufactured with one sharp edge and one rounded edge. When installing stamped circlips in a thrust situation, the sharp edge must face away from the part producing the thrust. When installing circlips, observe the following:

a. Remove and install circlips using circlip pliers. See *Circlip Pliers* in this chapter.
b. Compress or expand circlips only enough to install them.
c. After installing a circlip, make sure it seats in its groove completely.

Transmission circlips become worn with use and can result in excessive end play of a shaft or assembly. For this reason, always use new circlips whenever reassembling a transmission shaft.

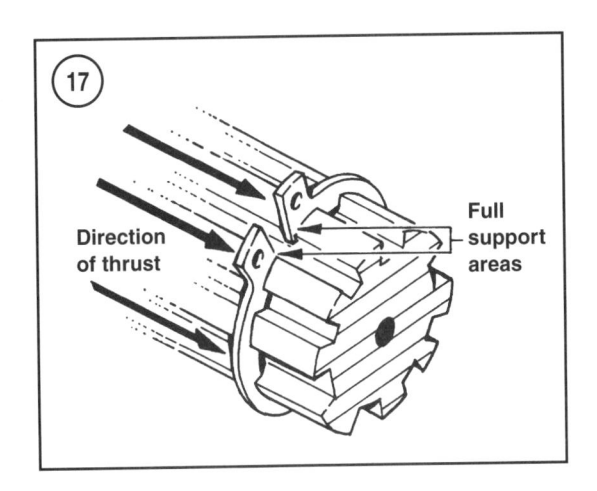

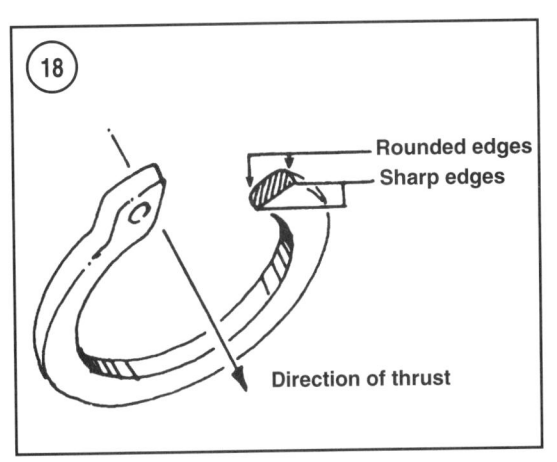

LUBRICANTS

Periodic lubrication helps ensure long life for any type of equipment. The type of lubricant used is just as important as the lubrication service itself, although in an emergency the wrong type of lubricant is better than none at all. The following paragraphs describe the types of lubricants most often used on motorcycles and other powersports equipment. Be sure to follow the manufacturer's recommendations for lubricant types.

Generally, all liquid lubricants are called oil. They may be mineral-based (including petroleum bases), natural-based (vegetable and animal bases), synthetic-based or emulsions (mixtures). Grease is an oil to which a thickening base has been added so that the end product is semi-solid. Grease is often classified by the type of thickener added; lithium soap is commonly used.

Engine Oil

Four-cycle oil for motorcycle and automotive engines is classified by the American Petroleum Institute (API) and the Society of Automotive Engineers (SAE) in several categories. Oil containers display these classifications on the top or label.

API oil classification is indicated by letters; oils for gasoline engines are identified by an S. Honda models described in this manual require SF or SG oil.

Viscosity is an indication of the oil's thickness. The SAE uses numbers to indicate viscosity. Thin oils have low numbers while thick oils have high numbers. A W after the number indicates that the viscosity testing was done at low temperature to simulate cold-weather operation. Engine oil falls into the 5W-30 and 20W-50 range.

Multigrade oil (for example 10W-40) is less viscous (thinner) at low temperature and more viscous (thicker) at high temperature. This allows the oil to perform efficiently across a wide range of engine operating conditions. The lower the number, the better the engine will start in cold climates. Higher numbers are usually recommended for engine running in hot weather conditions.

Grease

Grease is graded by the National Lubricating Grease Institute (NLGI). Grease is classified by number according to the consistency of the grease; these range from No. 000 to No. 6, with No. 6 being the most solid. A typical multipurpose grease is NLGI No. 2. For specific applications, equipment manufacturers may require grease with an additive such as molybdenum disulfide (MOS2) (**Figure 19**).

Antiseize Lubricant

An antiseize lubricant (**Figure 20**) may be specified in some assembly applications. The antiseize lubricant prevents the formation of corrosion that may lock parts together.

SEALANT, CEMENTS AND CLEANERS

Sealants and Adhesives

Many mating surfaces of an engine require a gasket or seal between them to prevent fluids and gases from passing through the joint. At times, the gasket or seal is installed as is. However, sometimes a sealer is applied to enhance the sealing capability of the gasket or seal. Note, however, that a sealing compound may be added to the gasket or seal during manufacturing and adding a sealant may cause premature failure of the gasket or seal.

RTV Sealants

One of the most common sealants is RTV (room temperature vulcanizing) sealant (**Figure 21**). This sealant hardens (cures) at room temperature over a period of several hours, which allows sufficient time to reposition parts if necessary without damaging the gaskets. RTV sealant is designed for different uses, including high temperature use. If in doubt as to the correct type to use, ask a vendor or read the sealant manufacturer's literature.

Cements and Adhesives

A variety of cements and adhesives are available (**Figure 22**). Their use is dependent on the type of materials to be sealed, and to some extent, the personal preference of the mechanic. Automotive parts stores offer cements and adhesives in a wide selec-

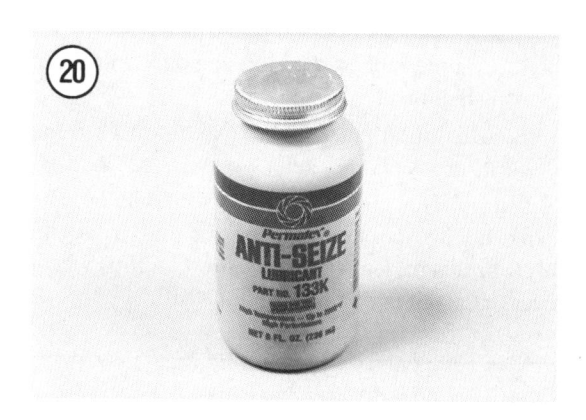

GENERAL INFORMATION

tion. Some points to consider when selecting cements or adhesives are: the type of material being sealed (metal, rubber, plastic, etc.), the type of fluid contacting the seal (gasoline, oil, water, etc.) and whether the seal is permanent or must be broken periodically, in which case a pliable sealant might be desirable.

Threadlocking Compound

A threadlocking compound (**Figure 23**) is a fluid applied to fastener threads. After tightening the fastener, the fluid dries to a solid filler between the mating threads, thereby locking the threads in position and preventing loosening due to vibration.

Threadlocking compound is available in different strengths, so make sure to follow the manufacturer's recommendations when using their particular compound. Two manufacturers of threadlocking compound are ThreeBond of America and the Loctite Corporation.

Before applying a threadlocking compound, clean the contacting threads with an aerosol electrical contact cleaner. Use only as much compound as necessary, usually one or two drops depending on the size of the fastener. Excess fluid can work its way into adjoining parts.

Cleaners and Solvents

Cleaners and solvents are helpful for removing oil, grease and other residue when maintaining and overhauling your motorcycle. Before purchasing cleaners and solvents, consider how they will be used and disposed of, particularly if they are not water soluble. Local ordinances may require special procedures for the disposal of certain cleaners and solvents.

> *WARNING*
> *Some cleaners and solvents are harmful and may be flammable. Follow any safety precautions noted on the container or in the manufacturer's literature. Use petroleum-resistant gloves to protect hands and arms from the harmful effect of cleaners and solvents.*

Figure 24 shows a variety of cleaners and solvents. Cleaners designed for ignition contact cleaning are excellent for removing light oil from a part without leaving a residue. Some degreasers will wash off with water. Ease the removal of stubborn gaskets with a gasket removal compound.

One of the more powerful cleaning solutions is carburetor cleaner. It is designed to dissolve the varnish that may build up in carburetor jets and orifices. Good carburetor cleaner is usually expensive and requires special disposal. Carefully read directions before purchase; do not immerse non-metallic parts in carburetor cleaner.

Gasket Removal Compound

Stubborn gaskets can present a problem during engine service as they can take a long time to remove. Consequently, there is the added problem of secondary damage occurring to the gasket mating surfaces from the incorrect use of gasket scraping tools. To remove stubborn gaskets, use a spray gasket remover. Spray gasket remover can be purchased through automotive parts houses. Follow its manufacturer's directions for use.

EXPENDABLE SUPPLIES

Certain expendable supplies are required during maintenance and repair work. These include grease, oil, gasket cement, wiping rags and cleaning solvent. Ask your dealer for the special locking compounds, silicone lubricants and other products which make vehicle maintenance simpler and easier. Cleaning solvent or kerosene is available at some service stations, paint or hardware stores.

WARNING
Having a stack of clean shop rags on hand is important when performing engine and suspension service work. However, to prevent the possibility of fire damage from spontaneous combustion from a pile of solvent soaked rags, store them in a sealed metal container until they can be washed or discarded.

NOTE
To prevent absorbing solvent and other chemicals into your skin while cleaning parts, wear a pair of petroleum-resistant rubber gloves. These can be purchased through industrial supply houses or well-equipped hardware stores.

BASIC HAND TOOLS

Many of the procedures in this manual can be carried out with simple hand tools and test equipment familiar to the average home mechanic. Keep your tools clean and in a tool box. Keep them organized with the related tools stored together. After using a tool, wipe off dirt and grease with a clean cloth and return the tool to its correct place.

Top quality tools are essential. They are also more economical in the long run. If you are now starting to build your tool collection, avoid the advertised specials featured at some parts houses, discount stores and chain drug stores. These are usually a poor grade tool that can be sold cheaply and that is exactly what they are—*cheap*. They are usually made of inferior material, and are thick, heavy and clumsy. Their rough finish makes them difficult to clean and they usually do not last very long. If it is ever your misfortune to use such tools, you will probably find out that the wrenches do not fit the heads of bolts and nuts correctly and damage the fastener.

Quality tools are made of alloy steel and are heat treated for greater strength. They are lighter and better balanced than cheap ones. Their surface is smooth, making them a pleasure to work with and easy to clean. The initial cost of good quality tools may be more but they are less expensive in the long run.

Screwdrivers

The screwdriver is a very basic tool, but if used improperly it can do more damage than good. The slot on a screw has a definite dimension and shape. A screwdriver must be selected to conform with that shape. Use a small screwdriver for small screws and a large one for large screws or the screw head will be damaged.

Two basic types of screwdriver are required: common (flat-blade) screwdrivers (**Figure 25**) and Phillips screwdrivers (**Figure 26**).

Screwdrivers are available in sets which often include an assortment of common and Phillips blades. If you buy them individually, buy at least the following:

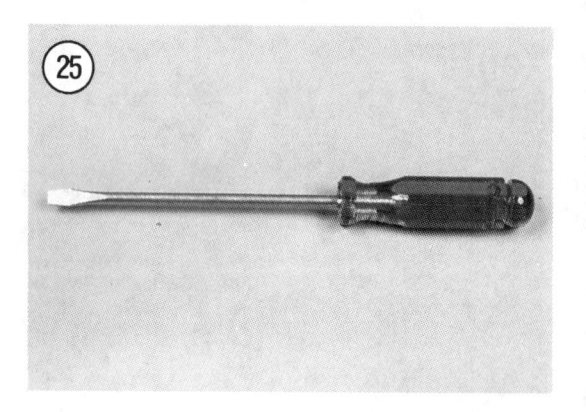

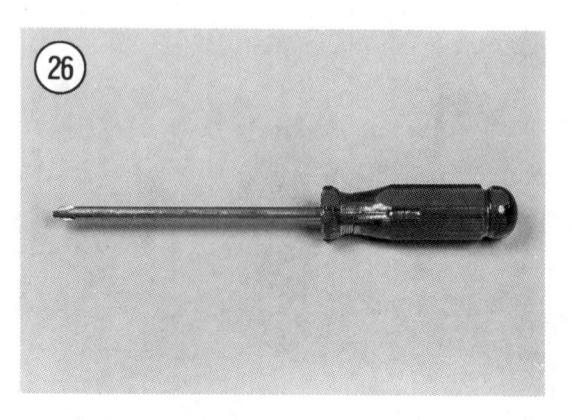

GENERAL INFORMATION

a. Common screwdriver—5/16 × 6 in. blade.

b. Common screwdriver—3/8 × 12 in. blade.

c. Phillips screwdriver—size 2 tip, 6 in. blade.

d. Phillips screwdriver—size 3 tip, 6 and 10 in. blade.

Use screwdrivers only for driving screws. Never use a screwdriver for prying or chiseling metal. Do not try to remove a Phillips or Allen head screw with a common screwdriver (unless the screw has a combination head that will accept either type); you can damage the head so even the proper tool will be unable to remove it.

Keep screwdrivers in the proper condition and they will last longer and perform better. Always keep the tip of a common screwdriver in good condition. **Figure 27** shows how to grind the tip to the proper shape if it becomes damaged. Note the symmetrical sides of the tip.

Pliers

Pliers come in a wide range of types and sizes. Pliers are useful for cutting, bending and crimping. Do not use them to cut hardened objects or to turn bolts or nuts. **Figure 28** shows several pliers useful in motorcycle repair.

Each type of pliers has a specialized function. Slip-joint pliers are general purpose pliers and are used mainly for holding things and for bending.

Needlenose pliers are used to hold or bend small objects. Adjustable pliers can be adjusted to hold various sizes of objects; the jaws remain parallel to grip around objects such as pipe or tubing. There are many more types of pliers. The ones described here are most suitable for vehicle repairs.

Locking Pliers

Locking pliers (**Figure 29**) are used to hold objects very tightly like a vise. But avoid using them

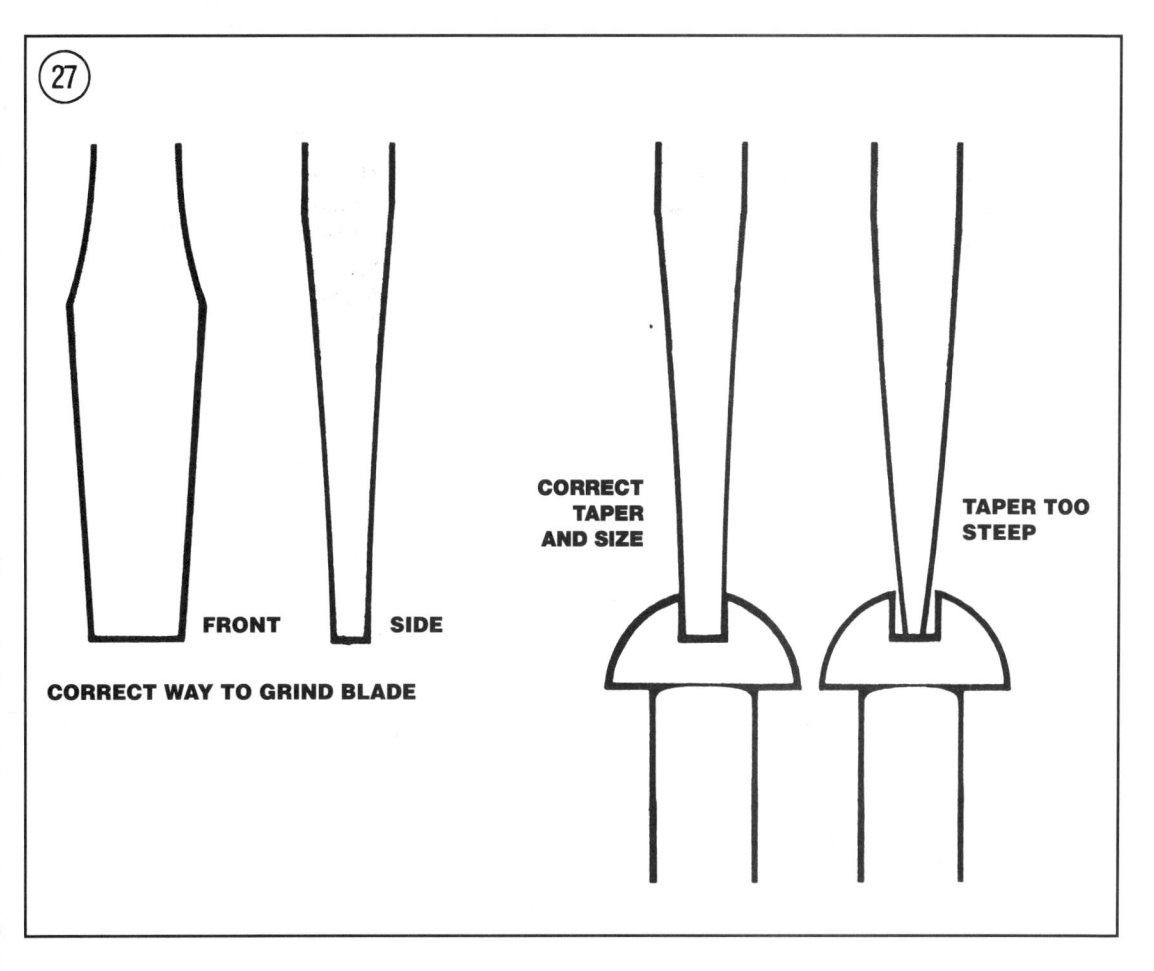

27

FRONT SIDE

CORRECT WAY TO GRIND BLADE

CORRECT TAPER AND SIZE

TAPER TOO STEEP

unless absolutely necessary since their sharp jaws will permanently scar any objects which are held. Locking pliers are available in many types for more specific tasks.

Circlip Pliers

Circlip pliers (**Figure 30**) are special in that they are only used to remove circlips from shafts or within engine or suspension housings. When purchasing circlip pliers, there are two kinds to distinguish from. External pliers (spreading) are used to remove circlips that fit on the outside of a shaft. Internal pliers (squeezing) are used to remove circlips which fit inside a gear or housing.

WARNING
Because circlips can sometimes slip and fly off when removing and installing them, always wear safety glasses.

Box-, Open-end and Combination Wrenches

Box-end, open-end and combination wrenches are available in sets or separately in a variety of sizes. On open and box end wrenches, the number stamped near the end refers to the distance between 2 parallel flats on the hex head bolt or nut. On combination wrenches, the number is stamped near the center.

Box-end wrenches require clear overhead access to the fastener but can work well in situations where the fastener head is close to another part. They grip on all six edges of a fastener for a very secure grip. They are available in either 6-point or 12-point. The 6-point gives superior holding power and durability but requires a greater swinging radius. The 12-point

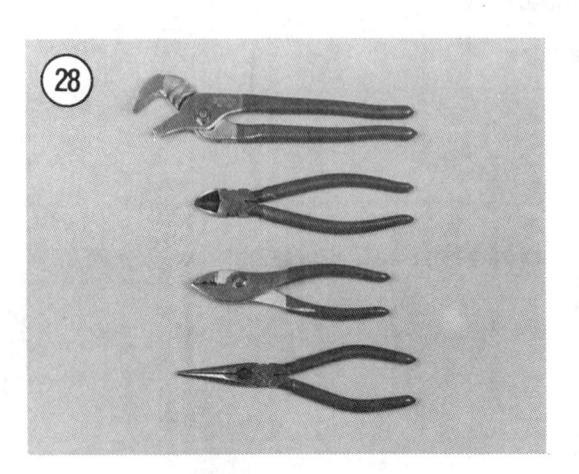

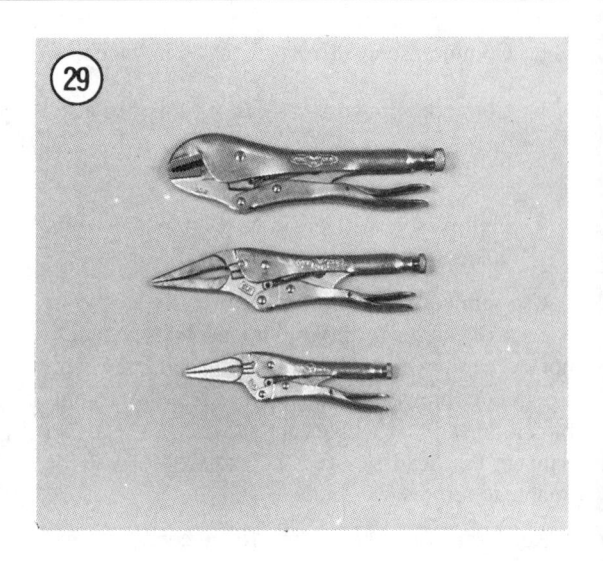

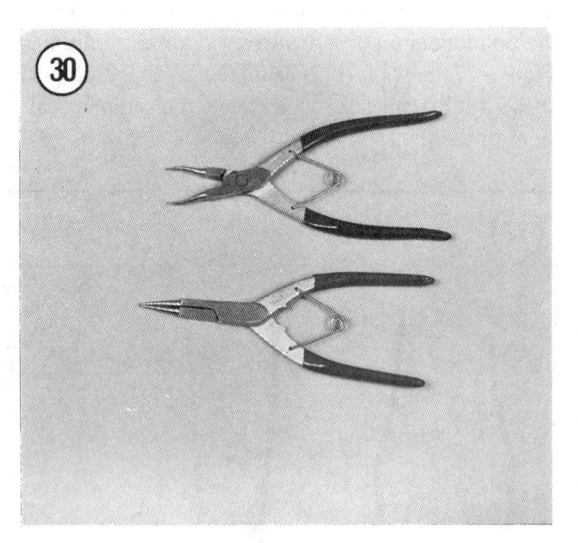

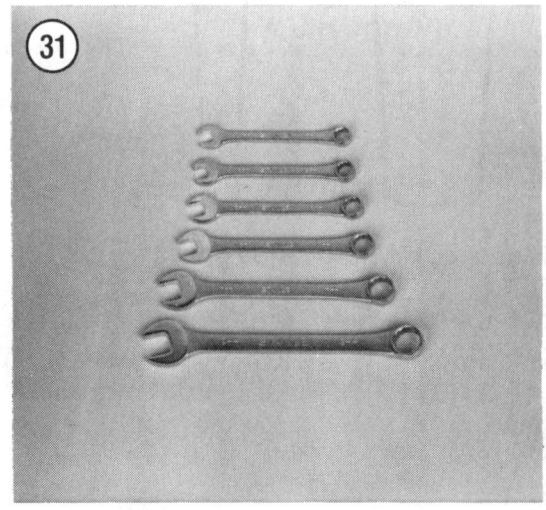

GENERAL INFORMATION

works better in areas with limited room for turning the wrench.

Open-end wrenches are speedy and work best in areas with limited overhead access. Their wide flat jaws make them unsuitable for situations where the bolt or nut is sunken in a well or close to the edge of a casting. These wrenches grip only two flats of a fastener so if either the fastener head or the wrench jaws are worn, the wrench may slip off.

Combination wrenches (**Figure 31**) have open-end on one side and box-end on the other with both ends being the same size. These wrenches are favored by professionals because of their versatility. **Figure 32** shows a set of open-end wrenches.

Adjustable Wrenches

An adjustable wrench (sometimes called crescent wrench) can be adjusted to fit nearly any nut or bolt head which has clear access around its entire perimeter. Adjustable wrenches (**Figure 33**) are best used as a backup wrench to keep a large nut or bolt from turning while the other end is being loosened or tightened with a proper wrench.

Adjustable wrenches have only 2 gripping surfaces, which makes them more subject to slipping off the fastener and damaging the part and possibly injuring your hand. The fact that one jaw is adjustable only aggravates this shortcoming.

These wrenches are directional; the solid jaw must be the one transmitting the force. If you use the adjustable jaw to transmit the force, it will loosen and possibly slip off.

Adjustable wrenches come in all sizes. A wrench in the 8 to 12 in. range is recommended as an all-purpose wrench.

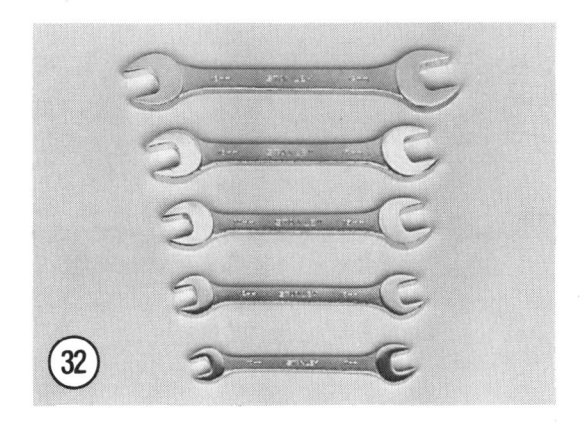

Socket Wrenches

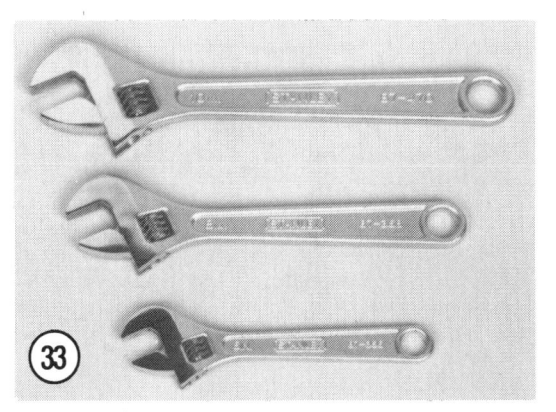

This type is undoubtedly the fastest, safest and most convenient to use. Sockets which attach to a ratchet handle (**Figure 34**) are available with 6-point or 12-point openings and 1/4, 3/8 and 3/4 in. drives. The drive size indicates the size of the square hole which mates with the ratchet handle (**Figure 35**).

Allen Wrenches

Allen wrenches are available in sets or separately in a variety of sizes. These sets come in U.S. standard and metric size, so be sure to buy a metric set. Allen bolts are sometimes called socket bolts. Some times the bolts are difficult to reach and it is suggested that a variety of Allen wrenches be purchased such as socket driven, T-handle and extension type, as shown in **Figure 36**.

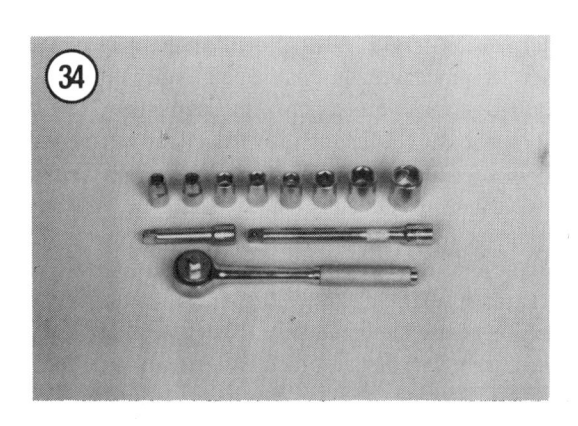

Torque Wrench

A torque wrench is used with a socket to measure how tightly a nut or bolt is installed. They come in a wide price range and with either 1/4, 3/8 or 1/2 in. square drive (**Figure 37**). The drive size indicates the size of the square drive which mates with the socket.

Impact Driver

This tool might have been designed with the motorcycle rider in mind. This tool makes removal of fasteners easy and eliminates damage to bolts and screw slots. Impact drivers and interchangeable bits (**Figure 38**) are available at most large hardware, motorcycle or auto parts stores. Sockets can also be used with a hand impact driver. However, make sure that the socket is designed for use with an impact driver or air tool. Do not use regular hand sockets, as they may shatter during use.

Hammers

The correct hammer (**Figure 39**) is necessary for certain repairs. Use only a hammer with a face (or head) of rubber or plastic or the soft-faced type that is filled with lead or steel shot. These are sometimes necessary during engine disassembly. *Never* use a metal-faced hammer on engine or suspension parts, as severe damage will result in most cases. You can always produce the same amount of force with a soft-faced hammer. A metal-faced hammer, however, is required when using a hand impact driver or cold chisel.

PRECISION MEASURING TOOLS

Measurement is an important part of engine and suspension service. When performing many of the service procedures in this manual, you will be required to make a number of measurements. These include basic checks such as valve clearance, engine compression and spark plug gap. As you get deeper into engine disassembly and service, measurements will be required to determine the size and condition of the piston and cylinder bore, valve and guide wear, camshaft wear, crankshaft runout and so on. When making these measurements, the degree of accuracy necessary will dictate which tool is required. Precision measuring tools are expensive. If this is your

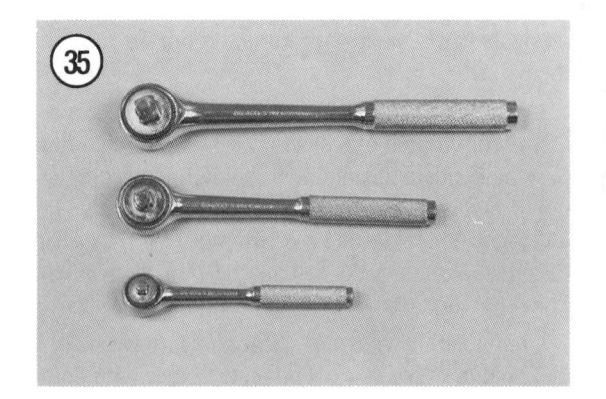

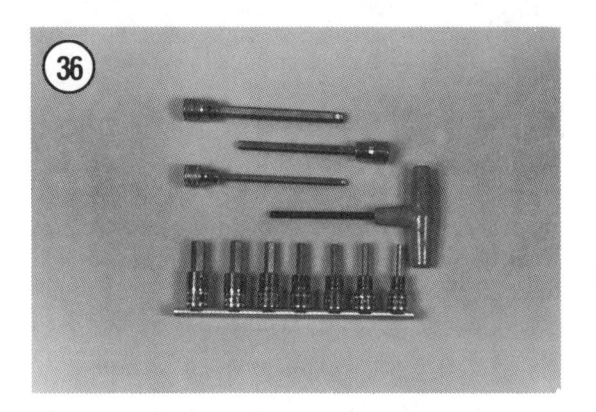

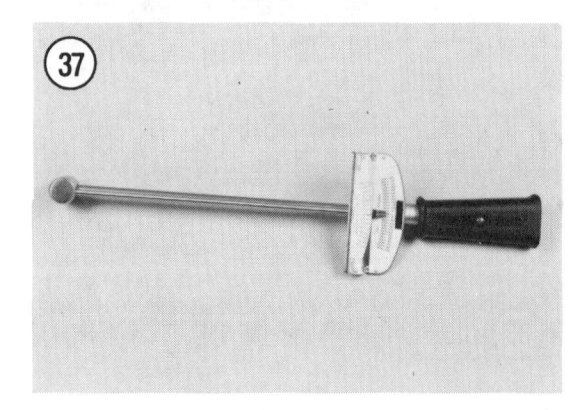

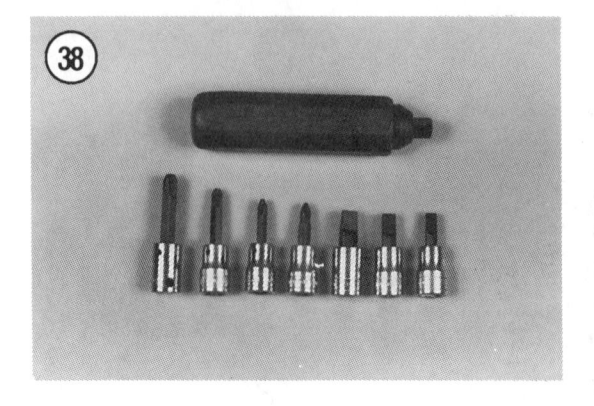

GENERAL INFORMATION

first experience at engine or suspension service, it may be worthwhile to have the checks made at a Honda dealership or machine shop. However, as your skills and enthusiasm increase for doing your own service work, you may want to begin purchasing some of these specialized tools. The following is a description of the measuring tools required during engine and suspension overhaul.

Feeler Gauge

Feeler gauges come in assorted sets and types (**Figure 40**). The feeler gauge is made of either a piece of flat or round hardened steel of a specified thickness. Wire gauges are used to measure spark plug gap. Flat gauges are used for all other measurements. Feeler gauges are also designed for specialized uses, such as for measuring valve clearances. On these gauges, the gauge end is usually small and angled to make checking valve clearances easier.

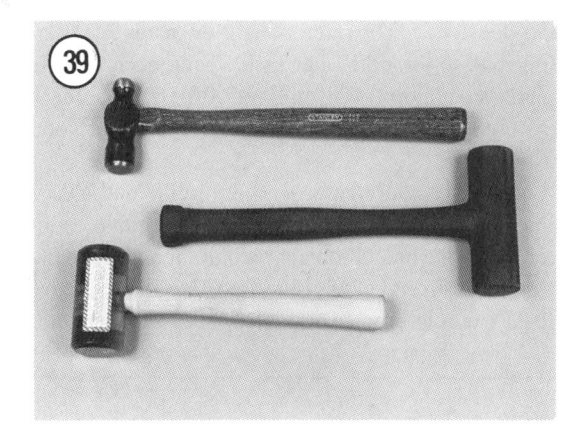

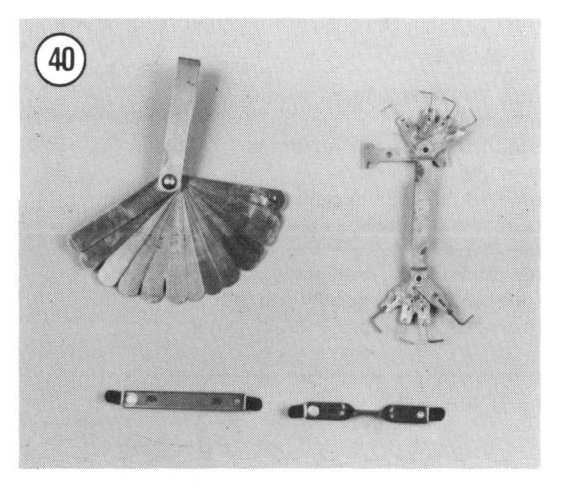

Vernier Caliper

This tool (**Figure 41**) is invaluable when reading inside, outside and depth measurements to close precision. Although this tool is not as precise as a micrometer, they allow measurements typically to within 0.025 mm (0.001 in.). Common uses of a vernier caliper are measuring the length of clutch springs, the thickness of clutch plates, shims and thrust washers, brake pad thickness or the depth of a bearing bore. The jaws of the caliper must be clean and free of burrs at all times to obtain an accurate measurement. There are several types of vernier calipers available. The standard vernier caliper has a highly accurate graduated scale on the handle with which the measurements must be calculated. The dial indicator caliper is equipped with a small dial and needle that indicates the measurement reading, and the digital electronic type with an LCD display that shows the measurement on the small display screen. Some vernier calipers must be calibrated prior to making a measurement to ensure an accurate measurement. Refer to the manufacturer's instructions for this procedure.

Outside Micrometers

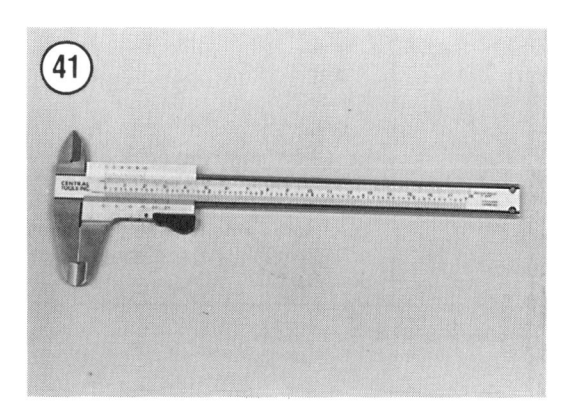

An outside micrometer is a precision tool used to accurately measure parts using the decimal divisions of the inch or meter (**Figure 42**). While there are many types and styles of micrometers, this section describes steps on how to use the outside micrometer. The outside micrometer is the most common type of micrometer used when servicing motorcycles. It is useful to accurately measure the outside diameter, length and thickness of parts used on your motorcycle. These parts include the piston, piston pin, crankshaft, piston rings and various shims. The outside micrometer is also used to measure the dimension taken by a small hole gauge or a telescoping gauge described later in this section. After the small hole gauge or telescoping gauge has been carefully expanded to a limit within the bore of the component being measured, carefully remove the gauge and measure the distance across its arms with the micrometer.

Other types of micrometers include the depth micrometer and screw thread micrometer. **Figure 43** illustrates the various parts of an outside micrometer with its part names and markings identified.

Micrometer Range

A micrometer's size indicates the minimum and maximum size of a part that it can measure. The usual sizes are: 0-1 in., 1-2 in., 2-3 in. and 3-4 in., 0-25 mm, 25-50 mm, 50-75 mm and 75-100 mm. These micrometers use fixed anvils.

Some micrometers use the same frame with interchangeable anvils of different lengths. This allows you to install the correct length anvil for a particular job. For example, a 0-4 in. interchangeable micrometer is equipped with four different length anvils. The large frame size typical of this type of micrometer makes it unsuitable for certain situations, however.

How to Read a Micrometer

When reading a micrometer, numbers are taken from different scales and then added together. The following sections describe how to read the standard inch micrometer, the vernier inch micrometer, the standard metric micrometer and the metric vernier micrometer.

Standard inch micrometer

The standard inch type micrometer is accurate to one-thousandth of an inch (0.001 in.). The heart of the micrometer is its spindle screw with 40 threads per inch. Every turn of the thimble will move the spindle 1/40 of an inch or 0.025 in. (to change 1/40 of an inch to a decimal: 1/40 = 0.025 in.).

Before you learn how to read a micrometer, study the markings and part names in **Figure 43**. Then turn the thimble until its zero mark aligns with the zero mark on the sleeve line. Now turn the thimble counterclockwise and align the next thimble mark with the sleeve line. The micrometer now reads 0.001 in. (one one-thousandth of an inch). Thus, each thimble mark is equal to 0.001 in. Every fifth thimble mark is numbered to help with reading: 0, 5, 10, 15 and 20.

Reset the micrometer so the thimble and sleeve line zero marks align. Then turn the thimble counterclockwise one complete revolution and align the thimble zero mark with the first line in the sleeve line. The micrometer now reads 0.025 in. (twenty-

---

(42)

DECIMAL PLACE VALUES*	
0.1	Indicates 1/10 (one tenth of an inch or millimeter)
0.01	Indicates 1/100 (one one-hundredth of an inch or millimeter)
0.001	Indicates 1/1,000 (one one-thousandth of an inch or millimeter)

* This chart represents the values of figures placed to the right of the decimal point. Use it when reading decimals from one-tenth to one one-thousandth of an inch or millimeter. It is not a conversion chart (for example: 0.001 in. is not equal to 0.001 mm).

five thousandths of an inch). Thus, each sleeve line represents 0.025 in.

Now turn the thimble counterclockwise while counting the sleeve line marks. Every fourth mark on the sleeve line is marked with a number ranging from 1 through 9. Manufacturers usually mark the last mark on the sleeve line with a 0. This indicates that you have reached the end of the micrometer's measuring range. Each sleeve number represents 0.100 in. For example, the number 1 represents 0.100 in. The number 9 represents 0.900 in.

When reading a standard micrometer, you take the following 3 measurements described and add them together. You take the first 2 readings from the sleeve. You take the last reading from the thimble. The sum of the 3 readings is the measurement in thousandths of an inch.

To read a micrometer, perform the following steps while referring to the example in **Figure 44**.
1. Read the sleeve line to find the largest number visible—each sleeve number equals 0.100 in.
2. Count the number of sleeve marks visible between the numbered sleeve mark and the thimble edge—each sleeve mark equals 0.025 in. If there is no visible sleeve mark, continue with Step 3.
3. Read the thimble mark that lines up with the sleeve line—each thimble mark equals 0.001 in.

NOTE
If a thimble mark does not align exactly with the sleeve line but falls between 2 lines, estimate the fraction or decimal amount between the lines. For a more accurate reading, you must use a vernier inch micrometer.

4. Add the micrometer readings in Steps 1, 2 and 3 to obtain the actual measurement.

Vernier inch micrometer

A vernier micrometer can accurately measure in ten-thousandths of an inch (0.0001 in.) increments. While it has the same markings as a standard micrometer, a vernier scale scribed on the sleeve (**Figure 45**) makes it unique. The vernier scale consists of eleven equally spaced lines marked 0-10 or 1-9 with a 0 on each end. These lines run parallel on the top of the sleeve where each line is equal to 0.0001 in. Thus, the vernier scale divides a thousandth of an inch (0.001 in.) into ten-thousandths of an inch (0.0001 in.).

To read a vernier inch micrometer, perform the following steps while referring to the example in **Figure 46**.
1. Read the micrometer in the same way as on the standard micrometer. This is your initial reading.
2. If a thimble mark aligns exactly with the sleeve line, reading the vernier scale is not necessary. If a thimble mark does not align exactly with the sleeve line, read the vernier scale in Step 3.

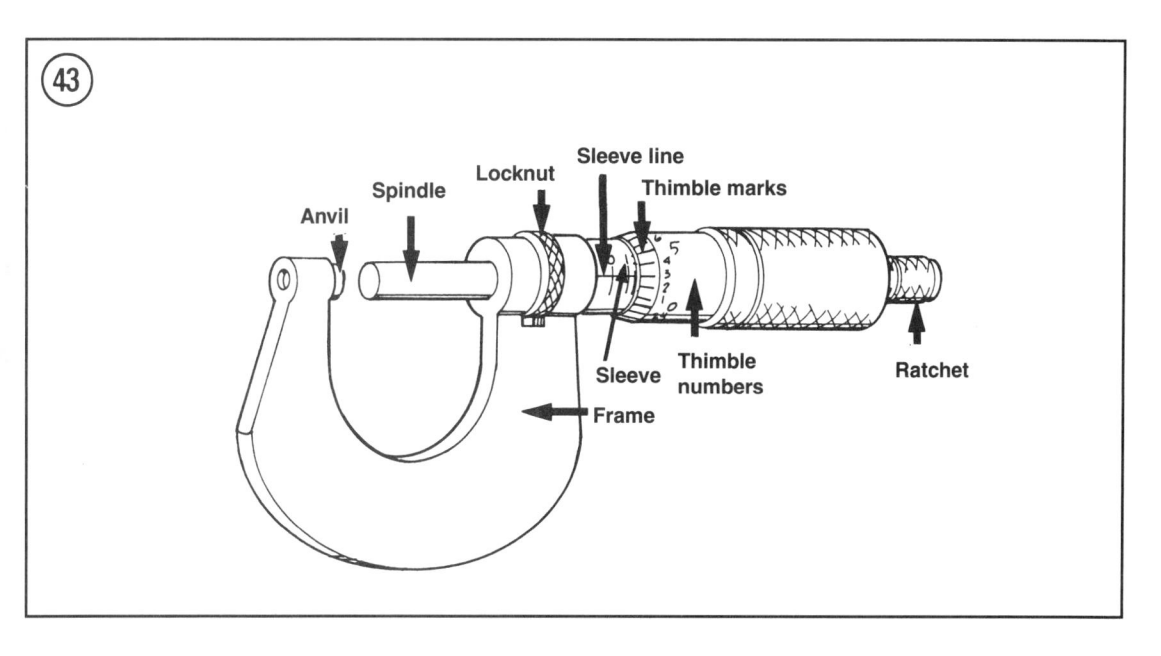

⃝43

3. Read the vernier scale to find which vernier mark aligns with one thimble mark. The number of that vernier mark is the number of ten-thousandths of an inch to add to the initial reading taken in Step 1.

Standard metric micrometers

The standard metric micrometer is very similar to the standard inch type. The differences are the graduations on the thimble and sleeve as shown in **Figure 47**.

The standard metric micrometer is accurate to one one-hundredth of a millimeter (0.01 mm). On the metric micrometer, the spindle screw is ground with a thread pitch of one-half millimeter (0.5 mm). Thus, every turn of the thimble will move the spindle 0.5 mm.

The sleeve line is graduated in millimeters and half millimeters. The marks on the upper side of the sleeve line are equal to 1.00 mm. Every fifth mark above the sleeve line is marked with a number. The actual numbers depend on the size of the micrometer. For example, on a 0-25 mm micrometer, the sleeve marks are numbered 0, 5, 10, 15, 20 and 25. On a 25-50 mm micrometer, the sleeve marks are numbered 25, 30, 35, 40, 45 and 50. This numbering sequence continues with larger size metric micrometers (50-75 and 75-100). Each mark on the lower side of the sleeve line is equal to 0.5 mm.

The thimble scale is divided into fifty graduations where one graduation is equal to 0.01 mm. Every fifth thimble graduation is numbered to help with reading from 0-45. The thimble edge is used to indicate which sleeve markings to read.

To read a metric micrometer, add the number of millimeters and half-millimeters on the sleeve line to the number of one one-hundredth millimeters on the thimble. To do so, perform the following steps while referring to the example in **Figure 48**.

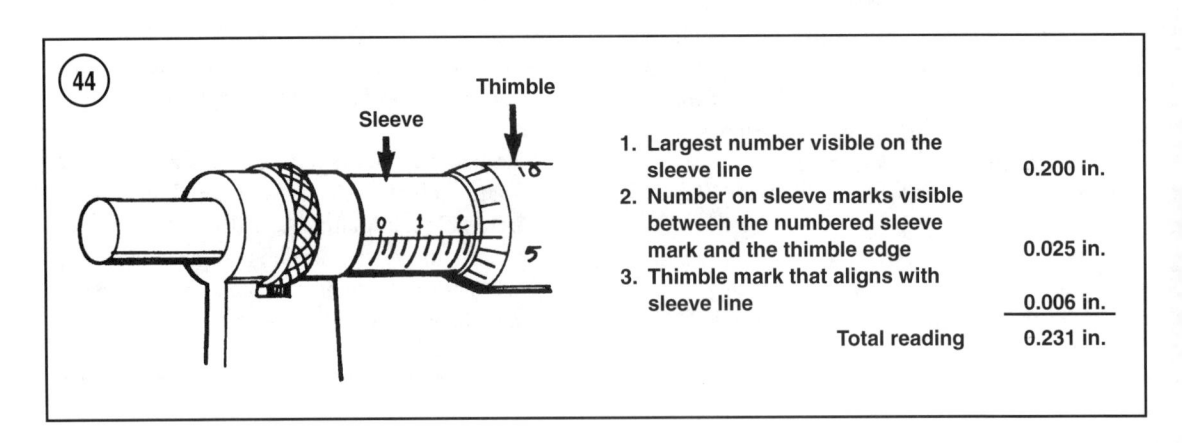

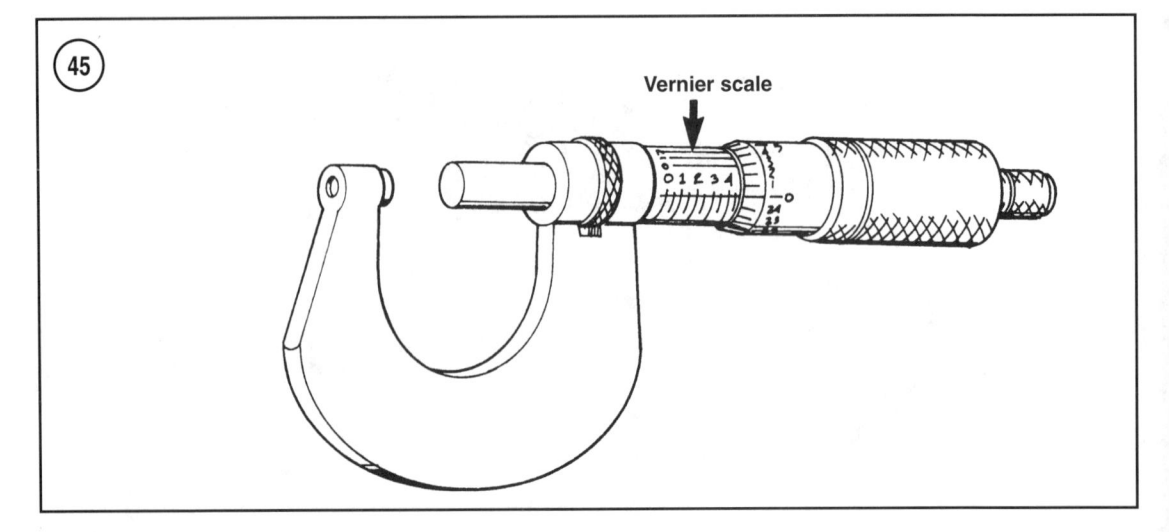

1. Largest number visible on the sleeve line	0.200 in.
2. Number on sleeve marks visible between the numbered sleeve mark and the thimble edge	0.025 in.
3. Thimble mark that aligns with sleeve line	0.006 in.
Total reading	0.231 in.

GENERAL INFORMATION

⑥

Vernier scale ↓
Sleeve ↑   **Thimble** ↑

Vernier scale ↓

| Sleeve | Thimble |

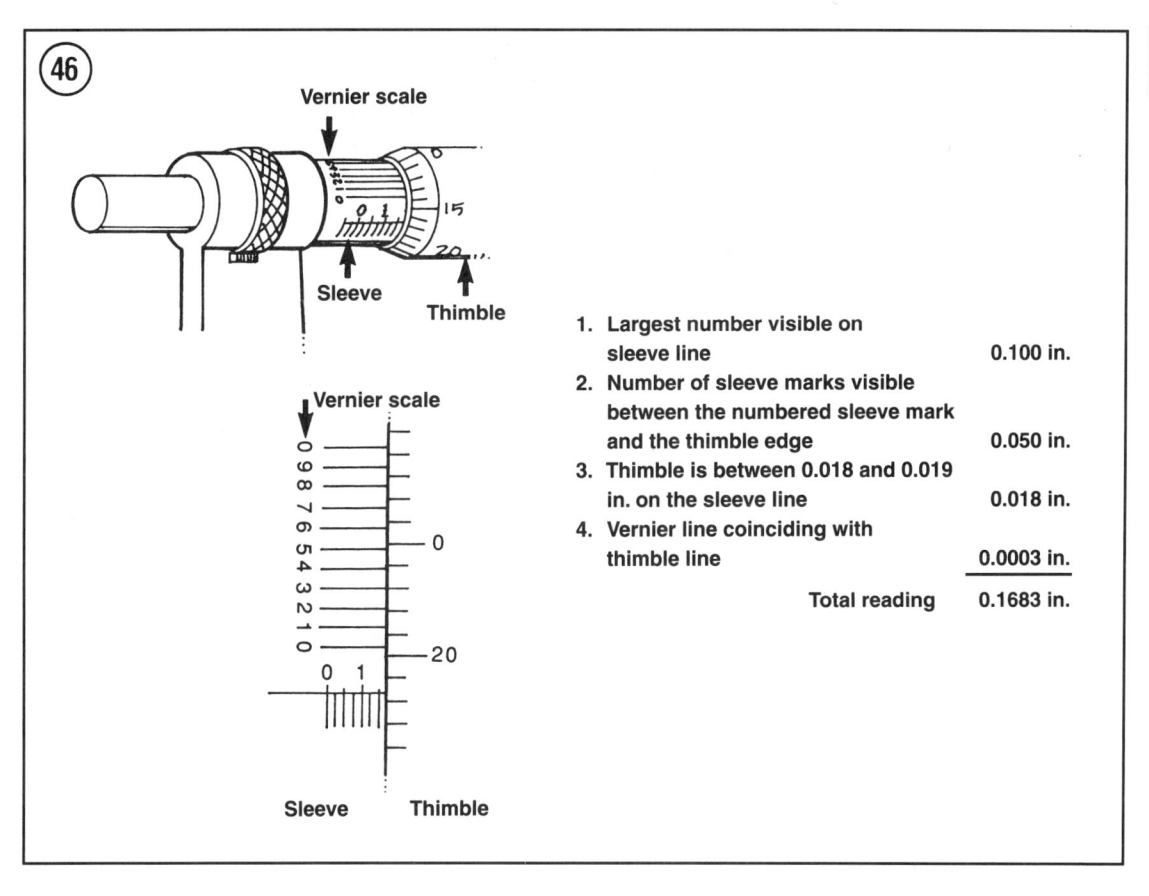

1. Largest number visible on sleeve line — 0.100 in.
2. Number of sleeve marks visible between the numbered sleeve mark and the thimble edge — 0.050 in.
3. Thimble is between 0.018 and 0.019 in. on the sleeve line — 0.018 in.
4. Vernier line coinciding with thimble line — 0.0003 in.

   Total reading 0.1683 in.

㊼

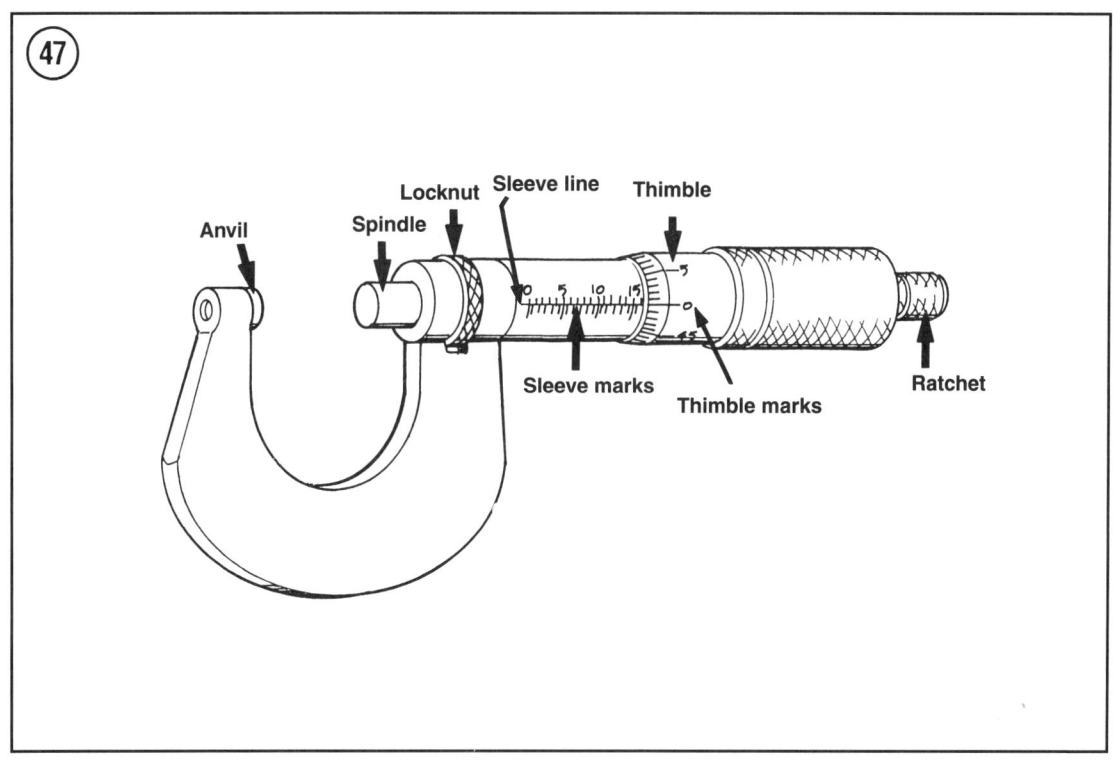

Anvil — Spindle — Locknut — Sleeve line — Thimble — Sleeve marks — Thimble marks — Ratchet

1. Take the first reading by counting the number of marks visible on the upper sleeve line. Record the reading.
2. Look below the sleeve line to see if a lower mark is visible directly past the upper line mark. If so, add 0.50 to the first reading.
3. Now read the thimble mark that aligns with the sleeve line. Record this reading.

NOTE
If a thimble mark does not align exactly with the sleeve line but falls between 2 lines, estimate the decimal amount between the lines. For a more accurate reading, you must use a metric vernier micrometer.

4. Add the micrometer readings in Steps 1, 2 and 3 to provide the actual measurement.

Metric vernier micrometers

A metric vernier micrometer can accurately measure to 2 thousandths of a millimeter (0.002 mm). While it has the same markings as a standard metric micrometer, a vernier scale scribed on the sleeve (**Figure 49**) makes it unique. The vernier scale consists of 5 equally spaced lines marked 0, 2, 4, 6 and 8. These lines run parallel on the top of the sleeve where each line is equal to 0.002 mm.

To read a metric vernier micrometer, perform the following steps while referring to the example in **Figure 50**:
1. Read the micrometer in the same way as on the standard metric micrometer. This is the initial reading.
2. If a thimble mark aligns exactly with the sleeve line, reading the vernier scale is not necessary. If a thimble mark does not align exactly with the sleeve line, read the vernier scale in Step 3.
3. Read the vernier scale to find which vernier mark aligns with one thimble mark. The number of that vernier mark is the number of thousandths of a millimeter to add to the initial reading taken in Step 1.

Micrometer Accuracy Check

You must check a micrometer frequently for accuracy. The following steps show you how to do this.
1. Make sure the anvil and spindle faces (**Figure 43**) are clean and dry.
2. To check a 0-1 in. (0-25 mm) micrometer, perform the following:
   a. Turn the thimble until the spindle contacts the anvil. If the micrometer has a ratchet stop, use

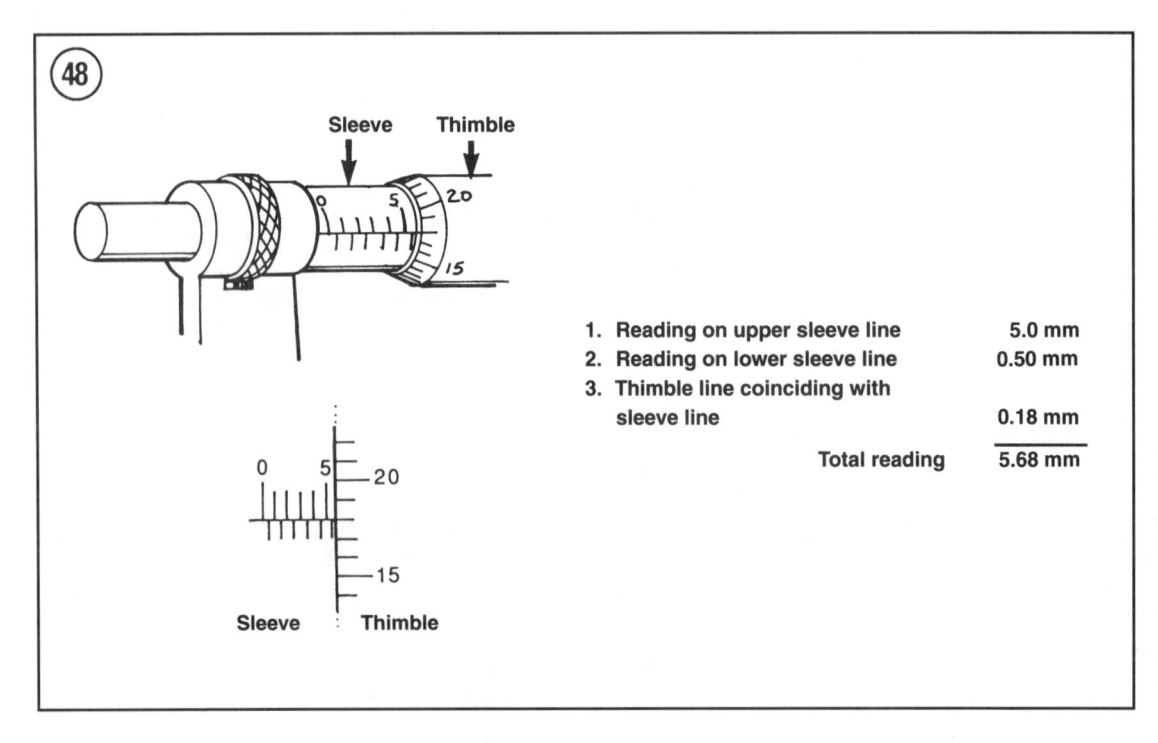

---

(48)

Sleeve   Thimble

1. Reading on upper sleeve line	5.0 mm
2. Reading on lower sleeve line	0.50 mm
3. Thimble line coinciding with sleeve line	0.18 mm
Total reading	5.68 mm

Sleeve : Thimble

GENERAL INFORMATION 23

it to ensure that the proper amount of pressure is applied against the contact surfaces.

b. Read the micrometer. If the adjustment is correct, the 0 mark on the thimble will align exactly with the 0 mark on the sleeve line. If the 0 marks do not align, the micrometer must be calibrated.

c. To adjust the micrometer, follow its manufacturer's instructions given with the micrometer.

3. To check the accuracy of micrometers above the 1 in. (25 mm) size, perform the following:

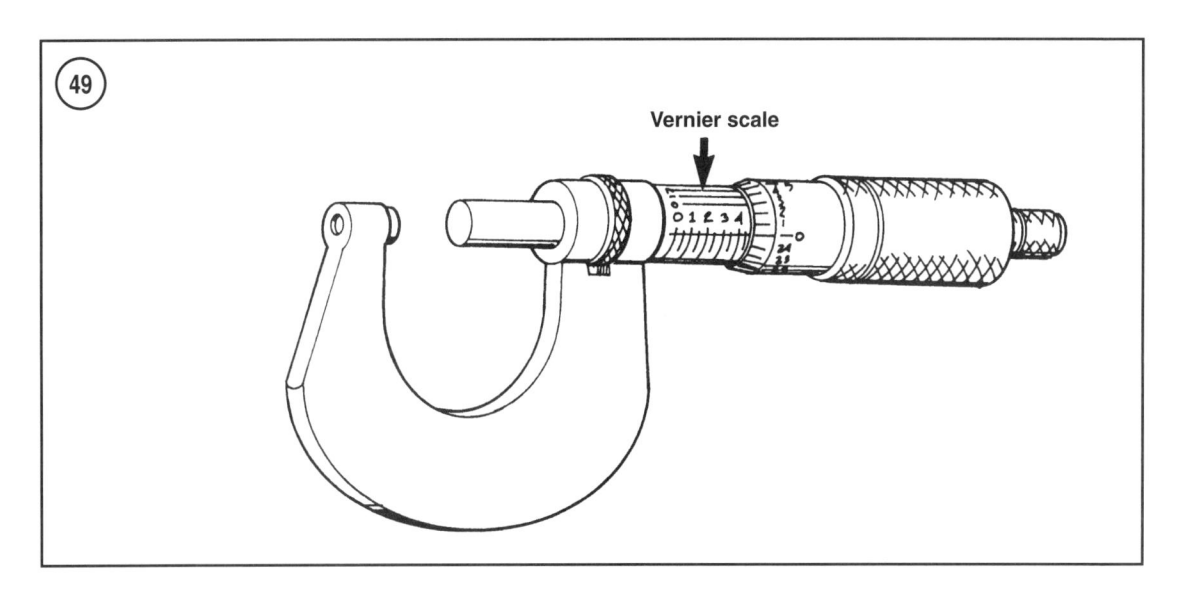

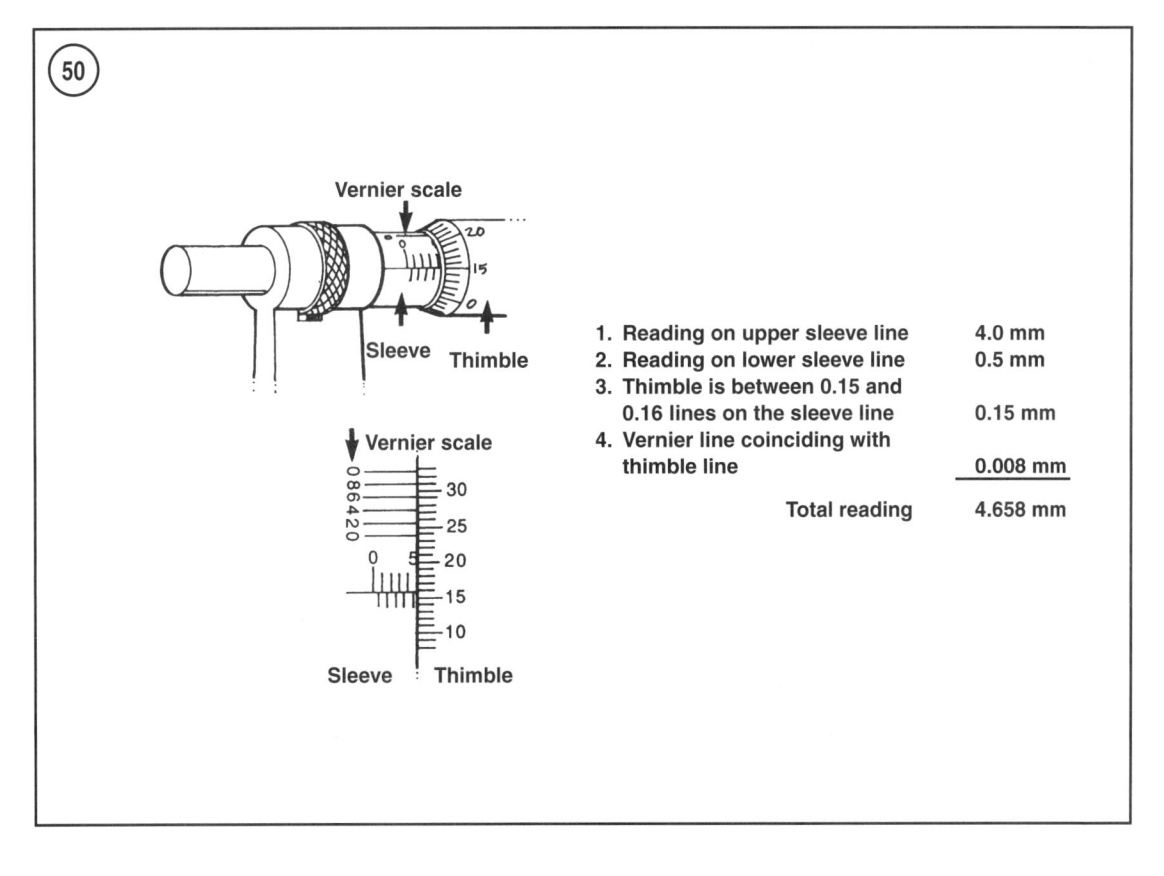

○49

Vernier scale

○50

Vernier scale

Sleeve   Thimble

Vernier scale

Sleeve   Thimble

1. Reading on upper sleeve line	4.0 mm
2. Reading on lower sleeve line	0.5 mm
3. Thimble is between 0.15 and 0.16 lines on the sleeve line	0.15 mm
4. Vernier line coinciding with thimble line	0.008 mm
Total reading	4.658 mm

a. Manufacturers usually supply a standard gauge with these micrometers. A standard is a steel block, disc or rod that is ground to an exact size to check the accuracy of the micrometer. For example, a 1-2 in. micrometer is equipped with a 1 inch standard gauge. A 25-50 mm micrometer is equipped with a 25 mm standard gauge.

b. Place the standard gauge between the micrometer's spindle and anvil and measure its outside diameter or length. Read the micrometer. If the adjustment is correct, the 0 mark on the thimble will align exactly with the 0 mark on the sleeve line. If the 0 marks do not align, the micrometer is out of adjustment.

c. To adjust the micrometer, follow its manufacturer's instructions given with the micrometer.

Proper Care of the Micrometer

Because the micrometer is a precision instrument, you must use it correctly and with great care.
1. Store a micrometer in its box or in a protected place where dust, oil, and other debris cannot come in contact with it. Do not store micrometers in a drawer with other tools or hang them on a tool board.
2. When storing a 0-1 in. (0-25 mm) micrometer, the spindle and anvil must not contact each other. If they do, the contact may cause rust to form on the contact ends or spindle damage from temperature changes.
3. Do not clean a micrometer with compressed air. Dirt forced into the tool can cause premature wear.
4. Occasionally lubricate the micrometer with a light oil to prevent rust and corrosion.
5. Before using a micrometer, check its accuracy. Refer to *Micrometer Accuracy Check* in this section.

Dial Indicator

Dial indicators (**Figure 51**) are precision tools used to check dimension variations on machined parts such as transmission shafts and axles, to check crankshaft and axle shaft end play and to measure lash between 2 gears. Dial indicators are available with various dial types. For motorcycle repair, select an indicator with a continuous dial face (**Figure 52**).

Cylinder Bore Gauge

The cylinder bore gauge is a very specialized precision tool. The gauge set shown in **Figure 53** is comprised of a dial indicator, handle and a number of length adapters to adapt the gauge to different bore sizes. The bore gauge can be used to make cylinder bore measurements such as bore size, taper

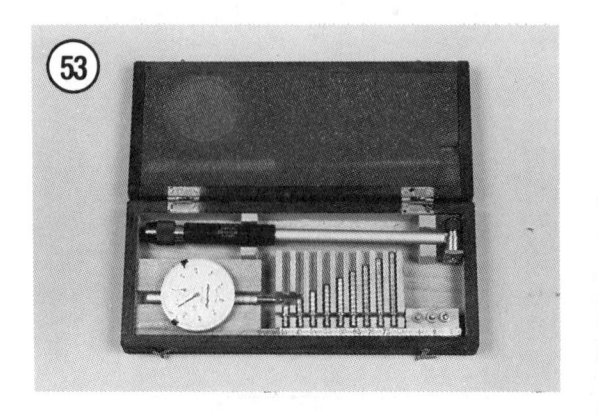

GENERAL INFORMATION

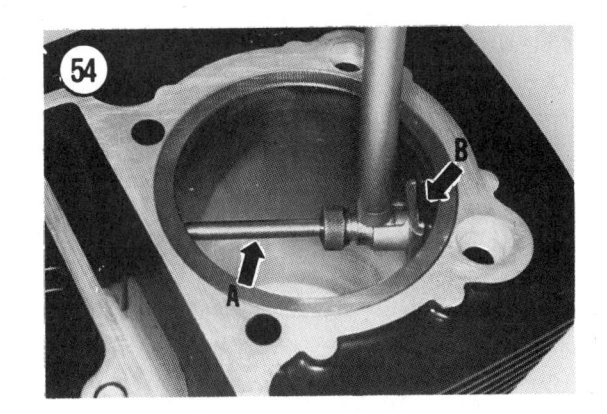

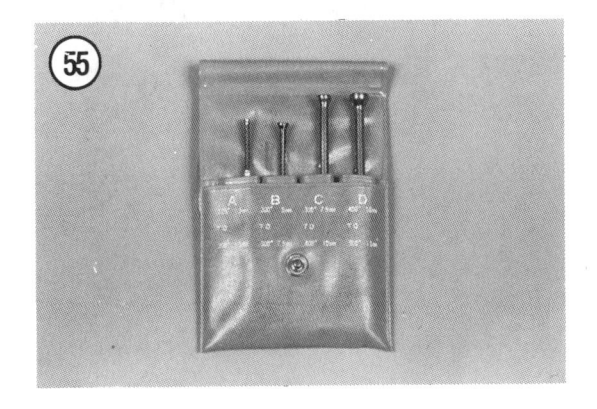

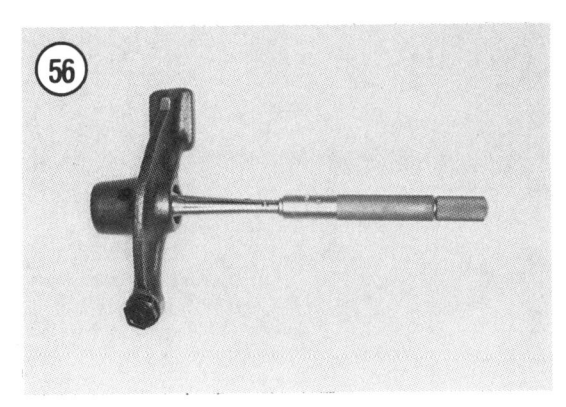

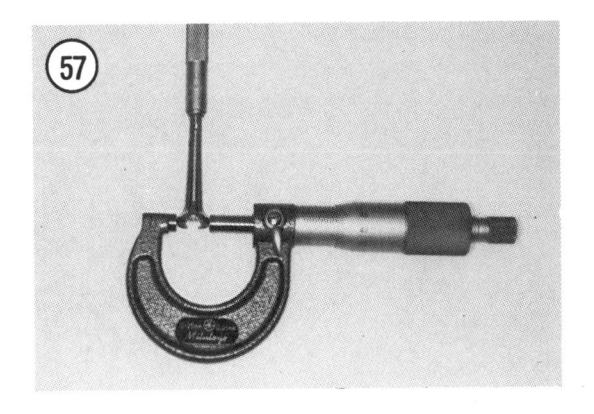

and out-of-round. Depending on the bore gauge, it can sometimes be used to measure brake caliper and master cylinder bore sizes. In some cases, an outside micrometer must be used to calibrate the bore gauge to a specific bore size.

Select the correct length adapter (A, **Figure 54**) for the size of the bore to be measured. Zero the bore gauge according to its manufacturer's instructions, insert the bore gauge into the cylinder, carefully move it around in the bore to make sure it is centered and that the gauge foot (B, **Figure 54**) is sitting correctly on the bore surface. This is necessary to obtain a correct reading. Refer to the manufacturer's instructions for reading the actual measurement obtained.

Small Hole Gauges

A set of small hole gauges (**Figure 55**) allows you to measure a hole, groove or slot ranging in size up to 13 mm (0.500 in.). A small hole gauge is required to measure valve guide, brake caliper and brake master cylinder bore diameters.

The small hole gauge does not have a scale for direct readings. An outside micrometer must be used to measure the small hole gauge to determine the bore size.

Carefully insert the small hole gauge into the bore of the component to be measured. Tighten the knurled end of the gauge to carefully expand the gauge fingers to the limit within the bore (**Figure 56**)—do not overtighten the gauge as there is no built-in release feature. If tightened too much, the gauge fingers can damage the bore surface. Carefully remove the gauge and measure the outside dimension of the gauge with a micrometer (**Figure 57**). See *Outside Micrometer* in this chapter.

Telescoping Gauges

A telescoping gauge (**Figure 58**) is used to measure hole diameters from approximately 8 mm (5/16 in.) to 150 mm (6 in.). Like the small hole gauge, the telescoping gauge does not have a scale for direct readings. An outside micrometer must be used to measure the telescoping gauge to determine the bore dimension.

Select the correct size telescoping gauge for the bore to be measured. Compress the movable side of the gauge post and carefully install the gauge into the bore of the component to be measured, then release the movable post against the bore. Carefully move the gauge around in the bore to make sure it is centered. Tighten the knurled end of the gauge to hold the movable gauge post in this position. Carefully remove the gauge and measure the outside dimension of the gauge posts with a micrometer. See *Outside Micrometer* in this chapter.

Screw Pitch Gauge

A screw pitch gauge (**Figure 59**) determines the thread pitch of threaded fasteners. The gauge is made up of a number of thin plates. Each plate has a thread shape cut on one edge to match one thread pitch. When using a screw pitch gauge to determine a thread pitch size, try to fit different blade sizes onto the bolt thread until both threads match exactly(**Figure 60**).

Magnetic Stand

A magnetic stand (**Figure 61**) holds a dial indicator securely when checking the runout of a round object or when checking the end play of a shaft.

V-Blocks

V-blocks (**Figure 62**) are precision ground blocks used to hold a round object when checking its runout or condition. Use V-blocks to check the runout of such items as valve stems, camshaft, crankshaft and other shafts and collars.

TEST EQUIPMENT

Compression Gauge

An engine with low compression cannot be properly tuned and will not develop full power. A compression gauge (**Figure 63**) measures cylinder compression. The one shown has a flexible stem with an extension that can allow you to hold it while cranking the engine. Open the throttle all the way when checking engine compression. See Chapter Three.

Cylinder Leak-Down Tester

Certain engine problems (leaking valve, broken, worn or stuck piston rings or leaking gasket) can be isolated by performing a cylinder leak-down test. An air compressor and a cylinder leak-down tester (**Figure 64**) are required to perform a leak-down test. This procedure is fully explained in Chapter Two. You can purchase a cylinder leak-down tester

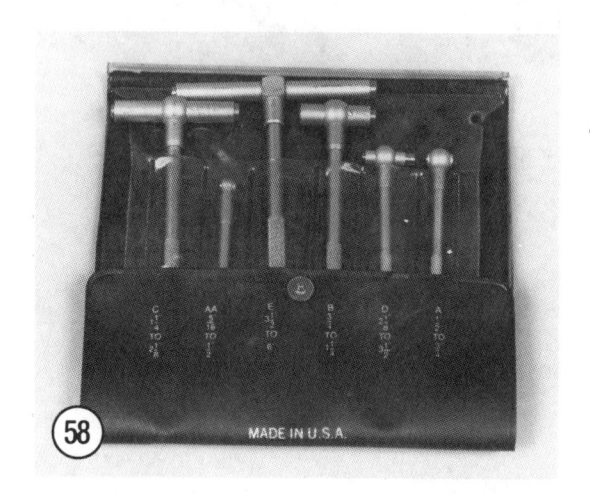

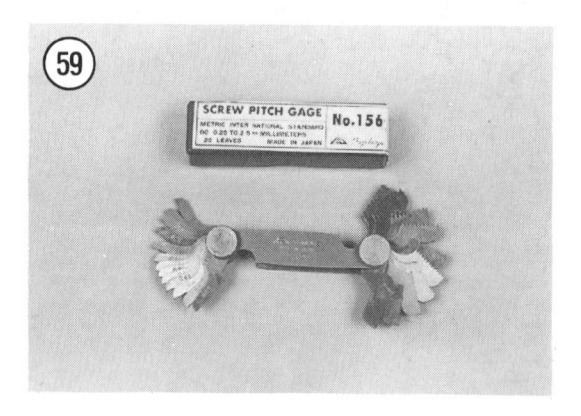

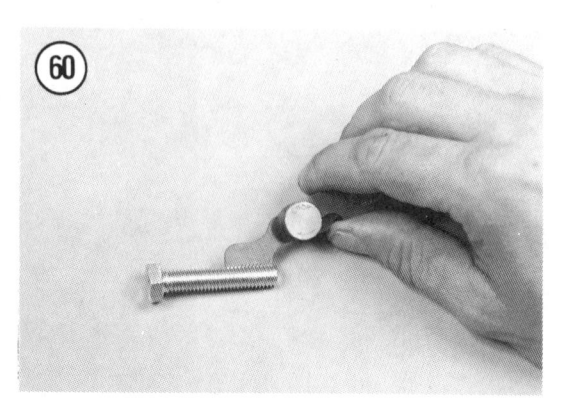

GENERAL INFORMATION

through Honda dealerships, tool manufacturers and tool suppliers. A typical set is shown in **Figure 65**.

When you purchase a cylinder leak-down tester, make sure it is equipped with a hose adapter that matches the spark plug thread size for your Honda. Leak-down testers purchased through automotive suppliers are usually equipped with 14 mm and 18 mm adapters.

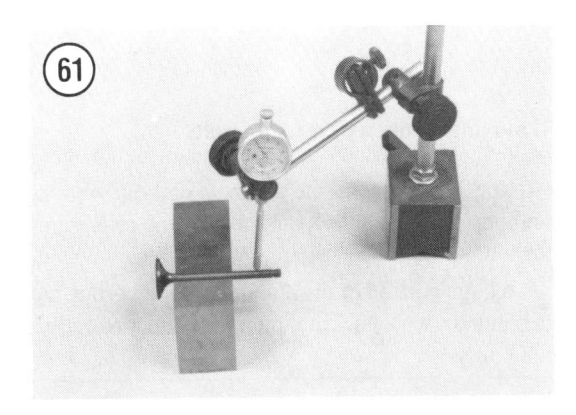

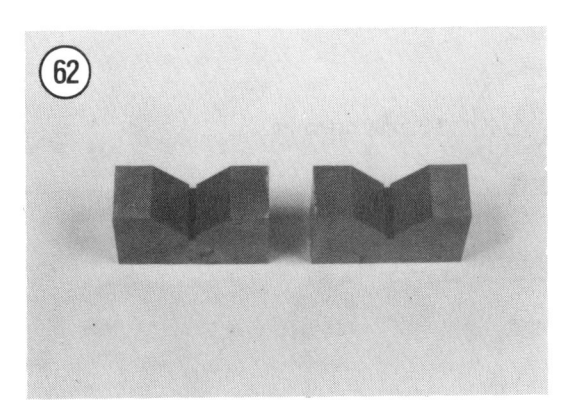

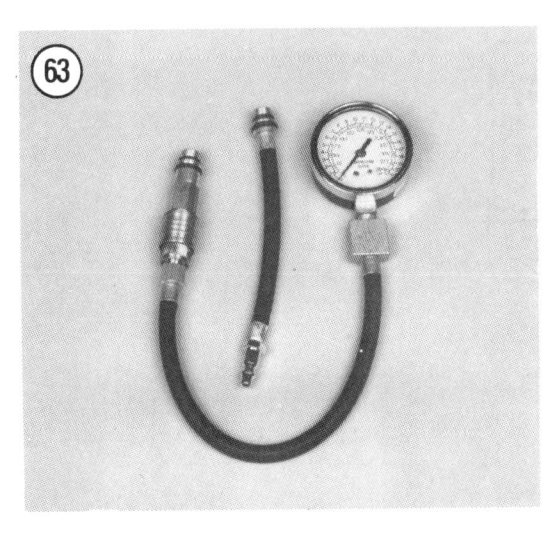

Strobe Timing Light

This instrument is used to check ignition timing. By flashing a light at the precise instant the spark plug fires, the position of the timing mark can be seen. The flashing light makes a moving mark appear to stand still opposite a stationary mark.

Suitable lights range from inexpensive neon bulb types (**Figure 66**) to powerful xenon strobe lights. A light with an inductive pickup is recommended to eliminate any possible damage to ignition wiring.

Multimeter or VOM

This instrument (**Figure 67**) is invaluable for electrical system troubleshooting. See *Electrical Troubleshooting* in Chapter Two for its use.

SPECIAL TOOLS

A few special tools may be required for major service. These are described in the appropriate chapters and are available either from a Honda dealership or other manufacturer as indicated.

This section describes special tools unique to this type of vehicle.

Flywheel Puller

A flywheel puller (**Figure 68**) is required to remove the flywheel from the crankshaft. There is no satisfactory substitute for this tool. Because the flywheel is a taper fit on the crankshaft, makeshift removal often results in crankshaft and flywheel damage. Do not attempt to remove the flywheel without this tool. This tool can be ordered through Honda dealerships.

Support Jack

Because the Honda ACE is not equipped with a centerstand, some type of support jack is required for many routine service procedure or major component replacement. An excellent tool for this purpose is the K&L centerstand scissors jack (**Figure 69**). This jack is designed so you can vary its width and height adjustments to securely contact the frame rails. The feature works well on the Honda ACE because of the way the engine drops below the frame.

NOTE
K&L Supply Co. is a manufacturer and distributor of motorcycle, ATV and watercraft tools, parts and accessories. You can order the centerstand scissors jack and other supplies through your Honda dealership.

MECHANIC'S TIPS

Removing Frozen Nuts and Screws

If a fastener rusts and cannot be removed, several methods may be used to loosen it. First, apply penetrating oil such as Liquid Wrench or WD-40 (available at hardware or auto supply stores). Apply it liberally and let it penetrate for 10-15 minutes. Rap the fastener several times with a small hammer; do not hit it hard enough to cause damage. Reapply the penetrating oil if necessary.

For frozen screws, apply penetrating oil as described, then insert a screwdriver in the slot and rap the top of the screwdriver with a hammer. This loosens the rust so the screw can be removed in the normal way. If the screw head is too damaged to use this method, grip the head with locking pliers and twist the screw out.

Avoid applying heat unless specifically instructed, as it may melt, warp or remove the temper from parts.

Removing Broken Screws or Bolts

If the head breaks off a screw or bolt, several methods are available for removing the remaining portion.

If a large portion of the remainder projects out, try gripping it with locking pliers. If the projecting

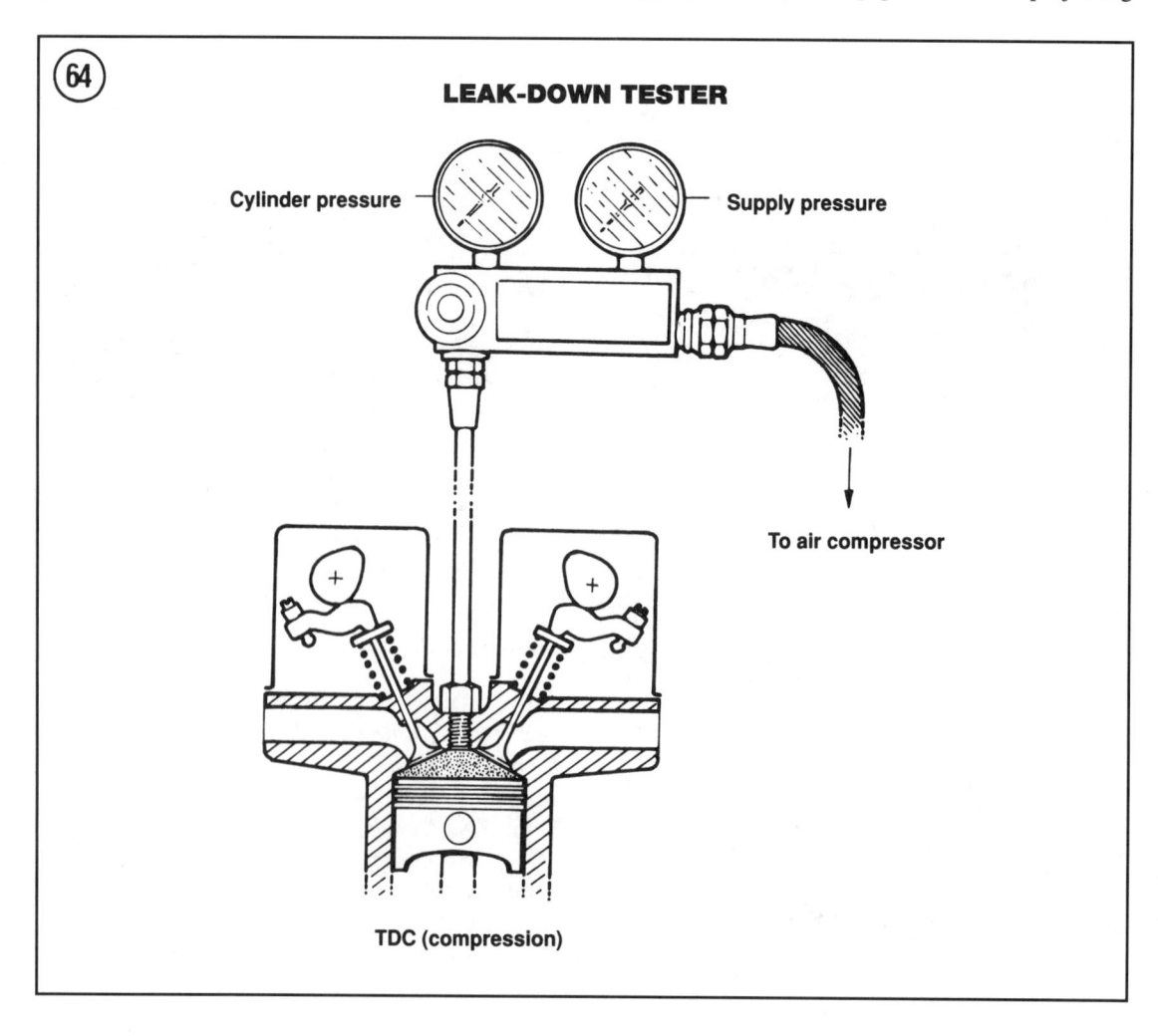

LEAK-DOWN TESTER

Cylinder pressure — Supply pressure

To air compressor

TDC (compression)

GENERAL INFORMATION

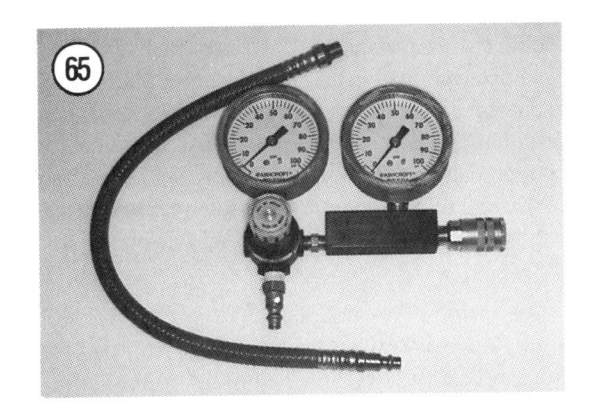

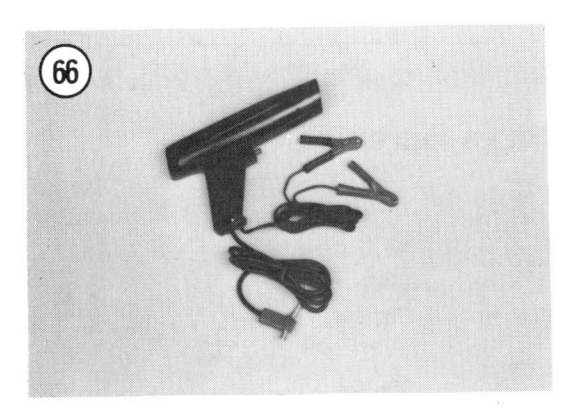

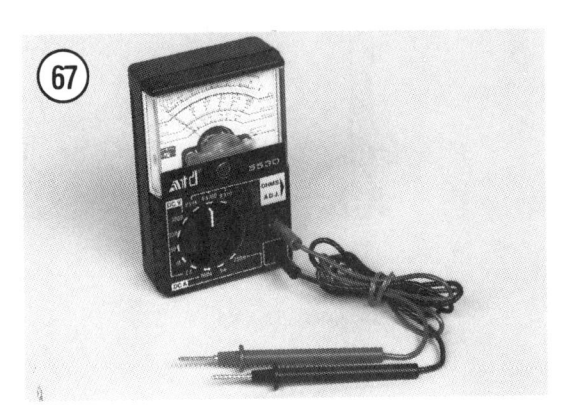

portion is too small, file it to fit a wrench or cut a slot in it to fit a screwdriver. See **Figure 70**.

If the head breaks off flush, use a screw extractor. To do this, centerpunch the exact center of the remaining portion of the screw or bolt. Drill a small hole in the screw and tap the extractor into the hole. Back the screw out with a wrench on the extractor. See **Figure 71**.

Remedying Stripped Threads

Occasionally, threads are stripped through carelessness or impact damage. Often the threads can be cleaned up by running a tap (for internal threads on nuts) or die (for external threads on bolts) through the threads. See **Figure 72**. To clean or repair spark plug threads, use the correct size spark plug tap (**Figure 73**).

NOTE
*Tap and dies can be purchased individually or in a set as shown in **Figure 74**.*

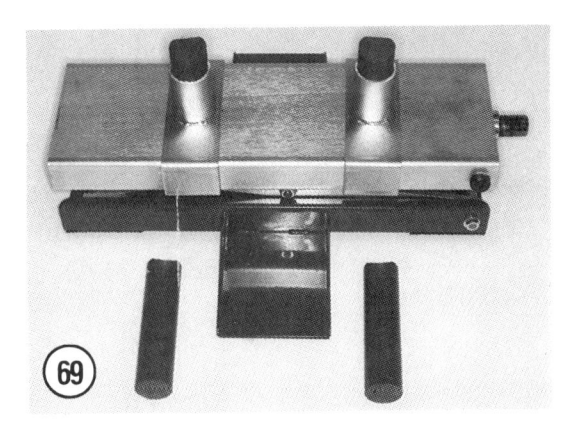

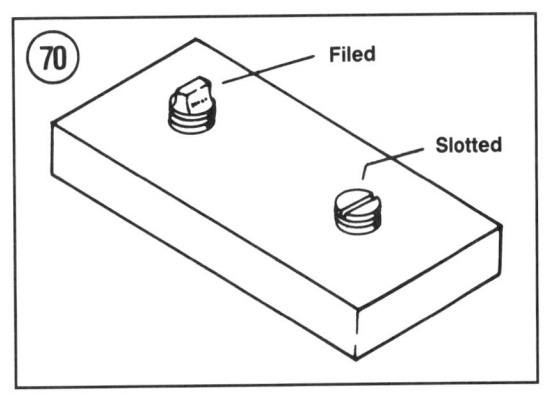

If an internal thread is damaged, it may be necessary to install a thread insert. See **Figure 75**, typical. Follow the insert manufacturer's instructions when installing their insert.

If it is necessary to drill and tap a hole, refer to **Table 8** for metric tap drill sizes.

BALL BEARING REPLACEMENT

Ball bearings (**Figure 76**) are used throughout the engine and chassis to reduce power loss, heat and noise resulting from friction. Because ball bearings are precision-made parts, they must be maintained by proper lubrication and maintenance. If a bearing is damaged, replace it immediately. However, when installing a new bearing, you must take care to prevent damage to the new bearing. While bearing replacement is covered in the individual chapters, use the following information as a basic guideline.

NOTE
Unless otherwise specified, install bearings with their manufacturer's mark or number facing outward.

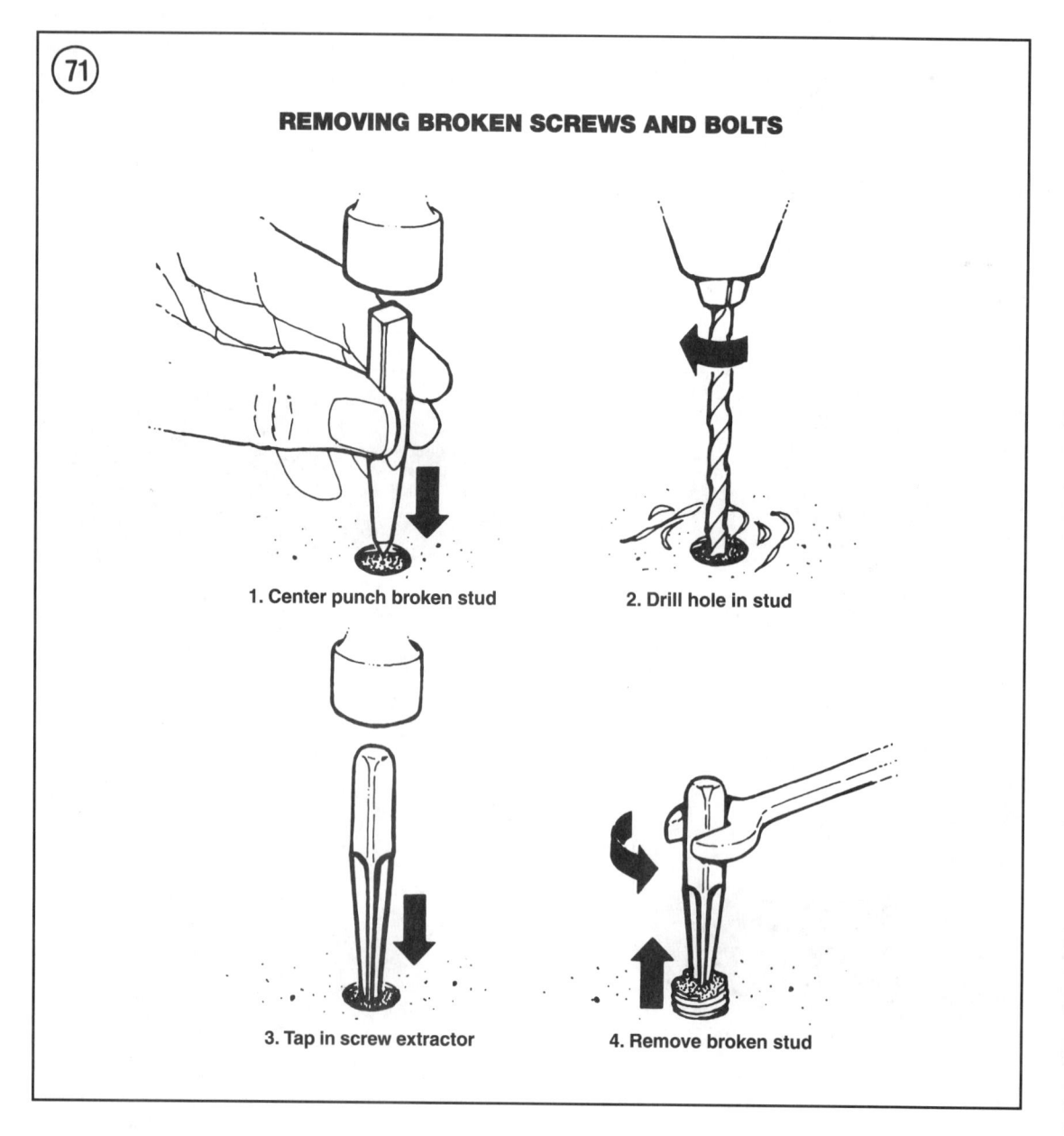

REMOVING BROKEN SCREWS AND BOLTS

1. Center punch broken stud
2. Drill hole in stud
3. Tap in screw extractor
4. Remove broken stud

GENERAL INFORMATION

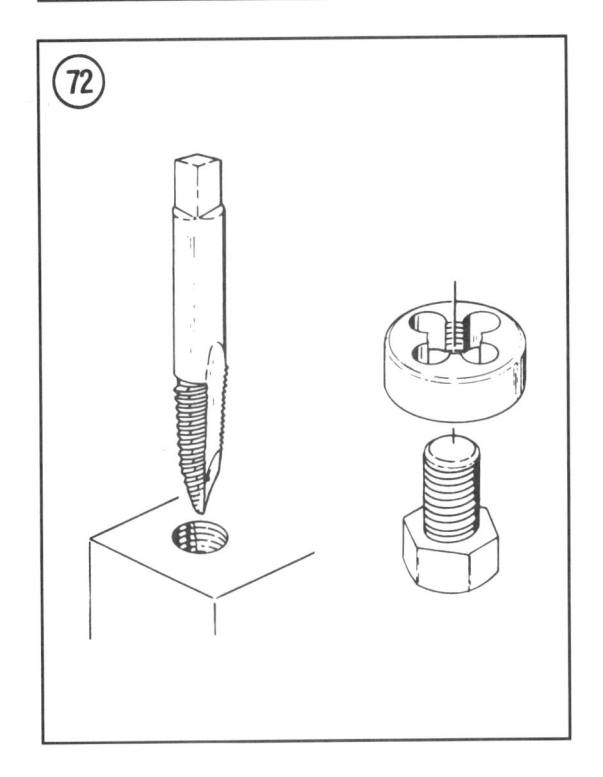

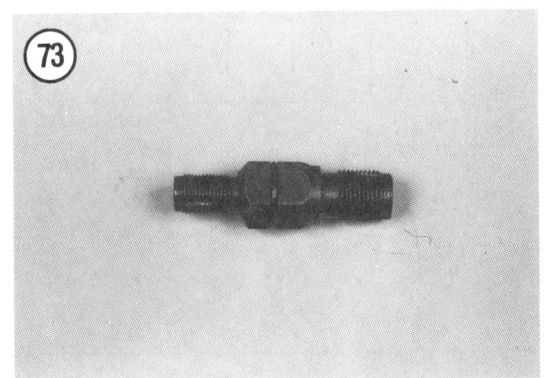

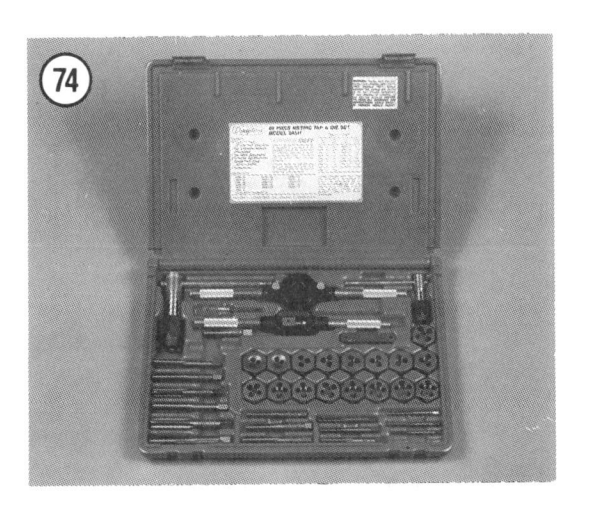

Bearing Removal

While you normally remove bearings only when damaged, there may be times when removing a bearing that is in good condition is necessary. However, improper bearing removal will damage the bearing and maybe the shaft or case half. Note the following when removing bearings.

1. When using a puller to remove a bearing on a shaft, you must take care so that shaft damage does not occur. Always place a piece of metal between the end of the shaft and the puller screw. In addition, place the puller arms next to the inner bearing race. See **Figure 77**.

2. When using a hammer to remove a bearing from a shaft, do not strike the hammer directly against the shaft. Instead, use a brass or aluminum driver between the hammer and shaft (**Figure 78**). In addition, support both bearing races with wooden blocks as shown in **Figure 78**.

3. The ideal method of bearing removal is with a hydraulic press. However, you must follow certain procedures or damage may occur to the bearing,

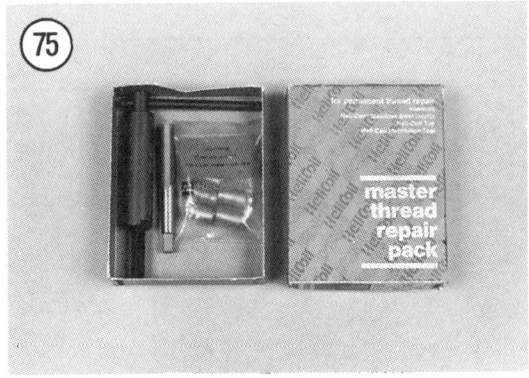

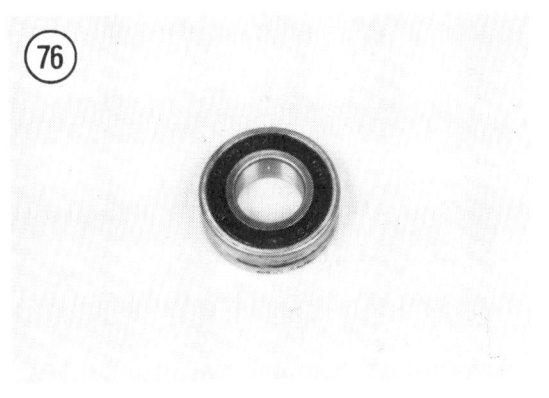

shaft or bearing housing. Note the following when using a press:

a. Always support the inner and outer bearing races with a suitable size wooden or aluminum spacer (**Figure 79**). If you only support the outer race, pressure applied against the balls and/or the inner race will damage them.

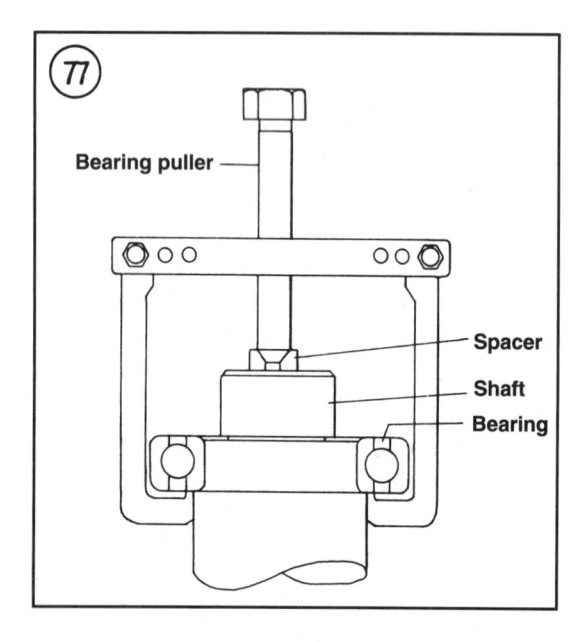

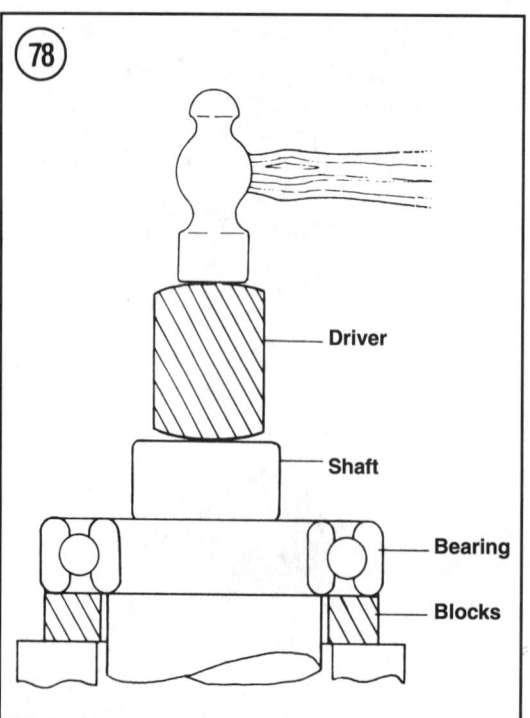

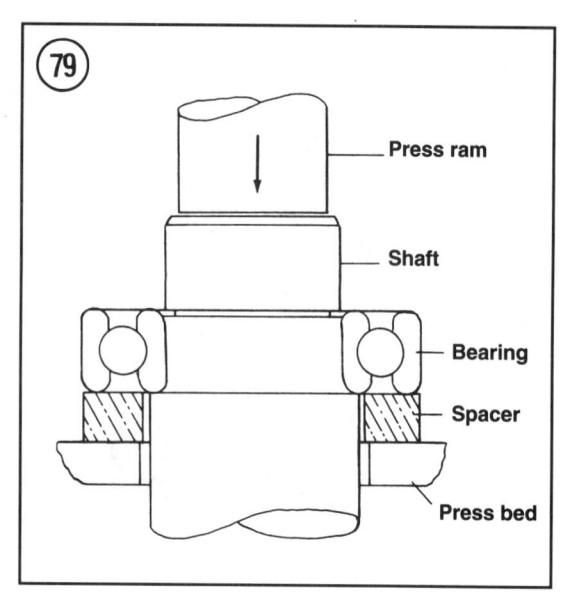

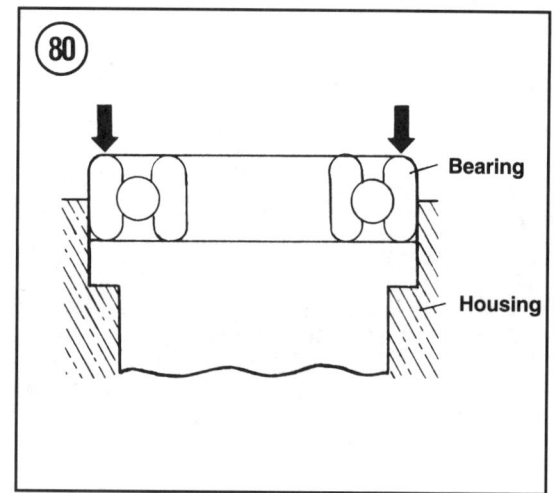

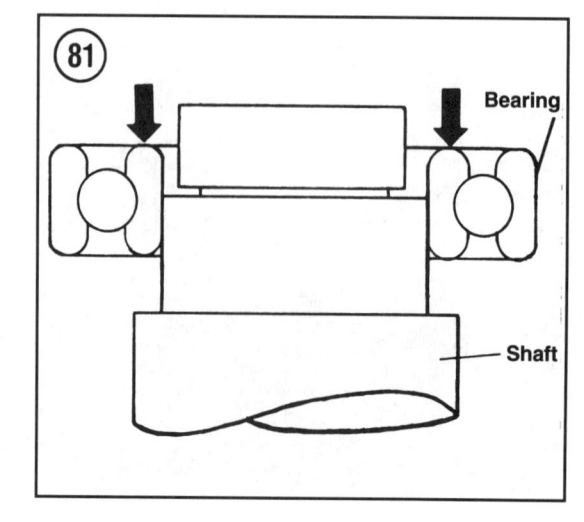

GENERAL INFORMATION 33

b. Always make sure the press ram (**Figure 79**) aligns with the center of the shaft. If you do not center the ram, it may damage the bearing and/or shaft.

c. The moment the shaft is free of the bearing, it will drop to the floor. Secure or hold the shaft to prevent it from falling.

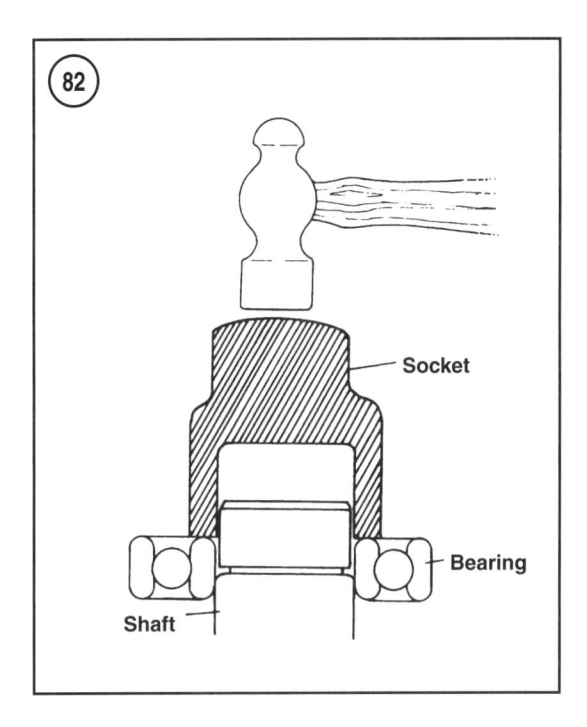

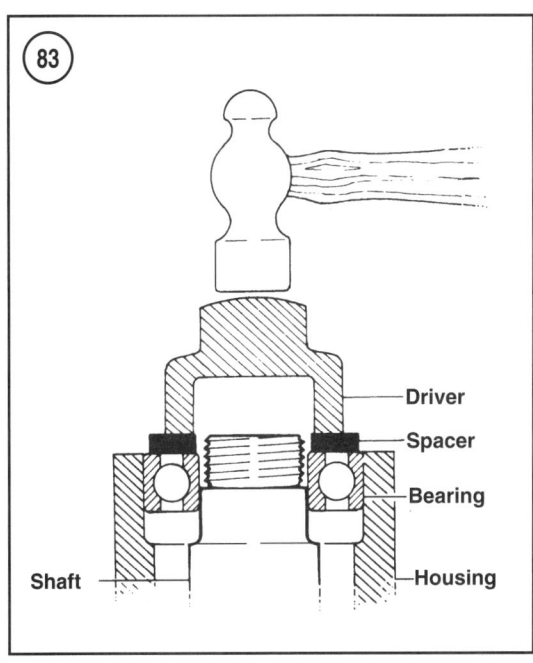

Bearing Installation

1. When installing a bearing in a housing, apply pressure to the *outer* bearing race (**Figure 80**). When installing a bearing on a shaft, apply pressure to the *inner* bearing race (**Figure 81**).

2. When installing a bearing as described in Step 1, some type of driver will be required. Never strike the bearing directly with a hammer or the bearing will be damaged. When installing a bearing, use a bearing driver with an outside diameter that matches the bearing race. **Figure 82** shows the correct way to use a bearing driver and hammer when installing a bearing over a shaft.

3. Step 1 describes how to install a bearing in a case half or over a shaft. However, when installing a bearing over a shaft and into a housing at the same time, a snug fit is required for both outer and inner bearing races. In this situation, a spacer must be installed underneath the driver tool so pressure is applied evenly across *both* races. See **Figure 83**. If you do not support the outer race as shown in **Figure 83**, the balls will push against the outer bearing track and damage it.

Shrink Fit

1. *Installing a bearing over a shaft:* When a tight fit is required, the bearing inside diameter is smaller than the shaft. In this case, driving the bearing on the shaft may damage the bearing. Instead, heat the bearing before installation. Note the following:

   a. Secure the shaft so it is ready for bearing installation.
   b. Clean the bearing surface on the shaft of all residue. Remove burrs with a file or sandpaper.
   c. Fill a suitable pot or beaker with clean mineral oil. Place a thermometer (rated higher than 120° C [248° F]) in the oil. Support the thermometer so it does not rest on the bottom or side of the pot.
   d. Secure the bearing with a piece of heavy wire bent to hold it in the pot. Hang the bearing in the pot so it does not touch the bottom or sides of the pot.
   e. Turn the heat on and monitor the thermometer. When the oil temperature rises to approximately 120° C (248° F), remove the bearing from the pot and quickly install it. If

necessary, place a driver on the inner bearing race and tap the bearing into place. As the bearing chills, it will tighten on the shaft so you must work quickly when installing it. Make sure you install the bearing all the way.

2. *Installing a bearing in a housing*: Bearings are generally installed in a housing with a slight interference fit. Driving the bearing into the housing may damage the housing or bearing. Instead, heat the housing before installing the bearing. Note the following:

CAUTION
Before heating the housing in this procedure to remove the bearings, wash the housing thoroughly with detergent and water. Rinse and rewash the housing as required to remove all traces of oil and other chemical deposits.

a. The housing must be heated to a temperature of about 212° F (100° C) in an oven. An easy way to determine if it is at the proper temperature is to place tiny drops of water on the housing as it heats up; if they sizzle and evaporate immediately, the temperature is correct. Heat only one housing at a time.

CAUTION
Do not heat the housing with a torch (propane or acetylene)—never bring a flame into contact with the bearing or housing. The direct heat will destroy the case hardening of the bearing and will likely warp the housing.

b. Remove the housing from the oven or hot plate and hold onto the housing with a kitchen pot holder, heavy gloves, or heavy shop cloths—*it is hot*.

NOTE
A suitable size socket and extension work well for removing and installing bearings.

c. Hold the housing with the bearing side down and tap the bearing out. Repeat for all bearings in the housing.

d. Before heating the housing, place the new bearings in a freezer, if possible. Chilling them will slightly reduce their overall diameter while the hot housing assembly is larger due to heat expansion. This will make installation much easier.

NOTE
Always install bearings with their manufacturer's mark or number facing outward.

e. While the housing is still hot, install the new bearing(s) into the housing. Install the bearing(s) by hand, if possible. If necessary, lightly tap the bearing(s) into the housing with a driver placed on the outer bearing race. *Do not install new bearings by driving on the inner bearing race.* Install the bearing(s) until it seats completely.

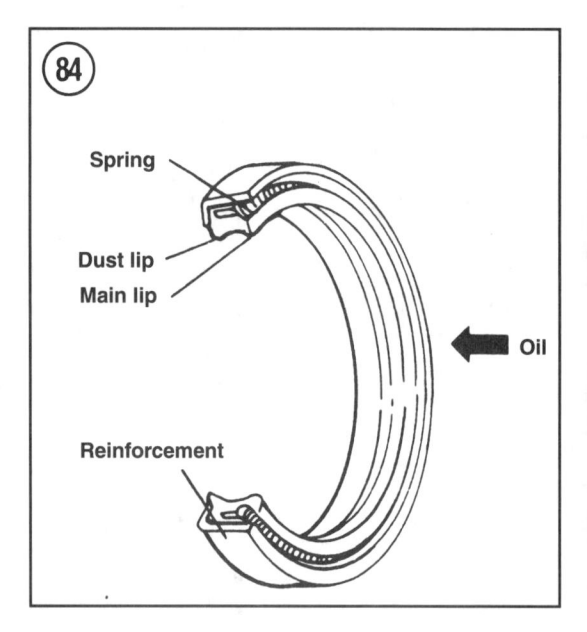

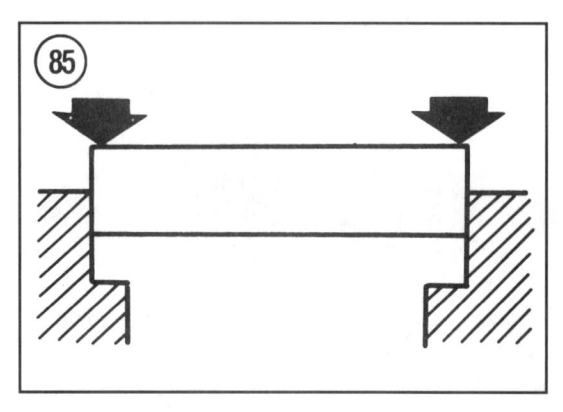

GENERAL INFORMATION

SEALS

Seals (**Figure 84**) are used to contain oil, water, grease or combustion gases in a housing or shaft. Improper installation of the seal can damage the housing or shaft. Improper installation of the seal can damage the seal. Note the following:

a. Prying is generally the easiest and most effective method to remove a seal from a housing. However, always place a rag underneath the pry tool to avoid damaging the housing.
b. Pack grease in the seal lips before installing the seal.
c. Unless specified otherwise in the text, install seals with the manufacturer's numbers or marks facing out.
d. Install seals with a driver placed on the outside of the seal as shown in **Figure 85**.

Make sure the seal is driven squarely into the housing. Never install a seal by hitting against the top of the seal with a hammer.

Table 1 ENGINE AND FRAME SERIAL NUMBERS

Model	Engine serial number (start to end)	Frame serial number (start to end)
1995 VT1100C2		
49-state	SC32E-2000001-on	SC320SA000001-on
California	SC32E-2000001-on	SC321SA000001-on
1996 VT1100C2		
49-state	SC32E-2100001-on	SC320TA100001-on
California	SC32E-2100001-on	SC321TA100001-on
1997-1999 VT1100C2		
49-state	N/A	N/A
California	N/A	N/A

Table 2 GENERAL DIMENSIONS

	mm	in.
Overall length	2,435	95.9
Overall width	965	38.0
Overall height	1,150	45.2
Wheelbase	1,650	65.0
Seat height	700	27.6
Ground clearance	140	5.5

Table 3 WEIGHT SPECIFICATIONS

	kg	lb.
Dry weight		
49 state and Canada	260	573
California	261	575
Curb weight		
49 state and Canada	279	615
California	280	617

(continued)

Table 3 WEIGHT SPECIFICATIONS (continued)

	kg	lb.
Maximum weight capacity		
U.S. models	169	373
Canada	173	381

Table 4 DECIMAL AND METRIC EQUIVALENTS

Fractions	Decimal in.	Metric mm	Fractions	Decimal in.	Metric mm
1/64	0.015625	0.39688	33/64	0.515625	13.09687
1/32	0.03125	0.79375	17/32	0.53125	13.49375
3/64	0.046875	1.19062	35/64	0.546875	13.89062
1/16	0.0625	1.58750	9/16	0.5625	14.28750
5/64	0.078125	1.98437	37/64	0.578125	14.68437
3/32	0.09375	2.38125	19/32	0.59375	15.08125
7/64	0.109375	2.77812	39/64	0.609375	15.47812
1/8	0.125	3.1750	5/8	0.625	15.87500
9/64	0.140625	3.57187	41/64	0.640625	16.27187
5/32	0.15625	3.96875	21/32	0.65625	16.66875
11/64	0.171875	4.36562	43/64	0.671875	17.06562
3/16	0.1875	4.76250	11/16	0.6875	17.46250
13/64	0.203125	5.15937	45/64	0.703125	17.85937
7/32	0.21875	5.55625	23/32	0.71875	18.25625
15/64	0.234375	5.95312	47/64	0.734375	18.65312
1/4	0.250	6.35000	3/4	0.750	19.05000
17/64	0.265625	6.74687	49/64	0.765625	19.44687
9/32	0.28125	7.14375	25/32	0.78125	19.84375
19/64	0.296875	7.54062	51/64	0.796875	20.24062
5/16	0.3125	7.93750	13/16	0.8125	20.63750
21/64	0.328125	8.33437	53/64	0.828125	21.03437
11/32	0.34375	8.73125	27/32	0.84375	21.43125
23/64	0.359375	9.12812	55/64	0.859375	22.82812
3/8	0.375	9.52500	7/8	0.875	22.22500
25/64	0.390625	9.92187	57/64	0.890625	22.62187
13/32	0.40625	10.31875	29/32	0.90625	23.01875
27/64	0.421875	10.71562	59/64	0.921875	23.41562
7/16	0.4375	11.11250	15/16	0.9375	23.81250
29/64	0.453125	11.50937	61/64	0.953125	24.20937
15/32	0.46875	11.90625	31/32	0.96875	24.60625
31/64	0.484375	12.30312	63/64	0.984375	25.00312
1/2	0.500	12.70000	1	1.00	25.40000

Table 5 CONVERSION TABLES

Multiply	By	To get equivalent of
Length		
Inches	25.4	Millimeter
Inches	2.54	Centimeter
Miles	1.609	Kilometer
Feet	0.3048	Meter
Millimeter	0.03937	Inches
Centimeter	0.3937	Inches
Kilometer	0.6214	Mile
Meter	3.281	Mile
(continued)		

GENERAL INFORMATION

Table 5 CONVERSION TABLES (continued)

Multiply	By	To get equivalent of
Fluid volume		
U.S. quarts	0.9463	Liters
U.S. gallons	3.785	Liters
U.S. ounces	29.573529	Milliliters
Imperial gallons	4.54609	Liters
Imperial quarts	1.1365	Liters
Liters	0.2641721	U.S. gallons
Liters	1.0566882	U.S. quarts
Liters	33.814023	U.S. ounces
Liters	0.22	Imperial gallons
Liters	0.8799	Imperial quarts
Milliliters	0.033814	U.S. ounces
Milliliters	1.0	Cubic centimeters
Milliliters	0.001	Liters
Torque		
Foot-pounds	1.3558	Newton-meters
Foot-pounds	0.138255	Meters-kilograms
Inch-pounds	0.11299	Newton-meters
Newton-meters	0.7375622	Foot-pounds
Newton-meters	8.8507	Inch-pounds
Meters-kilograms	7.2330139	Foot-pounds
Volume		
Cubic inches	16.387064	Cubic centimeters
Cubic centimeters	0.0610237	Cubic inches
Temperature		
Fahrenheit	(F − 32) × 0.556	Centigrade
Centigrade	(C × 1.8) + 32	Fahrenheit
Weight		
Ounces	28.3495	Grams
Pounds	0.4535924	Kilograms
Grams	0.035274	Ounces
Kilograms	2.2046224	Pounds
Pressure		
Pounds per square inch	0.070307	Kilograms per square centimeter
Kilograms per square centimeter	14.223343	Pounds per square inch
Kilopascals	0.1450	Pounds per square inch
Pounds per square inch	6.895	Kilopascals
Speed		
Miles per hour	1.609344	Kilometers per hour
Kilometers per hour	0.6213712	Miles per hour

Table 6 GENERAL TORQUE SPECIFICATIONS

Fastener size or type	N•m	in.-lb.	ft.-lb.
5 mm screw	4	35	—
5 mm bolt and nut	5	44	—
6 mm screw	9	80	—
6 mm bolt and nut	10	88	—
6 mm flange bolt (8 mm head, small flange)	9	80	—
6 mm flange bolt (10 mm head) and nut	12	106	—
8 mm bolt and nut	22	—	16

(continued)

Table 6 GENERAL TORQUE SPECIFICATIONS (continued)

Fastener size or type	N·m	in.-lb.	ft.-lb.
8 mm flange bolt and nut	27	—	20
10 mm bolt and nut	35	—	25
10 mm flange bolt and nut	40	—	29
12 mm bolt and nut	55	—	40

Table 7 TECHNICAL ABBREVIATIONS

ABDC	After bottom dead center
ATDC	After top dead center
BBDC	Before bottom dead center
BDC	Bottom dead center
BTDC	Before top dead center
C	Celsius (Centigrade)
cc	Cubic centimeters
CDI	Capacitor discharge ignition
cu. in.	Cubic inches
F	Fahrenheit
ft.-lb.	Foot-pounds
gal.	Gallons
H/A	High altitude
hp	Horsepower
in.	Inches
kg	Kilogram
kg/cm2	Kilograms per square centimeter
kgm	Kilogram meters
km	Kilometer
L	Liter
m	Meter
MAG	Magneto
ml	Milliliter
mm	Millimeter
N·m	Newton-meters
oz.	Ounce
psi	Pounds per square inch
PTO	Power take off
pt.	Pint
qt.	Quart
rpm	Revolutions per minute

Table 8 METRIC TAP DRILL SIZES

Metric (mm)	Drill size	Decimal equivalent	Nearest fraction
3 × 0.50	No. 39	0.0995	3/32
3 × 0.60	3/32	0.0937	3/32
4 × 0.70	No. 30	0.1285	1/8
4 × 0.75	1/8	0.125	1/8
5 × 0.80	No. 19	0.166	11/64
5 × 0.90	No. 20	0.161	5/32
6 × 1.00	No. 9	0.196	13/64
7 × 1.00	16/64	0.234	15/64
8 × 1.00	J	0.277	9/32
8 × 1.25	17/64	0.265	17/64
9 × 1.00	5/16	0.3125	5/16

(continued)

GENERAL INFORMATION

Table 8 METRIC TAP DRILL SIZES (continued)

Metric (mm)	Drill size	Decimal equivalent	Nearest fraction
9 × 1.25	5/16	0.3125	5/16
10 × 1.25	11/32	0.3437	11/32
10 × 1.50	R	0.339	11/32
11 × 1.50	3/8	0.375	3/8
12 × 1.50	13/32	0.406	13/32
12 × 1.75	13/32	0.406	13/32

Table 9 WINDCHILL FACTORS

Estimated wind speed in mph	Actual thermometer reading (°F)											
	50	40	30	20	10	0	−10	−20	−30	−40	−50	−60
	Equivalent temperature (°F)											
Calm	50	40	30	20	10	0	−10	−20	−30	−40	−50	−60
5	48	37	27	16	6	−5	−15	−26	−36	−47	−57	−68
10	40	28	16	4	−9	−21	−33	−46	−58	−70	−83	−95
15	36	22	9	−5	−18	−36	−45	−58	−72	−85	−99	−112
20	32	18	4	−10	−25	−39	−53	−67	−82	−96	−110	−124
25	30	16	0	−15	−29	−44	−59	−74	−88	−104	−118	−133
30	28	13	−2	−18	−33	−48	−63	−79	−94	−109	−125	−140
35	27	11	−4	−20	−35	−49	−67	−82	−98	−113	−129	−145
40*	26	10	−6	−21	−37	−53	−69	−85	−100	−116	−132	−148

Little danger (for properly clothed person) | Increasing danger | Great danger

• Danger from freezing of exposed flesh •

*Wind speeds greater than 40 mph have little additional effect.

CHAPTER TWO

TROUBLESHOOTING

Diagnosing mechanical and electrical problems is simple if you use orderly procedures and keep a few basic principles in mind. The first step in any troubleshooting procedure is to define the symptoms as closely as possible and localize the problem. Subsequent steps involve testing and analyzing those areas which could cause the symptoms. A haphazard approach may eventually solve the problem, but it can be very costly in wasted time and unnecessary parts replacement.

Proper lubrication, maintenance and periodic tune-ups as described in Chapter Three will reduce the necessity for troubleshooting. Even with the best of care, however, all vehicles are prone to problems which will require troubleshooting.

Never assume anything. Do not overlook the obvious. If the engine will not start, is the engine stop switch shorted out? Is the engine flooded with fuel?

If the engine suddenly quits, what sound did it make? Consider this and check the easiest, most accessible problem first. If the engine sounded like it ran out of fuel, check the fuel level in the tank. If there is fuel in the tank, is it reaching the carburetors?

If nothing obvious turns up during a quick inspection, look a little further. Learning to recognize and describe symptoms will make repair easier for you or a mechanic at the shop. Describe problems accurately and fully.

Gather as many symptoms as possible to aid in diagnosis. Note whether the engine lost power gradually or all at once. Remember that the more complicated a machine is, the easier it is to troubleshoot because symptoms point to specific problems.

After you define the symptoms, test and analyze areas which could cause the problem. Guessing at the cause of a problem may provide the solution, but it can easily lead to frustration, wasted time and a series of expensive, unnecessary part replacements.

You do not need expensive equipment or complicated test gear to decide whether you can attempt repairs at home. A few simple checks could save a large repair bill and lost riding time. On the other hand, be realistic and do not attempt repairs beyond your abilities.

OPERATING REQUIREMENTS

An engine needs 3 basics to run properly: correct fuel/air mixture, compression and a spark at the right time (**Figure 1**). If one basic requirement is missing, the engine will not run. *Engine Principles* in Chapter Four describes the operation of a 4-stroke engine.

If you have not ridden the vehicle for any length of time and it refuses to start, check and clean the

TROUBLESHOOTING

spark plugs. If the plugs are not fouled, look to the fuel delivery system. This includes the fuel tank, fuel shutoff valve, fuel filter, fuel pump and fuel line. If you did not run the engine for more than a month with fuel in the carburetors, fuel deposits may have gummed up carburetor jets and air passages. Gasoline tends to lose its potency after standing for long periods, and as it evaporates the mixture becomes richer. Condensation may contaminate it with water. Drain the old gas and try starting with a fresh tankful.

STARTING THE ENGINE

If experiencing an engine starting problem, it is easy to work out of sequence and forget basic starting procedures. The following sections list factory recommended starting procedures for the VT1100C2 engine at the following ambient temperatures and engine conditions:

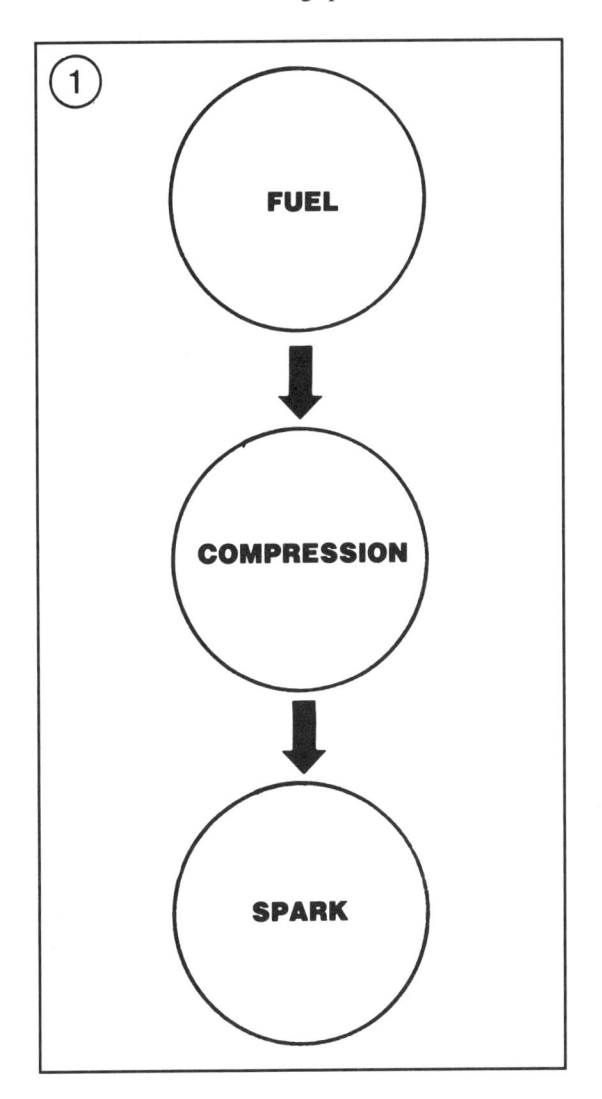

a. Cold engine with normal air temperature.
b. Cold engine with low air temperature.
c. Warm engine and/or high air temperature.
d. Flooded engine.

Starting Notes

1. A sidestand ignition cutoff system is used on all models. The position of the sidestand will affect engine starting. Note the following:

   a. The engine cannot start when the sidestand is down and the transmission is in gear.
   b. The engine can start when the sidestand is down and the transmission is in NEUTRAL. The engine will stop if the transmission is put in gear with the sidestand down.
   c. The engine can be started when the sidestand is up and the transmission is in NEUTRAL or in gear with the clutch lever pulled in.

2. Before starting the engine, shift the transmission into NEUTRAL and confirm that the engine stop switch is at RUN.

3. Turn the ignition switch to ON and confirm the following:

   a. The neutral indicator light is ON (when transmission is in NEUTRAL).
   b. The engine oil pressure warning light is ON.

4. The engine is now ready to start. Refer to the starting procedure in this section that best meets the air temperature and engine condition.

5. If the engine is idled at a fast idle speed for more than 5 minutes and/or the throttle is snapped on and off repeatedly at normal air temperature, the exhaust pipes may discolor.

6. Excessive choke use can cause an excessively rich fuel mixture. This condition can wash oil off of the piston and cylinder walls, causing piston and cylinder scuffing.

NOTE
Do not operate the starter motor for more than 5 seconds at a time. Wait approximately 10 seconds between starting attempts.

①
FUEL
↓
COMPRESSION
↓
SPARK

Starting Procedure

Cold engine with normal air temperature

Normal air temperature is considered to be between 50-90° F (10-35° C).
1. Perform the procedures under *Starting Notes*.
2. Turn the fuel valve (**Figure 2**) ON.
3. Install the ignition key and turn the ignition switch to ON.
4. Pull the choke lever (**Figure 3**) to the fully ON position.
5. Make sure the engine stop switch (A, **Figure 4**) is in the RUN position.
6. Depress the starter button (B, **Figure 4**) and start the engine. Do not open the throttle when pressing the starter button.

NOTE
If attempting to start a cold engine with the throttle open and the choke ON, a lean mixture will result and cause hard starting.

7. With the engine running, operate the choke lever as required to keep the engine idling at 1,500-2,500 rpm.
8. After approximately 30 seconds, push the choke lever (**Figure 3**) to the fully OFF position. If the engine is idling roughly, open the throttle lightly until the engine warms up.

Cold engine with low air temperature

Low air temperature is considered to be 50° F (10° C) or lower.
1. Perform the procedure under *Starting Notes*.
2. Turn the fuel valve (**Figure 2**) ON.
3. Turn the ignition switch to ON.
4. Pull the choke lever (**Figure 3**) to the fully ON position.
5. Make sure the engine stop switch (A, **Figure 4**) is in the RUN position.
6. Depress the starter button (B, **Figure 4**) and start the engine. Do not open the throttle when pressing the starter button.
7. Once the engine is running, open the throttle slightly to help warm the engine. Continue warming the engine until the choke can be turned to the fully OFF position and the engine responds to the throttle cleanly.

Warm engine and/or high air temperature

High air temperature is considered to be 95° F (35° C) or higher.
1. Perform the procedures under *Starting Notes*.
2. Turn the fuel valve (**Figure 2**) ON.
3. Install the ignition key and turn the ignition switch to ON.
4. Open the throttle slightly and depress the starter button (B, **Figure 4**). Do not use the choke.

Flooded engine

If the engine will not start after a few attempts it may be flooded. If you smell gasoline after attempting to start the engine, the engine is probably flooded. To start a flooded engine:
1. Turn the engine stop switch off (A, **Figure 4**).
2. Push the choke lever (**Figure 3**) to the OFF position.
3. Open the throttle completely and depress the starter button (B, **Figure 4**) for 5 seconds. Then release the starter button and close the throttle.
4. Wait 10 seconds, then continue with Step 5.

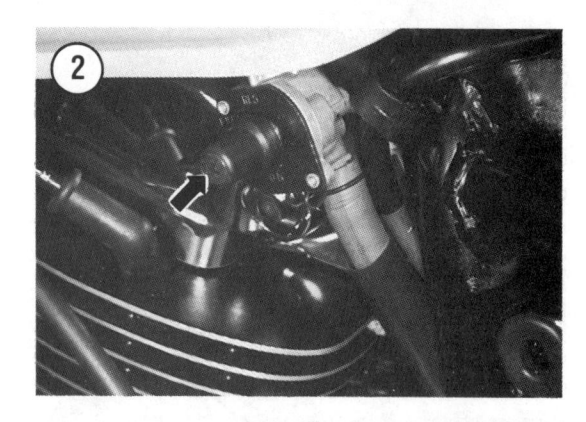

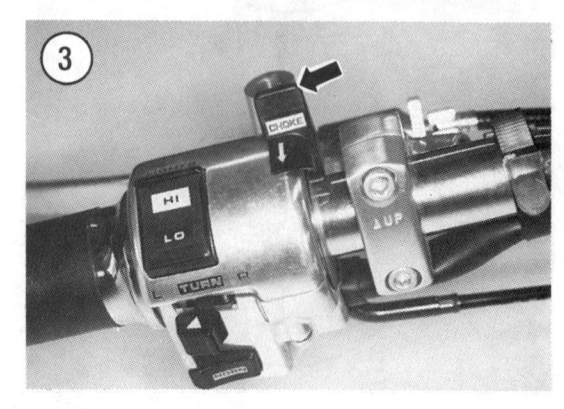

TROUBLESHOOTING

5. Turn the engine stop switch (A, **Figure 4**) on.
6. Turn the ignition switch on.
7. Open the throttle slightly and depress the starter button to start the engine. Do not use the choke.

STARTING DIFFICULTIES

If the engine cranks but is difficult to start, or will not start at all, it does not help to drain the battery. Check for obvious problems even before getting out your tools. Go down the following list step by step. Do each one while remembering the engine operating requirements described under *Operating Requirements* earlier in this chapter. If the engine still will not start, refer to the appropriate troubleshooting procedures which follow in this chapter.

1. Is the choke (**Figure 3**) in the right position? Open the choke for a cold engine and close it for a warm or hot engine.

WARNING
Do not use an open flame to check fuel in the tank. A serious explosion is certain to result.

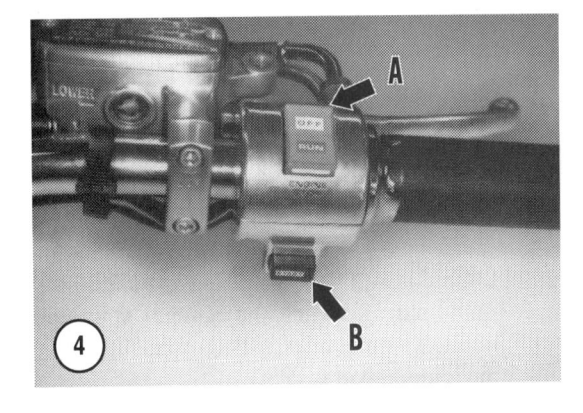

2. Is the fuel supply valve (**Figure 2**) in the ON position? Turn the valve to the ON position (or the RES position).
3. Make sure the engine stop switch (A, **Figure 4**) is not stuck or working improperly. Also make sure the stop switch wire is not shorted. If necessary, test the engine stop switch as described in Chapter Nine.
4. Are all 4 spark plug wires (**Figure 5**) on tight? Push the spark plug caps on each spark plug and slightly rotate them to clean the electrical connection between the plug and the connector.
5. Perform a spark test as described under *Engine Fails to Start (Spark Test)* in this chapter. If there is a strong spark, perform Step 6. If there is no spark or if the spark is very weak, test the ignition system as described in this chapter.
6. Check cylinder compression as follows:
   a. Turn the fuel valve (**Figure 2**) OFF.
   b. Remove each spark plug and ground them against the engine (**Figure 6**).

   CAUTION
   The ignition system can be permanently damaged if the spark plugs are not grounded when performing the following steps.

   c. Put your finger tightly over one of the spark plug holes.
   d. Operate the starter button. As the piston comes up on the compression stroke, rising pressure in the cylinder will force your finger off the spark plug hole. This shows that the cylinder compression is sufficient to start the engine.
   e. Repeat for the other cylinder.

   NOTE
   *You may still have a compression problem though it seems acceptable with the previous test. Check engine compression more accurately using a compression gauge as described under **Tune-up** in Chapter Three.*

Engine Fails to Start (Spark Test)

Perform the following spark test to determine if the ignition system is capable of producing sufficient spark.

CAUTION
Before removing the spark plug in Step 1, clean all dirt and debris away from the plug base. Dirt that falls into the cylinder will cause rapid piston, piston ring and cylinder wear.

1. Remove the spark plugs from each cylinder head as described in Chapter Three.

NOTE
A spark tester is a useful tool to check the ignition system. **Figure 7** *shows the Motion Pro Ignition System Tester (part No. 08-122). This tool is inserted in the spark plug cap and its base is set against the cylinder head for ground. The tester's air gap is adjustable and it allows you to see and hear the spark while testing the intensity of the spark. This tool is available through most motorcycle dealerships.*

2. Connect each spark plug wire and connector to a spark plug (or tester) and touch each spark plug base or tester to a good engine ground. Position the spark plugs so you can see the electrodes. Position the spark tester to you can see the terminals.

WARNING
Do not hold the spark plug, tester, wire or connector or a serious electrical shock may result.

3. Push the starter button to crank the engine. A fat blue spark must be evident across the spark plug electrodes or between the tester terminals. If the spark is good at each spark plug, continue with Step 4. If the spark is weak or if there is no spark at one or all plugs, perform Step 9.
5. Check engine compression as described in Chapter Three. If the engine compression is good, perform Steps 6-8. If the compression is low, perform a leak-down test as described in this chapter. Then check for one or more of the following conditions:
   a. Leaking cylinder head gasket(s).
   b. Cracked or warped cylinder head.
   c. Worn piston rings, pistons and cylinders.
   d. Valve stuck open.
   e. Worn or damaged valve seat(s).
   f. Incorrect valve timing.
6. Turn the fuel valve to the OFF position (**Figure 2**).
7. Disconnect the fuel hose from the fuel valve. Then connect a separate hose to the fuel valve and insert the open end into a clear container.
8. Turn the fuel valve to the ON, RES and OFF positions. A steady flow of fuel should be noticed with the fuel valve in the ON and RES positions. The fuel flow must stop with the fuel valve in the OFF position. If the fuel flow is good, perform Step 8. If there is no fuel flow or if the flow is slow and intermittent, check for one or more of the following conditions:
   a. Empty fuel tank.
   b. Plugged fuel tank cap vent hole.
   c. Clogged fuel filter or fuel line.
   d. Stuck or clogged carburetor fuel valve.
9. If the spark is weak or if there is no spark at one or both plugs, note the following:
   a. If there is no spark at all of the plugs, there may be a problem in the input side of the ignition system or ignition control module (ICM), ignition pulse generators, sidestand switch or neutral switch. Test these parts as described in Chapter Nine.
   b. If there is no spark at one spark plug, the spark plug is probably faulty or there is a problem with the spark plug wire or plug cap. Retest with a spark tester, or use a new spark plug. If there is still no spark at that one plug, make sure the spark plug cap is attached to its wire tightly.
   c. If there is still no spark at one cylinder (both spark plugs), switch the ignition coils and retest. If there is now spark (both spark plugs), the ignition coil is faulty.

TROUBLESHOOTING

Engine is Difficult to Start

Check for one or more of the following possible malfunctions:
a. Fouled spark plug(s).
b. Improperly adjusted choke.
c. Intake manifold air leak.
d. Contaminated fuel system.
e. Improperly adjusted carburetors.
f. Ignition system malfunction.
g. Weak ignition coil(s).
h. Poor compression.
i. Engine oil too heavy.

Engine Will Not Crank

Check for one or more of the following possible malfunctions:
a. Blown fuse.
b. Discharged battery.
c. Defective starter motor, starter solenoid or start switch.
d. Seized piston(s).
e. Seized crankshaft bearings.
f. Broken connecting rod.
g. Binding or locked transmission or clutch assembly.
h. Defective starter clutch.

ENGINE PERFORMANCE

In the following checklist, it is assumed that the engine runs, but is not operating at peak performance. This section will serve as a starting point from which to isolate a performance malfunction. Where ignition timing is mentioned as a problem, remember that there is no method of adjusting the ignition timing. If you check the ignition timing with a timing light as described in Chapter Three and it is incorrect, there is a faulty part (pulse generator or spark unit) within the ignition system. The individual parts must be checked and the faulty part(s) replaced.

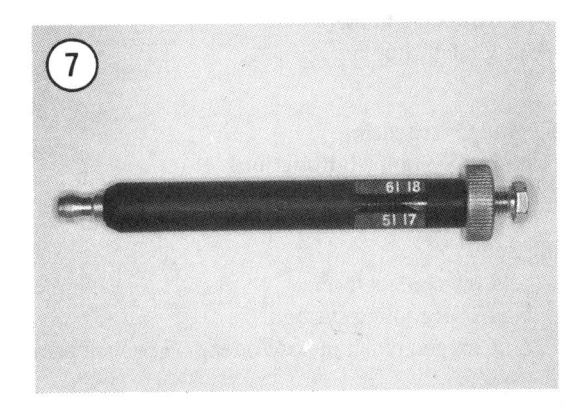

Engine Is Hard to Start

a. Obstructed fuel line, fuel shutoff valve or fuel filter.
b. Sticking float valve in carburetor(s).
c. Carburetors incorrectly adjusted.
d. Improper starter valve (choke) operation.
e. Improper throttle operation.
f. Fouled or improperly gapped spark plug(s).
g. Ignition timing incorrect.
h. Broken or shorted ignition coil(s).
i. Weak or faulty spark unit(s) or pulse generator(s).
j. Improper valve timing.
k. Clogged air filter element.
l. Contaminated fuel.
m. Engine flooded with fuel.

Engine Starts but Then Stops

a. Incorrect choke adjustment or operation.
b. Incorrect carburetor adjustment.
c. Incorrect ignition timing (caused by damaged ICM or ignition pulse generators).
d. Contaminated fuel.
e. Intake manifold air leak.

Engine Will Not Idle

a. Incorrect carburetor adjustment.
b. Fouled or improperly gapped spark plug(s).
c. Leaking head gasket(s) or vacuum leak.
d. Ignition timing incorrect (caused by damaged ICM or ignition pulse generators).
e. Incorrect valve timing.
f. Obstructed fuel line or fuel shutoff valve.
g. Low engine compression.
h. Starter valve (choke) stuck in the open position.
i. Incorrect pilot screw adjustment.
j. Clogged slow jet(s) in the carburetor(s).
k. Clogged air filter element.
l. Plugged tappet oil holes.
m. Damaged tappet.

Poor High-Speed Performance

1. Check ignition timing as described in Chapter Three. If ignition timing is correct, perform Step 2. If the timing is incorrect, test the following ignition system components as described in Chapter Nine:
    a. ICM unit.
    b. Pulse generators.
    c. Ignition coils.
2. Disconnect the fuel hose from the carburetor and insert the open end into a clear, glass container. Turn the fuel valve to ON, RES and OFF. A steady flow of fuel should be noticed with the fuel valve in the ON and RES positions. The fuel flow should stop with the fuel valve in the OFF position. If the fuel flow is good, perform Step 4. If there is no fuel flow or if the flow is slow or intermittent, check for one or more of the following conditions:
    a. Empty fuel tank.
    b. Plugged fuel tank cap vent hole.
    c. Clogged fuel filter or fuel line.
    d. Stuck or clogged carburetor fuel valve.
3. Check for a damaged fuel pump.
4. Remove the carburetors as described in Chapter Seven. Then remove the float bowls and check for contamination and plugged jets. If any contamination is found, disassemble and clean each carburetor. You should also pour out and discard the remaining fuel in the fuel tank and flush the fuel tank thoroughly. If no contamination is noted and the jets are not plugged, perform Step 6.
5. Incorrect valve timing and worn or damaged valve springs can cause poor high-speed performance. If the valve timing was set just prior to the bike experiencing this type of problem, the valve timing may be incorrect. If the valve timing was not set or changed, and you performed all of the other inspection procedures in this section without locating the problem area, the cylinder head should be removed and the valve train assembly inspected.
6. Check for plugged or damaged hydraulic tappets.

Low or Poor Engine Power

1. Support the bike with the rear wheel off the ground, then spin the rear wheel by hand. If the wheel spins freely, perform Step 2. If the wheel does not spin freely, check for the following conditions:
    a. Dragging rear brake.
    b. Excessive rear axle tightening torque.
    c. Worn or damaged rear wheel bearings.
    d. Final gear bearing damage.
    e. Damaged drive shaft assembly.
2. Check the clutch adjustment and operation. If the clutch slips, refer to *Clutch* in this chapter.
3. If Steps 1 and 2 do not locate the problem, test ride the bike and accelerate lightly. If the engine speed increases according to throttle position, perform Step 4. If the engine speed does not increase, check for one or more of the following problems:
    a. Clogged or damaged air filter.
    b. Restricted fuel flow.
    c. Clogged fuel tank cap vent.
    d. Incorrect choke adjustment or operation.
    e. Clogged or damaged muffler.
4. Check for one or more of the following problems:
    a. Low engine compression.
    b. Fouled spark plug(s).
    c. Clogged carburetor jet(s).
    d. Incorrect ignition timing (due to damaged ICM or ignition pulse generators).
    e. Plugged tappet oil holes.
    f. Incorrect oil level (too high or too low).
    g. Contaminated oil.
    h. Worn or damaged valve train assembly.
    i. Engine overheating.

Engine Overheating

   a. Incorrect coolant level.
   b. Incorrect carburetor adjustment or jet selection.
   c. Improper spark plug heat range.
   d. Cooling system malfunction (see below).
   e. Low oil level.
   f. Oil not circulating properly.
   g. Valves leaking.
   h. Heavy engine carbon deposits.
   i. Dragging brake(s).
   j. Clutch slipping.

Engine Overheating (Cooling System Malfunction)

Note the previous section, then check the following items:
   a. Low coolant level.
   b. Air in cooling system.
   c. Clogged radiator, hose or engine coolant passages.

TROUBLESHOOTING

d. Thermostat stuck closed.
e. Worn or damaged radiator cap.
f. Damaged water pump.
g. Damaged fan motor switch.
h. Damaged cooling fan.

Engine Runs Roughly

a. Clogged air filter element.
b. Carburetor adjustment incorrect—mixture too rich.
c. Incorrect starter valve (choke) adjustment.
d. Water or other contaminants in fuel.
e. Clogged fuel line.
f. Spark plugs fouled.
g. Ignition coil defective.
h. Loose or defective ignition circuit wire.
i. Short circuit from damaged wire insulation.
j. Loose battery cable connection(s).
k. Valve timing incorrect.

Engine Lacks Acceleration

a. Carburetor mixture too lean.
b. Clogged fuel line.
c. Incorrect ignition timing (due to damaged ICM or ignition pulse generators).
d. Dragging brake(s).
e. Slipping clutch.

Engine Backfires

a. Incorrect ignition timing (due to damaged ICM or ignition pulse generators).
b. Incorrect carburetor adjustment.

Engine Misfires During Acceleration

a. Incorrect ignition timing (damage or defective ICM or pulse generator).
b. Excessively worn or defective spark plug(s).
c. Damaged or defective spark plug wire(s).
d. Ignition system malfunction.
e. Incorrect carburetor adjustment.

ENGINE NOISES

Often the first evidence of an internal engine problem is a strange noise. That knocking, clicking or tapping sound which you never heard before may be warning you of impending trouble. While engine noises can indicate problems, they are difficult to interpret correctly; inexperienced mechanics can be seriously misled by them.

Professional mechanics often use a special stethoscope to isolate engine noise. You can do nearly as well with an ordinary piece of doweling or a section of small hose. By placing one end in contact with the area to which you want to listen and the other end to the front of your ear (not directly on your ear), you can hear sounds emanating from that area. The first time you do this, you may be confused at the strange sounds coming from even a normal engine. If you can, have an experienced friend or mechanic help you sort out the noises.

Consider the following when troubleshooting engine noises:

1. *Knocking or pinging during acceleration*—Caused by using a lower octane fuel than recommended. May also be caused by poor fuel. Pinging can also be caused by a spark plug of the wrong heat range or carbon buildup in the combustion chamber. Refer to *Correct Spark Plug Heat Range* and *Compression Test* in Chapter Three.

2. *Slapping or rattling noises at low speed or during acceleration*—May be caused by excessive piston-to-cylinder wall clearance (piston slap).

NOTE
Piston slap is easier to detect when the engine is cold and before the pistons have expanded. Once the engine has warmed up, piston expansion reduces piston-to-cylinder clearance.

3. *Knocking or rapping while decelerating*—Usually caused by excessive rod bearing clearance.

4. *Persistent knocking and vibration occurring every crankshaft rotation*—Usually caused by worn rod or main bearing(s). Can also be caused by broken piston rings or damaged piston pins.

5. *Rapid on-off squeal*—Compression leak around cylinder head gasket or spark plug(s).

6. *Valve train noise*—Check for the following:
   a. Clogged or damaged hydraulic tappet.
   b. Valve sticking in guide.
   c. Broken valve spring.
   d. Worn or damaged assist shaft and/or spring.
   e. Low oil pressure.
   f. Clogged cylinder oil hole or oil passage.

g. Excessively worn or damaged cam chain.

7. *Cylinder head noise (other than valve train noise)*—Check the following:
   a. Damaged cam chain tensioner.
   b. Excessively worn or damage cam chain.
   c. Excessively worn or damaged cam sprocket teeth.
   d. Damaged rocker arm follower or valve stem end.
   e. Damaged rocker arm and/or shaft.
   f. Excessively worn or damaged camshaft.

ENGINE LUBRICATION

An improperly operating engine lubrication system will quickly lead to engine seizure. Check the engine oil level before each ride and top off as described in Chapter Three. Oil pump service is described in Chapter Five.

Oil Consumption High or Engine Smokes Excessively

a. Worn valve guides.
b. Worn or damaged piston rings.

Engine Oil Leaks

a. Clogged air filter breather hose.
b. Loose engine parts.
c. Damaged gasket sealing surfaces.

Black Smoke

a. Clogged air filter.
b. Incorrect carburetor fuel level (too high).
c. Choke stuck ON.
d. Incorrect main jet (too large).

White Smoke

a. Worn valve guide.
b. Worn valve seal.
c. Worn piston oil ring.
d. Excessive cylinder and/or piston wear.

Oil Pressure Too High

a. Clogged oil filter.
b. Clogged oil gallery or metering orifices.
c. Pressure relief valve stuck closed.
d. Incorrect type engine oil being used.

Low Oil Pressure

a. Low oil level.
b. Damaged oil pump.
c. Clogged oil pump screen.
d. Clogged oil filter.
e. Internal oil leakage.
f. Pressure relief valve stuck open.
g. Incorrect type engine oil being used.

No Oil Pressure

a. Damaged oil pump.
b. Excessively low oil level.
c. Damaged oil pump drive chain and/or sprocket.
d. Damaged oil pump drive shaft.
e. Incorrect oil pump installation.

Oil Pressure Warning Light Stays On

a. Low oil pressure.
b. No oil pressure.
c. Damaged oil pressure switch.
d. Short circuit in warning light circuit.

Oil Level Too Low

a. Oil level not maintained at correct level.
b. Worn piston rings.
c. Worn cylinder.
d. Worn valve guides.
e. Worn valve stem seals.
f. Piston rings incorrectly installed.
g. External oil leakage.
h. Oil leaking into the cooling system.

Oil Contamination

a. Blown head gasket allowing coolant to leak into the engine.
b. Water contamination.
c. Oil and filter not changed at specified intervals.

TROUBLESHOOTING

HYDRAULIC TAPPETS

Noisy Tappet

1. If one or more tappets are noisy, check the oil level and bring to the correct level as required. Then ride the bike for five minutes with the engine speed over 3,000 rpm. Then stop and recheck the oil level. If the oil level is correct, check for a contaminated oil filter or contaminated oil.
2. Check the oil pressure as described in Chapter Six. Note the following:
   a. If the oil pressure reading is correct, continue with Step 3.
   b. If the oil pressure reading is incorrect, check for a clogged oil control orifice or a clogged engine oil passage.
3. Remove the cylinder head covers and oil hole caps and check the engine components for proper lubrication. Note the following:
   a. If it appears that the engine is being adequately lubricated, continue with Step 4.
   b. If the engine is not being adequately lubricated, check for a clogged oil pipe, a damaged O-ring or a damaged oil hole cap.
4. If you have not found the problem, remove the hydraulic tappets (Chapter Four) and check them for a sticking plunger, faulty one-way valve or other damage.

Engine Lacks Power

A clogged oiling system or damaged tappet(s) can cause hard starting and reduced engine performance. To isolate this problem, perform the following steps:
1. Try to start the engine with the starter. Note the following:
   a. If the engine does not start, continue with Step 2.
   b. If the engine starts, the engine oil may be foaming from engine over-rev.
2. Check the oil pressure as described in Chapter Six. Note the following:
   a. a. If the oil pressure reading is correct, continue with Step 3.
   b. If the oil pressure reading is incorrect, check for a low oil level. If the oil level is correct, check for a clogged oil control orifice, a clogged engine oil passage, contaminated oil or a contaminated oil filter.
3. Remove and inspect the tappets (Chapter Four).

ENGINE LEAKDOWN TEST

To pinpoint engine problems from compression leaks, you can perform an engine leakdown test. While a compression test (Chapter Three) can identify a weak cylinder, a leakdown test can determine where the leak is. Perform a cylinder leakdown test by applying compressed air through the spark plug hole (with the valves closed) using a leakage tester and then measuring the rate of leakage as a percent. Under pressure, air will leak past worn or damaged parts. You will need a cylinder leakage tester and air compressor to perform this test (**Figure 8**).

Follow the leakdown tester's manufacturer's directions along with the following information when performing a cylinder leakage test.

1. Start and run the engine until it is warm. Then turn the engine off.
2. Remove the air filter assembly. Open and secure the throttle in the wide-open position.
3. Set the front piston to TDC on its compression stroke.
4. Remove one of the front cylinder's spark plugs.
5. Install the cylinder leakage tester (**Figure 9**) into the front cylinder's spark plug. Connect a compressed-air hose to the tester fitting.
6. If the engine is not too hot, remove the radiator cap (**Figure 10**).

NOTE
To prevent the engine from turning as compressed air is applied to the cylinder, first shift the transmission into fifth gear and have an assistant apply the rear brake.

7. Apply compressed air to the leakage tester and make a cylinder leakage test following the manufacturer's instructions. Read the percent of leakage on the gauge. Note the following:
   a. For a new or rebuilt engine, a leakage rate of 2 to 4% per cylinder is desired.
   b. If you are testing a used engine, the critical rate is not the percent of leakage for each cylinder, but instead, the difference between the cylinders. On a used engine, a leakage rate of 10% or less between cylinders is satisfactory.
   c. A leakage rate exceeding 10% is considered excessive, and requires further inspection and possible engine repair.
8. After checking the percent of leakage, and with air pressure still applied to the combustion chamber,

listen for the sound of air escaping from the following areas:

a. Air leaking through the exhaust pipe indicates a leaking exhaust valve.

b. Air leaking through the carburetor indicates a leaking intake valve.

c. Air leaking through the crankcase breather tube suggests worn piston rings or a damaged cylinder.

d. Air bubbles in the radiator indicate a leaking cylinder head gasket or a cracked cylinder head or cylinder.

9. Remove the leakage tester and repeat these steps to test the rear cylinder.

CLUTCH

Common clutch problems and causes are listed in this section.

Excessive Clutch Lever Operation

If the clutch lever has become hard to pull in, check the following:

a. Dry and/or dirty clutch cable.

b. Kinked or damaged clutch cable.

c. Damaged clutch lifter mechanism.

d. Damaged clutch lifter plate bearing.

e. Improperly routed clutch cable.

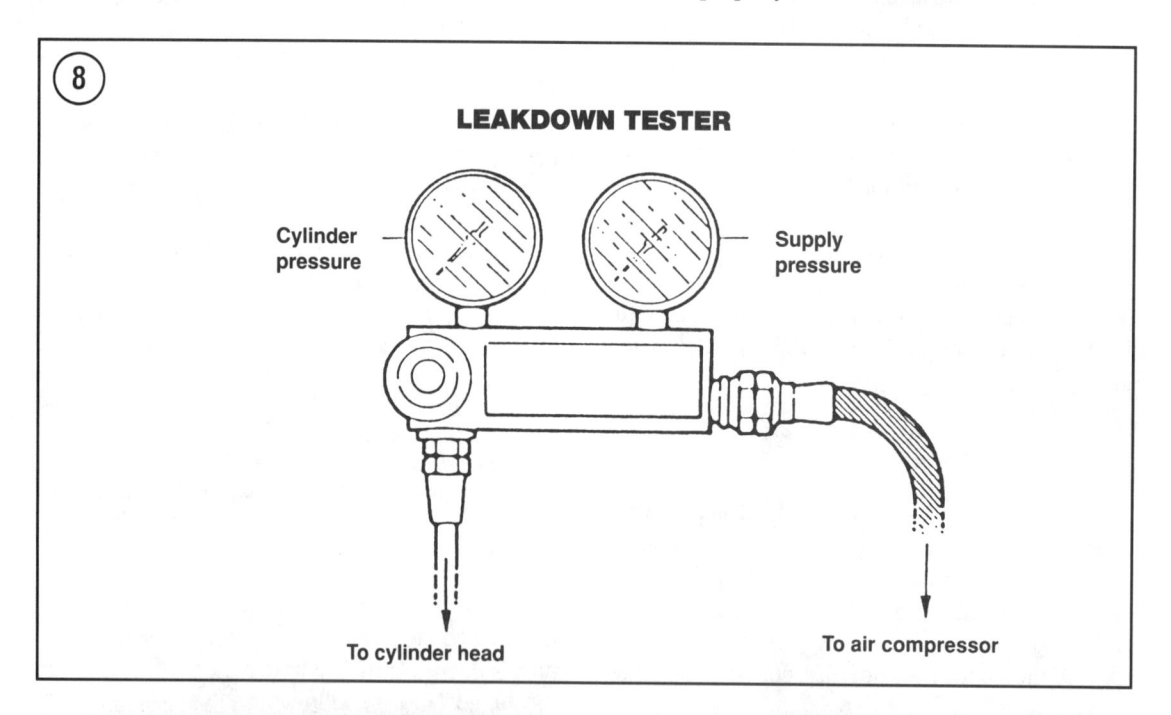

TROUBLESHOOTING

Rough Clutch Operation

This condition can be caused by excessively worn, grooved or damaged clutch housing slots.

Clutch Slippage

If the engine speed increases without a proportionate increase in motorcycle speed, the clutch is probably slipping. Some main causes of clutch slipping are:

a. Worn clutch plates.
b. Weak clutch springs.
c. No clutch lever free play.
d. Loose clutch lifter bolts.
e. Sticking or damaged clutch lifter assembly (**Figure 11**).
f. Engine oil additive being used (clutch plates contaminated).

Clutch Drag

If the clutch will not disengage or if the bike creeps with the transmission in gear and the clutch disengaged, the clutch is dragging. Some main causes of clutch drag are:

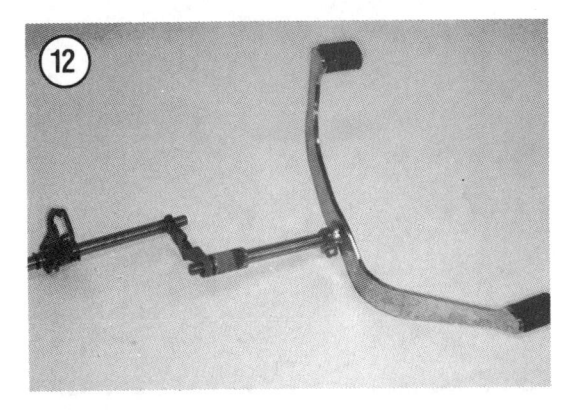

a. Excessive clutch lever free play.
b. Warped clutch plates.
c. Damaged clutch lifter assembly (**Figure 11**).
d. Loose clutch housing locknut.
e. Engine oil level too high.
f. Incorrect oil viscosity.
g. Engine oil additive being used.

GEARSHIFT LINKAGE

A 2-piece external gearshift linkage assembly is used. **Figure 12** shows the linkage assembly removed from the engine. The gearshift linkage assembly connects the gearshift pedal (external shift mechanism) to the shift drum (internal shift mechanism).

The external shift mechanism can be examined after removing the clutch assembly. The internal shift mechanism can be examined once the engine is removed from the frame and the crankcase disassembled. Common gearshift linkage problems are listed below.

Transmission Jumps out of Gear

a. Loose stopper arm bolt (**Figure 13**).
b. Damaged stopper arm.
c. Weak or damaged stopper arm spring.
d. Loose or damaged shift drum.
e. Bent shift fork shaft(s).
f. Bent or damaged shift fork(s).
g. Worn gear dogs or slots.
h. Damaged shift drum grooves.
i. Weak or damaged gearshift linkage springs.

Difficult Shifting

a. Incorrect clutch cable adjustment.
b. Incorrect oil viscosity.
c. Bent shift fork shaft(s).
d. Bent or damaged shift fork(s).
e. Worn gear dogs or slots.
f. Damaged shift drum grooves.
g. Weak or damaged gearshift linkage springs.
h. Incorrect gearshift linkage installation.

TRANSMISSION

Transmission symptoms are sometimes hard to distinguish from clutch symptoms. Common transmission problems are listed below. Refer to Chapter Seven for transmission service procedures. Prior to working on the transmission, make sure the clutch and gearshift linkage assembly are functioning properly.

Difficult Shifting

a. Incorrect clutch adjustment.
b. Incorrect clutch operation.
c. Bent shift fork(s).
d. Damaged shift fork guide pin(s).
d. Bent shift fork shaft(s).
e. Bent shift spindle.
f. Damaged shift drum grooves.

Jumps out of Gear

a. Loose or damaged shift drum stopper arm.
b. Bent or damaged shift fork(s).
c. Bent shift fork shaft(s).
d. Damaged shift drum grooves.
e. Worn gear dogs or slots.
f. Broken shift linkage return springs.

Incorrect Shift Lever Operation

a. Bent shift lever.
b. Stripped shift lever splines.
c. Damaged shift lever linkage.

Excessive Gear Noise

a. Worn bearings.
b. Worn or damaged gears.
c. Excessive gear backlash.

Excessive Output Gear Noise

The output gear assembly (**Figure 14**) is mounted on the left-side crankcase. The output gear (**Figure 15**) is mounted inside the engine.

a. Excessive output drive and driven gear backlash.
b. Excessively worn or damaged gear case bearings.
c. Excessively worn or damaged output drive and driven gears.
d. Incorrect shim adjustment (after final gear case reassembly).

ELECTRICAL TROUBLESHOOTING

This section describes the basics of electrical troubleshooting, how to use test equipment and the basic test procedures using the various test equipment.

Electrical troubleshooting can be very time-consuming and frustrating without proper knowledge and a suitable plan. Refer to the wiring diagrams at the end of the book and at the individual system diagrams included with the charging system, ignition system and starting system sections in this chapter. Wiring diagrams will help you determine how the circuit should work by tracing the current paths from the power source through the circuit components to ground. Also check any circuits that share the same fuse, ground or switch. If the other circuits work properly, the shared wiring is good. The cause

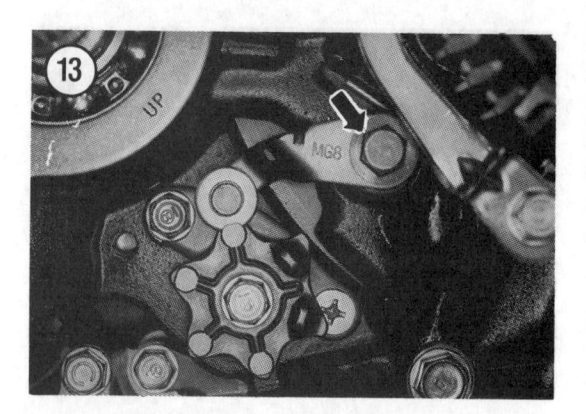

TROUBLESHOOTING

must be in the wiring used only by the suspect circuit. If all related circuits are faulty at the same time the probable cause is a poor ground connection or a blown fuse(s).

As with all troubleshooting procedures, analyze typical symptoms in a systematic procedure. Never assume anything and do not overlook the obvious like a blown fuse or an electrical connector that has separated. Test the simplest and most obvious cause first and try to make tests at easily accessible points on the bike.

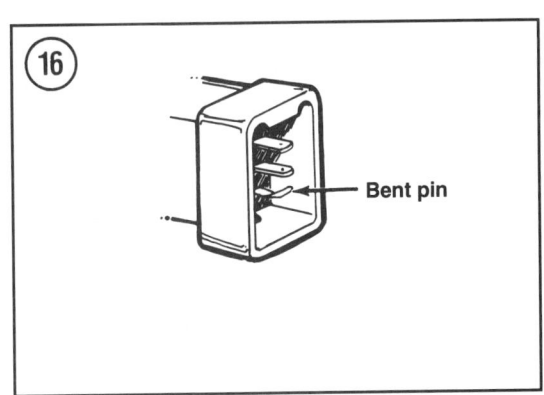

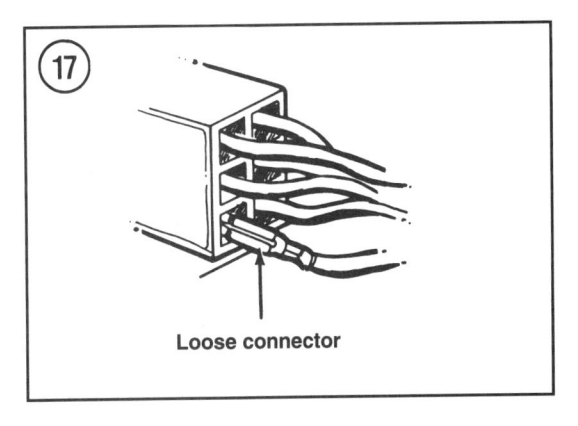

Preliminary Checks and Precautions

Prior to starting any electrical troubleshooting procedure perform the following:

a. Check the main fuse (Chapter Nine). If the fuse is blown, replace it.
b. Check the individual fuses mounted in the fuse box (Chapter Nine). Remove the suspected fuse and replace if blown.
c. Inspect the battery. Make sure it is fully charged, and that the battery leads are clean and securely attached to the battery terminals. Refer to *Battery* in Chapter Three.
d. Disconnect each electrical connector in the suspect circuit and check that there are no bent metal pins on the male side of the electrical connector (**Figure 16**). A bent pin will not connect to its mating receptacle in the female end of the connector, causing an open circuit.
e. Check each female end of the connector. Make sure that the metal connector on the end of each wire (**Figure 17**) is pushed all the way into the plastic connector. If not, carefully push them in with a narrow-blade screwdriver.
f. Check all electrical wires where they enter the individual metal connector in both the male and female plastic connector.
g. Make sure all terminals within the connector are clean and free of corrosion. Clean, if necessary, and pack the connectors with a dielectric grease.
h. After all is checked out, push the connectors together and make sure they are fully engaged and locked together (**Figure 18**).
i. Never pull on the electrical wires when disconnecting an electrical connector—pull only on the connector housing.
j. Never use a self-powered test light on circuits that contain solid-state devices. The solid-state devices may be damaged.

TEST EQUIPMENT

Test Light or Voltmeter

A test light can be purchased inexpensively or constructed of a 12-volt light bulb with a pair of test leads carefully soldered to the bulb. To check for battery voltage (12 volts) in a circuit, attach one lead to ground and the other lead to various points along the circuit. Where battery voltage is present the light bulb will light.

A voltmeter is used in the same manner as the test light to find out if battery voltage is present in any given circuit. The voltmeter will also indicate how much voltage is present at each test point. When using a voltmeter, attach the red lead (+) to the component or wire to be checked and the negative (–) lead to a good ground.

Self-powered Test Light and Ohmmeter

A self-powered test light can be purchased inexpensively or constructed of a 12-volt light bulb, a pair of test leads and a 12-volt battery. When the test leads are touched together the light bulb will illuminate.

Use a self-powered test light as follows:
a. Touch the test leads together to make sure the light bulb goes on. If not, correct the problem prior to using it in a test procedure.
b. Disconnect the bike's battery or remove the fuse(s) that protects the circuit to be tested.
c. Select 2 points within the circuit where there should be continuity.
d. Attach one lead of the self-powered test light to each point.
e. If there is continuity, the self-powered test light bulb will come on.
f. If there is no continuity, the self-powered test light bulb will not come on indicating an open circuit.

An ohmmeter can be used in place of the self-powered test light. The ohmmeter will also indicate how much resistance is present between each test point. Low resistance means good continuity in a complete circuit. Before using an ohmmeter (except a digital meter), it must first be calibrated. This is done by touching the leads together and turning the ohms calibration knob until the meter reads zero.

CAUTION
Never connect an ohmmeter to a circuit which has power applied to it. Always disconnect the battery negative lead before using the ohmmeter.

Jumper Wire

When using a jumper wire always install an inline fuse/fuse holder (available at most auto supply stores or electronic supply stores) to the jumper wire. Never use a jumper wire across any load (a component that is connected and turned on). This would result in a direct short and will blow the fuse(s).

BASIC TEST PROCEDURES

Voltage Testing

Unless otherwise specified, perform all voltage tests with the electrical connector still connected. Insert the test leads into the backside of the connector and make sure the test lead touches the electrical wire or metal connector within the connector. If the test lead only touches the wire insulation you will get a false reading.

Always check both sides of the connector as one side may be loose or corroded, thus preventing electrical flow through the connector. This type of test can be performed with a test light or a voltmeter. A voltmeter will give the best results.

NOTE
If using a test light, it does not make any difference which test lead is attached to ground.

1. Attach the negative test lead (if using a voltmeter) to a good ground (bare metal). If necessary, scrape away paint from the frame or engine (retouch later with paint). Make sure the part used for ground is not insulated with a rubber gasket or rubber grommet.
2. Attach the positive test lead (if using a voltmeter) to the point (electrical connector, terminal or wire) you want to check.
3. Turn the ignition switch on. If using a test light, the test light will come on if voltage is present. If using a voltmeter, note the voltage reading. The reading should generally be less than 1 volt of battery voltage (12 volts). If the voltage is 11 volts or

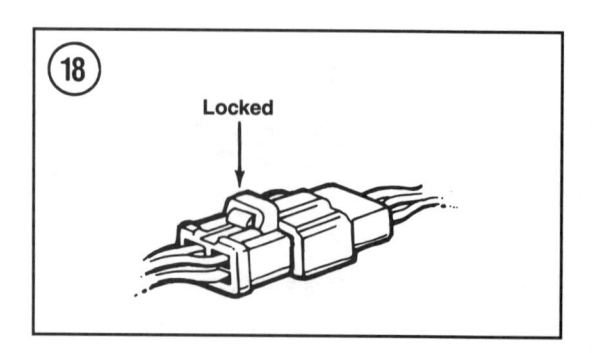

Locked

TROUBLESHOOTING

less, there may be an excessive voltage drop in the circuit.

Voltage Drop Test

A voltage drop of 1 volt or more means there is excessive resistance in the circuit. All components within the circuit are designed for low resistance in order to conduct electricity within a minimum loss of voltage.
1. Connect the voltmeter positive test lead to the end of the wire or switch closest to the battery.
2. Connect the voltmeter negative test lead to the other end of the wire or switch.
3. Turn the components on in the circuit.
4. The voltmeter should indicate 0 volts. If there is a drop of 1 volt or more, there is a problem within the circuit.
5. Check the circuit for loose or dirty connections within an electrical connector(s).

Continuity Test

A continuity test is made to determine if the circuit is complete with no opens in either the electrical wires or components.

Unless otherwise specified, perform all continuity tests with the electrical connector still connected. Insert the test leads into the backside of the connector and make sure the test lead touches the electrical wire or metal connector within the connector. If the test lead only touches the wire insulation you will get a false reading.

Always check both sides of the connectors as one side may be loose or corroded thus preventing electrical flow through the connector. This type of test can be performed with a self-powered test light or an ohmmeter. An ohmmeter will give the best results. If using an analog ohmmeter, calibrate the meter by touching the leads together and turning the ohms calibration knob until the meter reads zero.
1. Disconnect the battery negative lead.
2. Attach one test lead (test light or ohmmeter) to one end of the circuit to be tested.
3. Attach the other test lead to the other end of the circuit.
4. The self-powered test light will come on if there is continuity. The ohmmeter will indicate either a low or no resistance (means good continuity in a complete circuit) or infinite resistance (means an open circuit).

Testing for a Short Circuit with a Self-powered Test Light or Ohmmeter

Perform this test with either a self-powered test light or an ohmmeter.
1. Disconnect the battery negative lead.
2. Remove the blown fuse from the fuse panel.
3. Connect one test lead of the test light or ohmmeter to the load side (battery side) of the fuse terminal in the fuse panel.
4. Connect the other test lead to a good ground (bare metal). If necessary, scrape away paint from the frame or engine (retouch later with paint). Make sure the part used for a ground is not insulated with a rubber gasket or rubber grommet.
5. With the self-powered test light or ohmmeter attached to the fuse terminal and ground, wiggle the wiring harness relating to the suspect circuit at 6 in. (15.2 cm) intervals. Start next to the fuse panel and work your way away from the fuse panel. Watch the self-powered test light or ohmmeter as you progress along the harness.
6. If the test light blinks or the needle on the ohmmeter moves, there is a short-to-ground at that point in the harness.

Testing For a Short with a Test Light or Voltmeter

Perform this test using a 12-volt test lamp or a voltmeter.
1. Remove the blown fuse from the fuse panel.
2. Connect the test lamp or voltmeter across the fuse terminals in the fuse pane. Turn the ignition switch ON and note the voltmeter or test lamp. If the test lamp lights or the voltmeter indicates battery voltage, a short to ground is present in the respective circuit. If no voltage is present across the fuse terminals, a short circuit is not currently occuring. The short circuit could, however, be intermittent.
3. While watching the test lamp or voltmeter, wiggle the wiring harness related to the suspect circuit at 6 in. (15.2 cm) intervals, until the short circuit is located.

ELECTRICAL PROBLEMS

If bulbs burn out frequently, the cause may be excessive vibration, loose connections that permit sudden current surges or the installation of the wrong type of bulb. Most light and ignition problems are caused by loose or corroded ground connections. Check these prior to replacing a bulb or electrical component.

CHARGING SYSTEM

The charging system consists of the battery, alternator and a voltage regulator/rectifier (**Figure 19**). A 30 amp main fuse protects the circuit.

Alternating current generated by the alternator is rectified to direct current. The voltage regulator maintains the voltage to the battery and additional electrical loads at a constant voltage regardless of variations in engine speed and load.

The most common charging system complaints are:
 a. Battery discharging.
 b. Battery overcharging.

Battery Discharging

Before testing the charging system, the battery must be in good condition and fully charged. If necessary, inspect and charge the battery as described in Chapter Three.

1. Check all of the connections. Make sure they are tight and free of corrosion.
2. Perform the *Current Leakage Test* as described in Chapter Nine.
   a. If the current leakage exceeds 1 mA, perform Step 3.
   b. If the current leakage is 1 mA or less, perform Step 4.
3. Perform the *Regulator/Rectifier Unit Resistance Test* as described in Chapter Nine.
   a. If the resistance readings are within specification, perform the *Regulator/Rectifier Wiring Harness Test* as described in Chapter Nine. If the wiring harness is in good condition, the ignition switch is probably faulty; test the ignition switch as described in Chapter Nine.
   b. If the resistance readings are not as specified, the regulator/rectifier unit is probably faulty. Replace the regulator/rectifier unit and retest.
4. Perform the *Regulated Voltage Test* in Chapter Nine.
   a. If the voltage reading is between 13.9-14.9 volts, the battery is damaged. Install a new battery.
   b. If the voltage reading is more than 14.9 volts, test the voltage regulator/rectifier resistance as described in Chapter Nine (see Step 3).
   c. If the voltage reading is less than 14.0 volts, perform Step 5.
5. Perform the battery charging line and ground line tests as described under *Regulator/Rectifier Wiring Harness Test* in Chapter Nine. Note the following:
   a. If the test readings are correct, perform Step 6.
   b. If the test readings are incorrect, check for an open circuit in the wiring harness and for dirty or loose-fitting terminals. If these items are in acceptable condition, check for a damaged fuse.
6. Perform the charging coil line tests as described under *Regulator/Rectifier Wiring Harness Test* in Chapter Nine.

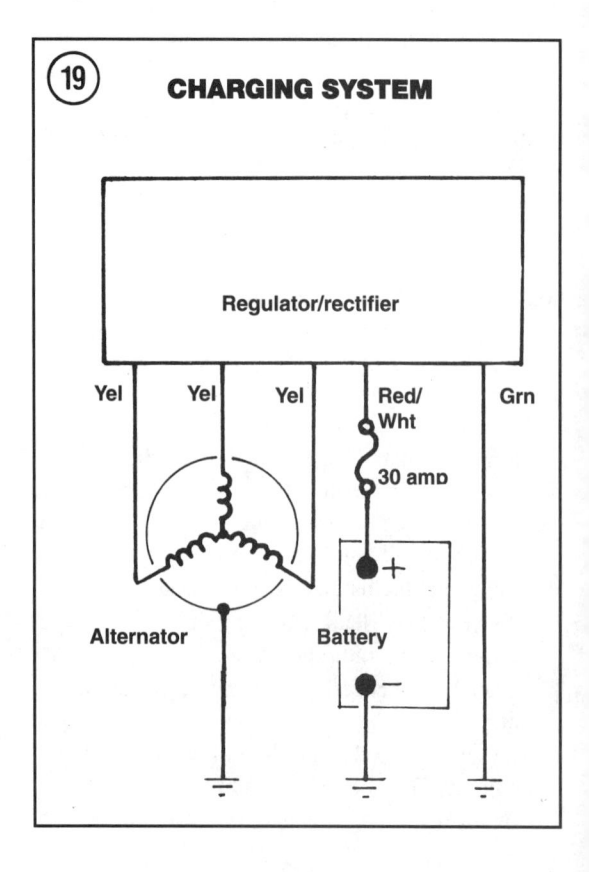

19 CHARGING SYSTEM

TROUBLESHOOTING

a. If the test readings are incorrect, perform Step 7.
b. If the test readings are correct, perform Step 8.

7. Perform the *Charging Coil Resistance Test* as described in Chapter Nine.
   a. If the charging coil resistance is within specification, check for a dirty or loose-fitting alternator electrical connector. If these items are in acceptable condition, perform Step 8.
   b. If the charging coil resistance is not as specified, replace the alternator assembly as described in Chapter Nine.

8. Perform the *Regulator/Rectifier Unit Resistance Test* as described in Chapter Nine. Note the following:
   a. If the resistance readings are within specification, the battery is faulty. Replace the battery and retest.
   b. If the resistance readings are not within specification, replace the regulator/rectifier unit and retest.

Battery Overcharging

If the battery is overcharging, the regulator/rectifier unit (**Figure 20**) is faulty. Replace the regulator/rectifier unit as described in Chapter Nine.

IGNITION SYSTEM TROUBLESHOOTING

Figure 21 shows the ignition system components and a schematic of the ignition system.

The most common ignition system complaints are:
a. No spark at all 4 spark plugs (2 per cylinder).
b. No spark at one cylinder only.

c. Engine starts and runs but sidestand switch does not operate.

Prior to troubleshooting the ignition system, perform the following:

1. Check the battery to make sure it is fully charged and in good condition. A weak battery will result in slow engine cranking speed.
2. Perform the spark test as described under *Engine Fails to Start (Spark Test)* in this chapter. Then refer to the appropriate ignition system complaint.
3. Because a loose or dirty electrical connector can prevent the ignition system from operating properly, check for dirty or loose-fitting connector terminals. The ignition system electrical diagram in **Figure 21** and the wiring diagram at the end of this book can be used to locate the appropriate electrical connectors. Also, refer to *Preliminary Checks and Precautions* under *Electrical Troubleshooting* in this chapter for additional information.

No Spark at All Spark Plugs

This section describes ignition system troubleshooting based on the results of the *Ignition Coil Primary Voltage Test* described in Chapter Nine. To make this test, you need the Honda peak voltage adapter (part No. 07HGJ-0020100) and a digital multimeter (impedance 10M ohms/DCV minimum). If you do not have these tools, refer testing to a Honda dealership.

1. Check for dirty or loose-fitting connector terminals as previously described. Clean and repair as required.

NOTE
If the ignition system does not operate properly after inspecting and cleaning the connector terminals, proceed with Step 2.

2. Perform the *Ignition Coil Primary Voltage Test* in Chapter Nine. After recording the test results, note the following before continuing with the diagnosis:
   a. If there is no initial voltage with the ignition and engine stop switch ON, go to Step 3.
   b. If the initial voltage is normal, but then drops to 2-4 volts while cranking the engine, go to Step 4.
   c. If the initial voltage reading is normal, but there is no peak voltage while the engine is cranked, go to Step 5.

CHAPTER TWO

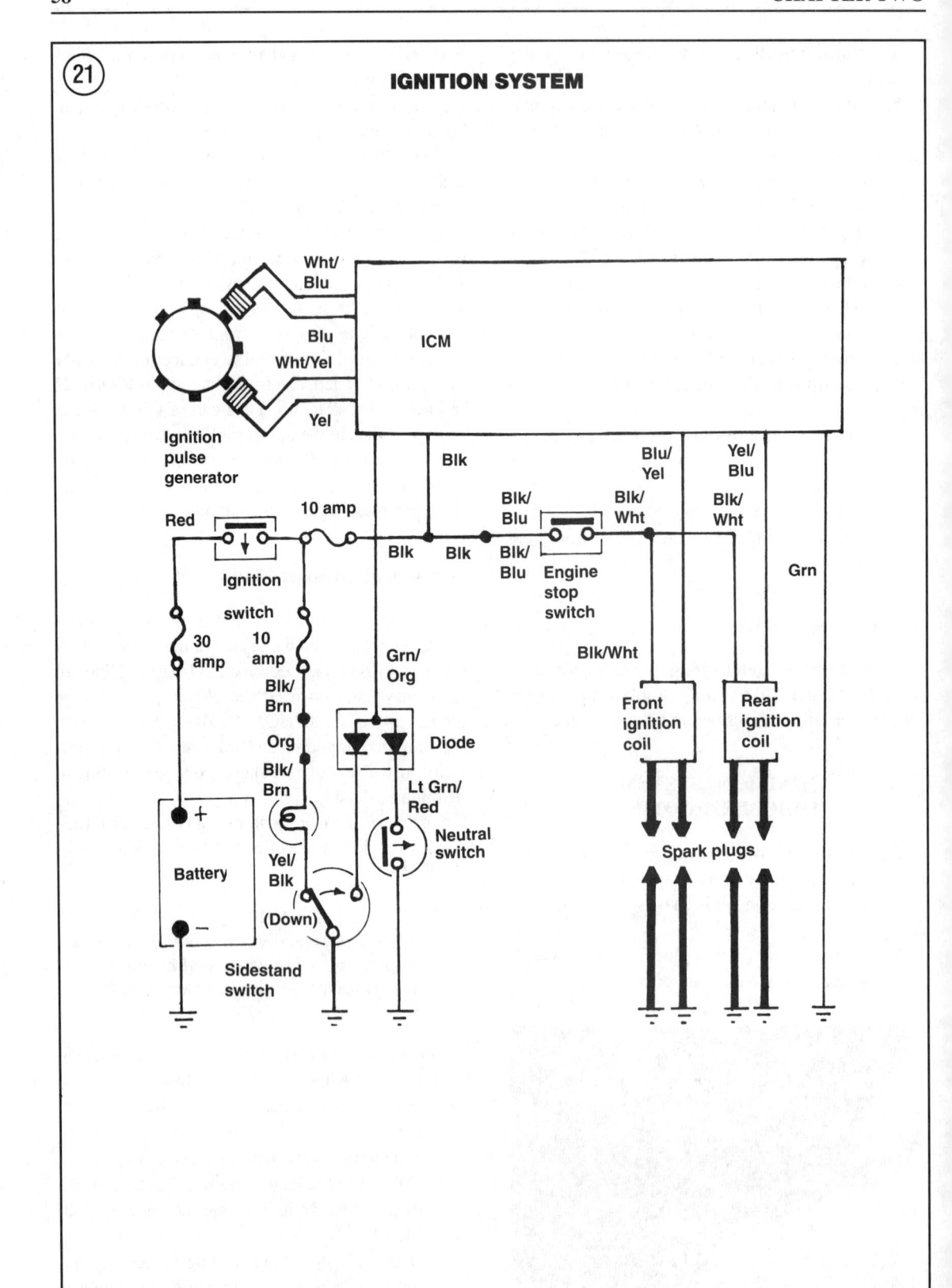

㉑ IGNITION SYSTEM

TROUBLESHOOTING

    d. If the initial and peak voltage readings are acceptable, but there is no spark, go to Step 6.

NOTE
For a description and location of the electrical components called out in the following steps, refer to the appropriate section in Chapter Nine and the wiring diagram for your model at the end of this book.

3. If there is no initial voltage with the ignition and engine stop switch ON, check for one or more of the following conditions in the order given:
    a. Incorrect peak voltage adapter connections.
    b. Battery undercharged.
    c. Loose ICM connection.
    d. No voltage between the black (+) and ground (−) side of the ignition control module (ICM) connector (**Figure 21**). Check for voltage with a voltmeter.
    e. A loose or damaged ICM ground wire (green).
    f. Loose connection or open circuit between the ICM and ignition coil(s) yellow/blue and/or blue/yellow wires.
    g. Short circuit in the ignition coil (primary side).
    h. Damaged sidestand switch.
    i. Damaged neutral switch.
    j. Loose connection or open circuit between the sidestand switch green/white and green wires.
    k. Loose connection or open circuit between the neutral switch light green and light green/red wires.
    l. If you cannot find a problem with one of the above listed items, the ICM is probably faulty.
4. If the initial voltage is normal, but then drops to 2-4 volts while cranking the engine, check for one or more of the following conditions in the order given:
    a. Incorrect peak voltage adapter connections.
    b. Damaged peak voltage adapter.
5. If the initial voltage reading is normal, but there is no peak voltage while the engine is cranked, check for one or more of the following conditions in the order given:
    a. The impedance of your digital multimeter is below 10 M ohms/DCV.
    b. The battery charge is low, causing a slow engine cranking speed.
    c. The multimeter and peak voltage adapter components are not working properly.

    d. If you cannot find a problem with one of the above listed items, the ICM is probably faulty.
6. If the initial and peak voltage readings are normal, but there is no spark, check for one or more of the following conditions in the order given:
    a. Damaged spark plug.
    b. Damaged spark plug wire or cap.
    c. Damaged ignition coils.

NOTE
If you could not find the spark problem after performing Steps 2-6, continue with Step 7.

7. Perform the *Ignition Pulse Generator Peak Voltage Test* in Chapter Nine. After recording the test results, note the following before continuing with the diagnosis:
    a. If the peak voltage reading is lower than the standard value (100 volts minimum), go to Step 8.
    b. If there is no peak voltage reading, go to Step 9.
8. If the peak voltage reading is lower than the standard value (100 volts minimum), check for one or more of the following conditions in the order given:
    a. The impedance of your digital multimeter is below 10 M ohms/DCV.
    b. The battery charge is low, causing a slow engine cranking speed.
    c. The multimeter and peak voltage adapter components are not working properly.
    d. If you cannot find a problem with one of the above listed items, the ICM is probably faulty.
9. If there is no peak voltage reading, check for one or more of the following conditions in the order given:
    a. The peak voltage adapter connection was incorrect.
    b. The peak voltage adapter is damaged.
    c. The ignition pulse generator is damaged.

No Spark at One Cylinder Only

If the spark test shows that there is spark at one cylinder only, switch the ignition coils and repeat the spark test. If the bad cylinder now sparks, its original ignition coil is damaged and must be replaced.

CHAPTER TWO

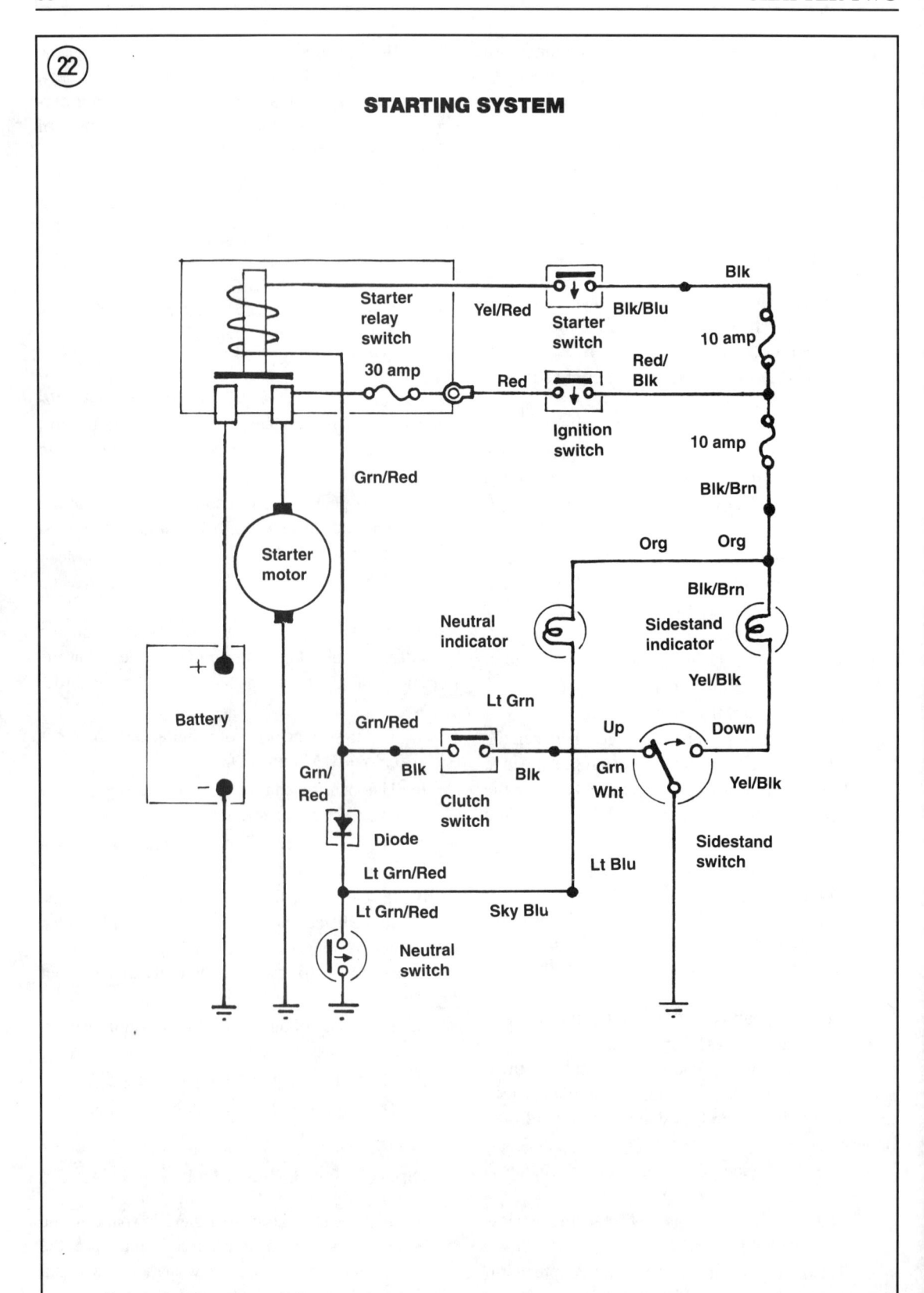

STARTING SYSTEM

TROUBLESHOOTING

Engine Starts and Runs but Sidestand Switch Does Not Operate

If the engine is running and the transmission is in NEUTRAL, it should continue to run when the sidestand is moved down. If the engine is running and the transmission is in gear, the engine should stop when the sidestand is moved down. If the engine does not run as described, test the sidestand switch as described in Chapter Nine.

STARTER SYSTEM TROUBLESHOOTING

The starter system consists of the starter motor, starter gears, solenoid, starter button, ignition switch, clutch switch, neutral switch, main and auxiliary fuses and battery. See **Figure 22**.

When the starter button is pressed, it allows current flow through the solenoid coil. The coil contacts close, allowing electricity to flow from the battery to the starter motor.

CAUTION
Do not operate the starter for more than 5 seconds at a time. Let it rest approximately 10 seconds, then use it again.

The starter should turn when the starter button is depressed when the transmission is in neutral and the clutch disengaged. If the starter does not operate properly, perform the following test procedures. Starter troubleshooting is grouped under the following conditions:

a. Starter motor does not turn.
b. Starter motor turns slowly.
c. Starter motor turns but the engine does not.
d. Starter relay switch clicks, but the engine does not turn.

Before going to one of the troubleshooting procedures, perform the following:

1. Check the battery to make sure it is fully charged and in good condition. Refer to Chapter Three for battery service.
2. Check the starter cables for loose or damaged connections.
3. Check the battery cables for loose or damaged connections. Then check the battery state of charge as described under *Battery Testing* in Chapter Three.
4. If the starter does not operate correctly after making these checks and adjustments, perform the test procedure that best describes the starting malfunction.

Starter Motor Does Not Turn

1. Check for a blown or damaged sub-fuse (Chapter Nine). If the fuses are good, continue with Step 2.
2. Check the starter motor cable for an open circuit or dirty or loose-fitting terminals.
3. Check the starter relay 4-pin connector (**Figure 23**) for dirty or loose-fitting terminals. Clean and repair as required.
4. Check the starter relay switch (**Figure 23**) as follows. Turn the ignition switch on and depress the starter switch button. When the starter button is depressed, the starter relay switch should click once. Note the following:
   a. If the relay clicks, continue with Step 4.
   b. If the relay does not click, go to Step 5.

CAUTION
Because of the large amount of current that will flow from the battery to the starter in Step 5, use a large diameter cable when making the connection.

5. Remove the starter from the motorcycle as described in Chapter Nine. Using an auxiliary battery, apply battery voltage directly to the starter. The starter should turn when battery voltage is directly applied. Note the following:
   a. If the starter motor does not turn, disassemble and inspect the starter motor as described in Chapter Nine. Test the starter components and replace worn or damaged parts as required.
   b. If the starter motor turns, check for loose or damaged starter motor cables. If the cables are good, check the starter relay switch as de-

scribed in Chapter Nine. Replace the starter relay switch if necessary.

6. Check the starter relay switch (**Figure 23**) ground line as described in Chapter Nine. Note the following:
   a. If there is continuity, continue with Step 7.
   b. If there is no continuity reading (high resistance), check for a loose or damaged connector or an open circuit in the wiring harness. If these items are okay, test the following items as described in Chapter Nine: neutral switch, clutch switch diode, clutch switch, and sidestand switch.
   c. Reconnect the starter relay switch electrical connector (**Figure 23**).

7. Check the starter relay (**Figure 23**) voltage as described in Chapter Nine. Note the following:
   a. If battery voltage (12 volts) is shown, continue with Step 8.
   b. If there is no battery voltage reading, check for a blown main or sub-fuse (Chapter Nine). If the fuses are okay, check for an open circuit in the wiring harness or for dirty or loose-fitting terminals. If the wiring and connectors are okay, check for a faulty ignition and/or starter switch (Chapter Nine).

8. Perform the starter relay switch (**Figure 23**) operational check as described in Chapter Nine. Note the following:
   a. If the starter relay switch is normal, check for dirty or loose-fitting terminals in its connector block.
   b. If the starter relay switch is faulty, replace it and retest.

Starter Motor Turns Slowly

If the starter motor turns slowly and all engine components and systems are normal, perform the following:
1. Test the battery as described in Chapter Three.
2. Check for the following:
   a. Loose or corroded battery terminals.
   b. Loose or corroded battery ground cable.
   c. Loose starter motor cable.
3. Remove, disassemble and bench test the starter as described in Chapter Nine.
4. Check the starter for binding during operation. Disassemble the starter and check the armature shaft for bending or damage. Also check the starter clutch as described in Chapter Five.

Starter Motor Turns but the Engine Does Not

If the starter motor turns but the engine does not, perform the following:
1. If the starter motor is running backward and the starter was just reassembled or if the starter motor cables were disconnected and then reconnected to the starter:
   a. The starter motor is reassembled incorrectly.
   b. The starter motor cables are incorrectly installed.
2. Check for a damaged starter clutch (Chapter Five).
3. Check for a damaged or faulty starter pinion gear (Chapter Five).
4. Check for damaged starter reduction gears (Chapter Five).

Starter Relay Switch Clicks but Engine Does Not Turn

1. Excessive reduction gear friction.
2. Crankshaft cannot turn because of mechanical failure.

Starter Motor Operates with the Transmission in Neutral but Does Not Turn with the Transmission in Gear with the Clutch Lever Pulled in and the Sidestand Up

1. Turn the ignition switch on and move the sidestand up and down while watching the sidestand switch indicator light.
   a. If the indicator light works properly, perform Step 2.
   b. If the indicator light does not work, check for a blown bulb, damaged sidestand switch (Chapter Nine) or an open circuit in the wiring harness.
2. Test the clutch switch as described in Chapter Nine.
   a. Clutch switch good, perform Step 3.
   b. Clutch switch faulty, replace switch and retest.
3. Test the sidestand switch as described in Chapter Nine.
   a. Sidestand switch good, perform Step 4.

TROUBLESHOOTING

b. Sidestand switch faulty, replace switch and retest.
4. Check for an open circuit in the wiring harness. Check for loose or damaged electrical connector.

WARNING
Before riding the bike, make sure the sidestand switch and its indicator light work properly. Riding your bike with the sidestand down can cause you to crash.

CARBURETOR TROUBLESHOOTING

The following lists isolate common carburetor problems under specific complaints.

Engine Will Not Start

If the engine will not start and you have determined that the electrical and mechanical systems are operating correctly, check the following:
1. If there is no fuel delivery to the carburetors, inspect the fuel system for:
   a. Clogged fuel tank breather tube.
   b. Clogged fuel line.
   c. Clogged fuel valve screen.
   d. Incorrect float adjustment.
   e. Stuck or clogged fuel valve in carburetor.
2. If the engine is flooded (too much fuel), inspect the fuel system for:
   a. Flooded carburetors. Fuel valve in carburetor stuck open.
   b. Clogged air filter element.
3. A faulty emission control system (if equipped) can cause fuel problems. Inspect the fuel system for:
   a. Faulty purge control valve (PCV).
   b. Faulty air vent control valve (AVCV).
   c. Loose, disconnected or plugged emission control system hoses.
4. If you have not located the problem in Steps 1-3, check for the following:
   a. Contaminated or deteriorated fuel.
   b. Intake manifold air leak.
   c. Clogged pilot or choke circuit.

Engine Starts but Idles and Runs Poorly or Stalls Frequently

An engine that idles roughly or stalls may have one or more of the following problems:

a. Partially plugged fuel line.
b. Incorrect fuel level adjustment.
c. Incorrect idle speed adjustment.
d. Incorrect pilot screw adjustment.
e. Intake manifold air leak.
f. Incorrect fuel mixture.
g. Contaminated or old fuel.
h. Plugged carburetor jets.
i. Partially plugged fuel tank breather tube on 49-state and Canada models.
j. Plugged choke circuit.
k. Faulty emission control system on California models.

Incorrect Fast Idle Speed

A fast idle speed can be due to one of the following problems:
a. Stuck choke valve.
b. Clogged starter air line.
c. Incorrect choke cable free play.
d. Incorrect carburetor synchronization.

Poor Gas Mileage and Engine Performance

Poor gas mileage and engine performance can be caused by infrequent engine tune-ups. Check your records to see when your bike was last tuned up and compare against the recommended tune-up service intervals in Chapter Three. If the last tune-up was within the specified service intervals, check for one or more of the following problems:
a. Clogged air filter.
b. Clogged fuel system.
c. Loose, disconnected or damaged fuel and emission control vacuum hoses.
d. Faulty evaporative emission control system hoses on California models.
e. Ignition system malfunction.

Rich Fuel Mixture

A rich carburetor fuel mixture can be caused by one or more of the following conditions:
a. Clogged or dirty air filter.
b. Worn or damaged fuel valve and seat.
c. Clogged air jets.
d. Incorrect float level (too high).
e. Choke valve damaged or stuck open.
f. Flooded carburetor(s).

g. Damaged vacuum piston.
h. Damaged evaporative emission purge control valve on California models.
i. Damaged emission control system hose(s) on California models.

Lean Fuel Mixture

A lean carburetor fuel mixture can be caused by one or more of the following conditions:
a. Incorrect float level adjustment (too low).
b. Partially restricted fuel line.
c. Clogged carburetor jet(s).
d. Worn or damaged fuel valve and seat.
e. Plugged carburetor air vent hose.
f. Damaged vacuum piston.
g. Damaged throttle valve.
h. Damaged evaporative emission carburetor air vent control valve on California models.
i. Damaged emission control system hose(s) on California models.

Engine Backfires or Misfires During Acceleration

Check for the following:
a. Lean fuel mixture.
b. Incorrect carburetor adjustment.
c. Ignition system malfunction.
d. Damaged air cutoff valve.
e. Ignition is intermittently stopped by ICM rev limiter circuit.
f. Faulty vacuum hoses; check for kinks, splits or bad connections.
g. Vacuum leak at the carburetor and/or intake manifold(s).
h. Fouled spark plug(s).
i. Low engine compression, especially at one cylinder only. Check engine compression as described in Chapter Three.

EXCESSIVE VIBRATION

If mounting hardware is in good condition, excessive vibration can be difficult to find without disassembling the engine. Usually, excessive vibration is caused by loose engine mounting hardware.

FRONT SUSPENSION AND STEERING

Poor handling may be caused by improper tire pressure, a damaged or bent frame or front steering components, a worn front fork assembly, worn wheel bearings or dragging brakes.

Steering is Sluggish

a. Incorrect steering stem adjustment (too tight).
b. Damaged steering head bearings.
c. Tire pressure too low.

Bike Steers to One Side

a. Bent front axle.
b. Bent frame.
c. Worn or damaged front wheel bearings.
d. Worn or damaged swing arm pivot bearings.
e. Damaged steering head bearings.
f. Bent swing arm.
g. Incorrectly installed wheels.
h. Front and rear wheels are not aligned.

Suspension Noise

a. Loose mounting fasteners.
b. Damaged fork(s) or rear shock absorber.
c. Incorrect front fork oil.

Wobble/Vibration

a. Loose front or rear axle.
b. Loose or damaged wheel bearing(s).
c. Damaged wheel rim(s).
d. Damaged tire(s).
e. Loose swing arm pivot bolts.
f. Unbalanced tire and wheel assembly.

Hard Suspension
(Front Forks)

a. Insufficient tire pressure.
b. Damaged steering head bearings.
c. Incorrect steering head bearing adjustment.
d. Bent fork tubes.
e. Binding slider.
f. Incorrect fork oil.
g. Plugged fork oil hydraulic passage.

TROUBLESHOOTING

Hard Suspension
(Rear Shock Absorbers)

a. Excessive tire pressure.
b. Bent damper rod.
c. Incorrect shock adjustment.
d. Damaged shock absorber bushing(s).
e. Damaged shock absorber bearing.
f. Damaged swing arm pivot bearing.

Soft Suspension
(Front Forks)

a. Insufficient tire pressure.
b. Insufficient fork oil level or fluid capacity.
c. Incorrect oil viscosity.
d. Weak or damaged fork springs.

Soft Suspension
(Rear Shock Absorbers)

a. Insufficient tire pressure.
b. Weak or damaged shock absorber spring.
c. Damaged shock absorber.
d. Incorrect shock absorber adjustment.
e. Leaking damper unit.

BRAKE PROBLEMS

Dragging disc brakes may be caused by a stuck piston(s) in a caliper assembly or warped pad shim(s).

Brake Drag

a. Clogged brake hydraulic system.
b. Sticking caliper pistons.
c. Sticking master cylinder piston.
d. Incorrectly installed brake caliper.
e. Warped brake disc.
f. Sticking caliper bolt pin.
g. Incorrect wheel alignment.

Brakes Grab

a. Contaminated brake pads.
b. Incorrect wheel alignment.
c. Warped brake disc.

Brake Squeal or Chatter

a. Contaminated brake pads.
b. Incorrectly installed brake caliper.
c. Warped brake disc.
d. Incorrect wheel alignment.

Soft or Spongy Brake Lever or Pedal

a. Low brake fluid level.
b. Air in brake hydraulic system.
c. Leaking brake hydraulic system.

Hard Brake Lever or Pedal Operation

a. Clogged brake hydraulic system.
b. Sticking caliper pistons.
c. Sticking master cylinder piston.
d. Glazed or worn brake pads.

CHAPTER THREE

LUBRICATION, MAINTENANCE AND TUNE-UP

This chapter covers all of the regular maintenance required to keep your Honda in top shape. Regular maintenance is something you cannot afford to ignore. Neglecting regular maintenance will reduce the life and performance of your Honda.

This chapter explains lubrication, maintenance and tune-up procedures required for the models described in this manual. **Table 1** is a suggested maintenance schedule. **Tables 1-11** are at the end of the chapter.

ROUTINE INSPECTION

Perform the following inspection before the first ride or the day.

Engine Oil Level

Refer to *Engine Oil Level Check* under *Periodic Lubrication* in this chapter.

Fuel

The Honda ACE engine is designed to use gasoline that has a pump octane rating of 86 or higher. The pump octane number is displayed on service station gas pumps. Using a gasoline with a lower octane number can cause pinging or spark knock. Either condition can lead to engine damage.

When choosing gasoline and filling the fuel tank, note the following:

a. When filling the tank, do not overfill it. Fuel expands in the tank due to engine heat or heating by the sun. Stop adding fuel when the fuel level reaches the bottom of the filler neck inside the fuel tank.

b. To help meet clean air standards in some areas of the United States and Canada, oxygenated fuels are being used. Oxygenated fuel is conventional gasoline that is blended with an ether compound to increase the gasoline's oxygen content.

c. Because oxygenated fuel can damage plastic and paint, make sure not to spill fuel onto the fuel tank during fuel stops.

d. An ethanol (ethyl or grain alcohol) gasoline that contains more than 10 percent ethanol by volume may cause engine starting and performance related problems.

e. A methanol (methyl or wood alcohol) gasoline that contains more than 5 percent methanol by volume may cause engine starting and performance related problems. Gasoline that contains methanol must have corrosion inhibitors to protect the metal, plastic and rubber parts in the fuel system from damage.

LUBRICATION, MAINTENANCE AND TUNE-UP

Coolant Level

Check the coolant level in the reservoir tank only when the engine is at normal operating temperature.

WARNING
Do not remove the radiator cap when the engine is HOT. The coolant is under pressure and scalding and severe burns could result.

1. Support the bike so that it is upright and parked on a flat surface. Do not check the coolant level with the bike resting on its sidestand.
2. The coolant must be between the UPPER and LOWER level marks (**Figure 1**) on the side of the tank. If necessary, add coolant to the coolant reserve tank.

NOTE
If the coolant level is very low, there may be a leak in the cooling system. If necessary, refer to Cooling System Inspection in this chapter.

3. Unscrew the cap (**Figure 2**) from the coolant reserve tank. Add a 50:50 mixture of distilled water and antifreeze to bring the level to the UPPER mark on the tank.
4. Install and tighten the cap securely.

Brake Operation

Make sure the brakes operate with full hydraulic advantage. Check the brake fluid level in both master cylinders as described in this chapter. Make sure there is no brake fluid leaking from the master cylinder, calipers or brake lines.

Throttle

Sit on the bike. With the rear brake applied, the transmission in NEUTRAL and the engine idling, move the handlebars from side to side. The engine idle speed must not increase or decrease as the handlebars are moved. Make sure the throttle moves

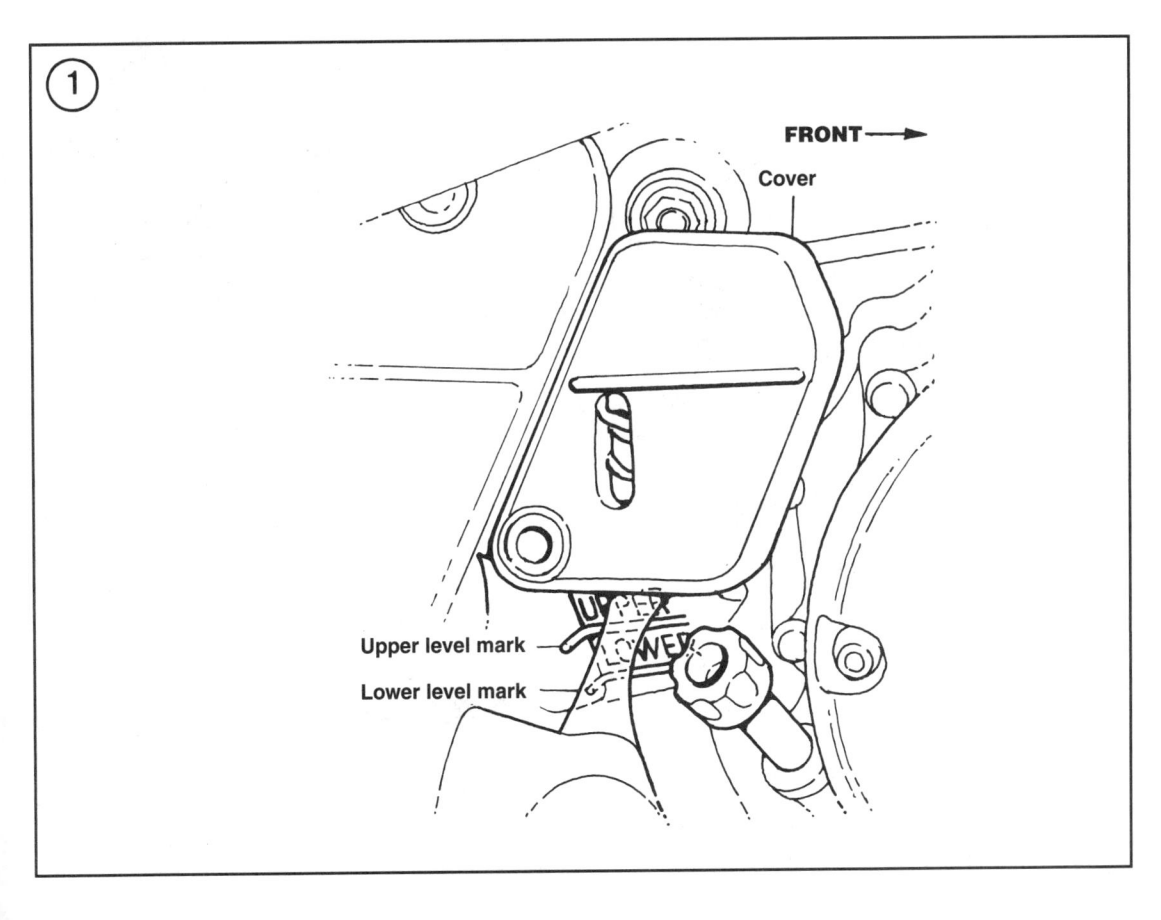

Figure 1
FRONT ➤
Cover
Upper level mark
Lower level mark

smoothly in all steering positions. Shut off the engine.

Engine Stop Switch

The engine stop switch (**Figure 3**) is designed primarily as an emergency or safety switch. It is part of the right-hand switch assembly next to the throttle housing and it has 2 operating positions: OFF and RUN. When the switch is in the OFF position, the engine will not start or run. In the RUN position, the engine should start and run with the ignition switch on, the clutch lever pulled in. With the engine idling, move the switch to OFF. The engine should turn off.

When stopping and parking the motorcycle, turn the ignition switch off. If you use the engine stop to turn off the ignition but leave the ignition switch on, the headlight and taillight will still be on, resulting in battery discharge.

Lights and Horn

1. With the engine running, pull the front brake lever and check that the brake light comes on.
2. Push the rear brake pedal down and check that the brake light comes on soon after you have begun depressing the pedal.
3. With the engine running, check to see that the headlight and taillight are on.
4. Move the dimmer switch up and down between the HI and LO positions and check to see that the headlight elements are working in the headlight.
5. On U.K. models, move the switch on and off and check to see that the headlight elements are working in the headlight and taillight.
6. Push the turn signal switch to the left and right positions and check that all 4 turn signals are working.
7. Push the horn button and make sure that the horn blows loudly.
8. If the rear brake pedal travels too far before the brake light came on, adjust the rear brake light switch as described in this chapter.
9. If the horn or any of the lights fail to operate properly, refer to Chapter Nine.

SERVICE INTERVALS

The factory recommends the services and intervals shown in **Table 1**. Strict adherence to these recommendations will help ensure long service from your Honda. However, if you run the vehicle in an area of high humidity or do much riding in the rain, perform the lubrication and service more frequently.

For convenience, this chapter describes most of the services shown in **Table 1**. However, when a procedure requires more than minor disassembly or adjustment, it is covered in the appropriate chapter. The *Table of Contents* and *Index* can help you locate a particular service procedure.

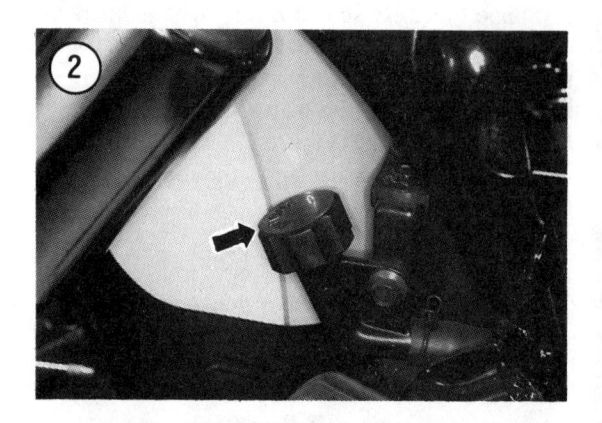

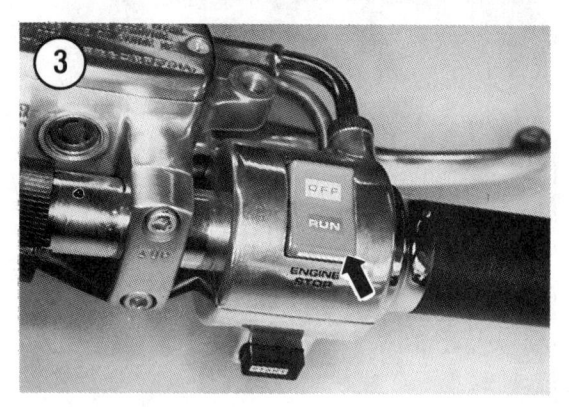

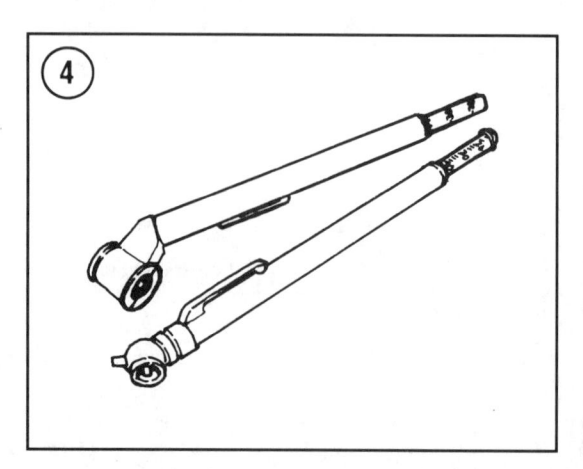

LUBRICATION, MAINTENANCE AND TUNE-UP

TIRES AND WHEELS

Tire Pressure

Check and adjust tire pressure to maintain the tire profile, good traction and handling and to get the maximum life out of each tire. Purchase an accurate tire gauge (**Figure 4**) and carry it in your motorcycle tool kit. Check tire pressure when the tires are cold. Correct tire pressure varies with the load you are carrying or if you have a passenger. See **Table 2**.

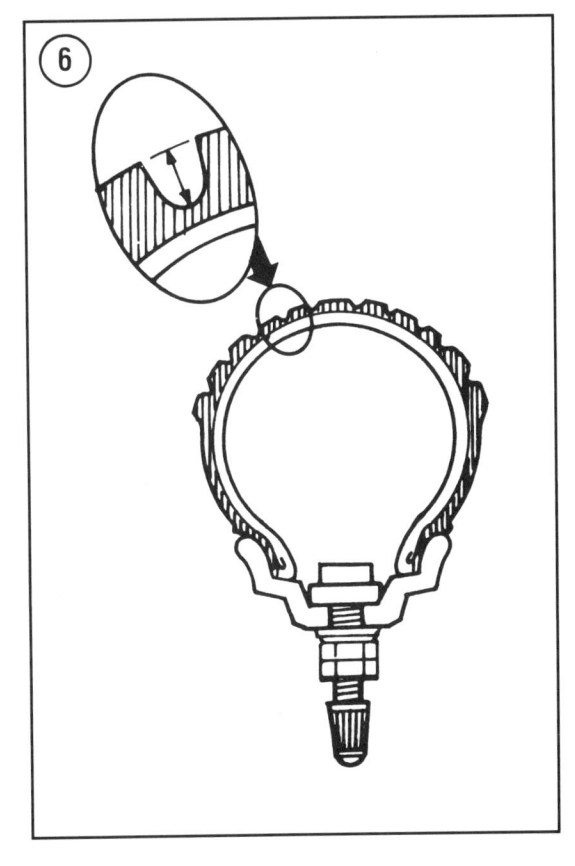

NOTE
*After checking and adjusting the air pressure, make sure to install the air valve cap (**Figure 5**). The cap prevents small pebbles and dirt from collecting in the valve stem.*

NOTE
A loss of air pressure may be due to a loose or damaged valve core. Put a few drops of water on the top of the valve core. If the water bubbles, tighten the valve core and recheck. If air is still leaking from the valve after tightening it, replace the valve core. If leakage is still present, replace the inner tube.

Tire Inspection

The tires take a lot of punishment and should be inspected prior to each ride. Inspect the tires for the following:

a. Deep cuts and imbedded objects such as stones, thorns or nails. If you find a nail or other object in the tire, mark its location with a light crayon before removing it. This will help you find the hole for repair. Refer to Chapter Eleven for tire changing and repair information.
b. Cracks.
c. Separating plies.
d. Sidewall damage.

Tread Depth

Honda recommends replacing original equipment tires before the tread depth at the center reaches 1.5 mm (0.06 in.) for the front tire or 2.0 mm (0.08 in.) for the rear tire or when tread wear indicators appear at the designated area on the tire indicating the minimum tread depth.

Measure the tread depth at the center of the tire and to the center of the tire tread (**Figure 6**) using a tread depth gauge (**Figure 7**) or small ruler.

WARNING
Do not ride the motorcycle with excessively worn tires. Excessively worn tires can cause you to lose control. Replace worn tires immediately.

Tire Wear Analysis

Abnormal tire wear must be analyzed to determine the causes. The most common causes are:
  a. Incorrect tire pressure. Check tire pressure as described in this chapter.
  b. Overloading.
  c. Incorrect wheel balance. The tire/wheel assembly must be balanced when installing a new tire and or tube and balanced again each time the tire is removed and reinstalled.
  d. Worn or damaged wheel bearings.

Incorrect tire pressure is the biggest cause of abnormal tire wear (**Figure 8**). Under-inflated tires will result in higher tire temperatures, hard or imprecise steering and abnormal tire wear. Overinflated tires will result in a hard ride and abnormal tire wear. Examine the tire tread, comparing the wear in the center of the contact patch with the tire wear at the edge of the contact patch. Note the following:
  a. If a tire shows excessive wear at the edge of the contact patch, but the wear at the center of the contact patch is good, the tire has been under-inflated.
  b. If a tire shows excessive wear in the center of the contact patch, but the wear at the edge of the contact patch is good, the tire has been overinflated.

Wheel Spoke Tension

Check each spoke (**Figure 9**) for bending or other damage, then check each spoke for tightness with a spoke wrench (**Figure 10**). If the spokes are loose, tighten them as described in Chapter Eleven.

NOTE
Most spokes loosen as a group rather than individually. Tighten loose spokes carefully. Burying just a few spokes tight into the rim will put improper pressure across the wheel. Never tighten spokes to the point that the spoke wrench rounds off the nipple flats.

Rim Inspection and Runout

Inspect the rims for cracks, warpage or dents. Replace damaged rims.

Wheel rim runout is the amount of wobble a wheel shows as it rotates. You can check runout with the wheels on the bike by simply supporting the wheel off the ground and turning the wheel slowly while

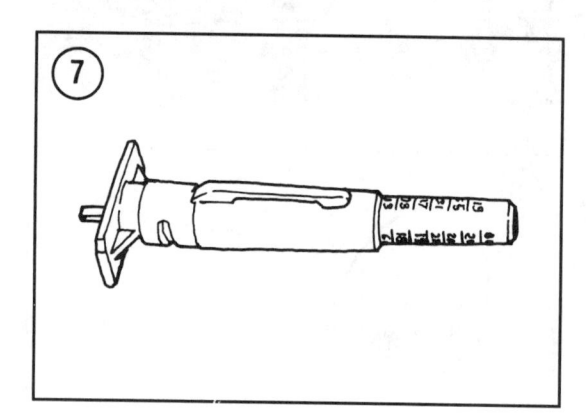

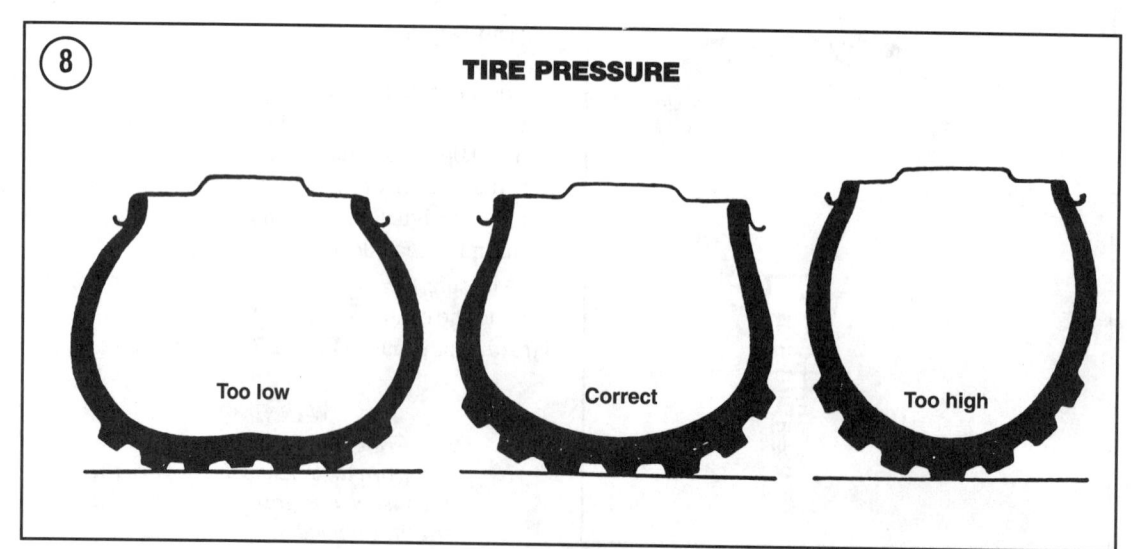

LUBRICATION, MAINTENANCE AND TUNE-UP

you hold a pointer solidly against a fork leg or the swing arm.

NOTE
Chapter Eleven describes a more accurate method of measuring wheel runout.

The maximum allowable runout with the tire installed on the rim is:

a. 2 mm (1/16 in.) axial play (side-to-side).
b. 2 mm (1/16 in.) radial play (up-and-down).

If the runout is excessive, true the wheel as described in Chapter Eleven.

BATTERY

While the battery is one of the easier components to maintain on a vehicle, it is also one of the most neglected components. Most no-start and electrical system problems can be traced to battery neglect.

To keep the battery in good condition, check and correct the battery electrolyte level on a weekly basis. Inspect, clean and test the battery at the service intervals specified in **Table 1**. The battery capacity for all models is listed in **Table 3**.

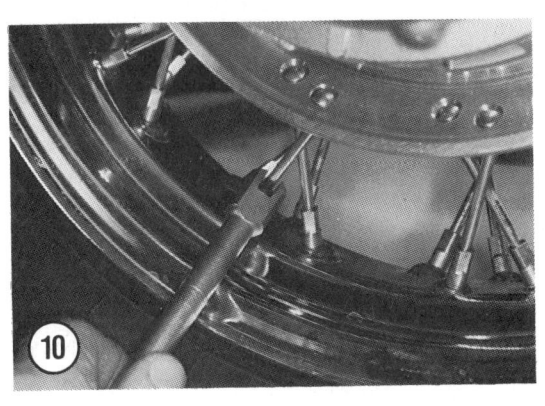

Safety Precautions

When working with batteries, use extreme care to avoid spilling or splashing the electrolyte. This solution contains sulfuric acid, which can ruin clothing and cause serious chemical burns. If any electrolyte is spilled or splashed on clothing or skin, immediately neutralize with a solution of baking soda and water, then flush with an abundance of clean water.

WARNING
Electrolyte splashed into the eyes is extremely harmful. Always wear safety while working with batteries. If you get electrolyte in your eyes, call a physician immediately and force your eyes open and flood them with cool, clean water for approximately 15 minutes.

Note the following when handling batteries:
1. Always wear a face shield or safety glasses when servicing and testing batteries.
2. To protect your hands and arms from acid burns, wear rubber gloves when handling batteries.
3. To protect your clothes from acid damage, wear a shop apron or similar protective clothing.
4. If electrolyte is spilled or splashed onto any surface, neutralize it immediately with a baking soda and water solution and then rinse with clean water.
5. Keep children and pets away from batteries and charging equipment.

While a battery is being charged, highly explosive hydrogen gas forms in each cell. Some of this gas escapes through filler cap openings and may form an explosive atmosphere in and around the battery. This condition can persist for several hours. Sparks, an open flame or a lighted cigarette can ignite the gas, causing an explosion and possible serious personal injury.

Note the following precautions to prevent an explosion:
1. Do not smoke or permit any open flame near any battery being charged or which has been recently charged.
2. Do not disconnect live circuits at the battery terminals since a spark usually occurs when a live circuit is broken.
3. Take care when connecting or disconnecting any battery charger. Be sure its power switch is off before making or breaking connections. Poor connections are a common cause of electrical arcs which cause explosions.

For maximum battery life, check the battery periodically for electrolyte level, state of charge and corrosion. During hot weather periods, frequent checks are recommended. If the electrolyte level is below the bottom of the vent well in one or more cells, add distilled water as required. To ensure proper mixing of the water and acid, operate the engine immediately after adding water. Never add electrolyte to an activated battery.

On all models covered in this manual, the negative side is ground. When removing the battery, disconnect the negative (–) cable first, then the positive (+) cable. This minimizes the chance of a tool shorting to ground when disconnecting the battery positive cable.

Battery Removal

The battery is mounted behind the left side cover.
1. Remove the left side cover (Chapter Fourteen).
2. Disconnect the negative battery cable (A, **Figure 11**) from the battery.
3. Disconnect the positive battery cable (B, **Figure 11**) from the battery.
4. Remove the battery holder bolt (C, **Figure 11**) and pivot the holder away from the battery.
5. Disconnect the battery vent hose (A, **Figure 12**) at the battery.
6. Remove the battery (B, **Figure 12**).

CAUTION
Be careful not to spill battery electrolyte on painted or polished surfaces. The liquid is highly corrosive and will damage the finish. If it is spilled, wash it off immediately with baking soda and water and thoroughly rinse with clean water.

Cleaning and Inspection

1. Before cleaning the battery, turn each battery fill plug to make sure it is tight. This will prevent the cleaning solution from entering the cells and neutralizing the acid.
2. Inspect the battery box for contamination or damage. Clean with a solution of baking soda and water.
3. Check the entire battery case (**Figure 13**) for cracks or other damage. If the battery case is warped, discolored or has a raised top, the battery has been suffering from overcharging or overheating.

4. Check the battery mounting bracket for acid damage, cracks or other damage. Replace if damaged.

5. Check the battery terminal bolts, spacers and nuts for corrosion or damage. Clean parts thoroughly with a solution of baking soda and water. Replace severely corroded or damaged parts.

NOTE
Keep the cleaning solution out of the battery cells or the electrolyte level will be seriously weakened.

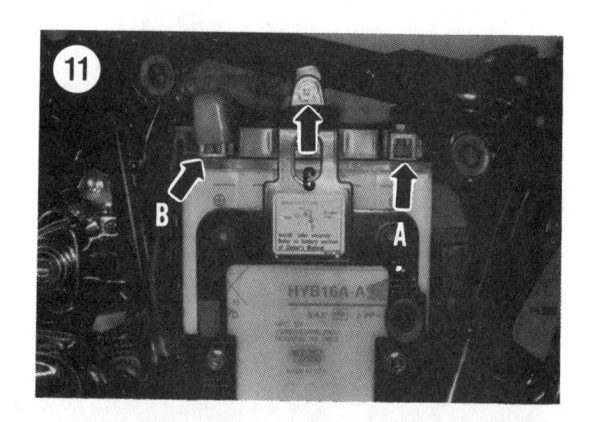

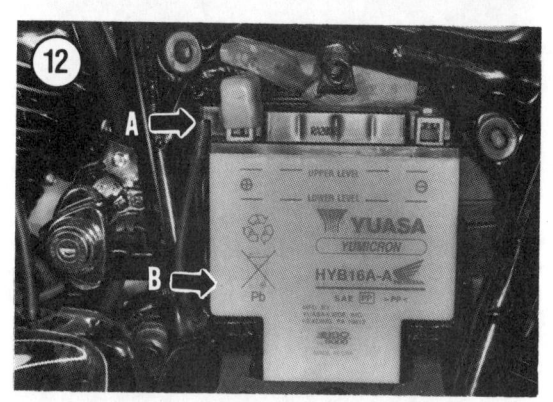

LUBRICATION, MAINTENANCE AND TUNE-UP

6. Clean the top of the battery with a stiff bristle brush.
7. Check the battery cable clamps for corrosion and damage. If corrosion is minor, clean the battery cable clamps with a stiff wire brush. Replace severely worn or damaged cables.

NOTE
Do not overfill the battery cells in Step 8. The electrolyte expands due to heat from charging and will overflow if the level is above the upper level line.

8. Place the battery on a level surface. Remove the battery fill caps (**Figure 14**) and check the electrolyte level. Add distilled water, if necessary, to bring the level within the upper and lower level lines on the battery case (**Figure 15**).
9. Install and tighten the battery fill plugs. Do not overtighten.

Battery Installation

1. Reinstall the battery into the battery compartment with as shown in **Figure 12**.

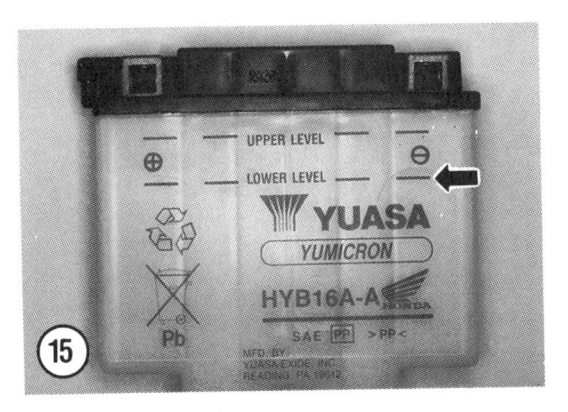

2. Reconnect the battery vent hose (A, **Figure 12**) to the battery, then slide the battery into position.

NOTE
*For further information on vent hose routing, refer to the **Battery Vent Hose Routing** decal mounted on the battery holder (**Figure 11**).*

WARNING
After installing the battery, make sure the vent hose is not pinched. A pinched or kinked hose will allow high pressure to accumulate in the battery and cause the electrolyte to overflow. If the vent hose is damaged, replace it.

3. Install and tighten the positive battery cable (B, **Figure 11**).
4. Install and tighten the negative battery cable (A, **Figure 11**).

CAUTION
Be sure the battery cables are connected to their proper terminals. Connecting the battery backward will reverse the polarity and damage the rectifier.

5. Coat the battery connections with dielectric grease or petroleum jelly.
6. Pivot the battery holder across the front of the battery and secure it with its mounting bolt (C, **Figure 11**).
7. Install the left side cover (Chapter Fourteen).

Battery Testing

Hydrometer testing is the best way to check battery condition. Use a hydrometer with numbered graduations from 1.100 to 1.300 rather than one with just color-coded bands. To use the hydrometer, squeeze the rubber ball, insert the tip into a cell and release the ball (**Figure 16**).

NOTE
Do not attempt to test a battery with a hydrometer immediately after adding water to the cells. Charge the battery for 15-20 minutes at a rate high enough to cause vigorous gassing and allow the water and electrolyte to mix thoroughly.

Draw enough electrolyte to float the weighted float inside the hydrometer. When using a temperature-compensated hydrometer, release the electrolyte and repeat this process several times to make sure the thermometer has adjusted to the electrolyte temperature before taking the reading.

Hold the hydrometer vertically and note the number in line with the surface of the electrolyte (**Figure 17**). This is the specific gravity for this cell. Return the electrolyte to the cell from which it came. The specific gravity of the electrolyte in each battery cell is an excellent indication of that cell's condition (**Figure 18**). A fully charged cell will read 1.260-1.280 while a cell in good condition reads from 1.230-1.250 and anything below 1.140 is discharged. Charging is also necessary if the specific gravity varies more than 0.050 points from cell to cell.

NOTE
If a temperature-compensated hydrometer is not used, add 0.004 to the specific gravity reading for every 10° above 80° F (25° C). For every 10° below 80° F (25° C), subtract 0.004.

Charging

A good state of charge must be maintained in batteries used for starting. When charging the battery, note the following:
 a. During charging, the cells will show signs of gas bubbling. If one cell has no gas bubbles or if its specific gravity is low, the cell is probably faulty. Replace the battery.
 b. If a battery not in use loses its charge within a week after charging, the battery is defective. A good battery should only self-discharge approximately 1% each day.

CAUTION
Always remove the battery from the vehicle before connecting charging equipment.

WARNING
During charging, highly explosive hydrogen gas is released from the battery. Charge the battery only in a well-ventilated area, away from all open flames and cigarettes. Never check the charge of the battery by arcing across the terminals; the resulting spark can ignite the hydrogen gas.

1. Remove the battery from the bike as described in this chapter.

2. Connect the positive (+) charger lead to the positive battery terminal and the negative (–) charger lead to the negative battery terminal.

3. Remove all vent caps (**Figure 14**) from the battery, set the charger at 12 volts, and switch it on. Normally, a battery should be charged at a slow

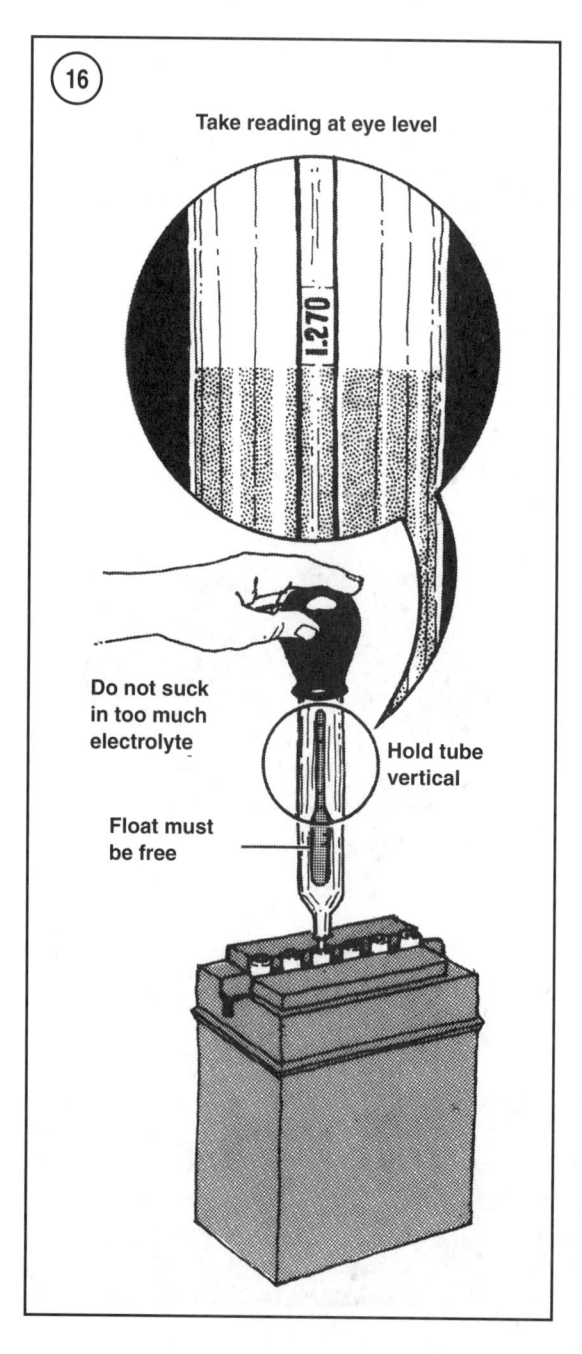

LUBRICATION, MAINTENANCE AND TUNE-UP

charge rate of 1/10 its given capacity. Refer to **Table 3** for battery capacity specifications.

CAUTION
The electrolyte level must be maintained at the upper level during the charging cycle. Check and refill with distilled water as necessary.

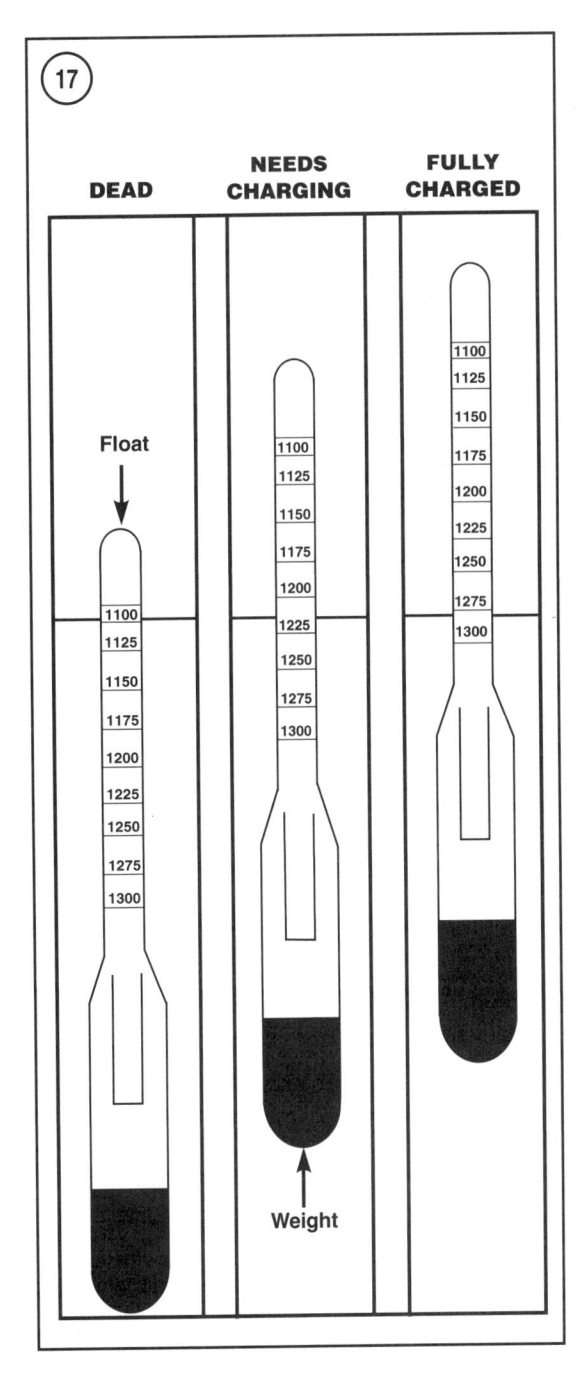

17

DEAD — Float

NEEDS CHARGING — Weight

FULLY CHARGED

4. The charging time depends on the discharged condition of the battery. Use the chart in **Figure 19** to determine approximate charging times at different specific gravity readings. For example, if the specific gravity of your battery is 1.180, the approximate charging time is 6 hours.

5. If the battery becomes hot to touch during charging, turn the charger off and allow the battery to cool off. Then resume charging.

6. After the battery has been charged for the predetermined time, turn the charger off, disconnect the leads and check the specific gravity. It should be within the limits specified in **Table 4**. If it is, and remains stable for one hour, the battery is charged.

NEW BATTERY INSTALLATION

A new battery must be charged (specific gravity reading of 1.260-1.280) before it is installed and put to use. When electrolyte is added to a new battery, its charge or capacity at that time is approximately 80%. To bring the battery to full charge, it must receive an initial or booster charge. Using a new battery without an initial charge will cause permanent battery damage. That is, the battery will never be able to hold more than an 80% charge. When purchasing a new battery from a dealer or parts store, verify its charge status.

NOTE
Recycle your old battery. When you replace the old battery, be sure to turn in the old battery at that time. The lead plates and the plastic case can be recycled. Most dealers will accept your old battery in trade when you purchase a new one. Never place an old battery in your household trash since it is illegal, in most states, to place any acid or lead (heavy metal) contents in landfills. There is also the danger of the battery being crushed in the trash truck and spraying acid on the truck or landfill operator.

LUBRICANTS

Engine Oil

Oil is classified according to its viscosity, which is an indication of how thick it is. The Society of

Automotive Engineers (SAE) system distinguishes oil viscosity by numbers, called weights. Thick (heavy) oil has higher viscosity numbers than thin (light) oil. For example, 5 weight (SAE 5) oil is a light oil while 90 weight (SAE 90) oil is relatively heavy. The viscosity of the oil has nothing to do with its lubricating properties. If the oil passes cold weather tests, it is denoted with a W after the number as SAE 10W.

Grease

Use a good quality waterproof grease when servicing your Honda. Water does not wash grease off parts as easily as it washes off oil. In addition, grease maintains its lubricating qualities better than oil on long rides.

PERIODIC LUBRICATION

Engine Oil Level Check

Check the engine oil level with the dipstick at the rear of the clutch cover.

1. Start the engine and let it warm up approximately 2-3 minutes.
2. Shut off the engine and position the bike upright. Allow the oil to settle.

CAUTION
Do not check the oil level with the bike resting on its sidestand. An incorrect reading will result.

3. After a few minutes, unscrew the dipstick (**Figure 20**) and wipe it clean. Reinsert it onto the threads in the hole but do not screw it in. Remove it and check the oil level.

4. The level is correct if it is between the 2 lines (**Figure 21**). If necessary, remove the oil fill cap (**Figure 20**) and add the recommended type oil (**Table 6**) to correct the level. Install the oil fill cap and tighten securely.

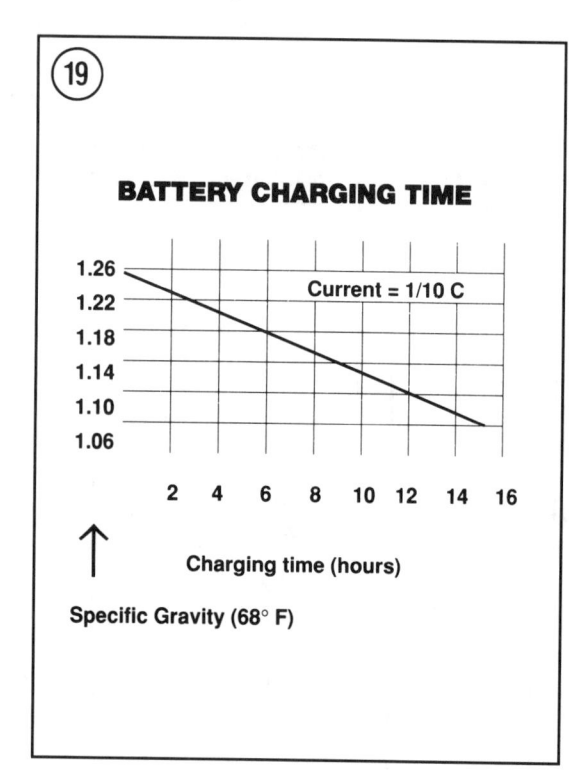

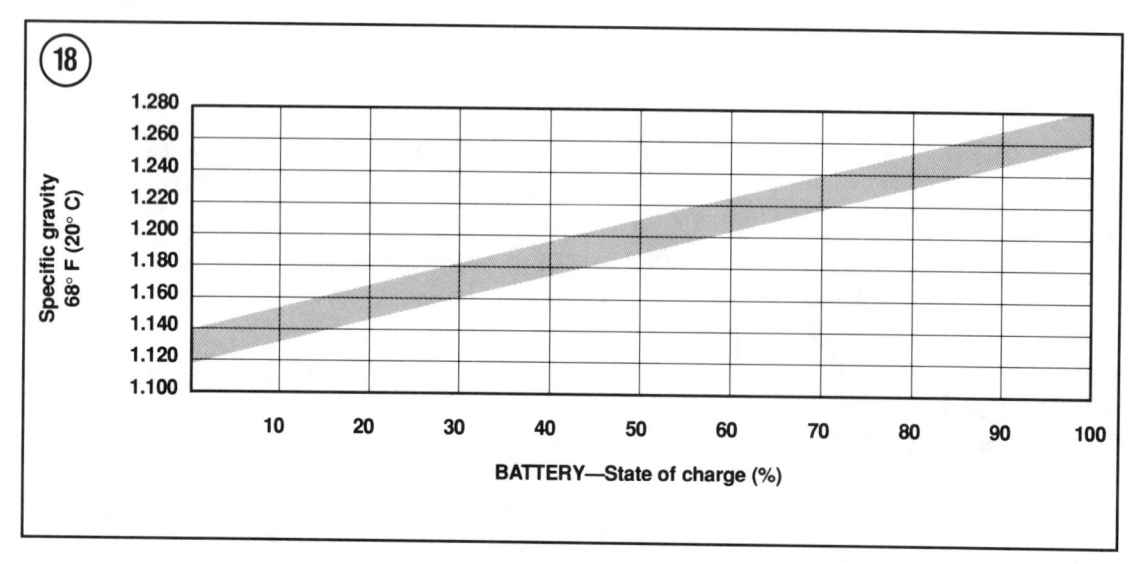

(19) BATTERY CHARGING TIME

Specific Gravity (68° F) vs Charging time (hours), Current = 1/10 C

(18) Specific gravity 68° F (20° C) vs BATTERY—State of charge (%)

LUBRICATION, MAINTENANCE AND TUNE-UP

Engine Oil and Filter Change

Table 1 lists the factory recommended oil and filter change intervals.

Use only a high-quality detergent motor oil with an API classification of SF or SG. The classification is stamped or printed on top of the can or label on plastic bottles (**Figure 22**). Try to use the same brand of oil at each oil change. Refer to **Figure 23** for the correct oil weight to use under anticipated ambient temperatures (not engine oil temperature).

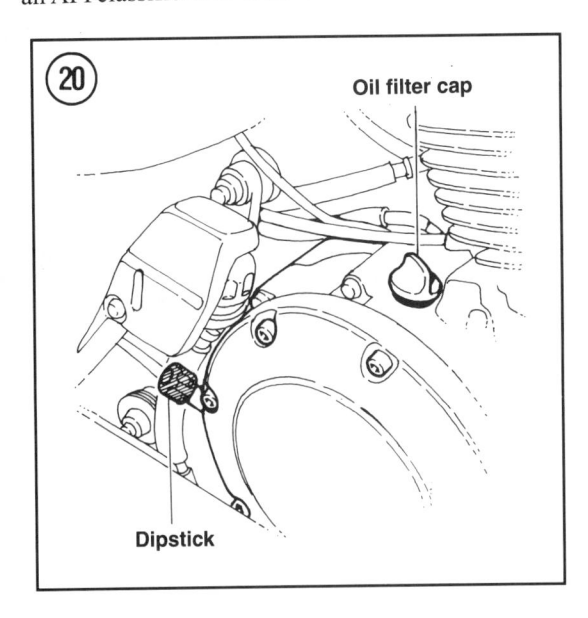

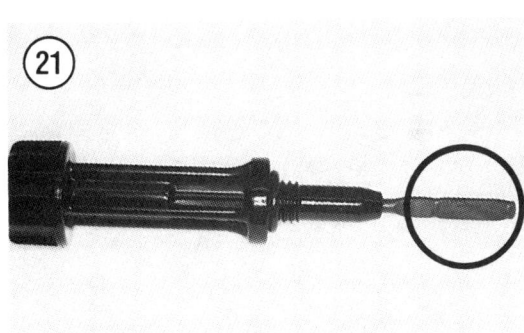

To change the engine oil and filter you need the following:

a. Drain pan.
b. Funnel.
c. Can opener or pour spout.
d. Wrench and sockets.
e. Engine oil (**Figure 24**).
f. New oil filter (**Figure 24**).

There are different ways to discard the old oil safely. Never drain the oil onto the ground.

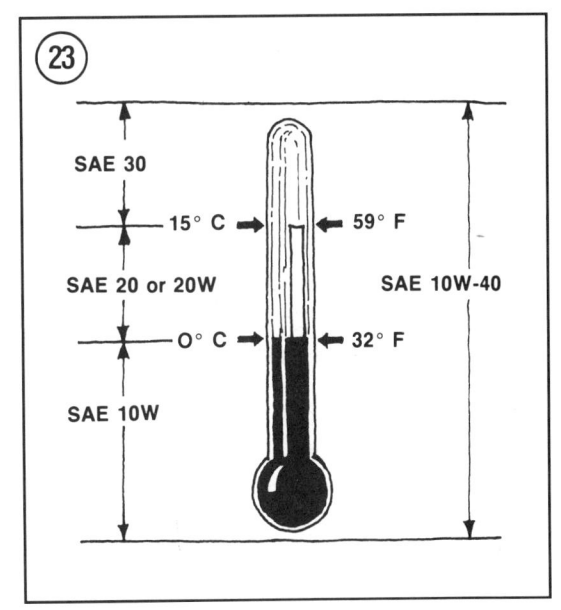

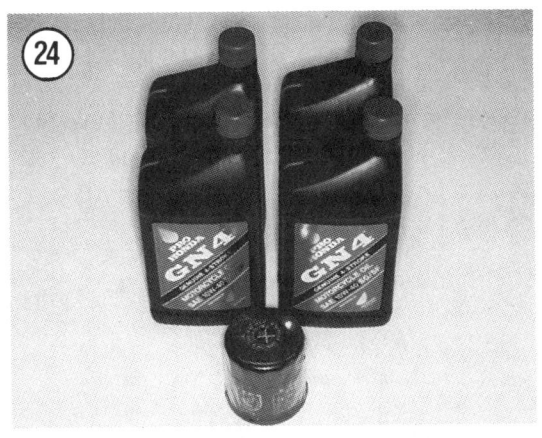

NOTE
Never dispose of motor oil in the trash, on the ground, or down the storm drain. Many service stations accept used motor oil and waste haulers provide curbside used motor oil collection. Do not combine other fluids with motor oil to be recycled. To locate a recycler, contact the American Petroleum Institute (API) at www.recycleoil.org..

NOTE
Warming the engine allows the oil to heat up; thus it flows freely and carries contamination and any sludge out with it.

1. Start the engine and let it reach operating temperature.
2. Park the bike on a level surface and support it on its sidestand.
3. Place a clean drain pan underneath the engine.
4. Remove the drain plug (**Figure 25**) and washer mounted in the bottom of the engine and allow the oil to drain.
5. Remove the oil fill cap (**Figure 20**) to help speed up the flow of oil.
6. Replace the drain plug washer (**Figure 26**) if leaking or damaged.
7. Remove and discard the oil filter (**Figure 27**).
8. Install the drain plug and washer (**Figure 25**) and tighten to the torque specification in **Table 5**.
9. Lubricate the oil filter O-ring (**Figure 28**) and threads with engine oil.
10. Install the new oil filter and tighten to the torque specification in **Table 5**.
11. Insert a funnel into the oil fill hole (**Figure 20**) and fill the engine with the correct oil. Refer to **Table 7** for engine oil capacity.
12. Screw in the oil fill cap securely (**Figure 20**).
13. Start the engine and run at idle speed.
14. Turn the engine off and check the drain bolt and oil filter for leaks.
15. Check the oil level and adjust if necessary.

WARNING
Prolonged contact with used oil may cause skin cancer. Wash your hands with soap and water after handling or coming in contact with motor oil.

Final Drive Oil Level Check

1. Park the bike on a level surface and support it so it is upright.

NOTE
The final drive oil level can be checked with the bike resting on its sidestand or in the upright position.

2. Wipe the area around the final drive oil filler plug and unscrew the oil filler plug (A, **Figure 29**).

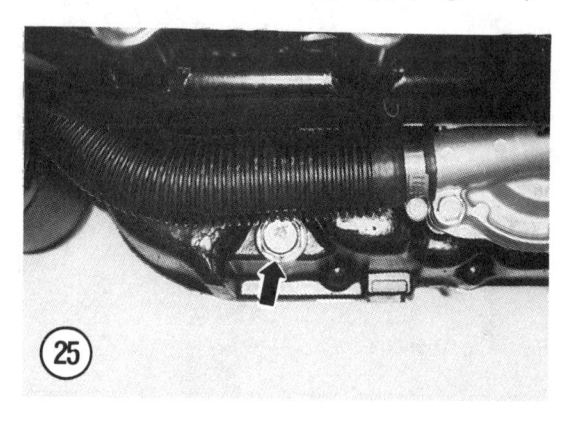

LUBRICATION, MAINTENANCE AND TUNE-UP

3. If the bike is resting on the sidestand, the final drive oil level must be even with the lower edge of the oil filter hole (**Figure 30**). If the bike is in the upright position, the oil level must be 13 mm (1/2 in.) below the lower edge of the filler hole. Refer to Table 6 for the correct oil viscosity.

4. Inspect the oil filler cap O-ring for leaks or damage. Lubricate the O-ring with grease (if dry or new).

5. Install the final drive oil filler plug (A, **Figure 29**) and tighten to the torque specification in **Table 5**.

6. Support the bike on its sidestand.

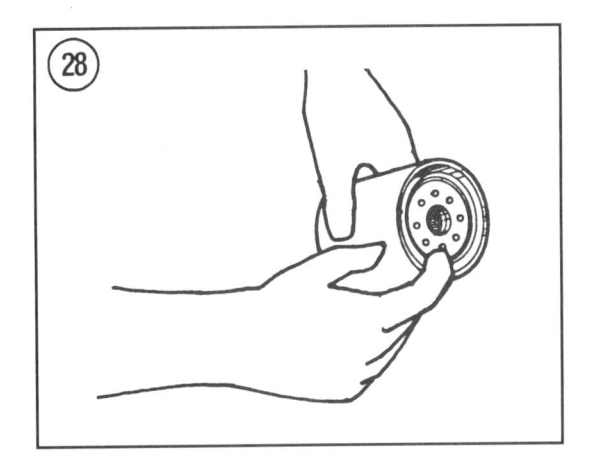

Final Drive Oil Change

The recommended oil change interval is listed in **Table 1**.

To drain the oil you need the following:

a. Drain pan.

b. The correct type (**Table 6**) and quantity (**Table 8**) final drive gear oil.

c. New gasket for the drain bolt.

1. Ride the bike until normal operating temperature is obtained.
2. Park the bike on a level surface and support it on a stand so the rear wheel clears the ground.
3. Place a drain pan underneath the drain plug.
4. Remove the oil filler plug (A, **Figure 29**) and drain plug (B, **Figure 29**).
5. With the transmission in NEUTRAL, slowly turn the rear wheel to drain the oil from the final drive unit.
6. Install a new washer on the drain plug, then install the drain plug and tighten to the torque specification in **Table 5**.
7. Add gear oil until the level is even with the lower edge of the filler plug hole (**Figure 30**) if the bike is resting on its sidestand. If the bike is in the upright position, add oil until the level is 13 mm (1/2 in.) below the lower edge of the filler plug hole.
8. Inspect the oil filler cap O-ring for leaks or damage. Lubricate the O-ring with grease (if dry or new).
9. Install the final drive oil filler plug (A, **Figure 29**) and tighten to the torque specification in **Table 5**.
10. Support the bike on its sidestand.
11. Discard the old oil as described under *Engine Oil and Filter Change* in this chapter.

Front Fork Oil Change

Honda does not list an oil change interval for the front forks. It is good practice to change the fork oil once per year, or more often if the bike is ridden often.

This procedure describes how to change the fork oil only. It does not include information on measuring the foil oil level. If you plan on measuring the fork oil level, remove and service the forks as described in Chapter Eleven. Because the forks must be in a vertical position to accurately measure and set the oil level, it is easier to do so with the forks removed from the bike. While it is possible to position the bike vertically with the forks mounted on the bike, it requires a suitable jack to prevent the bike from falling over.

1. Sit on the motorcycle and have an assistant hold a drain pan underneath one of the fork tube drain plugs (**Figure 31**) while they remove the drain bolt and allow the oil to drain.
2. When the oil flow starts to slow down, apply the front brake and pump the front forks up and down by applying pressure against the handlebars. Continue until the oil stops draining out of the hole.
3. Replace the drain plug gasket if leaking or damaged.
4. Reinstall the fork tube drain plug and gasket and tighten to the torque specification in **Table 5**.
5. Repeat Steps 1-4 for the other fork tube.

WARNING
Wipe up any oil that may have spilled onto the front tire or front brake caliper.

6. Support the bike with a stand so the front wheel is off the ground.
7. Loosen the fork tube upper pinch bolt (A, **Figure 32**).
8. Remove the fork cap (B, **Figure 32**), spacer, spring seat and fork spring from the fork tube. See **Figure 33**.
9. Pour the specified type (**Table 6**) and quantity (**Table 9**) of fork oil into the fork tube.
10. Lubricate fork cap O-ring and threads with fork oil.
11. Install the fork spring with its tighter wound coils (**Figure 34**) facing down.
12. Install the spring seat, spacer and fork cap (**Figure 33**). Tighten the fork cap to the torque specification in **Table 5**.
13. Tighten the fork tube upper pinch bolt (A, **Figure 32**) to the torque specification in **Table 5**.
14. Repeat Steps 7-13 for the other fork tube.

Control Cable Lubrication

Clean and lubricate the clutch and throttle cables at the intervals specified in **Table 1**. Also, check the cables for kinks, wear or damage that could cause a cable to stick or break. Cables are expendable items and will not last forever under the best of conditions.

The most positive method of control cable lubrication involves the use of a cable lubricator like the one shown in **Figure 35**. Lubricate the cables with cable lube or engine oil. Do *not* use chain lube to lubricate the cables.

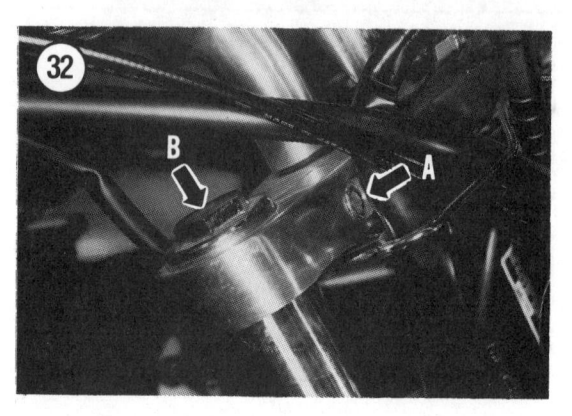

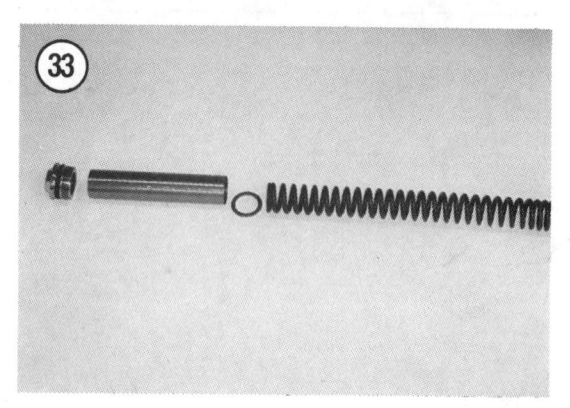

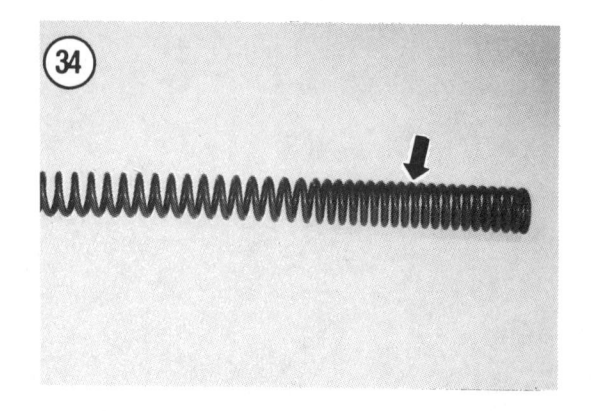

LUBRICATION, MAINTENANCE AND TUNE-UP

NOTE
It is not necessary to remove the cables when disconnecting them in Steps 1-3.

1. Disconnect both throttle cables from the throttle grip (**Figure 36**) as described under *Throttle Cable Replacement* in Chapter Eight.

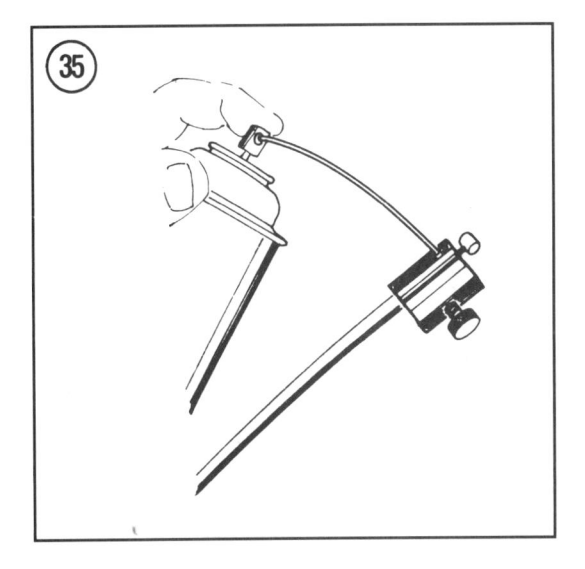

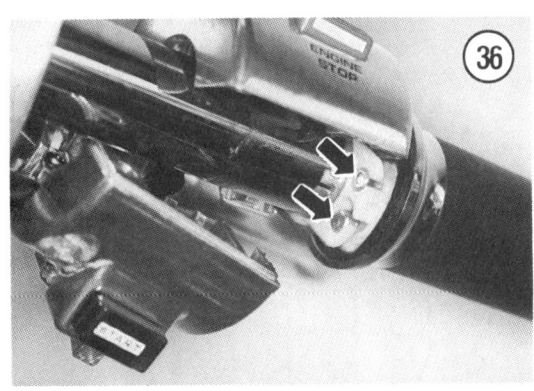

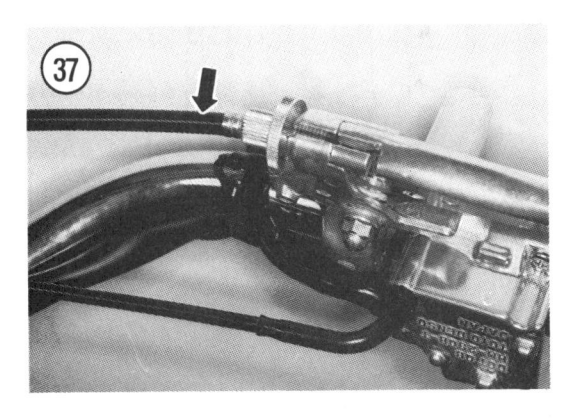

2. Disconnect the upper clutch cable end (**Figure 37**) as described *Clutch Cable Replacement* in Chapter Six.
3. Attach a cable lubricator to the end of the cable following its manufacturer's instructions (**Figure 35**).
4. Inject the lubricant into the lubricator until the lubricant begins to flow from the other end of the cable.

NOTE
Place a shop cloth at the end of the cable to catch the lubricant as it runs out. Do not allow the lubricant to contact any brake system component.

5. Disconnect the lubricator.
6. Apply a light coat of grease to the cable ends before reconnecting them.
7. Reconnect the cables by reversing Steps 1 and 2.
8. Adjust the cables as described in this chapter.
9. Operate each cable, making sure they move smoothly with no binding or roughness.

Steering Stem Bearings

Remove, clean and lubricate the steering stem bearings (**Figure 38**) as described in Chapter Eleven.

PERIODIC MAINTENANCE

Table 1 lists periodic maintenance items and intervals.

Disc Brake Hoses

Check the brake hoses between the master cylinder and the brake caliper. If there is any leakage,

CHAPTER THREE

tighten the bolt or hose and then bleed the brake as described in Chapter Thirteen. If this does not stop the leak or if a brake line is obviously damaged, cracked or chafed, replace the brake hose and bleed the system.

Brake Pad Wear

1. Inspect the front (**Figure 39**) and rear (**Figure 40**) brake pads for uneven wear, scoring, oil contamination or other damage. If there is no visible brake pad damage or contamination, perform Step 2.
2. Replace the brake pads as a set if either pad is worn to the bottom of the wear groove (**Figure 41**).
3. Replace the brake pads as described in Chapter Thirteen.

Front Brake Lever Adjustment

Brake pad wear in the caliper is automatically compensated for as the piston moves outward in the caliper. However, periodically slide the brake lever cover away from the lever and inspect the master cylinder bore (**Figure 42**) for brake fluid leakage. If necessary, service the front master cylinder as described in Chapter Thirteen.

Rear Brake Light Switch Adjustment

1. Turn the ignition switch on.
2. Depress the brake pedal. The brake light must activate just before the brake begins to work.
3. If the brake light activates too late, perform the following:
   a. Hold the brake light switch body (A, **Figure 43**).
   b. Turn the adjusting nut as required.

NOTE
Do not turn the switch body when adjusting the rear brake light switch.

4. Turn the ignition switch off.

Brake Fluid Selection

Use DOT 4 brake fluid in the front and rear master cylinder reservoirs.

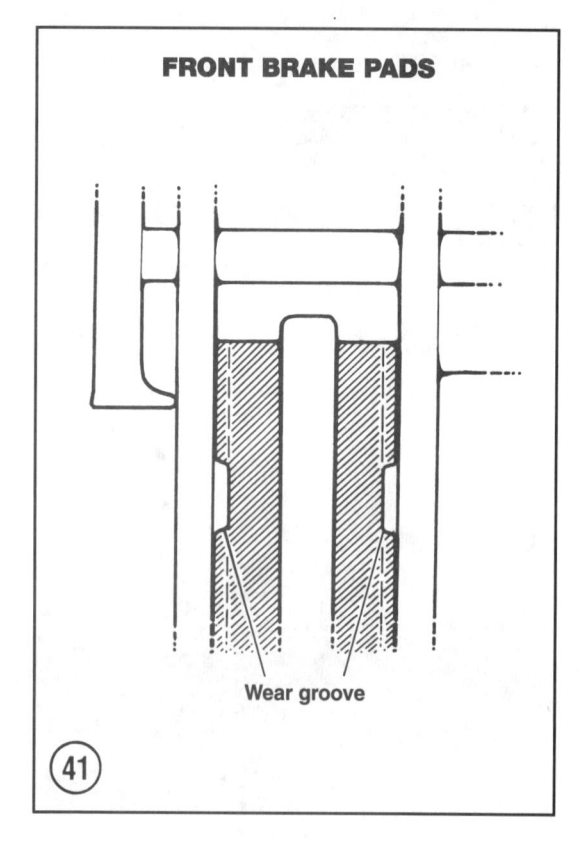

FRONT BRAKE PADS

Wear groove

LUBRICATION, MAINTENANCE AND TUNE-UP

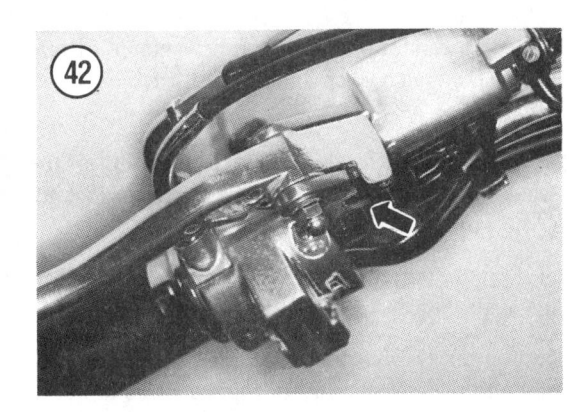

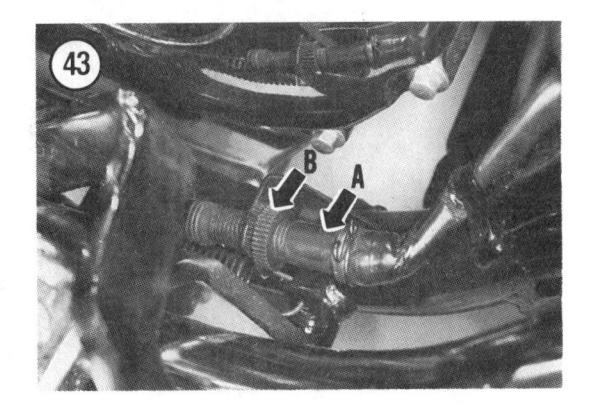

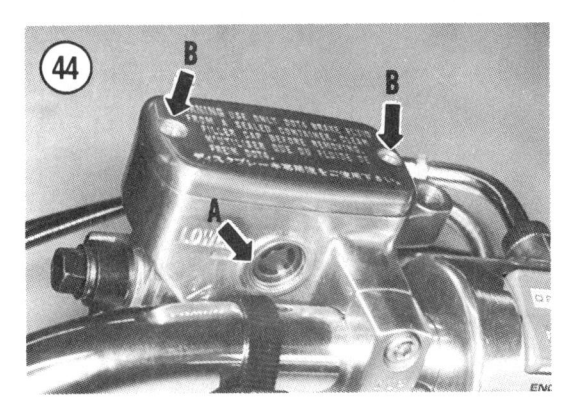

WARNING
Use brake fluid clearly marked DOT 4 as previously specified. Others may cause brake failure. Do not intermix different brands or types of brake fluid as they may not be compatible. Do not intermix silicone based (DOT 5) brake fluid as it can cause brake system failure.

CAUTION
Handle brake fluid carefully. Do not spill it on painted or plastic surfaces as it will destroy the surface. Wash the area immediately with soap and water and thoroughly rinse it off.

Front Brake Fluid Level Check

NOTE
If the brake fluid level lowers rapidly, check the brake hose and fittings.

1. Turn the handlebar so the front master cylinder is level.
2. The brake fluid level must be above the lower level line in the master cylinder window (A, **Figure 44**). If the brake fluid level is low, continue with Step 3.
3. Wipe off the master cylinder cover and remove the cover screws (B, **Figure 44**). Then remove the cover, set plate and diaphragm. Do not remove the float.
4. Add fresh DOT 4 brake fluid to fill the reservoir to the upper level mark in the reservoir (**Figure 45**).
5. Install the diaphragm, set plate and cover. Install and tighten the cover screws (B, **Figure 44**).

Rear Brake Fluid Level Check

NOTE
If the brake fluid level lowers rapidly, check the brake hose and fittings.

1. Park the vehicle on level ground. Then support it so it is upright.

WARNING
Do not check the rear brake fluid level with the bike resting on its sidestand. A false reading will result.

2. The brake fluid level must be between the upper and lower level marks (**Figure 46**) on the reservoir housing. If the brake fluid level is low, continue with Step 3.
3. Wipe off the master cylinder cover and unscrew the cover (**Figure 46**). Then remove the cover and diaphragm (**Figure 46**). Do not remove the float.
4. Add fresh DOT 4 brake fluid to fill the reservoir to the upper level mark on the reservoir (**Figure 46**).
5. Install the diaphragm and cover. Tighten the cover securely.

Disc Brake Fluid Change

Every time you remove the reservoir cap, a small amount of dirt and moisture enters the brake fluid. The same thing happens if a leak occurs or when you loosen and disconnect a brake hose. Dirt can clog the system and cause unnecessary wear. Water in the brake fluid vaporizes at high temperature, impairing the hydraulic action and reducing the brake's stopping ability. To maintain peak performance, change the brake fluid every year and whenever you overhaul a caliper or master cylinder. To change brake fluid, follow the brake bleeding procedure in Chapter Thirteen.

Clutch Adjustment

Clutch adjustment takes up slack caused by cable stretch and clutch plate wear. Insufficient free play will cause clutch slippage and rapid clutch disc wear.

NOTE
When checking and adjusting the clutch in the following steps, make sure the upper and lower clutch cable ends seat correctly in their respective positions. If not, the inspection and adjustment procedures will be incorrect.

1. With the engine off, pull the clutch lever and measure the clutch free play at the end of the clutch lever (**Figure 47**). The correct clutch free play measurement is 10-20 mm (3/8-3/4 in.). If the free play is incorrect, perform Step 2.
2. At the clutch lever, loosen the clutch adjuster locknut (A, **Figure 48**) and turn the adjuster (B, **Figure 48**) in or out to obtain the correct amount of free play. Tighten the locknut.

3. If you cannot obtain the proper amount of free play at the clutch lever adjuster, perform the following steps.
4. Turn the clutch adjuster (B, **Figure 48**) all the way in, then back out one turn and tighten its locknut (A, **Figure 48**).
5. Remove the left crankcase rear cover as described in Chapter Five.
6. Loosen the clutch cable locknut (A, **Figure 49**) and turn the adjuster nut (B, **Figure 49**) in or out to

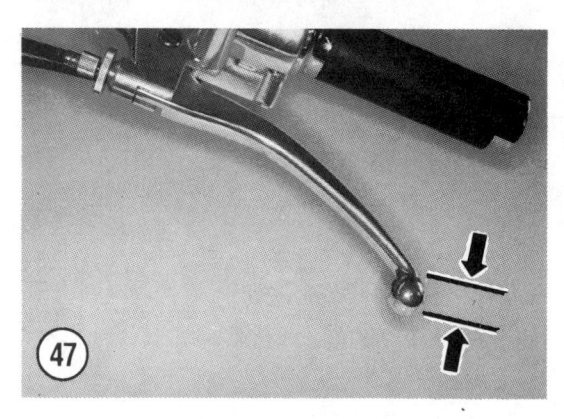

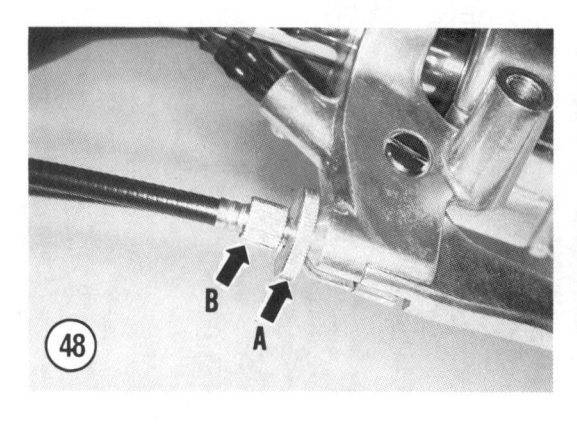

LUBRICATION, MAINTENANCE AND TUNE-UP

obtain the correct clutch free play measurement (Step 1).

7. Tighten the clutch cable locknut and remeasure the free play at the clutch lever (**Figure 47**).

8. If you are unable to obtain the proper free play, either the clutch cable or the clutch friction discs are excessively worn and must be replaced. Refer to Chapter Six for clutch cable replacement and clutch overhaul.

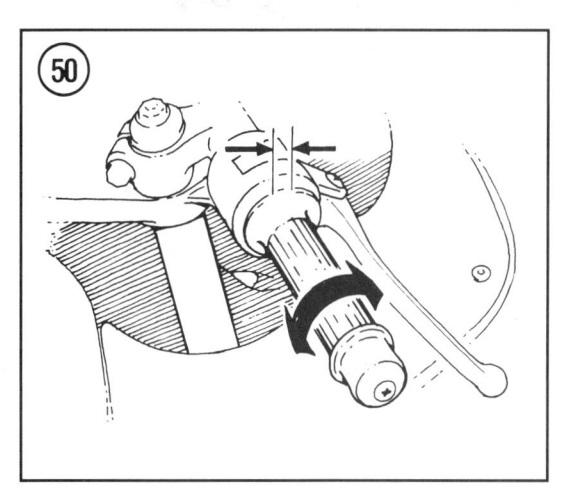

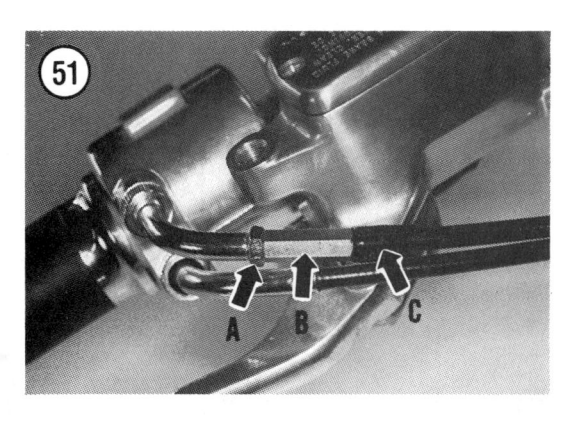

9. Install the left crankcase rear cover as described in Chapter Five.

Throttle Cable Adjustment and Operation

Some throttle cable play is necessary to prevent changes in the idle speed when you turn the handlebars. Honda specifies a throttle cable free play of 2-6 mm (1/8-1/4 in.), measured at the throttle grip flange (**Figure 50**).

In time, the throttle cable free play will become excessive from cable stretch. This will delay throttle response and affect low-speed operation. On the other hand, if there is no throttle cable free play, an excessively high idle can result.

1. Turn the throttle grip and measure free play as shown in **Figure 50**. The correct throttle free play measurement is 2-6 mm (1/8-1/4 in.). Note the following:

   a. If the free play measurement is incorrect, continue with Step 2.

   b. If the free play measurement is correct, go to Step 9.

2. Loosen the throttle cable adjuster locknut (A, **Figure 51**) and turn the adjuster (B, **Figure 51**) in or out to obtain the correct throttle cable free play measurement. Tighten the locknut and recheck free play. Reposition the adjuster boot (C, **Figure 51**) as required.

3. Recheck the throttle cable free play.

4. If you cannot obtain the correct throttle cable free play with the upper cable adjuster, make major adjustments at the lower adjuster; continue with Step 5.

5. Remove the fuel tank (Chapter Eight).

6. Loosen the lower adjuster locknuts (A, **Figure 52**) and turn the adjuster (B, **Figure 52**) to obtain the correct free play measurement (Step 1). Tighten the locknuts (A, **Figure 52**).

7. Install the fuel tank (Chapter Eight).

8. Recheck the throttle cable free play.

9. Make sure the throttle lever rotates freely from its fully closed to fully open position(s).

10. Start the engine and allow it to idle in NEUTRAL. Turn the handlebar from side to side. If the idle increases, the throttle cable is routed incorrectly or there is not enough cable free play.

NOTE
A damaged throttle cable(s) will prevent the engine from idling properly.

Choke Cable Adjustment

Choke cable adjustment is required if one or more of the following conditions occur:
   a. The engine is difficult to start when cold but easy to start once it has warmed (choke valve is not completely opened).
   b. Erratic idle speed occurs after the engine has warmed (choke valve not completely closing).
1. Remove the fuel tank (Chapter Eight).
2. Loosen the choke plunger cap (**Figure 53**) and remove the choke plunger (**Figure 54**) from each carburetor.
3. Push the choke lever (**Figure 55**) forward to its fully closed position.
4. Measure the distance between the choke plunger and the end of the plunger cap threads as shown in **Figure 56**). The correct distance is 10-11 mm (0.39-0.43 in.).
5. Adjust the choke cable as follows:
   a. Turn the handlebar all the way to the right side.
   b. Loosen the choke cable locknut (A, **Figure 57**).
   c. Turn the choke cable elbow (B, **Figure 57**) until the correct valve adjustment (Step 4) is obtained.
   d. Tighten the choke cable locknut and recheck the adjustment.
6. Insert the choke plunger (**Figure 54**) into the carburetor and tighten the plunger cap (**Figure 53**) until it contacts the carburetor housing, then tighten the plunger an additional 1/4 turn.
7. Repeat Step 6 for the other clutch cable end.

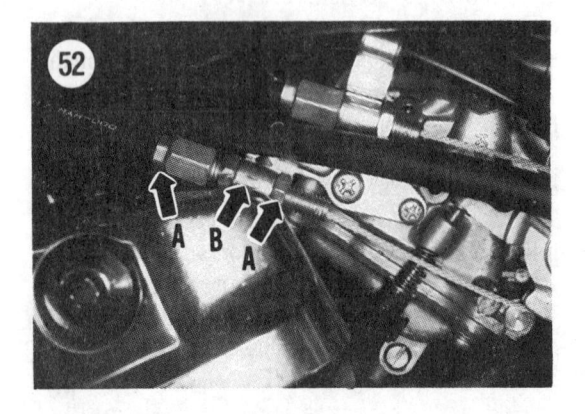

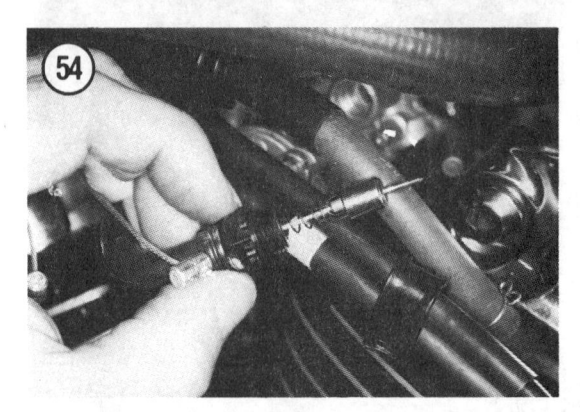

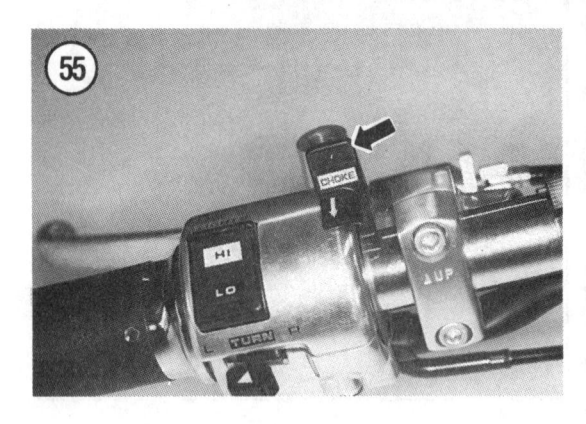

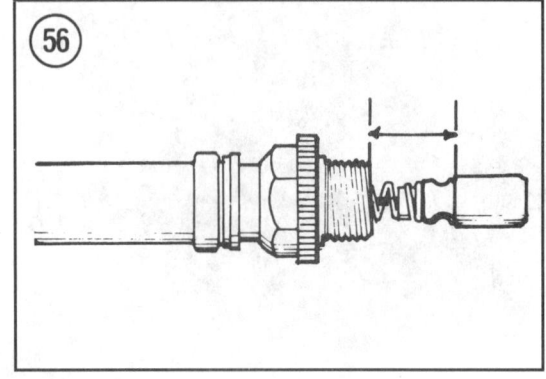

LUBRICATION, MAINTENANCE AND TUNE-UP

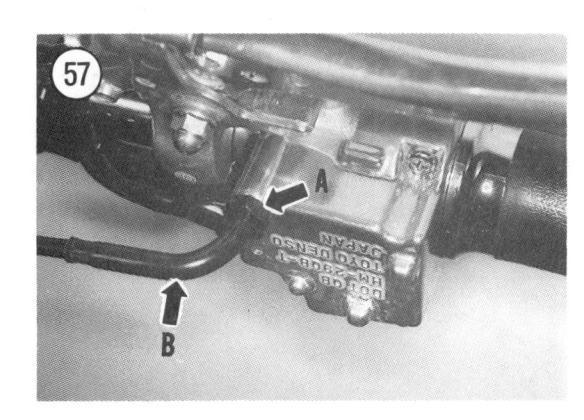

8. Operate the choke lever and make sure the choke plungers operate correctly. If the operation is incorrect or there is binding, make sure the cable is routed and attached correctly.

Air Filter

A clogged air filter will decrease the efficiency and life of the engine. Never run the bike without an air filter properly installed. Even minute particles of dust can cause severe internal engine wear and clogging of carburetor passages.

1. Remove the seat (Chapter Fourteen).

2. Remove the connector block mounting bolt (**Figure 58**) and move the connector assembly away from the air filter housing cover.

3. Remove the air filter housing cover (**Figure 59**) mounting screws and remove the cover (**Figure 60**).

4. Remove the air filter assembly (**Figure 61**).

5. Replace the air filter element (**Figure 62**) at the specified mileage intervals (**Table 1**) or if it is excessively dirty or damaged.

NOTE
*Because the stock air filter element (**Figure 62**) contains a dust adhesive, it cannot be cleaned. Replace the filter element when excessively dirty or damaged.*

6. Use a flashlight and check the air box-to-carburetor boot inside diameter for dirt or other contamination.

7. Wipe the inside of the air box with a clean rag. If you cannot clean the air box with it mounted on the bike, remove and clean the air box thoroughly with solvent. Then clean with hot soapy water and rinse with water from a garden hose. Remove and install the air box as described in Chapter Eight.

8. Inspect the seal installed around the perimeter of the air filter cover. Replace the seal if missing or damaged.

9. Reverse these steps to install the air filter element.

Crankcase Breather

At the service intervals in **Table 1** or after riding in wet weather, remove the plug (**Figure 63**) from the end of the breather tube and drain its contents into a suitable container. Reinstall the plug.

Fuel Line Inspection

1. Remove the fuel tank (Chapter Eight).
2. Remove the left side cover (Chapter Fourteen).
3. Remove the exhaust system (Chapter Fourteen).
4. Replace any leaking or damaged fuel hoses (**Figure 64** and **Figure 65**). Make sure the fuel hose clamps are in place and holding securely.
5. Reverse Steps 1-3.

WARNING
A damaged or deteriorated fuel line presents a very dangerous fire hazard to both the rider and the motorcycle.

Cooling System Inspection

Once a year, or whenever troubleshooting the cooling system, check the following items. If you do not have the test equipment, refer testing to a Honda dealership.

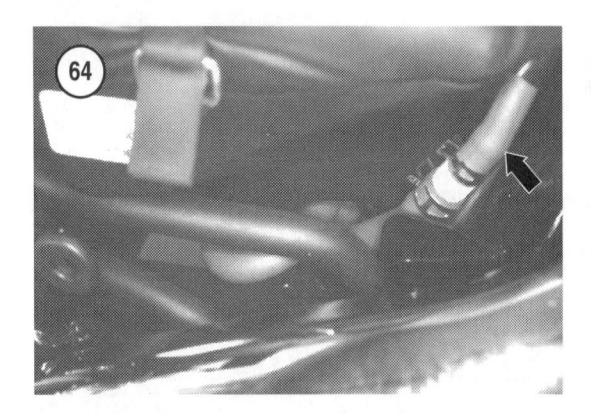

LUBRICATION, MAINTENANCE AND TUNE-UP

WARNING
When performing any service work to the engine or cooling system, never remove the radiator cap, coolant drain screws or disconnect any hose while the engine and radiator are hot. Scalding fluid and steam may be blown out under pressure and cause serious injury.

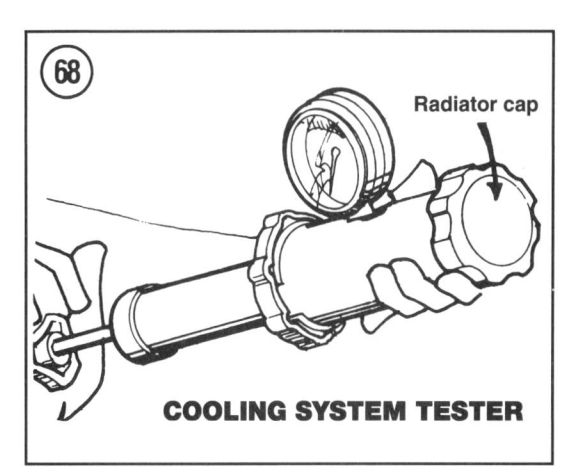

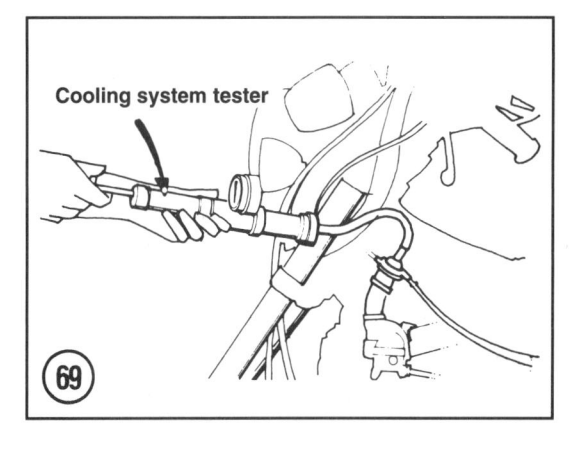

1. Remove the right side steering cover (Chapter Fourteen).
2. With the engine cold, remove the radiator cap (**Figure 66**).
3. Check the rubber washers inside the radiator cap (**Figure 67**). Replace the cap if the washers are cracked, damaged or deteriorated. If the radiator cap is good, perform Step 3.

CAUTION
When performing Steps 4 and 5, do not exceed the cooling system pressure specified in Step 3 or you can damage the cooling system components.

4. Pressure test the radiator cap (**Figure 68**) with a cooling system tester. The specified radiator cap relief pressure is 108-137 kPa (16-20 psi). The cap must be able to sustain this pressure for at least 6 seconds. Replace the radiator cap if it does not hold pressure.
5. Leave the radiator cap off and mount the cooling system tester onto the radiator (**Figure 69**). Then pressure test the cooling system as specified in Step 4. The system must be able to hold this pressure for at least 6 seconds. If the system fails to hold the specified pressure, check for the following conditions:
   a. Leaking or damaged hoses.
   b. Leaking water pump seal.
   c. Loose water pump mounting bolts.
   d. Warped water pump sealing surface.
   e. Warped cylinder head or cylinder mating surfaces.
6. Check all cooling system hoses for damage or deterioration. Replace any hose that is questionable. Make sure all hose clamps are tight.
7. Carefully clean any dirt, mud, bugs or other material from the radiator core. Use a whisk broom, compressed air or low-pressure water. Straighten bent radiator fins with a screwdriver.

Hydrometer Test

WARNING
When performing any service work to the engine or cooling system, never remove the radiator cap, coolant drain screws or disconnect any hose while the engine and radiators are hot. Scalding fluid and steam may be blown out under pressure and cause serious injury.

1. Remove the right side steering cover (Chapter Fourteen).
2. Remove the radiator cap (**Figure 66**).
3. Test the specific gravity of the coolant with a hydrometer (**Figure 70**). The system must have at least a 50:50 mixture of antifreeze and distilled water.
4. Install the radiator cap and the right steering side cover.

Coolant Change

Use only a high-quality ethylene glycol-based antifreeze compounded for aluminum engines. Mix the antifreeze with water in a 50:50 ratio. **Table 10** lists coolant capacity. When mixing antifreeze with water, use only soft or distilled water. Never use tap or saltwater as this will damage engine parts. You can purchase distilled water at supermarkets in gallon containers.

Change the engine coolant at the intervals specified in **Table 1**.

> *WARNING*
> *Antifreeze is classified as an environmental toxic waste by the EPA and cannot be legally disposed of by flushing down a drain or pouring it onto the ground. Place antifreeze in a suitable container and dispose of it according to local EPA regulations. Do not store coolant where it is accessible to children or animals.*

Perform the following procedure when the engine is *cold*.

> *CAUTION*
> *Be careful not to spill antifreeze on painted surfaces as it will destroy the surface. Wash immediately with soapy water and rinse thoroughly with clean water.*

1. Remove the right steering side cover (Chapter Fourteen).
2. Remove the radiator cap (**Figure 66**).
3. Place a clean container under the water pump.
4. Remove the coolant drain plug (**Figure 71**) from the water pump and drain the engine coolant.
5. Flush the cooling system with clean tap water directed through the radiator filler neck. Allow this water to drain completely.
6. Install the coolant drain plug and a new washer (**Figure 71**) and tighten to the torque specification in **Table 5**.
7. Place the drain pan underneath the siphon tube joint mounted on the coolant reserve tank. Then remove the siphon tube and drain the reserve tank coolant.
8. Flush the reserve tank with clean tap water directed through the reserve tank's coolant filler hole.

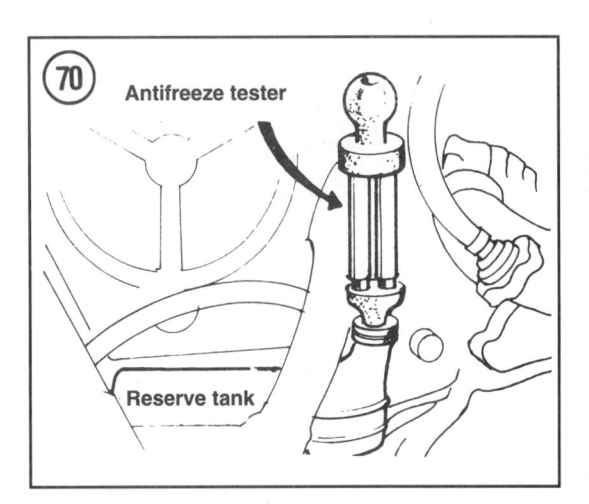

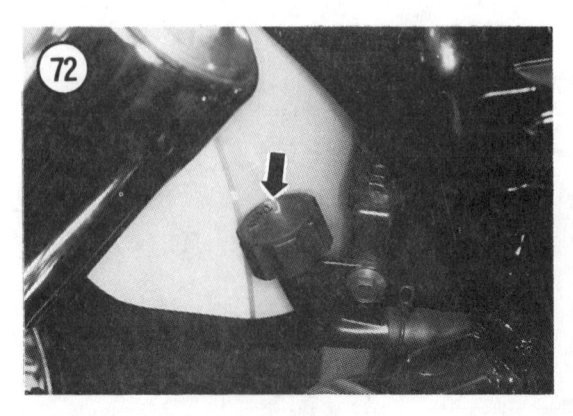

LUBRICATION, MAINTENANCE AND TUNE-UP

9. Reconnect the siphon tube and its hose clamp.
10. Refill the radiator by adding a 50:50 mixture of antifreeze and distilled water through the radiator filler neck (**Figure 66**). See **Table 10** for coolant capacity. Do not install the radiator cap at this time.
11. Remove the reserve tank cap (**Figure 72**) and fill the reserve tank to its upper level line (**Figure 73**).
12. Bleed air from the cooling system as follows:
   a. Shift the transmission into NEUTRAL.
   b. Start the engine and allow to idle for 2-3 minutes.
   c. Snap the throttle open 3-4 times to bleed air from the cooling system.
   d. Turn the engine off.
   e. Check the coolant level in the radiator. Add coolant to bring its level up to the filler neck opening. Install and tighten the radiator cap (**Figure 66**).
   f. Check the coolant level in the reserve tank (**Figure 73**). Add coolant to bring its level to the upper lever line (**Figure 73**). Install the reserve tank cap (**Figure 72**).
13. Install the right side steering cover (Chapter Fourteen).
14. Test ride the bike and readjust the coolant level in the reserve tank, if necessary.
15. Check the drain bolt for leaks.

Emission Control System (California Models)

At the service intervals in **Table 1**, check all of the emission control tubes and the EVAP canister for loose connections or damage. Refer to *Evaporative Emission Control System* in Chapter Eight.

Sidestand

At the service intervals in **Table 1**, check the sidestand and the ignition cutoff system operation as follows:

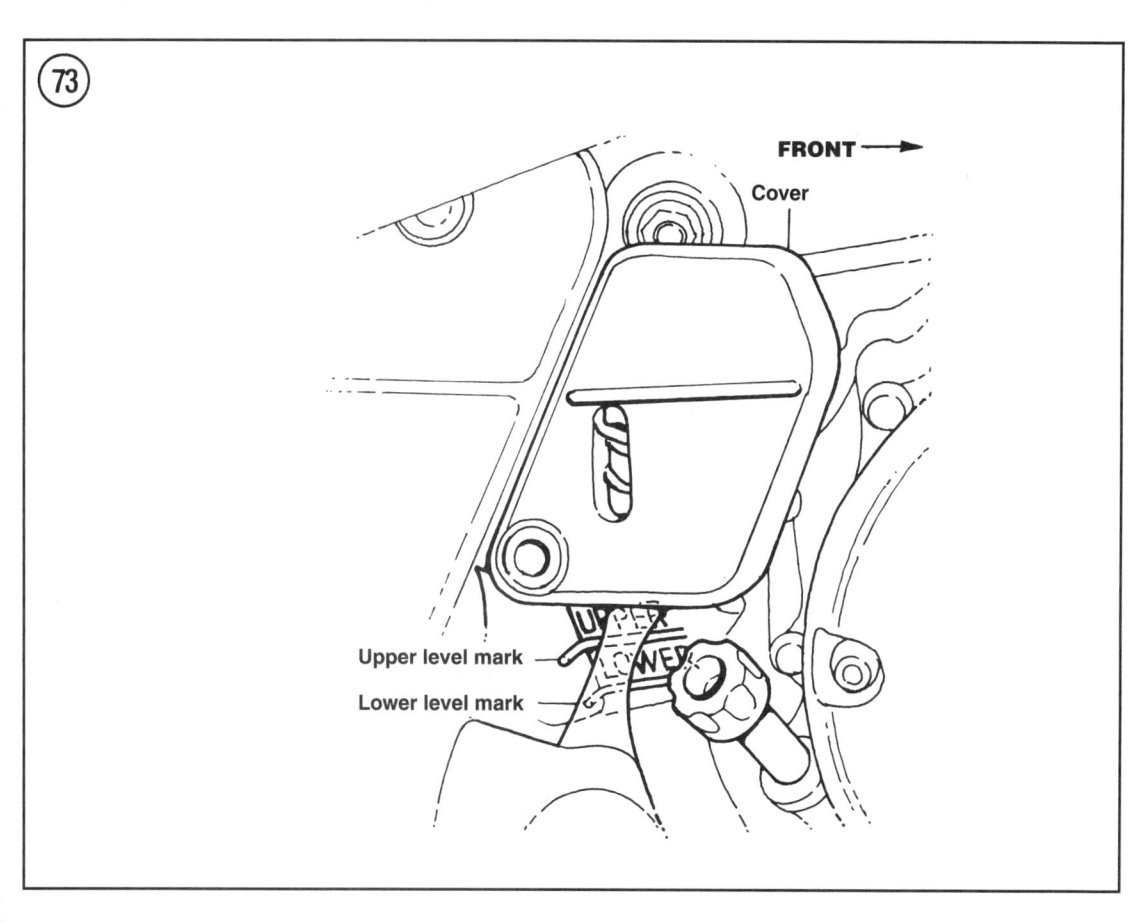

73

FRONT →
Cover
Upper level mark
Lower level mark

1. Park the bike on a level surface and support it with a suitable stand, or have an assistant support it for you.
2. Operate the sidestand (**Figure 74**) and check its movement and spring tension. Replace the spring if weak or damaged.
3. Lubricate the sidestand pivot bolt if necessary.
4. Check the sidestand ignition cutoff system as follows:
    a. Park the bike so both wheels are on the ground.
    b. Sit on the motorcycle and raise the sidestand.
    c. Shift the transmission into NEUTRAL.
    d. Start the engine, then squeeze the clutch lever and shift the transmission into gear.
    e. Move the sidestand down. When doing so, the engine should stop.
    f. If the engine does not stop as the sidestand is lowered, inspect the sidestand switch as described in Chapter Nine.
5. If removed, tighten the sidestand bolt and nut to the torque specification in **Table 5**.

Headlight Aim

Adjust the headlight as described in Chapter Nine.

Steering Stem Bearings

Inspect the steering bearing adjustment at the intervals specified in **Table 1**.
1. Support the bike on a stand with the front wheel off the ground.

NOTE
When performing Step 2, make sure the control cables do not interfere with handlebar movement.

2. Hold onto the handlebars and move them from side to side. Note any binding or roughness.
3. Support the bike so both wheels are on the ground.
4. Sit on the motorcycle and hold onto the handlebars. Apply the front brake lever and try to push the front forks forward. Try to detect any movement in the steering head area. If any movement is noted, the bearing adjustment is loose and requires adjustment.
5. If you feel any roughness, binding or looseness when performing Step 2 or Step 4, service the steering stem bearings as described in Chapter Eleven.

Front Suspension Check

1. Check the front forks for leaks or damage.
2. Apply the front brake and pump the forks up and down as vigorously as possible. Check for smooth operation.
3. Make sure the upper and lower fork tube pinch bolts are tight.
4. Make sure the handlebar holder bolts are tight.
5. Make sure the front axle is tight.

CAUTION
If any of the previously mentioned bolts and nuts are loose, refer to Chapter Eleven for torque specifications.

Rear Suspension Inspection

1. Support the bike on a stand with the rear wheel off the ground.
2. Check the final drive unit for leaks.
3. With an assistant steadying the bike, push hard on the rear wheel (sideways) to check for side play in the rear swing arm bearings.
4. Check the tightness of the upper and lower shock absorber fasteners.
5. Make sure the rear axle nut and pinch bolt are tight.

CAUTION
If any of the previously mentioned bolts and nuts are loose, refer to Chapter Twelve for torque specifications.

Wheel Bearings

There is no factory-recommended mileage interval for inspecting the wheel bearings. Check the

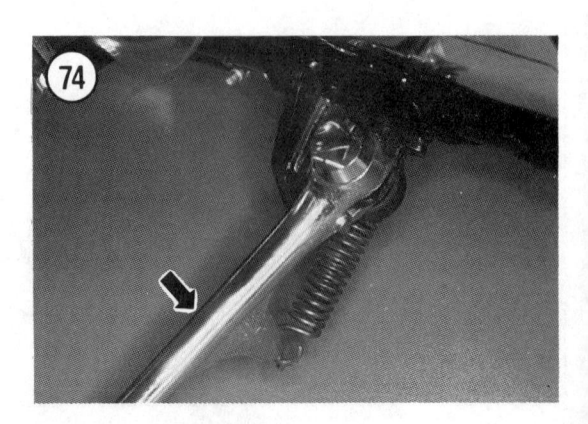

LUBRICATION, MAINTENANCE AND TUNE-UP

wheel bearings (**Figure 75**) whenever the wheel(s) is removed or if there is the likelihood of water or other contamination. See Chapter Eleven and Chapter Twelve for service procedures.

Nuts, Bolts, and Other Fasteners

Constant vibration can loosen many fasteners on your Honda. Check the tightness of all exposed fasteners.

ENGINE TUNE-UP

The number of definitions of the term tune-up is probably equal to the number of people defining it. For the purposes of this book, a tune-up is general adjustment and maintenance to ensure peak engine performance.

The cam chain tensioners are automatic and do not require periodic adjustment.

The engine is equipped with a hydraulic valve adjuster system and requires no periodic valve adjustment. The only time any type of adjustment is necessary is after a cylinder head overhaul or if damage has occurred. See Chapter Four.

The following paragraphs discuss each phase of a proper tune-up which you must perform in the order given. Have the new parts on hand before you begin.

To perform a tune-up on your Honda, you need the following tools and equipment:
 a. Spark plug wrench.
 b. Socket wrench and assorted sockets.
 c. Compression gauge.
 d. Spark plug feeler gauge and gap adjusting tool.
 e. Ignition timing light.
 f. Portable tachometer.
 g. Carburetor synchronization tool.
 h. Carburetor pilot screw adjusting tool.

Cylinder Compression

A cylinder compression test is one of the quickest ways to check the internal condition of the engine: piston, piston rings, valves, cylinder and head gasket. It is a good idea to check compression at each tune-up and compare it with the reading you get at the next tune-up. This will help you spot any developing problems.

1. Warm the engine to normal operating temperature, then turn it off.
2. Remove one of the spark plugs from each cylinder head.
3. Then insert each plug into its plug cap and ground the plug against the cylinder head.
4. Thread or insert the tip of a compression gauge into the front cylinder head spark plug hole (**Figure 76**). Make sure you seat the gauge properly.
5. Make sure the choke is completely OFF.
6. Hold the throttle wide open and crank the engine with the starter motor for several revolutions until the gauge gives its highest reading. Record the pressure reading and compare to the compression specification listed in **Table 11**.
7. Press the pressure release button on the compression tester, then remove the tester from the front cylinder head.
8. Repeat Steps 4-7 for the rear cylinder.
9. Reinstall the spark plugs and connect the spark plug caps.
10. When interpreting the results, actual readings are not as important as the difference between the readings. Standard compression pressure is listed in

Table 11. A maximum difference of 100 kPa (14 psi) between the 2 cylinders is acceptable. A greater pressure difference indicates worn or broken rings, leaking or sticking valves, blown head gasket(s) or a combination of all.

11. If the compression readings do not differ between the cylinders by more than 70 kPa (10 psi), the rings and valves are in good condition.

12. If a low reading (10% or more) is obtained on one of the cylinders, it indicates a leaking cylinder head gasket, valve(s) or piston ring trouble. To determine which, pour about a teaspoon of engine oil through the spark plug hole onto the top of the piston. Crank the engine over once to clear the excess oil, then make another compression test and record the reading. If the compression increases significantly, the rings are worn or damaged. If compression does not increase, the valves require servicing.

NOTE
If the compression is low, you cannot tune the engine to its maximum performance.

Correct Spark Plug Heat Range

Spark plugs are available in various heat ranges. They can be hotter or colder than the plug originally installed at the factory.

Select a plug of the heat range designed for the loads and conditions under which your Honda will be operated. Using a plug that is too cold will result in spark plug fouling. Using a plug that is too hot will result in preignition, detonation and piston damage.

In general, use a hot plug for low speeds and low temperatures. Use a cold plug for high speeds, high engine loads and high temperatures. The plug must operate hot enough to burn off unwanted deposits, but not so hot that it is damaged or causes preignition. A spark plug of the correct heat range will show a light tan color on the insulator after the plug has been in service.

The reach (length) (**Figure 77**) of a plug is also important. A plug that is too short will cause excessive carbon buildup, hard starting and plug fouling. A plug that is too long will cause overheating or may contact the top of the piston. Both conditions will cause engine damage.

Table 11 lists NGK and Denso spark plugs that you can use in your Honda.

Spark Plug Removal

CAUTION
Whenever you remove the spark plug, dirt around it can fall into the plug hole. This can cause expensive engine damage.

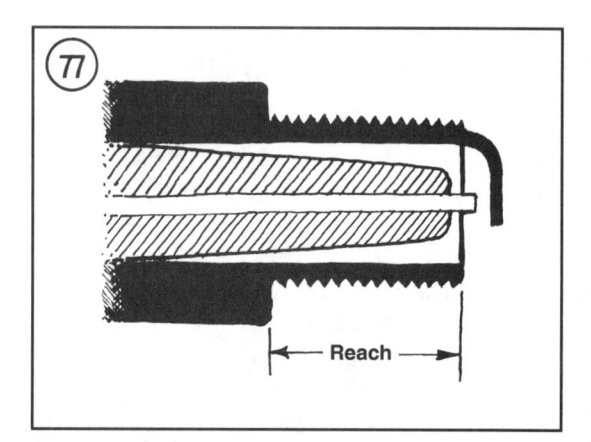

LUBRICATION, MAINTENANCE AND TUNE-UP

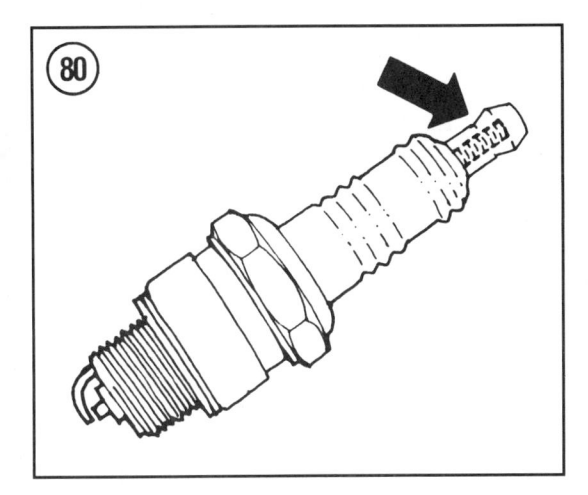

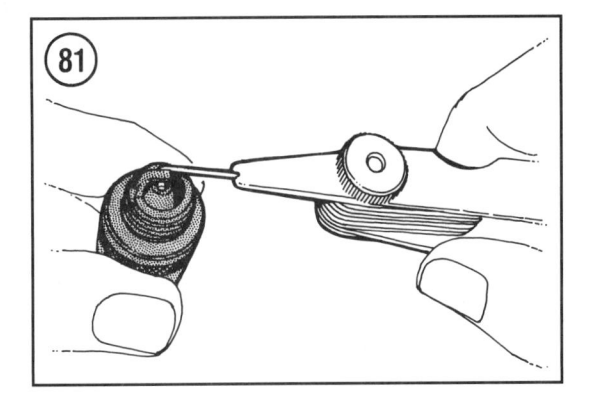

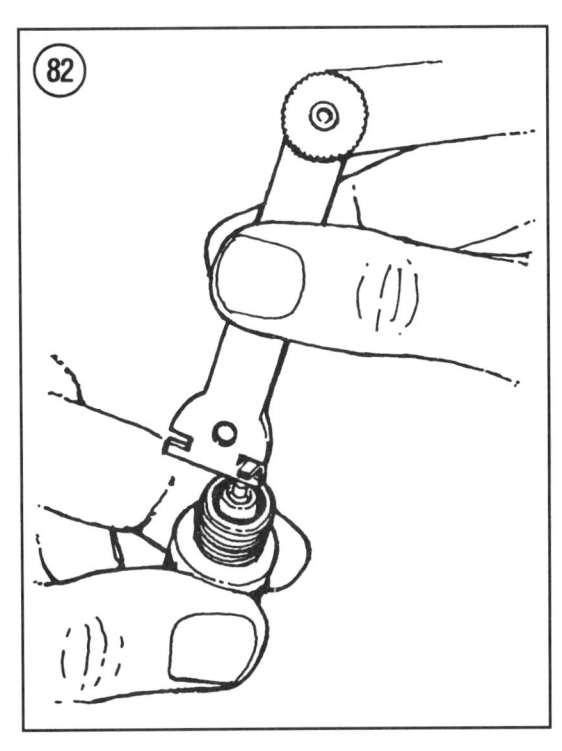

1. Grasp the spark plug lead as near the plug as possible and pull it off the plug. If the plug cap sticks to the plug, twist it slightly to break it loose.
2. Blow away any dirt collected inside the spark plug well (**Figure 78**) in the cylinder head.
3. Remove the spark plug with a spark plug socket (**Figure 79**).

NOTE
If the plug is difficult to remove, apply penetrating oil, like WD-40 or Liquid Wrench, around the base of the plug and let it soak in about 10-20 minutes.

4. Inspect the plug carefully. Look for a broken center porcelain, excessively eroded electrodes, and excessive carbon or oil fouling.
5. Repeat for each spark plug.

Gapping and Installing the Plug

Carefully adjust the electrode gap on a new spark plug to ensure a reliable, consistent spark. To do this, you must use a special spark plug gapping tool and a wire feeler gauge.

1. Remove the small terminal adapter from the end of the plug (**Figure 80**).

NOTE
The spark plug terminal adapter is not used with the stock Honda spark plug caps.

2. Insert a wire feeler gauge between the center and side electrode (**Figure 81**). The correct gap is listed in **Table 11**. If the gap is correct, you will feel a slight drag as you pull the wire through. If there is no drag, or the gauge will not pass through, bend the side electrode with a gapping tool (**Figure 82**) to set the proper gap.
3. Apply an antiseize compound to the plug threads before installing the spark plug. Do not use engine oil on the plug threads.
4. Screw the spark plug in by hand until it seats. This should require very little effort. If force is necessary, you may have the plug cross-threaded. Unscrew it and try again.
5. Use a spark plug wrench and tighten the spark plug to the torque specification in **Table 5**. If you do not have a torque wrench, tighten the plug an additional 1/4 to 1/2 turn after the gasket contacts the

cylinder head. If you are reusing a previously installed plug, only tighten an additional 1/4 turn.

NOTE
Do not overtighten the spark plug. This will crush the gasket and destroy its sealing ability.

6. Install the spark plug cap. Make sure it is on tight.
7. Repeat these steps for each spark plug.

Reading Spark Plugs

Careful examination of the spark plug can determine valuable engine and spark plug information. This information is more valid after performing the following steps.
1. Ride the vehicle at full throttle.

NOTE
You must ride the vehicle long enough to obtain an accurate reading or color on the spark plug. If your original plug is fouled, use a new plug.

2. Push the engine stop switch to OFF before closing the throttle and simultaneously pull in the clutch or shift to neutral then coast and brake to a stop.
3. Remove the spark plugs and examine them. Compare the plugs to **Figure 83** and note the following:

Normal condition

If the plug has a light tan- or gray-colored deposit and no abnormal gap wear or erosion, good engine, carburetion and ignition condition are indicated. The plug in use is of the proper heat range and may be serviced and returned to use.

Carbon fouled

Soft, dry, sooty deposits covering the entire firing end of the plug are evidence of incomplete combustion. Even though the firing end of the plug is dry, the plug's insulation decreases. An electrical path is formed that lowers the voltage from the ignition system. Engine misfiring is a sign of carbon fouling. Carbon fouling can be caused by one or more of the following:
 a. Too rich fuel mixture.
 b. Spark plug heat range too cold.
 c. Clogged air filter.
 d. Over-retarded ignition timing.
 e. Ignition component failure.
 f. Low engine compression.
 g. Prolonged idling.

Oil fouled

The tip of an oil fouled plug has a black insulator tip, a damp oily film over the firing end and a carbon layer over the entire nose. The electrodes will not be worn. Common causes for this condition are:
 a. Incorrect carburetor jetting.
 b. Low idle speed or prolonged idling.
 c. Ignition component failure.
 d. Spark plug heat range too cold.
 e. Engine still being broken in.

Oil fouled spark plugs may be cleaned in an emergency, but is better to replace them. It is important to correct the cause of fouling before you return the engine to service.

Gap bridging

Plugs with this condition exhibit gaps shorted out by combustion deposits between the electrodes. If you encounter this condition, check for an improper oil type or excessive carbon in the combustion chamber. Be sure to find and correct the cause of this condition.

Overheating

Badly worn electrodes and premature gap wear are signs of overheating, along with a gray or white blistered porcelain insulator surface. The most common cause for this condition is using a spark plug of the wrong heat range (too hot). If you have not changed to a hotter spark plug and the plug is overheated, consider the following causes:
 a. Lean fuel mixture.
 b. Ignition timing too advanced.
 c. Engine lubrication system malfunction.
 d. Engine air leak.
 e. Improper spark plug installation (overtightening).
 f. No spark plug gasket.

LUBRICATION, MAINTENANCE AND TUNE-UP

SPARK PLUG CONDITION

NORMAL
- Identified by light tan or gray deposits on the firing tip.
- Can be cleaned.

GAP BRIDGED
- Identified by deposit buildup closing gap between electrodes.
- Caused by oil or carbon fouling. If deposits are not excessive, the plug can be cleaned.

OIL FOULED
- Identified by wet black deposits on the insulator shell bore and electrodes.
- Caused by excessive oil entering combustion chamber through worn rings and pistons, excessive clearance between valve guides and stems or worn or loose bearings. Can be cleaned. If engine is not repaired, use a hotter plug.

CARBON FOULED
- Identified by black, dry fluffy carbon deposits on insulator tips, exposed shell surfaces and electrodes.
- Caused by too cold a plug, weak ignition, dirty air cleaner, too rich a fuel mixture or excessive idling. Can be cleaned.

LEAD FOULED
- Identified by dark gray, black, yellow or tan deposits or a fused glazed coating on the insulator tip.
- Caused by highly leaded gasoline. Can be cleaned.

WORN
- Identified by severely eroded or worn electrodes.
- Caused by normal wear. Should be replaced.

FUSED SPOT DEPOSIT
- Identified by melted or spotty deposits resembling bubbles or blisters.
- Caused by sudden acceleration. Can be cleaned.

OVERHEATING
- Identified by a white or light gray insulator with small black or gray brown spots and with bluish-burnt appearance of electrodes.
- Caused by engine overheating, wrong type of fuel, loose spark plugs, too hot a plug or incorrect ignition timing. Replace the plug.

PREIGNITION
- Identified by melted electrodes and possibly blistered insulator. Metallic deposits on insulator indicate engine damage.
- Caused by wrong type of fuel, incorrect ignition timing or advance, too hot a plug, burned valves or engine overheating. Replace the plug.

CHAPTER THREE

Worn out

Corrosive gases formed by combustion and high voltage sparks have eroded the electrodes. Spark plugs in this condition require more voltage to fire under hard acceleration. Replace with a new spark plug.

Preignition

If the electrodes are melted, preignition is almost certainly the cause. Check for carburetor mounting or intake manifold leaks and advanced ignition timing. It is also possible that a plug of the wrong heat range (too hot) is being used. Find the cause of the preignition before returning the engine into service.

Ignition Timing

All models are equipped with a capacitor discharge ignition system (CDI). On these models, the ignition timing is fixed and is not adjustable. While the ignition timing can be checked, its purpose is to check the operation of the ignition system, not to adjust it.

Incorrect ignition timing can be caused by dirty or loose connectors or a faulty component in the ignition system. Incorrect ignition timing will cause the engine to backfire, overheat and make it difficult to start.

Before starting this procedure, check all electrical connections related to the ignition system. Make sure all connections are tight and free from corrosion and that all ground connections are clean and tight.

1. Start the engine and let it warm up approximately 2-3 minutes.

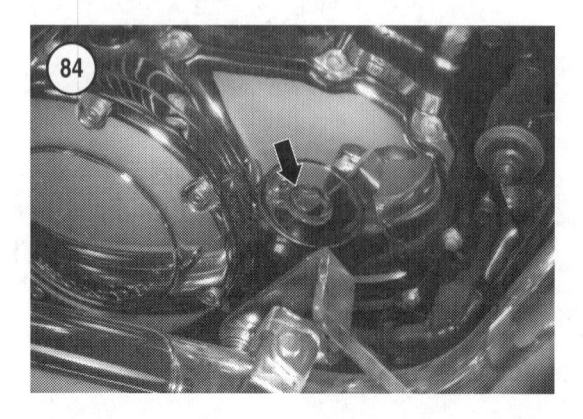

2. Park the motorcycle on level ground. Shut off the engine.

3. Remove the timing hole cap (**Figure 84**) from the right side of the engine.

4. Connect a portable tachometer following its manufacturer's instructions.

5. Connect a timing light to the No. 1 cylinder spark plug wire (rear plug wire) following its manufacturer's instructions.

6. Restart the engine and let it idle at the idle speed indicated in **Table 11**.

7. Adjust the idle speed as described in this chapter.

8. Aim the timing light at the timing window and pull the trigger. The timing is correct if the F mark

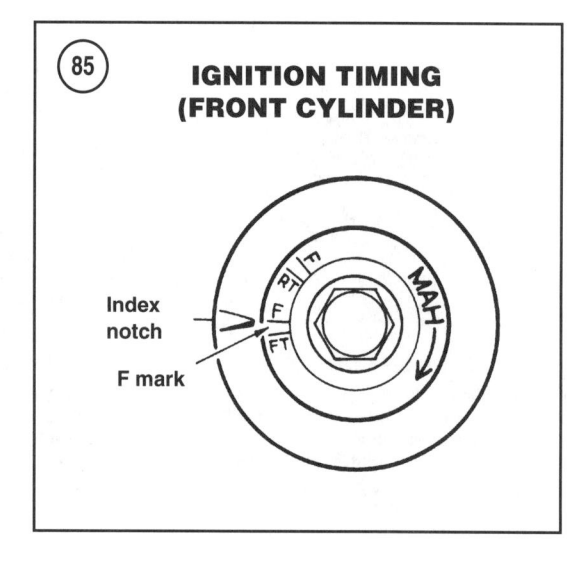

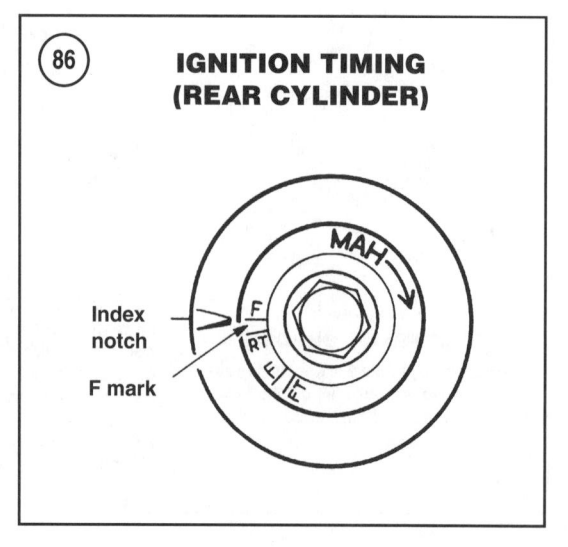

LUBRICATION, MAINTENANCE AND TUNE-UP

aligns with the fixed index mark (**Figure 85**) on the crankcase.
9. Turn the engine off and disconnect the timing light.
10. Connect the timing light to the No. 2 cylinder spark plug wire (front plug wire).
11. Restart the engine and let it idle. Aim the timing light at the timing window and pull the trigger. The timing is correct if the F mark aligns with the fixed index mark (**Figure 86**) on the crankcase.
12. Turn the engine off.
13. If ignition timing is incorrect, test the ignition system electrical components as described in Chapter Nine.
14. Disconnect the timing light and portable tachometer.
15. Install the timing hole cap and O-ring (**Figure 84**).

Carburetor Idle Mixture

The idle mixture (pilot screw) is preset at the factory and should not be reset during engine tune-up. Do not adjust the pilot screws unless the carburetors are overhauled. Refer to *Pilot Screw Adjustment* in Chapter Eight.

Carburetor Synchronization

When the carburetors are properly synchronized, the engine will warm up faster and there will be an improvement in throttle response, performance and mileage.

Before synchronizing the carburetors, the air filter element must be clean.

This procedure requires special tools. You need a carburetor tuner (mercury or vacuum gauge set) and an offset pilot screw adjusting tool.

These tools can be purchased through a Honda dealership.

1. Start the engine and let it warm up to normal operating temperature. Turn the engine off.
2. Support the bike on level ground on its sidestand.
3. Remove the screw and washer (**Figure 87**) from each cylinder head intake port.
4. Install the vacuum gauge adapters into the intake ports.
5. Connect the carburetor tuner to the vacuum gauge adapters.
6. Remove the fuel tank mounting bolts but do not disconnect the fuel tube (see Chapter Eight).
7. Start the engine and set the idle speed as described in this chapter.
8. Check the gauge readings. If the difference in gauge readings is 40 mm Hg (1.6 in. Hg) or less between the 2 cylinders, the carburetors are considered synchronized.

NOTE
***Figure 88** shows the carburetor synchronization adjusting screw with the carburetors removed for clarity. The base carburetor is the No. 1 (rear) carburetor.*

9. Using the pilot screw adjusting tool, turn the synchronization screw (**Figure 88**) to adjust the carburetors so the gauge readings are as close to each other as possible.
10. Turn the engine off and remove the vacuum lines and adapters. Install the screws and washers (**Figure 87**) into the vacuum ports in the cylinder heads. Make sure the screws are tight to prevent a vacuum leak.

11. Tighten the fuel tank mounting bolts as described in Chapter Eight.

12. Restart the engine and readjust the idle speed, if necessary, as described in this chapter.

Idle Speed Adjustment

Before making this adjustment, the air filter element must be clean and the engine must have adequate compression. See *Compression Test* in this chapter.

1. Start the engine and let it warm up approximately 2-3 minutes.
2. Park the vehicle on level ground and support it on its sidestand. Turn the engine off.
3. Connect a portable tachometer following its manufacturer's instructions.
4. Restart the engine and set the idle speed by turning the throttle stop screw (**Figure 89**). **Table 11** lists the correct idle speed.
5. Open and close the throttle a couple of times and check for variation in idle speed. Readjust if necessary.

WARNING
With the engine idling, move the handlebar from side to side. If idle speed increases during this movement, the throttle cable needs adjusting or may be incorrectly routed through the frame. Correct this problem immediately. Do not ride the vehicle in this unsafe condition.

6. Turn the engine off and disconnect the portable tachometer.

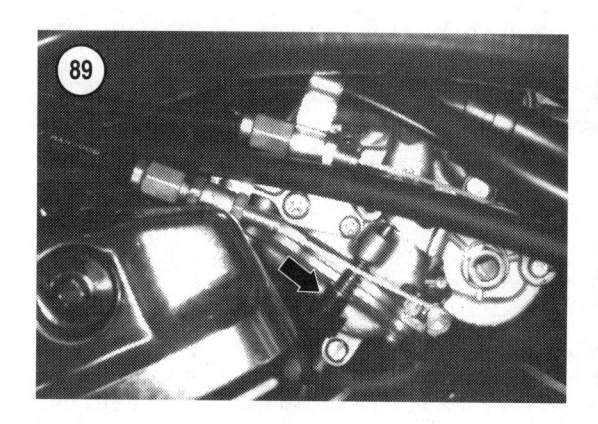

Table 1 MAINTENANCE AND LUBRICATION SCHEDULE*

Initial 600 miles (1,000 km):
Change engine oil and filter
Check and adjust engine idle speed
Check carburetor synchronization
Check brake system
Check clutch system
Check steering adjustment
Check wheels and tires
Check for loose or missing fasteners
Every 4,000 miles (6,400 km):
Clean crankcase breather (1)
Inspect spark plugs
Check and adjust engine idle speed
Check and clean battery
Inspect brake fluid level
Inspect brake pad wear
Inspect clutch system
Inspect tires and wheels

(continued)

LUBRICATION, MAINTENANCE AND TUNE-UP

Table 1 MAINTENANCE AND LUBRICATION SCHEDULE* (continued)

Every 8,000 miles (12,800 km):
  Replace spark plugs
  Inspect the fuel line
  Check the choke adjustment
  Inspect the throttle operation
  Check carburetor synchronization
  Inspect coolant level and condition
  Inspect cooling system
  Inspect final drive gear oil level
  Inspect brake system
  Inspect brake light switch
  Check headlight adjustment
  Check side stand operation
  Check side stand ignition cut-off system operation
  Check front and rear suspension
  Check steering adjustment
  Check for loose or missing fasteners
Every 2 years or 12,000 miles (19,200 km), whichever comes first:
  Replace brake fluid
  Replace engine coolant
Every 12,000 miles (19, 200 km):
  Replace air filter element (2)
  Inspect the evaporative emission control system (3)
Every 24,000 miles (38,400 km):
  Replace final drive gear oil

* This Honda Factory maintenance schedule must be considered a guide to general maintenance and lubrication intervals. Harder than normal use and exposure to mud, water, and, high humidity, etc. will require more frequent attention to most maintenance items. (1) Increase service intervals when riding in wet or dusty areas. (2) Replace more often when riding at full throttle (touring) or in wet areas. (3) California models.

Table 2 TIRE INFLATION PRESSURE*

	psi	kPa
Up to 200 lbs. (90 kg) load		
Front		
1995-1996	33	225
1997-1999	29	200
Rear	33	225
Up to maximum weight capacity		
Front	33	225
Rear	41	280

*The tire inflation pressures listed here are for original equipment tires. Aftermarket tires may require different inflation pressure; refer to tire manufacturer's specifications.

Table 3 BATTERY SPECIFICATIONS

Capacity	12 volts, 16 amp hours

Table 4 BATTERY STATE OF CHARGE

Specific gravity	State of charge
1.110-1.130	Discharged
1.140-1.160	Almost discharged
1.170-1.190	One-quarter charged
1.200-1.220	One-half charged
1.230-1.250	Three-quarters charged
1.260-1.280	Fully charged

Table 5 MAINTENANCE TORQUE SPECIFICATIONS

	N•m	in.-lb.	ft.-lb.
Coolant drain bolt	13	115	—
Engine oil drain bolt	30	—	22
Engine oil filter	10	88	—
Final drive oil drain bolt	12	106	—
Final drive oil filler cap	12	106	—
Front fork drain bolt	8	71	—
Fork cap	23	—	17
Side stand			
Bolt	10	88	—
Nut	30	—	22
Spark plug	14	—	10
Timing hole cap	18	—	13
Upper fork tube pinch bolt	11	97	—

Table 6 RECOMMENDED LUBRICANTS AND FUEL

Battery refilling	Distilled water
Brake fluid	DOT4
Control cables	Cable lubricant
Cooling system	Ethylene glycol
Engine oil	
Grade	API SF or SG
Viscosity	SAE10W-40
Final drive gear oil	Hypoid gear oil, SAE 80
Fork oil	SAE 10W fork oil
Fuel	See text
Speedometer cable	Cable lubricant

Table 7 ENGINE OIL CAPACITY

	Liters	U.S. qt.	Imp. qt.
Drain engine oil only	3.3	3.5	2.9
Engine oil and filter	3.5	3.7	3.1
After engine disassembly	4.2	4.4	3.7

LUBRICATION, MAINTENANCE AND TUNE-UP

Table 8 FINAL DRIVE OIL CAPACITY

	cc	U.S. oz.	Imp. oz.
At oil change	130	4.4	4.6
After disassembly	150	5.1	5.3

Table 9 FORK OIL CAPACITY

	cc	U.S. oz.	Imp. oz.
1995-1998	482	16.3	16.9
1999	495	16.7	17.4

Table 10 ENGINE COOLANT CAPACITY

	Liters	U.S. qt.	Imp. qt.
Radiator and engine capacity	2.0	2.1	1.8
Reserve tank capacity	0.39	0.41	0.34

Table 11 TUNE-UP SPECIFICATIONS

Carburetor vacuum difference	Within 40 mm HG (1.6 in. HG)
Engine compression	1,275 ± 196 kPa (185 +/- 28 psi)
Engine idle speed	1,000 ± 100 rpm
Spark plug type	
Standard heat range	NGK DPR7EA-9 or Denso X22EPR-U0
Cold (below 5° C/41° F)	NGK DPR6EA-9 or Denso X20EPR-U9
Hot (extended high speed riding)	NGK DPR8EA-9 or Denso X24EPR-U9
Spark plug gap	0.8-0.9 mm (0.031-0.035 in.)

CHAPTER FOUR

ENGINE TOP END

The engine is a V-twin liquid-cooled, 4-stroke design. The cylinders are offset at a 45° angle and fire on alternate crankshaft rotations. Each cylinder is equipped with a single camshaft and 3 valves. The single pin crankshaft is supported by 2 main bearings in a vertically split crankcase.

Both engine and transmission share a common case and the same wet sump oil supply. The clutch is a wet-type located on the right side of the engine. Refer to Chapter Five for service to the engine bottom end components. Refer to Chapter Six for clutch service.

This chapter provides information for disassembly, removal, inspection, service and reassembly of the engine top end components. These include the cylinder head covers, camshafts, cylinder heads, valves, cylinder blocks, pistons and piston rings.

Before starting any work, read the service hints in Chapter One. You will do a better job with this information fresh in your mind.

Before servicing any of the components in this chapter, you must first remove the engine from the frame. This procedure is described in Chapter Five.

Table 1 lists general engine specifications and **Tables 2-4** list engine service specifications. **Tables 1-6** are at the end of the chapter.

ENGINE PRINCIPLES

Figure 1 explains basic 4-stroke engine operation. Use the information in **Figure 1** when troubleshooting or repairing the engine.

SERVICE NOTES

Read this section before servicing any component described in this chapter.

1. Before removing and servicing the engine, perform an engine compression test (Chapter Three) and an engine leakdown test (Chapter Two). Record the results from each test so you can compare them with the test results made after servicing the engine.
2. When servicing both the front (A, **Figure 2**) and rear (B, **Figure 2**) cylinder assemblies, store the components in separate containers so you do not mix them up during reassembly.

CYLINDER HEAD COVER AND ROCKER ARMS

The aluminum cylinder head cover is machined with integral bearing surfaces for the camshaft. It is also equipped with 3 rocker arms and shafts, and 3

ENGINE TOP END

1

Carburetor
Intake valve

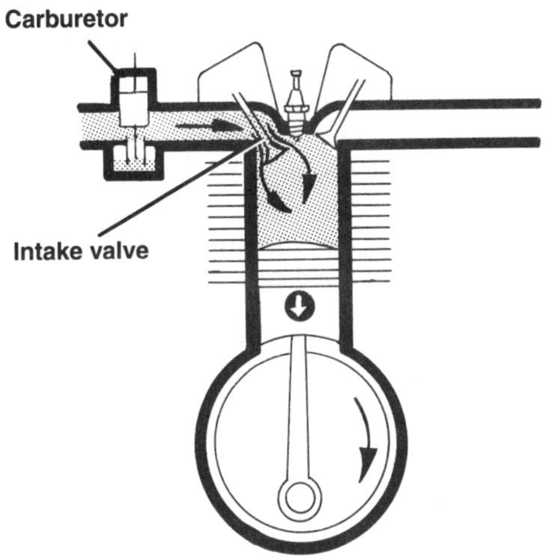

As the piston travels downward, the exhaust valve is closed and the intake valve opens, allowing the new air/fuel mixture from the carburetor to be drawn into the cylinder. When the piston reaches the bottom of its travel (BDC) the intake valve closes and remains closed for the next 1 1/2 revolutions of the crankshaft.

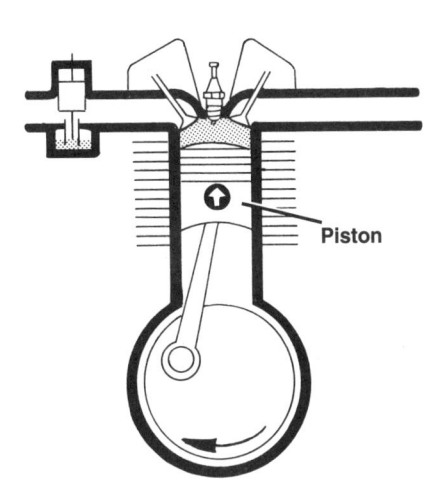

Piston

While the crankshaft continues to rotate, the piston moves upward, compressing the air-fuel mixture.

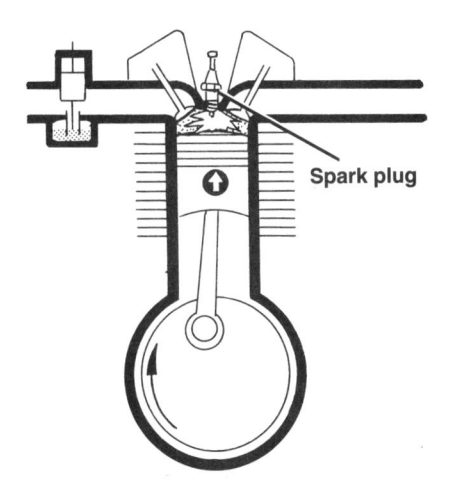

Spark plug

As the piston almost reaches the top of its travel, the spark plug fires, igniting the compressed air/fuel mixture. The piston continues to top dead center (TDC) and is pushed downward by the expanding gases.

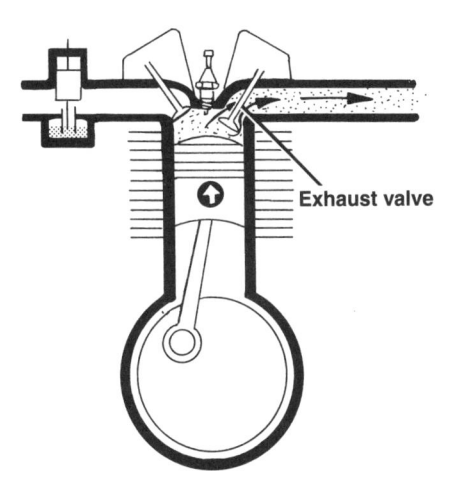

Exhaust valve

When the piston almost reaches BDC, the exhaust valve opens and remains open until the piston is near TDC. The upward travel of the piston forces the exhaust gses out of the cylinder. After the piston has reached TDC, the exhaust valve closes and the cycle starts all over again.

assist springs and assist shafts that are part of the hydraulic tappet assembly. The cylinder head cover is sealed to the cylinder head with a semi-drying gasket sealer.

Refer to **Figure 3** when servicing the cylinder head cover.

Removal

1. Read the information listed under *Service Notes* in this chapter.
2. Remove the engine from the frame (Chapter Five).
3. Plug the opening of each intake manifold.

NOTE
The cylinder head cover is sealed to the cylinder head with a semi-drying gasket sealer. When removing and servicing these components, be careful that you do not damage the mating gasket surfaces.

NOTE
When removing the cylinder head cover nuts and bolts in Step 4, do not loosen the 3 assist shaft caps (A, Figure 4).

4. Loosen the 8 mm and 10 mm cap nuts and the 8 mm cylinder head cover bolts.
5. Remove the nuts, bolts and water pipe from the cylinder head cover.

NOTE
Before removing the cylinder head cover in Step 6, tilt the engine as described in the procedure to prevent the hydraulic tappets and shims from coming out with the cover and possibly falling into the lower crankcase.

6A. To remove the front cylinder head cover (A, **Figure 2**), first tilt the engine 45° to its right side and support it there with wooden blocks. Then tap the cylinder head cover and carefully remove it from the cylinder head.
6B. To remove the rear cylinder head cover (B, **Figure 2**), first tilt the engine 45° toward its left side and support it there with wooden blocks. Then tap the cylinder head cover and carefully remove it from the cylinder head.

NOTE
If a hydraulic tappet and its shim(s) come out of their receptacle in the cylinder head, reinstall them into their original mounting position. They must be kept in their respective pairs and in their original position. If 2 or more of the tappets came out and you cannot identify their original mounting position, you must perform the hydraulic tappet adjustment procedure before assembling the engine.

7. Remove the hydraulic tappets (**Figure 5**) and shims (**Figure 6**) and store them in a container labeled so you do not mix them up.

NOTE
The shims will either stick to the base of the tappet or in the receptacle in the cylinder head. Make sure no shims are left in the cylinder head.

8. Locate and remove the 2 dowel pins. They may be stuck in the cylinder head cover (A, **Figure 7**).
9. Remove the camshaft plugs from the grooves in the cylinder head.

Disassembly

To remove the rocker arms and shafts, perform the following.
1. Remove the assist shaft caps and O-rings (A, **Figure 8**), springs (**Figure 9**) and shafts (**Figure 10**).
2. Remove the 2 rocker arm shaft plugs (B, **Figure 8**) and O-rings.

ENGINE TOP END

③ **CYLINDER HEAD COVER**

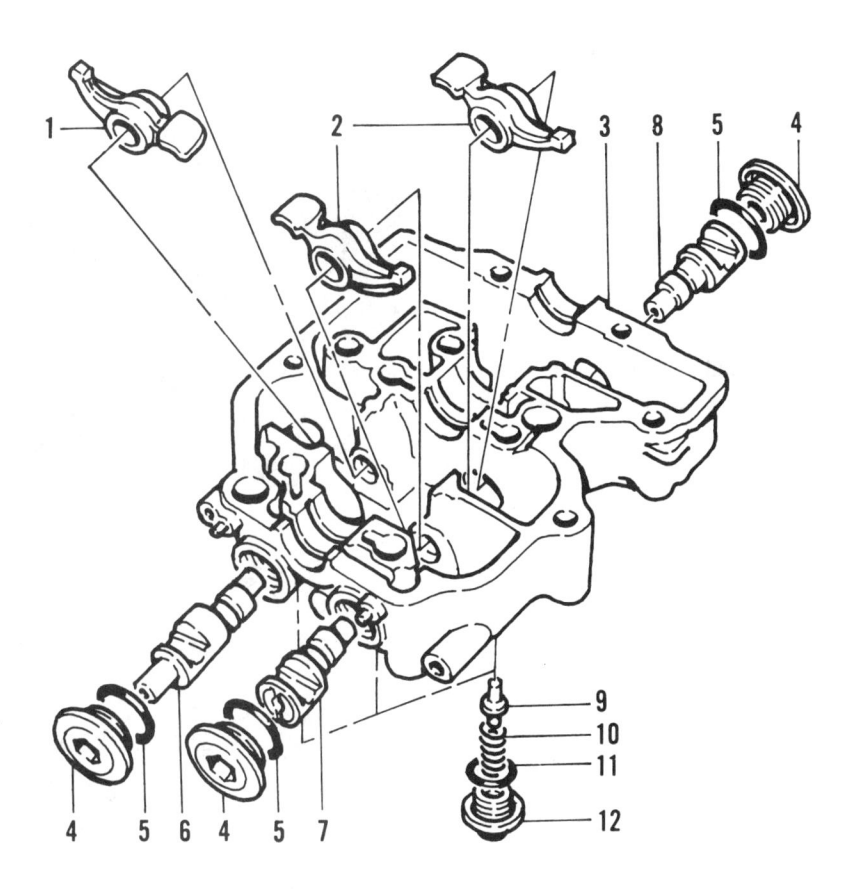

1. Exhaust rocker arm
2. Intake rocker arms
3. Cylinder head cover
4. Rocker arm shaft plugs
5. O-rings
6. Exhaust rocker arm shaft
7. Intake rocker arm shaft
8. Intake rocker arm shaft
9. Assist shafts
10. Assist springs
11. O-rings
12. Assist shaft caps

NOTE
Store each rocker arm and its shaft in a marked bag so that they can be installed in their original operating position.

3. Using a rubber mallet, tap on the end of the cylinder head cover to work the intake rocker arm shafts partially out of the cover. Then remove the rocker arm shafts and rocker arms.

4. Thread a 6 mm bolt or screw into the exhaust rocker arm shaft (**Figure 3**) and remove the shaft (**Figure 11**) and rocker arm.

Cylinder Head Cover
Cleaning and Inspection

1. Remove all gasket residue from the cylinder head cover and cylinder head gasket surfaces.

2. Clean the cylinder head cover in solvent then dry thoroughly. Clean the cylinder head cover oil passages with compressed air.

3. Inspect the camshaft bearing surfaces (**Figure 12**) in the cylinder head cover for cracks or wear.

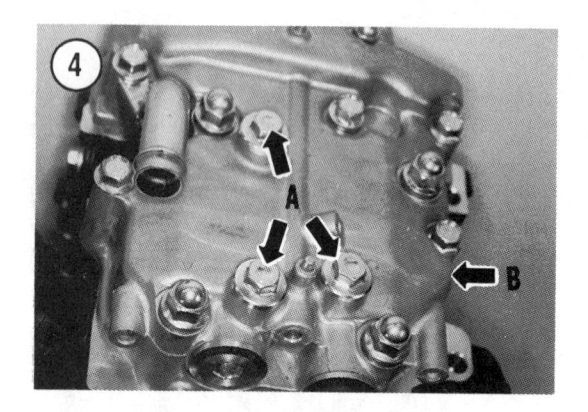

NOTE
If the cylinder head cover bearing surfaces are excessively worn or damaged, inspect the camshaft and cylinder head bearing surfaces for the same condition.

4. Replace the cap O-rings if leaking or damaged.
5. Measure camshaft oil clearance as described under *Camshaft* in this chapter.
6. Replace the cylinder head cover if damaged.
7. Repeat for the other cylinder head cover.

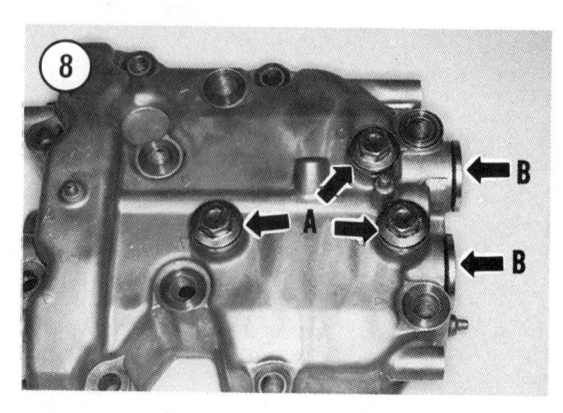

ENGINE TOP END

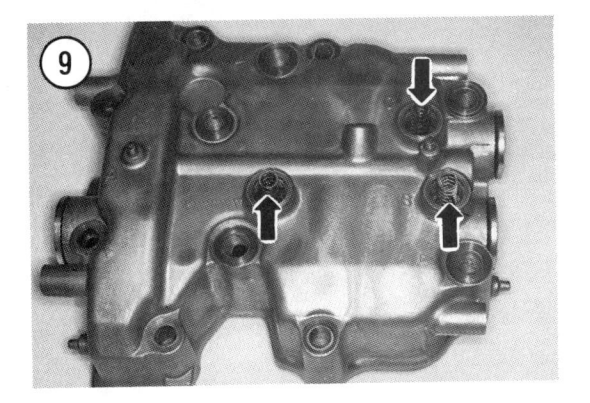

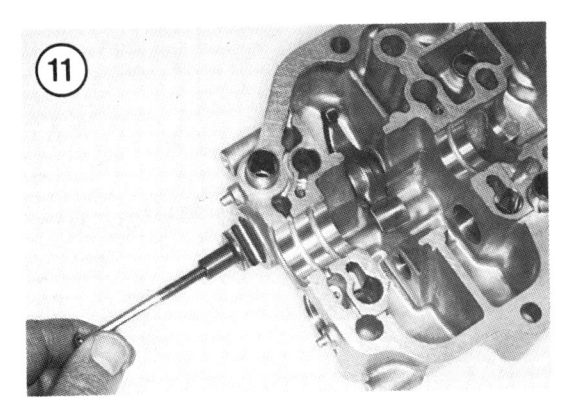

Rocker Arms and Shafts
Inspection

When measuring the rocker arm components in this section, compare the actual measurements to the specifications in **Table 2**. Replace parts that are out of specification or show signs of excessive wear, cracks, seizure or other damage.

1. Clean all parts (**Figure 13**) in solvent and dry with compressed air.
2. Clean the rocker arm and rocker arm shaft oil holes with compressed air.
3. Inspect both rocker arm contact surfaces (**Figure 14**). Check for scratches, flat spots, uneven wear and scoring.
4. Inspect the rocker arm shafts (**Figure 15**) for scoring, cracks or other damage.
5. Measure the rocker arm bore inside diameter (A, **Figure 16**) with a snap gauge. Measure the snap gauge with a micrometer and check against the specification in **Table 2**.
6. Measure the rocker arm shaft outside diameter (B, **Figure 16**) and check against the specification in **Table 2**.

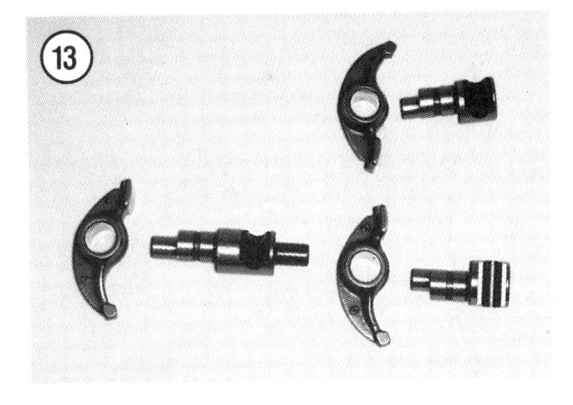

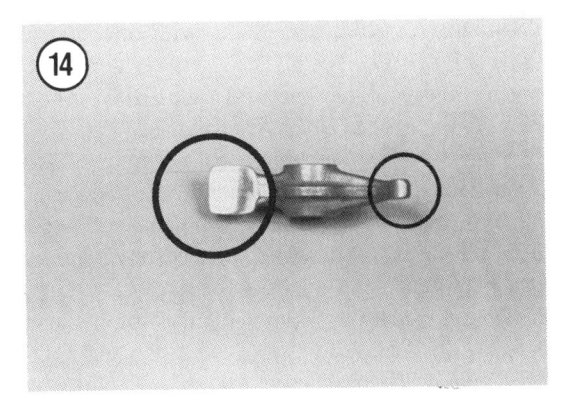

7. Calculate the rocker arm-to-rocker arm shaft clearance as follows:

   a. Subtract the rocker arm shaft outside diameter (Step 6) from the rocker arm bore inside diameter (Step 5).
   b. Replace the rocker arm and shaft and/or the rocker arm shaft if the clearance is too large (**Table 2**).

8. Repeat for the other rocker arm and shaft assemblies.

Assist Springs and Shafts
Inspection

1. Clean the assist springs and shafts (**Figure 17**) in solvent and dry thoroughly.
2. Inspect each assist shaft (**Figure 17**) for wear or bending. Replace if necessary.
3. Measure the free length of each assist spring (**Figure 18**) and compare to the service limit in **Table 2**. Replace the spring if it is too short.
4. To service the tappets, refer to *Hydraulic Tappets* in this chapter.

Assembly

To install the rocker arms and shafts, perform the following:

1. Coat the rocker arm shafts, rocker arm bores and the bearing surfaces in the cover with molybdenum disulfide grease or engine oil.

> *NOTE*
> *Make sure to install the rocker arms and rocker arm shafts in their original mounting positions.*

2. Install the rocker arm shafts with their rocker arms (**Figure 19**). Position each rocker arm so its notch (**Figure 20**) faces toward the assist shaft hole in the cylinder head cover. See **Figure 21**.
3. Using a screwdriver, rotate the rocker arm shafts so their arms move in toward the center of the cover.
4. If you replaced valve train components, adjust the hydraulic tappets as described under *Hydraulic Tappets* in this chapter.
5. Do not install the assist shafts and springs until after the cylinder head cover is installed and tightened onto its cylinder head.

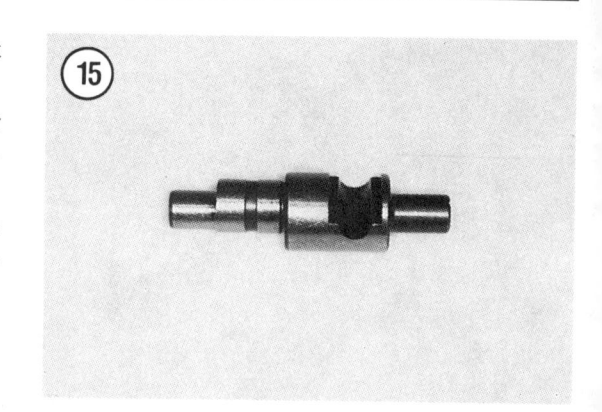

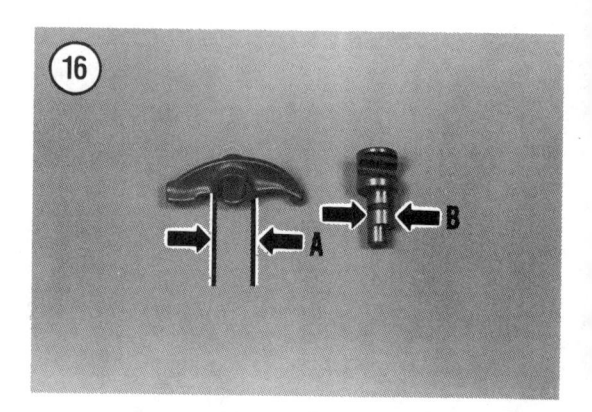

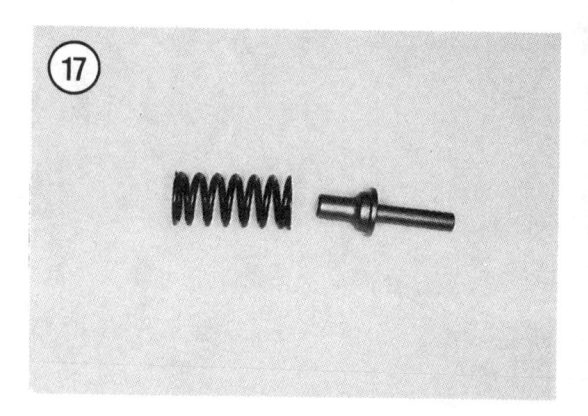

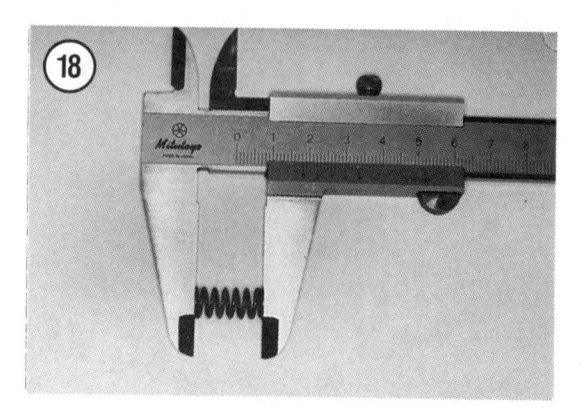

ENGINE TOP END

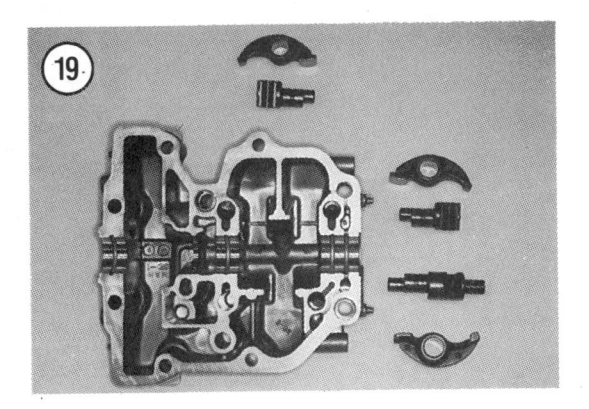

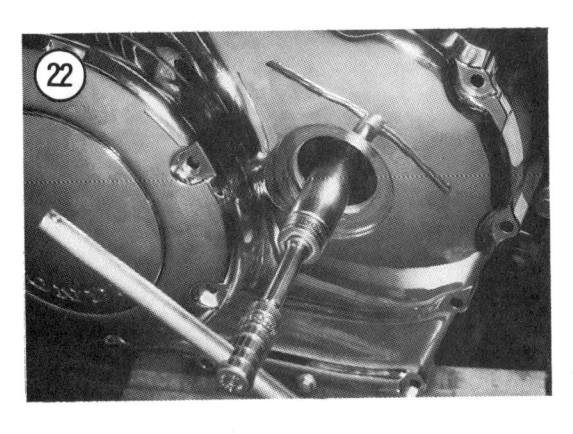

Installation

1. Bleed the hydraulic tappets as described under *Hydraulic Tappets* in this chapter. Then set them aside until installation.

2. Remove the timing hole cap from the left side of the engine. Then turn the crankshaft (**Figure 22**) clockwise and align the FT (front cylinder) or RT (rear cylinder) mark with the index notch on the right crankcase cover (**Figure 23**). Make sure the camshaft lobes for the cylinder you are working on are facing down (**Figure 24**).

CAUTION
If the cam lobes are not facing down, turn the crankshaft clockwise and re-align the timing marks.

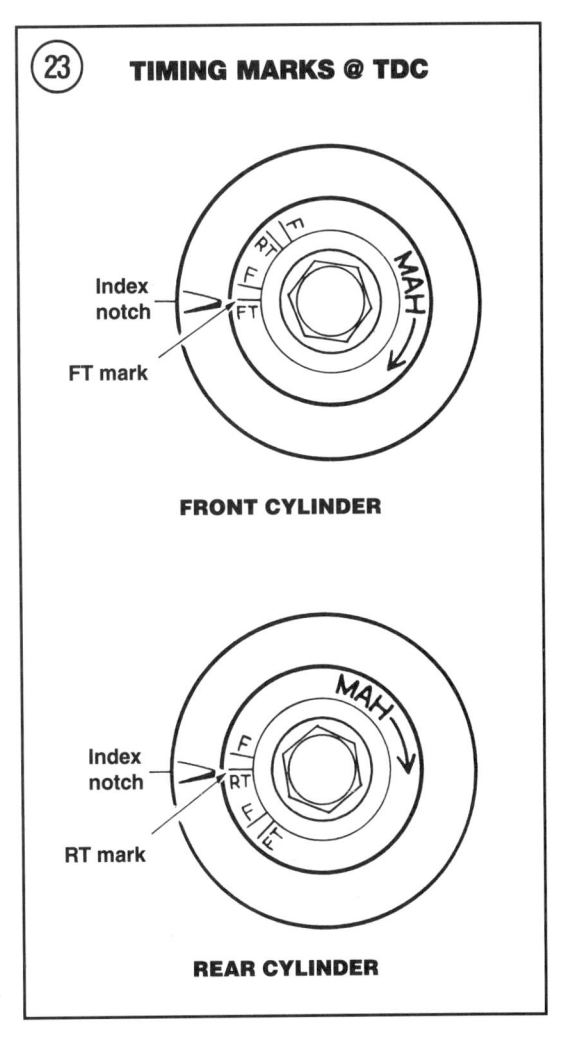

3. Install the correct number of shims (**Figure 25**) into each hydraulic tappet hole in the cylinder head.
4. Install the hydraulic tappets (**Figure 26**) into the cylinder head tappet holes.
5. Fill the cylinder head oil pockets with engine oil to cover the cam lobes.
6. Clean the cylinder head and cylinder cover mating surfaces of all oil or grease residue.

NOTE
Use a semi-drying liquid gasket sealer (ThreeBond Liquid Gasket 1104, Yamabond 4 or equivalent) when gasket sealer is called for in the following steps.

7. Apply gasket sealer to the camshaft plugs where they contact the cylinder head, then install them into the cylinder head. **Figure 27** shows one of the plugs.

CAUTION
*Do not apply gasket sealant around the 3 hydraulic tappet holes identified in **Figure 28**; otherwise, the sealant could cause hydraulic tappet failure.*

8. Apply a thin even coat of gasket sealer onto the cylinder head cover mating surface (except for the 3 areas identified in **Figure 28**).
9. If removed, install the 2 dowel pins into the cylinder head.
10. Install the cylinder head cover (**Figure 29**) and press it into position. Note the following:
  a. Make sure the cylinder head cover correctly engages the 2 dowel pins.
  b. Make sure the 2 outer seals seat squarely between the cylinder head cover and cylinder head mating surfaces.

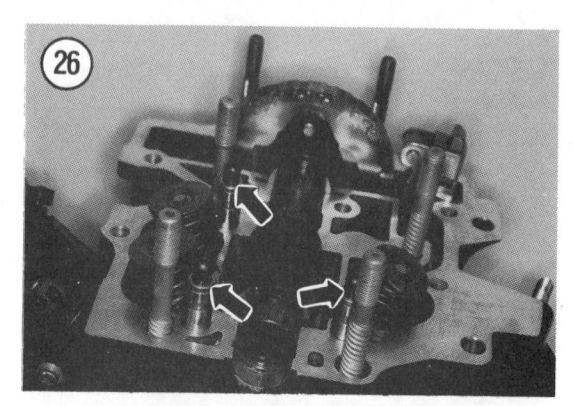

ENGINE TOP END

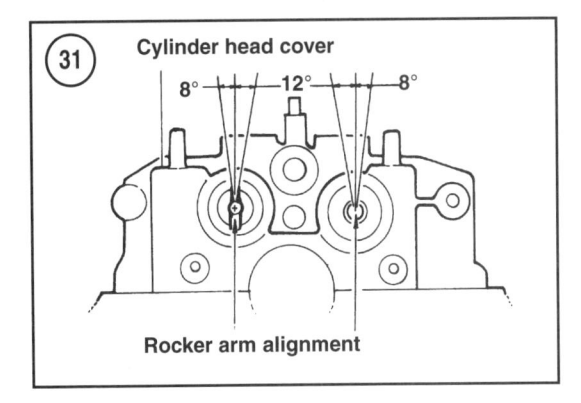

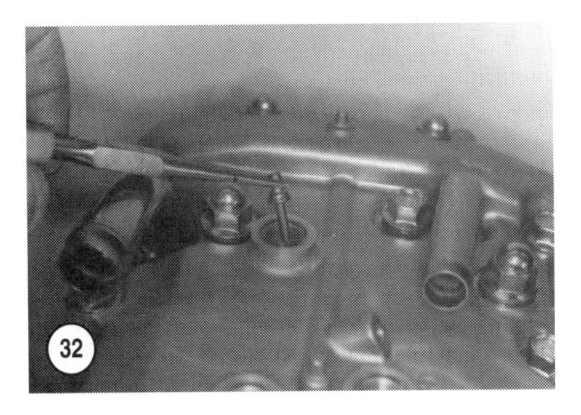

11. With the cylinder head cover seated firmly against the cylinder head, make sure the slots in the exhaust and intake rocker arm shafts (**Figure 30**) fall within the limits shown in **Figure 31**. If not, remove the cylinder head cover and check the position of the camshaft lobes. They must face down as described in Step 2. If the rocker arm slot positions are correct, continue with Step 12.

12. Install the cylinder head cover mounting bolts, nuts, water pipe and copper washers. Install the copper washers onto the bolts whose holes are marked with a triangle.

13. Tighten the cylinder head cover mounting bolts and nuts in a crisscross pattern to the torque specification in **Table 6**.

14. Install an assist shaft—long end facing down (**Figure 32**)—into each cylinder head cover hole.

15. Install an assist spring (**Figure 33**) over each assist shaft.

16. Lubricate the assist shaft cap O-rings with oil, then install and tighten the caps to the torque specification in **Table 6**.

17. Lubricate the rocker arm shaft hole plug O-rings with oil, then install and tighten the plugs to the torque specification in **Table 6**.

18. Install and tighten the timing hole cap.

19. Install the engine in the frame as described in Chapter Five.

HYDRAULIC TAPPETS

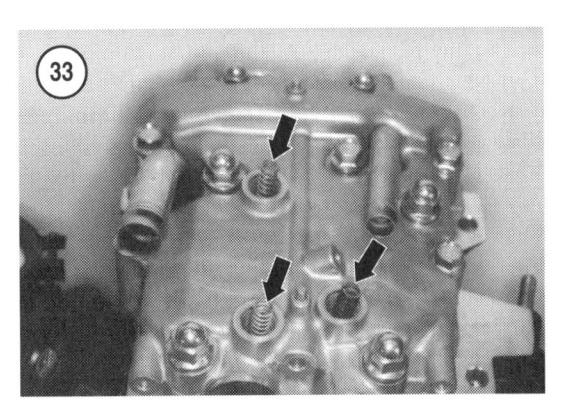

The hydraulic valve adjuster system is designed to create an automatic zero valve clearance throughout the engine's speed range, thus eliminating any routine valve adjustment. Valve clearance remains the same when the engine is cold or hot. The system is basically a tensioning system and does not contain hydraulic valve lifters like those used in many automobile engines.

Each rocker arm is installed on an eccentric rocker arm shaft. The rocker arm shaft has a notch on top of it where an assist shaft and spring are positioned. There is also a notch on the bottom of the rocker arm shaft that accepts the hydraulic tappet. The hydraulic tappets are supplied with air-free engine oil from the defoaming chambers in the cylinder head cover. The combined effect of these components is designed to maintain zero valve clearance.

Refer to **Figure 34** for the following description of the system:

a. When there is no cam lift on the rocker arm, the hydraulic tappet, assist shaft and spring are in the at-rest position (A, **Figure 34**).

b. As the cam lobe starts to lift the rocker arm, the eccentric rocker arm shaft also moves and begins to compress the hydraulic tappet, assist shaft and spring.

c. When the hydraulic tappet is compressed, the oil pressure in the tappet's high-pressure chamber increases and moves the check ball onto its seat to the closed position.

d. When the cam lobe reaches its maximum lift, the oil pressure within the tappet high-pressure chamber is very high and keeps the check ball seated.

e. As the rocker arm is pressing on the tappet, some of the oil within the high pressure chamber is forced out. This allows the plunger in the tappet to absorb some of the load when the cam lobe is at its maximum lift (B, **Figure 34**).

f. As the cam lobe moves past its maximum lift, the valve springs apply force on the other end of the rocker arm and move the rocker arm back in the other direction.

g. As the rocker arm shaft reverses direction, the springs within the tappet push the plunger upward (C, **Figure 34**).

h. The oil pressure within the high-pressure chamber has now decreased, allowing the check ball to leave its seat. This allows the oil to re-enter the high-pressure chamber.

i. The sequence starts over.

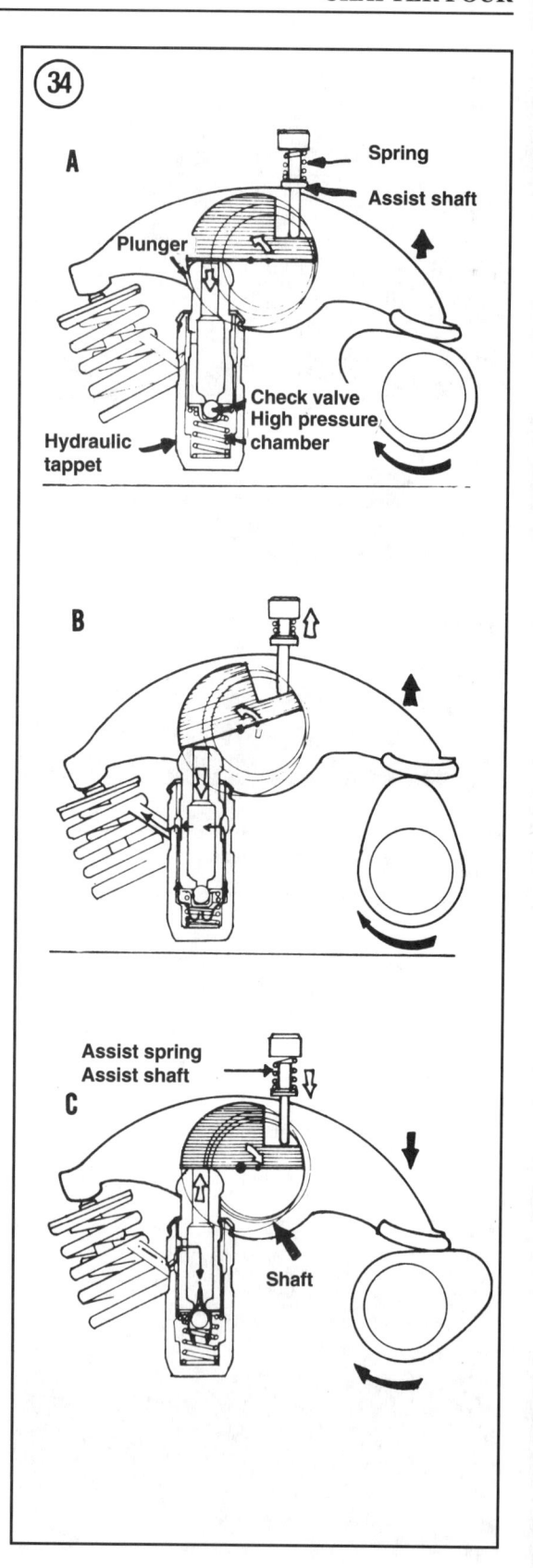

ENGINE TOP END

Inspection

1. Inspect the exterior of the tappet (A, **Figure 35**) for excessive wear, scoring or damage. Replace if necessary.
2. Make sure the oil hole (B, **Figure 35**) in the tappet is open and free of any oil sludge.
3. If the tappet is in acceptable condition, bleed it before installing it into the cylinder head.

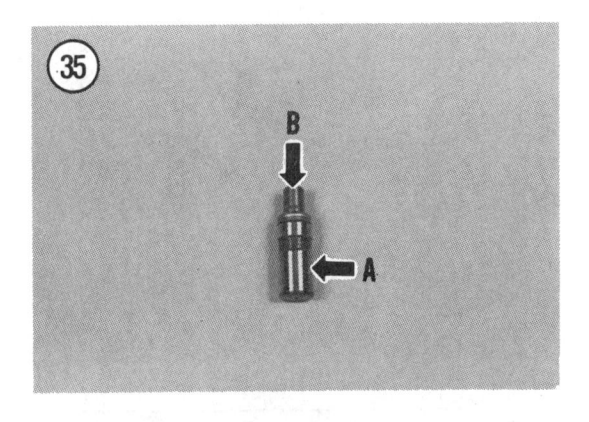

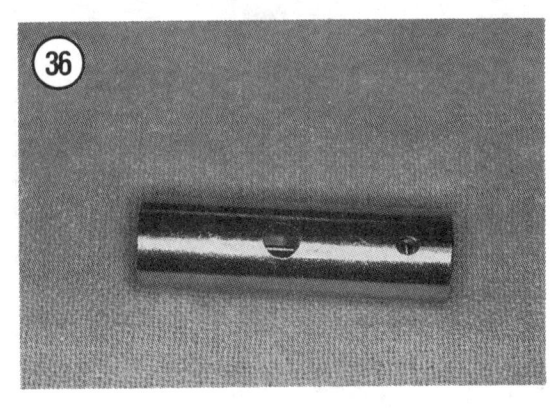

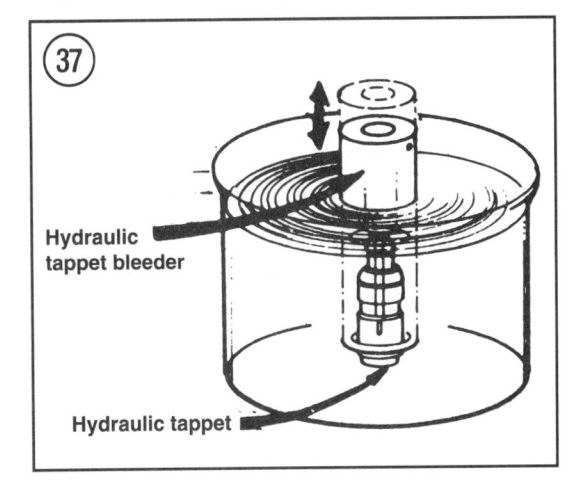

Bleeding

For proper operation, the hydraulic tappets must be free of air in the high-pressure chamber. The Honda Hydraulic Tappet Bleeder (part No. 07973-MJ00000 [**Figure 36**]) or an improvised tool setup may be used for this procedure. You also need a transparent container filled with kerosene and a dial indicator and magnetic stand.

CAUTION
Be sure to note the correct location in the cylinder head from which the tappet and shim(s) were removed.

1. Remove the tappet and shim(s) from the cylinder head as described under *Cylinder Head Cover and Rocker Arms* in this chapter.
2. Fill a transparent container with new kerosene. Fill the container with enough kerosene to completely submerge the tappet.

CAUTION
Keep the tappet submerged and upright during this procedure.

3A. To bleed the tappets with the Honda Hydraulic Tappet Bleeder (**Figure 36**), perform the following:
   a. With the tappet facing right side up, install the tool's bleed shaft into the tappet's oil hole.
   b. Place the tool and tappet into the container filled with kerosene (**Figure 37**).
   c. Hold the tappet and tool upright, then push down on the tool and pump the tappet as shown in **Figure 37**.
   d. Continue pumping the tappet until air bubbles stop coming from the high pressure chamber in the tappet.
   e. Remove the tappet and set it onto the workbench.

3B. If the special tool is not available, perform the following:
   a. Insert a 1/16 in. drill bit into the oil hole in the top of the tappet (**Figure 38**).
   b. Place the tappet and drill bit into a container filled with kerosene.
   c. Hold the tappet upright, then push down on the drill bit with a piece of metal or a wooden dowel and pump the tappet (**Figure 38**).
   d. Continue to pump the tappet until air bubbles stop coming from the high pressure chamber in the tappet.

e. Remove the tappet and set it onto the workbench.

NOTE
After removing the tappet from the container filled with kerosene, keep the tappet upright. If the tappet is laid down at an angle or on its side air will enter the high pressure chamber and the tappet will have to be bled again.

NOTE
The small amount of kerosene left in the tappet's high pressure chamber will not contaminate the engine oil.

4. With the tappet sitting on a flat surface and facing up, try to quickly compress the tappet with your fingers. Any compression felt must be minimal. To confirm, place the tappet underneath a dial indicator (**Figure 39**) and compress the tappet with your fingers while watching the dial gauge. If you can compress the tappet more than 0.20 mm (0.008 in.), you must bleed it again. If you cannot bleed the tappet so its compression is less than this limit, replace the tappet.

5. Reinstall the tappet and shim(s) into the correct receptacle in the camshaft holder as described in this chapter.

6. Repeat this procedure for all tappets.

Tappet Shim Measurement and Adjustment

To achieve zero clearance in the valve train, the tappet must provide the correct amount of pressure on the rocker arm (**Figure 34**). To compensate for manufacturing tolerance in valve train parts, one or more shims (**Figure 25**) are installed underneath each tappet. This procedure determines the correct number of shims to use. While this procedure is not a routine adjustment, you must perform it after replacing one of the following parts or after refacing the valve seats.

a. Cylinder head cover.
b. Cylinder head.
c. Camshaft.
d. Rocker arm and rocker arm shaft.
e. Valve or valve guide.

1. If removed, install the cylinder head and camshaft as described in this chapter.
2. Bleed the tappets as described in this chapter.
3. Install the tappets (without shims) and cylinder head cover as described in this chapter.
4. Install the assist shafts and their springs as described in this chapter.
5. Mount a dial indicator onto the cylinder head cover. Then center the indicator's plunger against the top of one assist shaft (**Figure 40**). Zero the dial on the dial indicator.

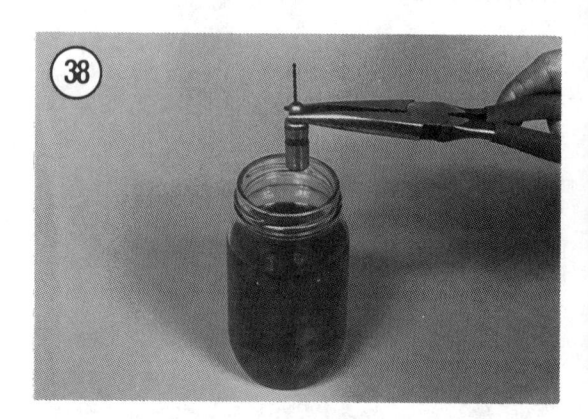

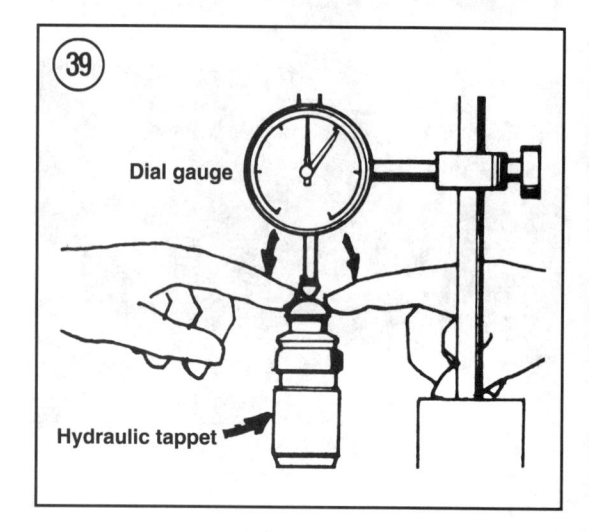

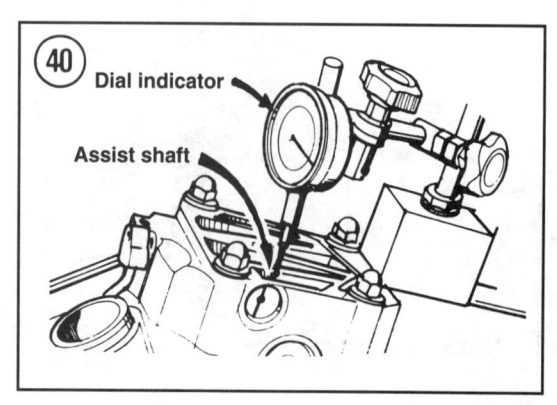

ENGINE TOP END

6. Have an assistant rotate the crankshaft clockwise 2 complete revolutions (**Figure 22**).
7. Record the assist shaft's stroke movement during these 2 revolutions.
8. Determine the number of shim(s) required for that tappet by referring to the stroke movement specifications in **Table 5**.

NOTE
You can purchase additional shims from your Honda dealership. The shim thickness is 0.5 mm (0.02 in.).

9. Repeat this procedure for all tappets affected by any replaced parts or services.
10. After replacing the shims and installing the tappets into the cylinder head, repeat this procedure (with shims in place) and make sure that the stroke movement for each tappet is within the 0-1.20 mm (0-0.047 in.) range.
11. Remove the dial indicator.

CAMSHAFTS

Either camshaft can be removed without first removing the other one.

Refer to **Figure 41** when servicing the camshafts in this chapter.

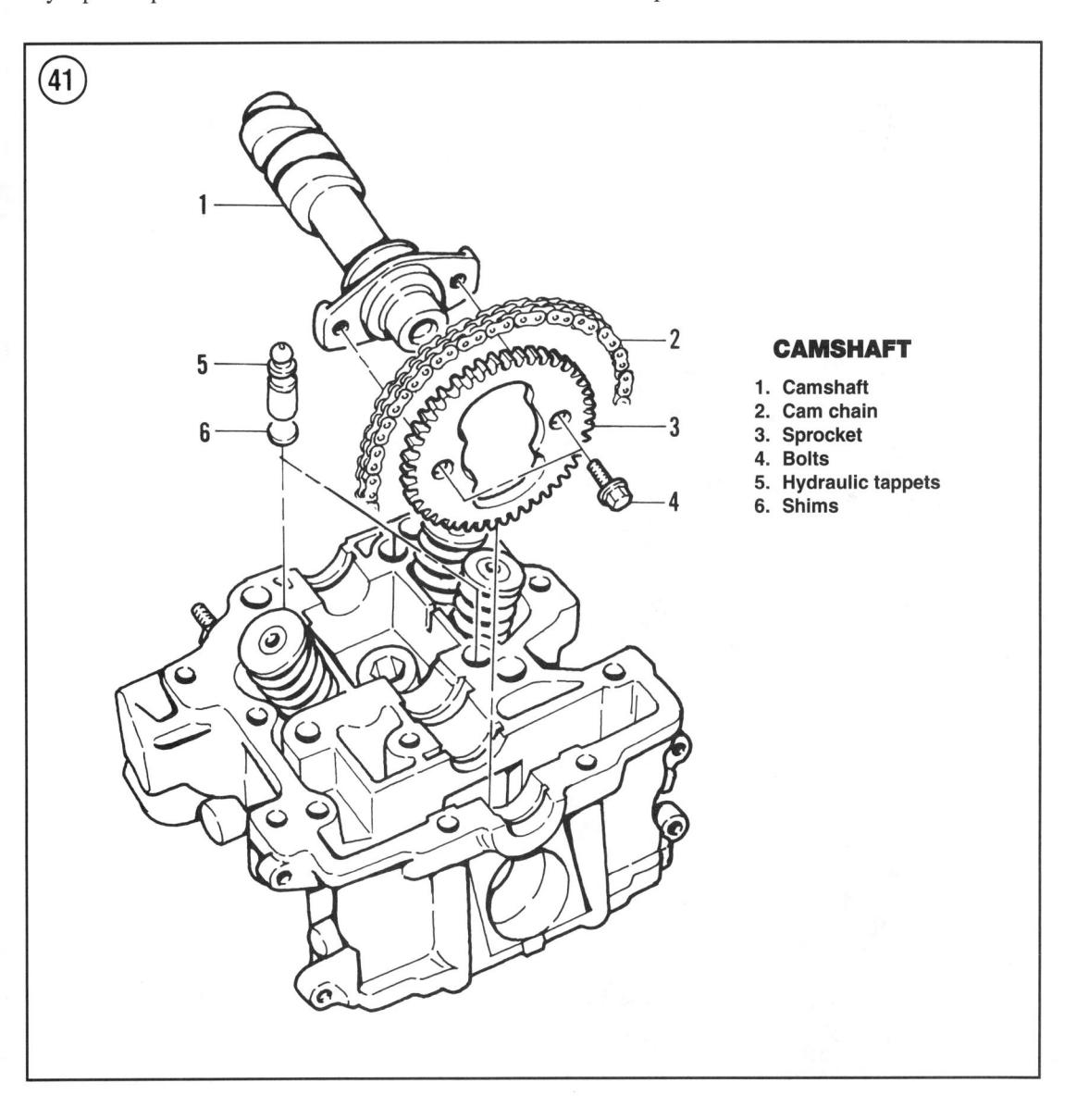

CAMSHAFT
1. Camshaft
2. Cam chain
3. Sprocket
4. Bolts
5. Hydraulic tappets
6. Shims

Removal

This procedure pertains to both camshafts (front and rear).

1. Remove the engine as described in Chapter Five.
2. Remove the cylinder head cover, tappets and shims as described in this chapter.
3. Remove the spark plug sleeve with the Honda fork tube holder attachment (part No. 07930-KA50100 [**Figure 42**]) or a bolt that is 27 mm (1 1/16 in.) across the flats of the head. **Figure 43** shows a flywheel puller used to remove the sleeve. Also see **Figure 44**.
4. Before removing the camshaft, inspect the cam chain wear as follows:

   a. Measure the amount that the cam chain tensioner wedge A projects above its bracket as shown in **Figure 45**.

   b. If the measurement exceeds 9.0 mm (0.35 in.), the cam chain is excessively worn and must be replaced.

5. To reduce cam chain tension before removing the cam sprocket, perform the following:

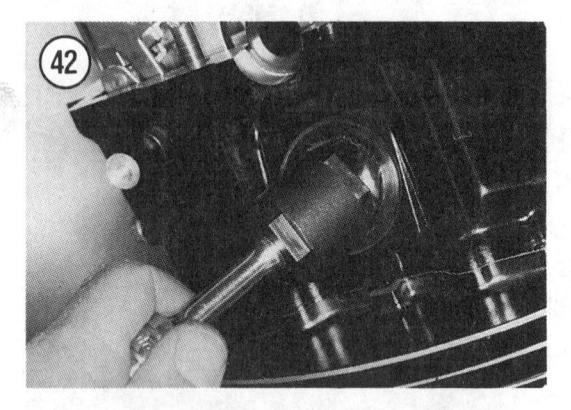

   a. Pull wedge A up with a pair of pliers, then push wedge B down and hold in this position (**Figure 46**).
   b. Install a 2 mm (5/64 in.) pin through the hole in wedge A (**Figure 47**), then release wedge B.

NOTE
Leave the pin in place until after the camshaft and its sprocket have been re-installed.

6. Remove the exposed cam sprocket bolt (**Figure 48**).

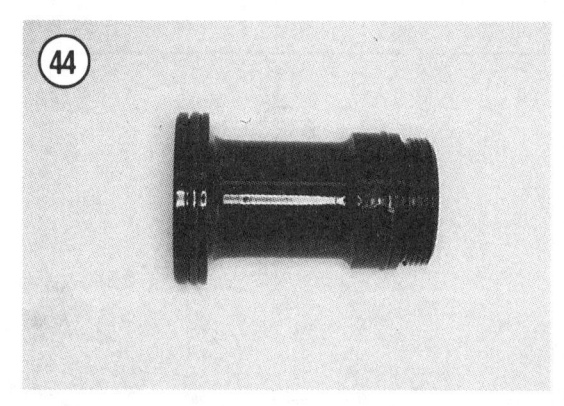

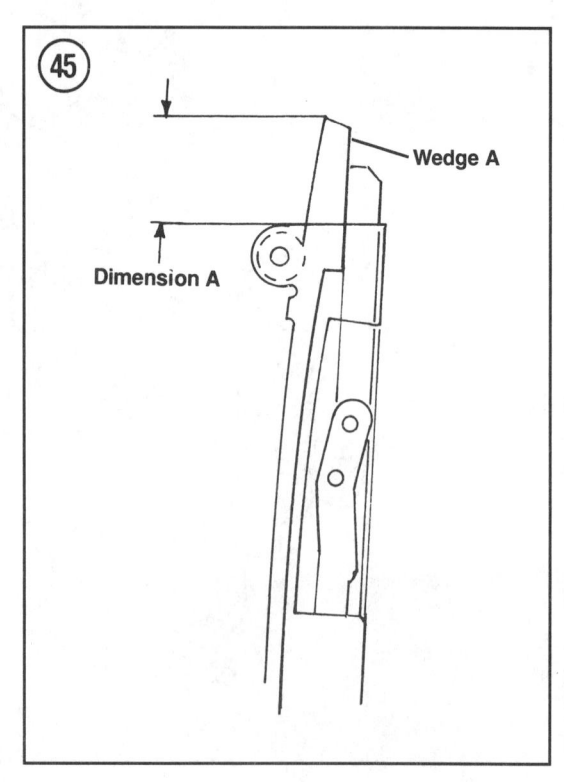

ENGINE TOP END

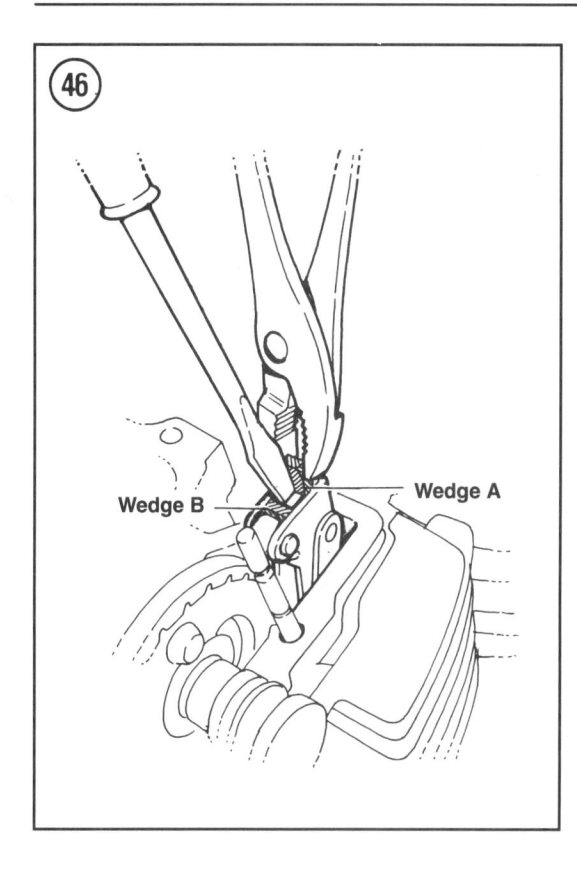

7. Rotate the engine clockwise and remove the other exposed sprocket bolt.

8. For easy cam removal, rotate the engine clockwise until the cam sprocket opening is positioned as shown in **Figure 49**.

9. Slide the cam sprocket and cam chain off the shoulder on the cam, then remove the cam (**Figure 50**).

10. Remove the cam sprocket and tie a piece of wire to the cam chain.

11. Repeat these steps to remove the opposite camshaft.

CAUTION
If you have to rotate the crankshaft after removing the camshaft(s), pull up on the cam chain(s) and keep it taut. Make certain that the cam chain(s) is meshing with its lower sprocket(s) or the cam chain(s) may become kinked, resulting in cam chain and sprocket damage.

Camshaft Inspection

When measuring the camshaft in this section, compare the actual measurements to the specifications in **Table 2**. Replace the camshaft if it is out of specification or shows excessive wear, cracks, seizure or other damage.

1. Remove all thread sealer residue from the camshaft sprocket bolt and camshaft threads.
2. Clean the camshaft, cam sprocket and its mounting bolts in solvent, and then dry thoroughly.
3. Check the cam lobes (A, **Figure 51**) and bearing journals (B, **Figure 51**) for scoring or other damage.
4. Measure the cam lobe height with a micrometer (**Figure 52**) and check against the specification in **Table 2**.
5. Measure the cam bearing journal outside diameter with a micrometer (**Figure 53**) at the points marked A, B and C in **Figure 54** and check against the specifications listed in **Table 2**.
6. Measure camshaft runout with a dial indicator and V-blocks as shown in **Figure 55** and check against the specification in **Table 2**.
7. Check the camshaft bearing journals (A-C, **Figure 56**) in the cylinder head cover and cylinder head for wear and scoring. The journal surfaces must be smooth with no visible seizure, scoring or other damaged areas. If excessive wear is noted, replace the cylinder head cover and cylinder head. To measure bearing journal wear, perform the *Camshaft Bearing Clearance Measurement* in this chapter.

Camshaft Sprocket Inspection

Inspect the camshaft sprocket (**Figure 57**) for excessive wear, broken or chipped teeth. If the sprocket is damaged or excessively worn, also inspect the crankshaft sprocket and cam chain for damage.

Camshaft Bearing Clearance Measurement

This procedure requires the use of a Plastigage set. The cylinder head must be installed on the engine when performing this procedure.

1. Drop the cam chain (with its attached wire) down the chain tunnel so it will not be pinched between any gasket surfaces later in this procedure.
2. Install all locating dowel pins into the cylinder head.
3. Wipe all oil from the upper and lower cam bearing journals prior to using the Plastigage.

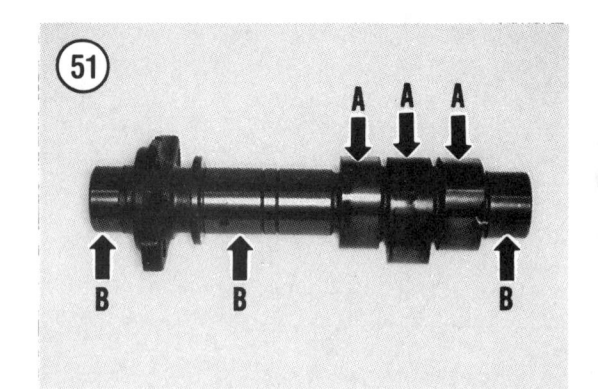

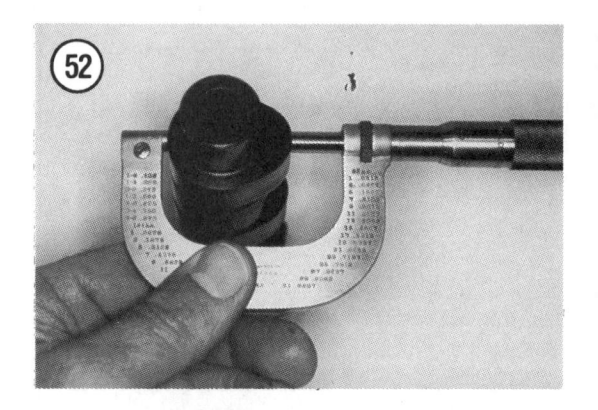

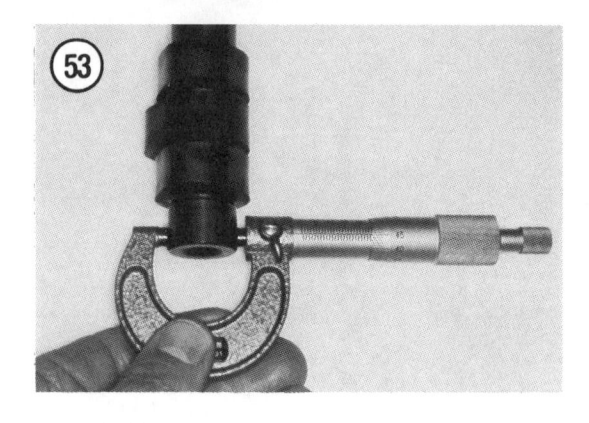

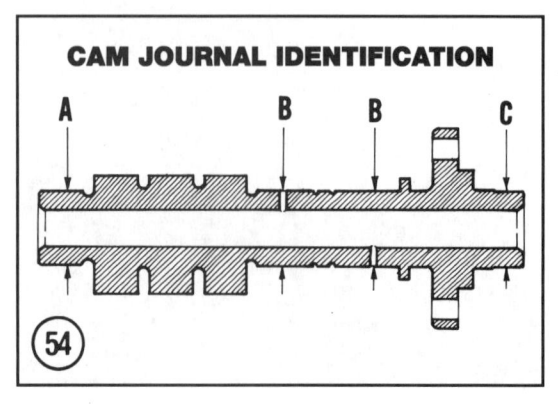

ENGINE TOP END

4. Install the camshaft into the cylinder head with its lobes facing down.

5. Place a strip of Plastigage material on top of each cam bearing journal (**Figure 58**), parallel to the cam journal.

6. Carefully place the cylinder head cover into position on the engine.

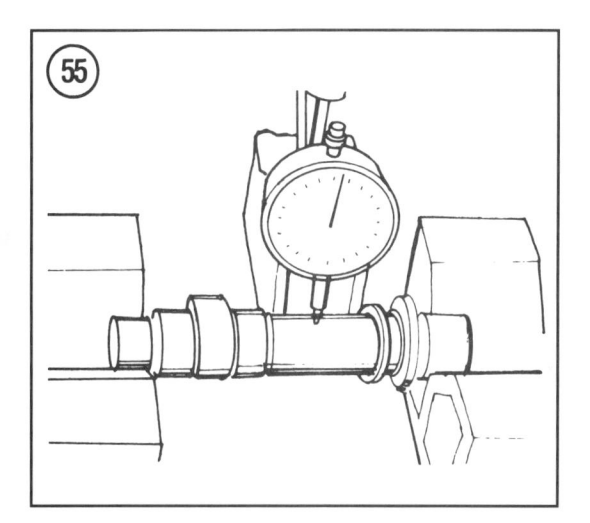

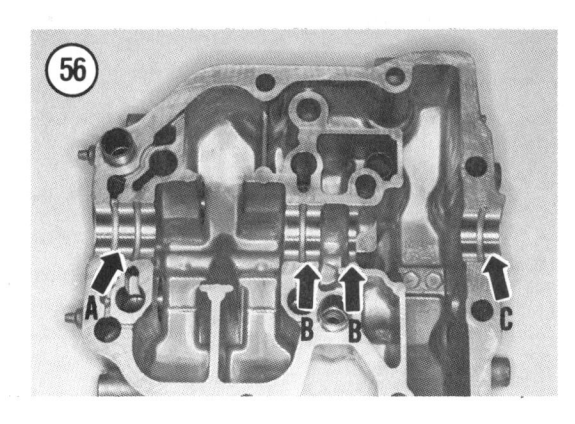

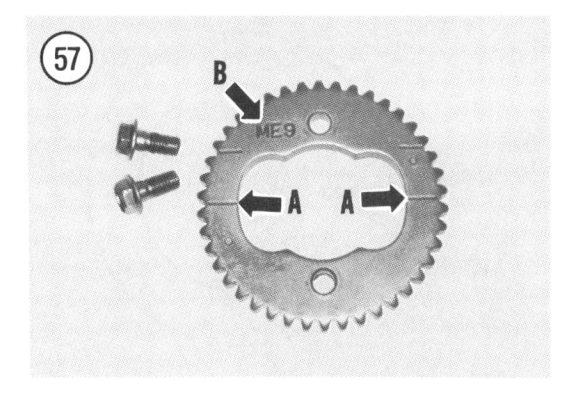

NOTE
The rocker arms and shafts do not have to be installed in the cylinder head cover when performing this procedure.

7. Install all cylinder head cover nuts and bolts and tighten in 2-3 stages in a crisscross pattern to the torque specification listed in **Table 6**.

CAUTION
Do not rotate the camshaft with the Plastigage material in place.

8. Loosen the cylinder head cover bolts in a crisscross pattern in 2-3 steps, then remove it while holding the camshaft in position.

9. Measure the width of the flattened Plastigage according to its manufacturer's instructions (**Figure 59**). The widest compressed thickness determines the oil clearance. Compare each Plastigage measure-

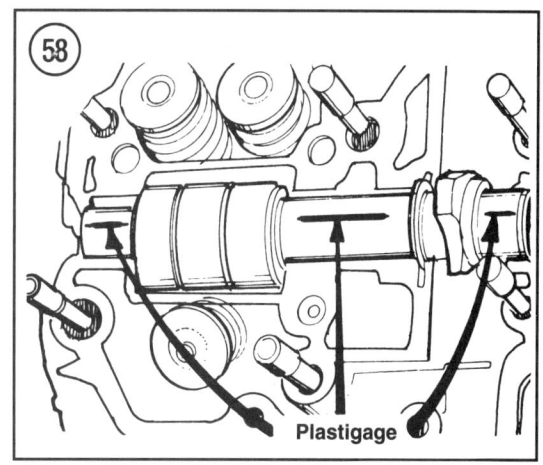

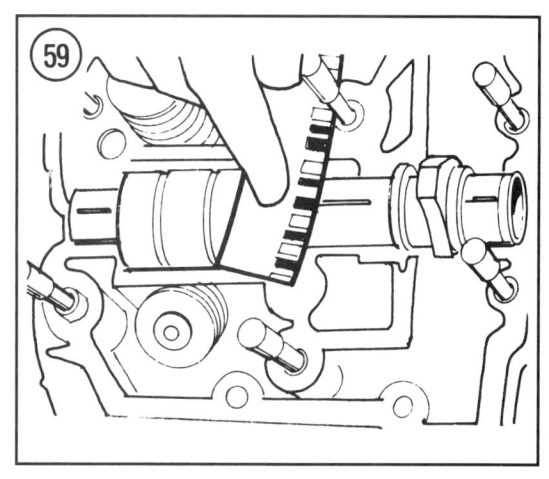

ment point (A, B and C in **Figure 56**) with the specifications in **Table 2**.

10. If the clearance is out of specification, measure the camshaft journals with a micrometer as described in this chapter. Replace the camshaft if its bearing journals are out of specification. If the camshaft journals are within specification, replace the cylinder head cover and cylinder head as a set.
11. Remove the camshaft.
12. Clean the camshaft, cylinder head cover and cylinder head of all Plastigage material.

CAUTION
Any Plastigage material left in the engine can plug up an oil orifice and cause severe engine damage.

Camshaft Installation

If both camshafts are removed, install the front camshaft first, then the rear. If only one camshaft is removed, you must remove the other cylinder head cover to observe the position of its camshaft marks during this procedure.

Each camshaft is marked with an F (front) or R (rear) on its sprocket boss (**Figure 60**). Make sure to install each camshaft correctly.

Front camshaft

1. Coat all camshaft lobes and bearing journals with molybdenum disulfide grease or assembly oil.
2. Remove the timing hole cap from the clutch cover.

CAUTION
When you rotate the crankshaft in the following steps, keep the cam chain taut and meshed with the timing sprocket on the crankshaft; otherwise, the chain may bind against the crankshaft sprocket, possibly damaging the chain and crankshaft sprocket.

3A. If the rear camshaft has not been removed, perform the following:
   a. Remove the rear cylinder head cover as described in this chapter.
   b. Turn the crankshaft clockwise (**Figure 61**) until the RT mark on the rotor aligns with the fixed pointer on the crankcase cover (**Figure 62**). Check the position of the R mark on the camshaft (**Figure 63**).
   c. If the R mark faces up, turn the crankshaft clockwise 1 1/8 turn (405°) and align the FT mark on the rotor with the fixed pointer on the crankcase cover (**Figure 64**).
   d. If the R mark faces down (you cannot see it), turn the crankshaft 1/8 turn (45°) clockwise

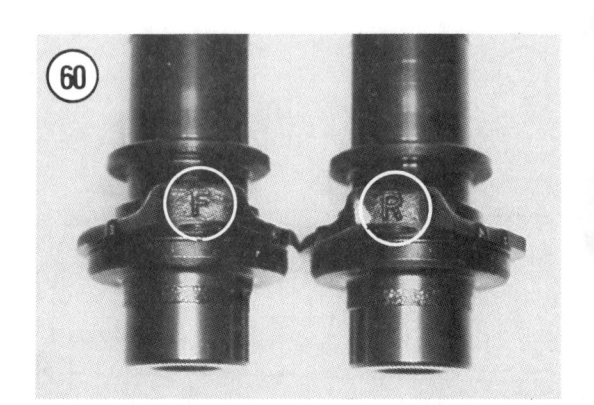

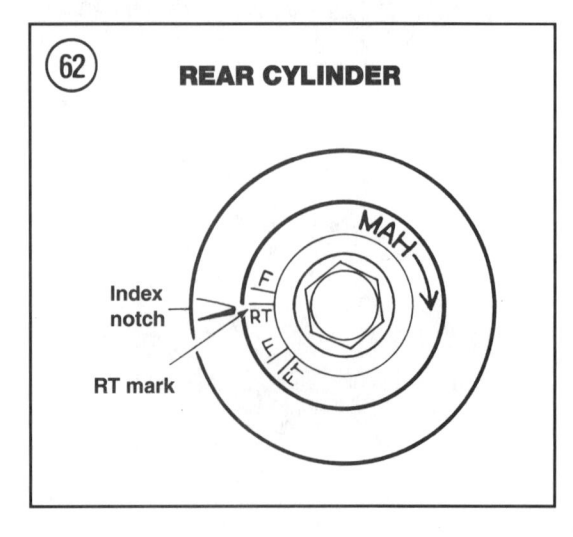

ENGINE TOP END

and align the FT mark on the rotor with the fixed pointer on the crankcase cover (**Figure 64**).

3B. If the rear camshaft was removed, turn the crankshaft (**Figure 61**) clockwise and align the FT mark on the rotor with the fixed pointer on the crankcase cover (**Figure 64**).

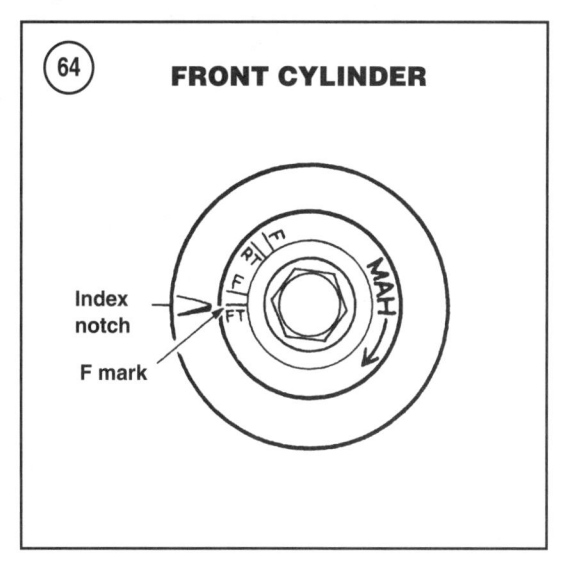

4. Install the cam sprocket with its index marks (A, **Figure 57**) facing out and aligned with the cylinder head gasket surface as shown in **Figure 65**. The ME9 mark on the camshaft (B, **Figure 57**) must be facing up. Mesh the cam sprocket with the cam chain.

NOTE
Positioning the cam sprocket as described in Step 5 makes it easier to install the cam through the sprocket.

5. Hold the sprocket so it is meshed with the cam chain, then turn the crankshaft (**Figure 61**) 1/2 turn (180°) clockwise to position the cam sprocket opening as shown in **Figure 66**.

6. Install the front camshaft (**Figure 60**) into the cylinder head and through the sprocket opening (**Figure 67**).

7. Hold the sprocket so it is meshed with the cam chain, then turn the crankshaft (**Figure 61**) 1/2 turn (180°) counterclockwise and realign the 2 sprocket index marks (A, **Figure 57**) with the cylinder head gasket surface as shown in **Figure 68**. Make sure the FT mark on the rotor aligns with the fixed pointer on the crankcase cover (**Figure 64**).

8. Turn the camshaft so its F mark faces up (**Figure 69**), then slide the sprocket onto the camshaft's shoulder. Again check the timing mark alignment as described in Step 7. If the alignment is incorrect, correct it at this time.

NOTE
*If you cannot slide the cam sprocket onto the camshaft, you will need to provide some additional slack in the cam chain. You can do this by holding the lower part of the front cam chain tensioner wedge against its engine boss guide with a large adjustable wrench (**Figure 70**). Tightening the tensioner wedge against the engine boss guide will straighten the tensioner wedge enough to allow the sprocket to be installed onto the camshaft. To access this part of the front chain tensioner, remove the starter clutch assembly as described in Chapter Five.*

9. Apply a medium strength threadlock to the camshaft sprocket bolts.
10. Install the first sprocket bolt (A, **Figure 71**) hand-tight.
11. Turn the crankshaft clockwise 1 turn (360°) and install the second sprocket bolt. Tighten this bolt to the torque specification in **Table 6**.
12. Turn the crankshaft clockwise 1 turn (360°) and align the FT mark on the rotor with the fixed pointer on the crankcase cover (**Figure 64**). Then make sure the sprocket index marks (**Figure 68**) align with the cylinder head gasket surface. If the camshaft timing is correct, continue with Step 13. If not, retime the camshaft.
13. Tighten the first sprocket bolt to the torque specification in **Table 6**.
14. Remove the 2 mm pin (B, **Figure 71**) installed through the chain tensioner. Turn the engine clockwise again and recheck the timing marks.
15. Lubricate the spark plug sleeve threads and both O-rings (**Figure 44**) with molybdenum oil. Then install and tighten the sleeve (**Figure 42**) to the torque specification in **Table 6**.
16A. Install the rear camshaft as described in the following procedure.
16B. If the rear camshaft is already installed, perform the following steps to complete engine assembly.

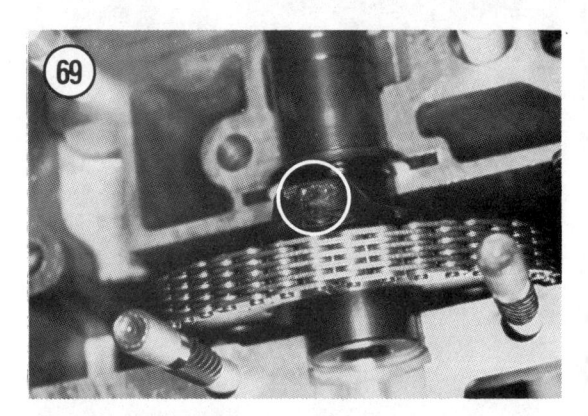

ENGINE TOP END

a. Install the shims, hydraulic lifters and cylinder head covers as described in this chapter.

b. Install the engine in the frame (Chapter Five).

Rear camshaft

1. Coat all camshaft lobes and bearing journals with molybdenum disulfide grease or assembly oil.
2. Remove the timing hole cap from the clutch cover.
3. If removed, install the front camshaft (**Figure 72**) before installing the rear camshaft. Refer *Front Camshaft* in this section.

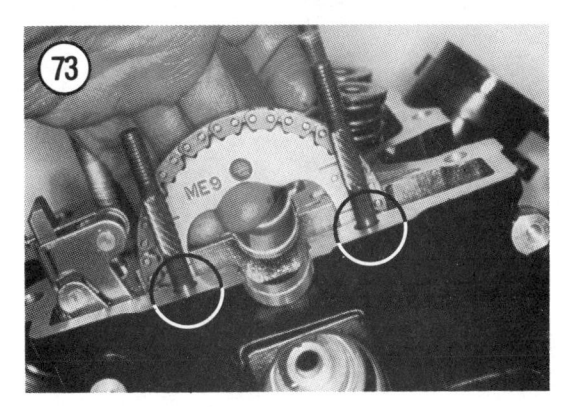

CAUTION
When you rotate the crankshaft in the following steps, keep the cam chain taut and meshed with the timing sprocket on the crankshaft; otherwise, the chain may bind against the crankshaft sprocket, possibly damaging the chain and crankshaft sprocket.

4. Perform the following:
   a. If installed on the engine, remove the front cylinder head cover as described in this chapter.
   b. Turn the crankshaft clockwise (**Figure 61**) until the FT mark on the rotor aligns with the fixed pointer on the crankcase cover (**Figure 64**). Check the position of the F mark on the camshaft (**Figure 69**).
   c. If the F mark faces up, turn the crankshaft clockwise 7/8 turn (315°) and align the RT mark on the rotor with the fixed pointer on the crankcase cover (**Figure 62**).
   d. If the F mark faces down (you cannot see it), turn the crankshaft 1 7/8 turn (675°) clockwise and align the RT mark on the rotor with the fixed pointer on the crankcase cover (**Figure 62**).
5. Install the cam sprocket with its index marks (A, **Figure 57**) facing out and aligned with the cylinder head gasket surface as shown in **Figure 73**. The ME9 mark on the camshaft (B, **Figure 57**) must face up. Mesh the cam sprocket with the cam chain.

NOTE
Positioning the cam sprocket as described in Step 6 makes it easier to install the cam through the sprocket.

6. Hold the sprocket so it is meshed with the cam chain, then turn the crankshaft (**Figure 61**) 1/2 turn (180°) clockwise to position the cam sprocket opening as shown in **Figure 74**.
7. Install the rear camshaft (**Figure 60**) into the cylinder head and through the sprocket opening (**Figure 75**).
8. Hold the sprocket so it is meshed with the cam chain, then turn the crankshaft (**Figure 61**) 1/2 turn (180°) counterclockwise and realign the 2 sprocket

index marks (A, **Figure 57**) with the cylinder head gasket surface as shown in **Figure 76**. Make sure the RT mark on the rotor aligns with the fixed pointer on the crankcase cover (**Figure 62**).

9. Turn the camshaft so its R mark faces up (**Figure 63**), then slide the sprocket onto the camshaft's shoulder. Again check the timing mark alignment as described in Step 8. If the alignment is incorrect, correct it at this time.

10. Apply a medium strength threadlock to the camshaft sprocket bolts.

11. Install the first sprocket bolt (A, **Figure 77**) hand-tight.

12. Turn the crankshaft clockwise 1 turn (360°) and install the second sprocket bolt. Tighten this bolt to the torque specification in **Table 6**.

13. Turn the crankshaft clockwise 1 turn (360°) and align the RT mark on the rotor with the fixed pointer on the crankcase cover (**Figure 62**). Then make sure the sprocket index marks (**Figure 76**) align with the cylinder head gasket surface. If the camshaft timing is correct, continue with Step 14. If not, correct it at this time.

14. Tighten the first sprocket bolt to the torque specification in **Table 6**.

15. Remove the 2 mm pin (B, **Figure 77**) installed through the chain tensioner. Turn the engine clockwise again and recheck the timing marks.

16. Lubricate the spark plug sleeve threads and both O-rings (**Figure 44**) with molybdenum oil. Then install and tighten the sleeve (**Figure 42**) to the torque specification in **Table 6**.

17. Install the shims, hydraulic lifters and cylinder head covers as described in this chapter.

18. Install the engine in the frame (Chapter Five).

CYLINDER HEAD

Either cylinder head (**Figure 78**) can be removed without first removing the other one. If both cylinder heads are going to be removed, either one can be removed first. This section pertains to both cylinder heads.

Removal

1. Remove the engine from the frame (Chapter Five).

2. Remove the cylinder head cover and camshaft as described in this chapter.

ENGINE TOP END

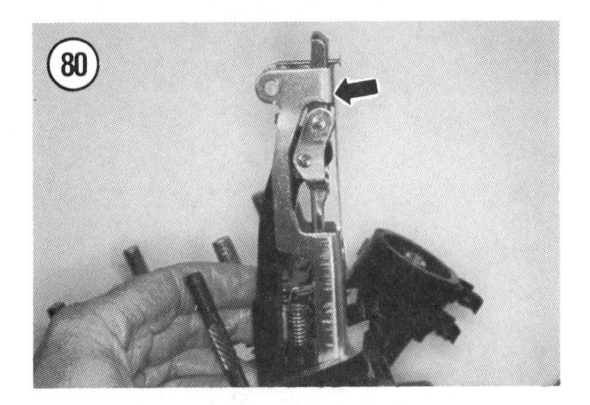

3. Remove the Allen bolts and the cylinder head fins.
4. Remove the bolts that hold the cylinder head to the cylinder block.
5. Remove the cam chain tensioner mounting bolts and washers (**Figure 79**), then remove the tensioner assembly (**Figure 80**).
6. Insert a screwdriver between the cylinder head and cylinder pry points (**Figure 81**), then lift the screwdriver to break the head gasket seal.

CAUTION
Do not pry between any gasket surfaces or you may permanently damage the cylinder head and cylinder.

7. Carefully lift the cylinder head (**Figure 82**) off the cylinder and remove it. Allow the cam chain and its safety wire to fall into the cylinder's chain tunnel.
8. Remove the head gasket and both dowel pins (**Figure 83**). Discard the gasket.
9. Lift out and remove the chain guide (**Figure 84**).
10. Cover the cylinder with a clean shop rag or paper towels.
11. Repeat for the opposite cylinder head.

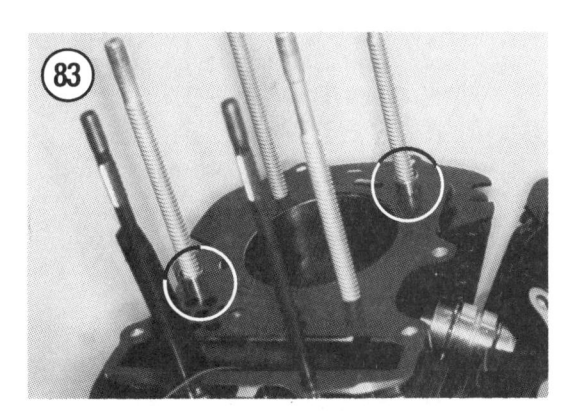

Cylinder Head Inspection

1. Remove all gasket residue from the head and cylinder mating surfaces. Do not scratch the gasket surface.

2. Without removing the valves, remove all carbon deposits from the combustion chamber (**Figure 85**). Use a fine wire brush dipped in solvent or make a scraper from hardwood. Take care not to damage the head, valves or spark plug threads.

CAUTION
If you clean the combustion chamber after removing the valves, you may damage the valve seats. A lightly scratched or damaged valve seat will cause poor valve seating.

3. Examine the spark plug threads in the cylinder head for damage. If damage is minor or if the threads are dirty or clogged with carbon, use a spark plug thread tap to clean the threads. If thread damage is severe, restore the threads with a steel thread insert.

NOTE
When using a tap to clean spark plug threads, coat the tap with an aluminum thread cutting fluid or kerosene.

NOTE
Aluminum spark plug threads are commonly damaged due to galling, cross-threading and overtightening. To prevent galling, apply an antiseize compound to the plug threads before installation and do not overtighten the spark plugs.

4. After you remove the carbon from the combustion chamber and valve ports and clean the spark plug thread hole, clean the entire head in solvent.

NOTE
If the cylinder head is cleaned using a bead blaster, make sure to clean the head first with solvent, and then with hot

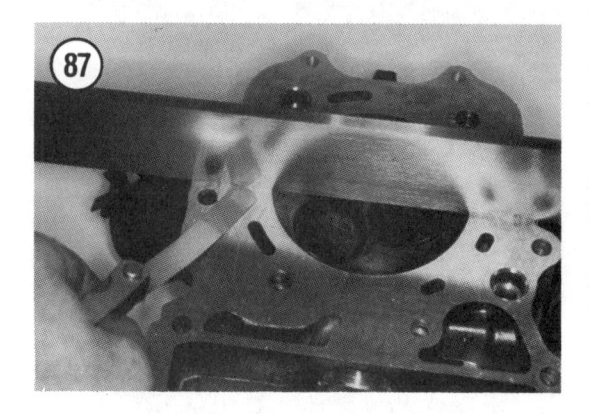

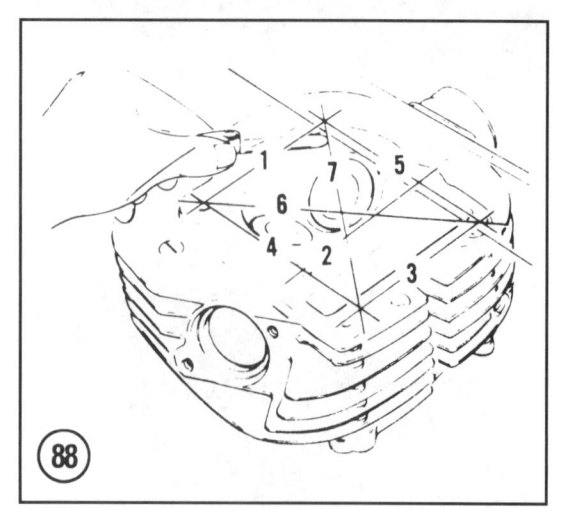

ENGINE TOP END

soapy water. Residue grit that seats in small crevices and other areas can be hard to get out. Also, chase each exposed thread with a tap to remove grit trapped between the threads. Grit left in the engine will cause premature piston, ring and bearing wear.

5. Examine the piston crown. The crown must show no wear or damage. If the crown appears pecked or spongy-looking, also check the spark plug, valves and combustion chamber for aluminum deposits. If these deposits are found, the cylinder is suffering from excessive heat caused by a lean fuel mixture or preignition.

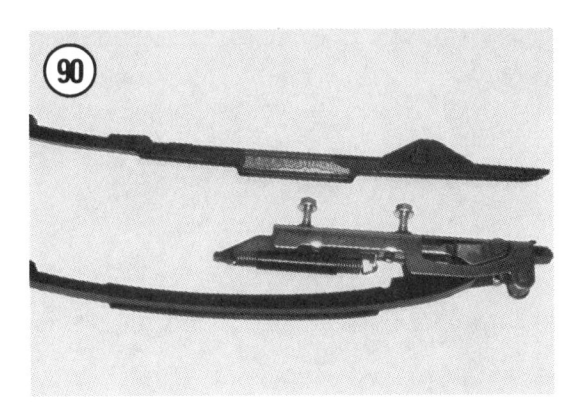

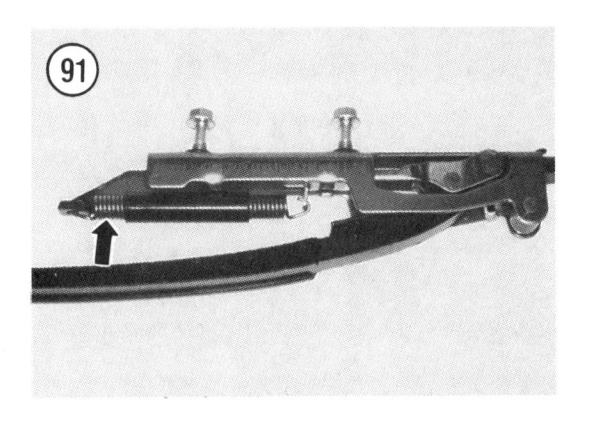

6. Inspect the intake manifold (**Figure 86**) for cracks or other damage that will allow unfiltered air to enter the engine. If you remove the intake manifold, discard its O-ring and install a new one during reassembly.

7. Check for cracks in the combustion chamber (**Figure 85**) and exhaust port. Replace the cylinder head if it cannot be repaired.

8. Place a straightedge across the gasket surface at several points (**Figure 87**). Measure warpage by inserting a feeler gauge between the straightedge and cylinder head at each location (**Figure 88**). **Table 2** lists the maximum allowable warpage. Warpage or nicks in the cylinder head surface could cause an air leak and overheating. If the cylinder is warped, resurface or replace the cylinder head. Consult a Honda dealer or a machine shop experienced in this type of work.

9. Inspect the camshaft bearing journals in the cylinder head (**Figure 89**) for cracks, seizure marks or other damage. Measure bearing journal wear by performing the *Camshaft Bearing Clearance Measurement* procedure in this chapter.

10. To service the valves, refer to *Valves and Valve Components* in this chapter.

11. Repeat for the opposite cylinder head.

Chain Tensioner and Chain Guide Inspection

1. Inspect the chain tensioner and guide (**Figure 90**) for excessive wear, cracks or other damage.

2. Inspect the chain tensioner spring assembly (**Figure 91**) for weakness or damage. If any parts are worn or damaged, replace the chain tensioner assembly.

3. If the chain tensioner and guide contact surfaces are excessively worn, also check the cam chain and both sprockets for wear or damage.

NOTE
*Refer to **Camshaft Removal** for information on measuring cam chain wear.*

Installation

Each cylinder head has a F (front) or R (rear) cast mark for identification (**Figure 92**). Make sure to install each cylinder head in its correct position.

1. Clean the cylinder head and cylinder mating surfaces of all gasket residue.
2. Insert the chain guide's lower end into the crankcase channel and its top bosses into the cylinder grooves (**Figure 93**). **Figure 94** (front cylinder) and **Figure 95** (rear cylinder) show how the guides fit into the crankcase.
3. Install the 2 dowel pins (**Figure 83**) and a new gasket.
4. Run the cam chain through the cylinder head chain tunnel. Then install the cylinder head onto the cylinder block (**Figure 82**). Make sure you seat the 2 dowel pins and head gasket against the cylinder head.
5. Install and tighten the bolts that hold the cylinder head to the cylinder block.
6. Install the chain tensioner (**Figure 80**) and secure it with its 2 mounting bolts and washers (**Figure 79**). Tighten the chain tensioner mounting bolts to the torque specification in **Table 6**.
7. Install the cylinder head fins and Allen bolts.
8. Install the camshaft as described in this chapter.
9. Repeat for the opposite cylinder head.
10. Install the cylinder head covers as described in this chapter.
11. Install the engine in the frame as described in Chapter Five.

VALVES AND VALVE COMPONENTS

Correct valve service requires many special tools. The following procedures describe how to check for valve component wear and to detect what type of service they require. A valve spring compressor is required to remove and install the valves.

Refer to **Figure 96** when servicing the valves in this section.

Solvent Test

Before removing the valves from the cylinder head, perform this solvent test to check the valve seal against its seat.
1. Remove the cylinder head as described in this chapter.

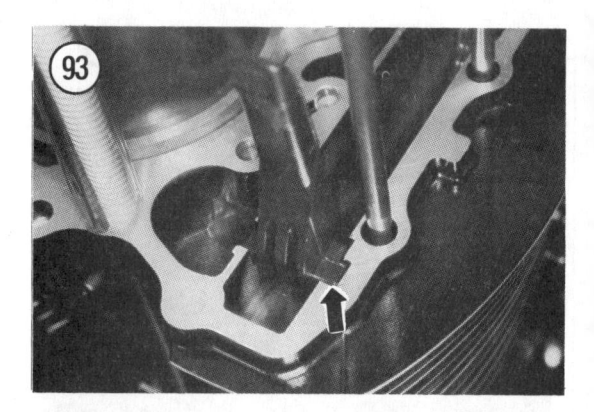

ENGINE TOP END

2. Support the cylinder head so the exhaust port faces up and pour solvent or kerosene into the port as shown in **Figure 97**. Then check the combustion chamber for fluid leaking past the exhaust valve.

3. Repeat Step 2 for the intake port and intake valves.

4. If there is fluid leakage around one or both sets of valves, one or both valves are leaking. The following conditions will cause poor valve seating:

   a. A bent valve stem.
   b. A worn or damaged valve seat (in cylinder head).
   c. A worn or damaged valve face.
   d. A crack in the combustion chamber.
   e. A piece of carbon trapped between the valve face and valve seat.

Valve Removal

1. Remove the cylinder head as described in this chapter.
2. Perform the solvent test for the intake and exhaust valves as described in this chapter.

CAUTION
*Keep all components of each valve assembly (**Figure 98**) together. Do not intermix components from the different valves.*

96 VALVES
1. Valve keepers
2. Upper spring seat
3. Outer spring
4. Inner spring
5. Valve stem seal
6. Lower spring seat
7. Valve guide
8. Exhaust valve
9. Intake valves
10. Cylinder head

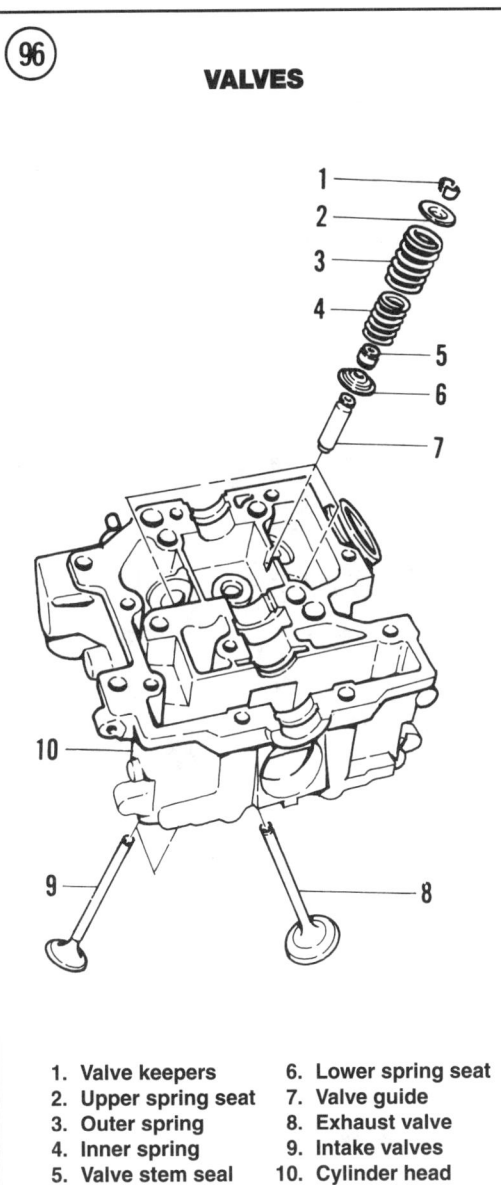

97 Port / Solvent or kerosene / Combustion chamber / Valve

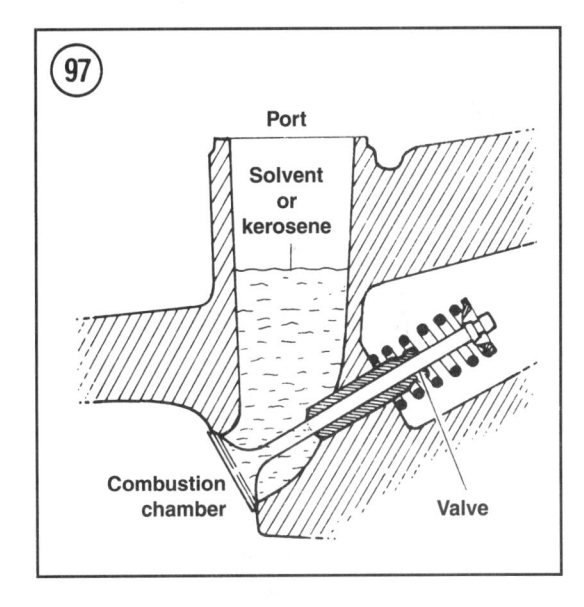

98

3. Install a valve spring compressor squarely over the valve spring seat with the other end of tool placed against the valve head (**Figure 99**).

4. Tighten the valve spring compressor until the valve keepers separate. Lift the valve keepers out through the valve spring compressor.

5. Gradually loosen the valve spring compressor and remove it from the head.

6. Remove the upper spring seat and both valve springs.

CAUTION
*Remove any burrs from the valve stem grooves before removing the valves (**Figure 100**); otherwise you will damage the valve guides as the valve stems are passed through them.*

7. Remove the valve.
8. Remove the lower spring seat.
9. Pull the valve stem seal off the valve guide.
10. Repeat Steps 3-9 for the other valves.

Inspection

Refer to the troubleshooting chart in **Figure 101** when performing the valve inspection procedure in this section. **Table 3** lists valve service specifications.

1. Clean each valve assembly in solvent. Do not gouge or damage the valve seating surface.

2. Inspect the contact surface (**Figure 102**) of each valve for burning. Lap the valves to remove minor roughness and pitting. Valve lapping is described in this chapter. Excessive unevenness to the contact surface is an indication that the valve is not serviceable.

3. Inspect the valve stems for wear and roughness. Then measure the valve stem diameter for wear using a micrometer (**Figure 103**). Compare with the specification in **Table 3**.

4. Remove all carbon and varnish from the valve guides with a stiff spiral wire brush before measuring wear.

NOTE
If you do not have the required measuring tools, go to Step 7.

5. Measure each valve guide at its top, center and bottom positions with a small hole gauge. Compare measurements with specification in **Table 3**.

6. Subtract the measurement made in Step 3 from the measurement made in Step 5. The difference is the valve stem-to-guide clearance. See **Table 3** for correct clearance. Replace any guide or valve that is not within tolerance. Valve guide replacement is described later in this chapter.

7. If a small hole gauge is not available, insert each valve in its guide. Hold the valve slightly off its seat and rock it sideways. If the valve rocks more than slightly, the guide is probably worn. However, to verify, take the cylinder head to a dealership or machine shop and have the valves and valve guides measured.

8. Check the inner and outer valve springs as follows:

 a. Check each of the valve springs for visual damage.

 b. Use a square and check each spring for distortion (**Figure 104**).

 c. Measure the valve spring length with a vernier caliper (**Figure 105**). All must be the length specified in **Table 3** with no bends or other distortion.

 d. Replace defective springs as a set.

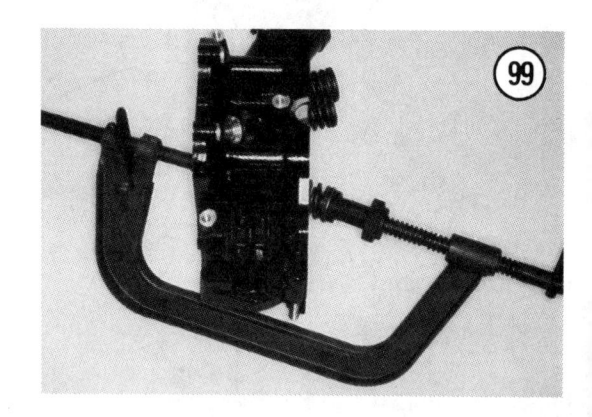

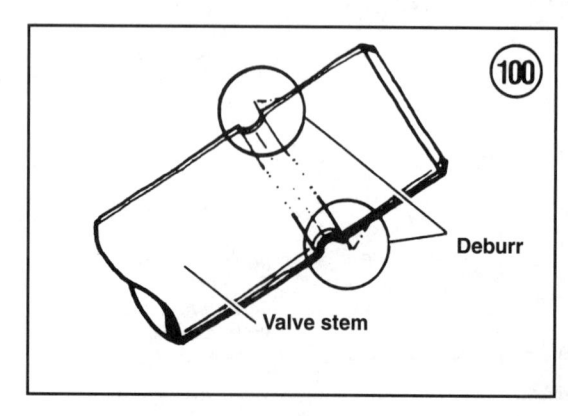

ENGINE TOP END

VALVE TROUBLESHOOTING

Valve deposits

Check:
- Worn valve guide
- Carbon buildup from incorrect engine tuning
- Carbon buildup from incorrect carburetor adjustment
- Dirty or gummed fuel
- Dirty engine oil

Valve sticking

Check:
- Worn valve guide
- Bent valve stem
- Deposits collected on valve stem
- Valve burning or overheating

Valve burning

Check:
- Valve sticking
- Cylinder head warped
- Valve seat distorted
- Valve clearance incorrect
- Incorrect valve spring
- Valve spring worn
- Worn valve seat
- Carbon buildup in engine
- Engine ignition and/or carburetor adjustments incorrect

Valve seat/face wear

Check:
- Valve burning
- Incorrect valve clearance
- Abrasive material on valve face and seat

Valve damage

Check:
- Valve burning
- Incorrectly installed or serviced valve guides
- Incorrect valve clearance
- Incorrect valve, spring seat and retainer assembly
- Detonation caused by incorrect ignition and/or carburetor adjustments

9. Check the valve spring seats and valve keepers for damage.

10. Inspect the valve seats in the cylinder head (**Figure 106**). Recondition the valve seats as described in this chapter if worn or burned. Lapping with fine carborundum paste can recondition seats and valves that are already in near-perfect condition. Check as follows:
   a. Clean the valve seat and valve mating areas with contact cleaner.
   b. Coat the valve seat with machinists' blue marking compound.
   c. Install the valve into its guide and rotate it against its seat with a valve lapping tool. See *Valve Lapping* in this chapter.
   d. Lift the valve out of the guide and measure the seat width with a vernier caliper.
   e. The seat width for intake and exhaust valves must measure within the specification listed in **Table 3** all the way around the seat. If the seat width exceeds the service limit (**Table 3**), regrind the seats as described in this chapter.
   f. Remove all residue from the seats and valves.

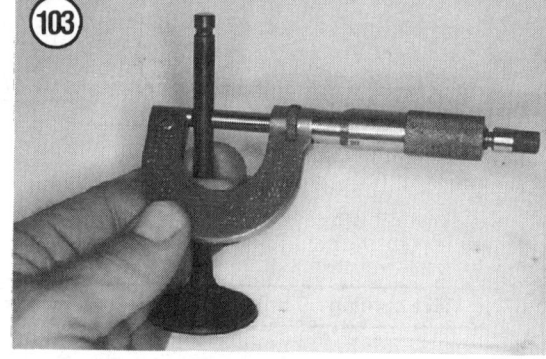

Valve Guide Replacement

Remove and install the valve guides with the following Honda tools (or equivalent):
   a. Valve guide remover, 6.6 mm: Honda part No. 07942-6570100.
   b. Valve guide driver: Honda part No. 07743-0020000.

NOTE
The Honda valve guide driver is not available in the United States. Install the valve guides to their correct depth as described in this chapter.

   c. Valve guide reamer, 6.612 mm: Honda part No. 07984-ZE2000D.

1. In the U.S. market, Honda does not sell a valve guide installer that installs and sets the valve guides to their correct projection height (**Figure 107**) above the cylinder head. If you do not have the Honda tool, mark the projection height on each new valve guide before installing it. The correct valve guide projection height dimensions for the VT1100C2 engine are:
   a. Intake: 14.5 mm (0.57 in.).
   b. Exhaust: 15.5 mm (0.61 in.).

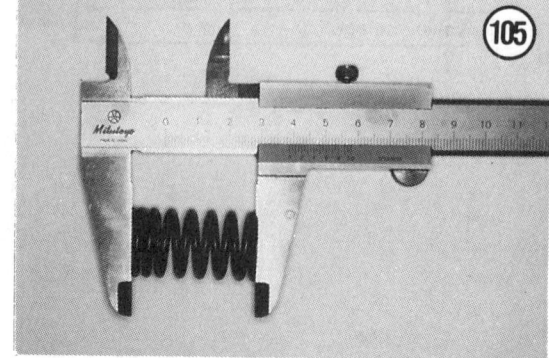

ENGINE TOP END

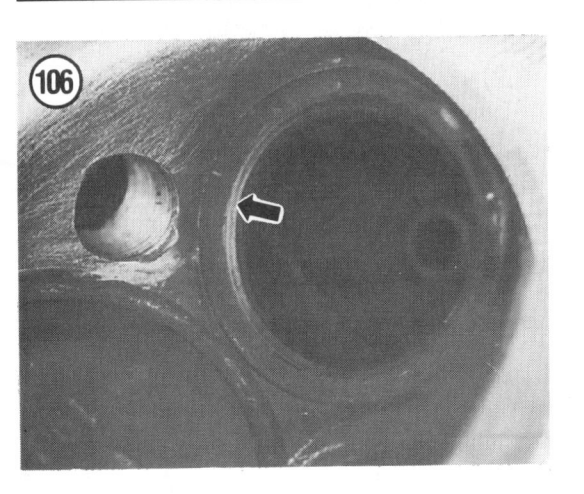

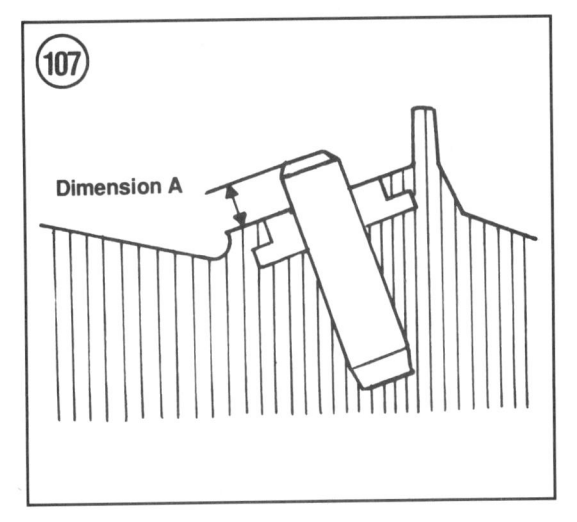

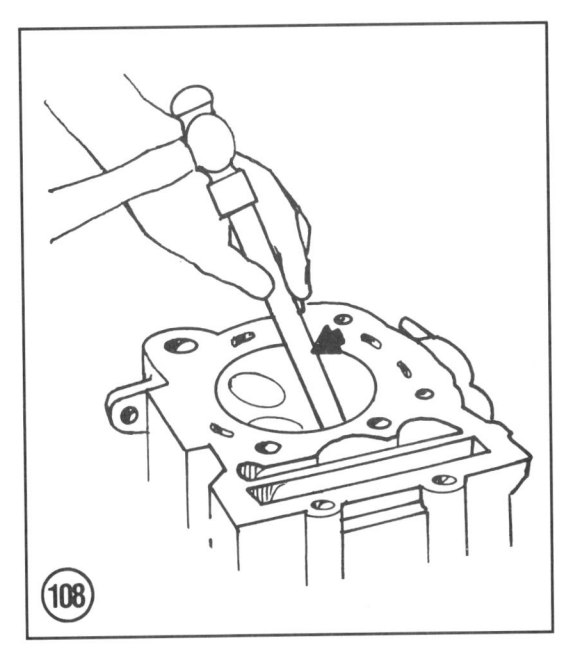

NOTE
*Projection height is the distance measured from the top of the valve guide to the cylinder head mating surface (**Figure 107**).*

2. After marking the projection height on each new valve guide (if necessary), place the valve guides in a freezer. The freezing temperature will shrink the new guides and ease installation.

3. The valve guides are a slight interference fit in the cylinder head. Heat the cylinder head in a shop oven or on a hot plate to 275-290° F (130-140° C)—do not exceed 300° F (150° C). To monitor cylinder head temperature, use temperature indicator sticks available at welding supply stores.

CAUTION
Do not attempt to remove the valve guides if the head is not hot enough; otherwise, you can enlarge the valve guide bore in the cylinder head and permanently damage the head.

CAUTION
Do not heat the cylinder head with a torch (propane or acetylene)—never bring a flame into contact with the cylinder head. The direct heat may warp the cylinder head.

WARNING
Wear welding gloves when performing this procedure. The cylinder head will be very hot.

4. Remove the cylinder head from the oven or hot plate and place onto wooden blocks with the combustion chamber facing *up*.

5. Drive the old valve guide out from the combustion chamber side of the cylinder head with the valve guide remover (**Figure 108**).

6. After the cylinder head cools, check the guide bores for carbon or other contamination.

7. Reheat the cylinder to 275-290° F (130-140° C).

8. Remove the cylinder head from the oven or hot plate and place it on wooden blocks with the combustion chamber facing *down*.

9. Remove the new valve guide from the freezer.

10A. If you are using the Honda valve guide installer (**Figure 109**), install the valve guide by following the directions included with the tool.

10B. If using a universal type valve guide installer, drive the new valve guide into the cylinder head until the projection height mark (made in Step 1) is even with the cylinder head mating surface. Then measure the valve guide's installed height and compare it to the dimension listed in Step 1.

11. If necessary, repeat these steps for the other valve guides.

12. After the cylinder head cools to room temperature, ream the new valve guide as follows:
   a. Coat the valve guide and valve guide reamer with cutting oil.

CAUTION
*Always rotate the valve guide reamer **clockwise** when installing and removing it from the guide. Rotating the reamer counterclockwise will damage the valve guide.*

   b. Insert the reamer from the combustion chamber side and rotate it *clockwise* through the valve guide. Continue to rotate the reamer and work it down through the entire length of the new valve guide. Add additional cutting oil during this procedure.
   c. While rotating the reamer *clockwise*, withdraw the reamer from the valve guide.
   d. Measure the valve guide's inside diameter with a small hole gauge. Then measure the small hole gauge with a micrometer. This measurement must be within the service specification listed in **Table 3**.

13. Repeat for the other valve guides.

14. Clean the cylinder head and valve guides with solvent to wash out all metal particles. Dry with compressed air.

15. Oil the valve guides to prevent rust.

16. Reface the valve seats with a 45° cutter after replacing valve guides. Reface the valve seats as described under *Valve Seat Reconditioning* in this chapter.

Valve Seat Reconditioning

A number of special tools are required to cut the valve seats. Valve seat cutters are available from Honda dealers and aftermarket tool and machine shop suppliers. Follow the manufacturer's instructions in regard to operating the cutters. You need the following tools:

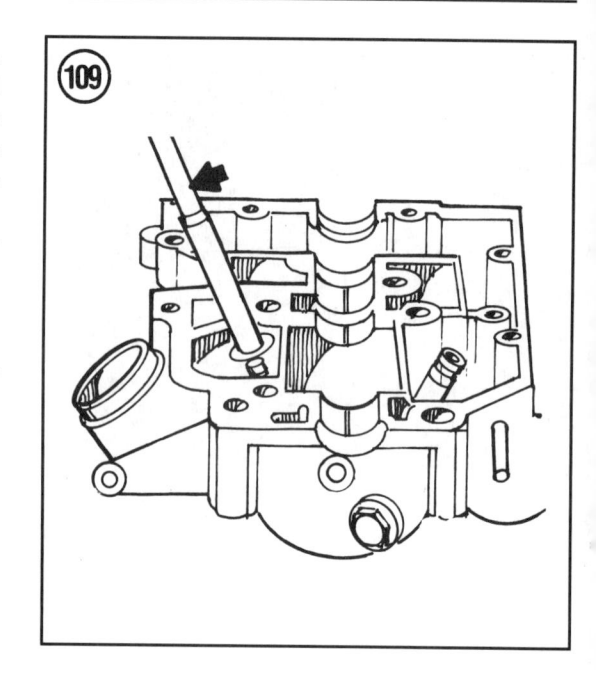

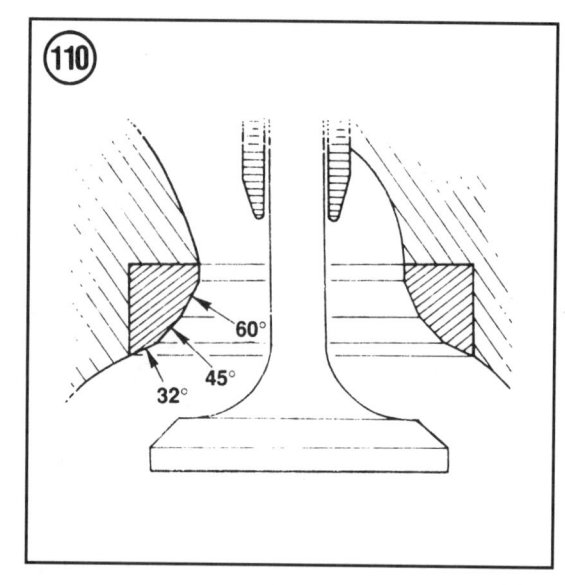

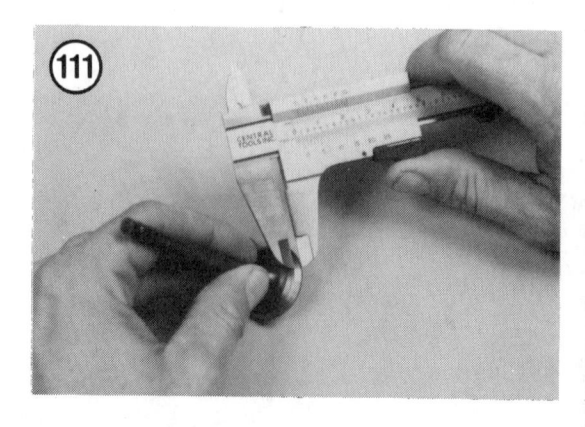

ENGINE TOP END

a. Valve seat cutters (**Figure 110**). See a Honda dealer for current part numbers.
b. A vernier caliper.
c. Machinists' blue (marking compound).
d. A valve lapping tool.

1. Inspect the valve seats (**Figure 106**). Recondition the valve seats if worn or burned. Lapping with fine carborundum paste can recondition seats and valves that are already in near-perfect condition. Lapping, however, is always inferior to precision grinding. Check as follows:

   a. Clean the valve seat and valve mating areas with contact cleaner.
   b. Coat the valve seat with machinists' blue.
   c. Install the valve into its guide and rotate it against its seat with a valve lapping tool. See *Valve Lapping* in this chapter.
   d. Lift the valve out of the guide and measure the seat width with a vernier caliper. See **Figure 111** and **Figure 112**.
   e. The seat width for intake and exhaust valves must be within the specification listed in **Table 3** all the way around the seat. If the seat width exceeds the service limit (**Table 3**), you must reface the seats as follows.

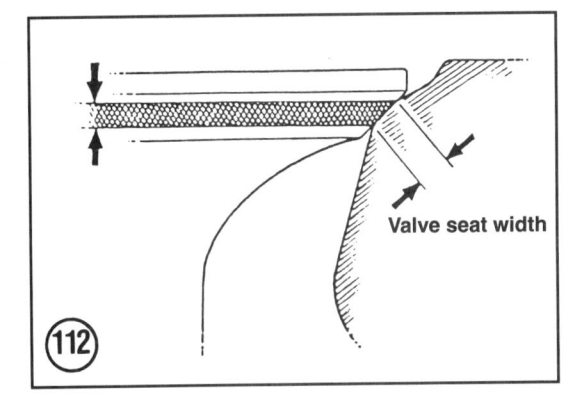

   CAUTION
   Cut the valve seats slowly to prevent overcutting them. Overcutting the valve seats can sink the valves too far into the cylinder head. If this happens, you must replace the cylinder head.

2. Install a 45° cutter onto the valve tool and lightly cut the seat to remove roughness.
3. Measure the valve seat with a vernier caliper (**Figure 112**). Use this measurement as a reference point when performing the following steps.

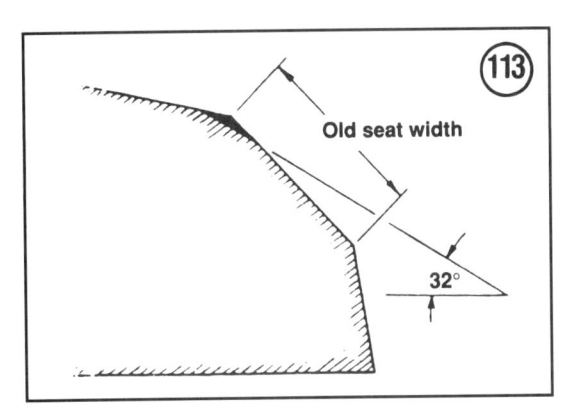

   CAUTION
   The 32° cutter removes material quickly. Work carefully and check your progress often.

4. Install a 32° cutter onto the valve tool and lightly cut the seat to remove 1/4 of the existing valve seat width (**Figure 113**).
5. Install a 60° cutter onto the valve tool and lightly cut the seat to remove the lower 1/4 of the existing valve seat width (**Figure 114**).
6. Measure the valve seat with a vernier caliper. Then fit a 45° cutter onto the valve tool and cut the valve seat to the specified seat width listed in **Table 2**. See **Figure 115**.
7. When the valve seat width is correct, check valve seating as follows.
8. Clean the valve seat and valve mating areas with contact cleaner.
9. Coat the valve seat with machinists' blue.

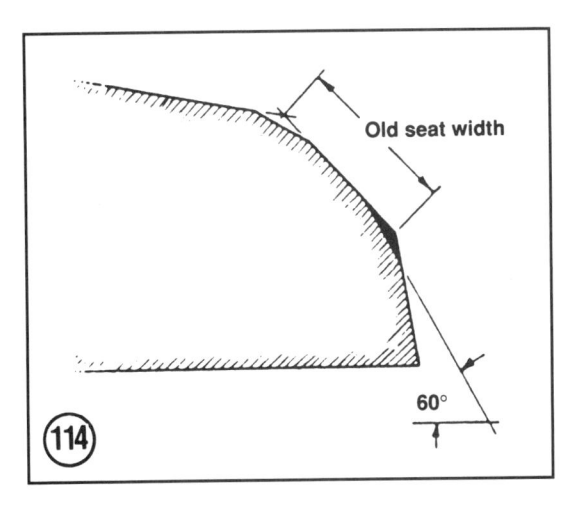

10. Install the valve into its guide and rotate it against its seat with a valve lapping tool. See *Valve Lapping* in this chapter.

11. Remove the valve and check the contact area on the valve (**Figure 116**). Interpret results as follows:

   a. The valve seat contact area should be in the center of the valve face.

   b. If the contact area is too high on the valve, lower the seat with a 32° flat cutter.

   c. If the contact area is too low on the valve, raise the seat with a 60° interior cutter.

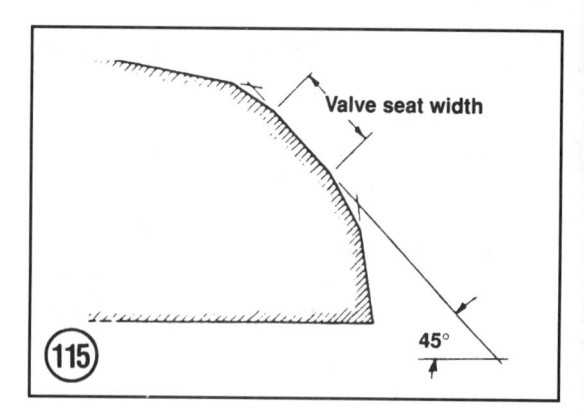

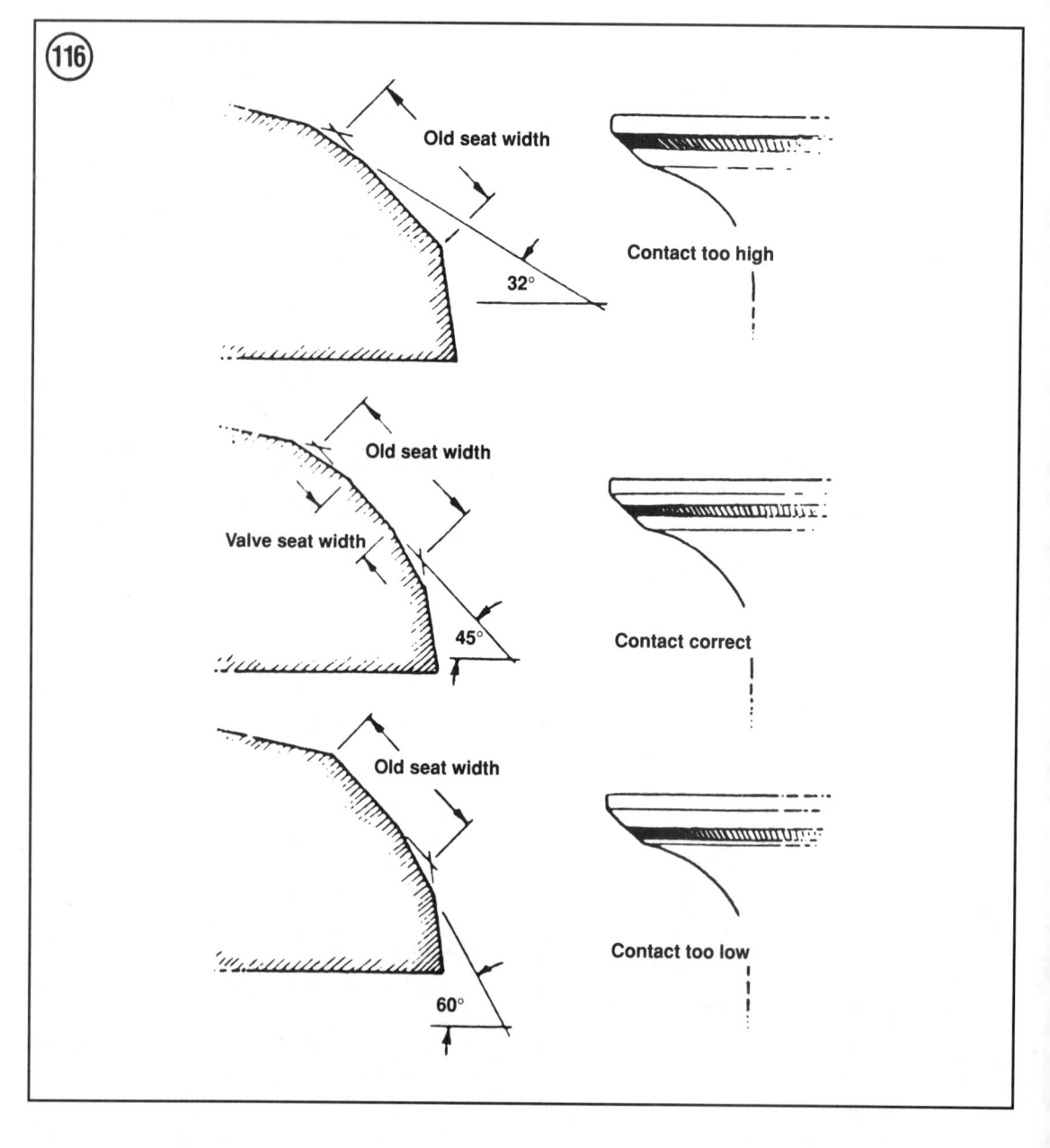

ENGINE TOP END

d. Refinish the seat using a 45° cutter.
12. When the contact area is correct, lap the valve as described in this chapter.

Valve Lapping

Valve lapping is a simple operation which can restore the valve seal without machining—if the wear or distortion is not too great.

Perform this procedure after determining that the valve seat width and outside diameter are within specification.

1. Smear a light coating of fine grade valve lapping compound onto the valve face.
2. Insert the valve into the head.
3. Wet the suction cup of the lapping tool and stick it to the head of the valve. Lap the valve to the seat by spinning the lapping tool in both directions. Every 5 to 10 seconds, rotate the valve 180° in the valve seat. Continue until the mating surfaces on the valve and seat are smooth and equal in size.
4. Examine the valve seat in cylinder head. It must be smooth and even with a smooth, polished seating ring.
5. Clean the valves and cylinder head in solvent to remove all of the grinding compound. Any compound left on the valves or cylinder head will cause excessive wear and damage.
6. After you have lapped the valves and installed the valves into the cylinder head, test the valve seal as described under *Solvent Test* in this chapter. If fluid leaks past any of the seats, remove that valve and repeat the lapping procedure until there is no leakage.

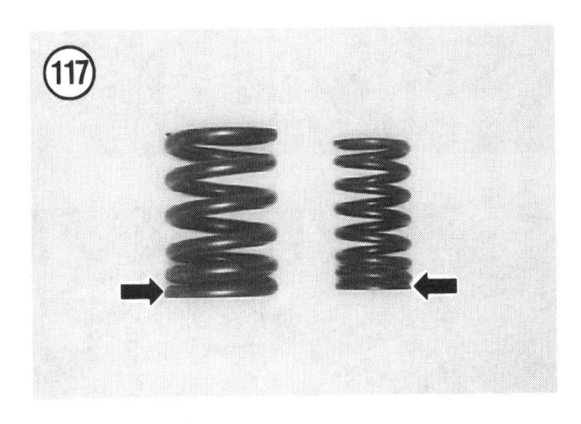

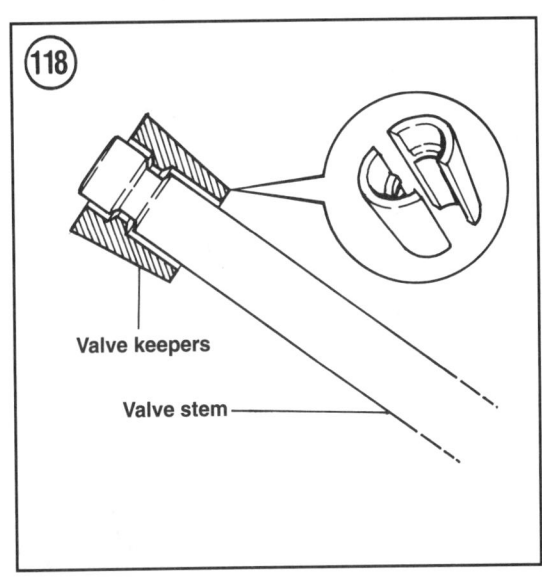

Installation

1. Clean the cylinder head thoroughly to remove all carbon residue. If the valve seats were refaced and new guides installed, clean these areas thoroughly to remove all chips and valve lapping compound.

> *CAUTION*
> *Lapping compound left in the engine will cause premature valve guide and valve wear.*

2. Install the lower spring seat.
3. Install a *new* valve guide seal by seating it onto the end of the guide.
4. Coat a valve stem with molybdenum disulfide paste and install into its correct guide. To prevent damaging the seal, turn the valve slowly as it enters and passes through the seal. Hold the valve in position.

> *NOTE*
> *Install valve springs with the narrow pitch end (end with coils closest together) facing the cylinder head. See* **Figure 117**.

5. Install the inner and outer valve springs.
6. Install the upper valve spring seat.
7. Push down on the upper valve seat with the valve spring compressor (**Figure 99**) and install the valve keepers (**Figure 118**). After releasing tension from the compressor, tap the end of the valve stem with a soft-faced hammer, then check that the valve keepers are seated (**Figure 118**) in the groove in the end of the valve. See **Figure 119**.

8. Repeat Steps 1-7 for the other valves.
9. Perform the *Solvent Test* in this chapter.

CYLINDERS

Each alloy cylinder block (**Figure 120**) has a pressed-in cast iron cylinder liner. Oversize piston and ring sizes are available through Honda dealerships and aftermarket piston suppliers.

Removal

1. Remove the cylinder head and cam chain guide as described in this chapter.
2. Remove the 2 bolts that secure the water hose joint (**Figure 121**) to the rear cylinder.
3. Remove the 2 water pipe clips (**Figure 122**).
4. Slide the water pipe off of one of the cylinder pipe joints (**Figure 123**).
5. Loosen the cylinder by tapping around the perimeter with a rubber or plastic mallet.
6. Pull the cylinder (**Figure 120**) straight up and off the crankcase for a short distance, then stop. Install a clean shop rag or paper towels underneath the cylinder to prevent any broken piston rings from falling into the crankcase.
7. Remove the cylinder from the engine.
8. Remove the base gasket and the 2 dowel pins. Discard the base gasket.
9. If necessary, remove the piston as described under *Piston Removal* in this chapter.
10. Slide a 1/2 in. rubber hose (**Figure 124**) down each stud to protect the piston and rings from damage.

Inspection

1. Remove the water pipe and discard the O-ring (**Figure 125**).
2. Carefully remove all gasket residue from the top (**Figure 126**) and bottom cylinder block gasket surfaces. If the bottom gasket is hard to remove, soak the gasket in solvent before trying to remove it.
3. Wash the cylinder and its coolant passages in solvent. Dry with compressed air.
4. Check the dowel pin holes for cracks or other damage.
5. Measure the cylinder bore with a bore gauge or inside micrometer (**Figure 127**) at the points shown in **Figure 128**. Measure in line with the piston pin

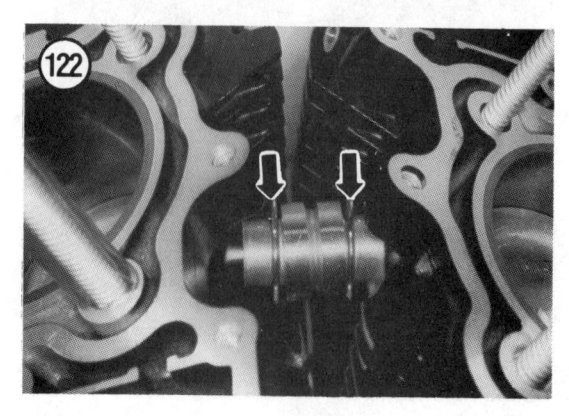

ENGINE TOP END

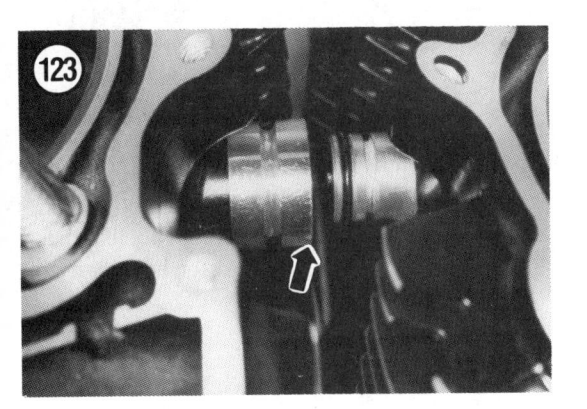

and 90° to the pin. This measurement determines the cylinder bore roundness. Now measure in 3 axes—in line with the piston pin and at 90° to the pin. If the taper or out-of-round is greater than specification (**Table 4**), bore the cylinder oversize and install a new piston and rings.

NOTE
*You must purchase the new piston before having the cylinder bored. Your machinist will bore the cylinder to match the piston size. **Table 2** lists piston-to-cylinder clearance.*

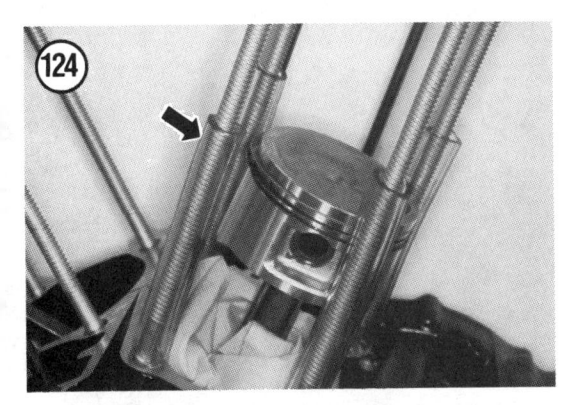

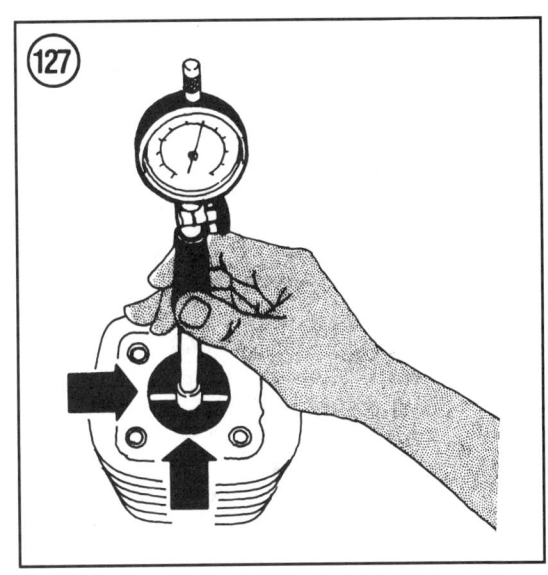

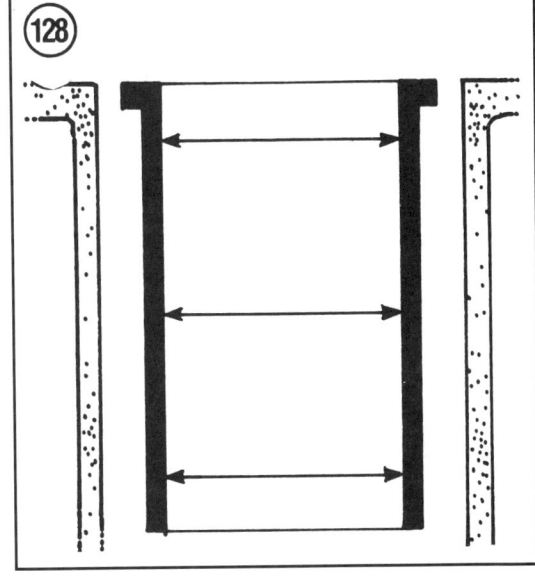

6. Check the bore (**Figure 126**) for scratches or gouges.

7. Place a straightedge across the upper cylinder block surface. Measure the warp by inserting a flat feeler gauge between the straightedge and the cylinder block at different locations (**Figure 129**). Compare the warpage to the service limit in **Table 2**. If this surface is out of specification, refer service to a Honda dealership or machine shop.

8. After servicing the cylinder, wash the bore in hot soapy water. This is the only way to clean the cylinder wall of the fine grit material left from the bore or honing job. After washing the cylinder wall, run a clean white cloth through it. The cylinder wall must be free of all grit and other debris. If the rag is dirty, rewash the cylinder wall. After the cylinder is clean, lubricate the cylinder wall with engine oil to prevent the cylinder liner from rusting.

CAUTION
Using soap and water as described in Step 8 is the only solution that can wash the fine grit residue out of the cylinder crevices. Solvent and kerosene cannot do this. Grit residue left in the cylinder will cause rapid and premature wear to the new rings and cylinder bore surface.

9. Repeat for the other cylinder.
10. Check for bent or damaged cylinder studs. If necessary, replace the studs as described in this chapter.

Installation

1. Make sure the top and bottom cylinder surfaces are clean of all gasket residue.
2. Lubricate a new cylinder water joint O-ring with coolant, then install it onto the cylinder (**Figure 125**).
3. Lubricate the water pipe with coolant, then slide it all the way onto one cylinder (**Figure 130**).
4. If removed, install the piston as described in this chapter. If you did not remove the piston, make sure both piston pin clips are seated correctly in the piston clip grooves—make sure the clip end gaps do not align with the piston cutouts.
5. If used, remove the hoses from around the cylinder studs.
6. Install the 2 dowel pins into the crankcase (**Figure 131**).

7. Install a new base gasket. Make sure all holes align.
8. Stagger the piston rings around the piston as shown in **Figure 132**.
9. Lubricate the cylinder wall, piston and rings with engine oil. Make sure the oil gets behind the rings and that the oil control ring is thoroughly lubricated.
10. Support the piston with a piston holding fixture (**Figure 133**).

NOTE
There are 2 ways to install the cylinder—with a ring compressor and by

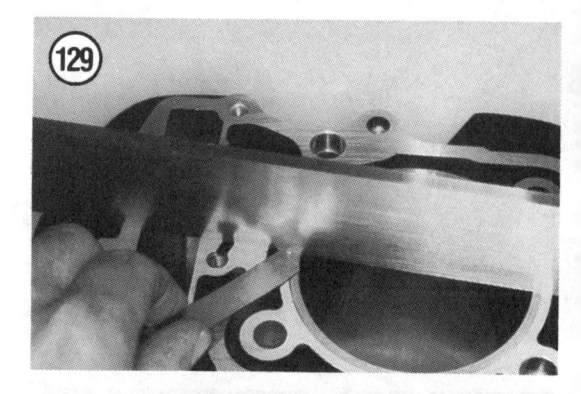

ENGINE TOP END

hand. Step 11A and Step 11B described both methods.

CAUTION
If you feel solid resistance when installing the cylinder over the piston and rings in the next step, stop immediately and remove the cylinder. A ring has probably slipped out and is binding against the bottom of the cylinder bore. Reposition the piston rings and start over.

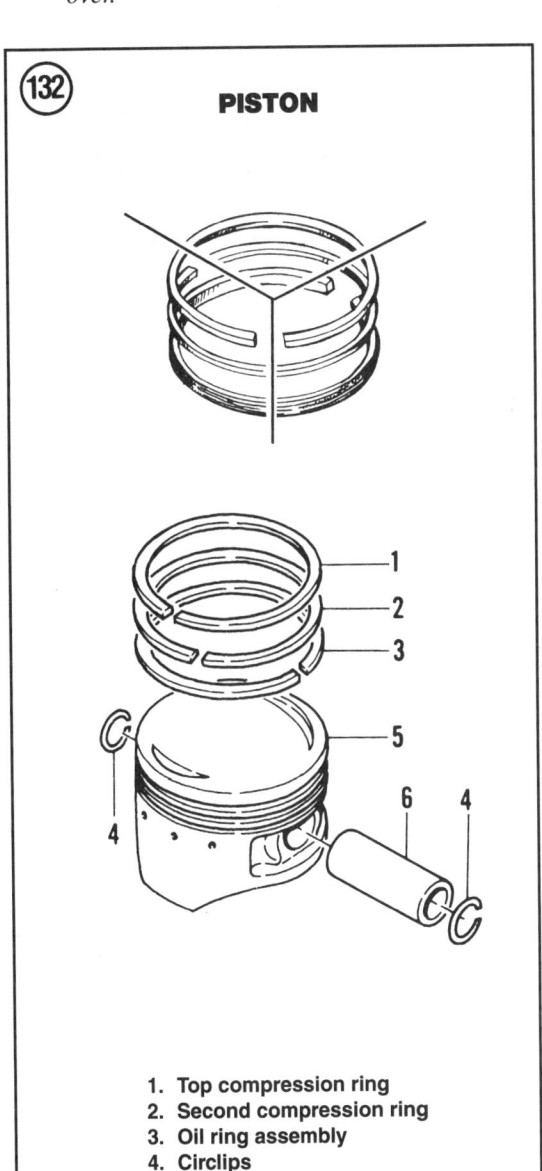

11A. Install a ring compressor (**Figure 134**) over the piston and rings following its manufacturer's instructions. Slide the cylinder over the cylinder studs until it contacts the piston squarely, then tap the cylinder to push the ring compressor past the rings and down onto the piston skirt. When the cylinder covers the rings, remove the ring compressor and the piston holding fixture, then slide the cylinder down until it bottoms on the crankcase (**Figure 135**).

11B. Align the cylinder with the piston and install the cylinder—compress each ring as it enters the cylinder with your fingers. When the cylinder covers the rings, remove the piston holding fixture and slide the cylinder down until it bottoms on the crankcase (**Figure 135**).

12. Run the chain and wire up through the chain tunnel.

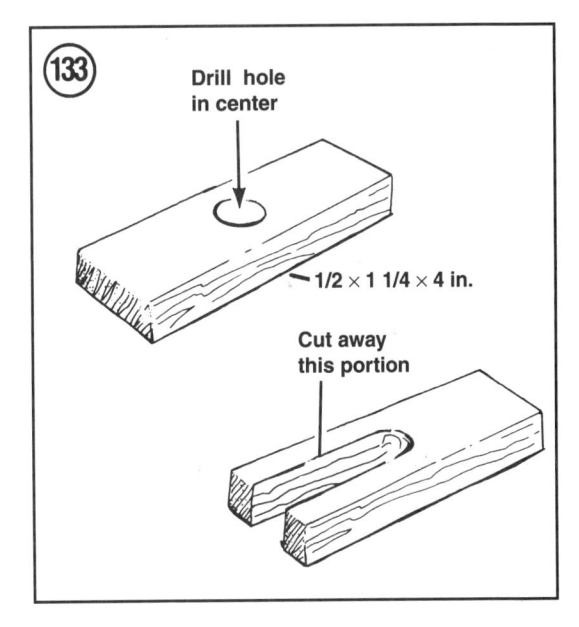

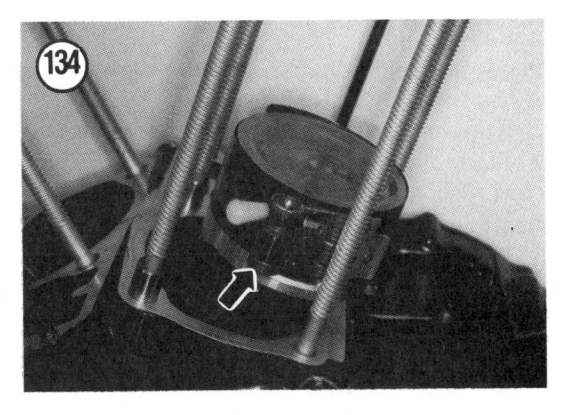

132 PISTON

1. Top compression ring
2. Second compression ring
3. Oil ring assembly
4. Circlips
5. Piston
6. Piston pin

133
Drill hole in center
1/2 × 1 1/4 × 4 in.
Cut away this portion

134

13. On the first cylinder installed, install a 1/2 in. hose and washer over one of its cylinder studs and secure it with a nut as shown in **Figure 136**. This will prevent the piston from pushing the cylinder up as you turn the crankshaft to position the other piston for its cylinder installation.
14. Repeat to install the other cylinder.

NOTE
When you turn the crankshaft in Step 15, have an assistant pull up on each cam chain to prevent them from binding against the crankshaft sprockets.

15. Turn the crankshaft with a wrench and check that each piston moves smoothly with no binding or roughness.
16. Lubricate the exposed cylinder water joint O-ring (**Figure 123**) with coolant, then slide the water pipe over it.
17. Install a clip in each water pipe clip groove (**Figure 122**).
18. Lubricate a new water hose joint O-ring with coolant and install it into the hose joint. Then install the water hose joint onto the rear cylinder and secure it with its 2 mounting bolts (**Figure 121**). Tighten the bolts securely.
19. Install the cylinder heads as described in this chapter.

PISTON AND PISTON RINGS

The piston is made of an aluminum alloy. The piston pin is made of steel and is a precision fit in the piston. The piston pin is held in place by a clip at each end.

Refer to **Figure 132** when servicing the piston and rings in the following section.

Piston Removal

1. Remove the cylinder as described in this chapter.
2. Block off the crankcase below the piston with clean paper towels to prevent the piston pin circlips from falling into the crankcase.
3. Before removing the piston, hold the rod and rock the piston (**Figure 137**). Any rocking motion (do not confuse with the normal sliding motion) indicates wear on the piston pin, rod bushing, pin bore, or a combination of all three.

4. Remove the circlips from the piston pin bore (**Figure 138**).

NOTE
Discard the piston circlips. You must install new circlips during reassembly.

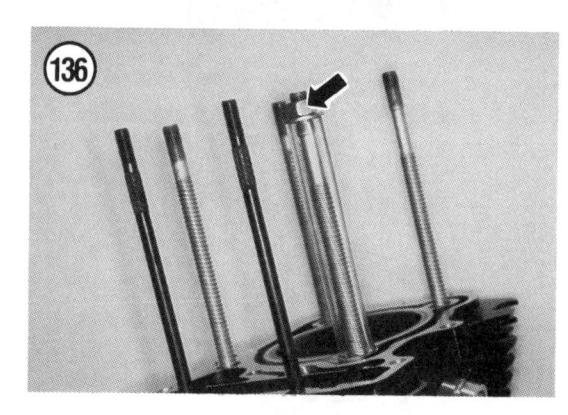

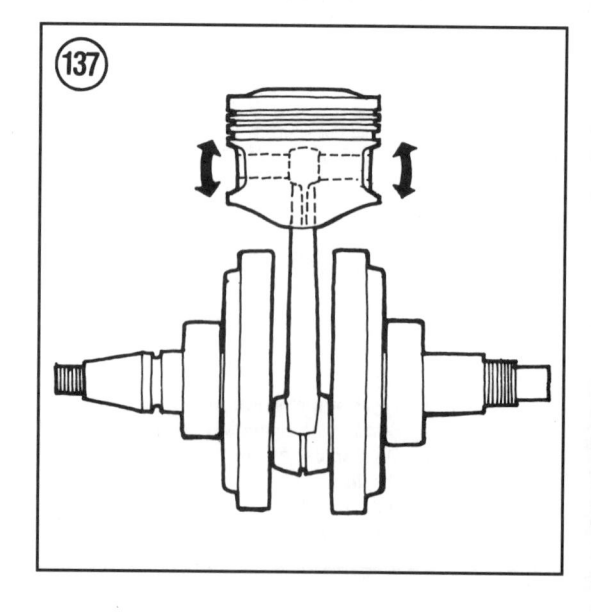

ENGINE TOP END

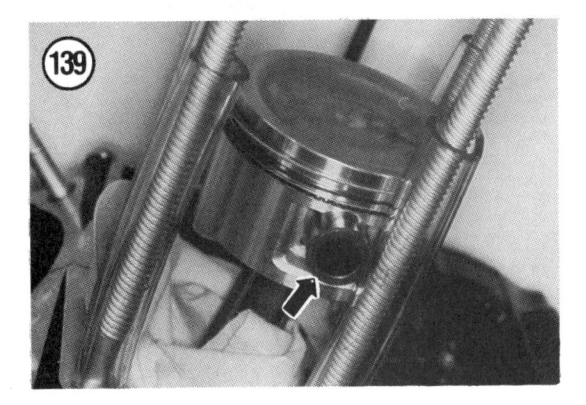

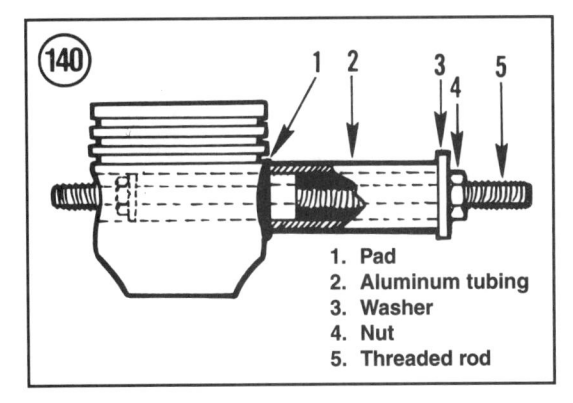

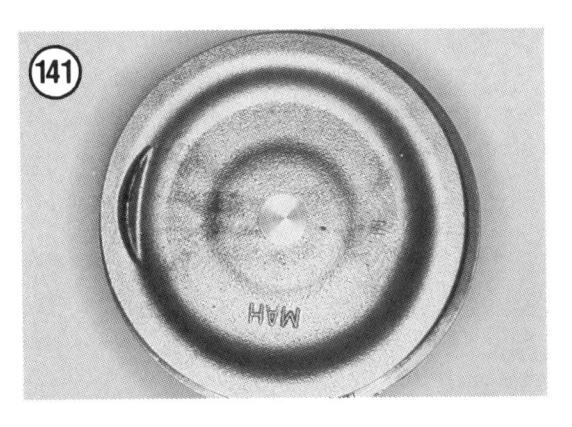

5. Push the piston pin (**Figure 139**) out of the piston by hand. If the pin is tight, use a homemade tool (**Figure 140**) to remove it. Do not drive the piston pin out as this may damage the piston pin, connecting rod or piston.
6. Lift the piston off the connecting rod.
7. Inspect the piston as described in this chapter.
8. Repeat for the other piston.
9. If necessary, remove and service the oil jets as described in this chapter.

Piston Inspection

1. Remove the piston rings as described in this chapter.
2. Clean the carbon from the piston crown with a soft scraper or wire wheel mounted in a drill. Large carbon accumulations reduce piston cooling and result in detonation and piston damage. Do not remove or damage the carbon ridge around the circumference of the piston above the top ring. If the piston, rings and cylinder are dimensionally correct, removal of the carbon ring from the top of the piston or the carbon ridges from the cylinder may promote excessive oil consumption.

> *CAUTION*
> *Do not wire brush piston skirts or ring lands. The wire brush removes aluminum and increases piston clearance. It also rounds the corners of the ring lands, which results in decreased support for the piston rings.*

3. After cleaning the piston, examine the crown (**Figure 141**). The crown must show no evidence of wear or damage. If the crown appears pecked or spongy-looking, also check the spark plug, valves and combustion chamber for aluminum deposits. If these deposits are found, the engine is overheating.
4. Examine each ring groove (**Figure 142**) for burrs, dented edges or other damage. Pay particular attention to the top compression ring groove as it usually wears more than the others. Because the oil rings are bathed in oil, these rings and grooves wear little compared to compression rings and their grooves. If there is evidence of oil ring groove wear or if the oil ring is tight and difficult to remove, the piston skirt may have collapsed due to excessive heat. Replace the piston.

1. Pad
2. Aluminum tubing
3. Washer
4. Nut
5. Threaded rod

5. Check the oil control holes in the piston (**Figure 143**) and clean of any carbon or oil sludge buildups.
6. Check the piston skirt (**Figure 144**) for cracks or other damage. If the piston shows evidence of partial seizure (bits of aluminum transferred onto the piston skirt), replace the piston.

NOTE
If the piston skirt is worn or scuffed unevenly from side to side, the connecting rod may be bent or twisted.

7. Check the piston circlip grooves (**Figure 145**) for wear, cracks or other damage. If necessary, check the circlip fit by installing a new circlip into each groove and then attempt to move the circlip from side to side. If the circlip has any side play, the groove is worn. Replace the piston. Discard these circlips after removing them.
8. Measure piston-to-cylinder clearance as described under *Piston Clearance* in this chapter.

Piston Pin
Inspection

1. Clean and dry the piston pin.

2. Inspect the piston pin for chrome flaking or cracks and replace if necessary.

3. Oil the piston pin and install it in the piston. Slowly rotate the piston pin and check for radial play (**Figure 146**). If any play exists, replace the piston pin and/or connecting rod. Confirm piston pin clearance by performing the following steps.

4. Measure the piston pin hole diameter (**Figure 147**) with a snap gauge. Then measure the snap gauge with a micrometer and check against the dimension in **Table 4**. Replace if worn to the service limit.

5. Measure the piston pin outside diameter (**Figure 148**) with a micrometer and check against the dimension in **Table 4**. Replace if worn to the service limit.

6. Subtract the measurement made in Step 5 from the measurement made in Step 4. The difference is the piston-to-piston pin clearance. See **Table 4** for the correct clearance.

7. Repeat for the other piston.

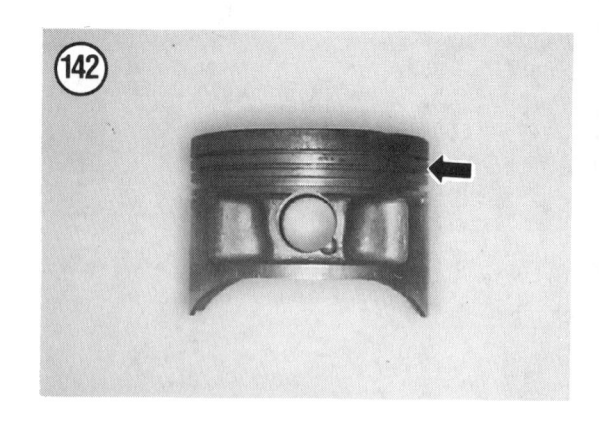

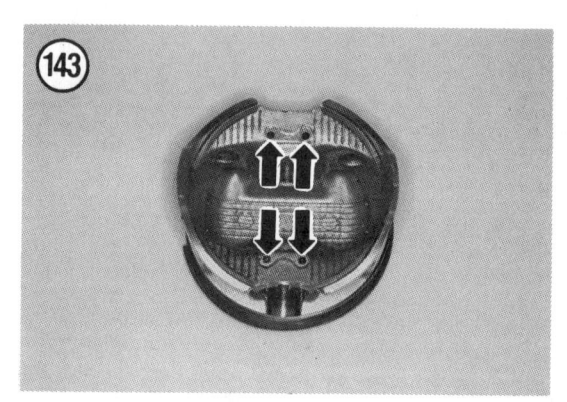

ENGINE TOP END

Connecting Rod
Small End Inspection

1. Inspect the connecting rod small end (**Figure 149**) for cracks, twisting or heat damage.
2. Measure the connecting rod bore inside diameter with a snap gauge (**Figure 150**). Then measure the snap gauge with a micrometer and check against the dimension in **Table 4**. Replace the connecting rod if worn to the service limit. Refer to Chapter Five for engine disassembly and connecting rod replacement.
3. Repeat for the other connecting rod.

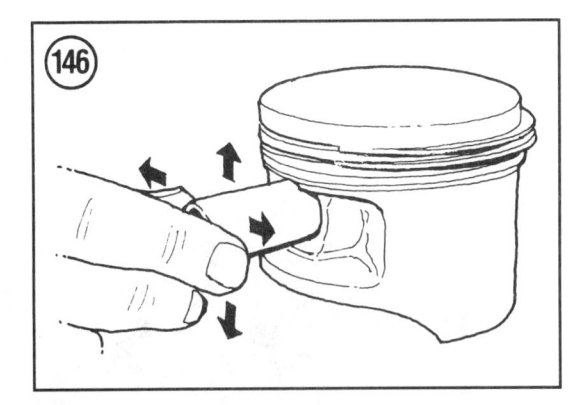

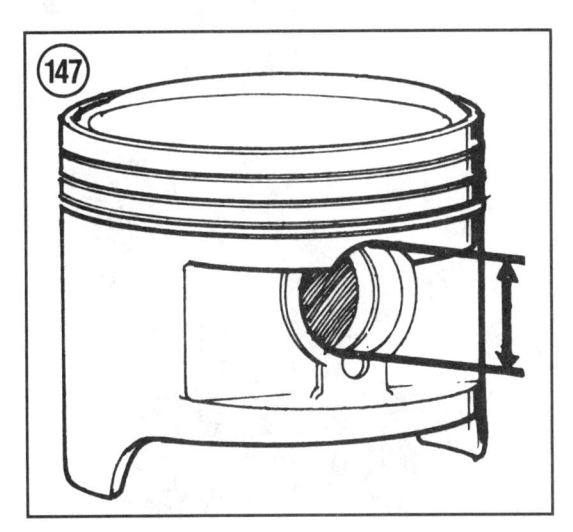

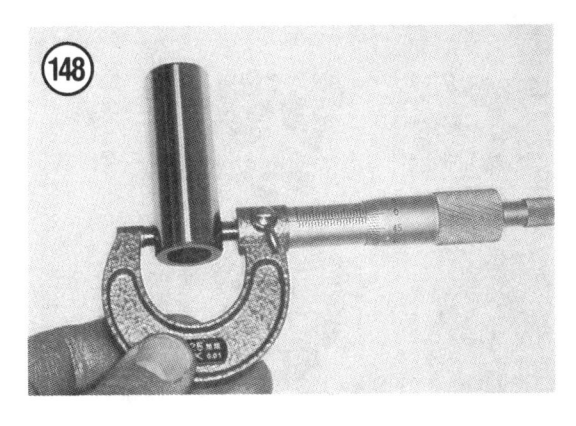

Piston Clearance Measurement

1. Make sure the piston and cylinder walls are clean and dry.
2. Measure the cylinder bore with a bore gauge or inside micrometer (**Figure 127**) at the points shown in **Figure 128**. Measure in line with the piston pin

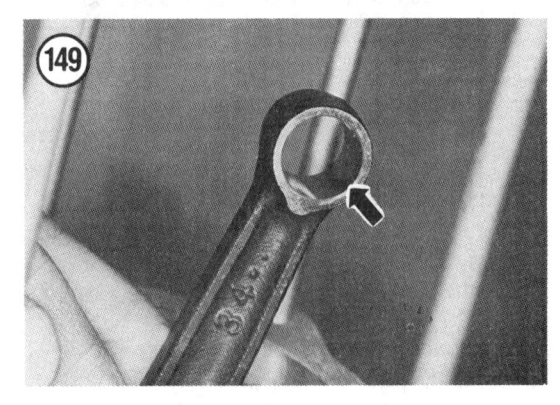

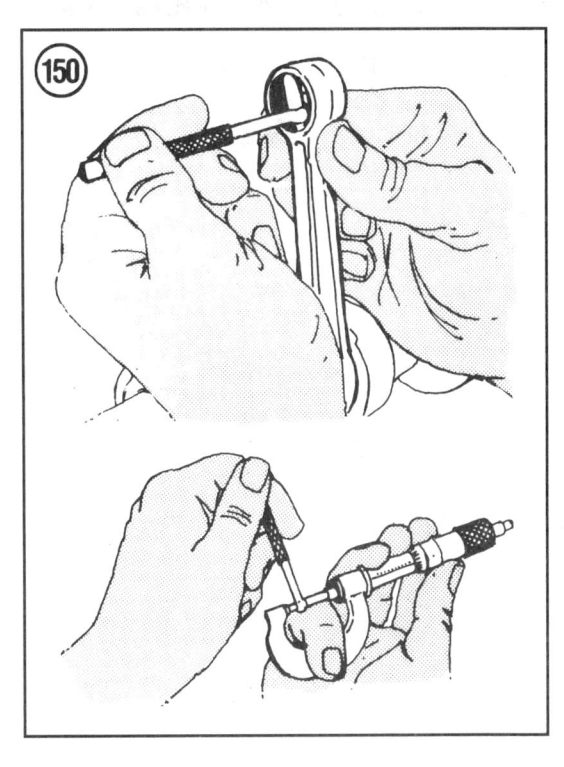

and 90° to the pin. Use the maximum cylinder bore measurement during this procedure.

3. Measure the piston diameter with a micrometer at a right angle to the piston pin bore (**Figure 151**). Measure up 10 mm (0.4 in.) from the bottom edge of the piston skirt (**Figure 151**). Write down the piston diameter measurement.

4. Subtract the piston diameter from the largest bore diameter; the difference is piston-to-cylinder clearance. If the piston clearance exceeds the service limit in **Table 4**, note the following:

   a. If the bore diameter is still within specification, it is possible to buy a new piston without reboring. The new piston will take up some of the excessive piston-to-cylinder clearance. Check carefully before deciding to rebore or just use a new piston.
   b. If the bore diameter is out of specification, bore the cylinder oversize and install a new piston.

5. Repeat for the other piston and cylinder.

Piston Installation

Install *new* piston pin circlips (**Figure 152**) when installing the pistons in this procedure.

1. If removed, install the oil jet as described in this chapter.
2. Slide a 1/2 in. hose over each cylinder stud (**Figure 153**). This will prevent the cylinder studs from scratching the piston and rings.
3. Install the piston rings onto the piston as described in this chapter.
4. Lubricate the connecting rod bushing, piston pin and piston with clean engine oil.
5. Install a new piston pin circlip into one of the piston clip grooves (**Figure 154**).

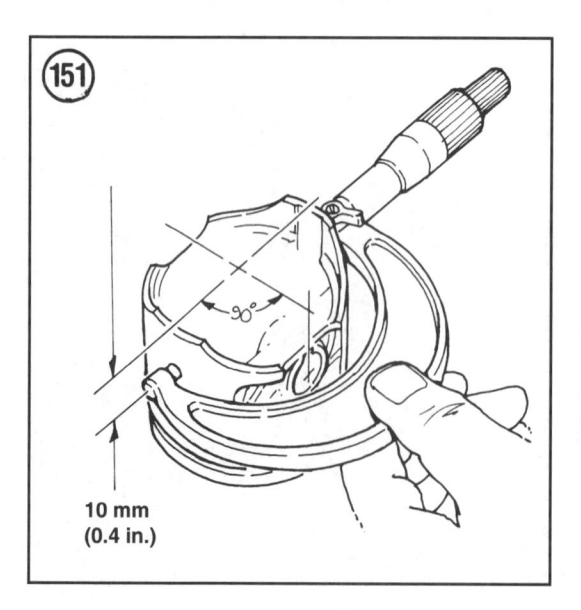

CAUTION
*Do not align the piston pin clip end gap with the cutout in the piston (**Figure 155**).*

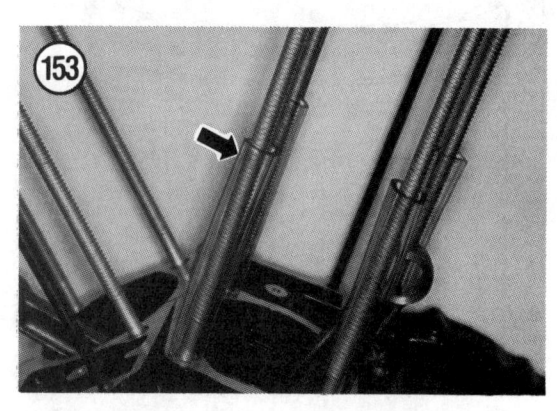

ENGINE TOP END

155

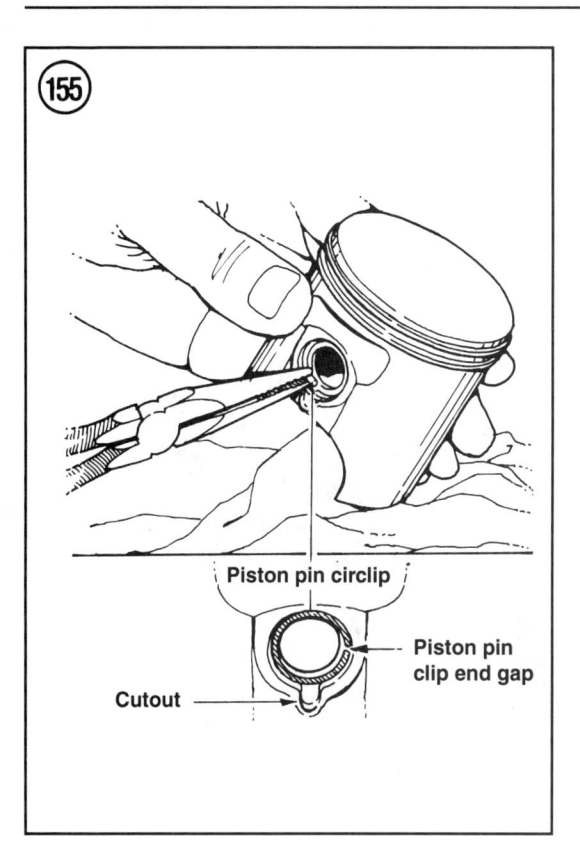

Piston pin circlip
Piston pin clip end gap
Cutout

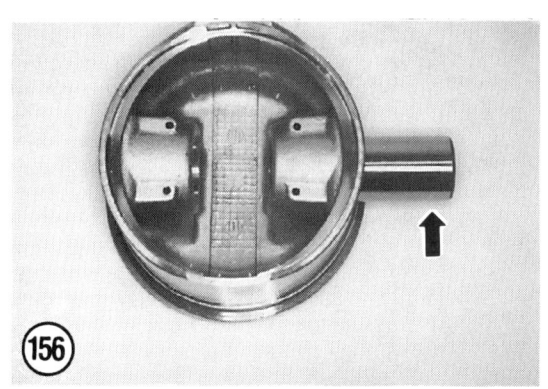

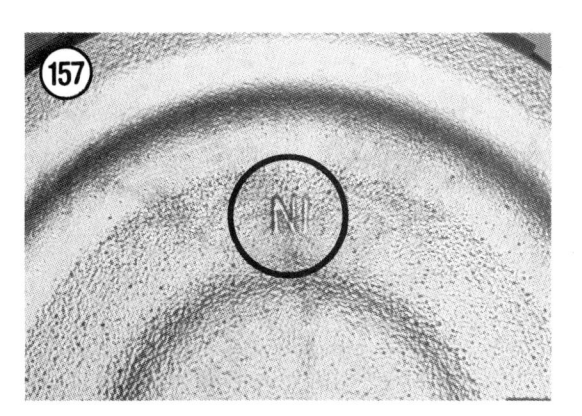

156

157

158

6. Slide the piston pin into the piston until its end is flush with the piston pin boss (**Figure 156**).
7. Place the piston over the connecting rod so the IN mark (**Figure 157**) on the piston crown faces toward the *intake* side of the engine.
8. Align the piston pin with the hole in the connecting rod. Push the piston pin (**Figure 139**) through the connecting rod and into the other side of the piston.
9. Install the second *new* piston pin clip (**Figure 138**) into the remaining piston clip groove.
10. Make sure both clips seat in their groove completely (**Figure 158**).
11. Install the cylinder as described in this chapter.
12. Repeat for the other piston.

Piston Ring
Inspection and Removal

A 3-ring type piston and ring assembly is used (**Figure 159**). The top and second rings are compression rings. The lower ring is an oil control ring assembly (consisting of 2 spacer rings and an expander spacer).

1. Measure the side clearance of each compression ring in its groove with a flat feeler gauge (**Figure 160**) and compare with the specifications in **Table 4**. If the clearance of one compression ring is out of specification, replace all 3 rings as a set. If the clearance is still excessive with the new ring, replace the piston.

WARNING
The edges of all piston rings are very sharp. Be careful when handling them to avoid cut fingers.

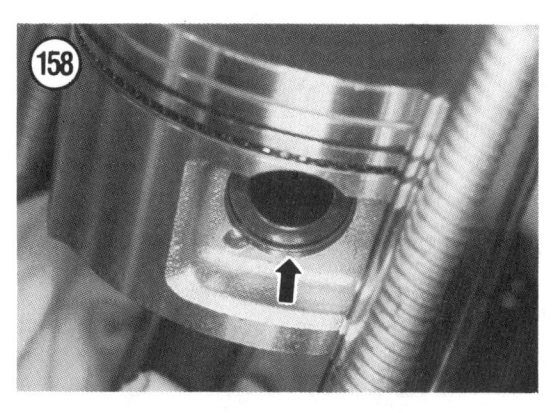

CHAPTER FOUR

NOTE
The stock Honda compression rings are different and must be reinstalled in their original operating positions.

2. Remove the compression rings with a ring expander tool (**Figure 161**) or spread the ring ends with your thumbs and lift the rings out of their grooves and up over the piston (**Figure 162**).
3. Remove the oil ring assembly (**Figure 163**) by first removing the upper (A, **Figure 164**) and then the lower (B, **Figure 164**) spacer rings. Then remove the expander spacer (C, **Figure 164**).
4. Using a broken piston ring, remove carbon and oil residue from the piston ring grooves (**Figure 165**). Do not remove aluminum material from the ring grooves as this will increase ring side clearance.
5. Inspect the ring grooves for burrs, nicks or broken or cracked lands. Replace the piston if necessary.
6. Check the end gap of each compression ring and both oil ring spacer rings. To check, insert the ring into the bottom of the cylinder bore and square it in the cylinder wall by tapping it with the piston. Meas-

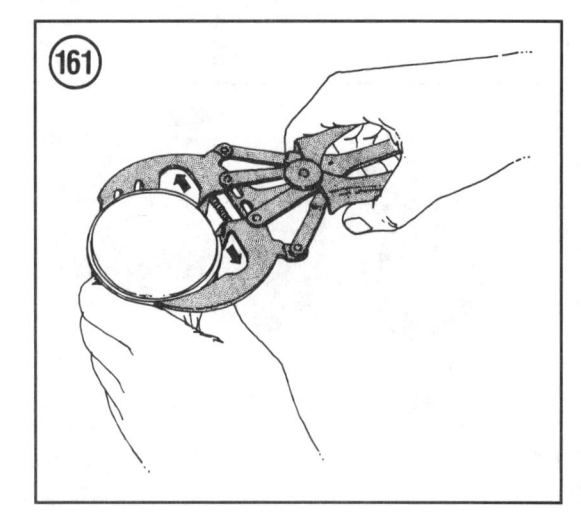

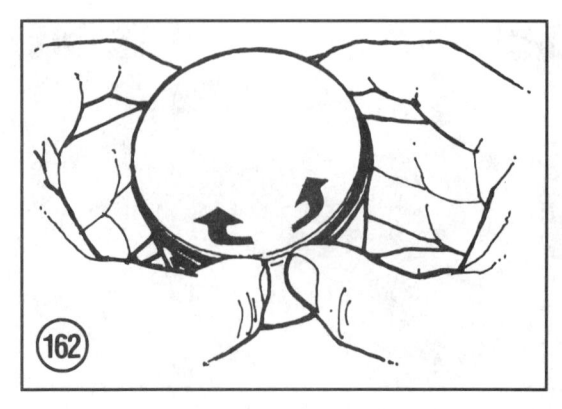

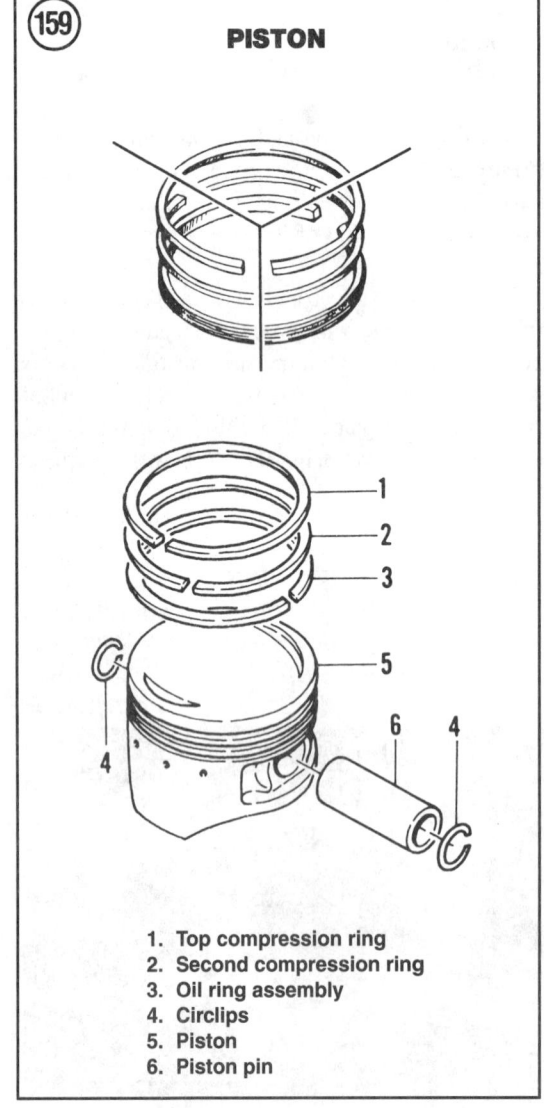

PISTON

1. Top compression ring
2. Second compression ring
3. Oil ring assembly
4. Circlips
5. Piston
6. Piston pin

ENGINE TOP END

ure the end gap with a feeler gauge (**Figure 166**) and compare with the specifications in **Table 4**. Replace the rings if the gap of any one ring is too large. If the gap on the new ring is smaller than specified, hold a small file in a vise, grip the ends of the ring with your fingers and enlarge the gap.

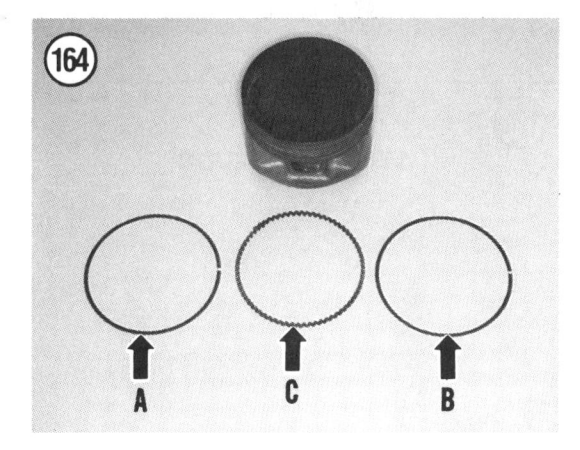

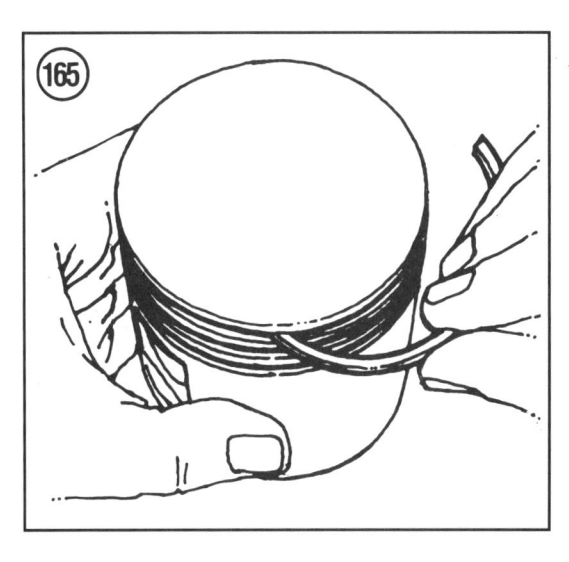

NOTE
*When measuring the oil control ring end gap, measure the upper and lower spacer ring end gaps only. Do not measure the expander spacer (C, **Figure 164**).*

7. Roll each compression ring around its piston groove as shown in **Figure 167** to check for binding.

Piston Ring Installation

1. When installing new rings, you must hone or deglaze the cylinder. This will help the new rings to seat in the cylinder. If necessary, refer honing service to a Honda dealership or motorcycle repair shop. After honing, measure the end gap of each ring (**Figure 166**) and compare to the specification in **Table 4**.

NOTE
*If you deglazed or honed the cylinder, clean the cylinder as described under **Cylinder Block Inspection** in this chapter.*

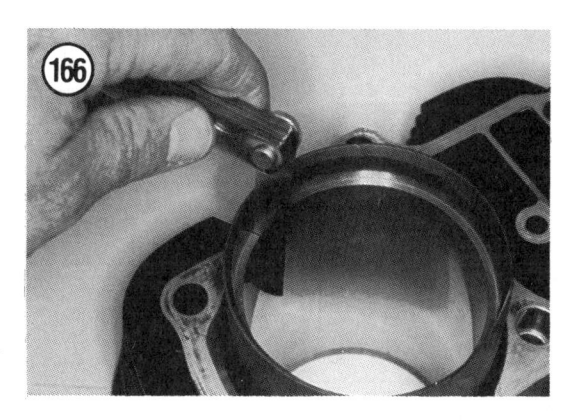

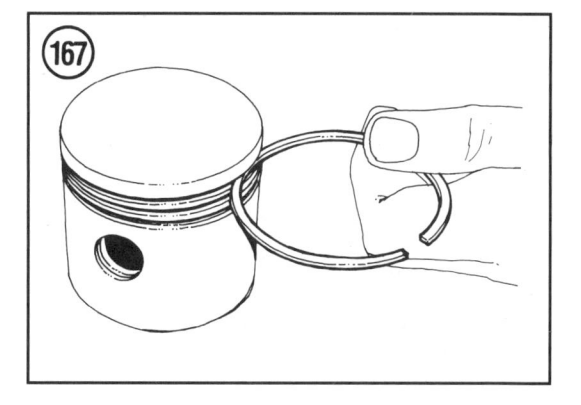

2. Clean the piston and rings in solvent. Dry with compressed air.

NOTE
*The top and second piston rings are different. The top ring is chrome-coated. The second ring is black (not coated). Refer to **Figure 168** to identify the shape of each ring.*

3. Install the piston rings as follows:

NOTE
Install the piston rings—first the bottom, then the middle, then the top ring—by spreading the ring ends with your thumbs or ring tool, and then slipping the rings over the top of the piston. Remember, you must install the piston rings with their marks facing toward the top of the piston or there is the possibility of oil pumping past the rings.

a. Install the oil ring assembly into the bottom ring groove. First install the expander spacer, then the bottom and top ring rails. See **Figure 163** and **Figure 164**.

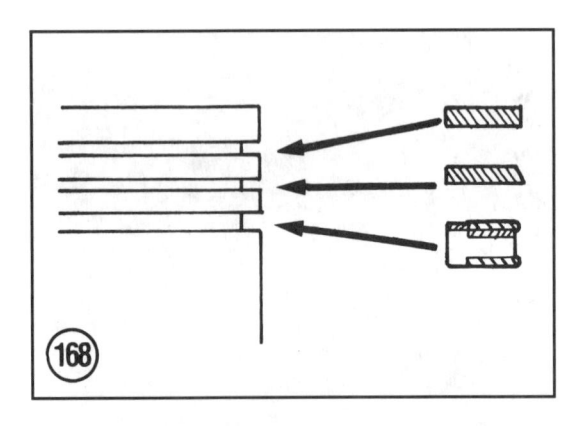

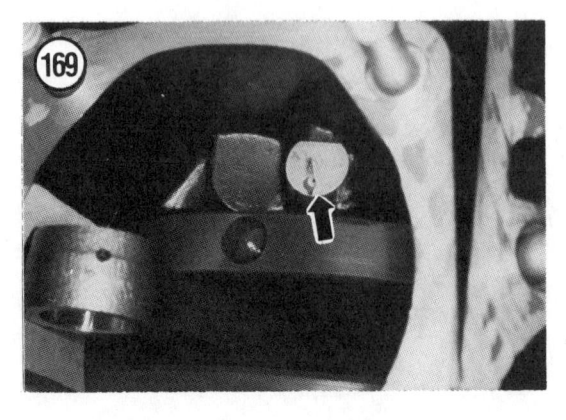

b. Install all rings with their manufacturer's markings facing up.

c. Install the second compression ring.

d. Install the top compression ring.

4. Make sure you seat the rings in their grooves and position the end gaps around the piston as shown in **Figure 159**.

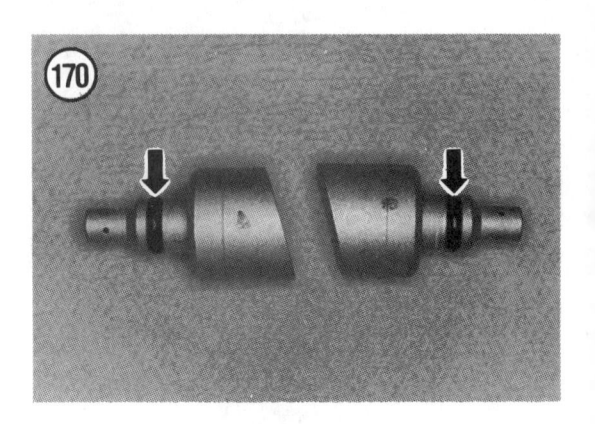

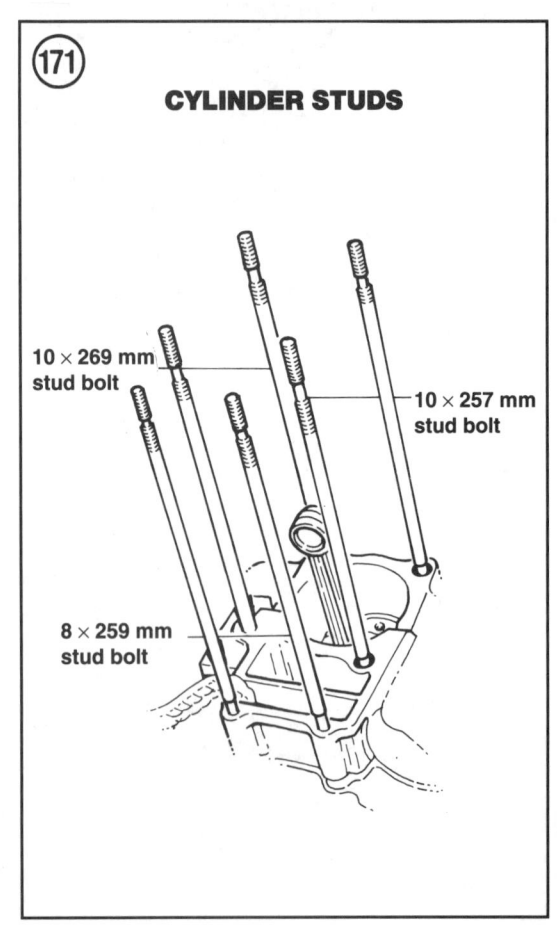

ENGINE TOP END

NOTE
The piston ring end gaps must not be aligned after installing the cylinder; otherwise, compression pressures can escape past them.

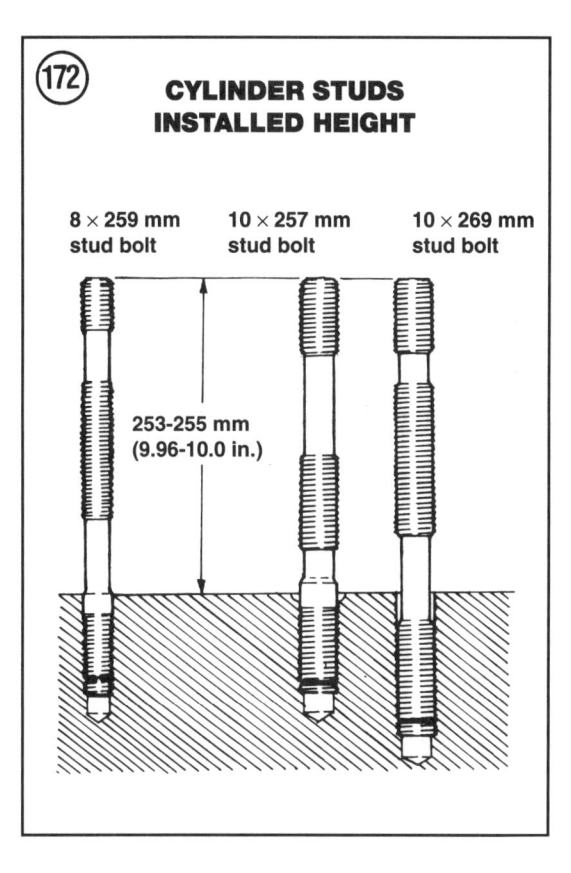

CYLINDER STUDS INSTALLED HEIGHT (Figure 172)

- 8 × 259 mm stud bolt
- 10 × 257 mm stud bolt
- 10 × 269 mm stud bolt

253-255 mm (9.96-10.0 in.)

OIL JET

An oil jet (**Figure 169**) is installed in the top of each crankcase bore and is accessible after removing the cylinder.

Removal/Installation

1. Remove the cylinder as described in this chapter.
2. Remove the oil jet (**Figure 169**) from the crankcase.
3. Remove and discard the O-rings (**Figure 170**).
4. Lubricate the new O-rings with engine oil and install them onto the oil jet.
5. Install the oil jet into the crankcase as shown in **Figure 169**.
6. Repeat for the other oil jet.

CYLINDER STUD REPLACEMENT

Three different length cylinder studs are used (**Figure 171**). The cylinder studs can be replaced without splitting the crankcase.

1. Remove the cylinder as described in this chapter.
2. Remove the damaged stud(s) with a stud remover.
3. Apply a thread sealer onto the threads of the new stud.
4. Install the new stud(s) to the dimensions shown in **Figure 172**. Refer to **Figure 171** to identify each stud.

Table 1 GENERAL ENGINE SPECIFICATIONS

Engine	
Type and number of cylinders	V-2 cylinder 45° V transverse, DOHC, liquid cooled
Bore × stroke	87.5 × 91.4 mm (3.44 × 3.60 in.)
Displacement	1099 cc (67.1 cu. in.)
Compression ratio	8.0:1
Valve timing	
Intake valve opens @ 1 mm lift	
Front	5° BTDC
Rear	2° BTDC
Intake valve closes @ 1 mm lift	
Front	30° ABDC
Rear	33° ABDC
Exhaust valve closes at 1 mm lift	
Front	30° BBDC
Rear	37° BBDC
(continued)	

Table 1 GENERAL ENGINE SPECIFICATIONS (continued)

Valve timing (continued)	
Exhaust valve opens at 1 mm lift	
Front	5° ATDC
Rear	–2° ATDC
Oil pump type	Trochoid
Cylinder number	
Front	No. 2
Rear	No. 1
Cylinder firing position	
Rear	405°
Front	315°
Engine weight	96.0 kg (212 lb.)

Table 2 CAMSHAFT AND ROCKER ARM SERVICE SPECIFICATIONS

	New mm (in.)	Service limit mm (in.)
Cylinder head warpage limit	–	0.05 (0.002)
Camshaft		
Runout limit	–	0.05 (0.002)
Lobe height		
Intake	38.021-38.181 (1.4969-1.5032)	37.99 (1.496)
Exhaust	38.027-38.187 (1.4971-1.5034)	38.00 (1.496)
Bearing oil clearance		
@ A and B measurement points*	0.050-0.111 (0.0020-0.0044)	0.130 (0.005)
@ C measurement point*	0.065-0.126 (0.0026-0.0050)	0.145 (0.006)
Camshaft journal diameter		
@ A and B measurement points*	23.949-23.970 (0.9429-0.9437)	23.92 (0.942)
@ C measurement point*	23.934-23.955 (0.9423-0.9431)	23.90 (0.941)
Rocker arms		
Inside diameter		
Intake and exhaust	13.750-13.768 (0.5413-0.5420)	13.778 (0.5424)
Rocker arm shaft diameter		
Intake and exhaust	13.716-13.734 (0.5400-0.5407)	13.706 (0.5396)
Rocker arm-to-rocker arm shaft clearance		
Intake and exhaust	0.016-0.052 (0.0006-0.0020)	0.072 (0.0028)
Tappets		
Assist spring free length	18.57 (0.731)	17.80 (0.701)
Tappet adjuster compression stroke with kerosene	–	0.2 (0.008)

* See text for measurement instructions.

ENGINE TOP END

Table 3 VALVE AND VALVE SPRING SERVICE SPECIFICATIONS

	New mm (in.)	Service limit mm (in.)
Valve stem diameter		
Intake	6.575-6.590 (0.2589-0.2594)	6.57 (0.259)
Exhaust	6.555-6.570 (0.2581-0.2587)	6.54 (0.257)
Valve guide inside diameter		
Intake	6.600-6.615 (0.2598-0.2604)	6.635 (0.2612)
Exhaust	6.600-6.615 (0.2598-0.2604)	6.655 (0.2620)
Valve stem-to-guide clearance		
Intake	0.010-0.040 (0.0004-0.0016)	0.08 (0.003)
Exhaust	0.030-0.060 (0.0012-0.0024)	0.12 (0.005)
Valve guide projection above cylinder head		
Intake	14.5 (0.57)	–
Exhaust	15.5 (0.61)	–
Valve seat width		
Intake and exhaust	0.09-1.10 (0.035-0.043)	1.50 (0.059)
Valve spring free length		
Inner spring		
Intake and exhaust	41.37 (1.629)	39.9 (1.57)
Outer spring		
Intake	45.70 (1.799)	43.90 (1.728)
Exhaust	43.50 (1.713)	41.80 (1.646)

Table 4 PISTON AND CYLINDER SERVICE SPECIFICATIONS

	New mm (in.)	Service limit mm (in.)
Cylinder		
Bore diameter (standard bore)	87.500-87.515 (3.4449-3.4455)	87.545 (3.4466)
Out of round limit	–	0.05 (0.002)
Taper limit	–	0.05 (0.002)
Warpage limit	–	0.05 (0.002)
Piston diameter (standard piston)*	87.470-87.490 (3.4437-3.4445)	87.41 (3.441)
Piston pin bore diameter	22.002-22.008 (0.8662-0.8665)	22.018 (0.8668)

Table 4 PISTON AND CYLINDER SERVICE SPECIFICATIONS (continued)

	New mm (in.)	Service limit mm (in.)
Piston pin outside diameter	21.994-22.000 (0.8695-0.8661)	21.984 (0.8655)
Piston-to-cylinder clearance	0.010-0.045 (0.0004-0.0018)	0.32 (0.013)
Connecting rod small end diameter	22.020-22.041 (0.8669-0.8678)	21.051 (0.8681)
Piston-to-piston pin clearance	0.002-0.014 (0.0001-0.0005)	0.034 (0.0013)
Connecting rod-to-piston pin clearance	0.020-0.047 (0.0008-0.0019)	0.07 (0.003)
Piston ring-to-groove clearance		
Top	0.020-0.050 (0.0008-0.0020)	0.25 (0.010)
Second	0.015-0.045 (0.0006-0.0018)	0.20 (0.008)
Piston ring end gap		
Top and second	0.20-0.35 (0.008-0.014)	0.50 (0.020)
Oil side rail	0.30-0.90 (0.012-0.035)	1.1 (0.04)

* Measured at 10 mm (0.4 in.) up from the bottom of the piston skirt. See text for information.

Table 5 HYDRAULIC TAPPET SHIM SELECTION

Assist shaft stroke	Number of shims required
0.00-1.20 mm (0-0.047 in.)	0
1.20-1.50 mm (0.047-0.059 in.)	1
1.50-1.80 mm (0.059-0.070 in.)	2
1.80-2.10 mm (0.070-0.083 in.)	3
2.10-2.40 mm (0.083-0.094 in.)	4
2.40-2.70 mm (0.094-01.069 in.)	5

Table 6 ENGINE TOP END TIGHTENING TORQUES

	N·m	in.-lb.	ft.-lb.
Assist shaft caps	22	—	16
Cam chain tensioner bolts	12	106	—
Cam sprocket bolts	18	—	13
Cylinder head cover			
Bolts	27	—	20
8 mm cap nuts	27	—	20
10 mm cap nuts	40	—	29
Rocker arm shaft hole plugs	40	—	29
Spark plugs	14	—	10
Spark plug sleeves	13	115	—

CHAPTER FIVE

ENGINE BOTTOM END

This chapter describes service procedures for the following lower end components:
 a. Left crankcase cover.
 b. Stator coil assembly.
 c. Flywheel.
 d. Starter clutch.
 e. Cam chain and tensioners.
 f. Flywheel.
 g. Crankcase.
 h. Crankshaft.
 i. Connecting rod.
 j. Transmission (removal and installation).
 k. Internal shift mechanism (removal and installation).

Before you begin work, read Chapter One again. You will do a better job with this information fresh in your mind.

Throughout the text there is frequent mention of the left and right side of the engine. This refers to the engine as it sits in the vehicle's frame, not as it sits on your workbench.

Tables 1-7 list engine service specifications. **Table 8** and **Table 9** list engine tightening torques. **Tables 1-9** are at the end of this chapter.

SERVICING ENGINE IN FRAME

You can service many engine components with the engine mounted in the frame (the frame is a great holding fixture—especially for breaking loose stubborn bolts and nuts):
 a. Oil pump.
 b. Clutch.
 c. Gearshift linkage.
 d. Alternator.
 e. Starter clutch and flywheel.
 f. Starter motor.
 g. Ignition pulse generator.

SUBFRAME

Refer to **Figure 1** when removing the subframe in this section.

Removal

1. Cover the front fender with a heavy blanket.
2. Remove the exhaust pipe assembly (Chapter Fourteen).
3. Remove the rear brake pedal (Chapter Thirteen).

CHAPTER FIVE

SUBFRAME

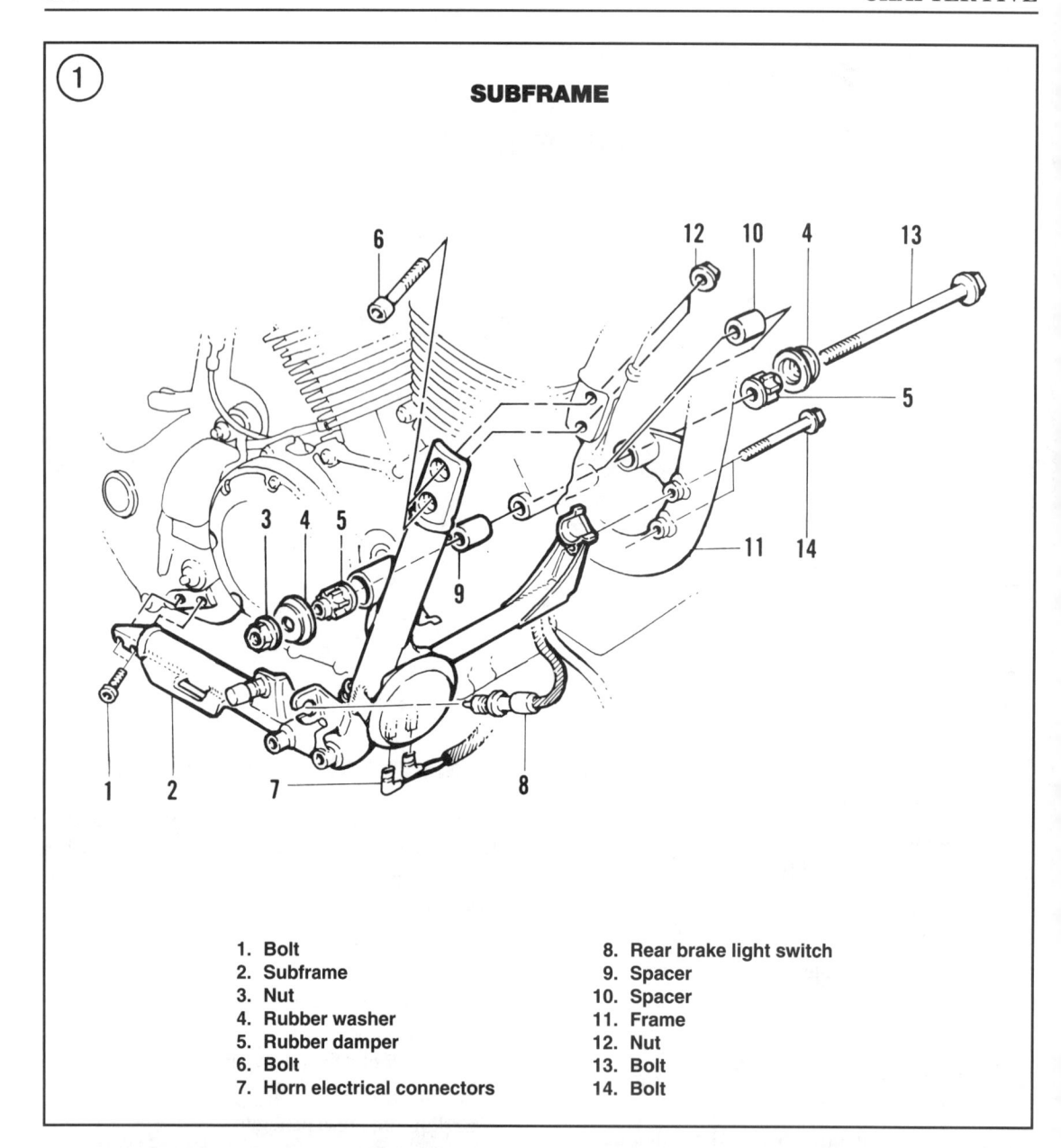

1. Bolt
2. Subframe
3. Nut
4. Rubber washer
5. Rubber damper
6. Bolt
7. Horn electrical connectors
8. Rear brake light switch
9. Spacer
10. Spacer
11. Frame
12. Nut
13. Bolt
14. Bolt

ENGINE BOTTOM END

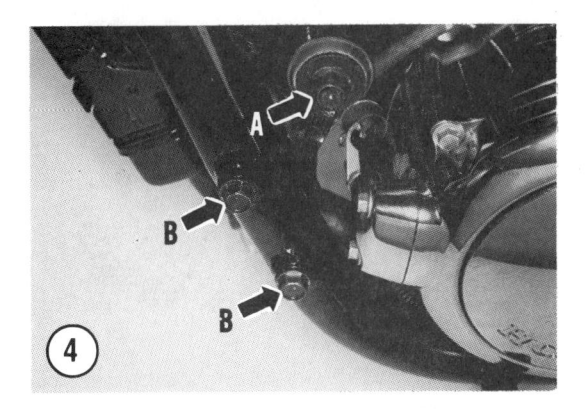

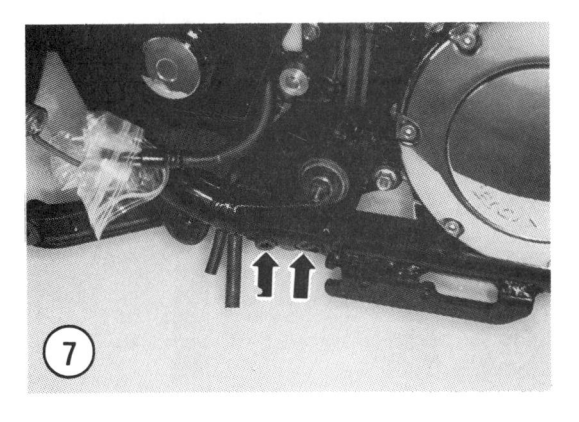

4. Remove the rear master cylinder (Chapter Thirteen).
5. On California models, remove the EVAP canister (Chapter Eight).
6. Disconnect the horn connectors from the horn (A, **Figure 2**).
7. Remove the rear brake light switch and its wiring harness from the subframe (B, **Figure 2**).
8. Remove the front lower engine mounting nut and rubber washer (**Figure 3**).
9. Pull the front lower engine mounting bolt (A, **Figure 4**) out and remove the right-side spacer (**Figure 5**).

NOTE
*If you remove the front lower engine mount bolt from the frame, also remove its left-side spacer and rubber washer (**Figure 1**).*

10. Remove the 2 left side subframe bolts (B, **Figure 4**).
11. Loosen the front subframe mounting bolts and nuts (**Figure 6**).
12. Loosen the rear subframe mounting bolts (**Figure 7**).
13. Hold the subframe in place and remove the nuts and bolts loosened in Steps 11 and 12. Then remove the subframe while releasing the radiator from the subframe. See **Figure 8**.

Inspection

1. Inspect all subframe nuts and bolts and replace if damaged.
2. Inspect the subframe (**Figure 9**) for cracks or other damage.

CHAPTER FIVE

3. Remove the rubber damper from the subframe mount (**Figure 10**).
4. Replace the rubber damper and the rubber washer (**Figure 11**) if worn or damaged.
5. Install the rubber damper (**Figure 10**)—shoulder side facing out—into the subframe.

Installation

CAUTION
To avoid cross-threading the subframe mounting bolts, install all of the bolts finger-tight. Then tighten all of the bolts as described in this procedure.

1. Install the subframe onto the frame while aligning the radiator mounting stays (on the subframe) with the radiator mounting dampers. Then hold the subframe in place against the frame.
2. Install the front subframe mounting bolts (**Figure 6**) as follows:
   a. Lubricate both bolts with engine oil.
   b. The upper bolt is longer than the lower bolt.
   c. Install both bolts. Do not install the nuts at this time.
3. Install the rear subframe mounting bolts (**Figure 7**).
4. Install the 2 left side subframe bolts (B, **Figure 4**).
5. Lubricate the front subframe mounting nuts with engine oil, then install them onto the 2 bolts (**Figure 6**).
6. If removed, install the front lower engine mount bolt (A, **Figure 4**) from the left side with its rubber washer and left side spacer (**Figure 5**).
7. Push the front lower engine mount bolt through and install its right-side spacer (B, **Figure 4**), then push the bolt through the subframe and install the rubber washer and nut (A, **Figure 4**).
8. Tighten all of the subframe mounting bolts and nuts in 2 or 3 stages to make sure the subframe seats squarely against the frame, then tighten the bolts in the following order to the torque specification listed in **Table 9**:
   a. Front lower engine mounting nut (**Figure 3**).
   b. Front subframe bolts and nuts (**Figure 6**).
   c. Rear subframe bolts (**Figure 7**).
   d. Left side subframe bolts (B, **Figure 4**).
9. Install the rear brake light switch and its wiring harness (B, **Figure 2**) onto the subframe.
10. Reconnect the horn connectors to the horn.

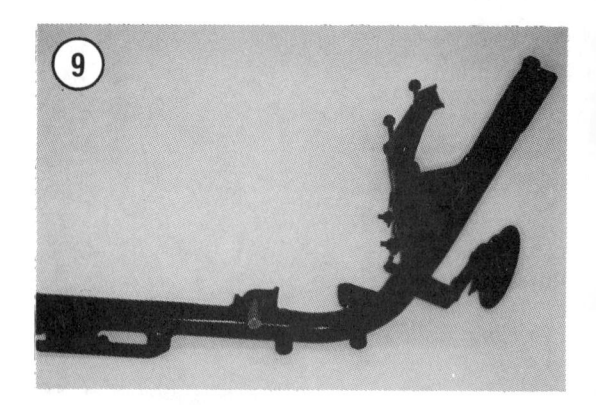

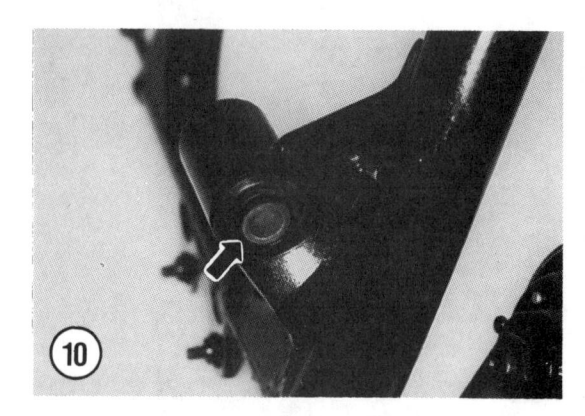

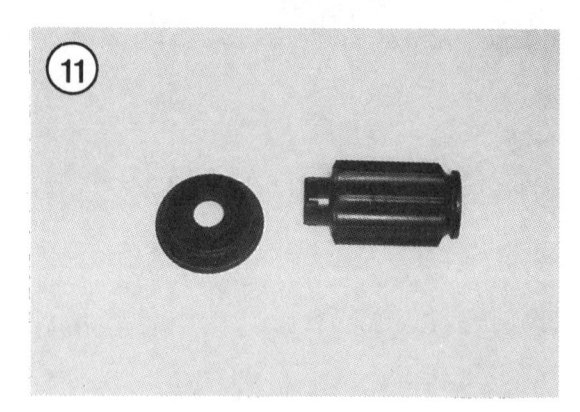

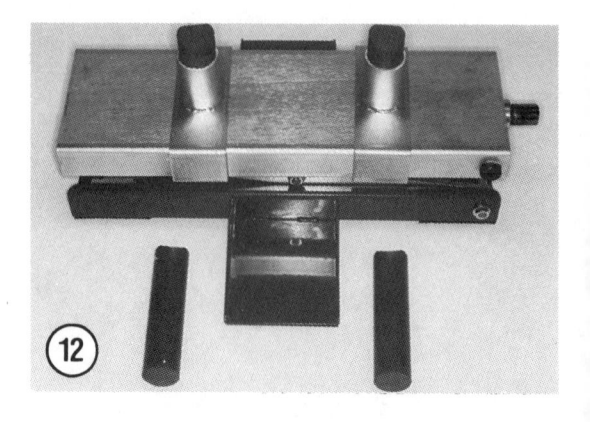

ENGINE BOTTOM END

11. On California models, install the EVAP canister (Chapter Eight).
12. Install the rear master cylinder (Chapter Thirteen).
13. Install the rear brake pedal (Chapter Thirteen).
14. Install the exhaust pipe assembly (Chapter Fourteen).
15. Adjust the rear brake light switch (Chapter Three).

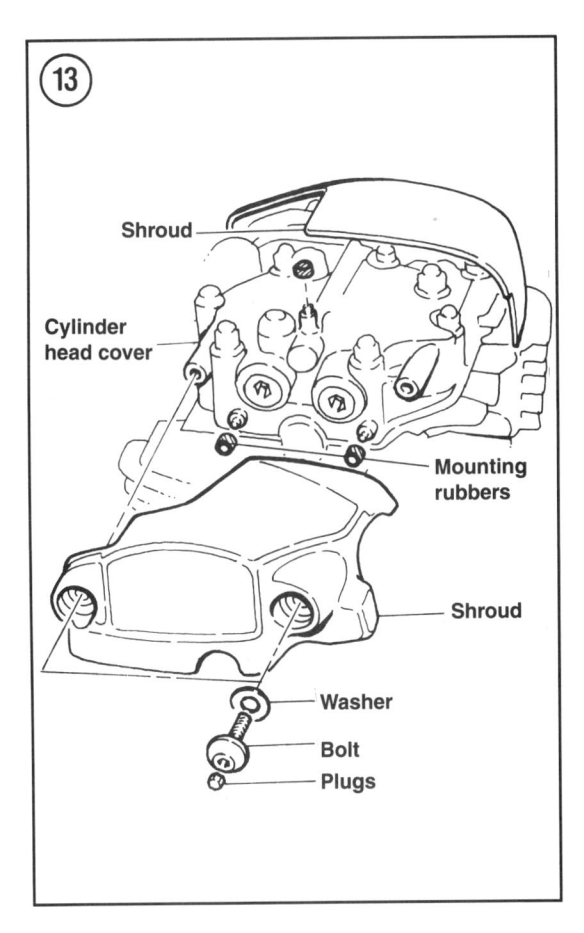

ENGINE REMOVAL

1. Park the bike on a level surface.
2. Before disassembling the engine, perform a leak down test (Chapter Two) and compression test (Chapter Three). Record the readings for future use.
3. Drain the engine oil (Chapter Three).
4. Drain the coolant (Chapter Three).
5. Drain the rear brake fluid (Chapter Thirteen).
6. Support the motorcycle behind the subframe with a jack or center stand that can contact the frame rails.

NOTE
A good jack for this purpose is the K&L MC450 Center Stand (Figure 12). This scissors-type jack is equipped with 2 movable slides and 2 different height rod sets for different frame width adjustments. This jack works well on motorcycles that must be supported by their lower frame rails. You can order this jack from K&L through your local motorcycle dealership.

7. Remove the right side cover (Chapter Fourteen).
8. Remove the battery holder as described under *Air Filter Housing Removal/Installation* in Chapter Eight.
9. Remove the carburetor (Chapter Eight).
10. Remove the radiator (Chapter Ten).
11. Remove the rear master cylinder reservoir (Chapter Thirteen).
12. Remove the left crankcase rear cover as described in this chapter.
13. Remove the spark plug caps and tie them out of the way.
14. Remove the subframe as described in this chapter.
15. Remove the head cover shrouds (**Figure 13**) as follows:
    a. Identify each head cover shroud for reassembly.
    b. Remove the rubber plug from each shroud bolt.
    c. Remove the shroud bolts, washer and shroud.
    d. Remove the mounting rubbers (**Figure 14**) that are installed behind each shroud.
16. Remove the water pump cover stud bolt (**Figure 15**) as follows:
    a. Screw 2 nuts onto the stud and lock them together.

b. Turn the inner nut to loosen and remove the stud (**Figure 16**).

17. Disconnect the starter motor cable (A, **Figure 17**) from the starter motor.

18. Disconnect the ground cable (B, **Figure 17**) from the engine.

19. Unhook and fold back the rubber cover protecting the electrical connector block mounted beside the air filter housing. Then disconnect the following electrical connectors:

  a. Ignition pulse generator 4-pin white connector (A, **Figure 18**).

  b. Alternator 3-pin white connector (B, **Figure 18**).

20A. When removing an assembled engine, disconnect the oil pressure and neutral switch electrical connectors from the group of connectors on the left side of the engine.

20B. If the left crankcase cover has been removed, perform the following:

  a. Disconnect the neutral switch electrical connector from the switch (**Figure 19**).

  b. Disconnect the oil pressure switch connector from the switch (**Figure 20**).

21. Disconnect the clutch cable (A, **Figure 21**) from the engine. Then disconnect the cable from its holder on the rear cylinder head.

22. Remove the clutch cable holder mounting bolts and remove the holder (B, **Figure 21**).

23. Remove the crankcase breather tube from the clamp at the front of the engine.

24. Install a rubber hose over each cylinder head exhaust pipe stud (**Figure 22**) to protect them from thread damage during engine removal.

25. Wrap the front exposed frame tubes with pieces of thin plastic or rubber (**Figure 22**) to protect them

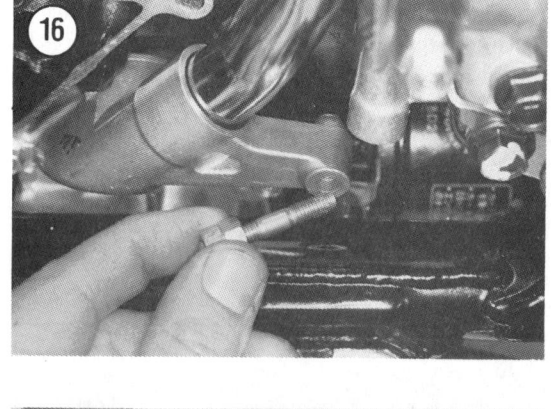

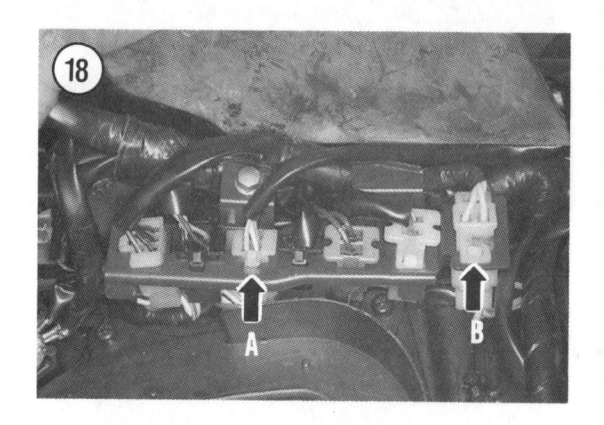

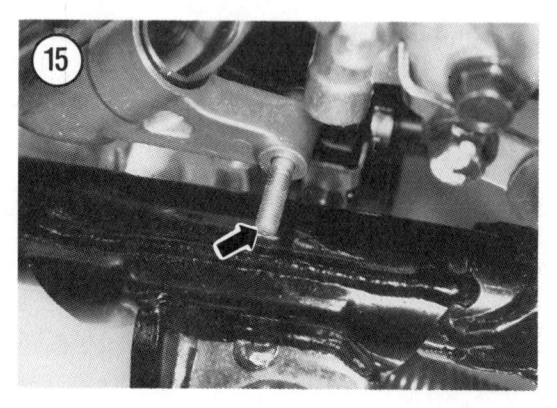

ENGINE BOTTOM END

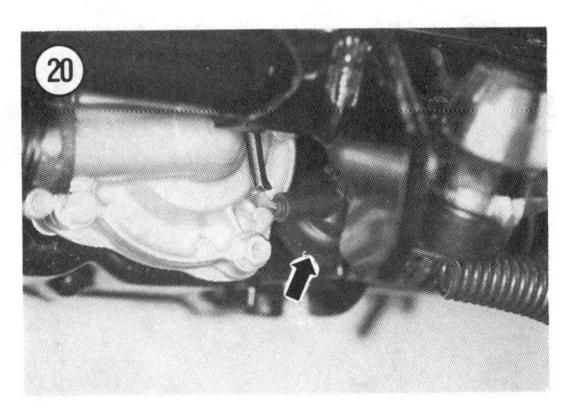

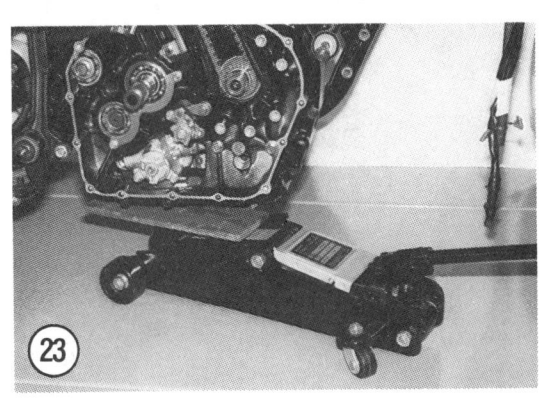

from scratches and other damage during engine removal.

26. Place a jack under the crankcase. Place a piece of wood between the jack pad and the engine to protect the crankcase. See **Figure 23**.

NOTE
Apply a slight amount of jack pressure against the engine as the engine mounting bolts are loosened and removed in the following steps.

27. Check the engine to make sure all hoses, cables and wires are either disconnected or removed (**Figure 24**).
28. Remove the front upper engine mounting bolts, brackets and rubber washers (**Figure 25**).
29. Remove the muffler bracket bolt (A, **Figure 26**).
30. Remove the rear lower engine mounting nut and rubber washer (B, **Figure 26**), then remove the mounting bolt and the other rubber washer (**Figure 27**).

CAUTION
The rear upper mounting bolt (removed in the next step) is the last bolt holding

*the engine in the frame. Steps 31-35 requires a minimum of 2, preferably 3 people to safely remove the engine from the frame and carry to a workbench. See **Table 1** for the weight of an assembled engine.*

31. With the engine supported on the jack and an assistant steadying the engine, remove the tube, nut and washer from the rear upper mounting bolt (**Figure 28**), then remove the bolt (**Figure 29**). The engine is now resting on the jack.

NOTE
There is very little clearance between the engine and the frame. Take your time and be careful not to drop the engine out of the frame.

32. Slowly pull the jack and engine forward to disconnect the engine's output driven gear shaft from the universal joint in the swing arm.
33. Carefully and slowly pivot the engine (on the jack) out of the right side of the frame. Move it far enough so everyone can get a good hand-hold on the engine.
34. Slide the engine out of the open frame area on the right side.
35. Take the engine to a workbench for further service (**Figure 30**).

ENGINE INSTALLATION

Refer to **Figure 31** when installing the engine in the frame.
1. Inspect the engine for cracks or damage.
2. Repair or replace any damaged wires or hoses.
3. Clean and inspect all engine mounting fasteners.

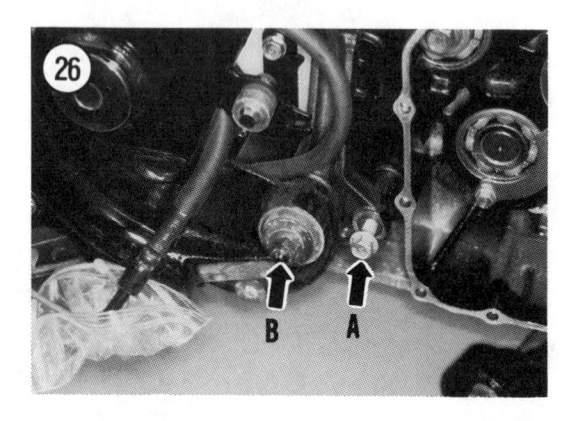

ENGINE BOTTOM END 165

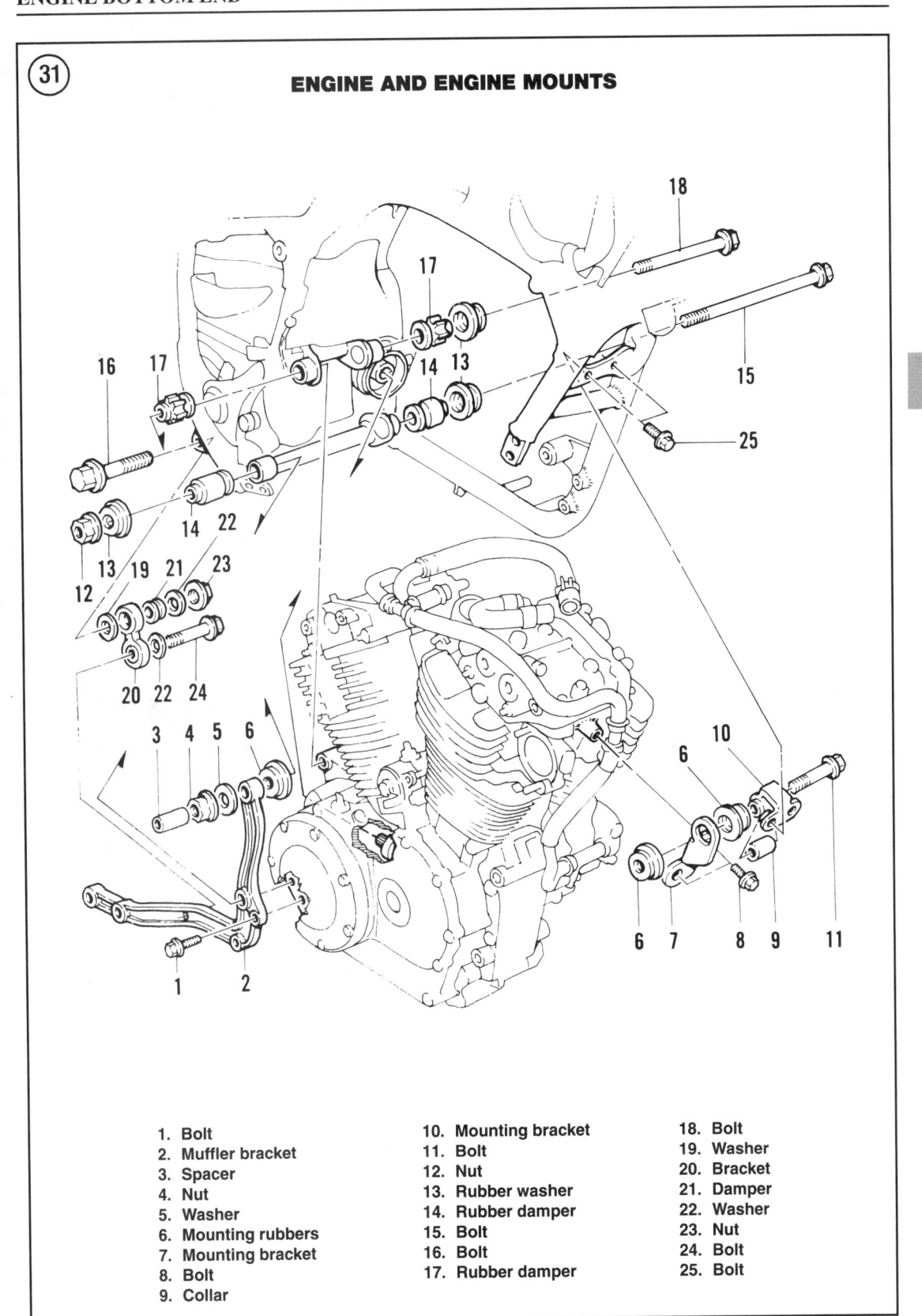

ENGINE AND ENGINE MOUNTS (31)

1. Bolt
2. Muffler bracket
3. Spacer
4. Nut
5. Washer
6. Mounting rubbers
7. Mounting bracket
8. Bolt
9. Collar
10. Mounting bracket
11. Bolt
12. Nut
13. Rubber washer
14. Rubber damper
15. Bolt
16. Bolt
17. Rubber damper
18. Bolt
19. Washer
20. Bracket
21. Damper
22. Washer
23. Nut
24. Bolt
25. Bolt

4. Inspect all of the engine mount rubber dampers and washers (**Figure 11**) and replace if severely worn or damaged.

5. Apply 1 gram (0.04 oz.) of molybdenum disulfide grease to the engine's output driven gear shaft splines.

CAUTION
*Step 6 requires a minimum of 2, preferably 3 people to safely remove the engine from the workbench and carry to the frame. See **Table 1** for the approximate weight of an assembled engine.*

6. Place the engine on a jack, then position the engine in the frame. Insert the output driven gear shaft into the universal joint in the swing arm.

NOTE
Tighten the engine mount fasteners finger-tight when installing them in the following steps.

7. Align the engine and frame mounting bolt holes, then install the rear upper mounting bolt assembly (**Figure 31**) from the left side. See **Figure 27**.
8. Install the rear lower mounting bolt assembly (**Figure 31**) from the left side. See **Figure 29**.
9. Install the muffler bracket bolt (A, **Figure 26**).
10. Assemble the front upper engine mounting brackets, rubber washers and center bolt as shown in **Figure 32**. Then install the mounting bracket in place and secure with its mounting bolts (**Figure 25**).
11. Pull the rubber boot over the output gear case shoulder (**Figure 33**).
12. Install the subframe (A, **Figure 34**) and tighten all of its mounting bolts and nuts, except the front lower engine mounting bolt (B, **Figure 34**), as described in this chapter.
13. Tighten all of the engine mounting bolts and nuts to the torque specification in **Table 9**. Tighten the bolts in the following order:

   a. Front upper engine mounting bolts (**Figure 25**).
   b. Front lower engine mounting nut (B, **Figure 34**).
   c. Rear upper engine mounting nut (**Figure 28**).
   d. Rear lower engine mounting nut (B, **Figure 26**).
   e. Muffler bracket engine attaching bolt (A, **Figure 26**).

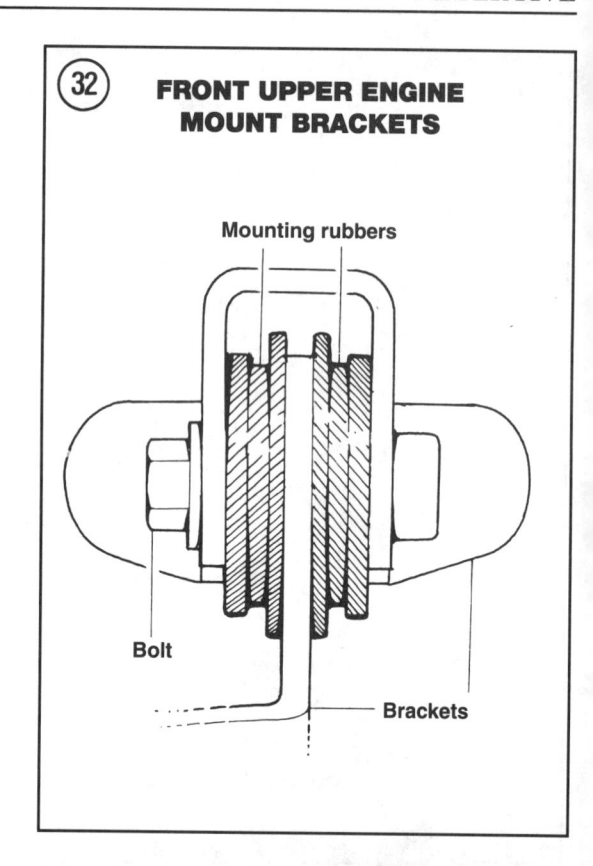

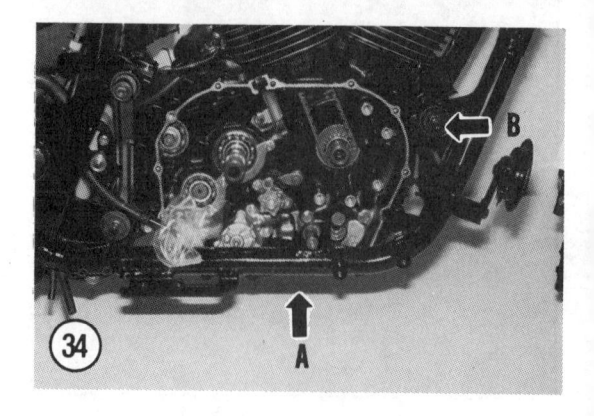

ENGINE BOTTOM END

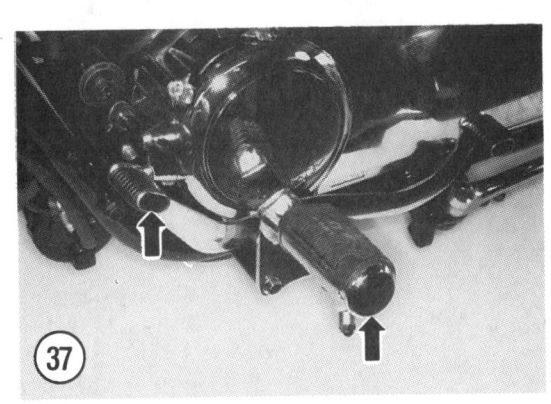

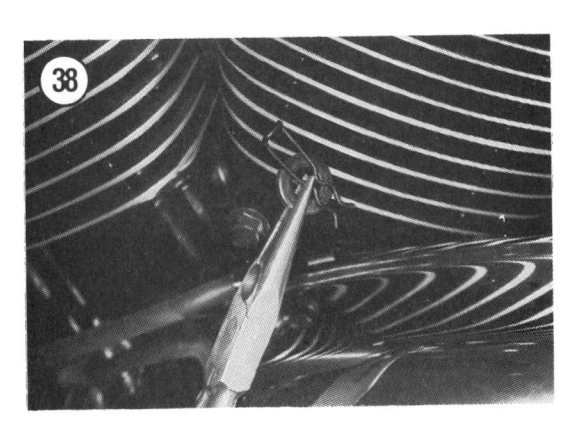

14. Install the water pump cover stud bolt (**Figure 16**) as follows:
    a. Clean the stud bolt and water pump cover threads with contact cleaner.
    b. Install the bolt until the distance from the bolt head to the water pump cover is 20 ±1 mm (0.8 ±0.004 in.). See **Figure 35**.
    c. Remove the 2 locknuts from the bolt stud threads. See **Figure 15**.
15. Remove the rubber hose installed over each cylinder head exhaust pipe stud (**Figure 22**).
16. Remove the plastic or rubber covers installed around the frame tubes.
17. Reverse Steps 1-23 under *Engine Removal* to complete engine installation. Tighten the cylinder head cover shroud bolts (**Figure 36**) to the torque specification in **Table 9**.
18. Bleed the rear brake (Chapter Thirteen).
19. Perform the following as described in Chapter Three:
    a. Refill the engine with oil.
    b. Adjust the rear brake light switch.
    c. Check and adjust the clutch.
    d. Adjust the throttle cables.
    e. Adjust the choke cable.
    f. Refill the engine with coolant.
20. Start the engine and check for leaks.
21. If you rebuilt the engine top end, perform a compression test (Chapter Three) and leak down test (Chapter Two). Record the test results to help monitor engine condition.

LEFT CRANKCASE REAR COVER

Removal/Installation

1. Support the bike securely on a stand.
2. Remove the left side footpeg (**Figure 37**) and the gearshift lever assembly.
3. Remove the clips and washers (**Figure 38**) securing the cover's upper bosses.
4. Remove the lower cover mounting nut, then pull the lower part of the cover out to release it from the 2 lower rubber dampers. Remove the left crankcase rear cover (**Figure 39**).
5. Inspect the cover and its mounting fasteners (**Figure 40**) for damage.
6. Inspect the cover mounting grommets (mounted on engine) and replace if worn or damaged.

7. Reverse these steps to install the left crankcase rear cover.
8. Install the clutch cable grommet into the notch in the top of the left crankcase rear cover.
9. Tighten the left crankcase rear cover mounting nut to the torque specification in **Table 8**.
10. Tighten the front footpeg bracket bolts to the torque specification in **Table 8**.

CLUTCH LIFTER ARM

The clutch lifter arm assembly (A, **Figure 41**) is mounted on the left side of the engine.

Removal

1. Remove the left crankcase rear cover as described in this chapter.
2. Loosen the clutch cable adjuster locknuts (B, **Figure 41**) and disconnect the clutch cable from the lifter arm.
3. Remove the bolts that holder the clutch lifter arm (A, **Figure 41**) to the engine. Then remove the clutch lifter arm, O-ring and lifter piece (**Figure 42**) and dowel pin.

Disassembly/Inspection/Assembly

1. Turn the lifter arm clockwise and remove the lifter piece (**Figure 43**).
2. Remove the lifter arm, spring and washer (**Figure 44**).
3. Clean and dry the clutch lifter arm assembly.
4. Replace the O-ring (A, **Figure 45**) and seal (B, **Figure 45**) if leaking or damaged.
5. Inspect the clutch lifter arm assembly and replace any worn or damaged parts.
6. Two needle bearings are installed in the lifter arm holder. Inspect the bearings as follows:
    a. Install the lifter arm into the holder and turn it back and forth. If the lifter arm turns roughly or if there is any noticeable binding, one or both bearings are damaged.
    b. The lifter arm holder bearings cannot be replaced. If damaged, replace the lifter arm holder assembly.
7. Lubricate both lifter arm holder bearings with engine oil.
8. Install a new seal (B, **Figure 45**) so its closed side faces out.

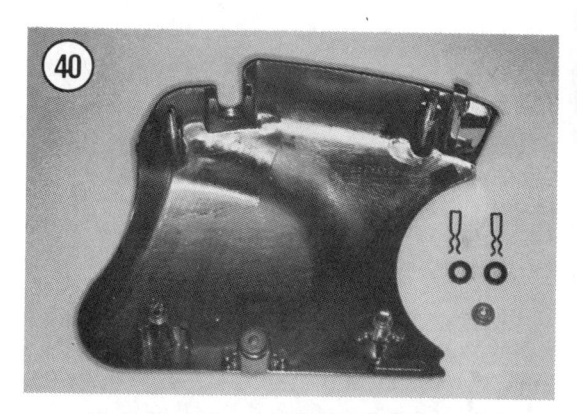

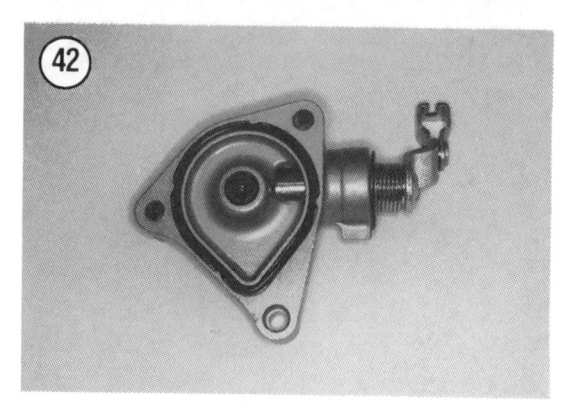

ENGINE BOTTOM END

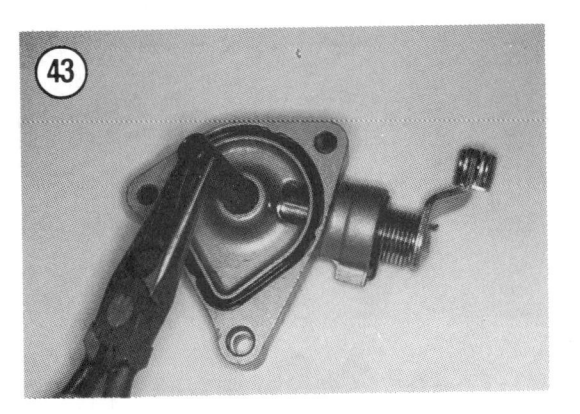

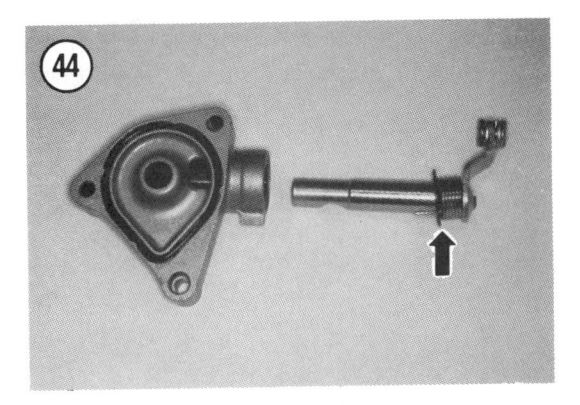

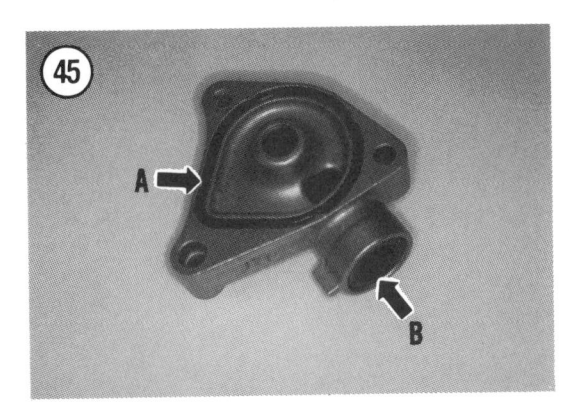

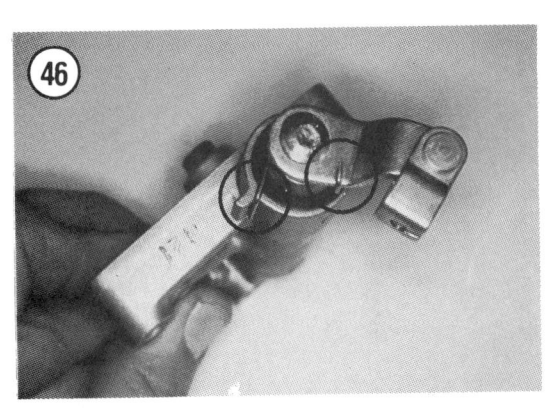

9. Lubricate the lifter arm holder seal lips with grease.
10. Install the spring and washer onto the lifter arm (**Figure 44**).
11. Install the lifter arm assembly into the lifter arm holder. Hook the spring arms against the lifter arm and holder as shown in **Figure 46**.
12. Turn the lifter arm clockwise to expose the notch in the lifter arm. Then install the lifter piece—open side facing out (**Figure 43**)—through the lifter arm holder into the lifter arm notch.

Installation

1. Lubricate the lifter arm holder O-ring with engine oil.
2. Install the dowel pin and lifter arm holder onto the crankcase.
3. Install and tighten the lifter arm holder mounting bolts as follows:
   a. Install the upper mounting bolt and clamp (A, **Figure 47**).
   b. Apply a medium strength threadlocking compound onto the lower mounting bolt threads, then install the bolt and its clamp (B, **Figure 47**).
   c. Install the middle mounting bolt (C, **Figure 47**), then tighten all bolts securely.
4. Route the No. 7 hose through the upper mounting bolt clamp (A, **Figure 47**).
5. Route the neutral and oil pressure switch wiring harness through the lower mounting bolt clamp (B, **Figure 47**).
6. Reconnect the clutch cable (B, **Figure 41**) to the lifter arm.
7. Adjust the clutch (Chapter Three).

8. Install the left crankcase rear cover as described in this chapter.

STARTER DRIVE GEAR AND TORQUE LIMITER

The starter drive gear and torque limiter assembly are mounted on the left side of the engine.

Removal/Installation

1. Remove the left crankcase rear cover as described in this chapter.
2. Remove the starter gear cover mounting bolts and remove the cover (A, **Figure 48**) and 2 dowel pins.
3. Remove the starter drive gear (A, **Figure 49**) and the starter torque limiter (B, **Figure 49**).
4. Refer to the *Inspection* procedure to clean and inspect all parts.
5. Reverse these steps to install the starter drive gear and starter torque limiter.
6. Install a new gasket during installation.
7. The 4 starter gear cover mounting bolts are different lengths. Note the the length of each bolt:
   a. B, **Figure 48** (6 × 75 mm).
   b. C, **Figure 48** (6 × 40 mm).
   c. D, **Figure 48** (6 × 45 mm).
   d. E, **Figure 48** (6 × 32 mm).
8. Tighten each bolt securely.

Inspection

1. Remove all gasket residue from the starter gear cover and crankcase mating surfaces.
2. Clean and dry all starter drive gear and torque limiter parts.
3. Check the starter gear cover bearings (A, **Figure 50**) for excessive wear or damage. Replace the bearings as follows:
   a. Remove the bearings with a blind bearing remover tool.
   b. Clean and inspect the cover bearing bores. Check for cracks and other damage.
   c. Press in the new bearings until they bottom. Install both bearings so that their manufacturer's marks face out (away from cover).
4. Inspect the starter gear cover rubber cap (B, **Figure 50**) and replace it if damaged.

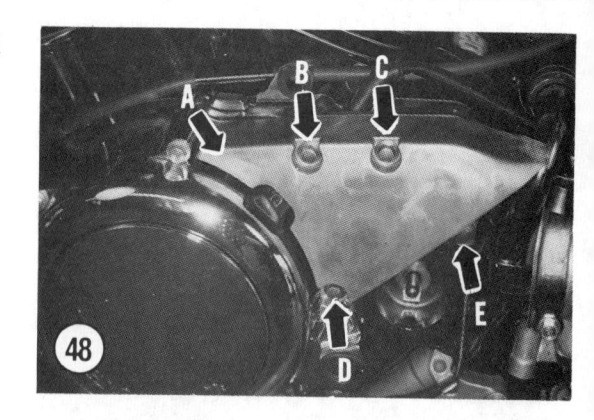

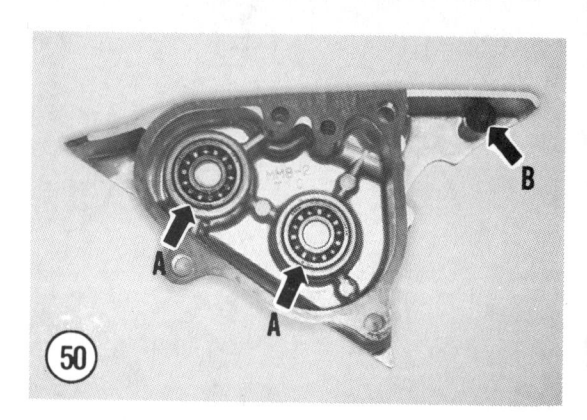

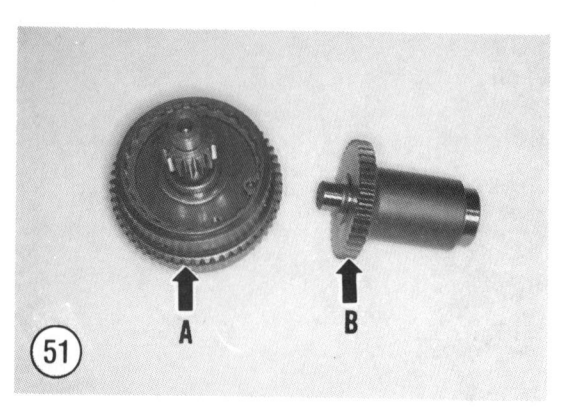

ENGINE BOTTOM END

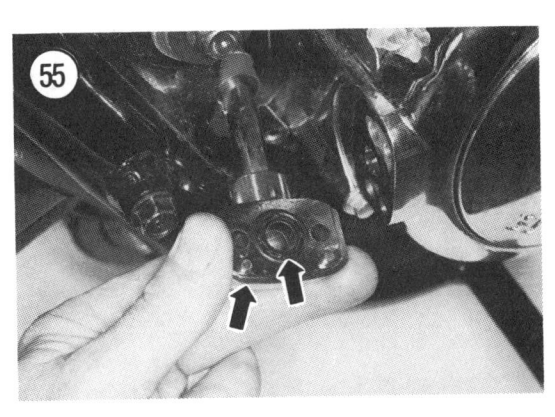

5. Inspect the torque limiter (A, **Figure 51**) and starter drive gear (B, **Figure 51**) for cracks, excessive gear wear or damage. Replace if necessary.

LEFT CRANKCASE COVER AND STATOR COIL

Left Crankcase Cover Removal/Installation

1. Remove the seat and the left side cover (Chapter Fourteen).
2. Disconnect the negative battery cable as described in Chapter Three.
3. Drain the engine oil (Chapter Three).
4. Remove the clutch lifter arm holder as described in this chapter.
5. Remove the starter drive gear and torque limiter as described in this chapter.
6. Remove the left side footpeg (**Figure 37**) and the gearshift lever assembly.
7. Unhook and fold back the rubber cover protecting the electrical connector block mounted beside the air filter housing. Then disconnect the alternator 3-pin white connector (**Figure 52**). Remove the connector and its wiring harness from its routing path through the frame. If you cannot remove the connector past the battery and battery box, perform Step 8. If you can remove the connector and wiring harness, go to Step 9.
8. If you cannot remove the alternator wiring harness and connector (A, **Figure 53**) because of its routing path behind the battery box, perform the following step:

   a. Remove the battery (Chapter Three).

   b. Remove the battery box bolts (B, **Figure 53**) so it can be moved in the frame, then remove the alternator wiring harness and connector.

9. Remove the bolts that hold the breather joint (**Figure 54**) to the crankcase. Then remove the breather joint and its O-ring (**Figure 55**).
10. Before removing the left crankcase cover mounting bolts, draw an outline of the cover on a piece of cardboard (**Figure 56**). Then punch holes along the outline for the placement of each mounting bolt.
11. Remove the left crankcase cover mounting bolts and cover stay and place them in the corresponding holes in the cardboard (**Figure 56**).

12. Remove the left crankcase cover (**Figure 57**) and gasket.
13. Remove the 2 dowel pins (**Figure 58**).
14. Perform the *Inspection* procedure in this section to clean the cover gasket surface and to replace its oil seal, if necessary.
15. Install the left crankcase cover by reversing these removal steps, while noting the following.
16. Install the 2 dowel pins (**Figure 58**) and a new gasket.
17. Install the left crankcase cover (**Figure 57**) and secure it with its mounting bolts. Install the cover stay at the lower mounting position shown in **Figure 56**. Tighten all of the mounting bolts.
18. Replace the breather O-ring (**Figure 55**) if worn or damaged. Lubricate the O-ring with engine oil, then install the breather cover (**Figure 54**) and secure it with its mounting bolts.
19. Route the alternator connector and its wiring harness through the frame by following its original path. Reconnect the alternator 3-pin-white connector (**Figure 52**).
20. Align the slit in the gearshift lever with the punch mark on the shift shaft spindle, then install the shift lever. Install and tighten the gearshift lever pinch bolt to the torque specification in **Table 8**.
21. Install the left side footpeg assembly and mounting bolts. Tighten the footpeg mounting bolts to the torque specification in **Table 8**.
22. Refill the engine with the correct type and quantity of oil (Chapter Three).
23. Start the engine and check for leaks.

Inspection

1. Remove all gasket residue from the left crankcase cover and crankcase gasket surfaces.
2. Check the shift shaft seal (**Figure 59**) for leaks or damage. Replace the seal as follows:
    a. Pry the seal out of the cover with a wide-blade screwdriver.
    b. Clean the seal bore.
    c. Pack the new seal lips with grease.
    d. Press the new seal into the crankcase cover.
3. If necessary, service the stator coils as described in this section.

Stator Coil Testing

Refer to Chapter Nine.

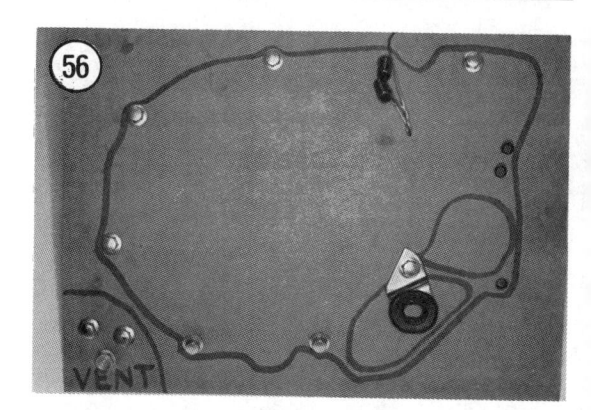

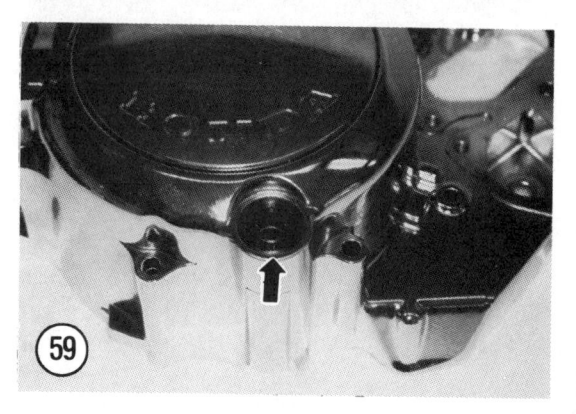

ENGINE BOTTOM END

Stator Coil
Removal/Installation

1. Remove the left crankcase cover as described in this section.
2. Remove the clamp bolt and clamp (A, **Figure 60**).
3. Pull the rubber plug (B, **Figure 60**) out of the cover. 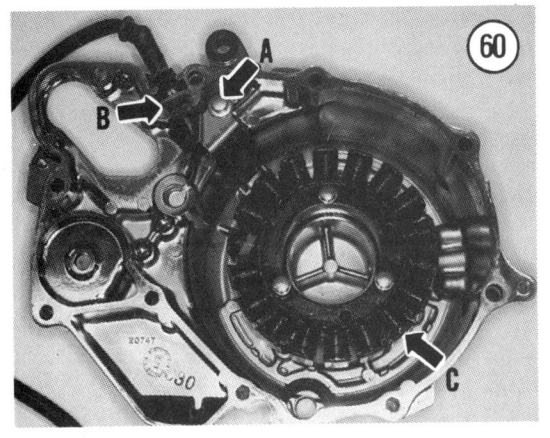
4. Remove the stator coil mounting bolts and remove the stator coil (C, **Figure 60**).
5. Install the stator coil by reversing these steps, while noting the following.
6. Remove all threadlocking compound from the mounting bolts and housing threads.
7. Apply a medium strength threadlocking compound to the stator coil mounting bolts, then install and tighten the bolts.
8. Apply Gasgacinch or RTV sealer to the wiring harness rubber plug, then insert the plug into the cover notch (B, **Figure 60**).
9. Install the clamp and its mounting bolt (A, **Figure 60**). Tighten the bolt securely.

FLYWHEEL (ROTOR)

Refer to **Figure 61** when servicing the flywheel rotor in this section.

ALTERNATOR

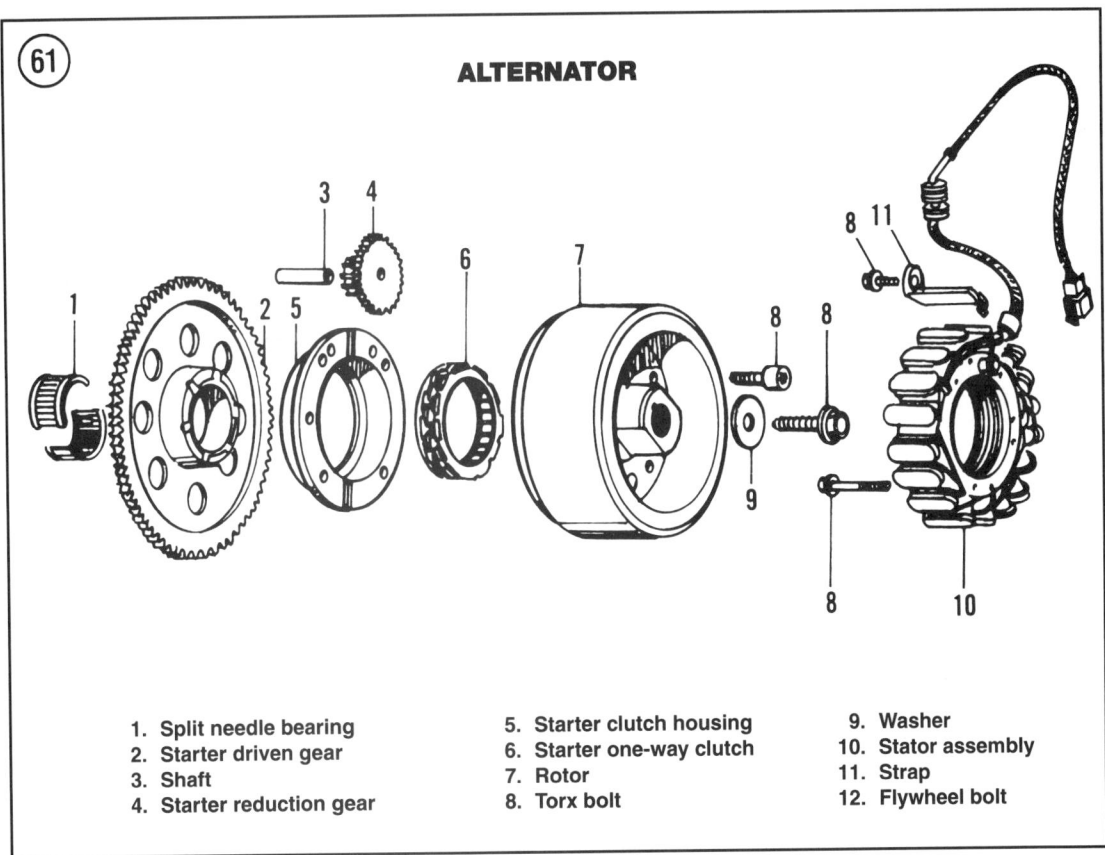

1. Split needle bearing
2. Starter driven gear
3. Shaft
4. Starter reduction gear
5. Starter clutch housing
6. Starter one-way clutch
7. Rotor
8. Torx bolt
9. Washer
10. Stator assembly
11. Strap
12. Flywheel bolt

CHAPTER FIVE

Special Tools

You need a flywheel puller (**Figure 62**) to remove the flywheel from the crankshaft. Use one of the following pullers to remove the flywheel:

a. Honda flywheel puller (part No. 07933-3290001).
b. Motion Pro flywheel puller (part No. 08-074).
c. K&N flywheel puller (part No. 82-0170).

You also need some type of holder to hold the flywheel when loosening and tightening the flywheel bolt and when using the flywheel puller. **Figure 63** and **Figure 64** show 2 holders that can be used to hold the flywheel.

Removal

1. Remove the left crankcase cover as described in this chapter.

CAUTION
*The flywheel mounting bolt has **left-hand** threads. Turn the bolt **clockwise** to loosening it.*

2. Hold the flywheel with a holding tool (**Figure 64**) and turn the flywheel bolt *clockwise* to loosen it. Then remove the flywheel bolt and washer (**Figure 65**).
3. Screw the flywheel puller (**Figure 66**) to the flywheel.

CAUTION
Do not try to remove the flywheel without a puller. Any attempt to do so may damage the flywheel and crankshaft.

CAUTION
If normal flywheel removal attempts fail, do not force the puller. Excessive force will strip the flywheel threads, causing expensive damage. Take the engine to a dealership for removal.

4. Hold the flywheel with the flywheel holder (**Figure 64**) and gradually tighten the flywheel puller until the flywheel pops off the crankshaft taper. See A, **Figure 67**.
5. Remove the puller from the flywheel.
6. If necessary, remove the Woodruff key (**Figure 68**) from the crankshaft.
7. If necessary, service the starter clutch (**Figure 69**) as described in this chapter.

Inspection

1. Clean the flywheel (A, **Figure 67**) in solvent and dry with compressed air.

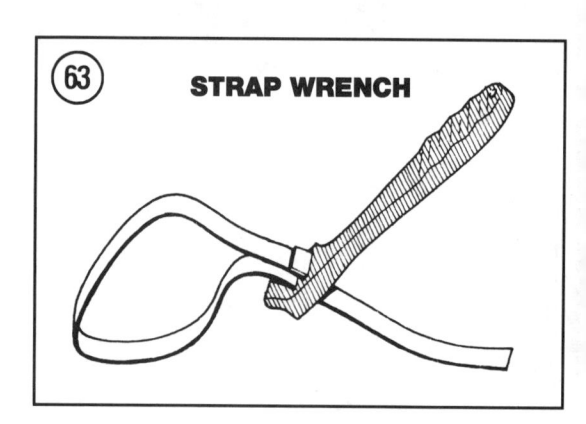

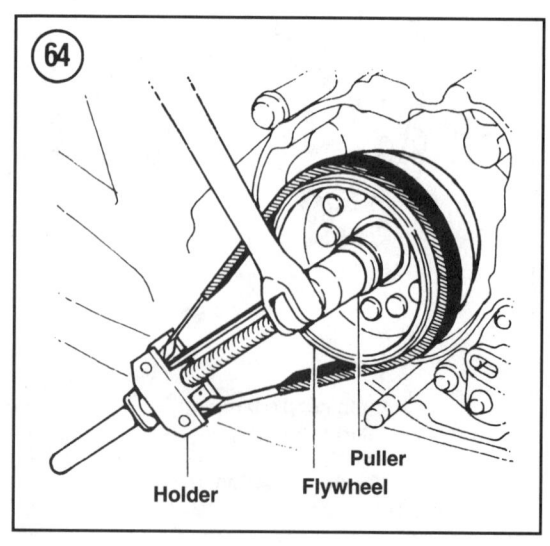

ENGINE BOTTOM END

2. Check the flywheel for cracks or breaks.

> **WARNING**
> *Replace a cracked or chipped flywheel. A damaged flywheel can fly apart at high speed, throwing metal fragments into the engine. Do not attempt to repair a damaged flywheel.*

3. Check the flywheel tapered bore and the crankshaft taper for damage.

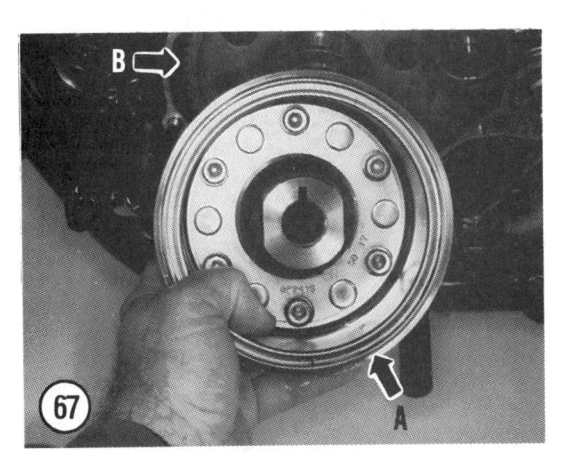

4. Replace damaged parts as required.

Installation

1. Apply engine oil to the one-way clutch rollers (**Figure 69**) and the starter drive gear shoulder.
2. Install the Woodruff key (**Figure 68**) into the crankshaft.
3. Align the keyway in the flywheel with the Woodruff key in the crankshaft and install the flywheel while turning the starter driven gear (B, **Figure 67**) clockwise.

> **CAUTION**
> *The flywheel mounting bolt has **left-hand** threads. Turn the bolt **counterclockwise** to tighten it.*

4. Lubricate the flywheel bolt threads and washer (**Figure 65**) with engine oil.
5. Use the same tool set used for removal and tighten the flywheel bolt *counterclockwise* to the torque specification listed in **Table 8**.
6. Install the left crankcase cover as described in this chapter.

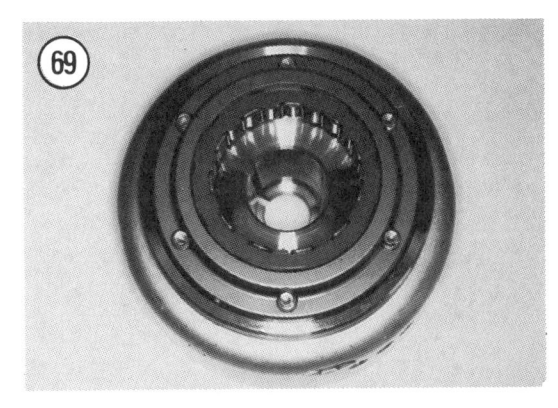

STARTER DRIVEN GEAR AND STARTER CLUTCH

Refer to **Figure 61**.

Starter Driven Gear and Starter Clutch Removal

1. Remove the flywheel as described in this chapter.
2. Remove the reduction gear and shaft (**Figure 70**).
3. Remove the neutral switch rubber plug (**Figure 71**) from the crankcase.
4. Using a screwdriver, pry the gearshift spindle guide plug (A, **Figure 72**) out of the crankcase.
5. Pull the gearshift spindle A (B, **Figure 72**) out to release it from the gearshift spindle B.

NOTE
Figure 73 shows how gearshift spindles A and B mesh together.

6. Remove the starter driven gear and its needle bearing (**Figure 74**).
7. Remove gearshift spindle assembly A (**Figure 75**) from the crankcase.

Inspection

1. Clean and dry all parts.
2. Inspect the starter driven gear for the following conditions:
   a. Excessively worn or damaged bearing shoulder (A, **Figure 76**).
   b. Excessively worn or damaged gear teeth (B, **Figure 76**).
3. Inspect the needle bearing (C, **Figure 76**). The needles must not show flat spots, cracks or other

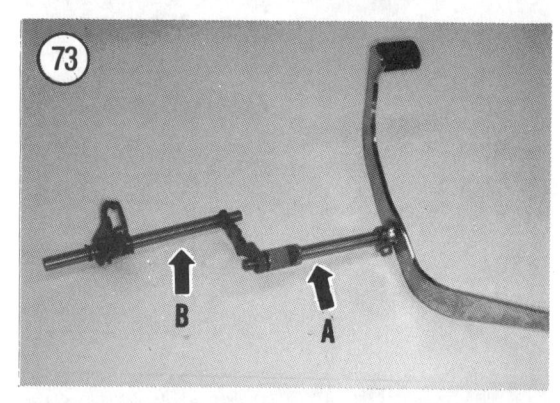

ENGINE BOTTOM END

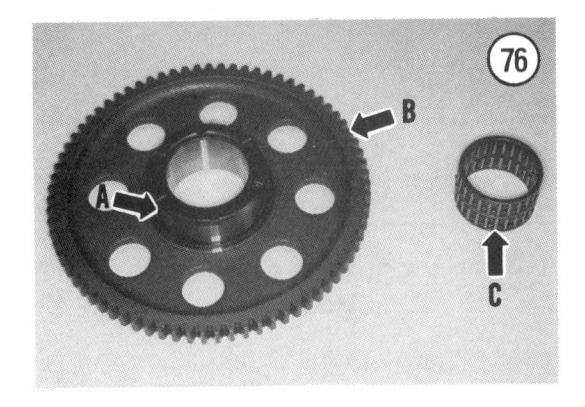

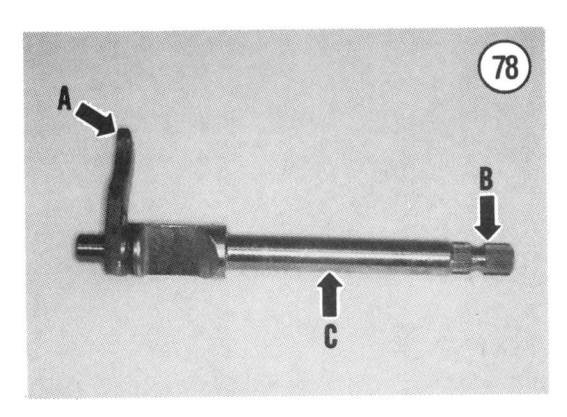

damage. Inspect the bearing cage for cracks or other damage. Replace the bearing if necessary.

4. Measure the starter driven gear outside diameter as shown in **Figure 77** and compare to the specification in **Table 2**. Replace the gear if the measurement is out of specification.

5. Inspect the gearshift spindle A for the following conditions:

   a. Excessively worn or damaged gear teeth (A, **Figure 78**).
   b. Damaged splines (B, **Figure 78**).
   c. Bent spindle shaft (C, **Figure 78**).

6. Inspect the starter reduction gear and shaft (**Figure 79**) for excessive wear or damage. Replace if necessary.

7. Inspect the spindle guide plug (**Figure 80**) if damaged. Replace the plug's O-ring if it is leaking or damaged.

Starter Clutch
Disassembly/Inspection/Reassembly

Refer to **Figure 61**.

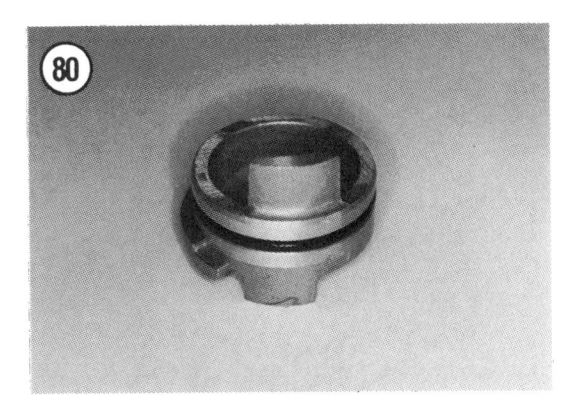

1. Secure the flywheel with the flywheel holder used during flywheel removal. Then remove the Torx bolts (**Figure 81**) securing the starter clutch assembly to the flywheel. Remove the housing and one-way clutch (**Figure 82**).
2. Clean and dry all parts. Remove all thread sealer residue from the Torx bolts and clutch housing threads.
3. Inspect the one-way clutch (**Figure 82**) for excessive wear and roller damage. Replace if damaged.
4. Inspect the clutch housing (**Figure 82**) for excessive wear or damage, especially where the one-way clutch operates.
5. Measure the clutch housing inside diameter (**Figure 83**) and compare to the specification in **Table 2**. Replace the clutch housing if the measurement is out of specification.
6. Install the one-way clutch into the clutch housing with its arrow mark facing toward the flywheel (**Figure 82**).
7. Install the clutch housing (**Figure 69**) onto the flywheel.
8. Apply a medium strength threadlocking compound to the threads of each Torx bolt.
9. Install the Torx bolts (**Figure 81**) finger-tight, then tighten to the torque specification listed in **Table 8**.

Installation

1. Install the gearshift spindle A (**Figure 84**) into the crankcase, but do not mesh it with gearshift spindle assembly B.
2. Lubricate the needle bearing, crankshaft and driven gear inside diameter with engine oil.
3. Install the driven gear (A, **Figure 85**)—shoulder side facing out—over the crankshaft, then install the

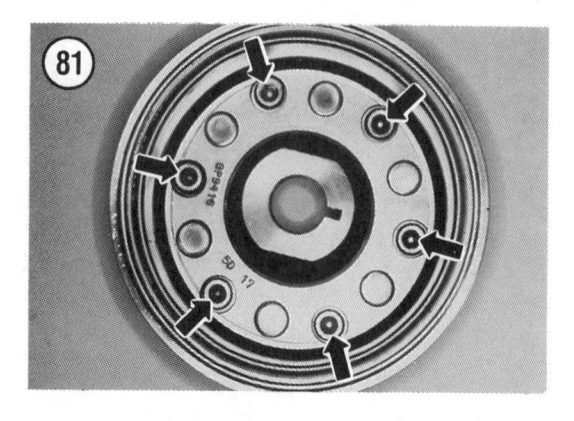

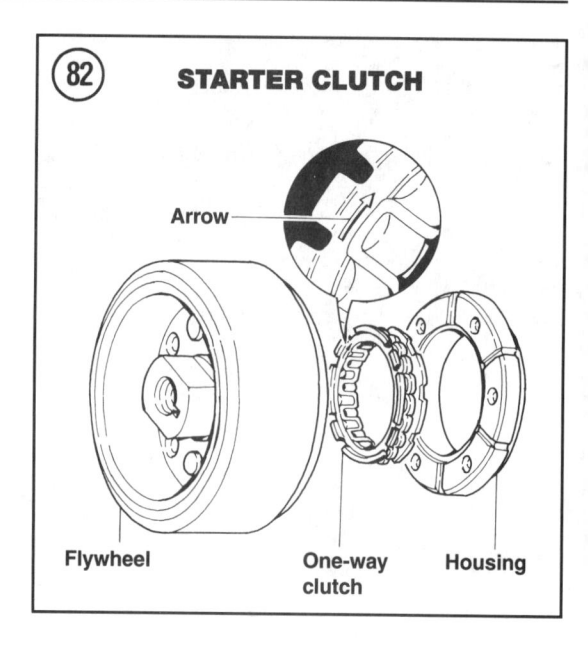

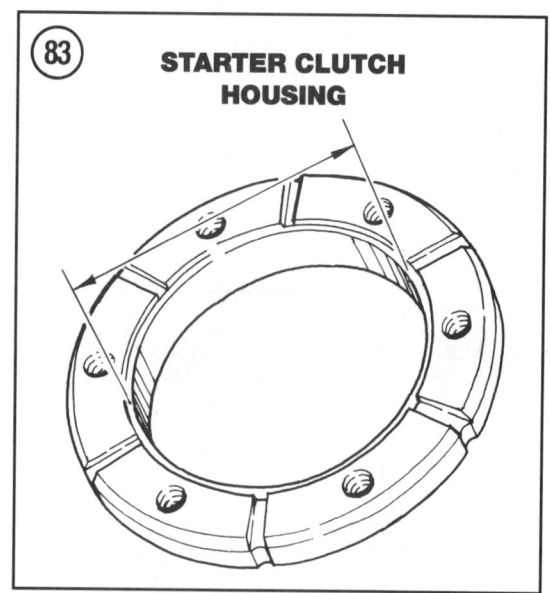

ENGINE BOTTOM END

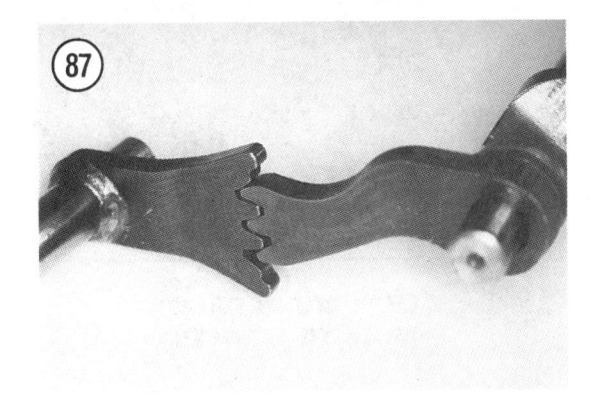

needle bearing (B, **Figure 85**) over the crankshaft and through the driven gear. Push the driven gear and needle bearing on all the way.

4. Align the gearshift spindle A gear teeth with the gearshift spindle B teeth and mesh both spindle gear teeth together as shown in **Figure 86**.

NOTE
Figure 87 shows how the gear teeth must mesh together.

5. Lubricate the spindle guide plug O-ring (**Figure 80**) with engine oil.

6. Install the spindle guide plug (**Figure 88**) into the crankcase until the plug's flange contacts the crankcase evenly. See **Figure 89**.

7. Reconnect the neutral switch electrical connector, then install its rubber plug (**Figure 71**) into the notch in the crankcase.

8. Lubricate the reduction gear shaft (**Figure 79**) with molybdenum oil, then install it into the crankcase (**Figure 70**).

9. Install the reduction gear—small gear facing in—and engage it with the driven gear (**Figure 70**).

10. Install the flywheel as described in this chapter.

CRANKCASE AND CRANKSHAFT

The crankcase is made in 2 halves of precision diecast aluminum alloy and is of the thin-walled type. To avoid damage to the crankcase, do not hammer or pry on any of the interior or exterior projected walls. These areas are easily damaged if stressed beyond what they are designed for. A gasket seals the crankcase halves while dowel pins align the crankcase halves when they are bolted together.

The procedure which follows is presented as a complete, step-by-step major lower end overhaul.

References to the left and right side of the engine, as used in the text, refers to the engine as it sits in the frame, not as it sits on your workbench.

Crankcase Disassembly

This procedure describes disassembly of the crankcase halves and removal of the crankshaft, transmission and internal shift mechanism.

1. With the engine mounted in the frame, remove the following components as described in Chapter Six:
   a. Clutch.
   b. Primary drive gear.
   c. Gearshift linkage.
   d. Oil pump.
2. With the engine mounted in the frame, remove the following components as described in this chapter:
   a. Left side crankcase cover.
   b. Flywheel.
   c. Starter clutch assembly.
3. Remove the engine from the frame as described in this chapter. Then remove the following components:
   a. Cylinder heads (Chapter Four).
   b. Cylinders and pistons (Chapter Four).
   c. Cam chain tensioners (Chapter Four).
   d. Ignition pulse generators (Chapter Nine).
   e. Water pump (Chapter Ten).
   f. Starter motor (Chapter Nine).
4. Remove the front (**Figure 90**) and rear (**Figure 91**) cam chains.
5. Remove the rear cylinder cam chain drive sprocket (**Figure 92**). 
6. Before removing the left and right side crankcase mounting bolts and washers, draw an outline of each crankcase on a piece of cardboard. Then punch holes along the outline for the placement of each mounting bolt. See **Figure 93** (left crankcase) and **Figure 94** (right crankcase).

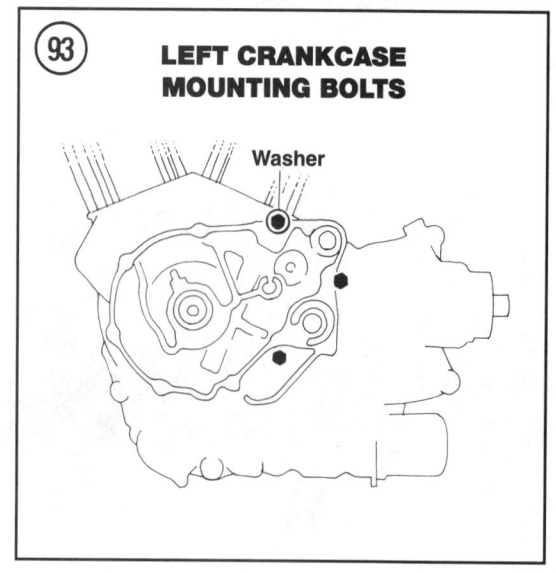

ENGINE BOTTOM END

7. Remove the 6 mm bolt and the two 8 mm bolts (and washers) from the left crankcase (**Figure 93**). Place them in the corresponding holes in the cardboard.

8. Hold the output driven gear shaft with the Honda shaft holder (part No. 07923-6890101) or equivalent (**Figure 95**). Then loosen and remove the output drive gear shaft bolt and washer (**Figure 95**).

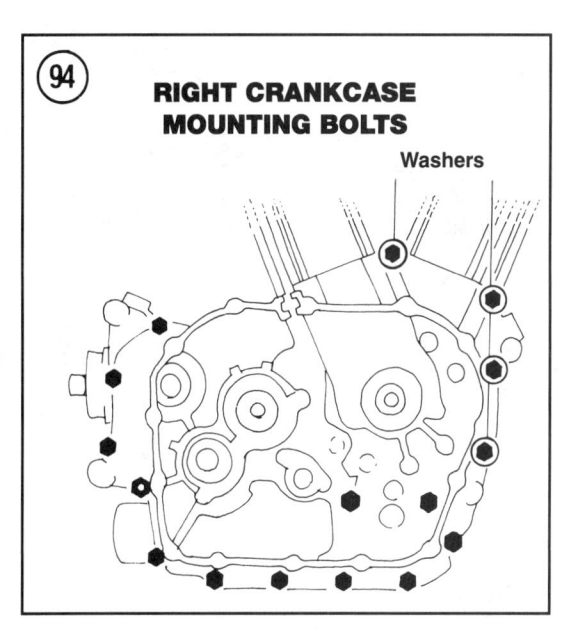

9. Loosen the right side crankcase bolts (**Figure 94**) in a crisscross pattern. Then remove all of the bolts and washers and place them in the corresponding holes in the cardboard.

10. Place the engine on 2 wooden blocks with the left side facing up.

11. Lightly tap the left crankcase half and remove it.

12. Remove the 2 dowel pins (A, **Figure 96**).

13. Remove the remaining dowel pin and O-ring (B, **Figure 96**).

14. Remove the output gear and bushing (**Figure 97**). Then remove its thrust washer (**Figure 98**).

NOTE
Steps 15-17 describes removal of the internal shift mechanism and transmission assembly. Refer to Chapter Seven to service these components.

15. Remove the shift fork shaft (**Figure 99**).

16. Remove the shift drum and the 3 shift forks (**Figure 100**).

NOTE
The mainshaft is equipped with an end washer on its left side. The countershaft is equipped with an end washer on its right side. Make sure you remove both washers during this procedure.

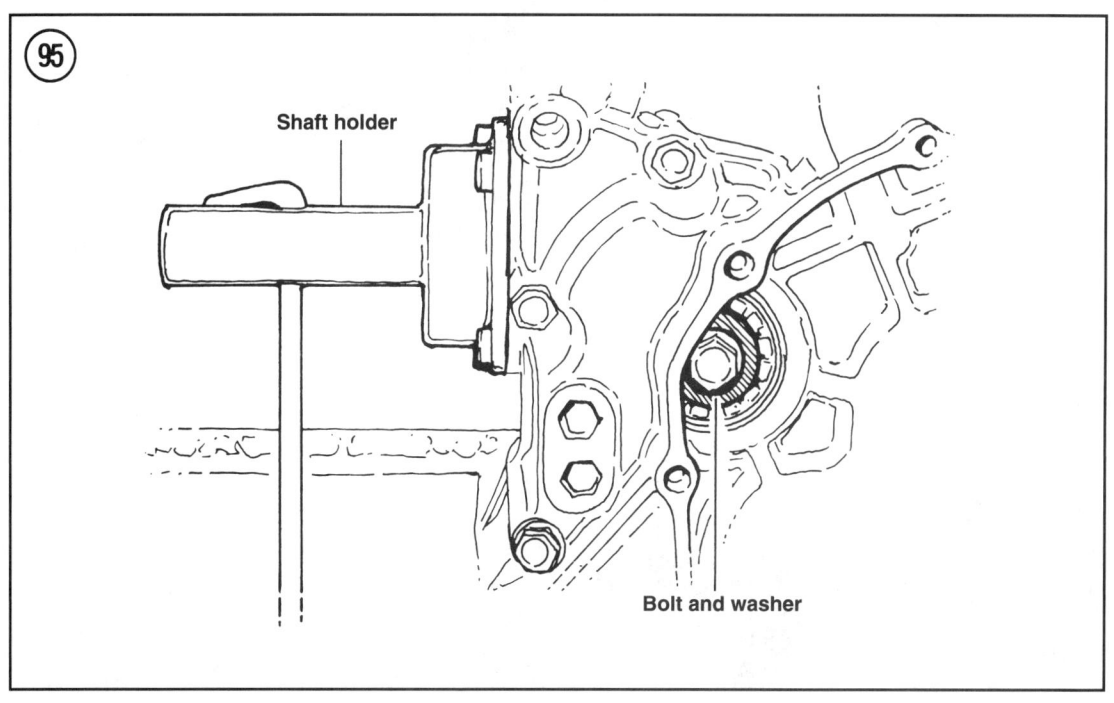

Figure 94 RIGHT CRANKCASE MOUNTING BOLTS — Washers

Figure 95 — Shaft holder; Bolt and washer

17. Remove the mainshaft (A, **Figure 101**) and countershaft (B, **Figure 101**) as an assembly. See **Figure 102**.
18. Lift the crankshaft (**Figure 103**) out of the crankcase and remove it.
19. To service the crankshaft, refer to *Crankshaft* in this chapter.
20. To service the connecting rods, refer to *Connecting Rods* in this chapter.
21. To service the output gear, refer to *Output Gear Assembly* in this chapter.
22. Refer to Chapter Seven to service the transmission and internal shift mechanism assemblies.

Crankcase Inspection

CAUTION
Do not pick up or hold the crankcase halves by their cylinder studs; otherwise, you may bend them, requiring their replacement.

1. Remove all sealer and gasket residue from the crankcase gasket surfaces.

CAUTION
When drying the crankcase bearings in Step 2, do not allow the inner bearing races to spin. The bearings are not lubricated and damage may result. When drying the bearings with compressed air, do not allow the air jet to spin the bearing. The air jet can rotate the bearings at excessive speeds. This could cause a bearing to fly apart.

2. Clean both crankcase halves (**Figure 104** and **Figure 105**) inside and out. Clean all crankcase

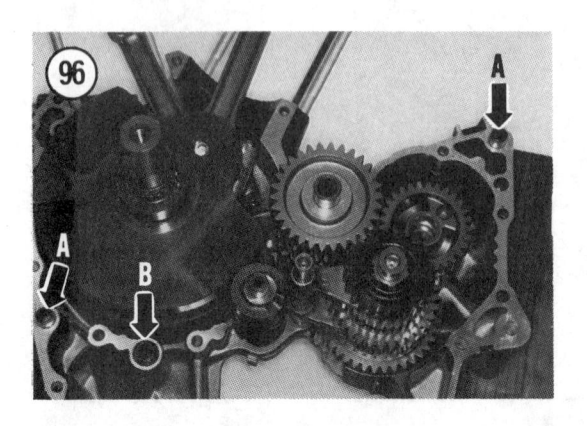

ENGINE BOTTOM END

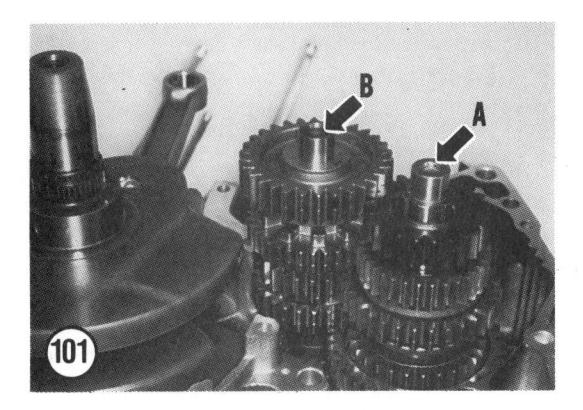

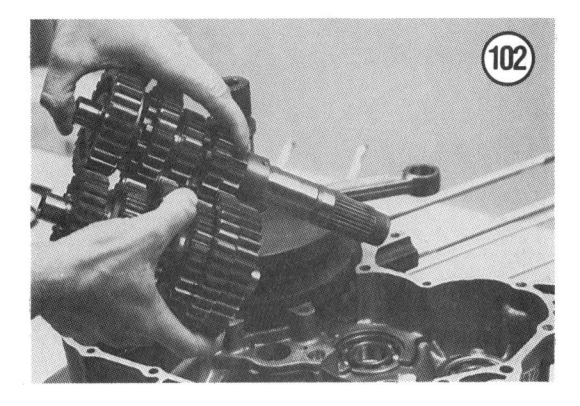

bearings with cleaning solvent. Thoroughly dry with compressed air.

3. Flush all crankcase oil passages with compressed air.

4. Lightly oil each crankcase bearing with engine oil before checking the bearings in Step 5.

5. Check the bearings for roughness, pitting, galling and play by rotating them slowly by hand. Replace any bearing that turns roughly or has excessive play (**Figure 106**).

6. Replace any worn or damaged bearings as described under *Crankcase Bearing Replacement* in this chapter.

7. Carefully inspect the cases for cracks and fractures, especially in the lower areas where they are vulnerable to damage.

8. Check the areas around the stiffening ribs, around bearing bosses and threaded holes for damage. Refer crankcase repair to a shop specializing in the repair of precision aluminum castings.

9. Check the threaded holes in both crankcase halves for thread damage, dirt or oil buildup. If necessary, clean or repair the threads with the correct size metric tap. Coat the tap threads with kerosene or an aluminum tap fluid before use.

10. Check for loose, damaged or bent cylinder studs (**Figure 107**). To replace or retighten the cylinder studs, refer to *Cylinder Stud Replacement* in Chapter Four.

Crankcase Bearing Replacement

When replacing bearings in the following steps, note the following:

  a. Identify the bearings used in the left (**Figure 108** and **Figure 109**) and right (A, **Figure 110**) crankcase halves before or immediately after

removing them. Identify the bearings by referring to their size code marks.
b. Refer to *Ball Bearing Replacement* in Chapter One for information on replacing the bearings.
c. Before removing the bearings, note and record the direction in which the bearings' size codes face for proper reinstallation.
d. Use a hydraulic press or a set of bearing drivers to remove and install the bearings. Use a blind bearing remover to remove bearings installed in blind holes (**Figure 111**).
e. On the right crankcase, remove the screws securing the bearing retainers (B, **Figure 110**) and remove the bearing retainers. When installing the retainers, apply a medium strength threadlocking compound to the retainer mounting bolts, then tighten the bolts securely.
f. To service the crankshaft bearing inserts (C, **Figure 110**), refer to *Crankshaft* in this chapter.

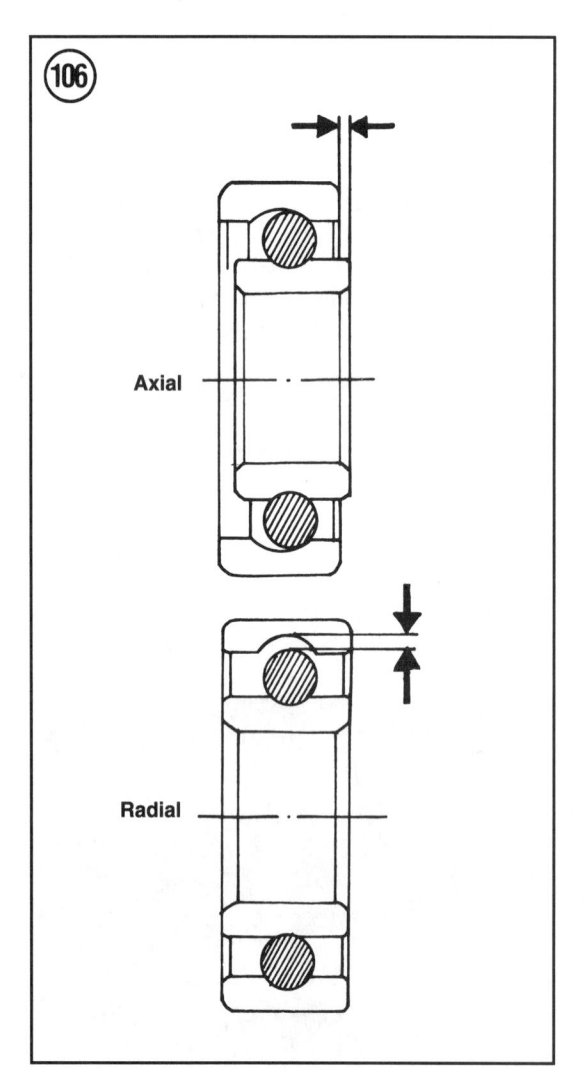

Crankcase Assembly

1. If removed, install the output gear as described under *Output Gear Assembly* in this chapter.
2. Lightly oil all of the crankcase bearings.
3. Check each of the following components as described in Chapter Seven. Check that all washers and

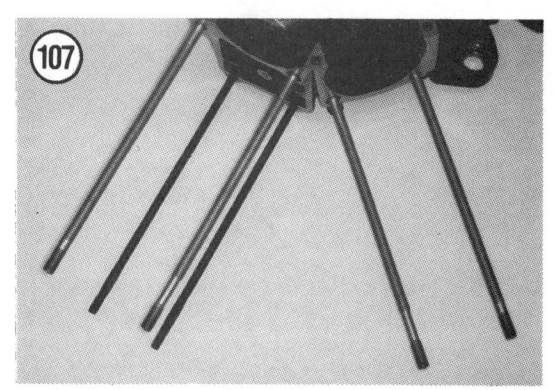

ENGINE BOTTOM END

circlips are in their correct position. Then set each assembly aside until reassembly:

a. Mainshaft.

b. Countershaft.

c. Shift drum.

4. Place the left crankcase (A, **Figure 112**) on 2 wooden blocks.

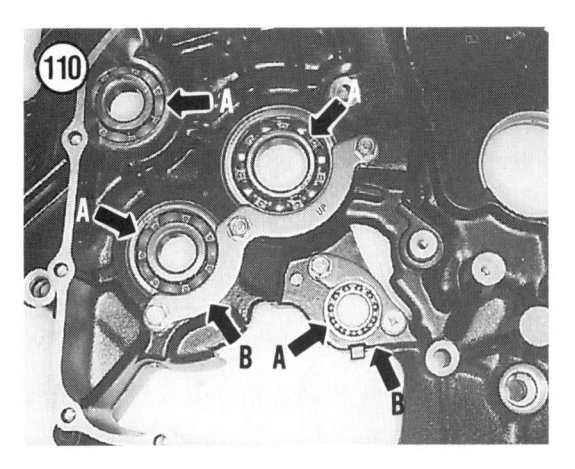

5. Make sure both crankcase gasket surfaces are clean and dry.

6. Lubricate the right crankcase main bearing insert (B, **Figure 112**) and the right side crankshaft race with engine oil.

7. Install the crankshaft into the crankcase (**Figure 103**).

8. Install the transmission shafts as follows:

   a. If removed, install the countershaft flat washer (**Figure 113**) with its flat edge facing away from the final drive gear.

   b. If removed, install the mainshaft flat washer (**Figure 114**) with its flat edge facing away from fifth gear.

   c. Mesh the countershaft and mainshaft together as shown in **Figure 102**.

   d. Install the countershaft and mainshaft into the left crankcase half (**Figure 101**). Make sure the outer washer on each shaft did not fall off.

NOTE
To identify the shift forks when installing them in Step 9, refer to the letter

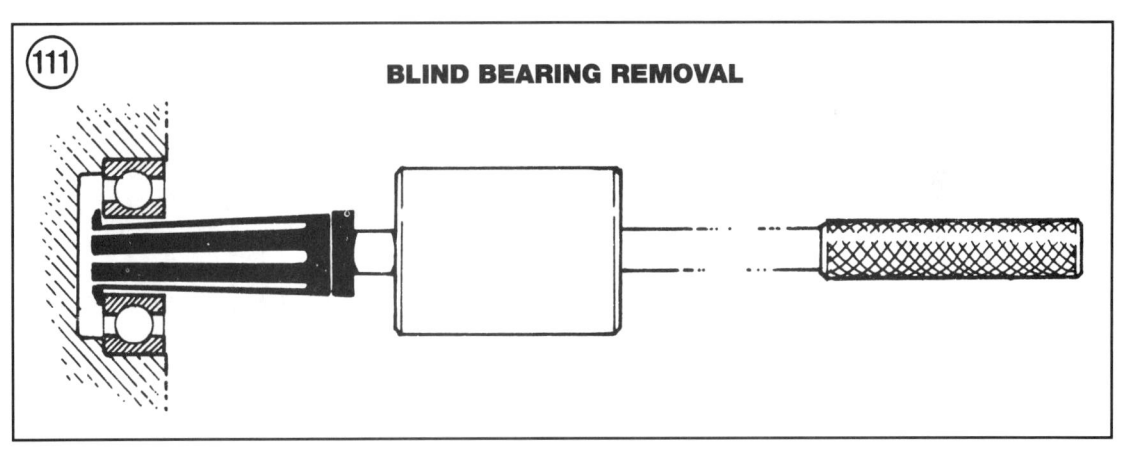

mark on each shift fork: L (left-hand), C (center) and R (right-hand). See Figure 115.

9. Install the shift forks (**Figure 115**) as follows:
   a. Install each shift fork with its letter mark (**Figure 115**) facing down (toward the right crankcase half).
   b. Install the R shift fork (**Figure 116**) into the countershaft third gear groove. See A, **Figure 117**.
   c. Install the C shift fork (**Figure 118**) into the mainshaft second/fourth combination gear groove. See B, **Figure 117**.
   d. Install the L shift fork (**Figure 119**) into the countershaft fifth gear groove. See C, **Figure 117**.

10. Install the shift drum and mesh the shift forks as follows:
    a. Lubricate the shift drum's right side shoulder with engine oil, then install the shift drum into the right crankcase bearing.
    b. Engage the R shift fork pin into the bottom shift drum groove (A, **Figure 120**).

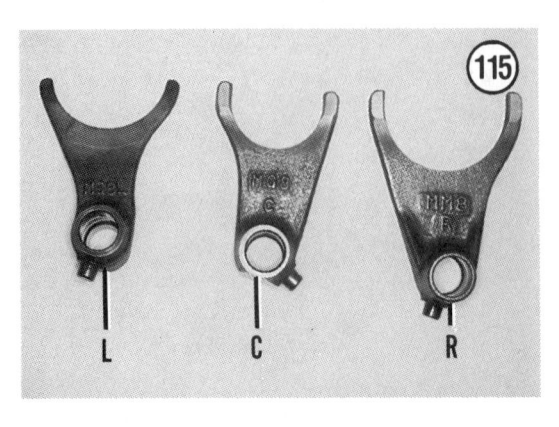

ENGINE BOTTOM END

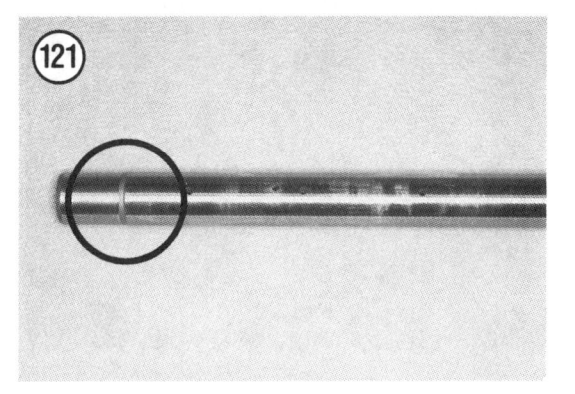

c. Engage the C shift fork pin into the center shift drum groove (B, **Figure 120**).
d. Engage the L shift fork pin into the upper shift drum groove (C, **Figure 120**).

CAUTION
The shift fork shaft is directional—one end is larger than the other. Make sure to install the shift fork shaft as described in Step 11.

11. Install the shift fork shaft as follows:
    a. The shift fork shaft has a groove on one end (**Figure 121**).
    b. Lubricate the shift fork shaft with molybdenum grease and oil solution (50:50) before installing it.
    c. Install the shift fork shaft with its grooved end facing up. Install it through the 3 shift forks until it bottoms in the right crankcase. See **Figure 122**.
    d. Check that each shift fork is still engaged with its respective gear and that its pin is in the correct shift drum groove.
12. Install the output gear assembly (**Figure 123**) as follows:
    a. Lubricate the washer, bushing and gear bore with engine oil.
    b. Install the washer and center it against the right crankcase bearing (**Figure 124**).
    c. Install the bushing into the gear, then install the gear into the right crankcase so its dog holes face up (**Figure 125**).
13. Spin the transmission shafts and shift through the gears using the shift drum. Check the shifting into each gear. This is the time to find that you may have installed a part incorrectly—not after you completely assemble the crankcase.

14. After making sure the transmission shifts into all of the gears correctly, shift the transmission assembly into NEUTRAL.
15. Lubricate a new O-ring with engine oil and install it and its dowel pin as shown in **Figure 126**.
16. Install the 2 dowel pins (**Figure 127**) into the right crankcase.
17. Lubricate all of the shafts and gears with engine oil.
18. Clean the mating surfaces of both crankcase halves with electrical contact cleaner. This will remove any traces of oil from the surfaces to achieve a better seal.

NOTE
Use a semi-drying liquid gasket sealer (ThreeBond Liquid Gasket 1104, Yamabond 4 or equivalent) to seal the crankcase.

19. Apply a thin even coat of a semi-drying liquid gasket sealer to the surface of one crankcase half.
20. Position the output gear (**Figure 125**) so its dog holes align with the 2 projections on the damper cam (**Figure 128**) when you install the left crankcase half in Step 21.
21. Install the left crankcase bolt over the right crankcase half so the damper cam engages the output gear (**Figure 128**) and the output drive gear shaft is installed through the output gear, bushing and washer.
22. Lightly tap the case halves together with a plastic mallet.

CAUTION
When the shafts align properly, the left crankcase can be installed without the use of force. If the crankcase halves do not fit together completely, do not pull them together with the crankcase screws. Remove the left crankcase and investigate the cause of the interference. If you disassembled the transmission shaft assemblies, make sure you did not install a gear backward. Also make sure the output gear, bushing and washer are aligned and installed correctly.

23. Turn all of the exposed shafts, crankshaft and shift drum. Each component must turn freely. If everything turns freely, continue with Step 24.

24. Referring to **Figure 129**, install the right crankcase bolts and washers. Install the washers on the 4 bolts as shown in **Figure 129**.
25. Tighten the right crankcase bolts in a crisscross pattern in 2-3 steps to the torque specification in **Table 8**.
26. Turn the engine over and install the left crankcase bolts and washer. Install the washer on the bolt indicated in **Figure 130**.

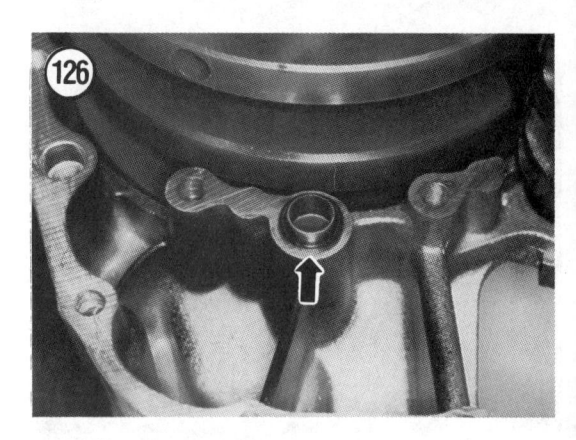

ENGINE BOTTOM END

27. Tighten the left crankcase bolts in a crisscross pattern in 2-3 steps to the torque specification in **Table 8**.
28. Rotate the transmission shafts and crankshaft to ensure there is no binding. If there is any binding, remove the crankcase mounting bolts and the left crankcase half and correct the problem.
29. Apply a medium strength threadlocking compound onto the output drive gear shaft bolt threads. Then hold the output driven gear shaft with the Honda shaft holder (part No. 07923-6890101) or equivalent (**Figure 131**) and tighten the bolt to the torque specification in **Table 8**.
30. Using your torque wrench, recheck the torque value of each crankcase half mounting bolt.
31. Check shifting as follows:
    a. Temporarily install the cam plate and stopper arm (**Figure 132**) as described in Chapter Six.
    b. Shift the shift drum into NEUTRAL as shown in **Figure 132** and turn the mainshaft. When the transmission is in NEUTRAL, the output driven gear shaft will not be engaged with the transmission.
    c. Turn the mainshaft while turning the cam plate to shift the transmission into each gear. The stopper arm roller will engage the cam plate notch at each gear position.
32. Slide the rear cylinder cam chain drive sprocket (**Figure 92**) onto the crankshaft by aligning the wide

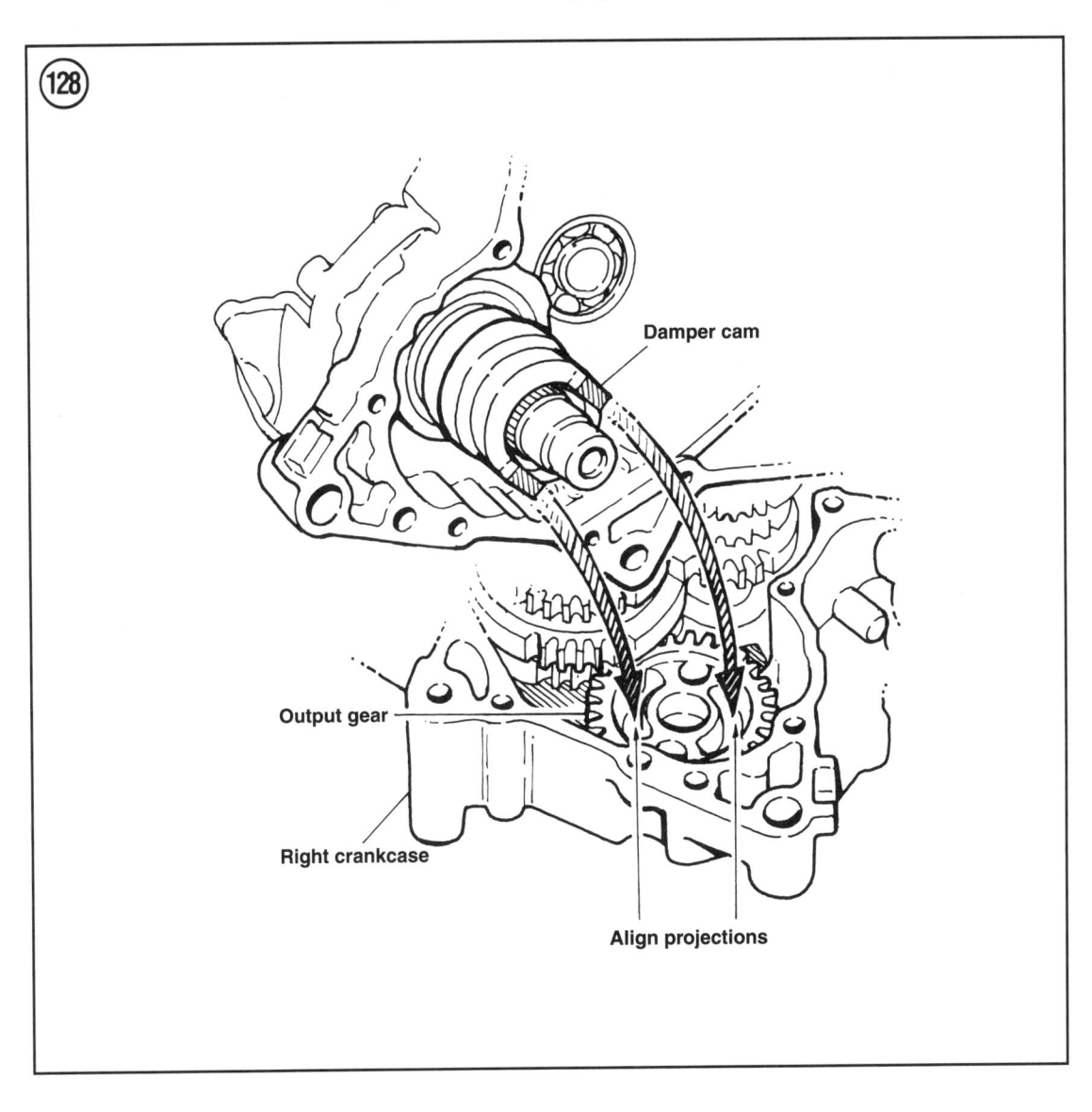

groove in the sprocket with the wide crankshaft tooth.

33. Install the front (**Figure 90**) and rear (**Figure 91**) cam chains.
34. Install the following components as described in the appropriate chapter:
    a. Starter motor (Chapter Nine).
    b. Water pump (Chapter Ten).
    c. Ignition pulse generators (Chapter Nine).
    d. Cam chain tensioners (Chapter Four).
    e. Cylinders and pistons (Chapter Four).
    f. Cylinder heads (Chapter Four).
35. Install the engine in the frame as described in this chapter.
36. Install the following components as described in this chapter:
    a. Starter clutch assembly.
    b. Flywheel.
    c. Left side crankcase cover.
37. Install the following components as described in Chapter Six:
    a. Oil pump.
    b. Gearshift linkage.
    c. Primary drive gear.
    d. Clutch.
38. Refill the engine with oil and coolant as described in Chapter Three.
39. Start the engine and check for leaks.

CRANKSHAFT

Removal/Installation

Remove and install the crankshaft as described under *Crankcase* in this chapter.

Inspection

1. Clean the crankshaft (**Figure 133**) thoroughly with solvent. Clean the crankshaft oil passageway with compressed air. Dry the crankshaft with compressed air. Then lubricate all bearing surfaces with a light coat of engine oil.
2. Check the crankshaft journals (**Figure 134**) for scratches, heat discoloration or other defects.
3. Check the flywheel taper, threads and keyway (**Figure 135**) for damage.
4. Check the crankshaft sprockets for excessive wear or tooth damage.
5. Place the crankshaft on a set of V-blocks or between lathe centers and measure runout with a dial indicator across each of the crankshaft's main journals. If the runout is out of specification (**Table 3**), take the crankshaft to a Honda dealership for service.

Crankshaft
Main Bearing Inspection

The crankshaft main bearing inserts in the crankcase (**Figure 136**) cannot be replaced. If excessively worn or damaged, the crankcase half must be replaced. Do not remove the inserts when inspecting them in the following steps.

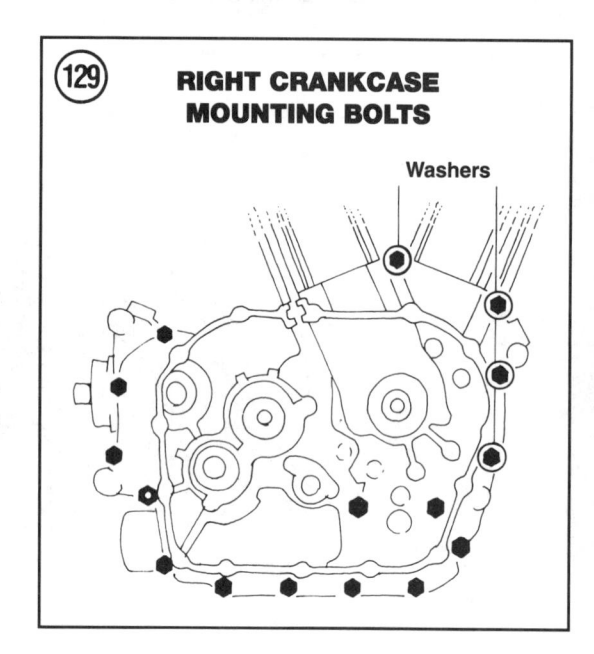

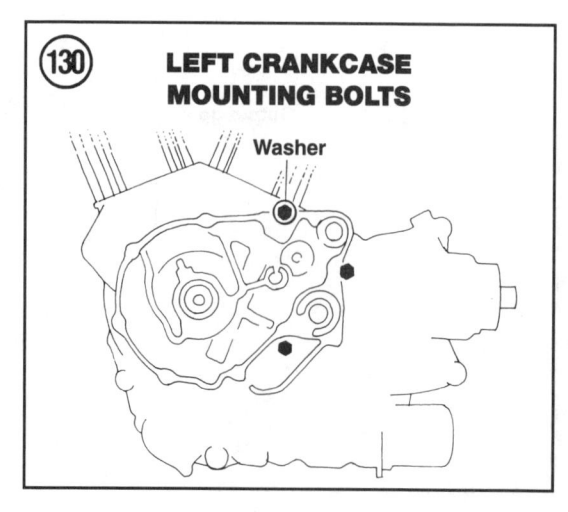

129 RIGHT CRANKCASE MOUNTING BOLTS

Washers

130 LEFT CRANKCASE MOUNTING BOLTS

Washer

ENGINE BOTTOM END

1. Inspect the inside surface of each bearing insert (**Figure 136**) for excessive wear, bluish or burned appearance, flaking and scoring. If the insert is questionable, replace the crankcase half.

2. Clean the crankshaft main bearing (**Figure 134**) and crankcase bearing insert (**Figure 136**) surfaces.

3. Measure the main bearing clearance by performing the following steps:

   a. Measure the inside diameter of the bearing insert with a bore gauge or inside micrometer (**Figure 137**).

   b. Measure the crankshaft main bearing journal outside diameter with a micrometer (**Figure 138**).

   c. Subtract the main bearing journal outside diameter from the bearing insert inside diameter to determine the main journal oil clearance. See **Table 3** for new and service limit specifications.

   d. If the bearing clearance is out of specification, replace the crankcase half.

4. Repeat these steps for the opposite bearing insert and crankshaft journal.

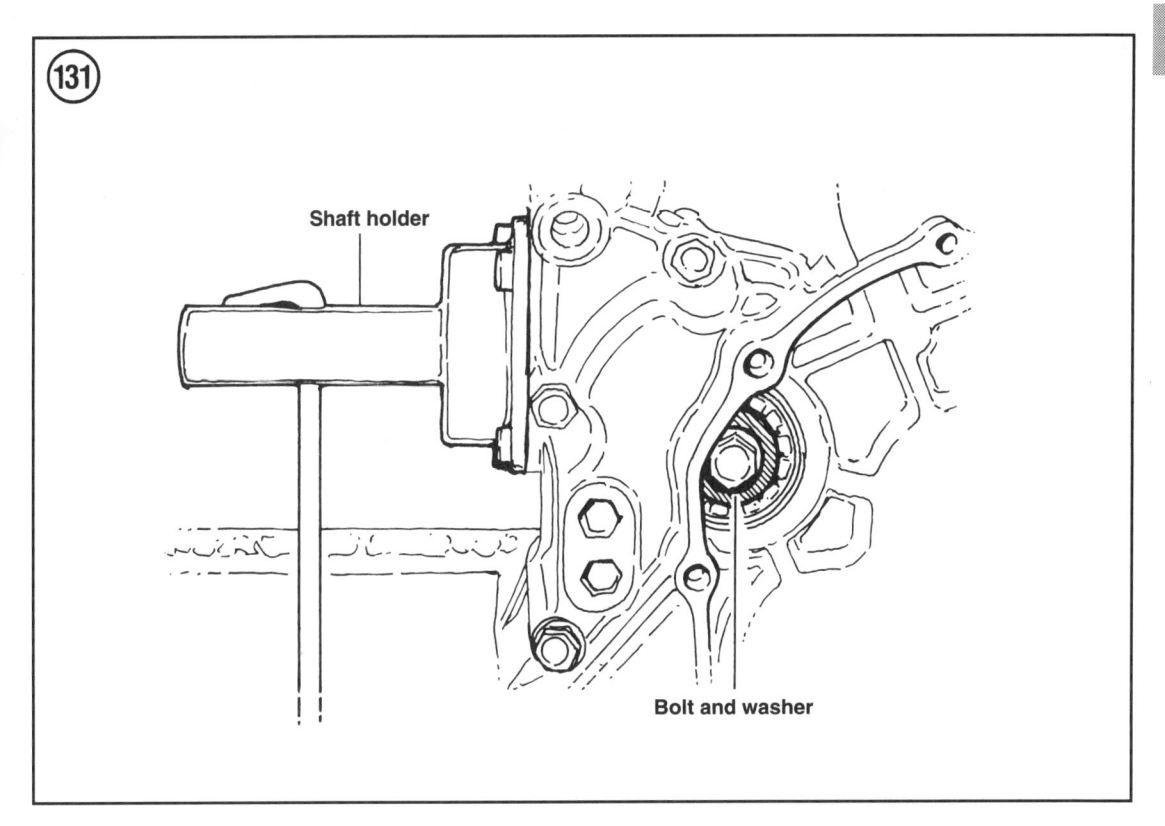

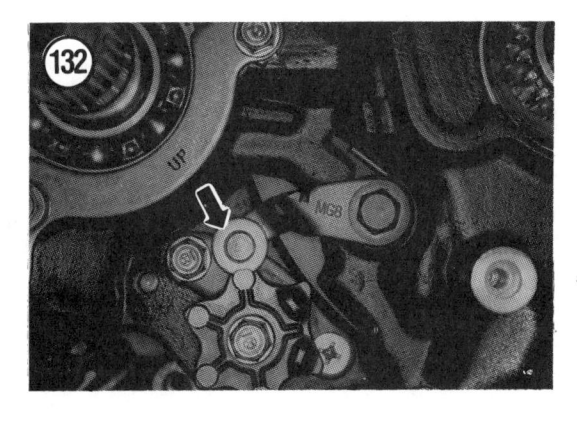

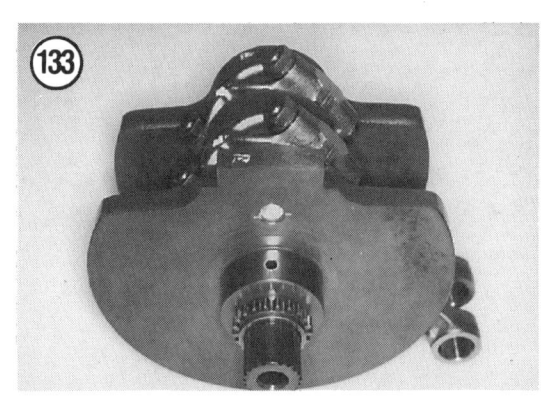

5. If you purchased a new crankcase half, check the clearance by repeating this procedure.

CONNECTING RODS

Removal/Installation

1. Split the crankcase and remove the crankshaft assembly as described under *Crankcase Disassembly* in this chapter.
2. Before removing the connecting rods from the crankshaft, measure the connecting rod side clearance as follows:

   a. Slide the connecting rod to one side and measure the connecting rod big end side clearance with a flat feeler gauge (**Figure 139**) and check against the specification in **Table 3**.
   b. Replace the connecting rod if out of specification.
   c. Repeat for the other connecting rod.

NOTE
When marking the connecting rods in Step 3, remember that the left side relates to the engine as it sits in the bike's frame, not as it sits on your workbench.

3. Mark the rods and caps with an L for left side (side with the flywheel keyway) or R for the right side (primary drive gear splines).
4. Remove the nuts securing the connecting rod caps and remove the caps (**Figure 140**).
5. Carefully remove the connecting rod from the crankshaft. Mark the rod, bearing and cap to show its correct cylinder and crankpin position for reassembly (**Figure 141**).

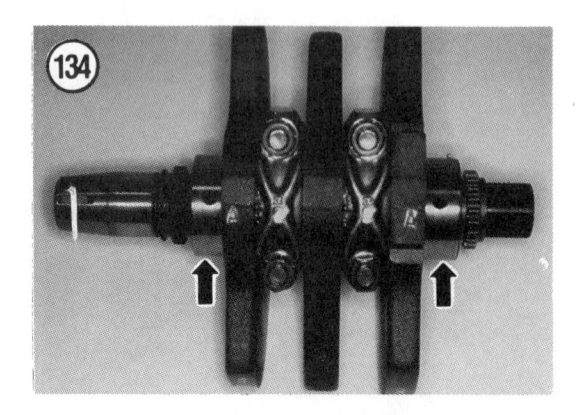

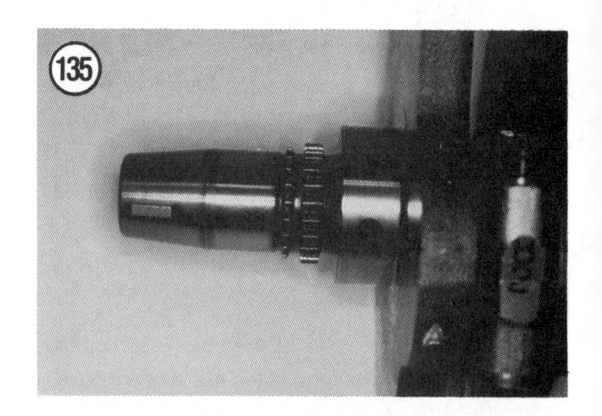

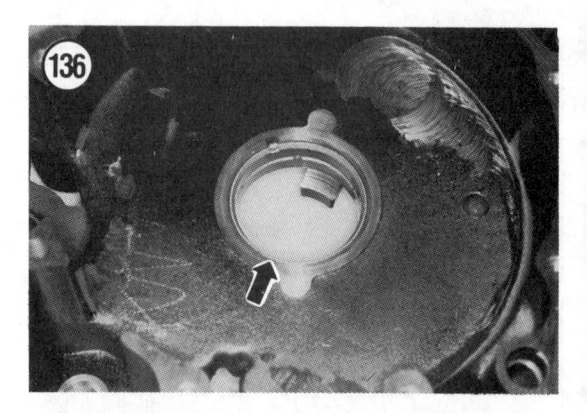

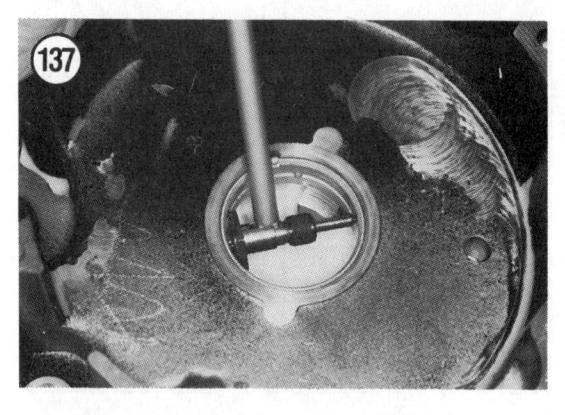

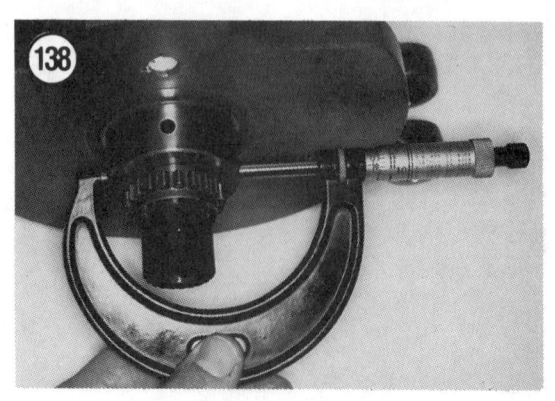

ENGINE BOTTOM END

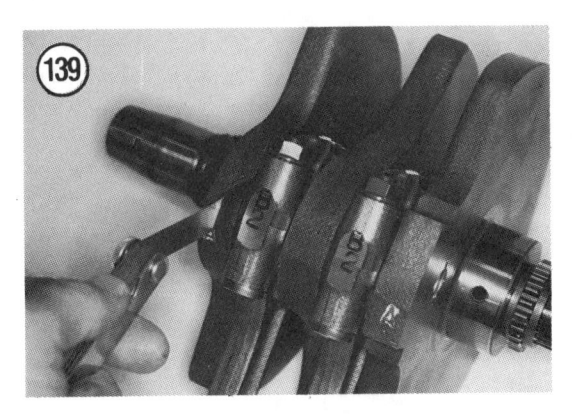

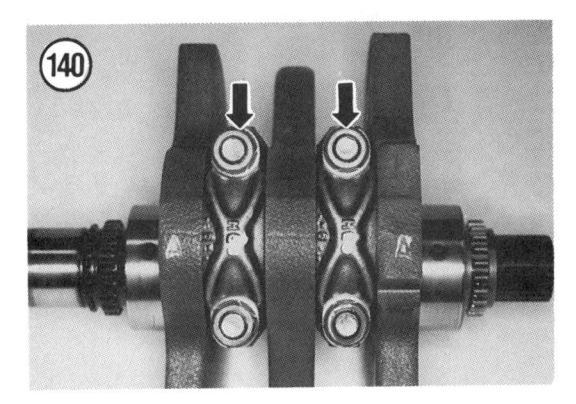

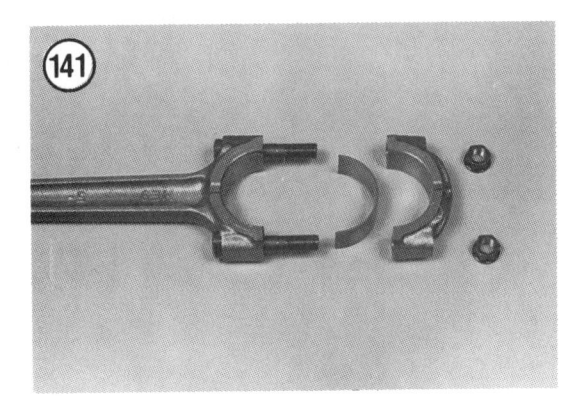

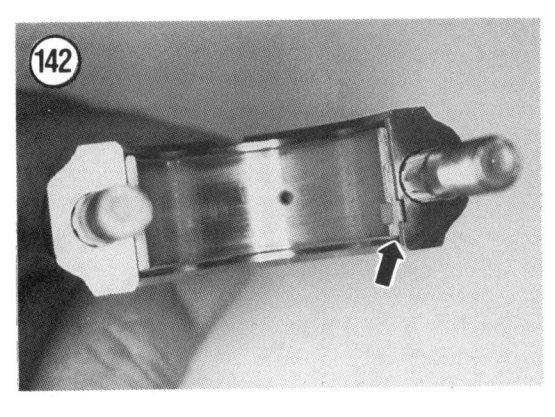

6. Remove and mark the back of each bearing insert (**Figure 141**). Mark each bearing insert as to its upper or lower position.
7. Clean these parts and the crankshaft in solvent and dry with compressed air.
8. Install by reversing these removal steps while noting the following.
9. Wipe off any oil from the bearing inserts, connecting rod and cap contact surfaces.
10. Install the bearing inserts into each connecting rod and cap. Make sure they are locked in place correctly (**Figure 142**).

CAUTION
If the old bearings inserts are reused, be sure they are installed in their original positions; refer to Steps 5 and 6.

11. Apply molybdenum disulfide grease to the bearing inserts and crankpin bearing thrust surfaces.
12. Install the connecting rod onto the crankshaft so it is facing in its original position, as noted during Step 5.
13. Match the code number on the end of the cap with the mark on the rod and install the cap.
14. Lubricate the bearing cap nut threads with engine oil and install the cap nuts. Tighten the cap nuts in 2-3 steps to the torque specification in **Table 8**.
15. Rotate the connecting rod several times to check that there is no binding or roughness.
16. Repeat for the other connecting rod.

Inspection

1. Remove the connecting rods from the crankshaft as described in this chapter.
2. Clean the connecting rods and inserts in solvent and dry with compressed air.
3. Carefully inspect each rod journal on the crankshaft for scratches, ridges, scoring and other damage.
4. Inspect each bearing insert (**Figure 141**) for excessive wear, cracks or other visible damage. If any insert is questionable, replace the entire set. Refer to *Crankpin Oil Clearance Measurement* in this section.
5. Measure the rod journal with a micrometer (**Figure 143**) and check for out-of-roundness and taper.
6. Check each connecting rod big end for signs of seizure, bearing or connecting rod damage.

7. Check each connecting rod small end (**Figure 144**) for signs of excessive heat (blue coloration) or other damage.
8. Measure the inside diameter of the small end of the connecting rod (**Figure 145**) with an inside micrometer or snap gauge. Check against the specification listed in **Table 3**. Replace the rod if this dimension is out of specification.
9. If all of the parts are within specification and do not show any type of visible damage, check the crankpin oil clearance as described in this section.

Crankpin Oil Clearance Measurement

1. Clean any oil from the bearing insert and crankpin surfaces.
2. Place a strip of Plastigage (**Figure 146**) over each rod bearing journal parallel to the crankshaft (**Figure 147**). Do not place the Plastigage material over an oil hole in the crankshaft.

NOTE
Do not rotate the connecting rod or crankshaft while the Plastigage strips are in place.

3. Install the bearing inserts into each connecting rod and end cap. Make sure they are locked in place correctly (**Figure 142**).

NOTE
Be sure the bearing inserts are installed in their original mounting positions.

4. Install the connecting rod onto the crankshaft so it is facing in its original position.
5. Match the code number on the end of the cap with the mark on the rod and install the cap.
6. Lubricate the bearing cap nut threads and seating surface with engine oil and install the cap nuts. Tighten the cap nuts (**Figure 140**) in 2-3 steps to the torque specification in **Table 8**.
7. Remove the rod cap nuts and rod cap.
8. Measure the width of the flattened Plastigage (**Figure 148**) following the manufacturer's instructions. Measure both ends of the Plastigage strip. A difference of 0.025 mm (0.001 in.) or more indicates a tapered journal. Confirm with a micrometer (**Figure 143**). See **Table 3** for crankpin oil clearance dimensions.

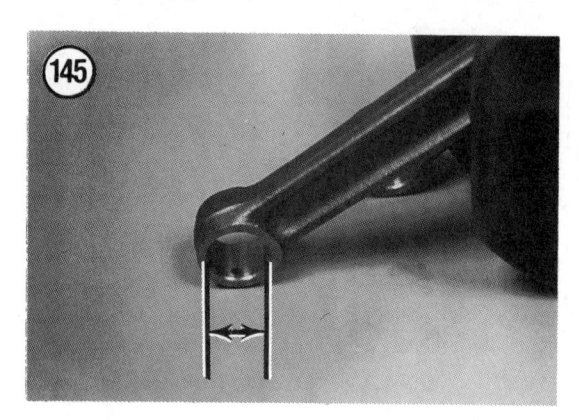

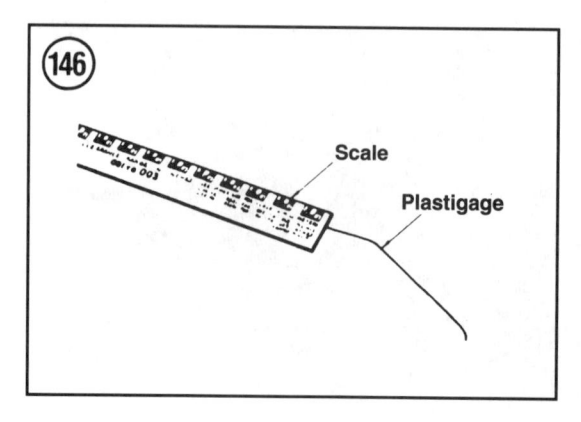

ENGINE BOTTOM END

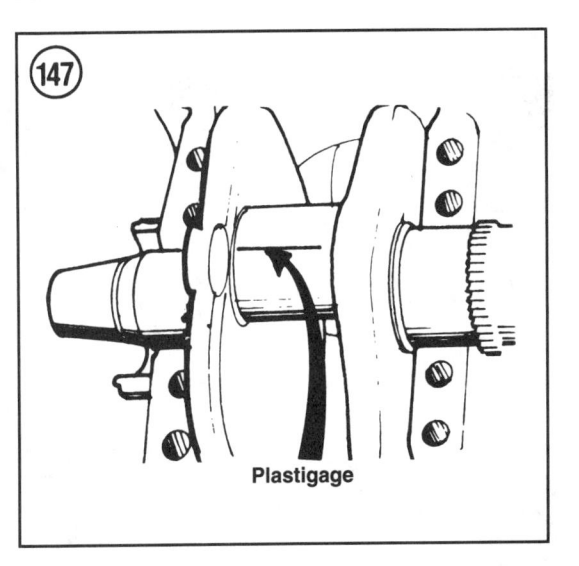

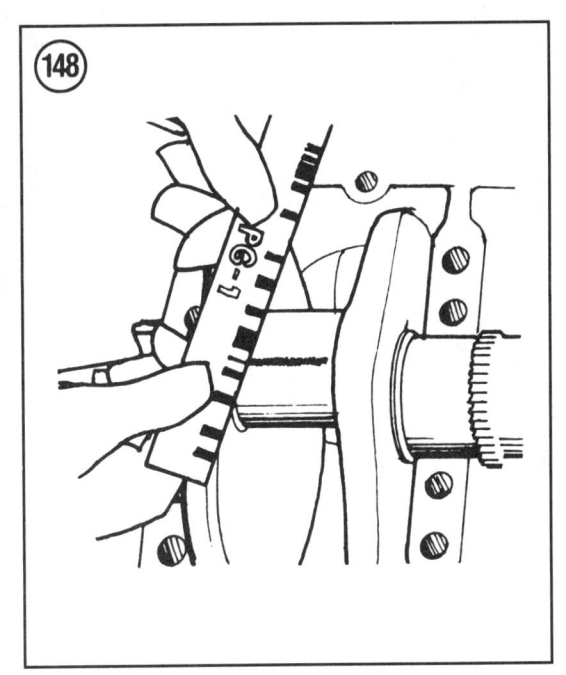

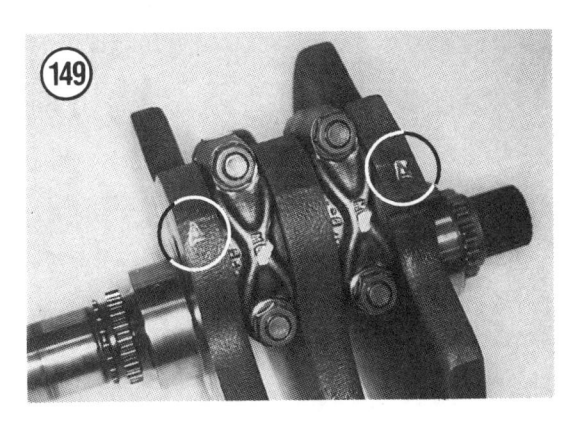

9. Remove all of the Plastigage material from the crankshaft journals and connecting rod caps.

If the bearing clearance is greater than specified, perform the following steps to select the new bearings.

10. The crankshaft connecting rod journals are marked with letters A or B (**Figure 149**). The letters represent the crankpin's outside diameter.

11. The connecting rod and cap are marked with the number 1 or 2 (**Figure 150**). These numbers represent the connecting rod's inside diameter.

NOTE
The letter mark on the connecting rod represents its weight code. Disregard the letter mark during this procedure.

12. Measure the rod journal with a micrometer (**Figure 143**). If the rod journal dimension is within the tolerance stated for each letter code in **Table 4**, the bearing can be selected by color code. If a dimension is not within the tolerance, refer the crankshaft to a Honda dealership for further inspection.

13. Select new bearings by cross-referencing the rod journal letters (**Figure 149**) in the horizontal column of **Table 4** to the rod bearing number (**Figure 150**) in the vertical column. Where the 2 columns intersect, the new bearing color is indicated. **Table 5** gives the bearing insert color and thickness.

14. After installing the new bearing inserts, recheck the bearing clearance by repeating this procedure.

15. Repeat for the other connecting rod.

Connecting Rod Replacement

An alphabetical weight code (A, B, C, D, or E) is marked on the side of each connecting rod (**Figure**

150). When replacing a connecting rod, replace it with the same weight code as the original rod. If the same weight code replacement rod is unavailable, cross-reference the front and rear connecting rods with the weight listings in **Table 6**. Where the 2 columns intersect with an × mark, the connecting rods are matched and can be used together.

OUTPUT GEAR ASSEMBLY

Special Tools

To disassemble and remove the damper spring assembly, the following Honda special tools or equivalent are required:

a. Assembly bolt (part No. 07965-1660200). See A, **Figure 151**.

b. Assembly collar (part No. 07965-1660300). See B, **Figure 151**.

c. Compressor seat (part No. 07967-9690200). See C, **Figure 151**.

d. Threaded adaptor (part No. 07965-KA30000). See D, **Figure 151**.

Removal

1. Split the crankcase and remove the output gear, bushing and thrust washer assembly (**Figure 152**) as described under *Crankcase Disassembly* in this chapter.
2. Place the left crankcase half on 2 wooden blocks with the damper spring assembly facing up (**Figure 153**).
3. Screw the threaded adaptor (A, **Figure 154**) into the output drive gear shaft.

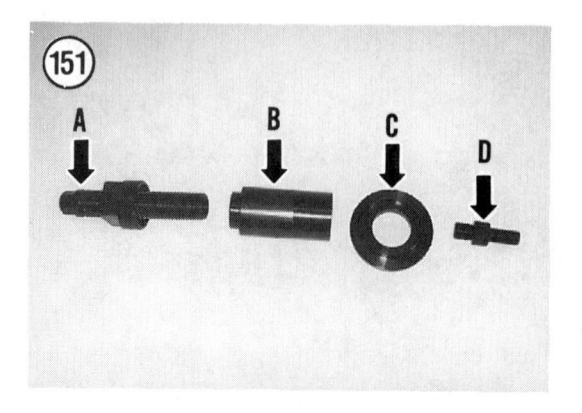

ENGINE BOTTOM END

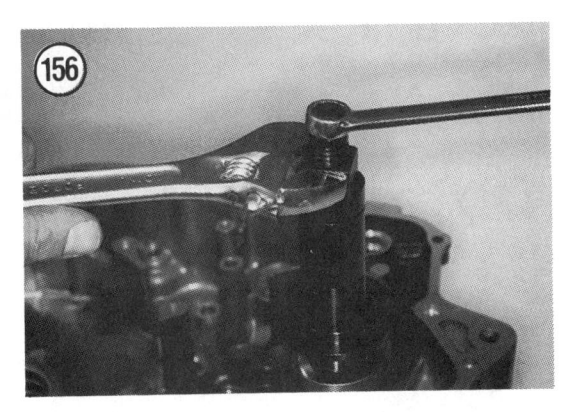

4. Install the compressor seat—shoulder side facing up—over the output drive gear shaft and seat it against the damper cam (B, **Figure 154**).
5. Install the assembly bolt through the assembly collar, then screw the assembly bolt onto the threaded adaptor (**Figure 155**).

CAUTION
When applying pressure against the damper spring in Step 6, make sure the assembly collar is centered on the damper cam. If not, loosen the tool and reposition the assembly collar.

6. Hold the assembly bolt, then tighten the assembly collar nut (**Figure 156**) to compress the damper spring. Continue until the circlip (**Figure 157**) installed on the output drive gear shaft is visible with enough room to remove it.
7. Using circlip pliers, remove the circlip from the output drive shaft groove and slide it up the shaft.
8. Slowly loosen the assembly collar nut (**Figure 156**) to release all of the tension from the damper spring. Then remove the tool assembly.
9. Remove the circlip, damper cam and spring (**Figure 158**). Discard the circlip as a new one must be installed during reassembly.
10. Turn the left crankcase over so that the output gear assembly faces up.
11. Remove the 3 bolts (**Figure 159**) and the output gear assembly. See **Figure 160**.
12. Remove the oil jet (**Figure 161**) and its 2 O-rings from the left crankcase.

Inspection

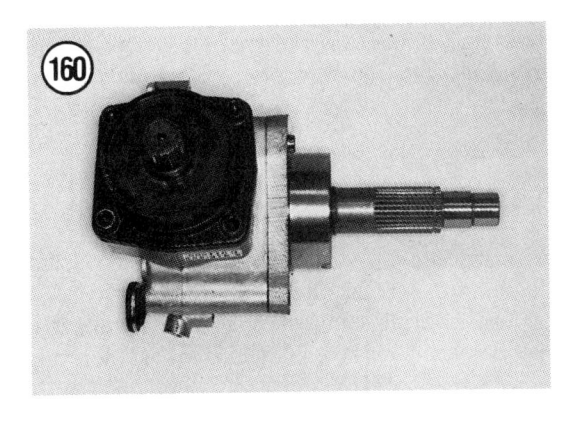

When measuring the output gear components in this section, compare the actual measurements to the new and service limit specifications in **Table 7**. Replace parts that are out of specification.

1. Clean and dry all of the output gear parts.
2. Clean the oil jet (**Figure 162**) with compressed air.
3. Install 2 new O-rings (**Figure 162**) onto the oil jet.
4. Inspect the output gear and bushing (**Figure 163**) for excessive wear or damage.
5. Measure the output gear (**Figure 163**) inside diameter and compare to the service limit in **Table 7**.
6. Measure the output gear bushing (**Figure 163**) outside diameter and inside diameter and compare to the service limit in **Table 7**.
7. Inspect the damper spring (**Figure 164**) for damage. Then measure the damper spring free length (**Figure 165**) and compare to the service limit in **Table 7**.
8. Inspect the damper cam ramps for excessive wear or damage.
9. Perform the following:

   a. Measure the output drive gear shaft outside diameter with a micrometer (**Figure 166**) and compare to the service limit in **Table 7**.

   b. Inspect the seal (**Figure 167**) for oil leaks or other damage.

   c. If the output drive gear shaft outside diameter is out of specification or if the oil seal is damaged, take the output gear housing to a dealership for further service.

Output Drive Gear Case Disassembly/Reassembly

Overhaul of the output drive gearcase requires a number of special Honda tools. The price of all of these tools is more than the cost of most repairs done at a dealership. Refer all service to a Honda dealership.

Installation

1. Lubricate 2 new O-rings with engine oil and install them onto the oil jet (**Figure 168**).
2. Install the oil jet into the crankcase (**Figure 161**) with its chamfered hole side facing toward the crankcase. See **Figure 169**.

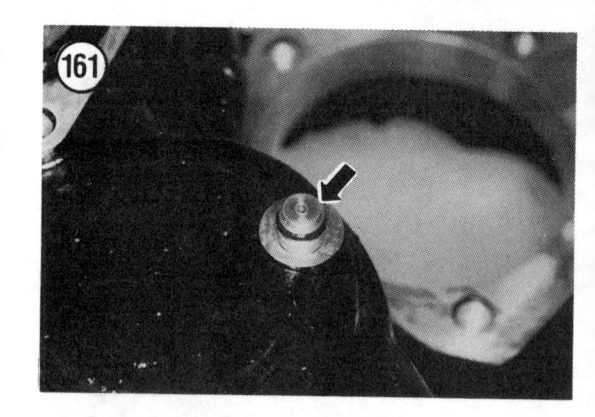

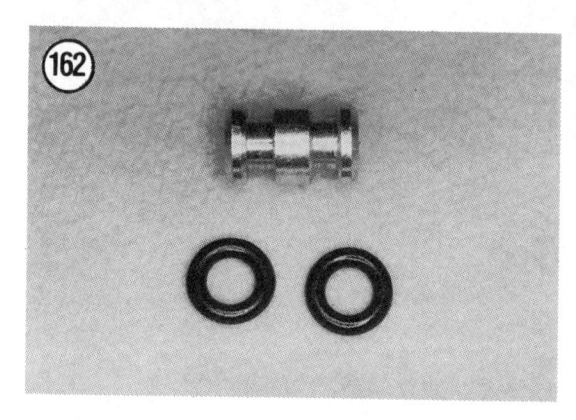

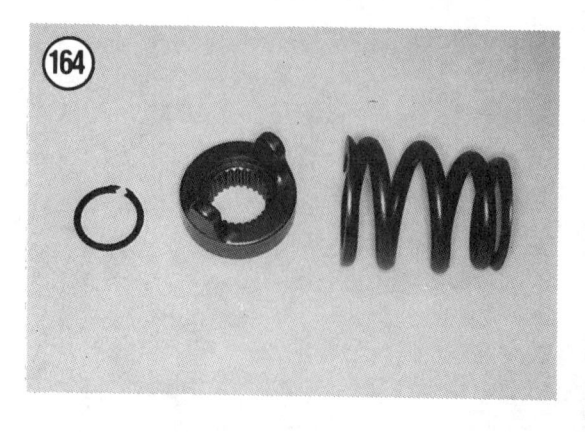

ENGINE BOTTOM END

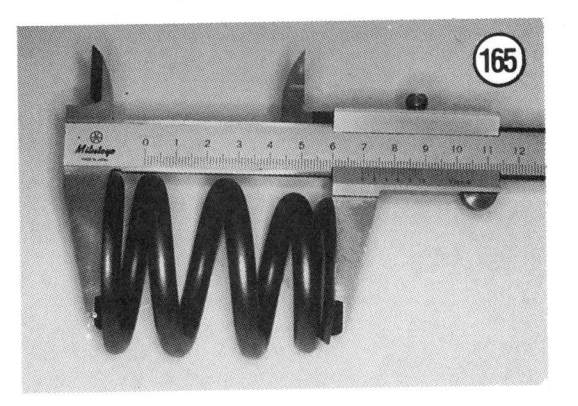

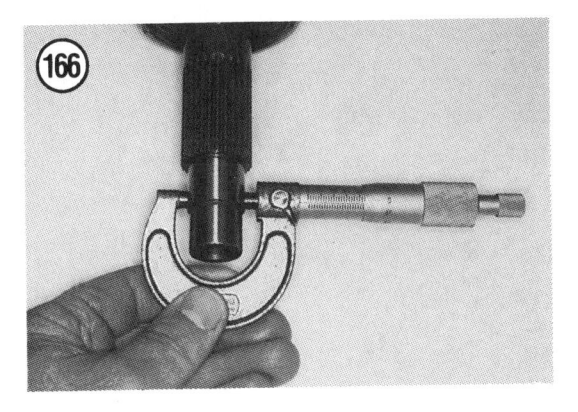

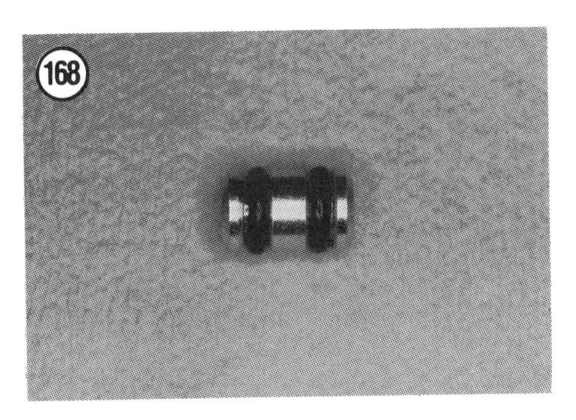

3. Lubricate a new O-ring with engine oil and install it into the groove in the bearing holder (A, **Figure 170**).
4. Install the dowel pin (B, **Figure 170**) into the bearing holder.
5. Install the output gear assembly (**Figure 159**) onto the left crankcase. Make sure the gearcase engages the oil jet and O-ring. Install and tighten the 3 bolts (**Figure 159**) hand-tight.
6. Turn the crankcase over so the drive gear shaft (**Figure 171**) faces up.
7. Install the damper spring over the drive gear shaft with its closely wound springs (**Figure 172**) facing down (toward left crankcase half). See **Figure 173**.
8. Install the damper cam (**Figure 158**) onto the damper spring.
9. Install a new circlip (**Figure 174**) over the drive gear shaft.
10. Thread the threaded adaptor (A, **Figure 154**) into the output drive gear shaft.
11. Install the compressor seat—shoulder side facing up—over the output drive gear shaft and seat it against the damper cam (B, **Figure 154**).

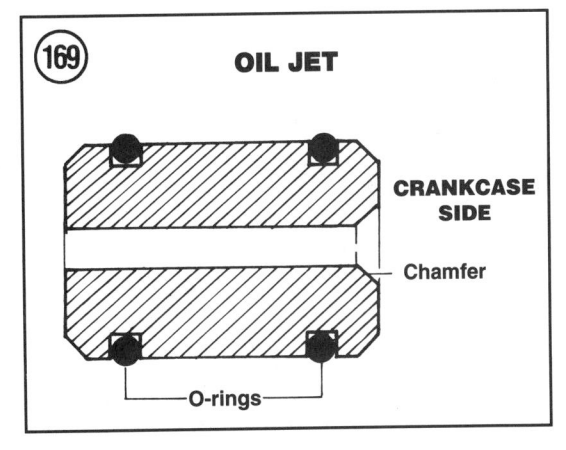

12. Install the assembly bolt through the assembly collar, then screw the assembly bolt onto the threaded adaptor (**Figure 155**).

CAUTION
When applying pressure against the damper spring in Step 6, make sure the assembly collar is centered on the damper cam. If not, loosen the tool and reposition the assembly collar.

13. Hold the assembly bolt, then tighten the assembly collar nut (**Figure 156**) to compress the damper

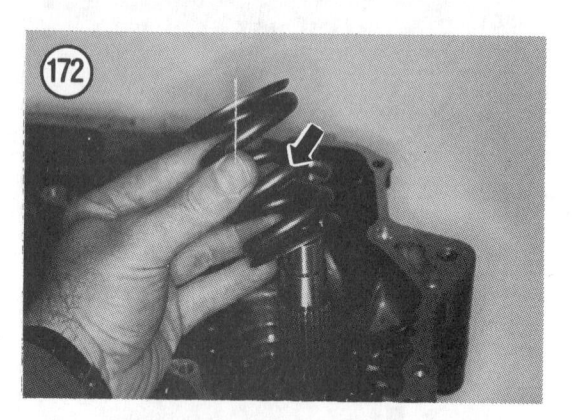

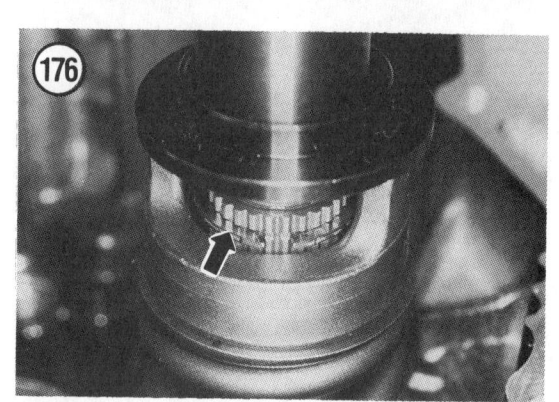

ENGINE BOTTOM END

spring. Continue until the circlip groove (**Figure 175**) on the output drive gear shaft is visible with enough room to install the circlip.

14. Using circlip pliers, install a new circlip into the output drive shaft groove (**Figure 176**). Make sure the circlip seats in the groove completely.
15. Slowly loosen the assembly collar nut (**Figure 156**) and allow the damper spring to unwind and for the damper cam to seat against the circlip.
16. When all tension has been removed from the tool assembly, remove the tool assembly from the engine.
17. Tighten the output gear case mounting bolts (**Figure 177**) to the torque specification in **Table 8**.
18. Install the output gear assembly (**Figure 152**) and assemble the engine as described in this chapter.

ENGINE BREAK-IN

If the rings were replaced, new pistons installed, the cylinders rebored or honed or major lower-end work performed, the engine must be broken in just as though it were new. The performance and service life of the engine depend greatly on a careful and sensible break-in.

For the first 600 miles (1,000 km), do not operate the motorcycle at more than 80% of its maximum speed in any gear. The engine speed must be varied as much as possible within this speed range. Prolonged steady running at one speed, no matter how moderate, must be avoided as well as hard acceleration.

During the break-in period, oil consumption will be higher than normal. It is therefore important to check and correct the oil level frequently. Do not allow the oil level to fall below the bottom line on the dipstick; if the oil level is low, the oil will become overheated resulting in insufficient lubrication and increased engine wear.

After the first 600 miles, change the engine oil and filter as described in Chapter Three.

Table 1 GENERAL ENGINE SPECIFICATIONS

Oil pump type	Trochoid
Engine weight	96.0 kg (212 lb.)

Table 2 STARTER CLUTCH SERVICE SPECIFICATIONS

	New mm (in.)	Service limit mm (in.)
One-way clutch housing inside diameter	–	74.50 (2.933)
Starter driven gear outside diameter	–	57.639 (2.2692)

Table 3 CRANKSHAFT SERVICE SPECIFICATIONS

	New mm (in.)	Service limit mm (in.)
Connecting rod big end side clearance	0.10-0.25 (0.004-0.010)	0.28 (0.011)
Connecting rod small end inside diameter	22.020-22.041 (0.8669-0.8678)	21.051 (0.8681)
Crankpin bearing oil clearance	0.038-0.062 (0.0015-0.0024)	0.070 (0.0028)
Crankshaft runout	–	0.05 (0.002)
Main bearing oil clearance	0.030-0.046 (0.0012-0.0018)	0.060 (0.0024)

Table 4 CONNECTING ROD BEARING SELECTION

	Crankpin journal outer diameter size code letter and dimension	
	Letter A 47.982-47.990 mm (1.8891-1.8894 in.)	**Letter B** 47.974-47.982 mm (1.8887-1.8891 in.)
Connecting rod inner diameter code number and dimension		
Number 1 51.000-51.008 mm (2.0079-2.0082 in.)	Pink	Yellow
Number 2 51.008-51.016 mm (2.0082-2.0085 in.)	Yellow	Green

Table 5 CONNECTING ROD BEARING INSERT THICKNESS

Color	mm	in.
Green	1.495-1.499	0.0589-0.0590
Yellow	1.491-1.495	0.0587-0.0589
Pink	1.487-1.491	0.0585-0.0587

TABLE 6 CONNECTING ROD WEIGHT SELECTION

	\multicolumn{5}{c}{Rear rod code marking}				
Front rod code marking	A	B	C	D	E
A	X	X			
B	X	X	X		
C		X	X	X	
D			X	X	X
E				X	X

Table 7 OUTPUT DRIVE TRAIN SERVICE SPECIFICATIONS

	New mm (in.)	Service limit mm (in.)
Backlash difference between measurements	–	0.10 (0.004)
Output gear inside diameter	25.000-25.021 (0.9843-0.9851)	25.031 (0.9855)
Output gear bushing		
Outside diameter	24.959-24.980 (0.9826-0.9835)	24.949 (0.9822)
Inside diameter	22.020-22.041 (0.8669-0.8678)	22.051 (0.8681)
Output drive gear shaft diameter	21.979-22.000 (0.8653-0.8661)	21.969 (0.8649)

(continued)

ENGINE BOTTOM END

Table 7 OUTPUT DRIVE TRAIN SERVICE SPECIFICATIONS (continued)

	New mm (in.)	Service limit mm (in.)
Gear-to-bushing clearance	0.020-0.062 (0.0008-0.0024)	0.082 (0.0032)
Gear bushing-to-shaft clearance	0.020-0.062 (0.0008-0.062)	0.082 (0.0032)
Output gear damper spring free length	69.3 (2.73)	68.1 (2.68)
Output drive gear backlash	0.08-0.23 (0.003-0.009)	0.40 (0.016)

Table 8 ENGINE LOWER END TIGHTENING TORQUES

	N•m	in.-lb.	ft.-lb.
Connecting rod bearing cap nut	60	—	44
Flywheel bolt	140	—	103
Footpeg mounting bolts	27	—	20
Front footpeg bracket bolts	27	—	20
Gearshift lever pinch bolt	23	—	17
Left crankcase rear cover mounting nut	12	106	—
Left side crankcase bolts			
6 mm	12	106	—
8 mm	27	—	20
Oil orifice bolt	10	88	—
Oil pressure switch	12	106	—
Oil pump assembly bolt	13	115	—
Oil pump driven sprocket bolt	18	—	13
Output drive/driven gear bearing locknut			
Inner	75	—	55
Outer	100	—	74
Output gear case mounting bolt	32	—	23
Output drive gear bearing holder bolt	32	—	23
Output driven gear bearing holder bolt	32	—	23
Output drive gear shaft bolt (@ right crankcase)	50	—	37
Right crankcase bearing setting plate			
Screw	9	80	—
Bolt	12	106	—
Right side crankcase bolts			
6 mm	12	106	—
8 mm	27	—	20
10 mm	40	—	29
Starter clutch Torx bolts	23	—	17

Table 9 ENGINE MOUNT TIGHTENING TORQUES

	N•m	in.-lb.	ft.-lb.
Cylinder head cover shroud bolts	12	106	—
Front lower engine mount nut	40	—	29
Front upper engine mount bolt	27	—	20
Muffler bracket			
At engine attaching bolt	27	—	20
Stay bolt	35	—	25
Rear lower engine mount nut	55	—	40
Rear upper engine mount nut	55	—	40
Sub-frame bolts			
Front	65	—	47
Left side	27	—	20
Rear	40	—	29

CHAPTER SIX

CLUTCH AND EXTERNAL SHIFT MECHANISM

This chapter describes service procedures for the following subassemblies mounted on the right side of the engine:

   a. Clutch cover.
   b. Clutch.
   c. Right crankcase cover.
   d. Primary drive gear.
   e. Gearshift linkage.
   f. Oil pump.
   g. Clutch cable.

You can remove these subassemblies with the engine mounted in the frame. **Table 1** lists clutch service specifications. **Tables 1-3** are found at the end of the chapter.

CLUTCH

All clutch components, except the clutch outer housing, can be removed by simply removing the clutch cover from the right crankcase cover. This section describes removal of the clutch cover and clutch.

Clutch Cover
Removal/Installation

1. Drain the engine oil (Chapter Three).
2. Remove the exhaust system (Chapter Fourteen).
3. Remove the bolts that hold the clutch cover (**Figure 1**) to the right crankcase cover, then remove the clutch cover.
4. Remove the 2 dowel pins (**Figure 2**) and gasket.

CLUTCH AND EXTERNAL SHIFT MECHANISM

5. Reverse these steps to install the clutch cover, plus the following.

6. Install a new clutch cover gasket.

7. Tighten the clutch cover mounting bolts to the torque specification in **Table 3**.

8. Refill the engine with oil (Chapter Three).

9. Check and adjust the clutch (Chapter Three).

10. Start the engine and check the cover for oil leaks.

Clutch Removal

Refer to **Figure 3**.

1. Remove the clutch cover as described in this chapter.

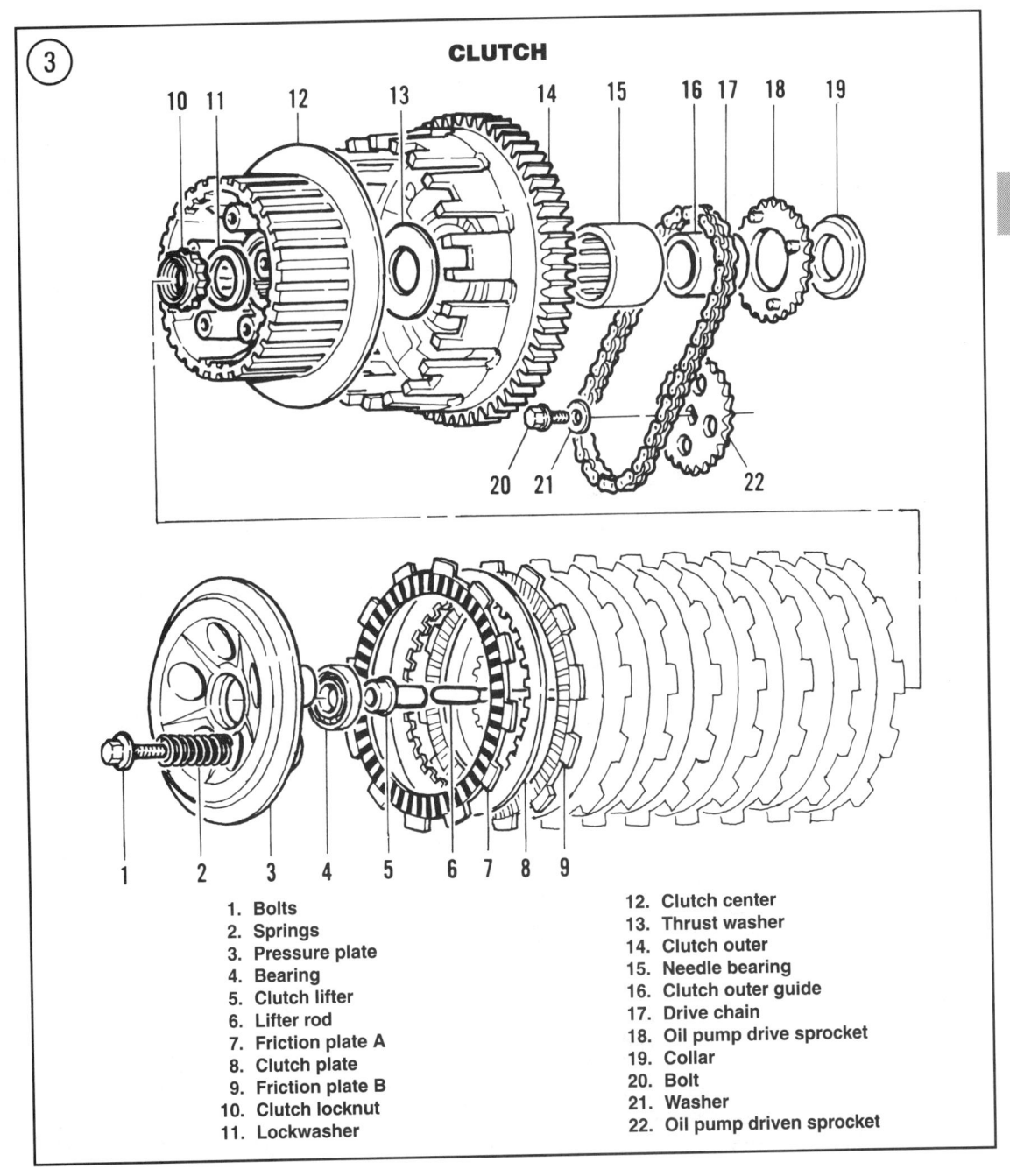

CLUTCH

1. Bolts
2. Springs
3. Pressure plate
4. Bearing
5. Clutch lifter
6. Lifter rod
7. Friction plate A
8. Clutch plate
9. Friction plate B
10. Clutch locknut
11. Lockwasher
12. Clutch center
13. Thrust washer
14. Clutch outer
15. Needle bearing
16. Clutch outer guide
17. Drive chain
18. Oil pump drive sprocket
19. Collar
20. Bolt
21. Washer
22. Oil pump driven sprocket

2. Loosen the pressure plate bolts (**Figure 4**) 1/4 turn at a time in a crisscross pattern. Then remove the bolts (**Figure 4**) and springs.

3. Remove the pressure plate (**Figure 5**) and its bearing.

4. Remove the clutch lifter (A, **Figure 6**) and the lifter rod (B, **Figure 6**).

5. Remove the clutch plates.

CAUTION
Do not loosen the clutch locknut until you unstake it from the mainshaft; otherwise, the nut may damage the mainshaft threads.

6. Unstake the clutch center locknut (**Figure 7**) from the groove in the mainshaft.

7. Hold the clutch center with a clutch holding tool (**Figure 8**), then loosen and remove the clutch locknut and lockwasher (**Figure 9**).

8. Remove the clutch center (**Figure 10**) and thrust washer (**Figure 11**).

9. To remove the clutch outer (**Figure 12**), refer to *Clutch Outer* in this chapter.

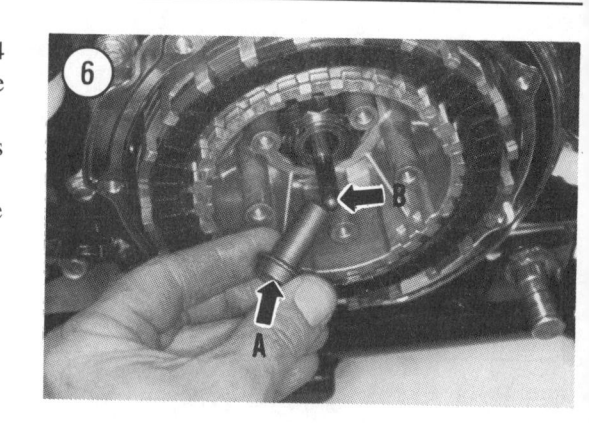

CLUTCH AND EXTERNAL SHIFT MECHANISM

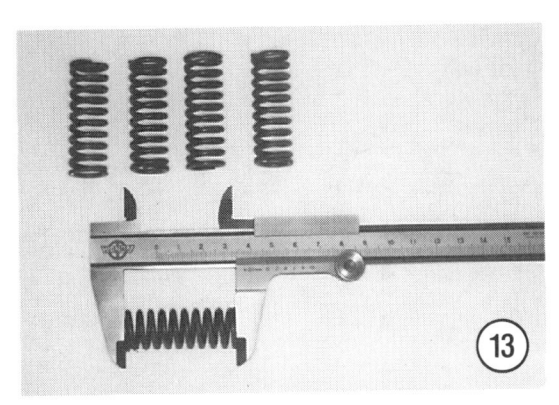

Inspection

When measuring the clutch components in this section, compare the actual measurements to the new and service limit specifications in **Table 1**. Replace parts that are out of specification or show signs of visible damage.

1. Clean and dry all parts.
2. Measure the free length of each clutch spring (**Figure 13**) with a vernier caliper. Replace the springs as a set if any one spring is too short.

NOTE
*A total of 9 friction plates are used. The first and last friction plates (plate A) are black and have a larger inside diameter (A, **Figure 14**) than the remaining 7 friction plates (plate B [B, **Figure 14**]) used in the clutch. These 7 inside friction plates are brown. The thicknesses of the A and B friction plates are the same.*

3. Measure the thickness of each friction plate at several places around the plate (**Figure 15**). Replace

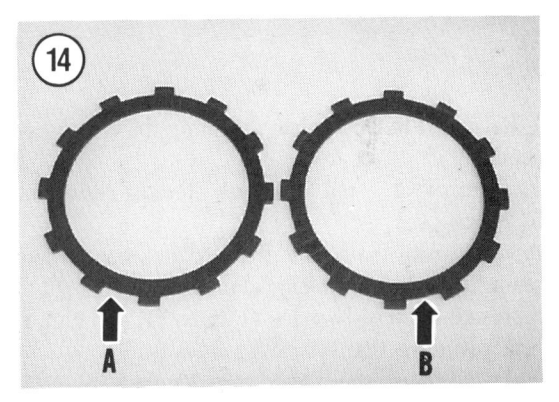

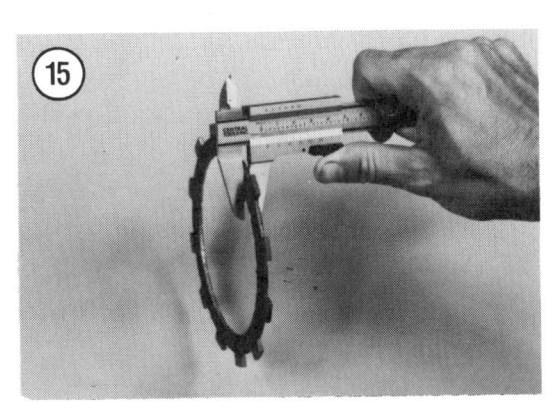

the friction plates as a set if any one plate is too thin or damaged. Do not replace only one or two plates.

4. Place each clutch plate (metal plates) on a surface plate or a thick piece of glass. Then measure warpage with a feeler gauge (**Figure 16**). Replace all of the clutch plates as a set if any one plate is warped more than specified. Do not replace only one or two plates.

5. The clutch plate inner teeth mesh with the clutch center splines (A, **Figure 17**). Check the splines for cracks or galling. If the clutch center splines are worn, check the clutch plate teeth for wear or damage.

6. Check the clutch center spring towers (B, **Figure 17**) for cracks or thread damage.

7. Inspect the clutch center shaft splines (C, **Figure 17**) for scoring or other damage.

8. Check the pressure plate (**Figure 18**) for warpage, cracked spring towers or other damage. Replace if you find any damage or excessive wear.

9. Replace the pressure plate bearing (**Figure 18**) if it turns roughly or is damaged.

10. Inspect the clutch lifter and lifter rod (**Figure 19**) and replace if damaged.

11. Inspect the clutch outer (**Figure 12**) as described under *Clutch Outer* in this chapter.

Assembly

Refer to **Figure 3** when installing the clutch assembly.

1. If removed, install the clutch outer as described in this chapter.
2. Coat all of the clutch plates, clutch center and mainshaft splines with engine oil.
3. Install the thrust washer (**Figure 11**) and clutch center (**Figure 10**).
4. Install the washer (A, **Figure 20**) with its *OUT* mark facing out. See **Figure 9**.

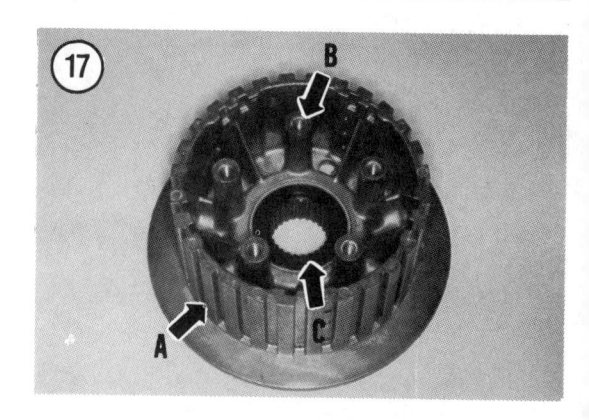

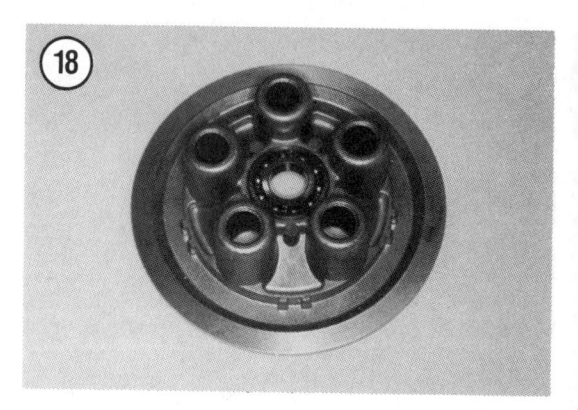

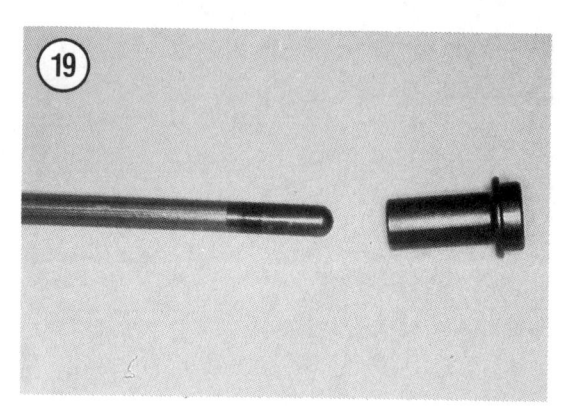

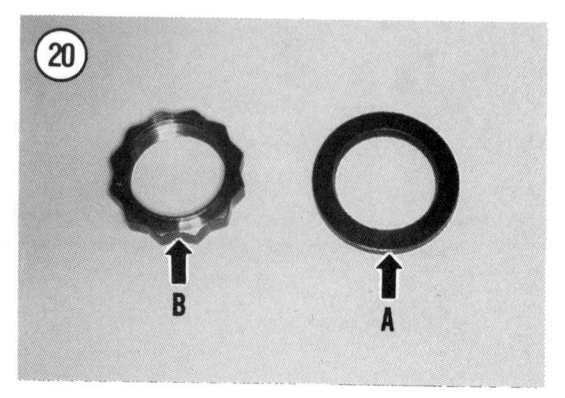

CLUTCH AND EXTERNAL SHIFT MECHANISM

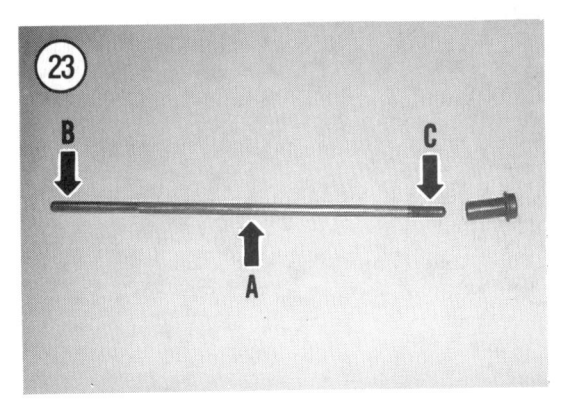

5. Lubricate the threads of a new clutch locknut (B, **Figure 20**) and install it onto the mainshaft. See **Figure 9**.
6. Hold the clutch center with the same tool used during disassembly, then tighten the clutch locknut to the torque specification in **Table 3**.
7. Using a punch, stake the clutch locknut into the mainshaft groove (**Figure 7**).
8. Install the clutch plates (**Figure 21**) as follows:

NOTE
A total of 9 friction plates are used. The first and last friction plates (plate A) are black in color and have a larger inside diameter (A, Figure 14) than the remaining 7 friction plates (plate B [B, Figure 14]) used in the clutch. The 7 inside friction plates are brown. The thicknesses of the A and B friction plates are the same.

   a. Install the first friction plate A.
   b. Install the clutch plates and the 7 inner friction plates (plate B), alternating between steel and friction plates.
   c. Install the outer friction plate A by aligning its plate tabs with the grooves in the clutch outer (**Figure 22**).

9. The lifter rod (A, **Figure 23**) has one long (B, **Figure 23**) and one short (C, **Figure 23**) end. Install the lifter rod so its short end (**Figure 6**) faces out of the engine.
10. Lubricate the clutch lifter with engine oil and install it over the lifter rod. See A, **Figure 6**.
11. Install the pressure plate and its bearing (**Figure 5**). Make sure the clutch lifter seats in the pressure plate bearing as shown in **Figure 24**.
12. Install the clutch springs and bolts (**Figure 25**). Tighten the bolts in a crisscross pattern in 2-3 steps to the torque specification in **Table 3**.

13. Install the clutch cover as described in this chapter.

RIGHT CRANKCASE COVER

Removal/Installation

1. Remove the subframe (Chapter Five).
2. Remove the clutch cover as described in this chapter.
3. Before removing the right crankcase cover mounting bolts, draw an outline of the cover on a piece of cardboard (**Figure 26**). Then punch holes along the outline for the placement of each mounting bolt.
4. Remove the right crankcase cover mounting bolts and place them in the corresponding holes in the cardboard (**Figure 26**).
5. Remove the right crankcase cover (**Figure 27**).
6. Remove the 2 dowel pins (A, **Figure 28**) and gasket.
7. Remove all gasket residue from the crankcase and crankcase mating surfaces.
8. Install the right crankcase cover by reversing these removal steps, while noting the following.
9. Install the 2 dowel pins (A, **Figure 28**) and a new gasket.
10. Install the right crankcase cover (**Figure 27**) and secure it with its mounting bolts. Install and tighten the mounting bolts securely.
11. Start the engine and check for oil leaks.

CLUTCH OUTER

Refer to **Figure 29** when servicing the clutch outer in this section.

Removal

1. Remove the clutch as described in this chapter.
2. Remove the right crankcase cover as described in this chapter.
3. Install, but do not tighten, a 6 × 20 mm Allen bolt into the primary drive gear as shown in **Figure 30**.
4. Insert a wide-blade screwdriver (**Figure 31**) between the clutch outer and primary drive gear teeth.
5. Pry the scissors gear (subgear teeth) to align it with the primary drive gear, then tighten the Allen bolt (**Figure 31**) to hold the gear in alignment.

6. Turn the primary drive gear to move all of the ignition pulse generator rotor tips (A, **Figure 32**) away from the clutch outer gear teeth (B, **Figure 32**).
7. Remove the clutch outer (**Figure 33**).
8. Remove the needle bearing (**Figure 34**) and the clutch outer guide (**Figure 35**).

Inspection

1. Clean and dry all parts.
2. Check the clutch outer for chipped or excessively worn gear teeth (A, **Figure 36**).

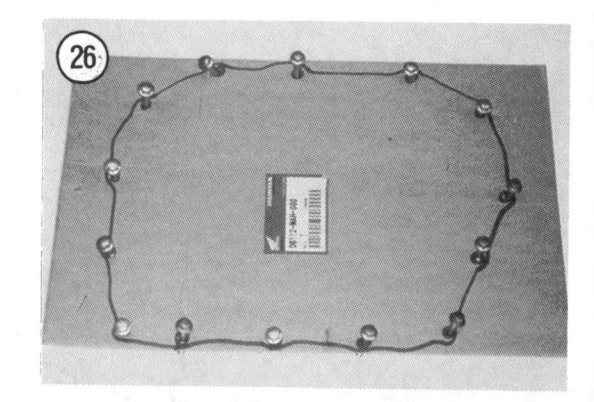

CLUTCH AND EXTERNAL SHIFT MECHANISM

29

CLUTCH OUTER ASSEMBLY

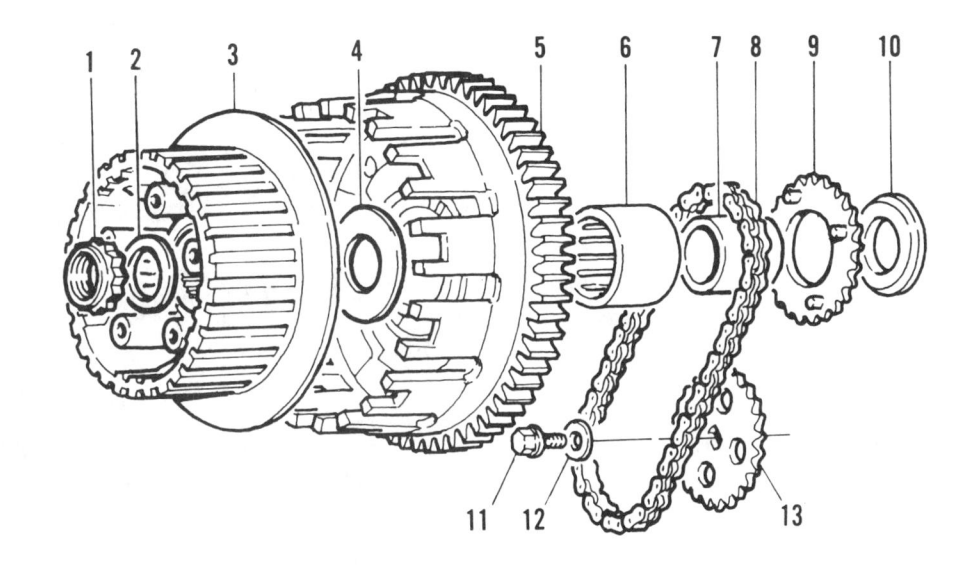

1. Clutch locknut
2. Lockwasher
3. Clutch center
4. Thrust washer
5. Clutch outer
6. Needle bearing
7. Clutch outer guide
8. Drive chain
9. Oil pump drive sprocket
10. Collar
11. Bolt
12. Washer
13. Oil pump driven sprocket

3. Check the clutch outer bore (B, **Figure 36**) for cracks, deep scoring, excessive wear or heat discoloration.
4. Check the clutch outer slots (C, **Figure 36**) for grooves or other damage caused by the friction plate tabs. Repair minor damage with a fine-cut file.
5. Check the holes in the back of the clutch outer (**Figure 37**) for cracks or damage. If these holes are damaged, check the oil pump drive gear pins for damage.
6. Check the needle bearing (A, **Figure 38**) for damage.
7. Check the clutch outer guide (B, **Figure 38**) for excessive wear, cracks or other damage. Then measure the clutch outer guide's inside diameter and check against the dimension in **Table 1**. Replace if out of specification.
8. Measure the mainshaft outside diameter (**Figure 39**) and check against the dimension in **Table 1**. If out of specification, replace the mainshaft.

Installation

Use a 50:50 molybdenum grease and engine oil solution when oil is called for in the following steps.
1. Lubricate the clutch outer guide outside diameter (B, **Figure 38**) with oil.
2. Install the clutch outer guide over the mainshaft and slide it into the oil pump drive sprocket (**Figure 35**).
3. Install the needle bearing (**Figure 34**) over the clutch outer guide.
4. If the crankshaft was turned over after the clutch outer was removed, reposition the primary drive gear sprocket as described under the *Removal* procedure.
5. Lubricate the clutch outer bore with oil.

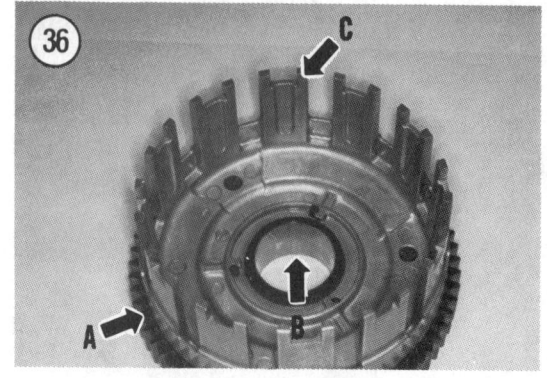

CLUTCH AND EXTERNAL SHIFT MECHANISM

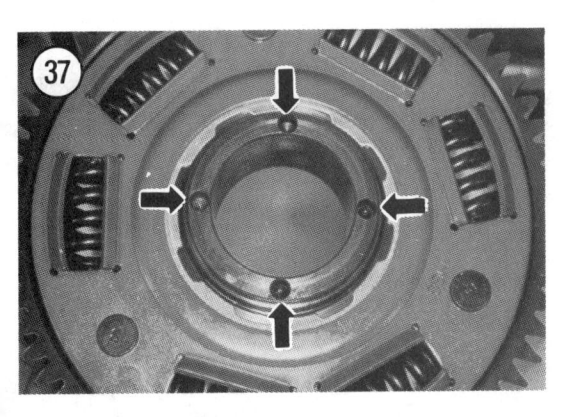

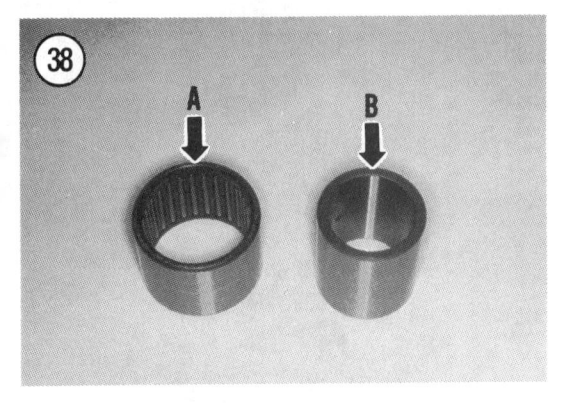

6. Align the 4 holes in the clutch outer (**Figure 37**) with the 4 pins on the oil pump drive sprocket (**Figure 40**) and install the clutch outer. See **Figure 33**.
7. Check that the clutch outer gear teeth are flush with the scissors gear as shown in **Figure 41**. If the gear teeth are not flush, remove the clutch outer and reinstall it.
8. Remove the Allen bolt (**Figure 30**) installed in the primary drive gear. This will release the scissors gear and allow it to turn and apply pressure against the clutch outer gear teeth.
9. Install the right crankcase cover as described in this chapter.
10. Install the clutch as described in this chapter.

PRIMARY DRIVE GEAR

Removal

1. Remove the clutch as described in this chapter.
2. Remove the right crankcase cover as described in this chapter.
3. Install, but do not tighten, a 6 × 20 mm Allen bolt into the primary drive gear as shown in **Figure 30**.
4. Insert a wide-blade screwdriver (**Figure 31**) between the clutch outer and primary drive gear teeth.
5. Pry the scissors gear (subgear teeth) to align it with the primary drive gear, then tighten the Allen bolt (**Figure 31**) to hold the gear in alignment.
6. Lock the clutch and primary gears together with a separate gear (**Figure 42**) or use the Honda gear holder (part No. 07724-0010100). Then loosen the primary drive gear bolt (**Figure 32**).
7. Remove the bolt and washer (**Figure 43**).

8. Remove the ignition pulse generator rotor (**Figure 44**).
9. Remove the primary drive gear assembly (**Figure 45**).
10. Remove the Allen bolt (installed in Step 3) and remove the scissors gear (A, **Figure 46**) from the primary drive gear (B, **Figure 46**).

Inspection

1. Clean and dry all parts.
2. Inspect the scissors gear (A, **Figure 46**) for:
   a. Missing, broken or chipped teeth.
   b. Damaged arms.
3. Inspect the primary drive gear (B, **Figure 46**) for:
   a. Missing, broken or chipped teeth.
   b. Worn or damaged splines.
   c. Weak, damaged or missing springs.
4. Inspect the ignition pulse generator rotor (**Figure 47**) for:
   a. Damaged splines.
   b. Damaged rotor tips.
5. Replace excessively worn or damaged parts.

Installation

1. If removed, install the springs into the primary drive gear grooves (B, **Figure 46**).
2. Align the hole in the scissors gear (C, **Figure 46**) with the threaded hole in the primary drive gear (D, **Figure 46**) and install the scissors gear into the primary drive gear. Align the gear teeth with a screwdriver, then install and tighten the Allen bolt (B, **Figure 48**).
3. Install the primary drive gear (**Figure 45**) by aligning the wide gear groove with the wide crankshaft tooth (**Figure 49**).

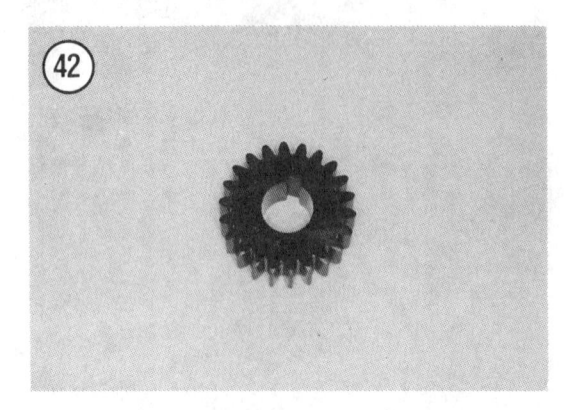

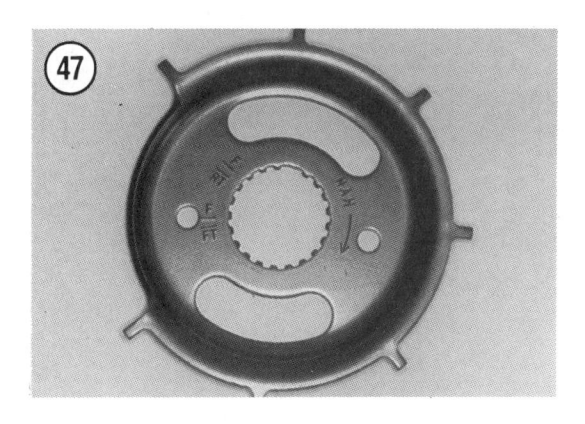

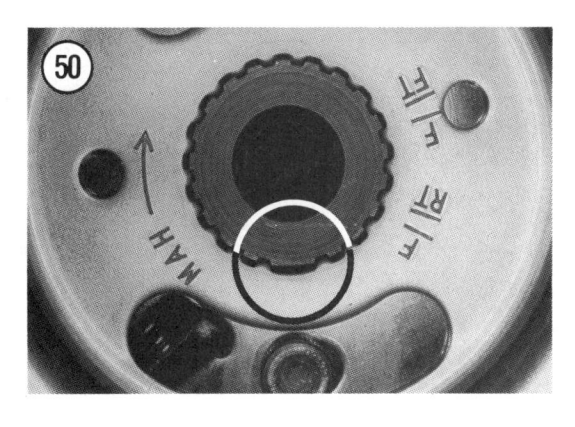

CLUTCH AND EXTERNAL SHIFT MECHANISM

4. Install the ignition pulse generator rotor (**Figure 44**) by aligning the wide gear groove with the wide crankshaft tooth (**Figure 50**).

5. Install the primary drive gear bolt and washer (**Figure 43**) and tighten hand-tight. Make sure the clutch outer gear teeth are flush with the scissors gear as shown in **Figure 41**.

6. Use the same tool to hold the clutch and primary drive gears and tighten the primary drive gear bolt to the torque specification in **Table 3**.

7. Remove the Allen bolt (**Figure 30**) installed in the primary drive gear. This will release the scissors gear and allow it to turn and apply pressure against the clutch outer gear teeth.

8. Install the right crankcase cover as described in this chapter.

9. Install the clutch as described in this chapter.

EXTERNAL SHIFT MECHANISM

Refer to **Figure 51** when servicing the external shift mechanism in this section.

Removal

1. Shift the transmission into NEUTRAL.
2. Remove the clutch as described in this chapter.

Figure 51 — EXTERNAL SHIFT MECHANISM

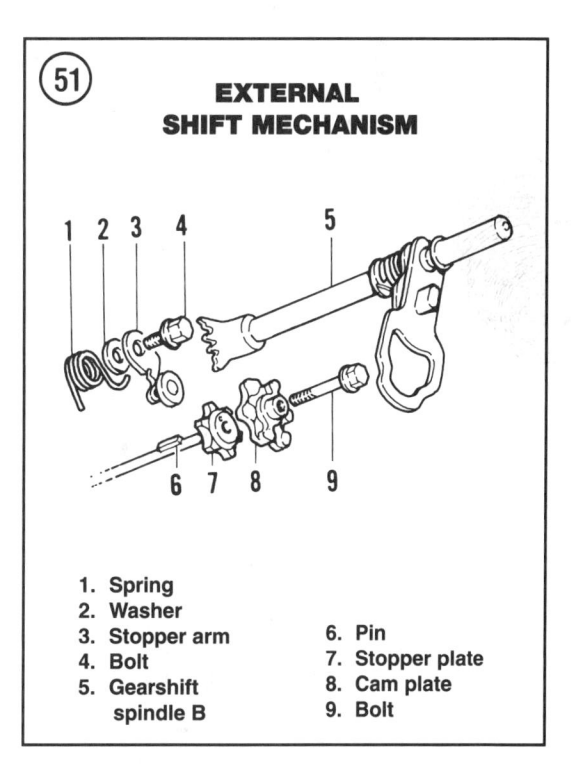

1. Spring
2. Washer
3. Stopper arm
4. Bolt
5. Gearshift spindle B
6. Pin
7. Stopper plate
8. Cam plate
9. Bolt

3. Remove the right crankcase cover as described in this chapter.

4. Remove the oil pipe (**Figure 52**) and both O-rings. Discard the O-rings as new ones must be installed.

5. Loosen the bolt and washer (**Figure 53**) securing the oil pump driven sprocket to the oil pump.

6. Remove the clutch center as described in this chapter.

7. Remove the bolt and washer (**Figure 53**) loosened in Step 5.

8. Remove the oil pump sprockets and chain (**Figure 54**) as a set.

9. Remove the distance collar (**Figure 55**) from the mainshaft.

10. Remove the gearshift spindle B (**Figure 56**) from the crankcase.

11. Remove the bolt, washer, return spring and the shift drum stopper arm (A, **Figure 57**).

12. Remove the bolt, cam plate, dowel pin, stopper plate and dowel pin (B, **Figure 57**).

13. To remove the gearshift spindle A installed on the left side of the engine, refer to *Starter Driven Gear and Starter Clutch* in Chapter Five.

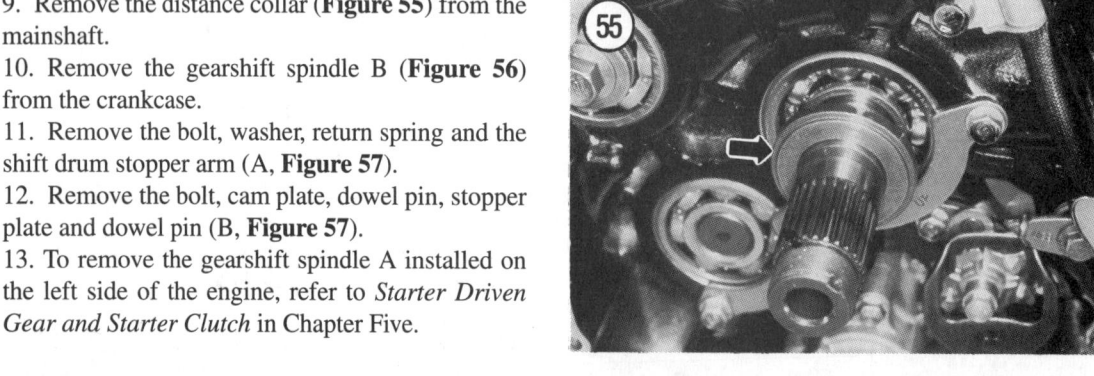

CLUTCH AND EXTERNAL SHIFT MECHANISM

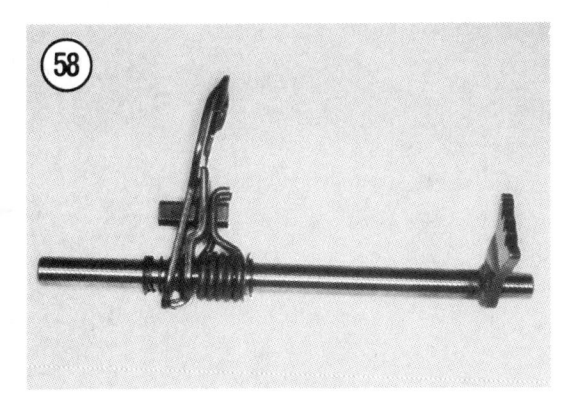

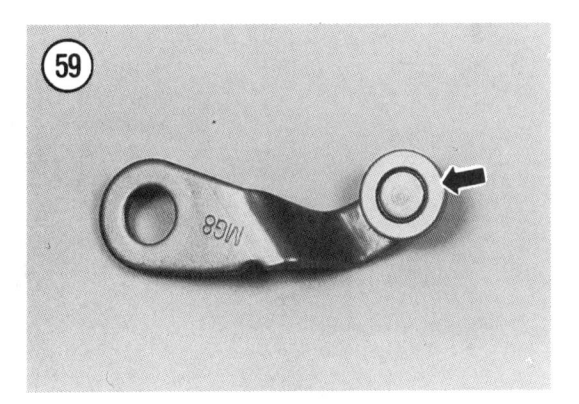

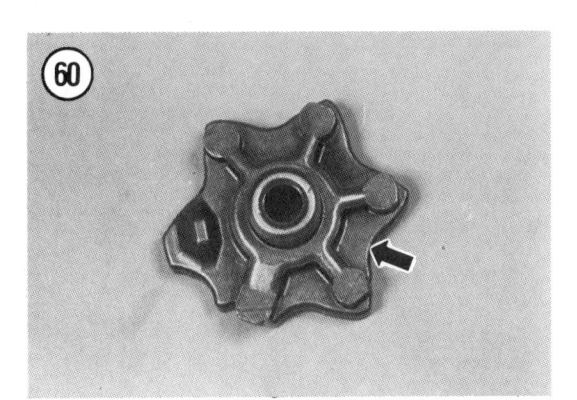

Inspection

1. Clean and dry all parts.
2. Inspect the gearshift spindle B (**Figure 58**) for bending, excessive wear and damage.
3. Inspect the shift drum stopper arm assembly (**Figure 59**) for excessive wear and damage.
4. Inspect the cam plate and stopper plate detents (**Figure 60**) for excessive wear and damage.

Installation

1. Assemble the spring, washer, stopper arm and bolt as shown in **Figure 51**, then install the assembly into the crankcase (**Figure 61**). Tighten the stopper arm mounting bolt to the torque specification in **Table 3**.
2. Install the dowel pin (**Figure 62**) into the shift drum hole.
3. Align the hole in the stopper plate with the dowel pin and install the stopper plate (A, **Figure 63**).
4. Install the dowel pin (B, **Figure 63**) into the stopper plate hole.
5. Align the hole in the cam plate with the dowel pin (**Figure 64**) and install the cam plate (B, **Figure 57**).

6. Apply a medium strength threadlocking compound onto the cam plate mounting bolt threads, then install and tighten the bolt (B, **Figure 57**) securely.
7. Make sure the transmission is shifted into NEUTRAL as shown in **Figure 65**.
8. Install the gearshift spindle B (**Figure 56**) and mesh it with the gearshift spindle A while centering the return spring around the crankcase pin. See **Figure 66** and **Figure 67**.

NOTE
*For additional information on meshing the gearshift spindle A with gearshift spindle B, refer to **Starter Driven Gear and Starter Clutch** in Chapter Five. **Figure 68** shows how the gear teeth must mesh together.*

9. Install the distance collar—shoulder side facing out—over the mainshaft. See **Figure 55**.
10. Mesh the oil pump drive and driven sprockets with the drive chain (**Figure 69**), then install them as an assembly (**Figure 54**). The long pins on the drive sprocket must face out (**Figure 54**). Install the drive sprocket against the distance collar and align the flat surfaces of the driven sprocket hole with the oil pump shaft.
11. Apply a medium strength threadlocking compound onto the oil pump sprocket bolt, then install the bolt and washer (**Figure 53**) and tighten finger-tight at this time.
12. Install the clutch center as described in this chapter.
13. Tighten the oil pump sprocket bolt (**Figure 53**) securely.
14. Coat the 2 new O-rings (**Figure 70**) with engine oil and install them onto the oil pipe.

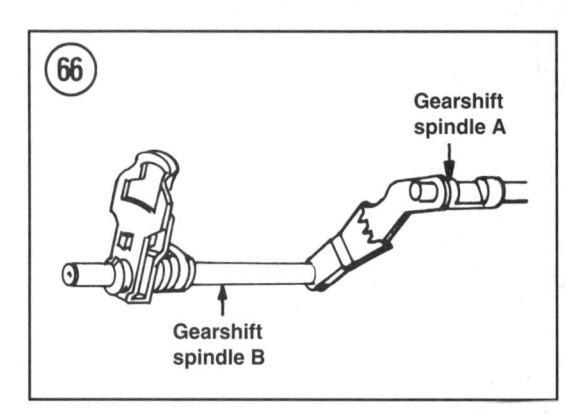

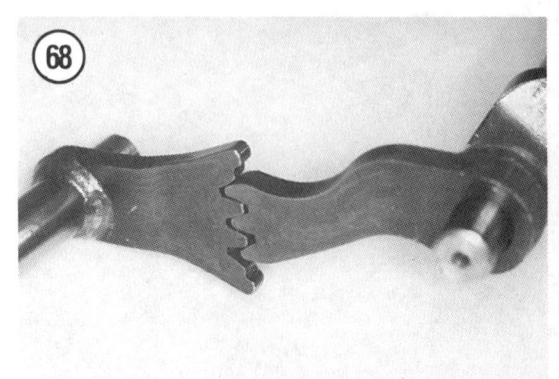

CLUTCH AND EXTERNAL SHIFT MECHANISM

15. Install the oil pipe (**Figure 52**) into the crankcase.
16. Install the right crankcase cover as described in this chapter.
17. Install the clutch as described in this chapter.

OIL PUMP

Removal

Refer to **Figure 71** when removing the oil pump.

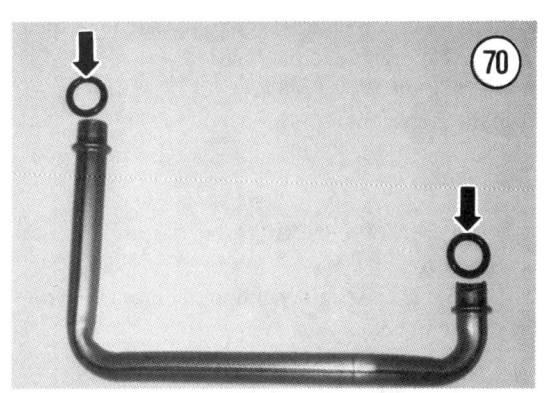

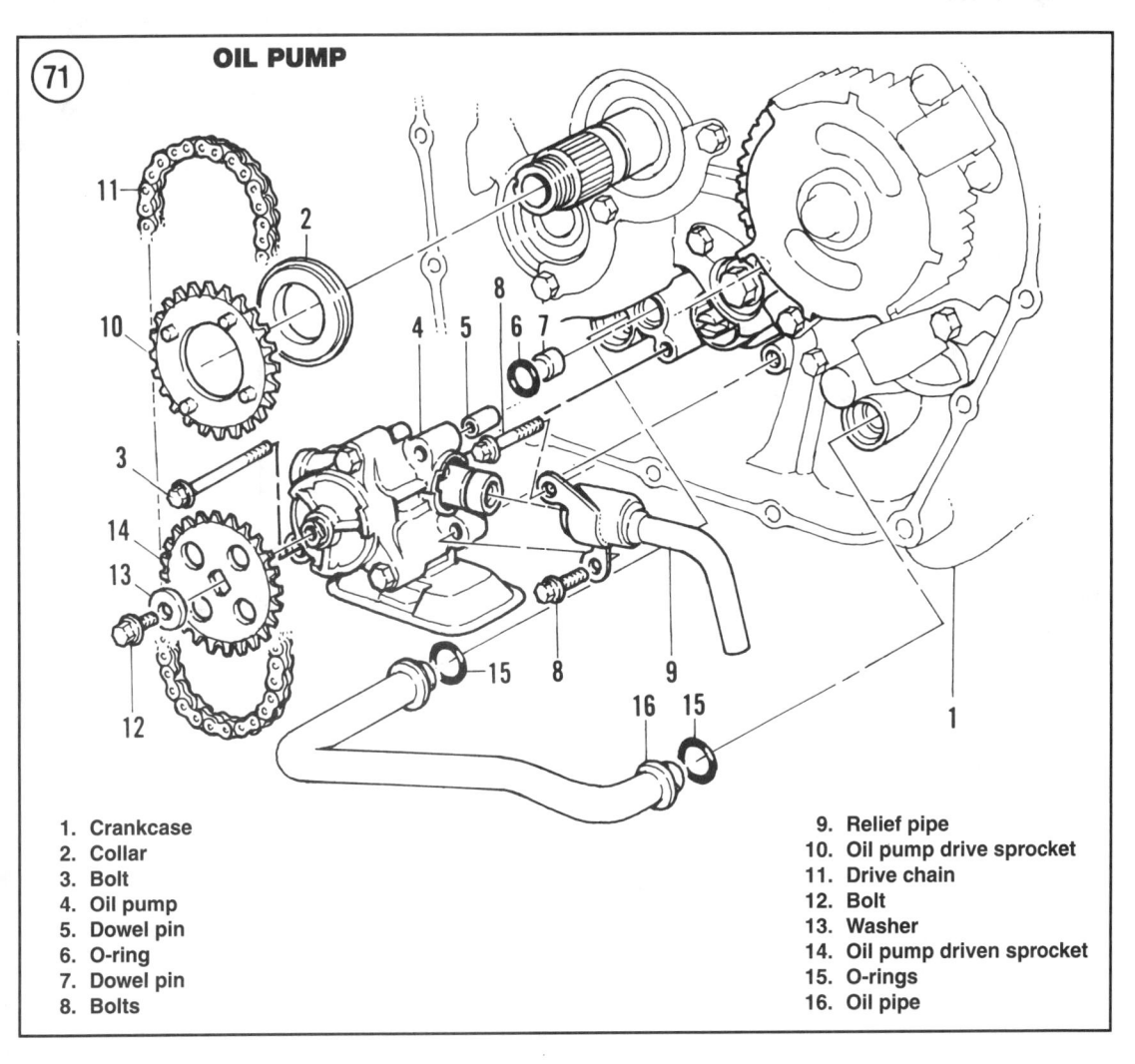

OIL PUMP

1. Crankcase
2. Collar
3. Bolt
4. Oil pump
5. Dowel pin
6. O-ring
7. Dowel pin
8. Bolts
9. Relief pipe
10. Oil pump drive sprocket
11. Drive chain
12. Bolt
13. Washer
14. Oil pump driven sprocket
15. O-rings
16. Oil pipe

1. Remove the external shift mechanism as described in this chapter.
2. Remove the 3 oil pump mounting bolts (A, **Figure 72**).
3. Remove the relief pipe (B, **Figure 72**) from the oil pump.
4. Remove the oil pump (**Figure 73**) and relief pipe (**Figure 74**) from the crankcase.
5. Remove the dowel pins and O-ring (**Figure 75**) from the crankcase.

Disassembly

1. Pull the relief valve (**Figure 76**) out of the oil pump.
2. Remove the oil strainer and seal (**Figure 77**) from the oil pump body.
3. Remove the 2 bolts (**Figure 78**) and disassemble the oil pump assembly. See **Figure 79**.

Inspection

When measuring the oil pump components in this section, compare the actual measurements to the new and service limit specifications in **Table 2**. If any measurement is out of specification, or if any component shows visual damage, the entire oil pump

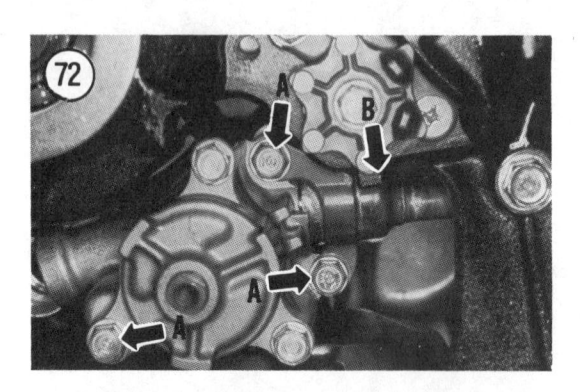

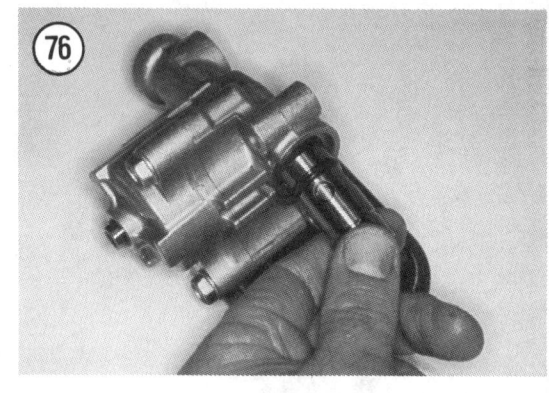

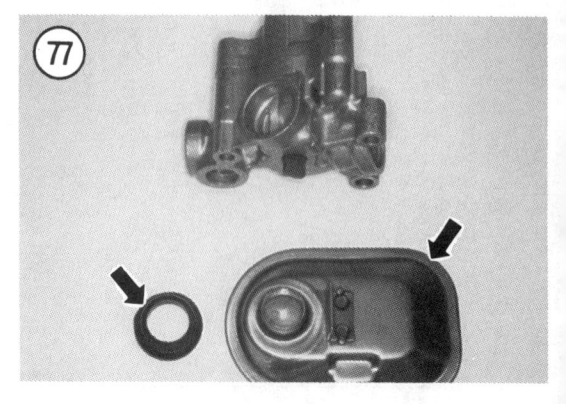

CLUTCH AND EXTERNAL SHIFT MECHANISM

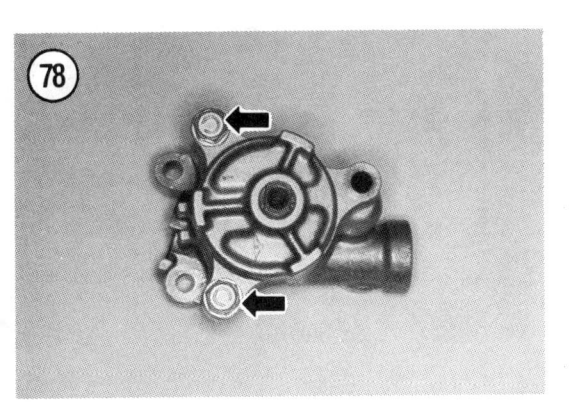

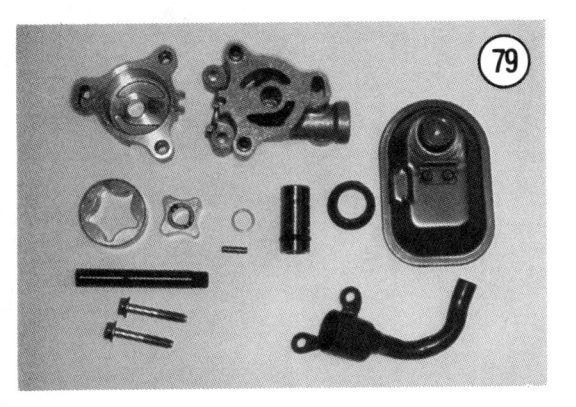

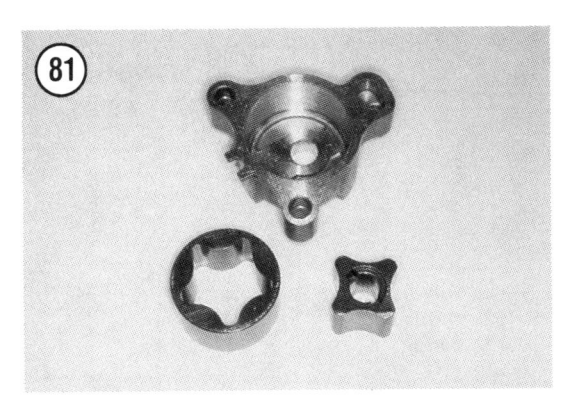

assembly must be replaced. Replacement parts are not available for the oil pump.
1. Clean and dry all parts.
2. Inspect the outer cover and body (**Figure 80**) for cracks.
3. Check the inner and outer rotors and the body (**Figure 81**) for deep scratches and wear.
4. Inspect the strainer screen (**Figure 82**) for broken areas. Replace if damaged.
5. Inspect the shaft, pin and shim (**Figure 83**) for cracks or other damage.
6. Inspect the relief pipe (**Figure 84**) and replace if damaged.
7. Install the outer rotor into the pump body with its dot mark (A, **Figure 85**) facing out.
8. Install the inner rotor into the pump body with its pin groove (B, **Figure 85**) facing out.
9. Measure the rotor end clearance with a straightedge and flat feeler gauge (**Figure 86**).
10. Install the pin into the shaft and install the shaft and pin into the inner rotor.
11. Measure the clearance between the inner tip and outer rotor with a flat feeler gauge (**Figure 87**).
12. Measure the clearance between the outer rotor and body with a flat feeler gauge (**Figure 88**).
13. Inspect the oil pressure relief valve as described in this section.

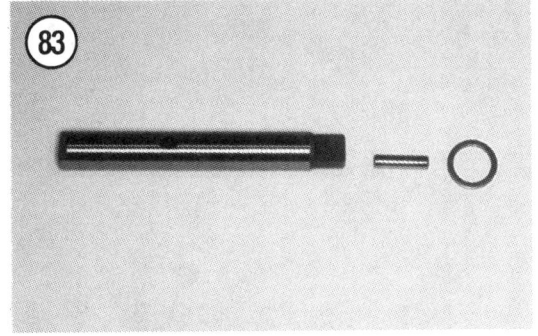

Oil Pressure Relief Valve Inspection

Refer to **Figure 89** for this procedure.
1. Remove the circlip and disassemble the oil pressure relief valve assembly.
2. Remove and discard the O-ring (**Figure 90**).
3. Clean and dry all parts.
4. Inspect the valve bore and piston outside diameter for scratches or wear. Replace if damaged.
5. Inspect the spring for cracks, distortion or other damage. Replace the spring if any damage is noted.
6. Make sure the holes in the valve body are not clogged.
7. Install the piston, spring, washer and circlip. Make sure the circlip seats in the groove completely.
8. Install a new O-ring (**Figure 90**) into the valve body groove.

Assembly

1. Lubricate the rotors, shaft and shim with engine oil, then place the parts on a clean, lint-free cloth until reassembly.
2. Install the outer rotor into the pump body with its dot mark (A, **Figure 85**) facing out.
3. Install the inner rotor into the pump body with its pin groove (B, **Figure 85**) facing out.

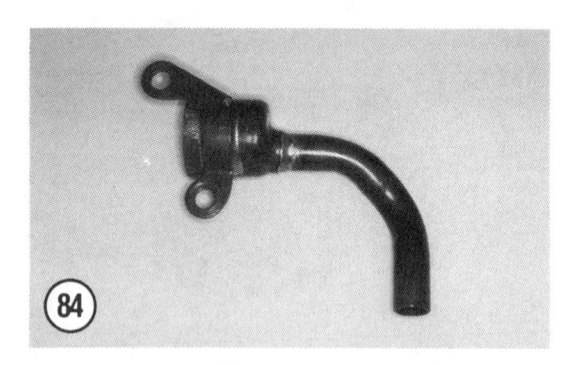

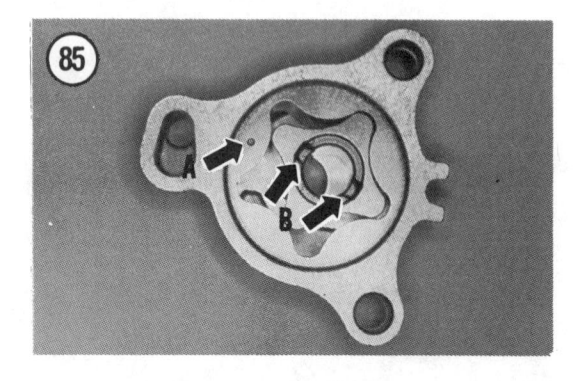

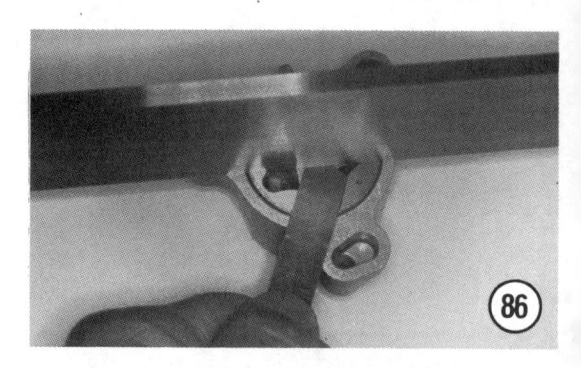

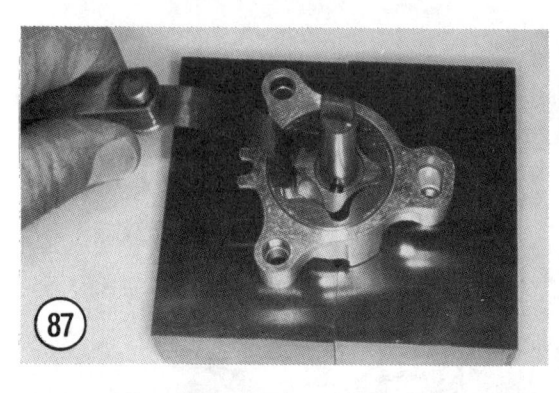

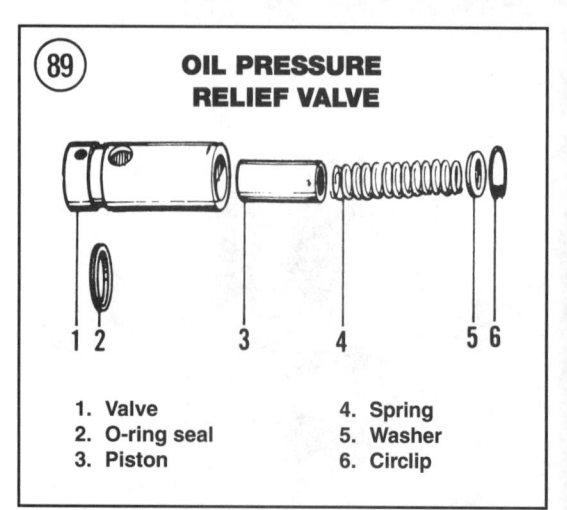

OIL PRESSURE RELIEF VALVE

1. Valve
2. O-ring seal
3. Piston
4. Spring
5. Washer
6. Circlip

CLUTCH AND EXTERNAL SHIFT MECHANISM

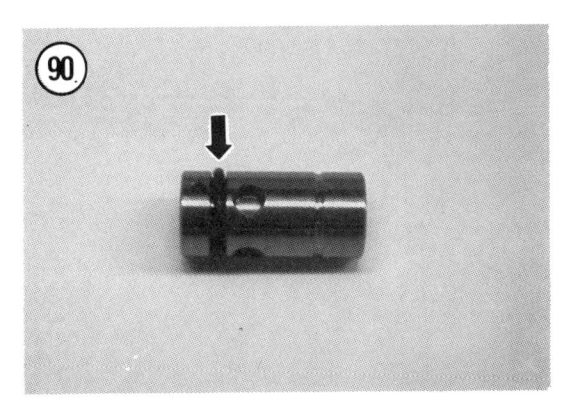

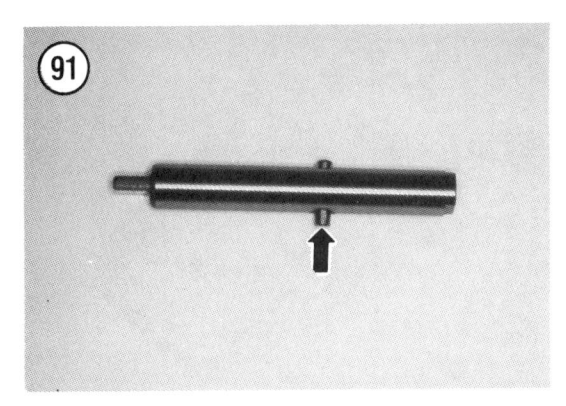

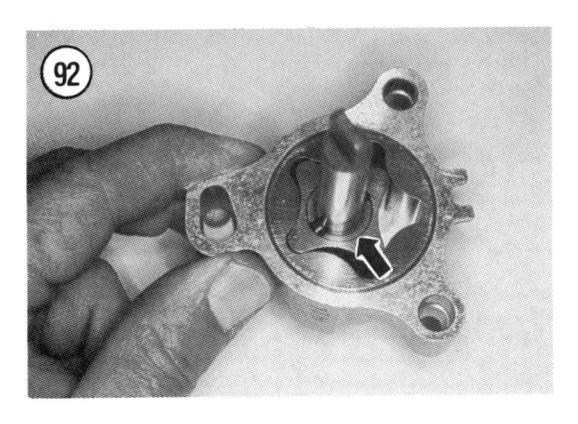

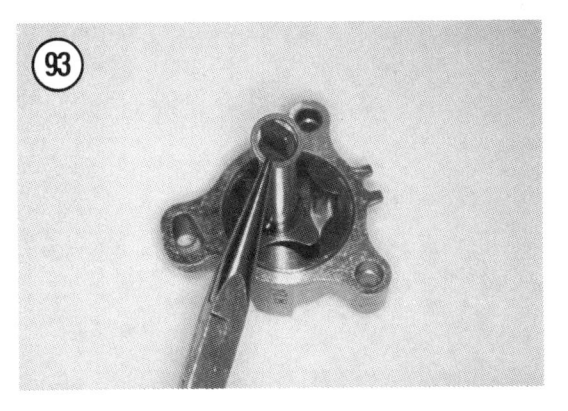

4. Install the pin into the shaft (**Figure 91**), then install the shaft and pin into the inner rotor (**Figure 92**).
5. Install the shim (**Figure 93**) over the shaft and seat it against the inner rotor.
6. Install the 2 dowel pins (**Figure 94**) into the body.
7. Lubricate the shaft with engine oil.
8. Install the pump body onto the cover (**Figure 95**).
9. Install and tighten the pump body mounting bolts (**Figure 78**) to the torque specification in **Table 3**.
10. Turn the shaft (**Figure 96**) and make sure the oil pump turns freely.
11. Lubricate a new seal with engine oil and install it into the groove in the oil pump (**Figure 97**).
12. Install the oil strainer into the seal in the oil pump (A, **Figure 98**).
13. Install the oil pressure relief valve—O-ring end first—into the oil pump. See **Figure 99**.
14. Install the oil pump as described in this chapter.

Installation

Refer to **Figure 71** when installing the oil pump.
1. Lubricate a new O-ring with engine oil and install it and its dowel pin (A, **Figure 100**) into the crankcase.

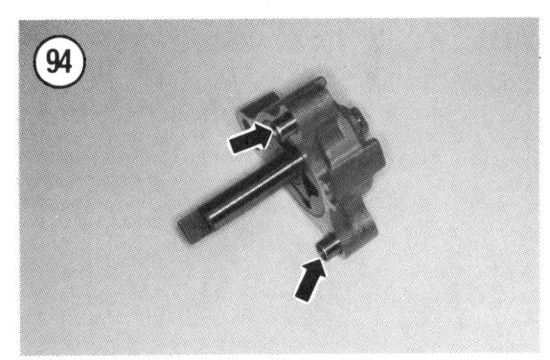

2. Install the small dowel pin (B, **Figure 100**).
3. Install the relief pipe (**Figure 74**) into the crankcase.
4. Align the oil pump shaft (B, **Figure 98**) with the notch in the end of the water pump shaft (C, **Figure 100**) and install the oil pump into the crankcase (**Figure 73**).
5. Connect the relief pipe over the oil pressure relief valve.
6. Make sure the oil screen is positioned against the raised crankcase boss as shown in **Figure 101**.
7. Install the oil pump mounting bolts (**Figure 72**) and tighten to the torque specification in **Table 3**.
8. Install the external shift mechanism as described in this chapter.

Oil Pump Pressure Test

1. Warm the engine to normal operating temperature. Shut the engine off.
2. Make sure the engine oil level is correct (Chapter Three).
3. Remove the oil pressure switch from the crankcase as described under *Switches* in Chapter Nine.
4. Mount a portable oil pressure gauge into the switch hole in the crankcase.
5. Start the engine and run it at 5,000 rpm. The standard pressure is 441 kPa (64 psi) with the engine

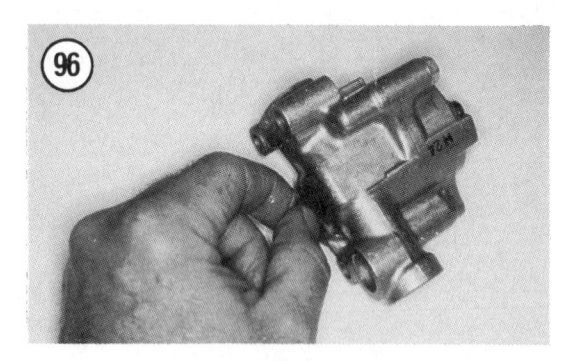

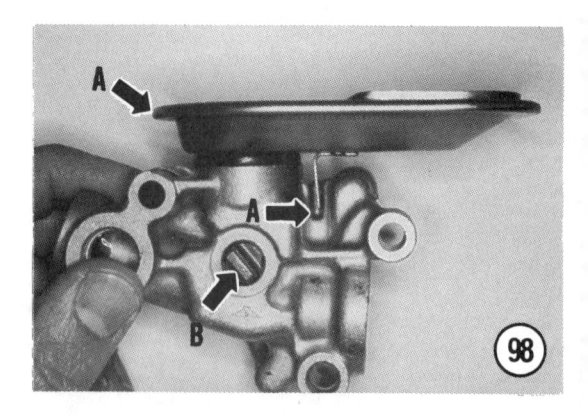

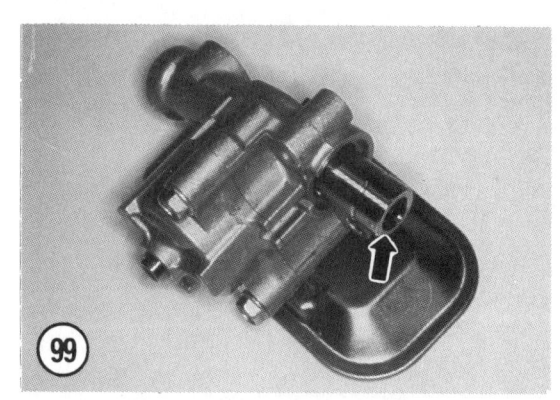

CLUTCH AND EXTERNAL SHIFT MECHANISM

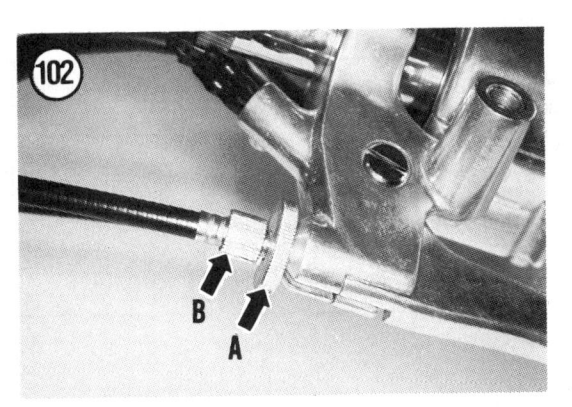

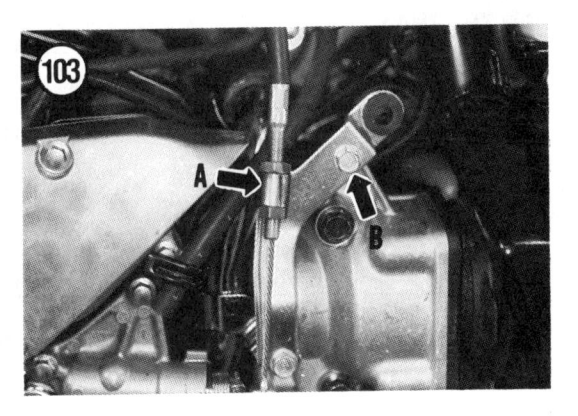

at normal operating temperature. If the oil pressure is less than this amount, replace the oil pump and retest.

6. Remove the oil pressure gauge.
7. Install the oil pressure switch as described in Chapter Nine.

CLUTCH CABLE REPLACEMENT

1. Remove the fuel tank as described in Chapter Eight.
2. Remove the left crankcase rear cover (Chapter Five).
3. Loosen the upper (**Figure 102**) and lower (**Figure 103**) clutch cable adjusters.
4. Make a drawing of the clutch cable as it is routed through the frame.
5. Remove the clutch cable from the vehicle.
6. Lubricate the new cable as described in Chapter Three.
7. Install the new cable by reversing these removal steps. Make sure you correctly route it with no sharp turns.
8. Adjust the clutch cable as described in Chapter Three.

Table 1 CLUTCH SERVICE SPECIFICATIONS

	New mm (in.)	Service limit mm (in.)
Clutch spring free length	44.0 (1.73)	42.5 (1.67)
Clutch friction disc thickness	3.72-3.88 (0.146-0.153)	3.1 (0.12)
Clutch plate (steel) warpage limit	—	0.30 (0.012)
Clutch outer guide inside diameter	27.955-28.012 (1.1022-1.1028)	28.08 (1.106)
Mainshaft outside diameter (at clutch outer guide position)	27.980-27.993 (1.1016-1.1021)	27.93 (1.100)

Table 2 OIL PUMP SERVICE SPECIFICATIONS

	New mm (in.)	Service limit mm (in.)
Body clearance	0.15-0.22 (0.006-0.009)	0.35 (0.014)
End clearance	0.02-0.07 (0.001-0.003)	0.10 (0.004)
Tip clearance	0.15 (0.006)	0.20 (0.008)

Table 3 TIGHTENING TORQUES

	N·m	in.-lb.	ft.-lb.
Clutch cover mounting bolts	12	106	—
Clutch center locknut	100	—	74
Clutch lifter plate bolt	12	106	—
Oil pump body bolts	12	106	—
Oil pump mounting bolts	12	106	—
Primary drive gear bolt	100	—	74
Shift stopper arm pivot bolt	10	88	—

# CHAPTER SEVEN

TRANSMISSION AND INTERNAL SHIFT MECHANISM

A 5-speed transmission unit is used on all models. You must remove the engine and split the crankcase (Chapter Five) to service the transmission and internal shift mechanism.

Table 1 lists transmission gear ratios. **Tables 1-4** are found at the end of the chapter.

TRANSMISSION IDENTIFICATION

This chapter describes service to the transmission assemblies identified in **Figure 1**:
 a. Mainshaft.
 b. Countershaft.
 c. Shift drum.
 d. Shift forks.

TRANSMISSION TROUBLESHOOTING

Refer to Chapter Two.

TRANSMISSION OVERHAUL

Removal/Installation

Remove and install the transmission and internal shift assemblies as described under *Crankcase Disassembly and Crankcase Assembly* in Chapter Five.

Transmission Service Notes

1. Parts with two different sides (such as gears, circlips and shift forks) can be installed backward. To maintain the correct alignment and position of the parts during disassembly, store each part in order and in a divided container.
2. The circlips are a tight fit on the transmission shafts and will bend and twist when you remove them. Install new circlips when you assemble the transmission.
3. To prevent bending and twisting the new circlips when you install them, use the following installation technique: Open the new circlip with a pair of circlip pliers while holding the back of the circlip with a pair of pliers (**Figure 2**). Then slide the circlip down

the shaft and seat it into its correct transmission groove.

Mainshaft
Disassembly/Assembly

Refer to **Figure 3** for this procedure.
1. Clean the assembled mainshaft (**Figure 4**) in solvent, then dry with compressed air.
2. Remove the flat washer.
3. Remove fifth gear and the fifth gear spline bushing.
4. Remove the spline washer and circlip.
5. Remove the second/fourth combination gear.
6. Remove the circlip and the spline washer.
7. Remove third gear and the third gear bushing.

NOTE
*Mainshaft first gear (**Figure 5**) is an integral part of the mainshaft.*

8. Inspect the mainshaft assembly as described under *Transmission Inspection* in this chapter.

NOTE
*Install new circlips when you assemble the mainshaft. The 2 mainshaft circlips (**Figure 3**) are identical (same part number).*

9. Lubricate all sliding surfaces with engine oil.
10. Install the third gear bushing and seat it against first gear (**Figure 6**).
11. Install third gear (**Figure 7**) with its gear dogs facing away from first gear.

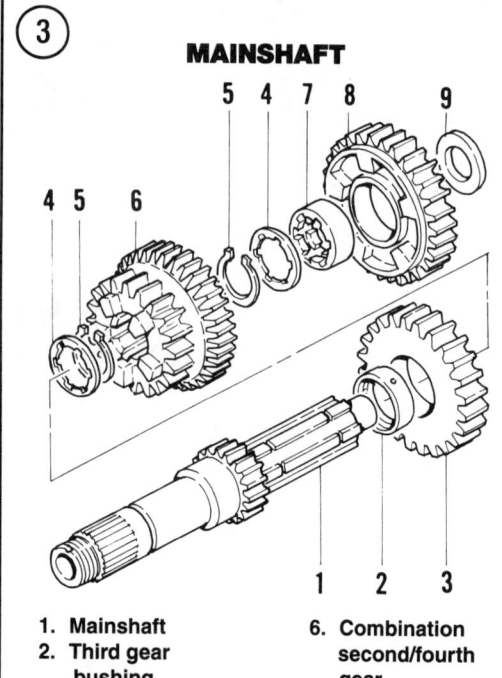

③ MAINSHAFT

1. Mainshaft
2. Third gear bushing
3. Third gear
4. Spline washer
5. Circlip
6. Combination second/fourth gear
7. Fifth gear spline bushing
8. Fifth gear
9. Washer

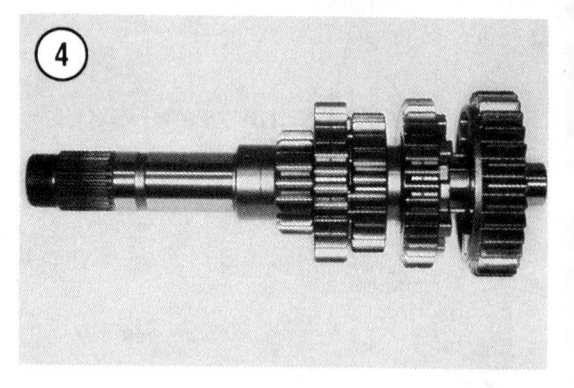

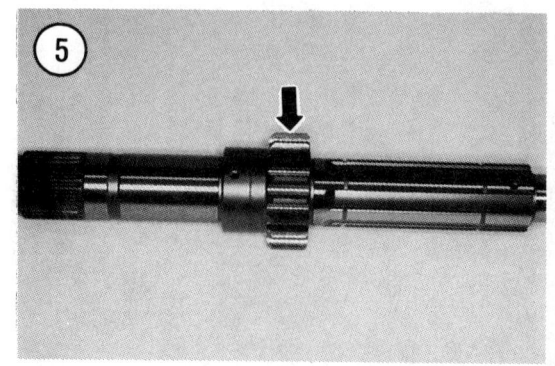

TRANSMISSION AND INTERNAL SHIFT MECHANISM

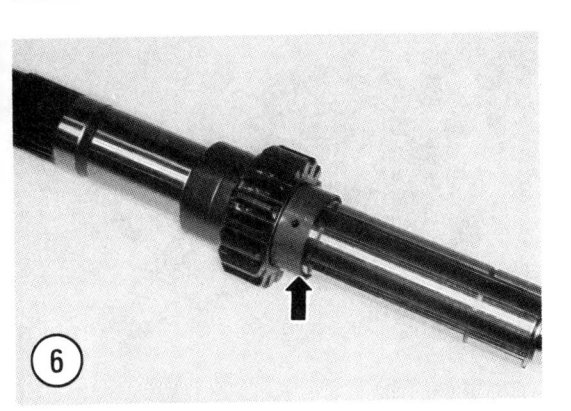

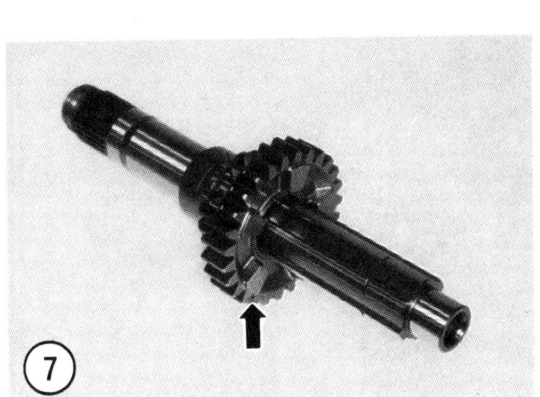

NOTE
In Step 12, install the spline washer and circlip with their flat edges facing away from third gear (Figure 8).

12. Install the spline washer and circlip (**Figure 9**). Seat the circlip in the groove next to third gear (**Figure 10**). Align the circlip gap with the shaft groove as shown in **Figure 11**.
13. Install the second/fourth combination gear with the small gear (**Figure 12**) facing toward third gear.

NOTE
In Step 14, install the circlip and spline washer with their flat edges facing toward the second/fourth combination gear (Figure 8).

14. Install the circlip and spline washer (**Figure 13**). Seat the circlip in the groove as shown in **Figure 14**. Align the circlip gap with the shaft groove as shown in **Figure 11**.
15. Align the oil hole in the fifth gear spline bushing with the oil hole in the mainshaft (**Figure 15**) and install the bushing.

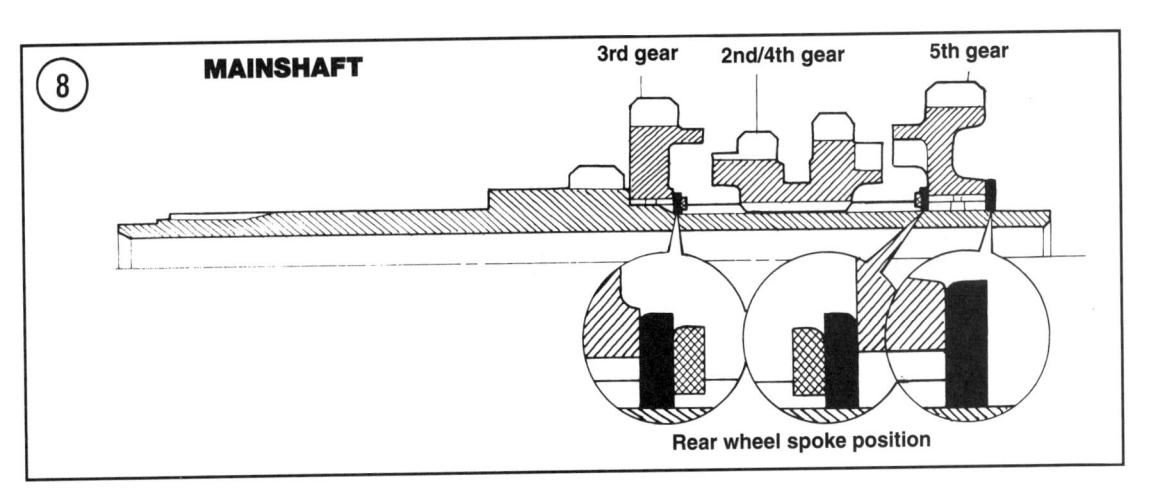

MAINSHAFT

3rd gear 2nd/4th gear 5th gear

Rear wheel spoke position

16. Install fifth gear with its gear dogs (**Figure 16**) facing toward the second/fourth combination gear. See **Figure 17**.

17. Install the flat washer (**Figure 18**) with its flat edge facing away from 5th gear. See **Figure 8**.

NOTE
Mainshaft assembly is now complete. Compare the mainshaft assembly with Figure 3 and Figure 4.

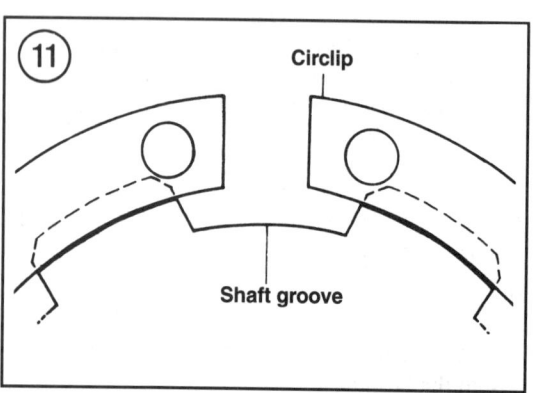

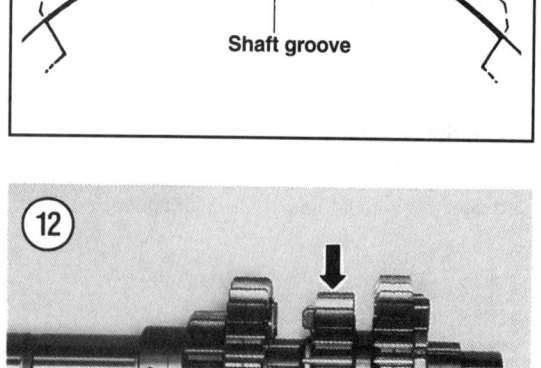

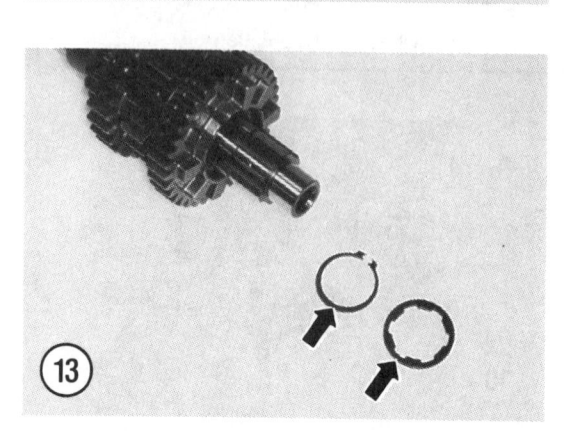

TRANSMISSION AND INTERNAL SHIFT MECHANISM

Countershaft
Disassembly/Assembly

Refer to **Figure 19** for this procedure.
1. Clean the assembled countershaft (**Figure 20**) in solvent, and then dry with compressed air.
2. From the left side of the countershaft, remove the following parts:

a. Fifth gear.
b. Circlip.
c. Spline washer.
d. Fourth gear.
e. Fourth gear bushing.

3. From the right side of the countershaft, remove the following parts:

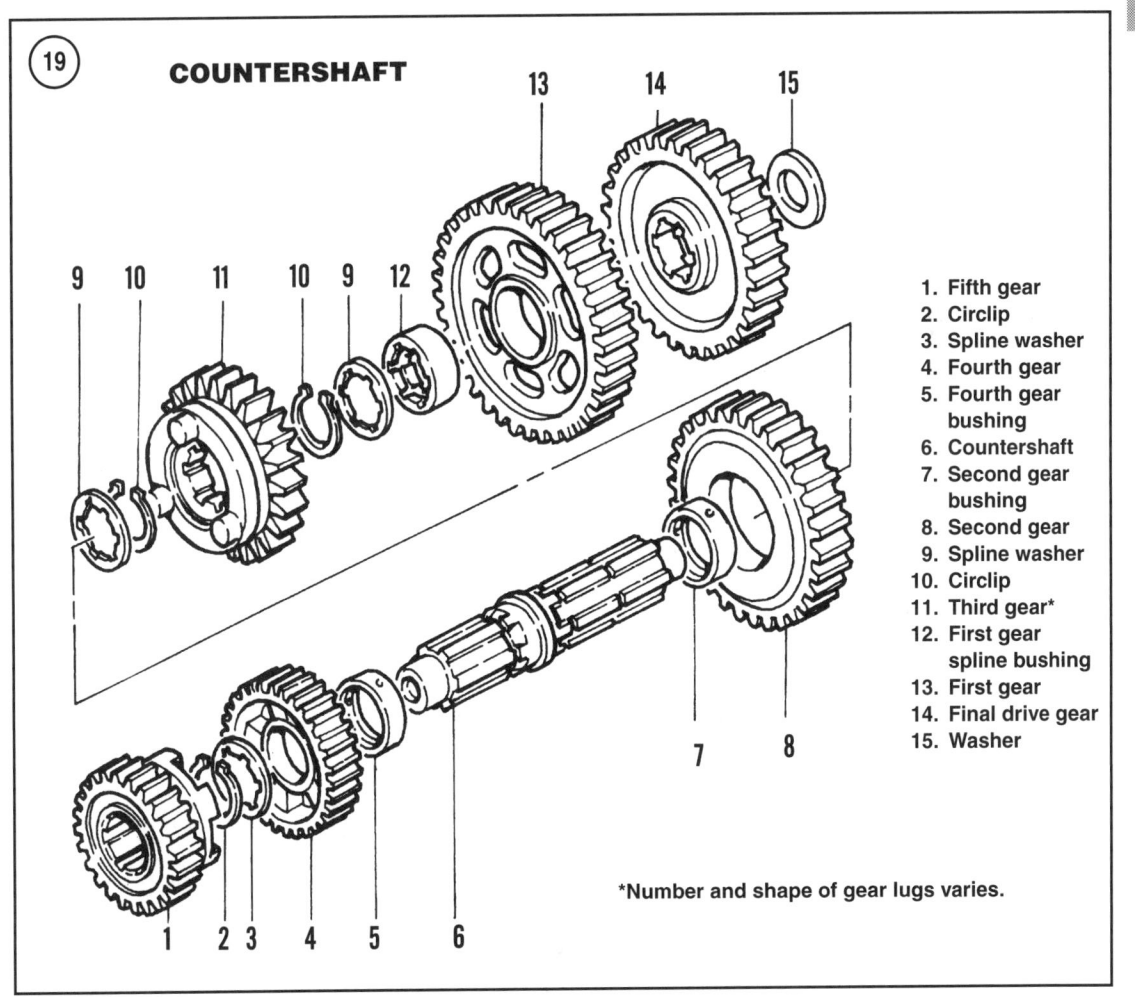

COUNTERSHAFT

1. Fifth gear
2. Circlip
3. Spline washer
4. Fourth gear
5. Fourth gear bushing
6. Countershaft
7. Second gear bushing
8. Second gear
9. Spline washer
10. Circlip
11. Third gear*
12. First gear spline bushing
13. First gear
14. Final drive gear
15. Washer

*Number and shape of gear lugs varies.

a. Flat washer.
b. Final drive gear.
c. First gear.
d. First gear bushing.
e. Spline washer.
f. Circlip.
g. Third gear.
h. Circlip.
i. Spline washer.
j. Second gear.
k. Second gear bushing.

4. Inspect the countershaft assembly as described under *Transmission Inspection* in this chapter.
5. Lubricate all sliding surfaces with engine oil.

NOTE
*Steps 6-9 assemble the gears on the left side of the countershaft (**Figure 21**).*

6. Install the fourth gear bushing (**Figure 22**) and seat it against the countershaft shoulder.
7. Install fourth gear (**Figure 23**) with its gear dogs facing away from the countershaft shoulder.

NOTE
*In Step 8, install the spline washer and circlip with their flat edges facing away from fourth gear. See **Figure 24**.*

8. Install the spline washer and circlip (**Figure 25**). Seat the circlip in the groove next to fourth gear

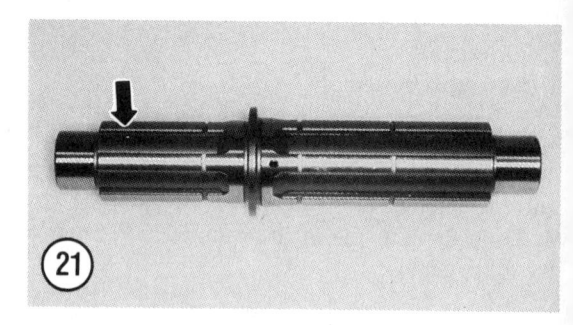

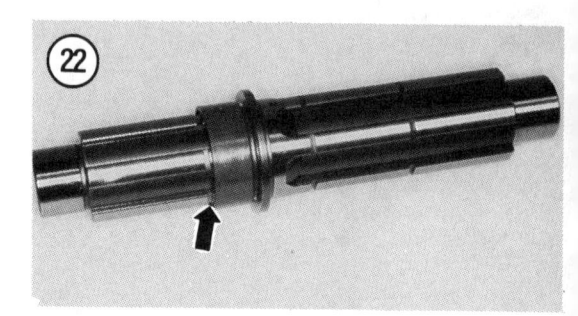

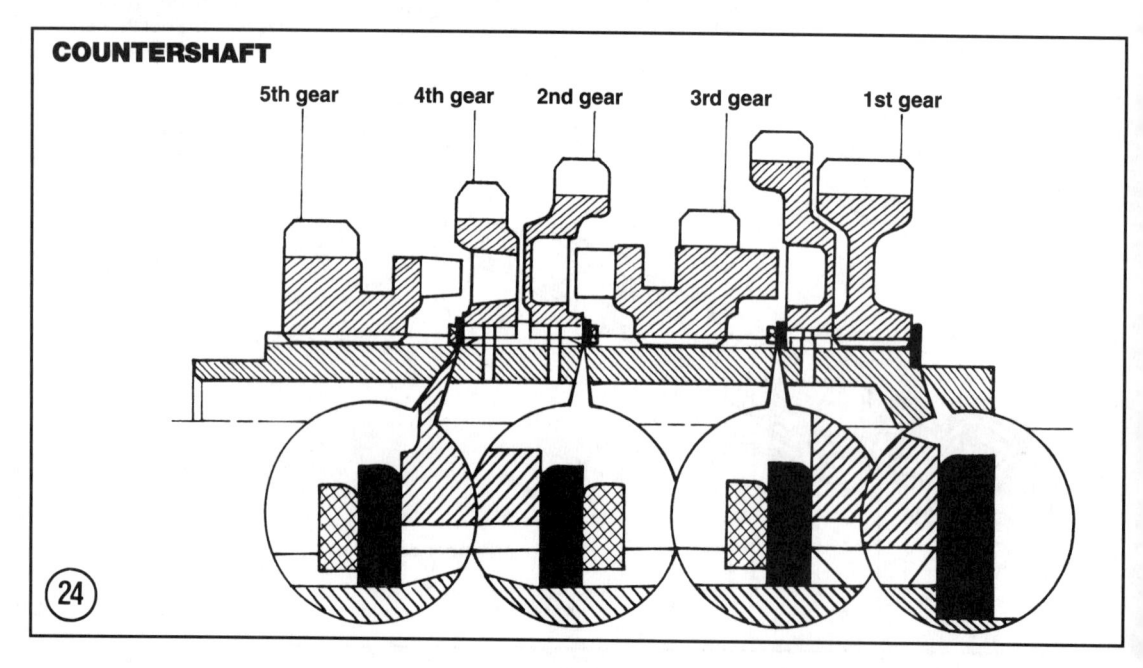

TRANSMISSION AND INTERNAL SHIFT MECHANISM

(**Figure 26**). Align the circlip gap with the shaft groove as shown in **Figure 27**.

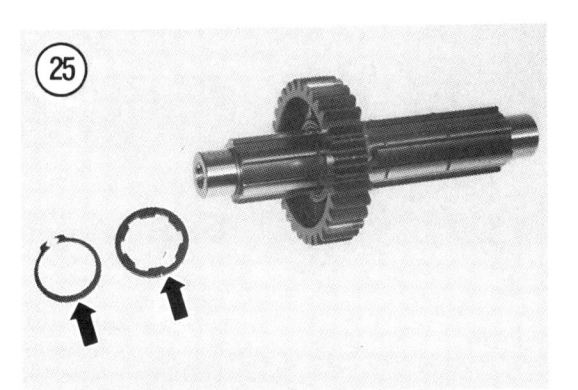

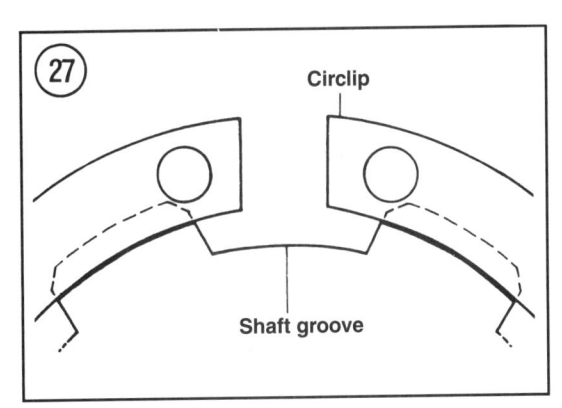

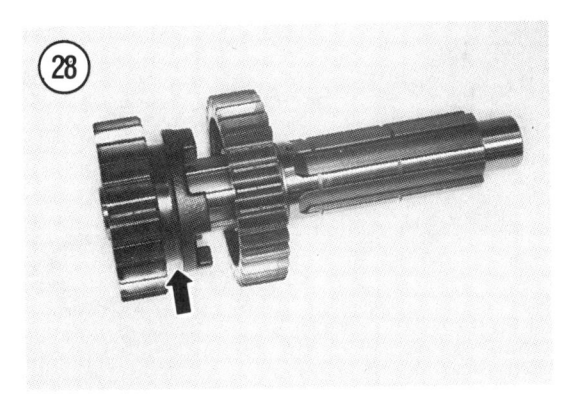

9. Install fifth gear with its gear dogs (**Figure 28**) facing toward fourth gear.

NOTE
*This complete assembly of the left side of the countershaft (A, **Figure 29**). Steps 10-18 assemble the gears on the right side of the countershaft (B, **Figure 29**).*

10. Install the second gear bushing and seat it against the countershaft shoulder (**Figure 30**).
11. Install second gear so that its gear dogs (**Figure 31**) face away from fourth gear. See **Figure 32**.

NOTE
*In Step 12, install the spline washer and circlip with their flat edges facing away from second gear. See **Figure 24**.*

12. Install the spline washer and circlip (**Figure 33**). Seat the circlip in the groove as shown in **Figure 34**. Align the circlip gap with the shaft groove as shown in **Figure 27**.

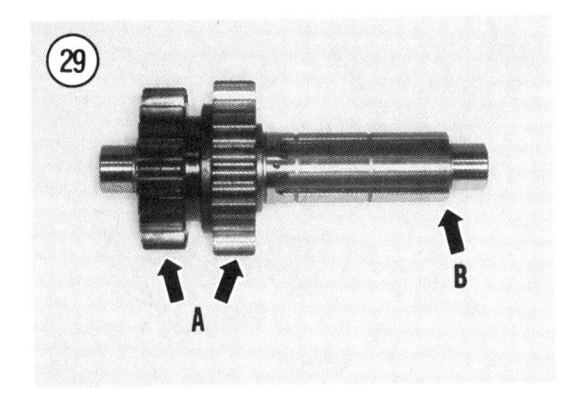

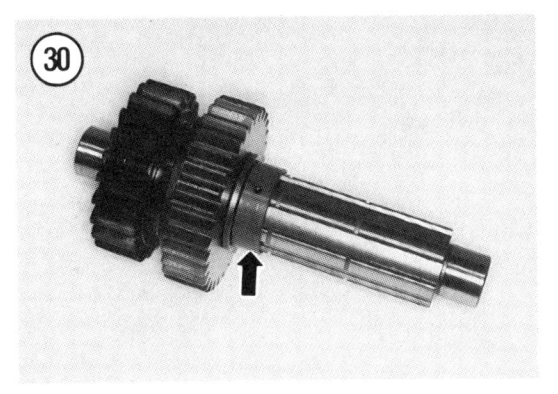

13. Install third gear so that its shift fork groove (**Figure 35**) faces toward second gear.

NOTE
*In Step 14, install the circlip and spline washer with their flat edges facing toward third gear. See **Figure 24**.*

14. Install the circlip and washer (**Figure 36**). Seat the circlip in the groove as shown in **Figure 37**. Align the circlip gap with the shaft groove as shown in **Figure 27**.
15. Align the oil hole in the first gear spline bushing with the oil hole in the countershaft (**Figure 38**) and install the bushing.
16. Install first gear with its shoulder side (**Figure 39**) facing toward third gear. See **Figure 40**.
17. Install the final drive gear (**Figure 41**) and seat it next to first gear.
18. Install the flat washer (**Figure 42**) with its flat edge facing away from the final drive gear. See **Figure 24**.

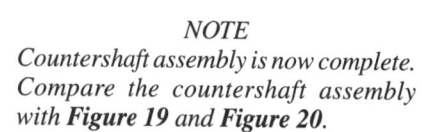

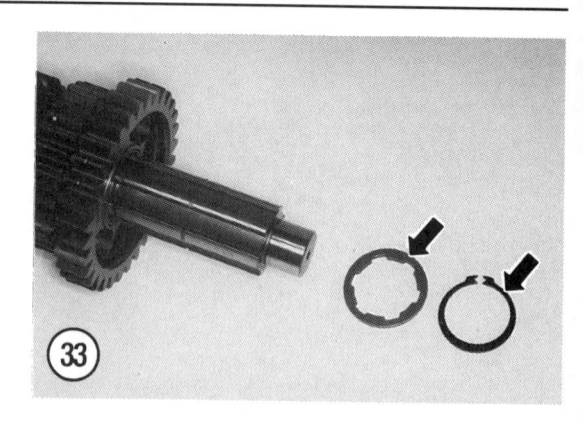

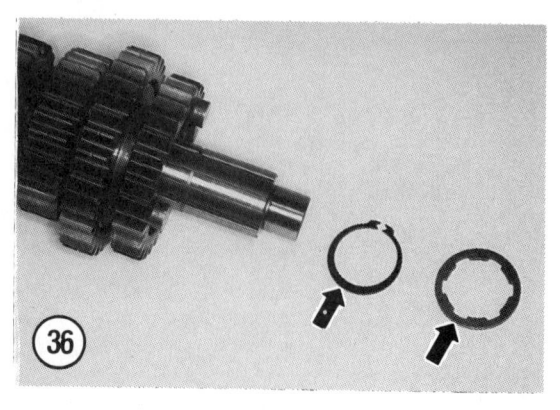

NOTE
*Countershaft assembly is now complete. Compare the countershaft assembly with **Figure 19** and **Figure 20**.*

TRANSMISSION AND INTERNAL SHIFT MECHANISM

TRANSMISSION INSPECTION

Mainshaft
Cleaning and Inspection

When measuring the mainshaft components (**Figure 43**) in this section, compare the actual measurements to the specifications in **Table 2**. Replace parts that are out of specification or show damage as described in this section.

NOTE
When you perform the following steps, maintain the alignment of the mainshaft components.

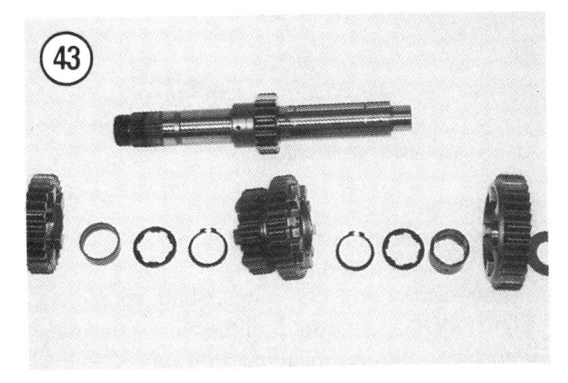

1. Clean the mainshaft assembly in solvent and dry with compressed air.
2. Flush the oil control holes through the mainshaft (**Figure 44**) with compressed air.
3. Inspect the mainshaft (**Figure 44**) for:
    a. Worn or damages splines.
    b. Missing, broken or chipped first gear teeth.
    c. Excessively worn or damaged bearing surfaces.
    d. Cracked or rounded-off circlip grooves.
4. Check each mainshaft gear (**Figure 43**) for:
    a. Missing, broken or chipped teeth.
    b. Worn, damaged, or rounded-off gear lugs.
    c. Worn or damaged splines.
    d. Cracked or scored gear bore.
5. Check the mainshaft bushings (**Figure 45**) for:
    a. Excessively worn or damaged bearing surface.
    b. Worn or damaged splines.
    c. Cracked or scored gear bore.
6. Measure the mainshaft outside diameter at the third gear operating position (**Figure 46**). Replace the mainshaft if out of specification.
7. Measure the mainshaft third and fifth gear inside diameters (**Figure 47**). Replace the mainshaft if out of specification.
8. Measure the mainshaft third and fifth gear bushing outside diameters (**Figure 48**). Replace the mainshaft if out of specification.
9. Measure the mainshaft third gear bushing inside diameter (**Figure 48**). Replace the mainshaft if out of specification.
10. Using the measurements recorded in the previous steps, determine the gear-to-bushing and shaft-to-bushing clearances specified in **Table 2**. Replace worn parts to bring the clearances within normal operating specifications.
11. Make sure each mainshaft gear slides or turns on the mainshaft without binding or roughness.

NOTE
Replace defective gears and their mating gear, though it may not show as much wear or damage.

Countershaft
Cleaning and Inspection

When measuring the countershaft components (**Figure 49**) in this section, compare the actual measurements to the specifications in **Table 3**. Replace

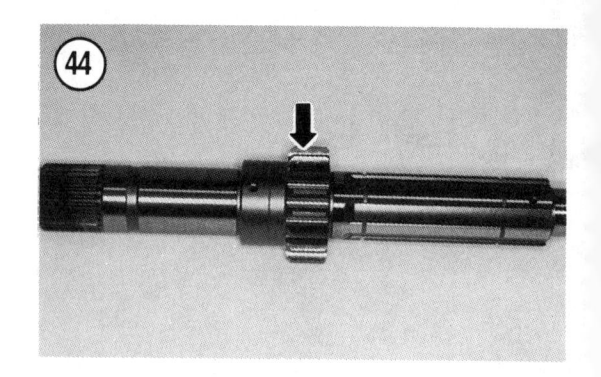

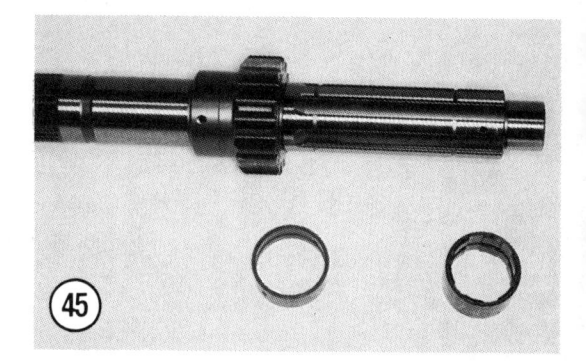

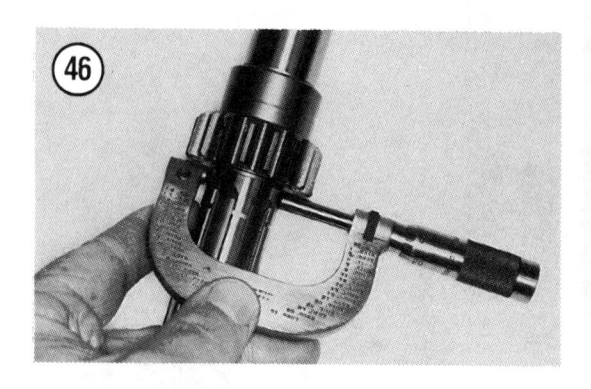

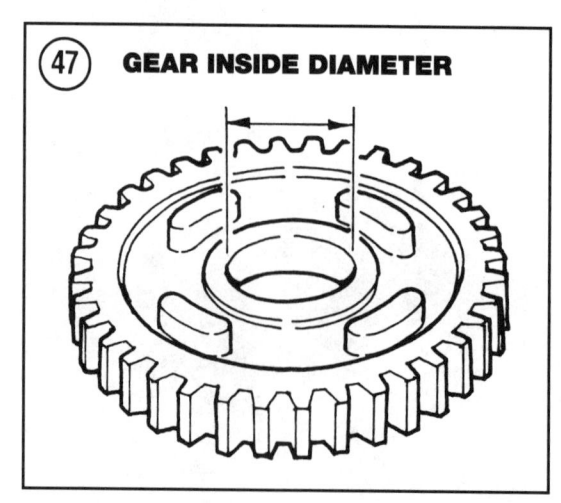

TRANSMISSION AND INTERNAL SHIFT MECHANISM

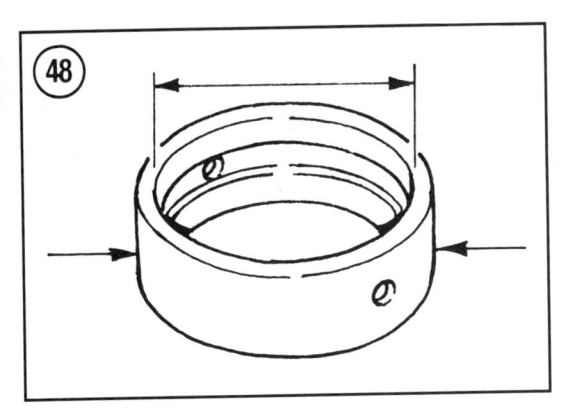

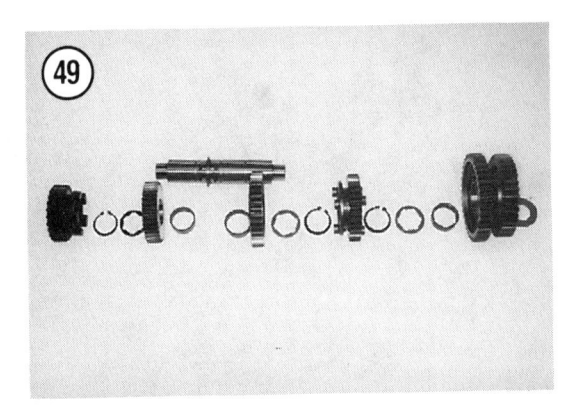

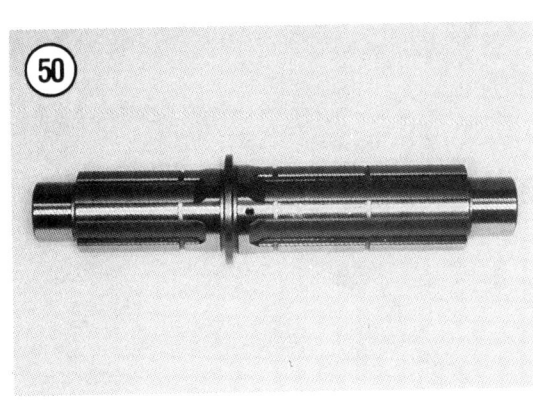

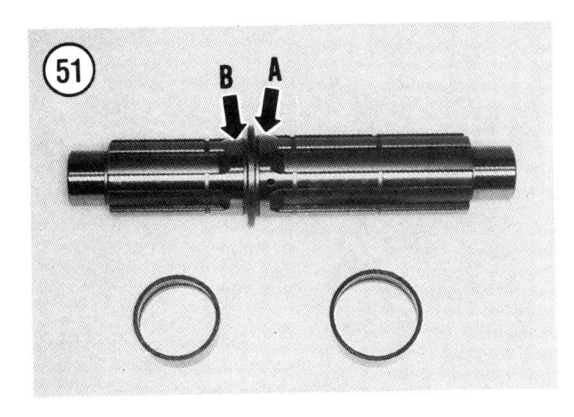

parts that are out of specification or show damage as described in this section.

NOTE
When you perform the following steps, maintain the alignment of the countershaft components.

1. Clean the countershaft assembly in solvent and dry with compressed air.
2. Flush the oil control holes through the countershaft (**Figure 50**) with compressed air.
3. Inspect the countershaft (**Figure 50**) for:

    a. Worn or damaged splines.

    b. Excessively worn or damaged bearing surfaces.

    c. Cracked or rounded-off circlip grooves.

4. Check each countershaft gear (**Figure 49**) for:

    a. Missing, broken or chipped teeth.

    b. Worn, damaged, or rounded-off gear lugs.

    c. Worn or damaged splines.

    d. Cracked or scored gear bore.

5. Check the countershaft bushings (**Figure 51**) for:

    a. Excessively worn or damaged bearing surface.

    b. Worn or damaged splines.

    c. Cracked or scored gear bore.

6. Measure the countershaft diameter at the second gear operating position (A, **Figure 51**). Replace the countershaft if out of specification.
7. Measure the countershaft diameter at the fourth gear operating position (B, **Figure 51**). Replace the countershaft if out of specification.
8. Measure the countershaft gear inside diameters (**Figure 47**) listed in **Table 3**. Replace the gears that are out of specification.
9. Measure the countershaft gear bushing outside diameters (**Figure 48**) listed in **Table 3**. Replace bushings that are out of specification.
10. Measure the countershaft gear bushing inside diameters (**Figure 48**) listed in **Table 3**. Replace bushings that are out of specification.
11. Using the measurements recorded in Steps 6-10, determine the gear-to-bushing and shaft-to-bushing clearances specified in **Table 3**. Replace worn parts to bring the clearances within normal operating specifications.
12. Make sure each countershaft gear slides or turns on the countershaft without binding or roughness.

NOTE
Replace defective gears and their mating gear, though it may not show as much wear or damage.

INTERNAL SHIFT MECHANISM

Removal/Installation

Remove and install the transmission assembly as described under *Crankcase Disassembly and Crankcase Assembly* in Chapter Five.

Shift Fork Inspection

When measuring the shift fork components in this section, compare the actual measurements to the new and service limit specifications in **Table 4**. Replace parts that are out of specification or show damage as described in this section.

1. Clean and dry the shift forks and shaft.
2. Inspect each shift fork (**Figure 52**) for wear or damage. Examine the shift forks at the points where they contact the slider gear (**Figure 53**). These surfaces must be smooth with no wear, bending, cracks, heat discoloration or other damage.
3. Check each shift fork for arc-shaped wear or burn marks. These marks indicate that the shift fork has contacted the gear.
4. Measure the thickness of each shift fork claw (**Figure 54**) and compare to the specification in **Table 4**. Replace if out of specification.
5. Check the shift fork shaft (**Figure 55**) for bending or other damage. Install each shift fork on the shaft and slide it back and forth. Each shift fork must slide smoothly with no binding or tight spots. If you notice

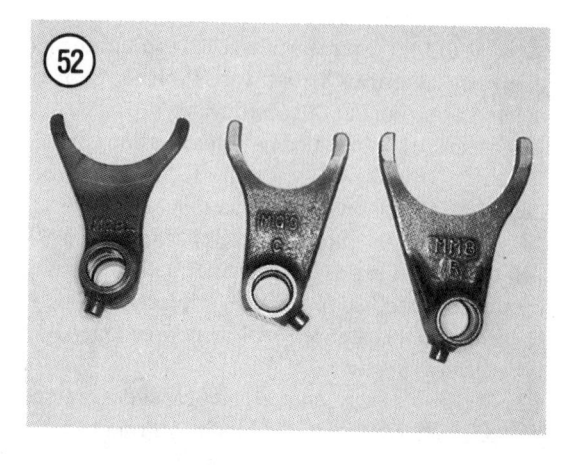

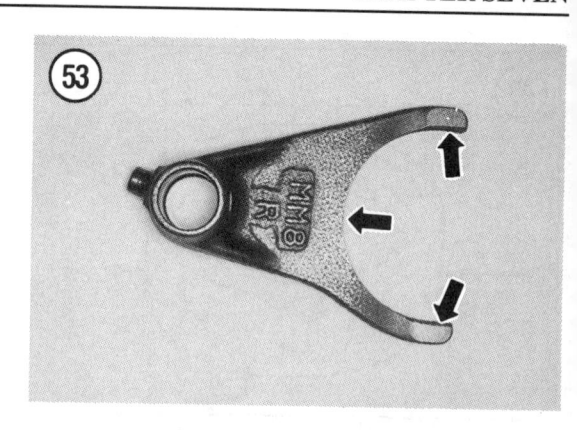

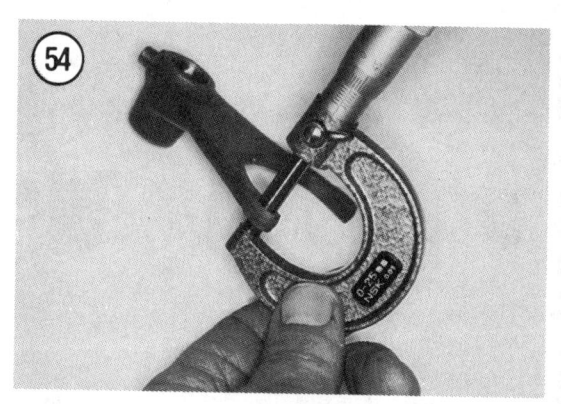

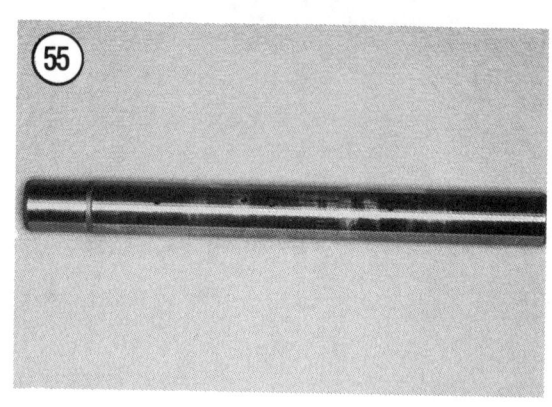

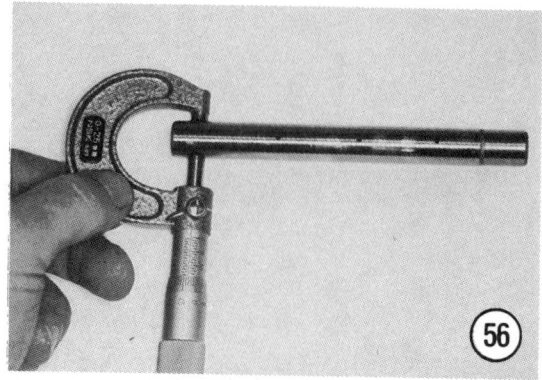

TRANSMISSION AND INTERNAL SHIFT MECHANISM

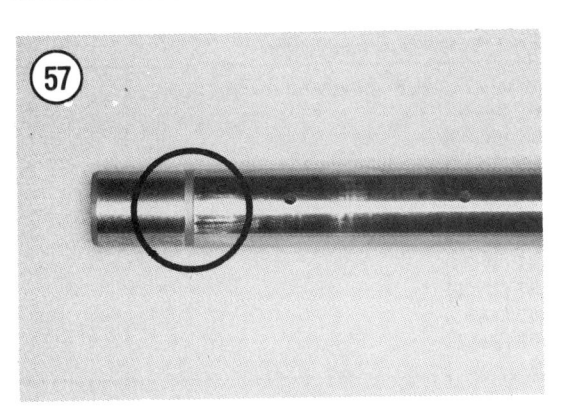

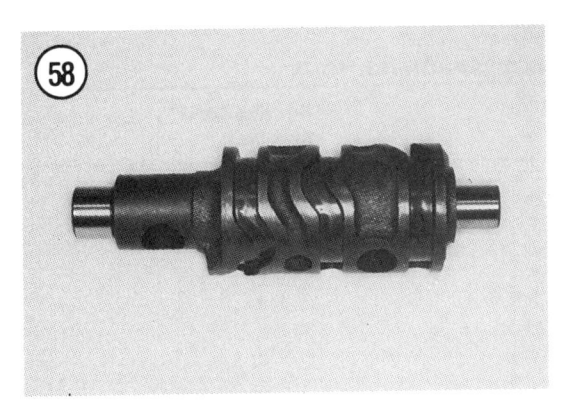

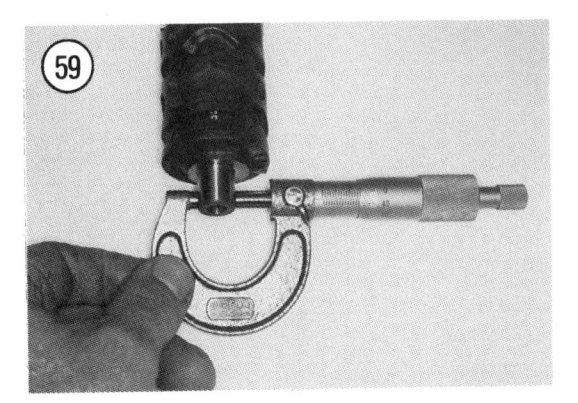

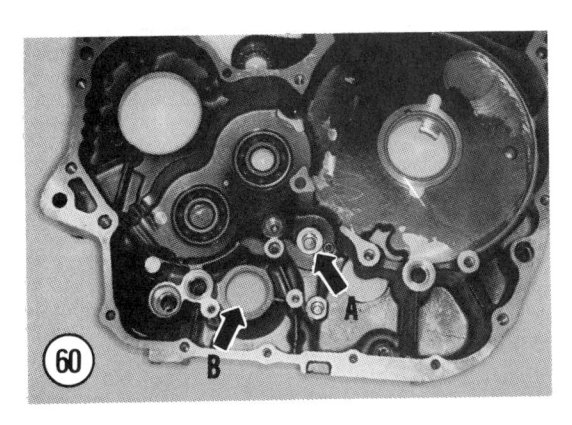

binding with all 3 shift forks, check the shaft closely for bending. If you note a binding condition with one shift fork only, check the shift fork closely.

6. Measure the left and right side shift fork shaft diameter (**Figure 56**) and compare to the dimensions in **Table 4**. Replace the shift fork shaft if out of specification.

NOTE
*The left side of the shift fork shaft has a machined groove (**Figure 57**).*

Shift Drum Inspection

1. Clean and dry the shift drum.
2. Check the shift drum (**Figure 58**) for:
   a. Excessively worn or damaged cam grooves.
   b. Excessively worn or damaged bearing surfaces.
3. Measure the shift drum's left end (**Figure 59**) and compare to the dimension in **Table 4**. Replace if out of specification.

Shift Shaft and Shift Drum Journals Inside Diameter Measurement

Using a bore gauge or inside micrometer, measure the following journal inside diameters and compare to the specification in **Table 4**. Replace one or both crankcase halves if any measurement is out of specification:

   a. Shift shaft left hand journal inside diameter (A, **Figure 60**).
   b. Shift shaft right hand journal inside diameter (**Figure 61**).
   c. Shift drum journal at left side crankcase (B, **Figure 60**).

Table 1 TRANSMISSION GENERAL SPECIFICATIONS

Transmission	Constant mesh, 5-speed and reverse
Shift pattern	1-N-2-3-4-5
Primary reduction ratio	1.692 (66/39)
Third reduction ratio (output drive reduction)	1.059 (18/17)
Final reduction ratio	3.091 (34/11)
Transmission gear ratios	
1st gear	2.235 (38/17)
2nd gear	1.391 (32/23)
3rd gear	1.037 (28/27)
4th gear	0.888 (32/66)
5th gear	0.766 (23/30)

Table 2 MAINSHAFT SERVICE SPECIFICATIONS

	New mm (in.)	Service limit mm (in.)
Gear inside diameter		
3rd and 5th gears	31.000-31.025 (1.2205-1.2215)	31.035 (1.2218)
Gear bushing outside diameter		
3rd gear	30.970-30.995 (1.2193-1.2203)	30.94 (1.218)
5th gear	30.950-30.975 (1.2185-1.2195)	30.94 (1.218)
Gear bushing inside diameter		
3rd gear	28.000-28.021 (1.1024-1.1032)	28.04 (1.104)
Mainshaft outside diameter		
@ 3rd gear position	27.959-27.980 (1.1007-1.1016)	27.94 (1.100)
Gear-to-bushing clearance		
3rd gear	0.005-0.055 (0.0002-0.0022)	0.075 (0.0030)
5th gear	0.025-0.075 (0.0010-0.0030)	0.095 (0.0037)
Gear bushing-to-shaft clearance	0.020-0.056 (0.0002-0.0022)	0.076 (0.0030)

Table 3 COUNTERSHAFT SERVICE SPECIFICATIONS

	New mm (in.)	Service limit mm (in.)
Gear inside diameter		
1st and 2nd gears	33.000-33.025 (1.2992-1.3002)	33.035 (1.3006)
4th gear	31.000-31.025 (1.2205-1.2215)	31.035 (1.2218)
Gear bushing outside diameter		
1st gear	32.950-32.975 (1.2972-1.2982)	32.94 (1.297)
2nd gear	32.955-32.980 (1.2974-1.2984)	32.94 (1.297)

(continued)

TRANSMISSION AND INTERNAL SHIFT MECHANISM

Table 3 COUNTERSHAFT SERVICE SPECIFICATIONS (continued)

	New mm (in.)	Service limit mm (in.)
Gear bushing outside diameter (continued)		
4th gear	30.970-30.995 (1.2193-1.2203)	30.94 (1.218)
Gear bushing inside diameter		
2nd gear	29.985-30.006 (1.1805-1.1813)	30.03 (1.182)
4th gear	28.000-28.021 (1.1024-1.1032)	28.04 (1.104)
Countershaft outside diameter		
@ 2nd gear	29.950-29.975 (1.1791-1.1801)	29.94 (1.179)
@ 4th gear	27.967-27.980 (1.1011-1.1016)	27.95 (1.100)
Gear-to-bushing clearance		
1st gear	0.025-0.075 (0.0010-0.0030)	0.095 (0.0037)
2nd gear	0.020-0.070 (0.0008-0.0028)	0.090 (0.0035)
4th gear	0.005-0.055 (0.0002-0.0022)	0.075 (0.0030)
Gear bushing-to-shaft clearance		
2nd gear	0.005-0.056 (0.0002-0.0022)	0.076 (0.0030)
4th gear	0.020-0.054 (0.0008-0.0021)	0.074 (0.0029)

Table 4 SHIFT FORK AND SHIFT DRUM SERVICE SPECIFICATIONS

	New mm (in.)	Service limit mm (in.)
Shift fork claw thickness		
Left side shift fork	5.93-6.00 (0.233-0.236)	5.83 (0.230)
Center and right side shift forks	6.43-6.50 (0.253-0.256)	6.33 (0.249)
Shift shaft outside diameter		
Left end	13.466-13.484 (0.5302-0.5309)	13.456 (0.5289)
Right end	13.966-13.984 (0.5498-0.5506)	13.956 (0.5494)
Shift shaft journal inside diameter		
Left side crankcase	13.500-13.527 (0.5315-0.5326)	13.537 (0.5330)
Right side crankcase	14.000-14.027 (0.5512-0.5522)	14.037 (0.5526)
Shift drum journal @ left side crankcase	14.000-14.018 (0.5512-0.5519)	14.028 (0.5534)
Shift drum outside diameter @ left end	13.966-13.984 (0.5498-0.5506)	13.956 (0.5494)

7

CHAPTER EIGHT

FUEL AND EMISSION CONTROL SYSTEMS

The fuel system consists of a fuel tank, shutoff valve, fuel pump and filter, 2 Keihin constant velocity carburetors and air filter.

This chapter includes service procedures for all parts of the fuel and emission control systems. See Chapter Three for air filter service.

Carburetor specifications are listed in **Table 1**. **Table 1** and **Table 2** are at the end of this chapter.

WARNING
Because of the explosive and flammable conditions that exist around gasoline, always observe the following:

1. Disconnect the negative battery cable before working on the fuel system.
2. Gasoline dripping onto a hot engine component may cause a fire. Always allow the engine to cool completely before working on any fuel system component.
3. Wipe up spilled gasoline immediately with dry rags. Then store the rags in a suitable metal container until they can be cleaned or disposed of.
4. Do not service any fuel system component while in the vicinity of open flames, sparks or while anyone is smoking next to the motorcycle.
5. Always have a fire extinguisher close at hand when working on the fuel system.

FUEL SYSTEM IDENTIFICATION

You must disconnect a number of fuel lines and hoses when removing many of the fuel system components for service. To help with reassembly, identify the hoses before disconnecting them. Many of the factory hoses are coded by number and/or color. Look for these marks and compare them with the fuel system hose diagram for your model. If a hose is not labeled, tag the hose with your own identification mark. As you disconnect a hose, write its name and connection point on the tag and immediately attach the tag to the hose. You can make tags with strips of masking tape and a permanent marking pen. Use a permanent marking pen as most ink marks, as well as lead pencil marks, fade on tape. This preparation will save a lot of inconvenience during reassembly.

AIR FILTER HOUSING

Air filter service is described in Chapter Three. The following section describes air filter housing removal and installation.

Removal/Installation

Refer to **Figure 1** for this procedure.
1. Read the information listed under *Fuel System Identification* in this chapter.

FUEL AND EMISSION CONTROL SYSTEMS

2. Remove the battery (Chapter Three).
3. Remove the seat (Chapter Fourteen).
4. Remove the fuse box cover screws and cover (**Figure 2**).
5. Remove the fuse box mounting bolts (A, **Figure 3**) and pull the fuse box (B, **Figure 3**) away from the frame.
6. Remove the ignition control module (ICM) from the right side of the battery holder (**Figure 4**).
7. Remove the starter motor and ground cables from the clips on the bottom of the battery holder.
8. Remove the battery holder mounting bolts and remove the upper seat rubber flap and battery holder from the frame.
9. Remove the right side crankcase cover (Chapter Five).
10. Remove the swing arm (Chapter Twelve).
11. Disconnect the 2-pin fuel pump (black) connector (A, **Figure 5**) from the connector holder mounted on top of the air filter housing.
12. Disconnect the crankcase breather tube from the air filter housing (front, right side).

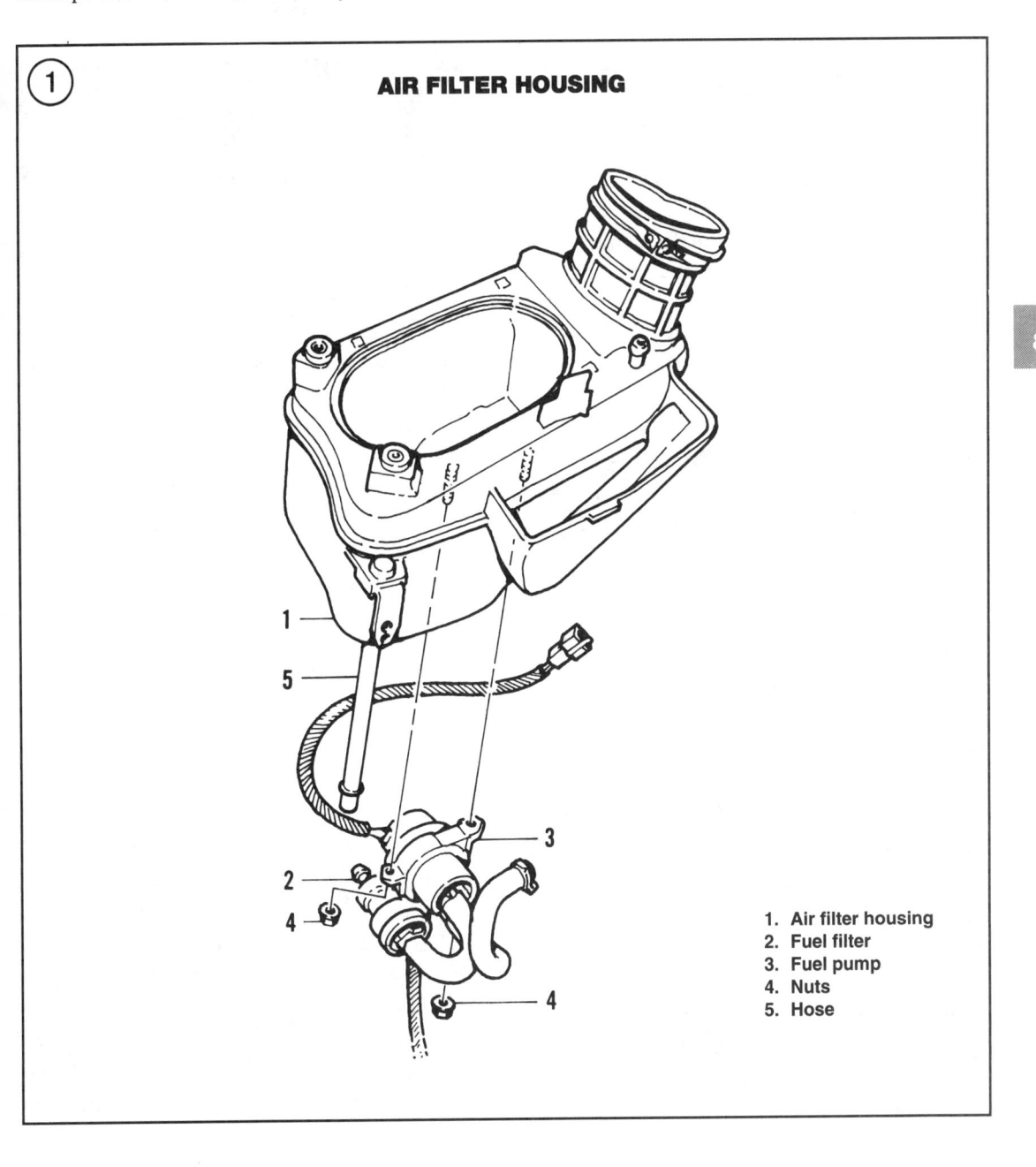

① AIR FILTER HOUSING

1. Air filter housing
2. Fuel filter
3. Fuel pump
4. Nuts
5. Hose

13. Remove the tool band from the air filter housing (middle, right side).

14. Disconnect the fuel pump breather tube (A, **Figure 6**) from the frame clamp.

15. Disconnect the fuel tube from the fuel filter (B, **Figure 6**).

16. Disconnect the fuel tube (**Figure 7**) from the fuel joint.

17. Remove the air filter housing mounting bolts. B, **Figure 5**. The ground terminal is connected to the left side upper mounting bolt.

18. Loosen the air filter hose clamp at the frame.

19. Disconnect the air filter hose from the frame, then remove the air filter housing (with the fuel filter and fuel pump assembly attached) from the frame.

20. If necessary, remove the 2 nuts and remove the fuel pump and fuel filter assembly (**Figure 8**) from the bottom of the air filter housing.

21. Reverse these steps to install the air filter housing, fuel pump and fuel filter assembly while noting the following.

22. When you install the ground terminal onto the left side upper air filter housing mounting bolt, position it against the stopper as shown in **Figure 9**.

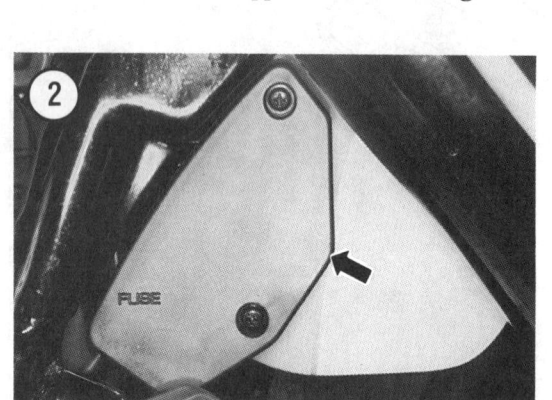

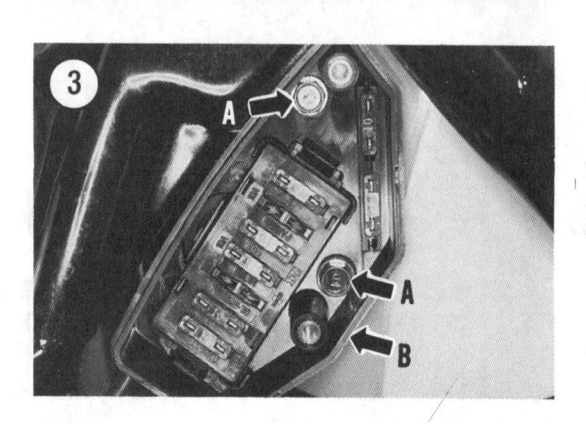

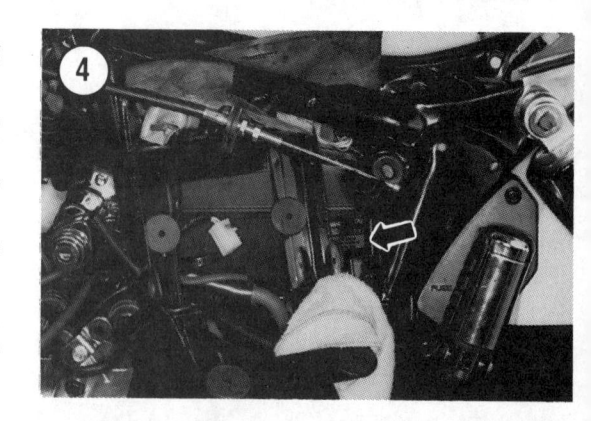

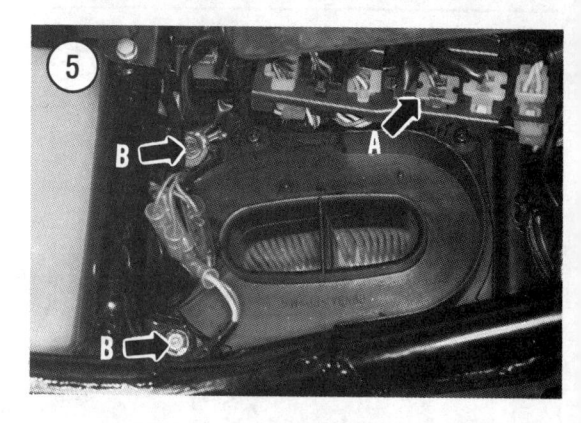

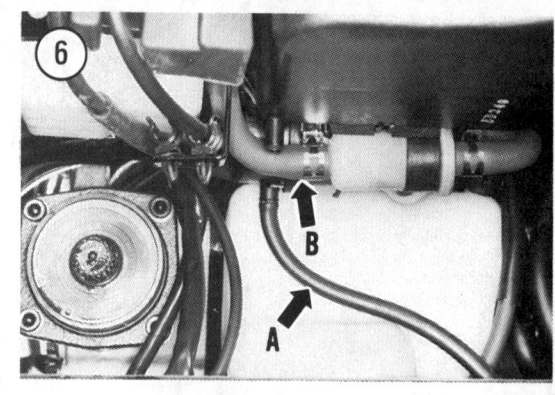

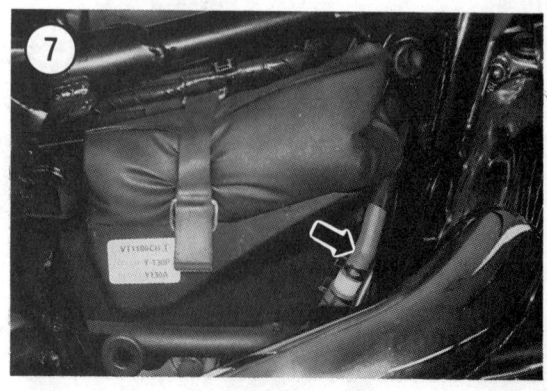

FUEL AND EMISSION CONTROL SYSTEMS

Tighten all of the air filter housing mounting bolts securely.

23. When you reconnect the air filter housing tube to the air box, note the following:

   a. Seal the air filter housing tube to the housing with Honda Bond A or equivalent.

   b. Align the air filter housing groove with the tube tab.

24. When you install the air filter housing tube onto the frame, align the groove in the tube with the tab on the tube hose clamp, then tighten the clamp securely.
25. Check the fuel hoses for leaks.
26. Make sure all hoses are connected and secured properly.

CARBURETOR OPERATION

Understanding the function of each of the carburetor components and their relationships to one another is a valuable aid for pinpointing carburetor trouble.

The carburetor's purpose is to supply and atomize fuel and mix it in correct proportions with air that is drawn in through the air intake. At the primary throttle opening (idle), a small amount of fuel is siphoned through the pilot jet by the incoming air. As the throttle is opened further, the air stream begins to siphon fuel through the main jet and needle jet. The tapered needle increases the effective flow capacity of the needle jet as it is lifted, in that it occupies less of the area of the jet.

At full throttle the carburetor venturi is fully open and the needle is lifted far enough to permit the main jet to flow at full capacity.

The choke circuit is a bystarter system in which the choke lever opens a choke valve and needle rather than closing a butterfly valve in the venturi area as on many carburetors. In the open position, the pilot jet discharges a stream of fuel into the carburetor venturi, enriching the mixture.

⑧ FUEL PUMP/FUEL FILTER

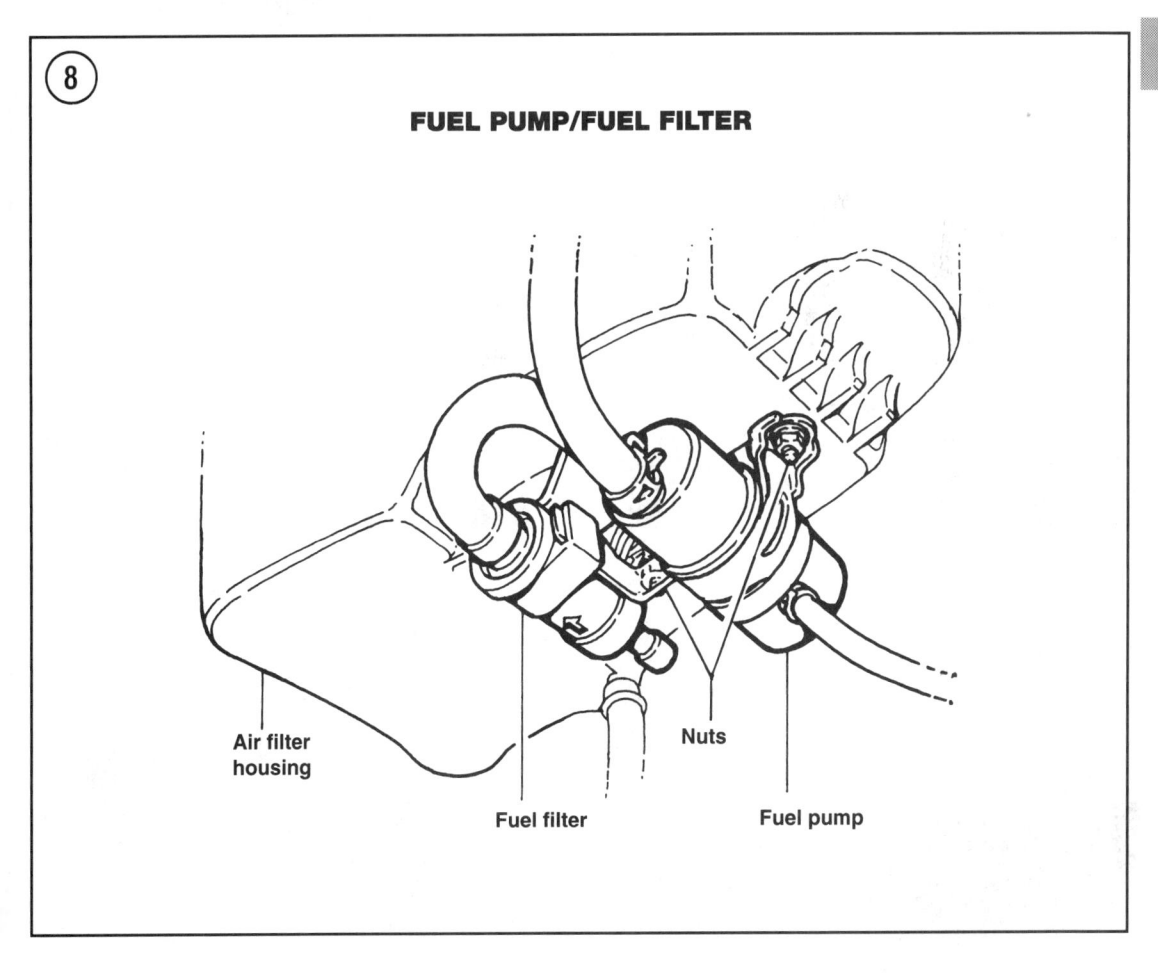

Air filter housing

Fuel filter

Nuts

Fuel pump

CARBURETOR SERVICE

Removal

NOTE
The rear carburetor is mounted on the left side of the bike; the front carburetor is mounted on the right side.

1. Read the information listed under *Fuel System Identification* in this chapter.
2. Disconnect the 2 tubes from the crankcase breather storage tank (**Figure 10**). Then remove the mounting bolt and the breather storage tank.
3. Remove the connecting tube clamps (**Figure 11**) at the carburetors and frame. Then remove the connecting tube assembly (**Figure 12**).
4. Disconnect the fuel hose from each carburetor (**Figure 13** and **Figure 14**).
5. On California models, disconnect the No. 6 carburetor air vent tube (**Figure 15**) from the carburetor hose nozzle.
6. Disconnect the 2 throttle cables and remove the cable holder from the rear carburetor. See **Figure 16**.

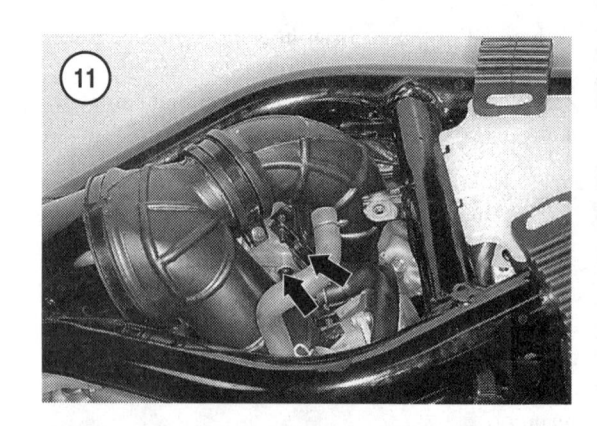

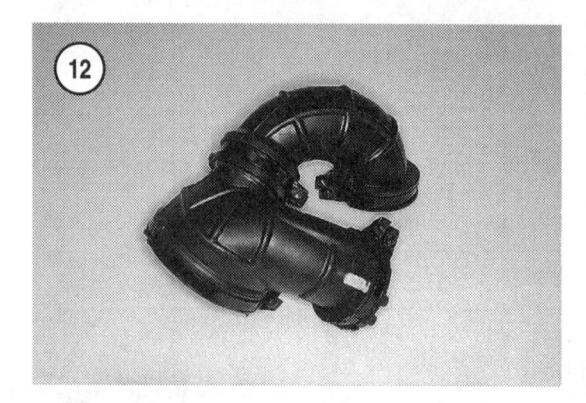

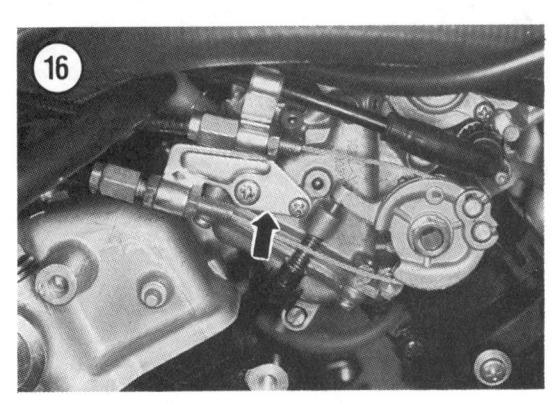

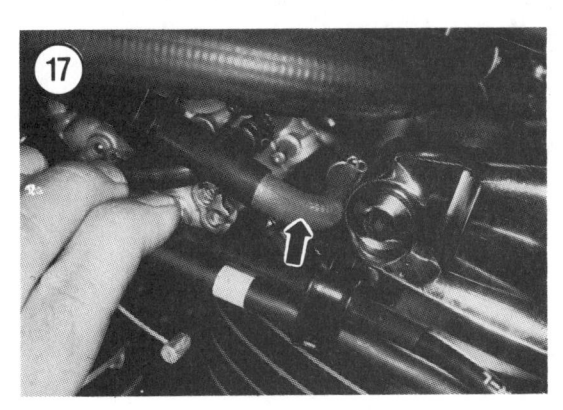

FUEL AND EMISSION CONTROL SYSTEMS

7. On California models, disconnect the No. 5 tube (**Figure 17**) from the rear carburetor.

8. Unscrew and remove the choke assembly (**Figure 18**) from the rear carburetor (**Figure 19**). Disconnect and store the choke plunger and spring (**Figure 20**) in a plastic bag to prevent their loss.

9. On California models, disconnect the following tubes from the front carburetor:

    a. No. 5 hose (A, **Figure 21**).
    b. No. 10 hose (B, **Figure 21**).

10. Unscrew and remove the choke assembly (**Figure 22**) from the front carburetor (**Figure 23**). Dis-

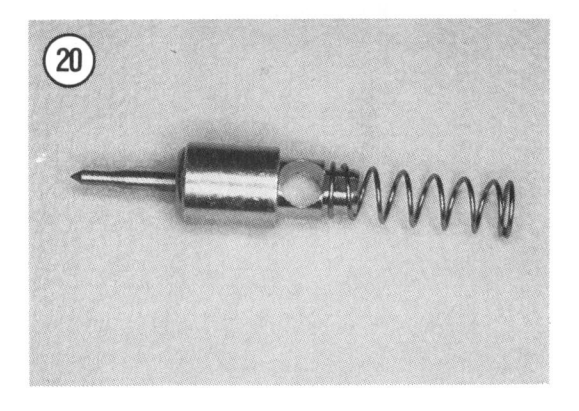

connect and store the choke plunger and spring (**Figure 20**) in a plastic bag to prevent their loss.

11. Remove the screw and the spark plug wire clamp (**Figure 24**) from the front carburetor.

12. On California models, remove the evaporative emission carburetor air vent (EVAP CAV) control valve (**Figure 25**) from the metal bracket on the carburetor. Do not disconnect any of the hoses from the EVAP CAV (**Figure 26**) unless you are going to remove it.

13. Loosen the hose clamp screw at the side of each carburetor (**Figure 27**). Do not loosen the manifold screws.

14. Pull up on the carburetors to release them from the intake manifolds, then remove them from between the upper frame tubes (**Figure 28**). On California models, disconnect the No. 11 tube from the carburetor (**Figure 29**).

15. Remove the carburetor assembly and take it to a workbench for service.

16. Cover the intake manifold openings to prevent objects from falling undetected into the engine.

17. Reverse these steps to install the carburetors, while noting the following.

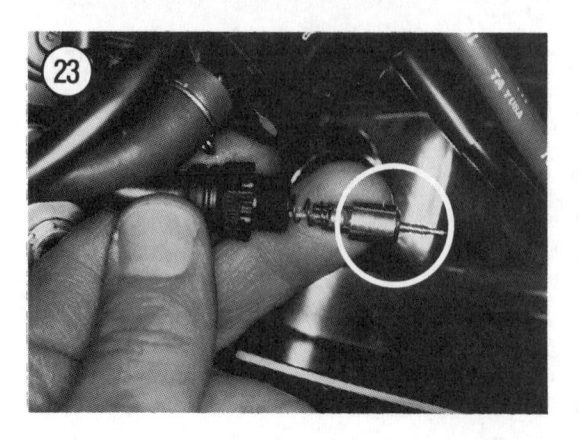

FUEL AND EMISSION CONTROL SYSTEMS

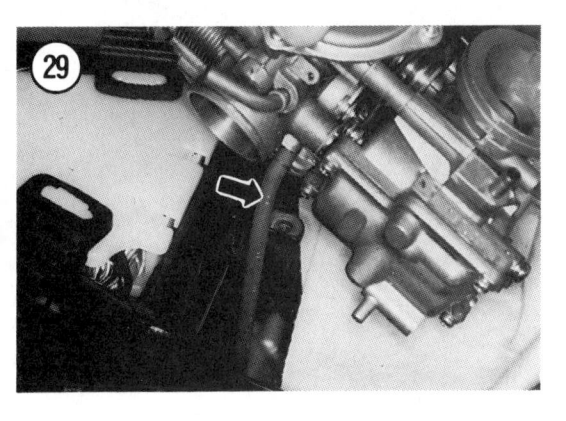

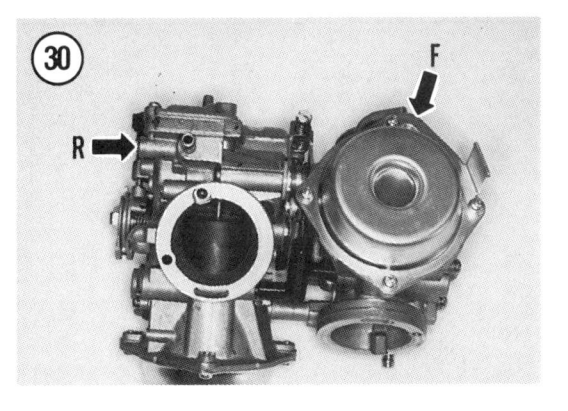

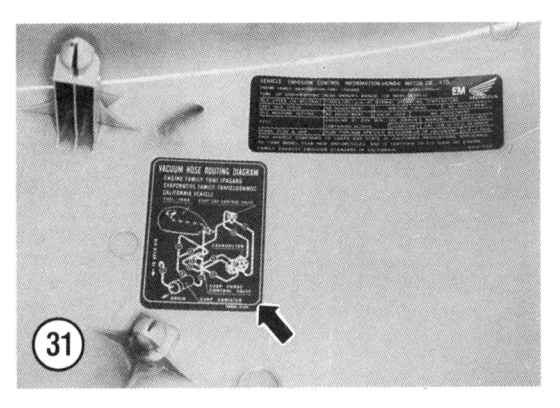

18. Refer to **Figure 30** to identify the carburetors:
    a. Front (F).
    b. Rear (R).

19. On California models, the evaporative emission control tubes can be identified by numbers printed on the tubes. Compare the actual tube numbers with the vacuum hose routing diagram mounted on the reverse side of the right side cover (**Figure 31**).

20. When installing the choke cables, note the following:

    a. Install the spring, then hook the choke plunger onto the cable as shown in **Figure 19** and **Figure 23**.

    b. Insert the choke plunger into the carburetor and tighten the plunger cap until it contacts the carburetor housing (**Figure 18** and **Figure 22**). Then tighten the plunger an additional 1/4 turn.

21. When installing the throttle cables, note the following:

    a. Attach the *pull* throttle cable (A, **Figure 32**) into the lower portion of the throttle drum. Then install and secure its cable holder (**Figure 33**) with the 2 screws.

CHAPTER EIGHT

b. Attach the *return* throttle cable (B, **Figure 32**) into the upper bracket and into the upper portion of the throttle drum.

c. Open and release the throttle a few times, making sure that the throttle drum opens and returns with no binding or roughness.

22. Before installing the connecting tube assembly (**Figure 12**), note the following:

   a. If you disconnected the connecting tube assembly, align their arrows (**Figure 34**) when reconnecting them. Tighten the clamps securely.

   b. Before you install the connecting tube assembly, position the hose clamp tabs into the grooves in the connecting tube assembly (**Figure 35**).

   c. Install the connecting tube assembly (**Figure 36**) through the frame tubes and connect it to each carburetor and to the large frame tube. Then align the notch in each connecting tube with the projection tab on each carburetor (**Figure 35**).

   d. Tighten each hose clamp securely.

23. Perform the following adjustments as described in Chapter Three:

   a. Adjust throttle cables.

   b. Check and adjust carburetor synchronization and idle speed.

   c. Adjust carburetor choke.

24. After installing the fuel tank and turning on the fuel valve, check the carburetors for fuel leaks. Repair any leak before starting the engine.

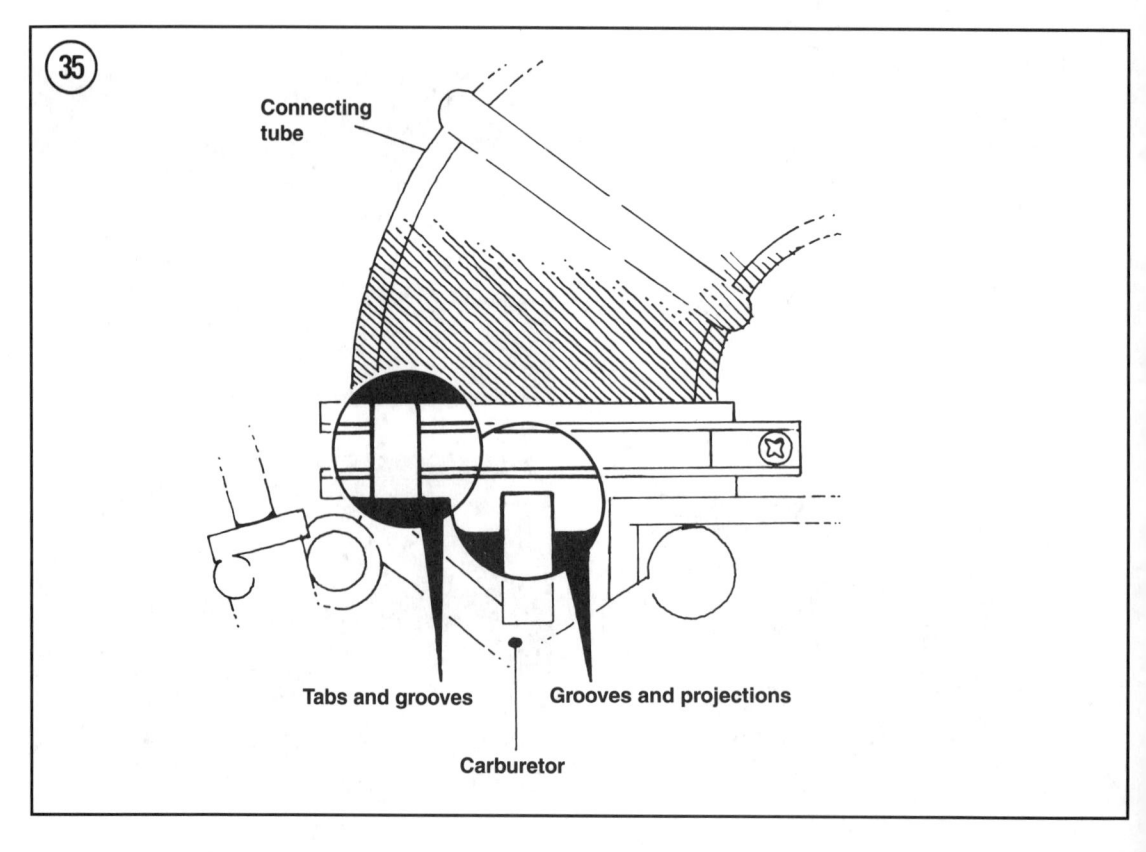

FUEL AND EMISSION CONTROL SYSTEMS

WARNING
Do not ride the motorcycle until the throttle cables are adjusted properly.

Air Cutoff Valve
Removal/Installation

The air cutoff valves can be removed without disassembling the carburetors.

Refer to **Figure 37** when performing this procedure.
1. Remove the carburetor as described in this chapter.
2. Remove the air cutoff valve cover screws, then remove the cover (**Figure 38**) and spring, diaphragm (**Figure 39**) and O-ring (**Figure 40**).
3. Inspect the spring (A, **Figure 41**) for weakness or damage.
4. Inspect the cover (B, **Figure 41**) for corrosion or damage. Clean the cover passages with compressed air.
5. Inspect the diaphragm (C, **Figure 41**) for deterioration or other damage.
6. Inspect the diaphragm needle (D, **Figure 41**) for excessive wear or damage.
7. Replace the O-ring if deteriorated or damaged.
8. Check the air vent passage in the carburetor (**Figure 40**) for dirt or other debris.
9. Replace excessively worn or damaged parts.
10. Install the O-ring (**Figure 40**).
11. Install the diaphragm and seat it into the carburetor groove as shown in **Figure 39**.
12. Install the spring and seat it into the cover (**Figure 42**), then install the cover and spring (**Figure 38**) and secure it with its mounting screws.
13. Repeat these steps for the remaining air cutoff valve assembly.

Carburetor Disassembly

Refer to **Figure 37** when servicing the carburetors in this section.

NOTE
Do not interchange parts between the front and rear carburetors. Keep both carburetors and their parts separate when performing the following procedures.

1. Remove the air cutoff valve as described in this chapter.
2. Remove the vacuum chamber cover screws and cover (A, **Figure 43**).
3. Remove the diaphragm/vacuum piston and spring (**Figure 44**).

CAUTION
*Do not damage the jet needle (**Figure 45**) installed in the vacuum piston.*

4. Remove the float bowl mounting screws, float bowl (**Figure 46**) and O-ring.
5. Remove the float pin (**Figure 47**), then remove the float and fuel valve. See **Figure 48**.
6. Remove the pilot jet (**Figure 49**).
7. Remove the main jet (**Figure 50**).
8. Remove the needle jet holder (**Figure 51**).

NOTE
The needle jet is pressed into place and cannot be removed.

9. Remove the fuel valve seat/screen and gasket assembly (**Figure 52**).
10. To remove the jet needle from the vacuum piston, perform the following:
   a. Insert a Phillips screwdriver into the vacuum piston cavity and turn the holder (**Figure 53**) 90° in either direction to unlock it from the tangs within the piston cavity.
   b. Remove the holder, spring and jet needle (**Figure 54**).
11. For complete cleaning of the carburetors, separate the carburetor assemblies as described in this chapter.

NOTE
Further disassembly is not recommended. If the throttle plate and shaft are damaged, the carburetor body must be replaced.

252　　　　　　　　　　　　　　　　　　　　　　　　　　　　　　　　　CHAPTER EIGHT

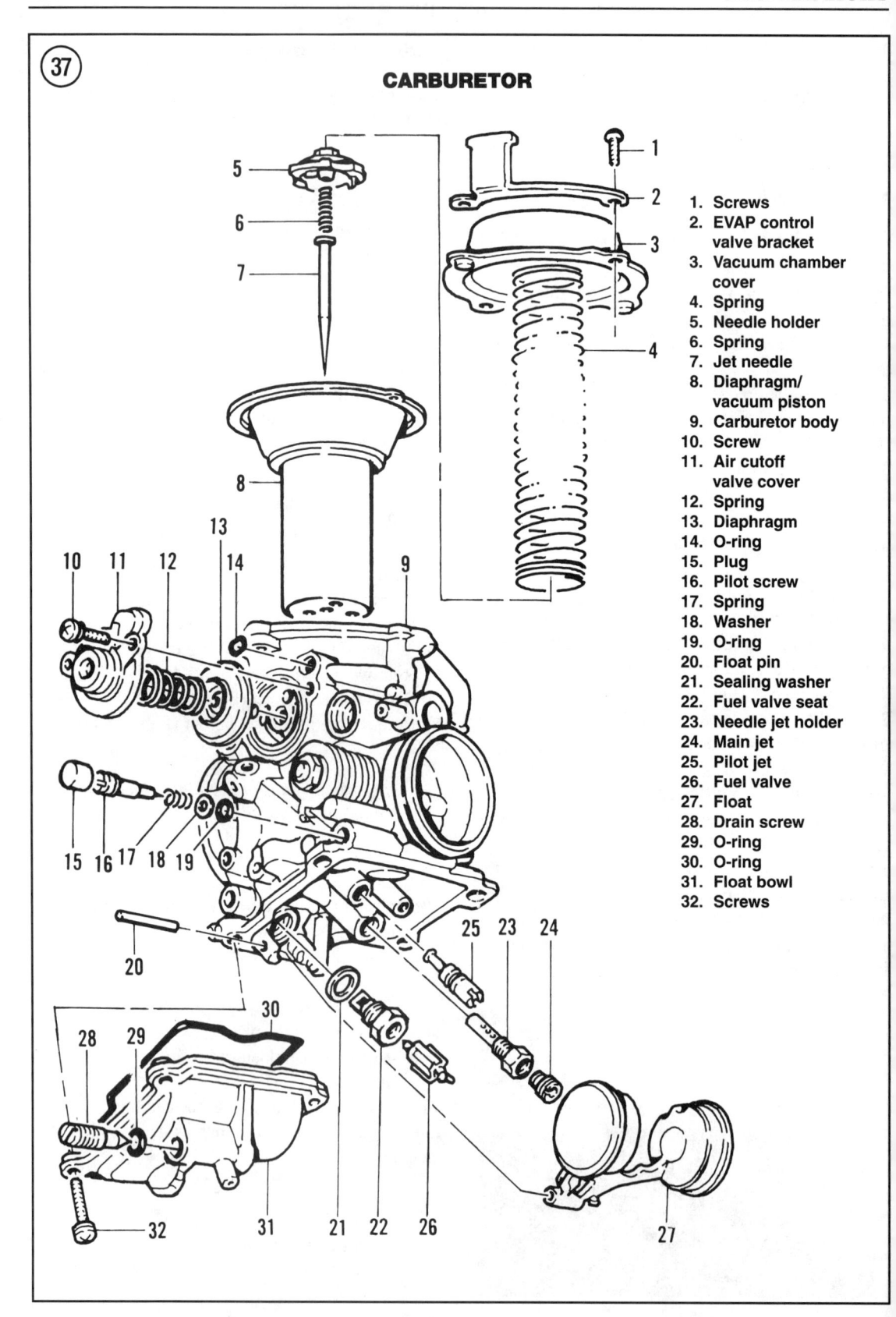

CARBURETOR

37

1. Screws
2. EVAP control valve bracket
3. Vacuum chamber cover
4. Spring
5. Needle holder
6. Spring
7. Jet needle
8. Diaphragm/vacuum piston
9. Carburetor body
10. Screw
11. Air cutoff valve cover
12. Spring
13. Diaphragm
14. O-ring
15. Plug
16. Pilot screw
17. Spring
18. Washer
19. O-ring
20. Float pin
21. Sealing washer
22. Fuel valve seat
23. Needle jet holder
24. Main jet
25. Pilot jet
26. Fuel valve
27. Float
28. Drain screw
29. O-ring
30. O-ring
31. Float bowl
32. Screws

FUEL AND EMISSION CONTROL SYSTEMS

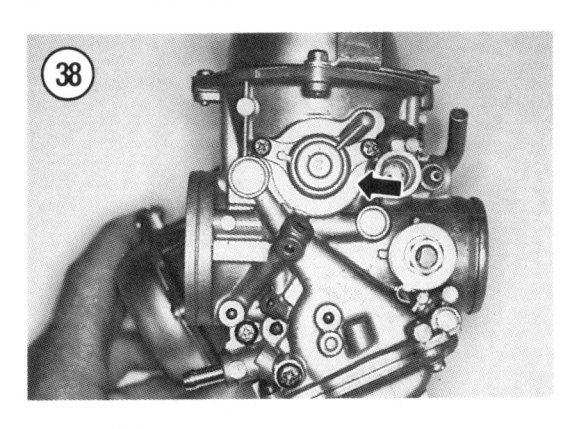

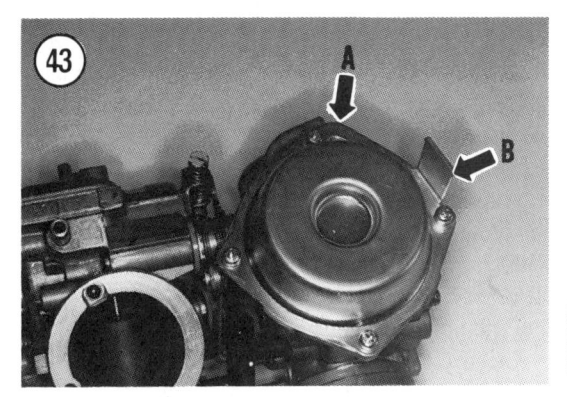

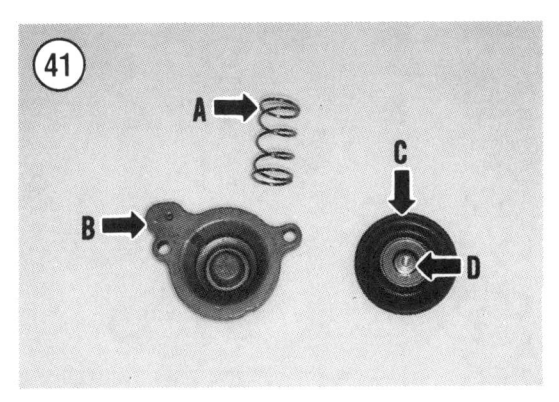

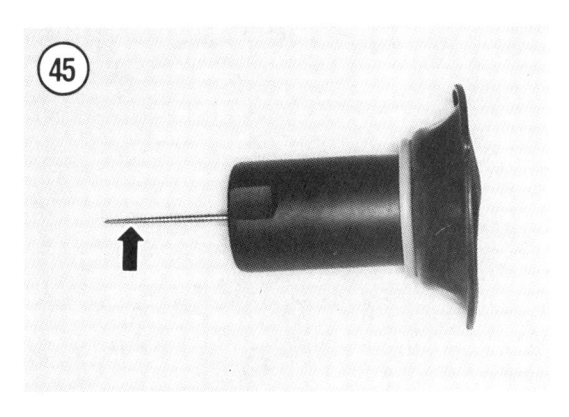

253

Carburetor
Cleaning and Inspection

The following steps list a step-by-step cleaning and inspection procedure for both carburetors. If the motorcycle has been in storage for more than a month and the float bowls were not drained, the carburetor passages and jets must be cleaned thoroughly to remove any varnish residue that is left from evaporating gasoline.

1. Clean all parts, except the carburetor housing, rubber and plastic parts, in a good grade of carburetor cleaner. This solution is available at most automotive supply stores in a small, resealable tank with a dip basket. If it is tightly sealed when not in use, the solution will last for several cleanings. Follow the manufacturer's instructions for correct soak time (usually about 1/2 hour).
2. After soaking the parts, rinse them in warm water and blow dry with compressed air. Blow out the jets with compressed air. Do not use a piece of wire to clean them as minor gouges in a jet can alter flow rate and upset the fuel/air mixture.
3. Clean the carburetor housing with compressed air.

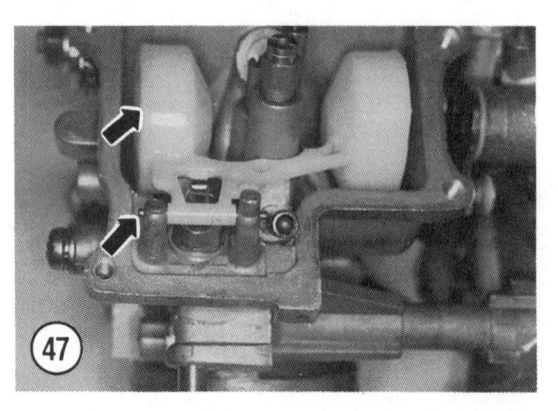

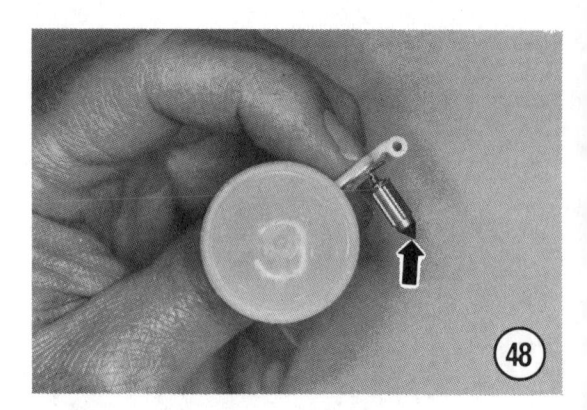

FUEL AND EMISSION CONTROL SYSTEMS

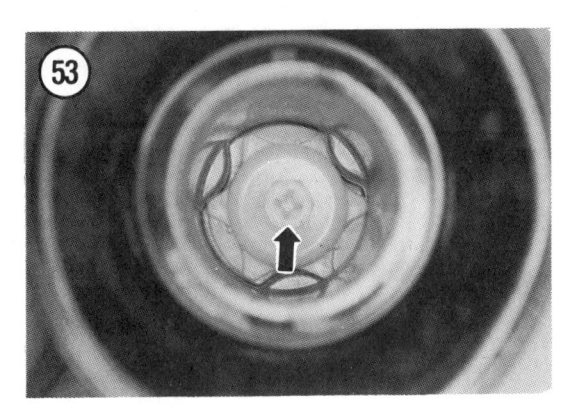

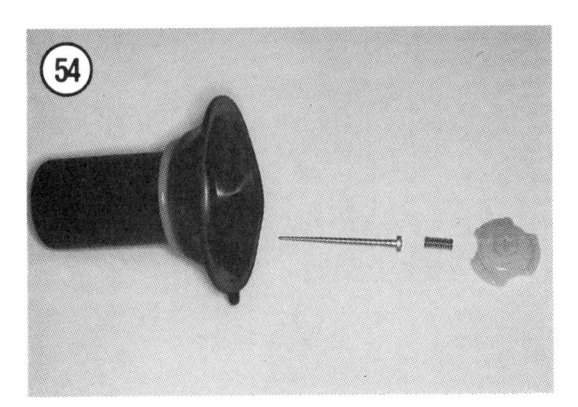

4. Inspect the end of the fuel valve (**Figure 55**) and fuel valve seat (A, **Figure 56**) for wear or damage. If the fuel valve is worn or damaged, replace the valve and seat at the same time.
5. Clean and inspect the fuel valve seat filter (B, **Figure 56**). If damaged, replace the fuel valve seat and valve as a set. Clean the filter with compressed air (low pressure).

NOTE
A worn fuel valve and seat assembly will cause engine flooding. If there is any doubt about the condition of these parts, replace them as a set.

6. Inspect the main jet (A, **Figure 57**), needle jet (B) holder and pilot jet (C) for contamination or thread damage.
7. Check the vacuum piston (A, **Figure 58**) for nicks, scoring or damage.
8. Check the vacuum piston diaphragm (B, **Figure 58**) for tearing, pin holes, age deterioration or other damage.
9. Inspect the jet needle (**Figure 59**) for excessive wear at the tip or other damage on the needle.

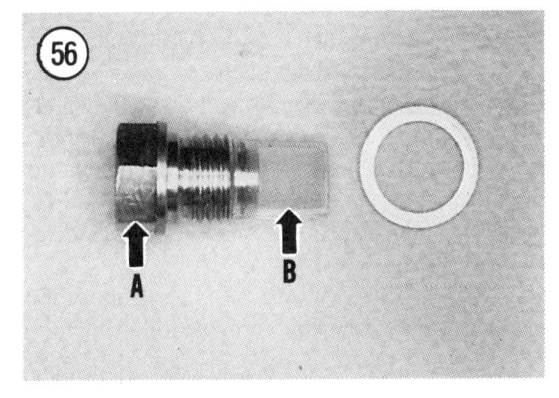

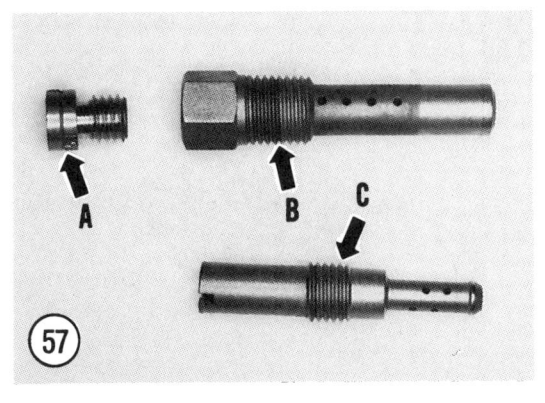

10. Inspect the jet needle spring and holder (**Figure 59**) for corrosion or damage.

11. Inspect the float (**Figure 60**) for deterioration or damage. If the float is suspected of leakage, place it in a container of water and push it down. If the float sinks or if bubbles appear (indicating a leak), replace the float.

12. Replace all O-rings (**Figure 61**) and gaskets upon assembly. O-rings tend to become hardened over time and therefore lose their ability to seal properly.

Assembly

1. If the pilot screw was removed, install as described under *Pilot Screw and Plug Removal/Installation* in this chapter.
2. Install a new gasket (**Figure 56**) onto the fuel valve seat/screen assembly, then install and tighten the seat (**Figure 52**).
3. Install and tighten the needle jet holder (**Figure 51**).
4. Install and tighten the main jet (**Figure 50**).
5. Install and tighten the pilot jet (**Figure 49**).
6. Hook the fuel valve onto the float (**Figure 48**), then install the float and secure it with its float pin (**Figure 47**).
7. Measure the float height as described under *Carburetor Adjustments* in this chapter.
8. If removed, install the O-ring into the float bowl groove (**Figure 61**).
9. Align the float bowl pin with the pin hole in the carburetor housing (**Figure 62**) and install the float. Install and tighten the float bowl (**Figure 46**) mounting screws securely.
10. To install the jet needle assembly (**Figure 59**) into the vacuum piston, perform the following:

   a. Install the jet needle into the vacuum piston.

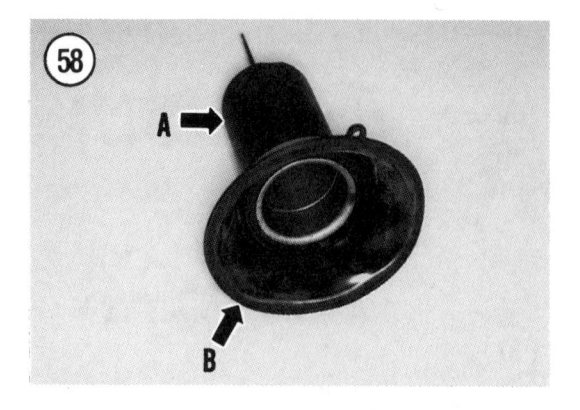

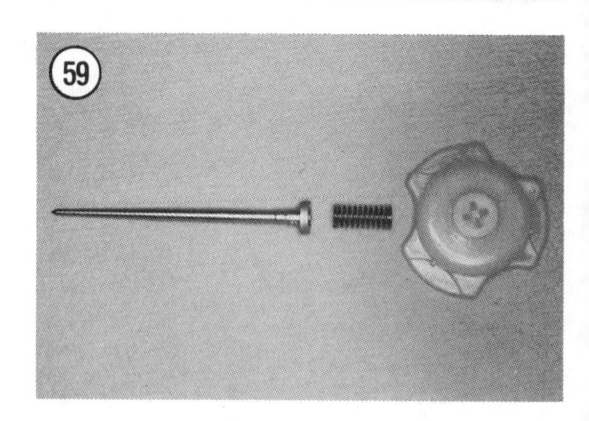

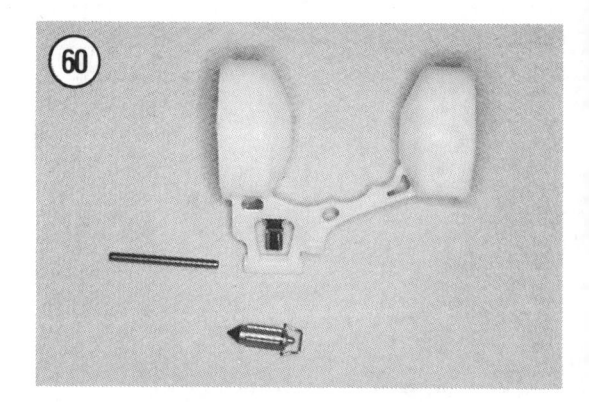

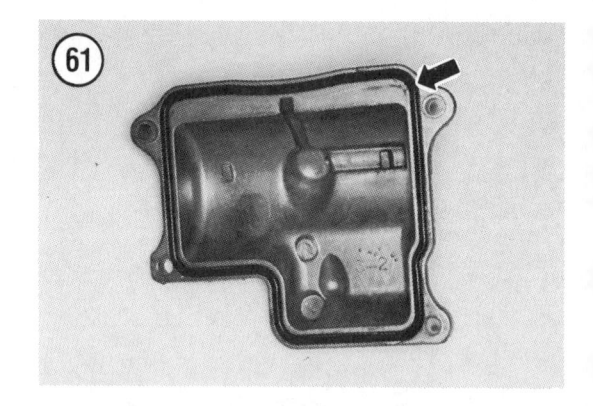

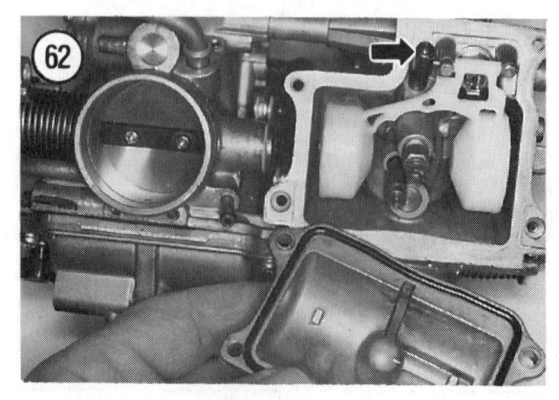

FUEL AND EMISSION CONTROL SYSTEMS

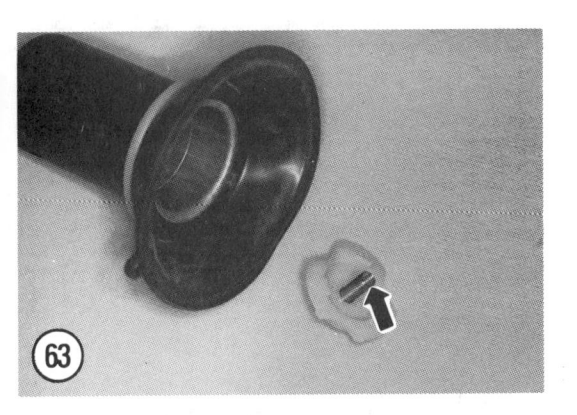

b. Install the spring onto the holder (**Figure 63**), then install the holder into the vacuum piston.

c. Press and turn the holder (**Figure 53**) clockwise until it locks in place.

11. Install the diaphragm/vacuum piston into the carburetor. Then align the diaphragm tab with the cavity in the carburetor housing (**Figure 64**).

12. Lift the vacuum piston (from the bottom) and seat the diaphragm rib (**Figure 65**) into the groove in the top of the carburetor housing.

13. Install the spring (**Figure 44**) into the vacuum piston.

14. Align the shoulder on the inside of the vacuum chamber cover with the spring, then install the cover (A, **Figure 43**). Align the diaphragm tab with the concave part of the cover (**Figure 66**) when installing the cover.

15. On California models, install the EVAP CAV control valve bracket (B, **Figure 43**) on the right side carburetor.

16. Install and tighten the vacuum chamber cover screws (**Figure 43**).

17. Install the air cutoff valve as described in this chapter.

18. If separated, assemble the carburetors as described in this chapter.

Carburetor Separation/Assembly

Refer to **Figure 67** for this procedure.

1. Loosen the synchronization screw (A, **Figure 68**) to remove all tension from the screw, then remove the synchronization spring (B, **Figure 68**).

2. Remove the 2 carburetor mounting screws (**Figure 69** and **Figure 70**).

3. Separate the carburetors while removing the thrust spring and the air vent joint (**Figure 71**).

4. Discard the 2 O-rings installed on the air vent joint.

5. Service the carburetors as described in this chapter.

6. Assemble by reversing these disassembly steps while noting the following.

7. Lubricate 2 new O-rings with engine oil and install them onto the air vent joint.

8. Install the thrust spring and air vent joint and join the 2 carburetors as shown in **Figure 67**.

9. Make sure there is no clearance or gap where the 2 carburetor housings join together, then install and tighten the screws (**Figure 69** and **Figure 70**) gradu-

CHAPTER EIGHT

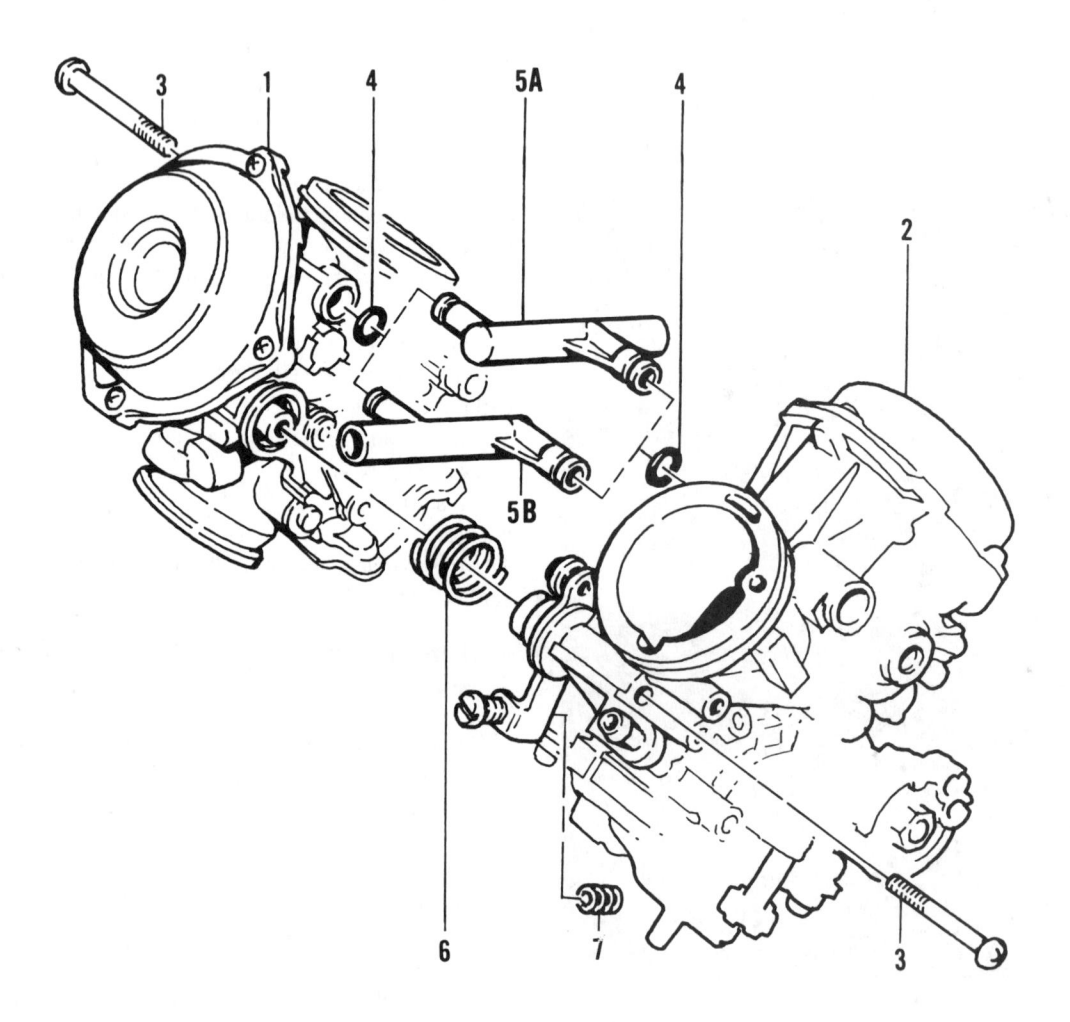

⑥⑦ CARBURETOR ASSEMBLY

1. Front carburetor
2. Rear carburetor
3. Screw
4. O-rings
5A. Air vent joint
    (California models)
5B. Air vent joint
    (except California models)
6. Thrust spring
7. Synchronization pin

FUEL AND EMISSION CONTROL SYSTEMS

ally, first one screw and then the other until they are both tight.

10. Install the synchronization spring (B, **Figure 68**).

11. Turn the throttle stop screw (A, **Figure 72**) and align the throttle valve (B, **Figure 72**) with the edge of the bypass hole in the No. 1 carburetor.

12. Turn the synchronization screw (A, **Figure 68**) to align the throttle valve (C, **Figure 68**) with the edge of the bypass hole in the No. 2 carburetor.

13. Open the throttle with the throttle linkage and then release it. The throttle should return smoothly with no drag.

14. If the throttle does not move smoothly or return properly, recheck all previous steps until the problem is solved.

Pilot Screw and Plug
Removal and Installation

The pilot screws are covered by a plug (**Figure 73**) that must be drilled out to remove or adjust the screw.

1. Use a small center punch and hammer and center punch the middle of the plug (**Figure 73**).

CHAPTER EIGHT

CAUTION
Be careful not to drill too far into the plug. You could damage the pilot screw.

2. Drill a hole into the plug (**Figure 74**) with a 4 mm (5/32 in.) drill bit. If available, attach a drill stop to the drill bit 3 mm (1.8 in.) from the end of the drill bit to prevent contacting the pilot screw.

NOTE
If you do not have a drill stop, wrap 8-10 layers of masking tape 3 mm (1/8 in.) from the end of the drill bit. Use the tape as a visual guide only as it will not stop the drill from penetrating too far into the plug.

3. Thread a 4 mm self-tapping screw into the drilled hole. Continue to turn the screw until the plug starts to turn with the screw.
4. Remove the plug and screw with a pair of pliers (**Figure 75**) and blow away all metal shavings from the area.

NOTE
Before removing the pilot screw, record the number of turns necessary to seat the screw lightly. Record the number of turns for each carburetor as the screws must be reinstalled to the exact same setting.

5. While noting the number of turns necessary, lightly seat the pilot screw.
6. Remove the pilot screw, spring, washer and O-ring.
7. Inspect the pilot screw for a worn or damaged tip. Replace the screw if damaged.
8. Slide the spring, washer and a new O-ring onto the pilot screw.

NOTE
Pilot screws must be installed into their original carburetor.

9. Screw the pilot screw into the carburetor until it lightly seats, then back it out the number of turns noted during disassembly.

NOTE
Do not install new plugs until after the carburetor is installed and adjusted.

10. Repeat these steps for the other carburetor.

CARBURETOR ADJUSTMENT

Float Adjustment

The carburetors must be removed and partially disassembled for this adjustment.

1. Remove the carburetors as described in this chapter.
2. Remove the screws securing the float bowls to the main bodies and remove them.
3. Hold the carburetor assembly so the float arm is just touching the float needle. Use a float level gauge

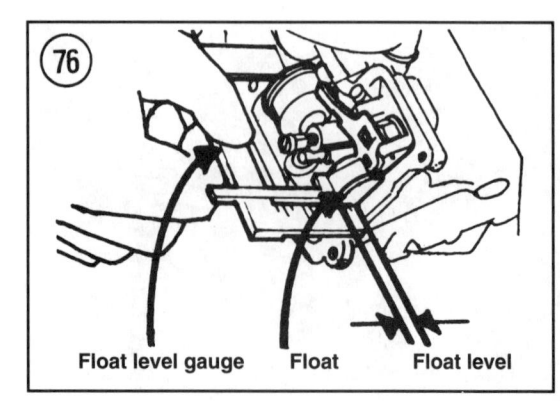

FUEL AND EMISSION CONTROL SYSTEMS

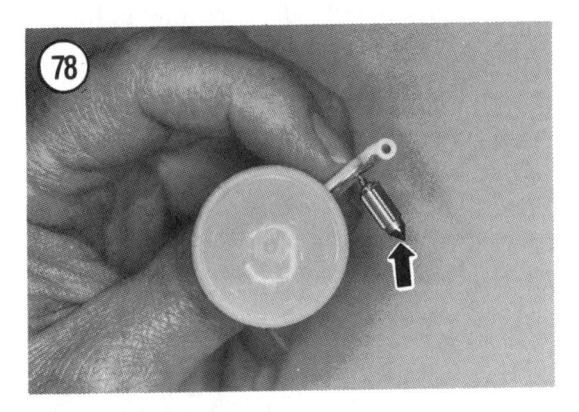

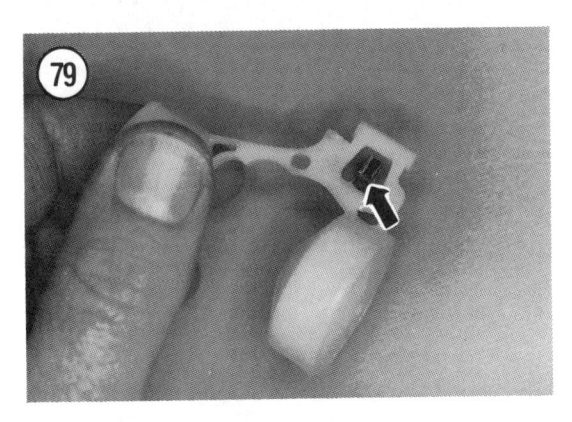

(Honda part No. 07401-0010001 or equivalent) and measure the distance from the carburetor body to the float arm (**Figure 76**). The correct float height is listed in **Table 1**. If the height is incorrect, perform Step 4.

4. To adjust the float height:
   a. Remove the float pin (**Figure 77**), then remove the float (**Figure 77**) and fuel valve.
   b. Remove the fuel valve from the float (**Figure 78**).
   c. Adjust by carefully bending the tang on the float arm (**Figure 79**).
   d. Reverse to install the float assembly.
   e. Install the float bowl as described under *Carburetor Assembly* in this chapter.

5. If the float level is too high, the result will be a rich fuel/air mixture. If it is too low, the mixture will be too lean.

NOTE
The floats on both carburetors must be adjusted to the same height position.

6. Reassemble and install the carburetors as described in this chapter.

Needle Jet Adjustment

The needle jet is not adjustable on all models.

Pilot Screw Adjustment
(Idle Drop Procedure)

The pilot screws are preset at the factory. Adjustment is not necessary unless the carburetors have been overhauled or the pilot screws were replaced.

The air filter element must not be clogged or the results will be inaccurate. If necessary, replace a clogged air filter element before performing this procedure.

1. Remove the pilot screw plugs (A, **Figure 80**) as described in this chapter.

NOTE
If you are going to remove the plugs with the carburetors installed on the bike, first remove the fuel tank and then plug the fuel line opening. Reinstall the fuel tank once both plugs are removed.

CAUTION
Make sure you lightly seat the pilot screws when performing Step 2 or you can damage the pilot screw and the pilot screw seat in the carburetor.

2. Carefully turn the pilot screw (A, **Figure 80**) on each carburetor in until it *lightly* seats then back it out the number of turns listed in **Table 1**.
3. Start the engine and let it reach normal operating temperature. Approximately 10-15 minutes of stop-and-go riding is sufficient.
4. Turn the engine off and support it on its sidestand.
5. Connect a portable tachometer (that can register a change of 50 rpm or less) to the engine following its manufacturer's instructions.
6. Start the engine and turn the throttle stop screw (B, **Figure 80**) in or out to achieve the idle speed listed in **Table 1**.
7. Read the tachometer scale and turn each pilot screw out 1/2 turn from the initial setting in Step 2. If the engine speed increases by 50 rpm or more, turn each pilot screw out an additional 1/2 turn until the engine speed does not increase.
8. Turn the throttle stop screw (B, **Figure 80**) in or out again to achieve the idle speed listed in **Table 1**.
9. Turn the pilot screw on the rear cylinder carburetor until the engine speed drops 50 rpm.
10. Turn the pilot screw on the rear cylinder out 3/4 turn from the position obtained in Step 9.
11. Turn the throttle stop screw (B, **Figure 80**) in or out again to achieve the idle speed listed in **Table 1**.
12. Repeat Steps 9-11 for the front cylinder carburetor pilot screw.
13. Turn the engine off and disconnect the portable tachometer.
14. Test ride the bike. Throttle response from idle should be rapid without any hesitation.
15. Drive in new limiter caps until their outer surface is recessed 1 mm (0.04 in.) into the pilot screw bore.

High-Elevation Adjustment

If the bike is going to be ridden for any sustained period of time at high elevation (2,000 m [6,500 ft.]), the carburetors must be readjusted to improve performance and decrease emissions.
1. Remove each pilot screw plug (A, **Figure 80**) as described in this chapter.

NOTE
If you are going to remove the plugs with the carburetors installed on the bike, first remove the fuel tank and then plug the fuel line opening. Reinstall the fuel tank once both plugs are removed.

2. Start the engine and let it reach normal operating temperature. Approximately 10-15 minutes of stop-and-go riding is sufficient.
3. Turn each pilot screw *clockwise* 1/2 turn as viewed from the side of the carburetor.
4. Turn the throttle stop screw (B, **Figure 80**) in or out again to achieve the idle speed listed in **Table 1**.
5. Drive in new limiter caps until their outer surface is recessed 1 mm (0.04 in.) into the pilot screw bore.
6. When the bike is returned to elevations below 2,000 m (6,500 ft.), adjust the pilot screws to their original position and reset the idle speed to the rpm specified in **Table 1**. Make sure to make these adjustments with the bike at a lower altitude and with the engine running at normal operating temperature.

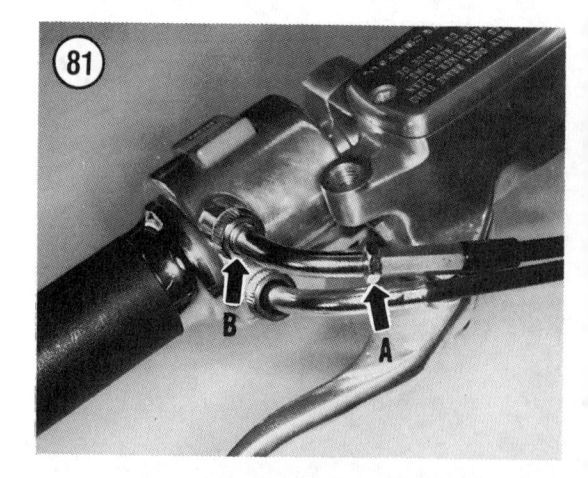

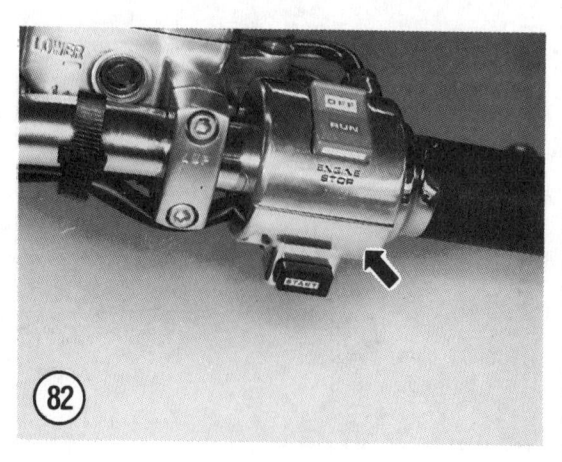

FUEL AND EMISSION CONTROL SYSTEMS

WARNING
The carburetors must be adjusted for the elevation that the bike is primarily operated in. If you run the bike at an altitude lower than 1,500 m (5,000 ft.) with the carburetors adjusted for high altitude, the engine will idle roughly and stall in traffic. Overheating may also cause engine damage.

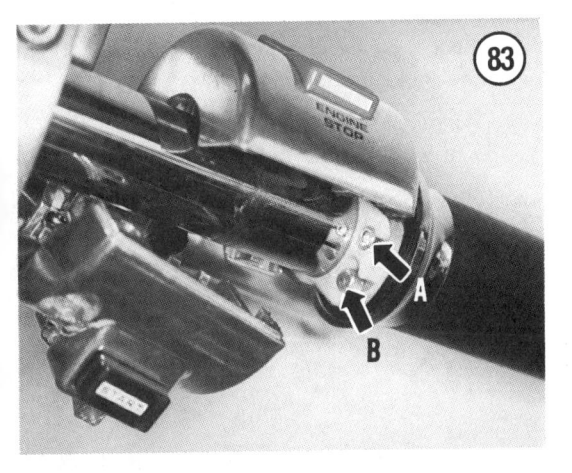

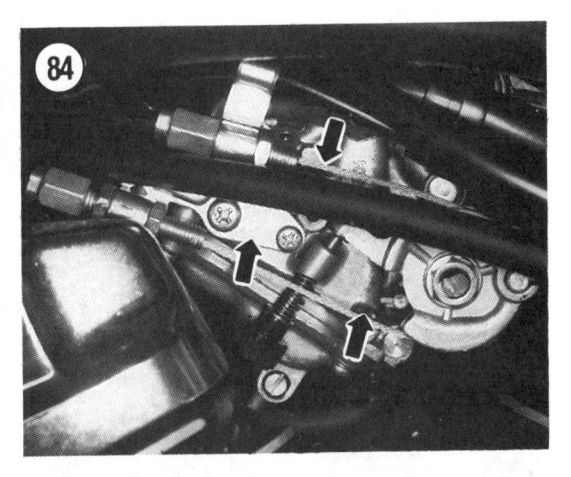

THROTTLE CABLE REPLACEMENT

1. Lubricate the new cables (Chapter Three) and set them aside until installation.
2. Remove the fuel tank as described in this chapter.
3. Note the routing of both cables from the throttle grip to the carburetors. Record this information on a piece of paper for proper installation. Then identify each cable's mounting position at the handlebar and carburetor for proper installation.
4. Loosen the throttle cable adjuster (A, **Figure 81**) and locknut (B, **Figure 81**) at the throttle grip.
5. Remove the 2 right side handlebar switch housing screws and separate the switch housing (**Figure 82**) from around the handlebar.
6. Disconnect the 2 throttle cables (**Figure 83**) from the throttle grip.
7. Disconnect the 2 throttle cables and remove the cable holder from the rear carburetor. See **Figure 84**.
8. Lubricate the new cables as described in Chapter Three.

CAUTION
Install the new cables carefully in Steps 9 and 10 to prevent bending or otherwise damaging them.

9. Hook one of the new cables to its matched old cable, then carefully pull the old cable out and replace it with the new one.
10. Repeat Step 9 for the other cable.
11. Make sure the new cables follow the original path of the old cables. Also make sure the cables are not kinked or binding against any part.
12. Connect the *pull* throttle cable as follows:
    a. Connect the *pull* throttle cable (A, **Figure 85**) into the upper hole (A, **Figure 83**) in the throttle grip.
    b. Attach the *pull* throttle cable (A, **Figure 85**) into the lower portion of the throttle drum. Then install and secure its cable holder (**Figure 84**) to the carburetor with the 2 screws.
13. Connect the *return* throttle cable as follows:
    a. Connect the *return* throttle cable into the lower hole (B, **Figure 83**) in the throttle grip.
    b. Attach the *return* throttle cable (B, **Figure 85**) into the upper bracket and into the upper portion of the throttle drum.

14. Install and tighten the right side switch housing as follows:
    a. Align the switch housing locating pin (**Figure 86**) with the hole in the handlebar and close the switch halves around the handlebar. Try to twist the switch; it must not turn.

    NOTE
    *The front switch housing screw is **longer** than the rear screw.*

    b. Install the front and rear switch housing screws and tighten securely.
15. Install the fuel tank as described in this chapter.
16. Operate the throttle grip and make sure the carburetor linkage is operating correctly with no binding. If operation is incorrect or if there is binding, carefully check that the cables are attached correctly and that there are no tight bends in the cables.
17. Adjust the throttle cables as described in Chapter Three.
18. Test ride the bike slowly at first and make certain the throttle is operating correctly.

WARNING
Do not ride the bike until the throttle cables are working correctly.

CHOKE CABLE REPLACEMENT

1. Remove the fuel tank as described in this chapter.
2. Note the routing of the choke cable at the handlebar to both lower cables where they mount at the carburetors. Record this information on a piece of paper for proper installation.
3. Unscrew and remove the choke assembly (**Figure 87**) from the rear carburetor (**Figure 88**). Disconnect and remove the choke plunger and spring (**Figure 89**).

NOTE
Separate the choke plungers so that you can install them into their original carburetor.

4. Repeat Step 3 for the front carburetor.
5. Loosen the choke cable locknut (A, **Figure 90**) at the left switch housing.
6. Remove the 2 left handlebar switch housing screws (B, **Figure 90**) and separate the switch housing from around the handlebar.
7. Disconnect the choke cable (A, **Figure 91**) from the choke lever mounted inside the switch housing.
8. Remove the choke cable assembly.
9. Install the new choke cable assembly, following the original path recorded in Step 2.
10. Connect the upper choke cable end and install the left side handlebar switch housing as follows:
    a. Reconnect the choke cable (A, **Figure 91**) to the choke lever.
    b. Align the switch housing locating pin (B, **Figure 91**) with the hole in the handlebar and

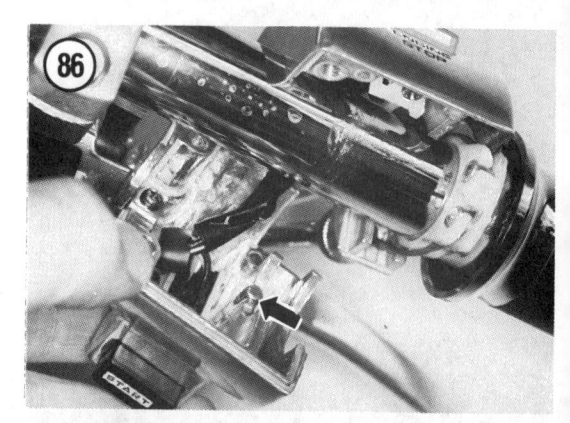

FUEL AND EMISSION CONTROL SYSTEMS

close the switch halves around the handlebar. Try to twist the switch; it must not turn.

NOTE
*The front switch housing screw is **shorter** than the rear screw.*

c. Install the front and rear switch housing screws. Tighten the front screw, then the rear screw. Tighten both screws securely.
11. Reconnect the choke cables to the carburetors as follows:

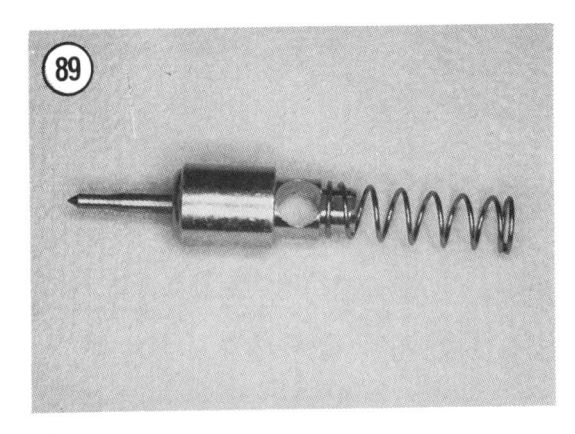

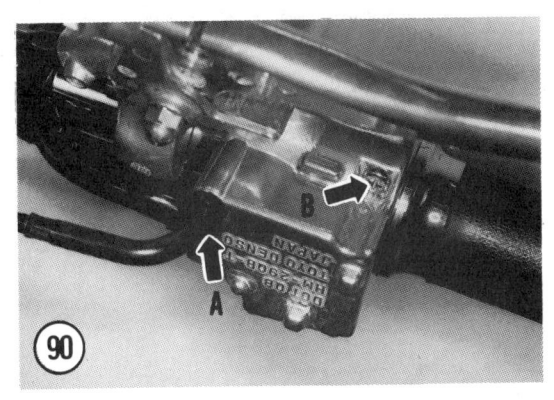

a. Install the spring and hook the choke plunger onto the cable as shown in **Figure 88**.

b. Insert the choke plunger into the carburetor and tighten the plunger cap until it contacts the carburetor housing (**Figure 87**). Then tighten the plunger an additional 1/4 turn.

c. Repeat for the other cable end and carburetor.
12. Operate the choke lever and make sure the choke plungers operate correctly. If the operation is incorrect or there is binding, first make sure the cable is routed and attached correctly. Make sure the cable works correctly before adjusting the choke in Step 14.
13. Install the fuel tank as described in this chapter.
14. Adjust the choke cable as described in Chapter Three.

FUEL FILTER

Removal/Installation

The fuel filter is mounted on the bottom of the air filter housing (**Figure 92**).
1. Read the *WARNING* at the beginning of this chapter before removing the fuel filter.
2. Disconnect the negative battery cable from the battery (Chapter Three).
3. Remove the rear wheel (Chapter Twelve).
4. Disconnect, then plug each hose at the fuel filter (**Figure 93**).
5. Remove the fuel filter and its rubber bracket from the mounting bracket on the bottom of the air filter housing.
6. Reverse these steps to install the new fuel filter, while noting the following.
7. Install the fuel filter with its arrow mark facing in the direction shown in **Figure 92**.
8. Reconnect the hoses to the fuel filter, then secure each hose with its metal hose clamp.
9. Check the fuel hoses for leaks.

FUEL PUMP

Testing

Fuel pump performance testing is covered in Chapter Nine.

Removal/Installation

The fuel pump is mounted on the bottom of the air filter housing (**Figure 92**). To remove the fuel pump, first remove the air filter housing as described in this chapter.

FUEL TANK

Refer to **Figure 94** when performing this procedure.

Removal/Installation

1. Read the *WARNING* at the beginning of this chapter.
2. Disconnect the battery negative cable as described in Chapter Three.
3. Turn the fuel valve off.
4. Remove the front mounting bolt and collar (**Figure 95**).
5. Remove the rear mounting bolt, washer and collar (**Figure 96**).
6. Lift up the rear of the fuel tank, then disconnect the tube (**Figure 97**) from underneath the fuel tank.
7. Disconnect the fuel hose (**Figure 98**) from the fuel valve. Plug the hose to prevent contamination.
8. Remove the fuel tank.
9. Install the fuel tank by reversing these removal steps while noting the following.
10. Secure the fuel hose and tube with their respective hose clamps.
11. Tighten the front (**Figure 95**) and rear (**Figure 96**) fuel tank mounting bolts to the torque specification in **Table 2**.
12. Turn the valve to the ON position and check for any fuel leaks. Repair any fuel leaks before riding the bike.

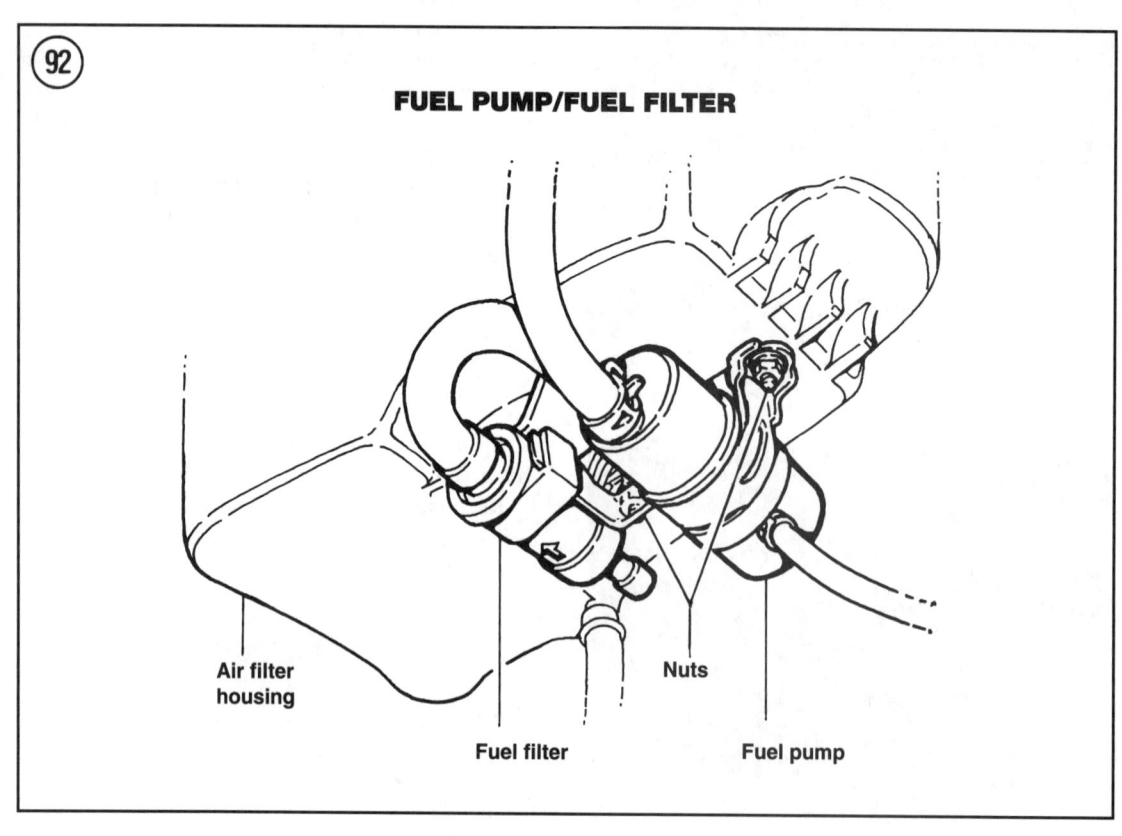

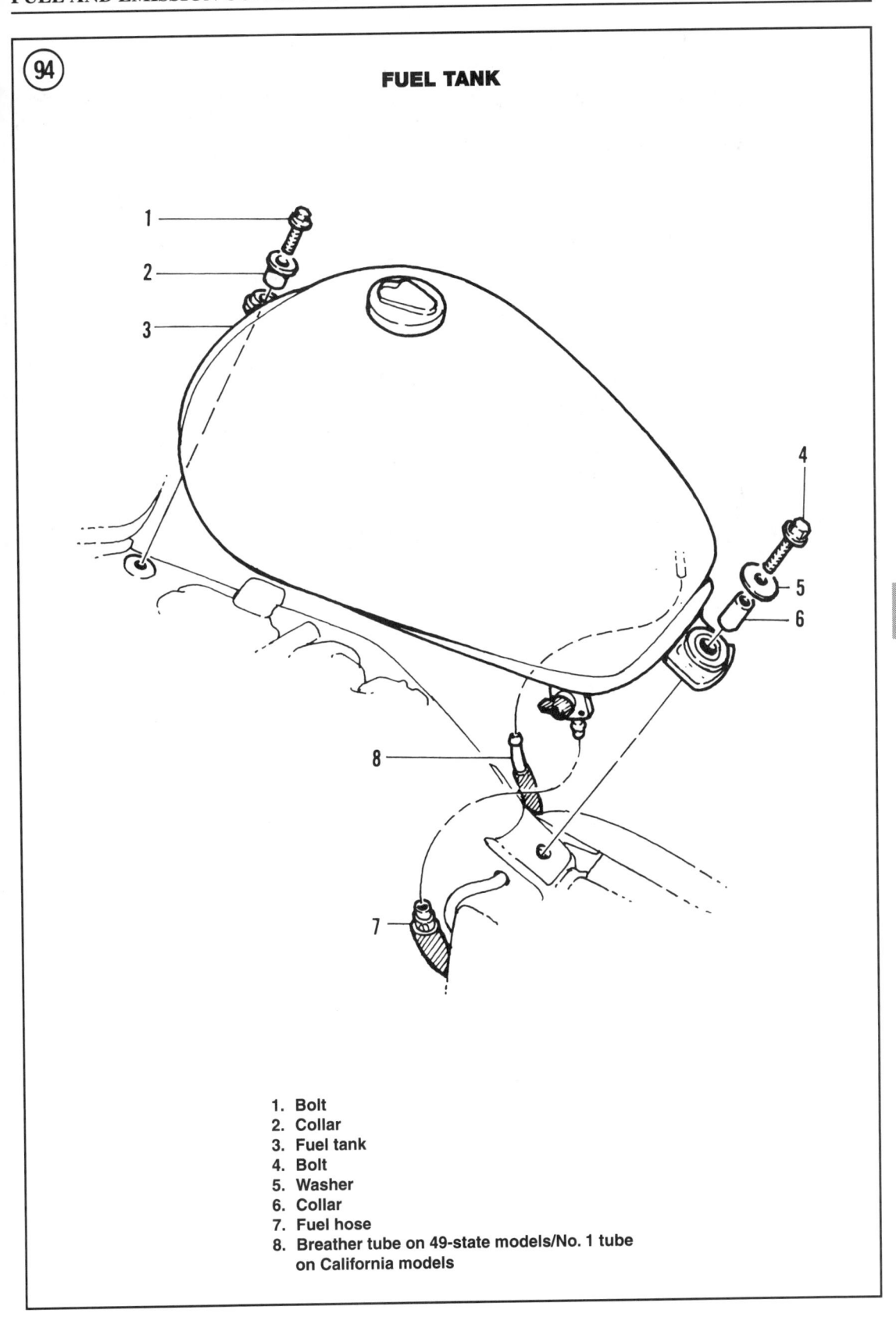

FUEL AND EMISSION CONTROL SYSTEMS

FUEL TANK

1. Bolt
2. Collar
3. Fuel tank
4. Bolt
5. Washer
6. Collar
7. Fuel hose
8. Breather tube on 49-state models/No. 1 tube on California models

CHAPTER EIGHT

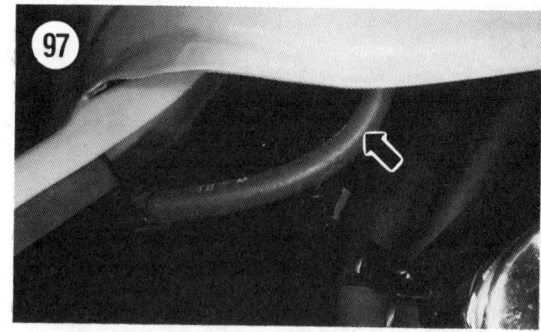

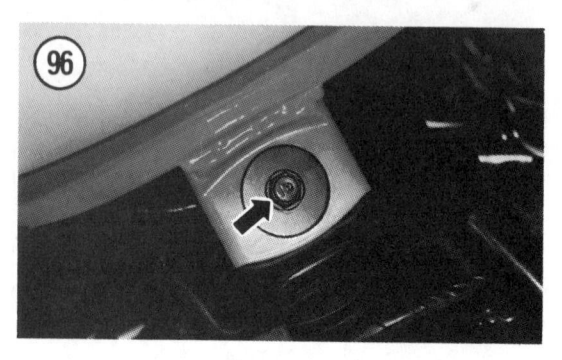

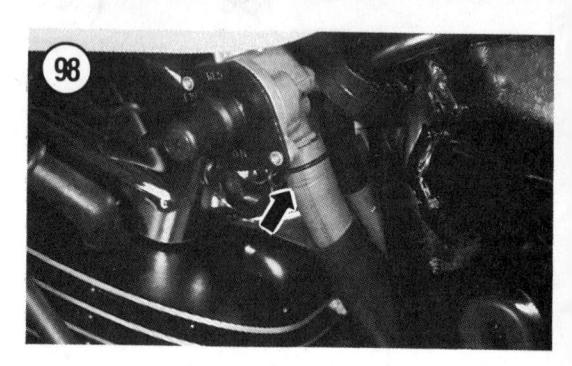

CRANKCASE EMISSION CONTROL SYSTEM

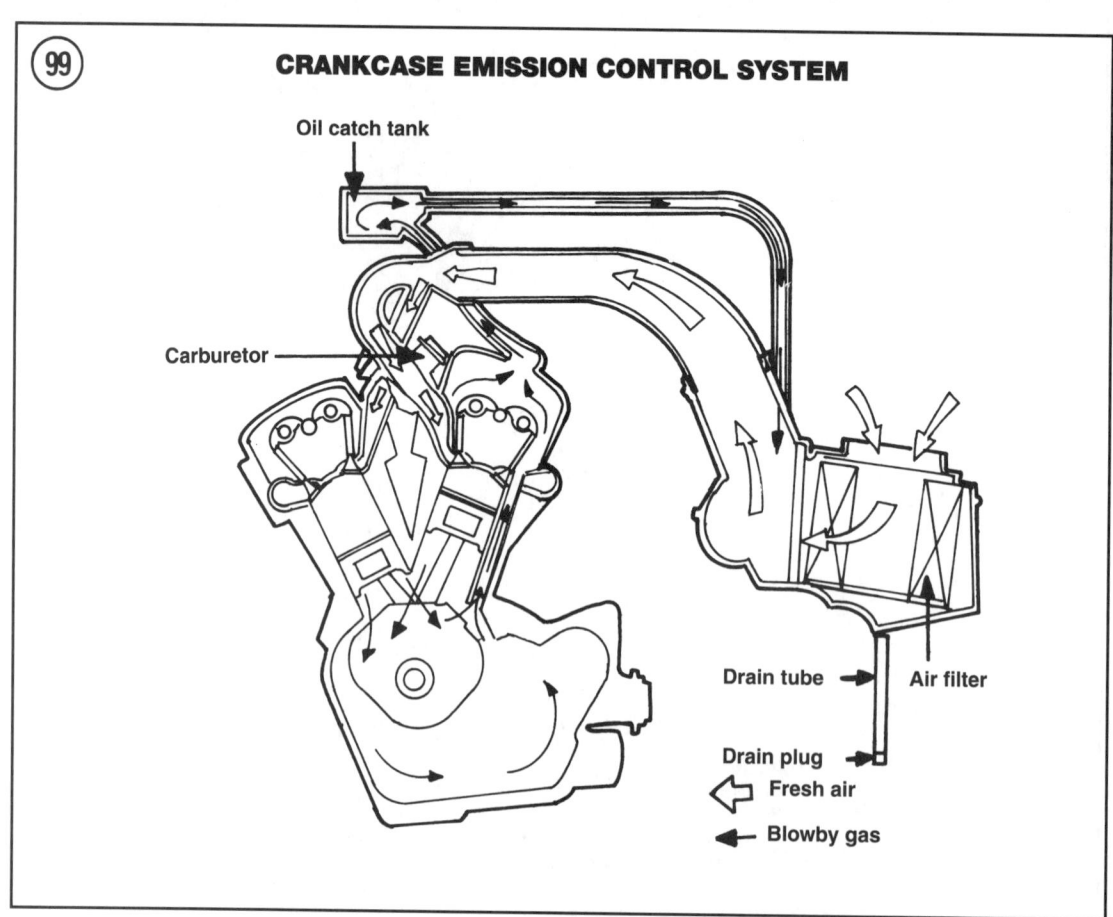

- Oil catch tank
- Carburetor
- Drain tube
- Air filter
- Drain plug
- ⇦ Fresh air
- ← Blowby gas

FUEL AND EMISSION CONTROL SYSTEMS

CRANKCASE BREATHER SYSTEM—U.S. ONLY

The engine is equipped with a closed crankcase breather system (**Figure 99**). The system draws blow-by gases from the crankcase and recirculates them into the combustion chamber to be burned.

Vapor collects in the crankcase breather storage tank and drain tube. These must be emptied at periodic intervals. See Chapter Three for service intervals and procedures.

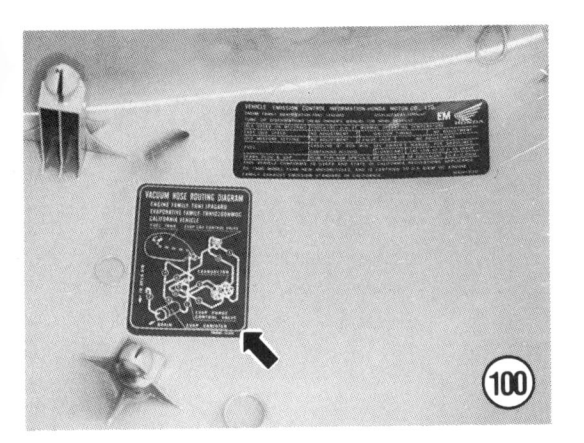

EVAPORATIVE EMISSION CONTROL SYSTEM—CALIFORNIA ONLY

Fuel vapor from the fuel tank is routed into a charcoal canister. This vapor is stored when the engine is not running. When the engine is running the vapor is drawn through a EVAP purge control valve and into the carburetor to be burned.

Make sure all hose clamps are tight. Check all hoses for deterioration and replace as necessary.

Refer to the emission control information and the vacuum hose routing diagram labels mounted on the back of the right side cover (**Figure 100**) and to the drawing in **Figure 101**.

Evaporative Emission (EVAP) Canister Removal/Installation

1. Disconnect the No. 2 tube (**Figure 102**) from the canister.
2. Disconnect the No. 1 (A, **Figure 103**) and No. 4 (B, **Figure 103**) tubes from the EVAP canister.
3. Remove the mounting bolts (C, **Figure 103**) and the EVAP canister. See **Figure 104**.

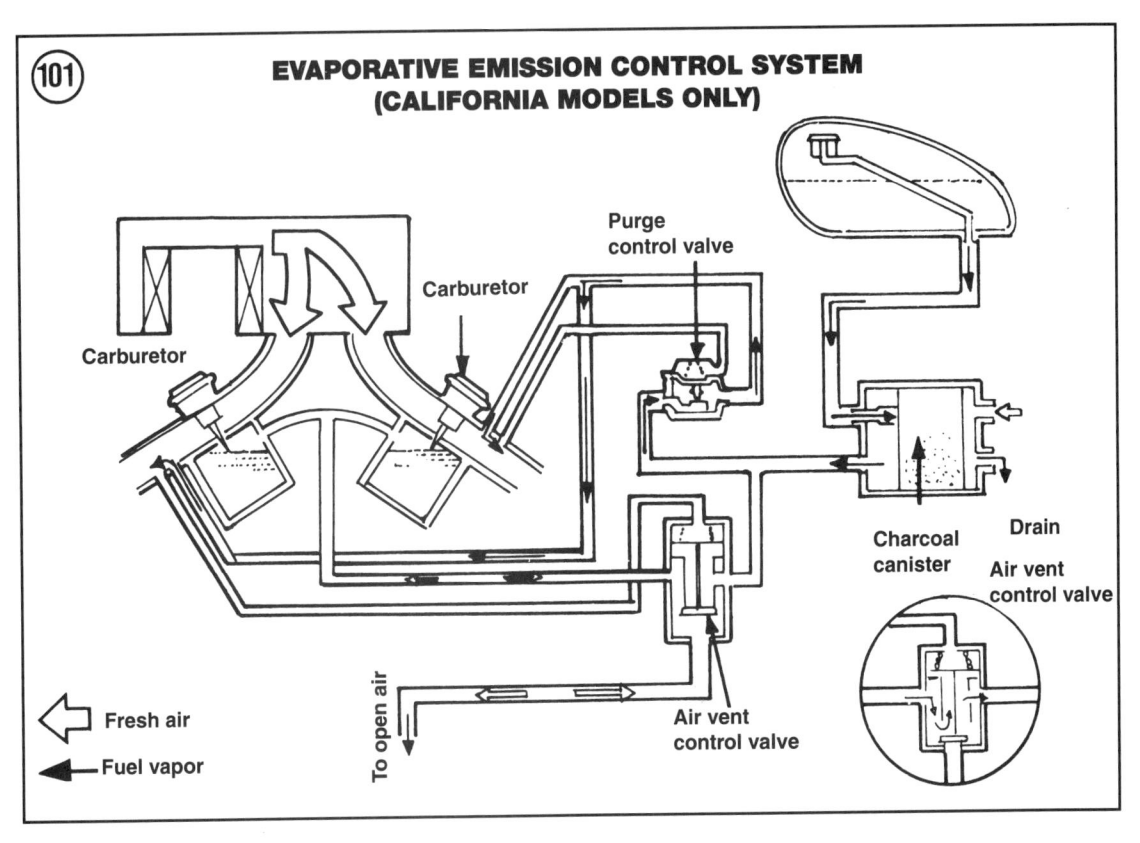

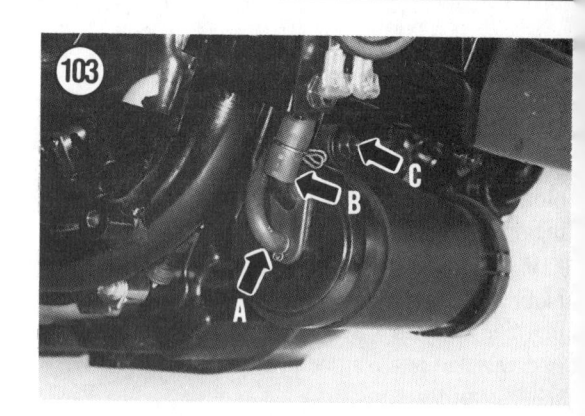

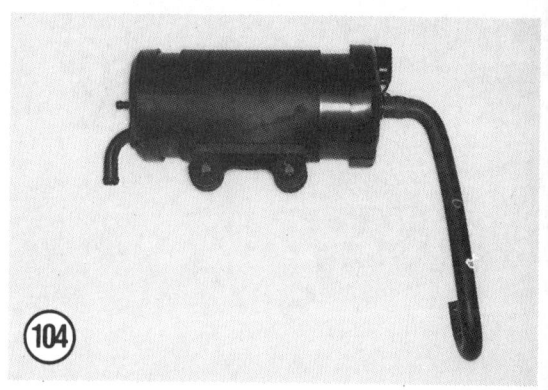

4. Reverse these steps to install the EVAP canister.

Evaporative Emission (EVAP) Purge Control Valve
Removal/Installation

1. Pull the EVAP purge control valve (**Figure 105**) off its mounting stay.
2. Disconnect the following tubes from the EVAP purge control valve (**Figure 105**):
    a. No. 4 tube.
    b. No. 5 tube.
    c. No. 11 tube.

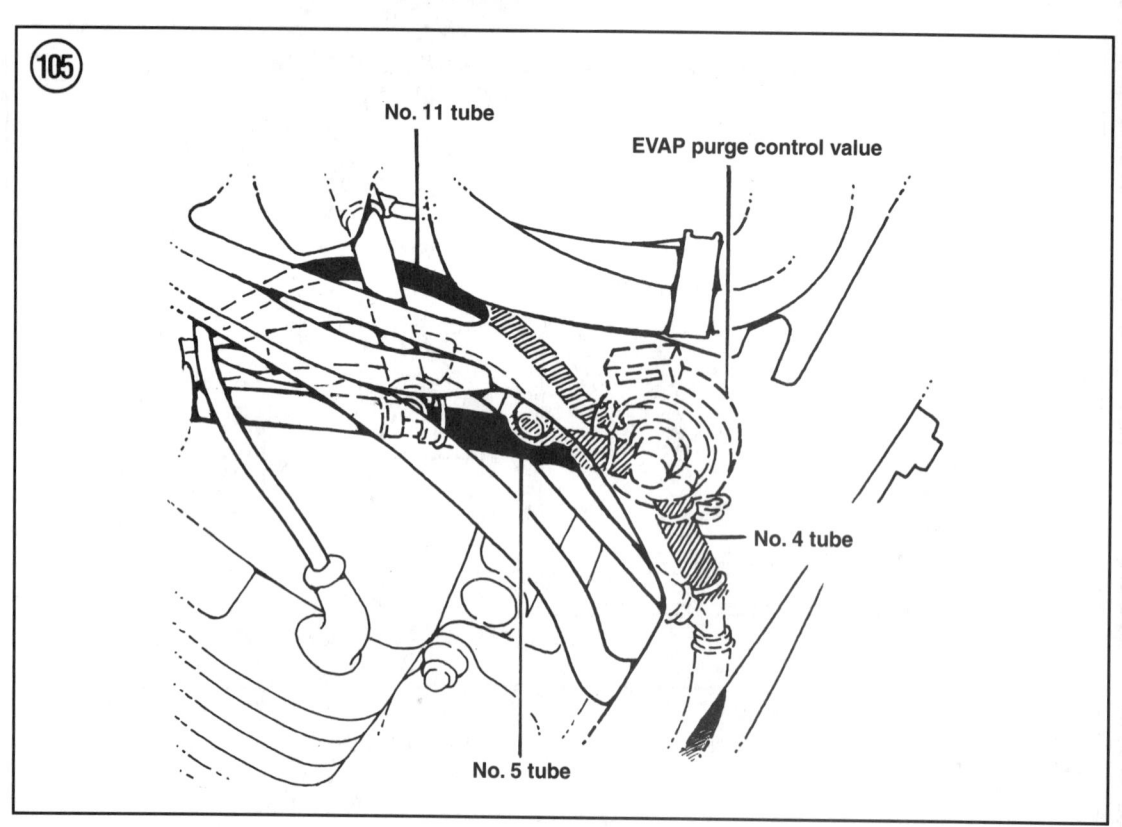

FUEL AND EMISSION CONTROL SYSTEMS

3. Reverse these steps to install the EVAP purge control valve.

Evaporative Emission (EVAP) Purge Control Valve Testing

If the engine is hard to restart when hot, test the EVAP purge control valve as follows. Refer to **Figure 106** to identify the tube fittings called out in this procedure.

1. Remove the EVAP purge control valve as described in this chapter.
2. Connect a vacuum pump to the No. 5 tube fitting (**Figure 106**) and apply 33 kPa (9.8 in.) Hg of vacuum. The vacuum must hold. If the valve loses vacuum, replace the EVAP purge control valve.
3. Disconnect the vacuum pump.
4. Connect the vacuum pump to No. 11 tube fitting (**Figure 106**) and apply 33 kPa (9.8 in.) Hg of vacuum. The vacuum must hold. If the valve loses vacuum, replace the EVAP purge control valve. If the vacuum holds, leave the vacuum pump connected to the No. 11 tube fitting and continue with Step 5.
5. Connect a pressure pump to the No. 4 tube fitting (**Figure 106**).
6. Apply 33 kPa (9.8 in.) Hg of vacuum to the No. 11 tube fitting, then pump air through the No. 4 tube fitting. When doing so, air must exit through the No. 5 tube fitting. If air does not exit through the No. 5 tube fitting, replace the EVAP purge control valve.
7. Disconnect the vacuum and pressure pumps.
8. Install the EVAP purge control valve as described in this chapter.

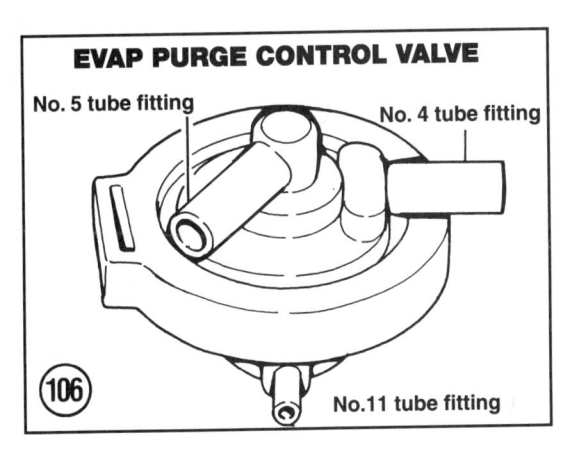

Evaporative Emission Carburetor Air Vent (EVAP CAV) Control Valve Removal/Installation

1. Remove the fuel tank as described in this chapter.
2. Pull the EVAP CAV control valve (**Figure 107**) off its mounting stay.

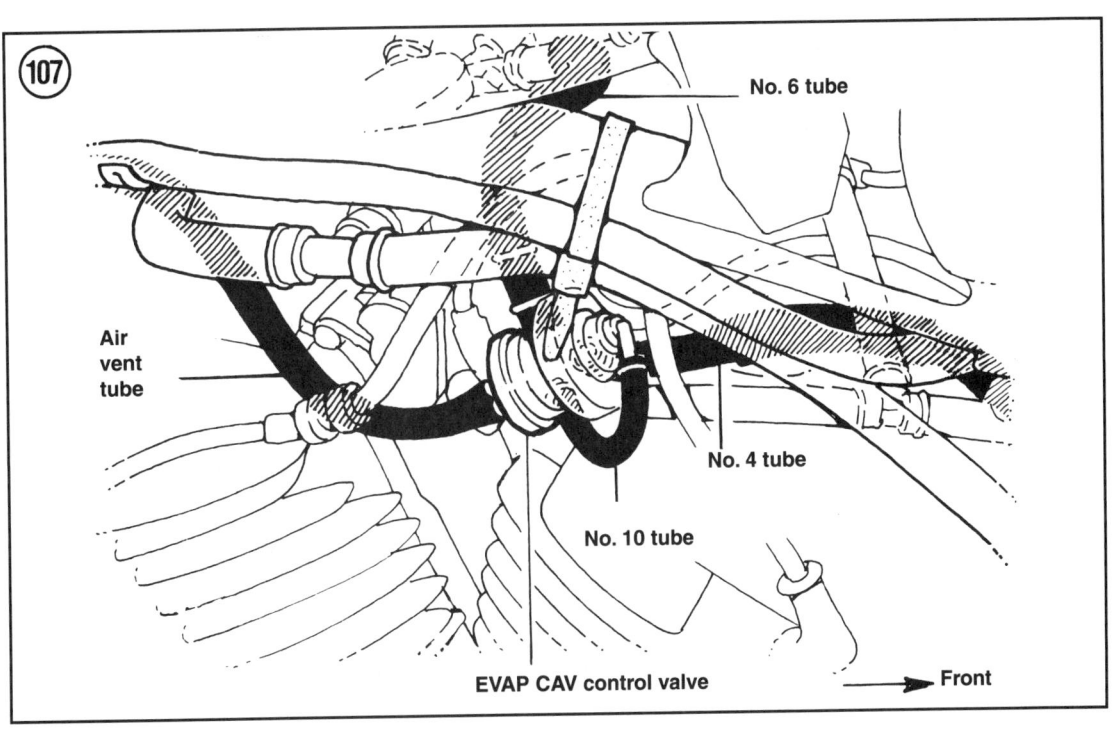

3. Disconnect the following tubes from the EVAP CAV control valve (**Figure 107**):
   a. No. 4 tube.
   b. No. 6 tube.
   c. No. 10 tube.
4. Reverse these steps to install the EVAP CAV control valve.

Evaporative Emission Carburetor Air Vent (EVAP CAV) Control Valve Testing

If the engine is hard to restart when hot, test the EVAP purge control valve as follows. Refer to **Figure 108** to identify the tube fittings called out in this procedure.

1. Remove the EVAP CAV control valve as described in this chapter.
2. Connect a vacuum pump to the No. 10 tube fitting (**Figure 108**) and apply 33 kPa (9.8 in.) Hg of vacuum. The vacuum must hold. If the valve loses vacuum, replace the EVAP CAV control valve.
3. Disconnect the vacuum pump.
4. Connect the vacuum pump to air vent tube fitting (**Figure 108**) and apply 33 kPa (9.8 in.) Hg of vacuum. The vacuum must hold. If the valve loses vacuum, replace the EVAP CAV control valve.
5. Remove the vacuum pump and reconnect it to the No. 10 tube fitting (**Figure 108**). Connect a pressure pump to the air vent tube fitting (**Figure 108**).
6. Apply vacuum to the No. 10 tube fitting, then pump air through the air vent tube fitting. Air must flow through the valve and exit through the No. 6 tube fitting.
7. Plug the No. 6 tube fitting. Then apply vacuum to the No. 10 tube fitting while pumping air through the air vent tube fitting. The pressure at both pumps should remain steady.
8. If the EVAP CAV control valve checked out okay, reinstall it. If the EVAP CAV control valve failed any one of these tests, install a new valve.

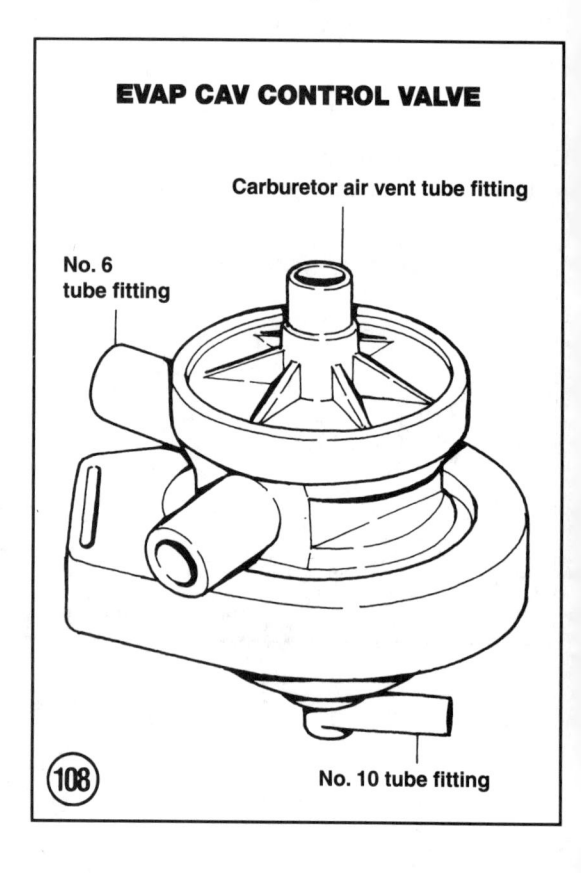

EVAP CAV CONTROL VALVE

Carburetor air vent tube fitting

No. 6 tube fitting

No. 10 tube fitting

108

FUEL AND EMISSION CONTROL SYSTEMS

Table 1 CARBURETOR SPECIFICATIONS

Carburetor	
Type	Constant venturi
Throttle bore size	26 mm (1.4 in.)
Carburetor identification number	
1995	
49-state	VDKBA
California	VDKCA
Canada	VDK2A
1996	
49-state	VDKBB
California	VDKCB
Canada	VDK2B
Main jet	
Front carburetor	
1995	180
1996	175
Rear carburetor	
1995	185
1996	180
Pilot jet	42
Pilot screw adjustment	see text
Float level	9.2 mm (0.36 in.)
Idle speed	1,000 ± 100 rpm
Pilot screw idle drop procedure	
Initial pilot screw setting	
1995	1 3/4 turns out
1996-on	1 1/2 turns out

Table 2 TIGHTENING TORQUES

	N·m	in.-lb.	ft.-lb.
Fuel tank mounting bolts			
Front	12	106	—
Rear	27	—	20
Fuel valve	35	—	25

CHAPTER NINE

ELECTRICAL SYSTEM

This chapter contains service and test procedures for all electrical and ignition components. Information regarding the battery and spark plugs are covered in Chapter Three.

The electrical system includes the following systems:

a. Charging system.
b. Ignition system.
c. Starting system
d. Lighting system.
e. Switches.
f. Electrical components.
g. Fuses.

Tables 1-7 are at the end of this chapter.

CHARGING SYSTEM

The charging system (**Figure 1**) consists of the battery, alternator and a voltage regulator/rectifier. A 30-amp main fuse protects the circuit.

Alternating current generated by the alternator is rectified to direct current. The voltage regulator maintains the voltage to the battery and additional electrical loads (such as lights and ignition) at a constant voltage despite variations in engine speed and load.

Troubleshooting

Refer to Chapter Two to troubleshoot the following charging system malfunctions:

a. Battery discharging.
b. Battery overcharging.

Current Leakage Test

Perform this test before performing the charging voltage test.

1. Remove the left side cover (Chapter Fourteen).
2. Turn the ignition switch off.
3. Disconnect the negative battery cable from the battery (**Figure 2**).

CAUTION
Before connecting the ammeter into the circuit in Step 3, set the meter to its highest amperage scale. This will prevent a large current flow from damaging the meter or blowing the meter's fuse, if so equipped.

4. Connect an ammeter between the battery ground cable and the negative battery terminal (**Figure 3**).
5. Adjust the ammeter between its highest and lowest amperage scale while reading the ammeter scale. The specified current leakage rate is 0.1 mA maximum.

ELECTRICAL SYSTEM

CHARGING SYSTEM

Regulator/rectifier

Yel Yel Yel Red/Wht Grn

30 amp

Alternator   Battery

①

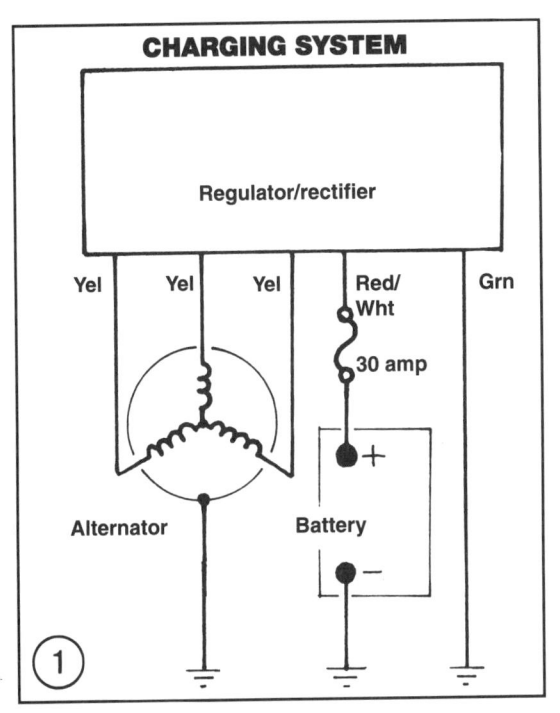

②

6. A higher current leakage rate suggests a continuous battery discharge (drain). Dirt and/or electrolyte on top of the battery or a crack in the battery case can cause this type of problem by providing a path for battery current to follow. Remove and clean the battery as described in Chapter Three. Then reinstall the battery and retest.

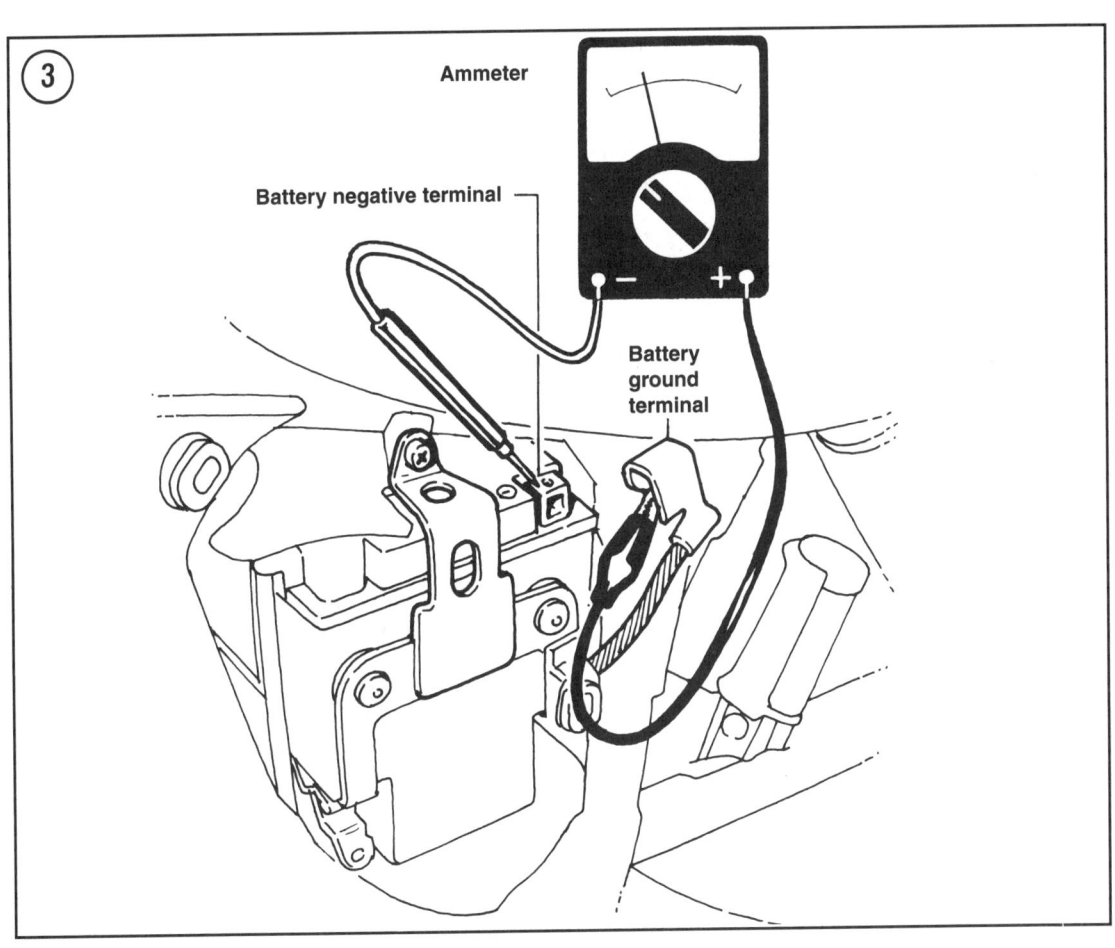

③

Ammeter

Battery negative terminal

Battery ground terminal

7. If the current leakage rate is still excessive, consider the following probable causes:

   a. Damaged battery.

   b. Short circuit in the system.

   c. Loose, dirty or faulty electrical connectors in the charging circuit.

8. To find a short circuit, refer to the wiring diagram for your model at the end of this book. Then measure the current leakage while disconnecting different connectors in the electrical system one by one. When the current leakage rate returns to normal, you have found the short circuit. Test the circuit further to find the problem.
9. Disconnect the ammeter from the battery and battery cable.
10. Reconnect the negative battery cable at the battery (**Figure 2**).
11. Install the left side cover (Chapter Fourteen).

Regulated Voltage Test

This procedure tests charging system operation. It does not measure maximum charging system output. **Table 1** lists charging system test specifications.

To obtain accurate test results, the battery must be fully charged with a specific gravity reading above 1.260. Measure the battery's specific gravity as described in Chapter Three.

1. Start and run the engine until it reaches normal operating temperature, then turn the engine off.
2. Connect a 0-20 DC voltmeter across the battery terminals as shown in **Figure 4**.

NOTE
Do not disconnect either battery cable when making this test.

3. Start the engine and allow it to idle. Turn the headlight to HI beam.
4. Gradually increase engine speed from idle to 5,000 rpm and read the voltage indicated on the voltmeter. Compare this with the specified voltage reading in **Table 1**.
5. If the voltage reading is not as specified, perform the *Regulator/Rectifier Wiring Harness Test* in this chapter.

Regulator/Rectifier Wiring Harness Test

This procedure tests the integrity of the wires and connectors attached to the regulator/rectifier (**Figure 5**) assembly.

1. Remove the seat (Chapter Fourteen).
2. Disconnect the following regulator/rectifier electrical connectors from the connector block mounted beside the air filter housing:

   a. 2-pin green connector (A, **Figure 6**).

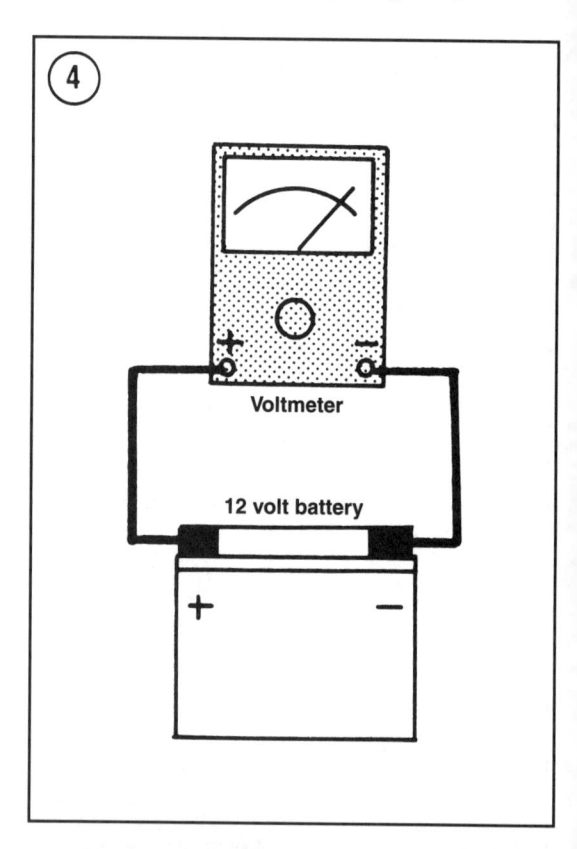

   b. 2-pin white connector (B, **Figure 6**).

ELECTRICAL SYSTEM

c. 3-pin white connector (C, **Figure 6**).

NOTE
Make all of the tests (Steps 3-5) on the wiring harness connector side, not on the regulator/rectifier connector side.

3. Check the battery charge lead as follows:
   a. Connect a voltmeter between the red/white (+) connector (on the wiring harness side) and a good engine ground.
   b. With the ignition switch off, read the voltage indicated on the voltmeter. It must be 13.0-13.2 volts (battery voltage).
   c. If the voltage is less than specified, check the red/white wire for damage.
   d. Disconnect the voltmeter leads.
4. Check the ground line as follows:
   a. Switch an ohmmeter to R × 1.
   b. Connect the ohmmeter between the green wire and a good engine ground.
   c. The ohmmeter must read continuity.
   d. If there is no continuity (high resistance), check the green wire for damage.
5. Check the charge coil line as follows:
   a. Switch an ohmmeter to R × 1.
   b. Touch one ohmmeter lead on one yellow wire and the other lead to another yellow wire and then to the other. Read the resistance on the ohmmeter after making each test connection.
   c. The ohmmeter must read 0.3-0.5 ohms (@ 20° C [69° F]). A higher reading indicates an open circuit. If the reading is out of specification, test the stator coil resistance as described in this chapter.
   d. If the resistance reading is excessive, check for dirty or loose-fitting terminals or damaged wires.

6. Reconnect the regulator/rectifier electrical connectors (**Figure 6**).
7. Install the seat (Chapter Fourteen).

Regulator/Rectifier Unit Resistance Test

Honda specifies the use of 2 multi-testers for accurate testing of the regulator/rectifier unit. These are the KOWA digital multimeter (part No. 07411-0020000) and the SANWA analog multimeter (part No. 07308-0020001). Because of the different resistance characteristics of the semiconductors used in these meters, the use of a different meter may give you a false reading. You can purchase these meters through a Honda dealership, or you can remove the regulator/rectifier unit and have the dealer bench test it for you.

1. Remove the seat (Chapter Fourteen).
2. Disconnect the following regulator/rectifier electrical connectors from the connector block mounted beside the air filter housing:
   a. 2-pin green connector (A, **Figure 6**).
   b. 2-pin white connector (B, **Figure 6**).
   c. 3-pin white connector (C, **Figure 6**).

3A. Set the SANWA tester (or your digital meter) to the R × 1000 ohms scale.
3B. Set the KOWA tester (or your analog meter) to the R × 100 ohms scale.
4. Refer to **Figure 7** for test connections and values. If any of the meter readings differ from the stated values, first check the condition of the battery in the multimeter; an old battery can cause inaccurate readings. If the readings are still incorrect with a new battery, replace the regulator/rectifier unit as described in this chapter.
5. Reconnect the electrical connectors and install the seat (Chapter Fourteen).

Regulator/Rectifier Removal/Installation

1. Remove the seat and the left side cover (Chapter Fourteen).
2. Disconnect the negative battery cable from the battery (**Figure 2**).
3. Disconnect the following regulator/rectifier electrical connectors from the connector block mounted beside the air filter housing:
   a. 2-pin green connector (A, **Figure 6**).
   b. 2-pin white connector (B, **Figure 6**).

c. 3-pin white connector (C, **Figure 6**).

4. Remove the bolts securing the voltage regulator/rectifier (**Figure 5**) to the frame and remove it.

5. Install by reversing these removal steps, while noting the following:

6. Make sure all electrical connectors are tight and free of corrosion.

7. Connect the negative battery cable to the battery (**Figure 2**).

ALTERNATOR

The alternator consists of the flywheel and stator coil assembly. Flywheel and stator removal and installation procedures are covered in Chapter Five.

Flywheel Testing

The flywheel is permanently magnetized and cannot be tested except by replacing it with a known good one. The flywheel can lose magnetism from old age or a sharp hit, such as dropping it onto a cement floor. Replace the flywheel if defective or damaged.

Stator Coil Resistance Test

The stator coil is mounted inside the left side cover (**Figure 8**). You can test the stator coil with it mounted on the engine.

1. Remove the seat (Chapter Fourteen).
2. Disconnect the alternator 3-pin white connector containing 3 yellow wires (C, **Figure 6**).
3. Use an ohmmeter set at R × 1 and measure resistance between each yellow wire on the alternator side of the connector. **Table 1** lists the specified stator coil resistance.
4. If there is continuity (indicated resistance) and it is within the specified resistance, the stator coil is

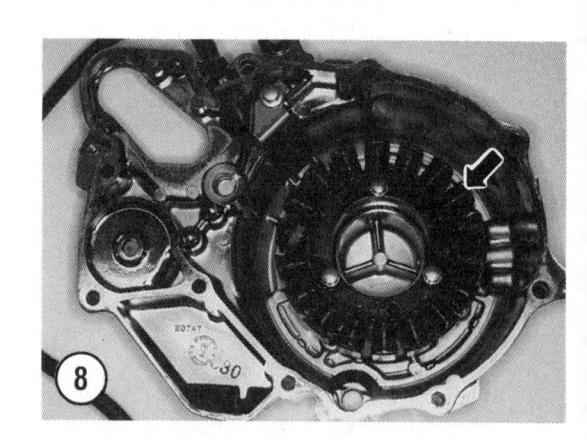

⑦ REGULATOR/RECTIFIER TESTING

Unit: Ω

±	RED/WHT	YEL	YEL	YEL	YEL
RED/WHT		∞	∞	∞	∞
YEL	500-15K		∞	∞	∞
YEL	500-15K	∞		∞	∞
YEL	500-15K	∞	∞		∞
GRN	500-20K	∞	500-15K	500-15K	

ELECTRICAL SYSTEM

good. If there is no continuity (infinite resistance) or the resistance is higher than specified, the coil is damaged. Replace the stator assembly.

5. Use an ohmmeter set at R × 1 and check continuity between each yellow stator and ground.

6. Replace the stator coil if any yellow terminal shows continuity (indicated resistance) to ground. Continuity indicates a short within the stator coil winding.

NOTE
Before replacing the stator assembly, check the electrical wires to and within the electrical connector for any opens or poor connections.

7. If the stator coil (**Figure 8**) fails either of these tests, replace it as described in Chapter Five.
8. Make sure the electrical connector is free of corrosion and properly connected.

IGNITION SYSTEM

All vehicle models are equipped with a capacitor discharge ignition (CDI) system.

Figure 9 shows a schematic of the ignition system.

CDI Troubleshooting

Refer to Chapter Two.

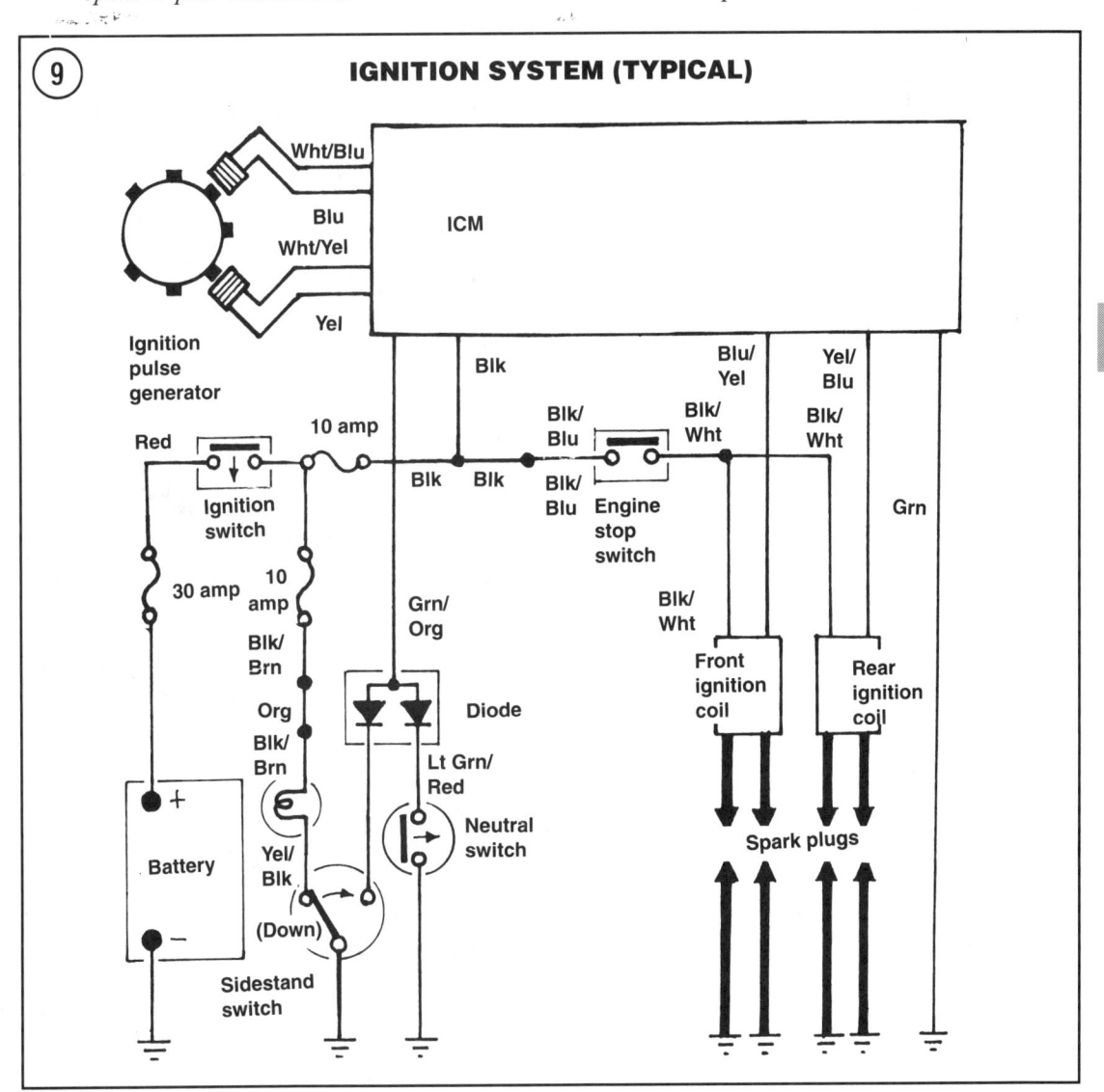

Figure 9 IGNITION SYSTEM (TYPICAL)

Ignition Test Tools

The test results determined under the *Ignition Coil Primary Voltage Test* and *Ignition Pulse Generator Peak Voltage Test* procedures in this section are based on the use of the Honda peak voltage adapter (part No. 07HGJ-0020100 [**Figure 10**]) and a digital multimeter (impedance 10M ohms/DCV minimum) or the Imrie Diagnostic Tester (Model 625). If you do not have these tools, refer testing to a Honda dealership.

> *NOTE*
> *Refer to the manufacturer's instructions when using these tools.*

Ignition Coil Primary Voltage Test

1. Refer to *Ignition Test Tools* in this section. Refer testing to a Honda dealership if you do not have one of the tools described.
2. Check engine compression as described in Chapter Three. If the compression is low in one or both cylinders, the following test results will be inaccurate.
3. Remove the left steering side cover (Chapter Fourteen).
4. Remove the spark plug cap from each spark plug and check that each spark plug (2 in each cylinder head) is tightened securely (**Figure 11**). Do not reconnect the spark plug caps to the spark plugs.
5. Connect 4 known good spark plugs to the spark plug caps and ground them against the cylinder as shown in **Figure 12**.
6. If you are using the peak voltage adapter (**Figure 10**), connect it to your multimeter.

> *NOTE*
> *If you are using the Imrie tester, follow its manufacturer's instructions for connecting the tester to the ignition coil.*

> *NOTE*
> *Do not disconnect the ignition coil primary wires (**Figure 13**) when performing Step 7.*

7. Connect the peak voltage adapter to one of the front or rear ignition coil primary wires (**Figure 14**) as follows:
   a. Front ignition coil: Connect the tester's positive (+) lead to the blue/yellow terminal and the negative (−) lead to a good ground.

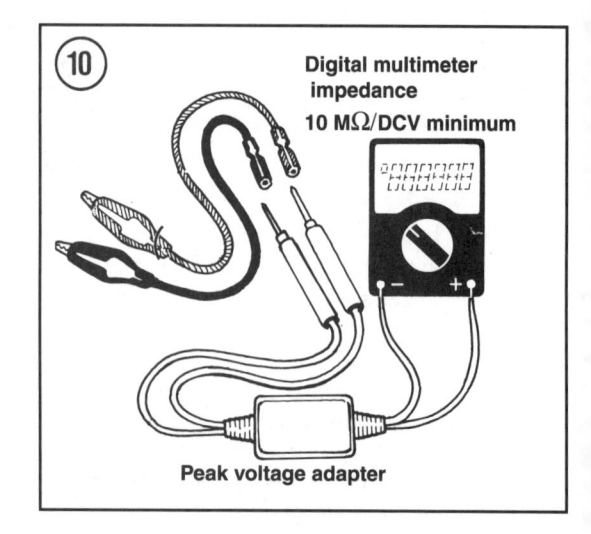

ELECTRICAL SYSTEM

b. Rear ignition coil: Connect the tester's positive (+) lead to the yellow/blue terminal and the negative (−) lead to a good ground.

8. Turn the ignition switch to ON and the engine stop switch to RUN.

9. Read the voltage on the meter's scale and note the following:

   a. If there is no battery voltage, refer to the *No Spark at All Four Spark Plugs* procedure under *Ignition Troubleshooting* in Chapter Two.
   b. If there is battery voltage, continue with Step 10.

10. Shift the transmission into NEUTRAL.

> **WARNING**
> *To prevent an electric shock, do not touch the spark plugs or the tester leads when cranking the engine in the following steps.*

11. Press the starter button while reading the voltage indicated on the meter's scale.

12. Release the starter button, then connect the test lead to the other ignition coil primary lead. Repeat Step 11.

13. Interpret the test results as follows:

   a. The minimum peak voltage reading is 100 volts.
   b. The individual peak voltage reading recorded for each ignition coil can vary as long as the voltage readings are higher than the specified minimum value.
   c. If the peak voltage reading for one or both ignition coils is less than 100 volts, perform the *No Spark at All Four Spark Plugs* procedure under *Ignition Troubleshooting* in Chapter Two.

14. Disconnect the test leads.

15. Remove the spark plugs from the plug caps, then reconnect the plug caps onto the spark plugs installed in the cylinder head.

Ignition Pulse Generator Peak Voltage Test

1. Refer to *Ignition Test Tools* in this section. Refer testing to a Honda dealership if you do not have one of the tools described.
2. Remove the seat (Chapter Fourteen).
3. Disconnect the ignition pulse generator 4-pin white connector (D, **Figure 6**).

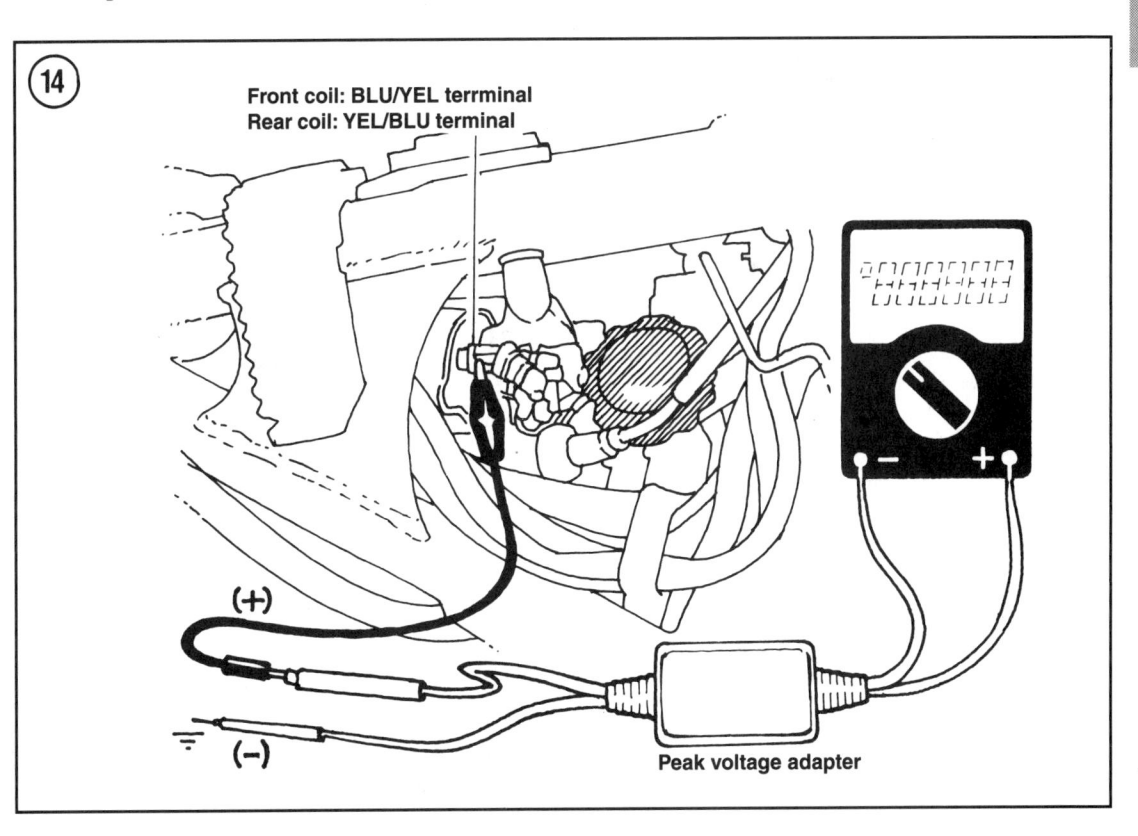

14

Front coil: BLU/YEL terrminal
Rear coil: YEL/BLU terminal

(+)

(−)

Peak voltage adapter

4. If you are using the peak voltage adapter (**Figure 10**), connect it to your multimeter.
5. Shift the transmission into NEUTRAL.

NOTE
If you are using the Imrie tester, follow its manufacturer's instructions for connecting the tester to the ignition coil.

WARNING
To prevent an electric shock, do not touch the spark plugs or the tester leads when cranking the engine in the following steps.

6. Perform the following:
   a. Connect the tester's positive (+) lead to the white/yellow terminal and the negative (–) lead to the yellow terminal (**Figure 15**).
   b. Turn the ignition switch to ON and the engine stop switch to RUN.
   c. Press the starter button while reading the voltage indicated on the tester.
   d. The minimum peak voltage reading is 0.7 volts.
   e. Release the starter button and turn the ignition switch OFF.

7. Perform the following:
   a. Connect the tester's positive (+) lead to the white/blue terminal and the negative (–) lead to the blue terminal.
   b. Turn the ignition switch to ON and the engine stop switch to RUN.
   c. Press the starter button while reading the voltage indicated on the tester.
   d. The minimum peak voltage reading is 0.7 volts.
   e. Release the starter button and turn the ignition switch OFF.

8. If the peak voltage reading is out of specification for either test (Steps 6 and 7), perform the *No Spark at All Four Spark Plugs* procedure under *Ignition Troubleshooting* in Chapter Two.

9. Disconnect the test leads and install all parts removed.

IGNITION PULSE GENERATOR

Ignition Pulse Generator Resistance Test

The ignition pulse generators are mounted on the right crankcase (A, **Figure 16**). You can test the

15 Ignition pulse generator AP white connector

Peak voltage adapter

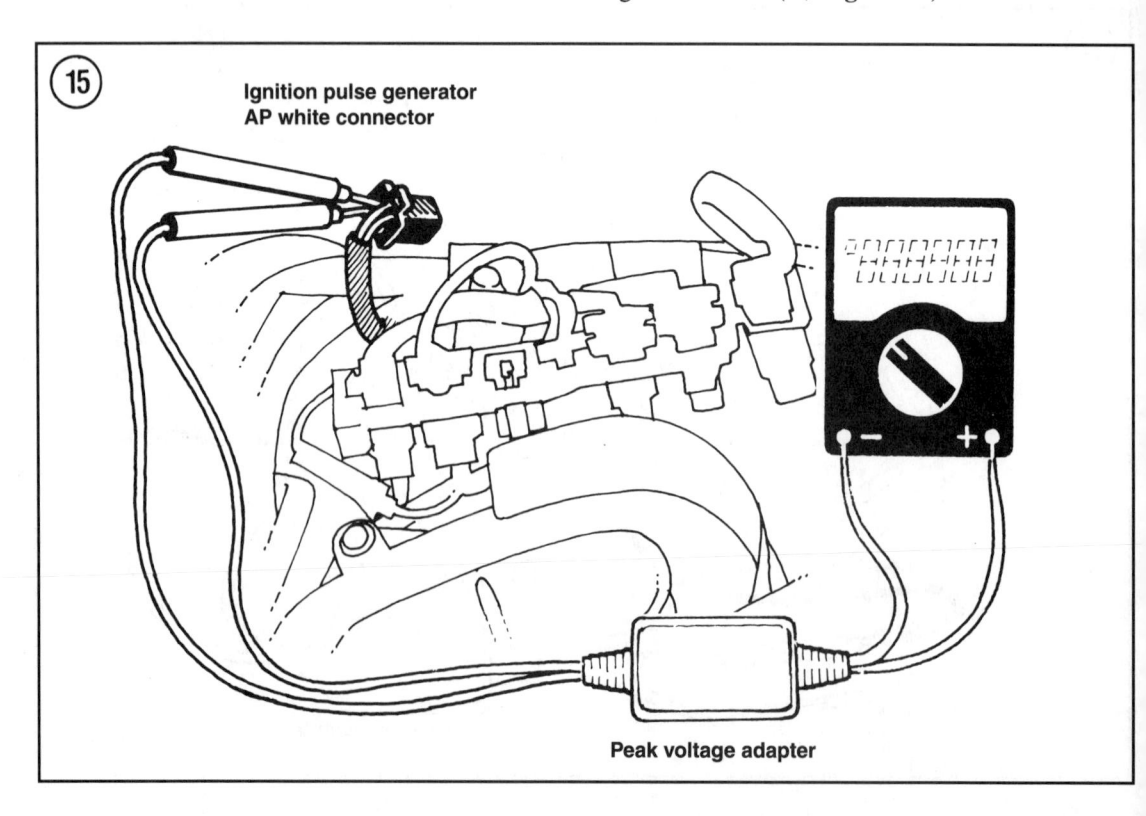

ELECTRICAL SYSTEM

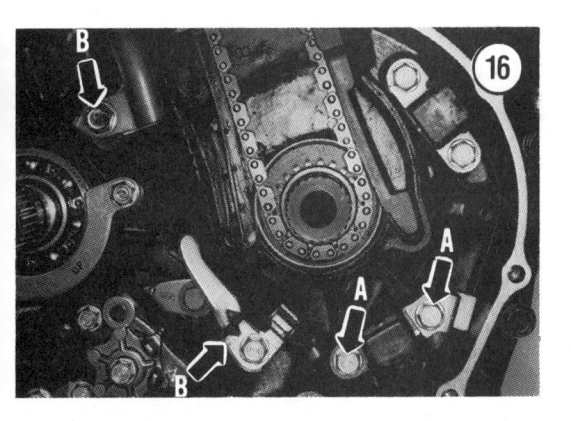

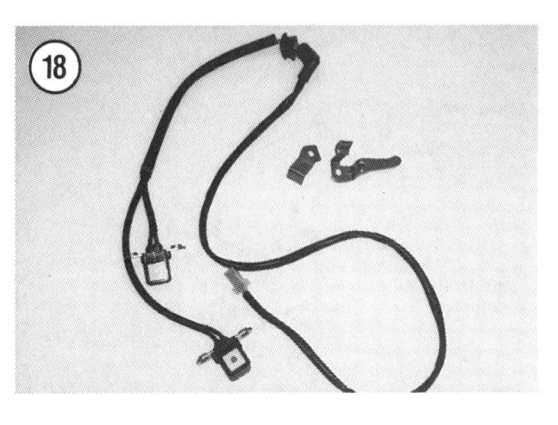

ignition pulse generators while they are mounted inside the engine.

1. Remove the seat (Chapter Fourteen).
2. Disconnect the ignition pulse generator 4-pin white connector (D, **Figure 6**).
3. Use an ohmmeter set at R × 100 and measure resistance between the white/yellow and yellow terminals, then between and the white/blue and blue terminals. The standard ignition pulse generator resistance is listed in **Table 2**.
4. If the reading is within the specified resistance, the ignition pulse generators are good. If there is no continuity (infinite resistance) or the resistance is higher than specified, one or both ignition pulse generators are damaged. Replace them as a set as described in this section.

NOTE
Before replacing the ignition pulse generators, check the electrical wires to and within the electrical connector for any opens or poor connections.

5. Make sure the electrical connector is free of corrosion and properly connected.

Removal/Installation

1. Remove the seat (Chapter Fourteen).
2. Disconnect the ignition pulse generator 4-pin white connector (D, **Figure 6**).
3. Remove the clutch outer (Chapter Six).

NOTE
You can remove the ignition pulse generators with the primary drive gear assembly installed on the crankshaft. The following photographs show the service performed with the primary drive gear assembly removed for clarity.

4. Remove the 2 wire clamp mounting bolts and clamps (B, **Figure 16**).
5. Pull the 2 wire grommets (**Figure 17**) out of the crankcase.
6. Remove the mounting bolts and the ignition pulse generators (A, **Figure 16**) from the crankcase. See **Figure 18**.
7. Reverse these steps to install the ignition pulse generators.
8. Apply a liquid sealant to the grommets (**Figure 19**) before installing them into the crankcase notches.

9. Tighten the ignition pulse generator 8 mm clamp bolt (right crankcase bolt) to the torque specification in **Table 7**.

10. When routing the ignition pulse generator wiring harness, make sure it does not contact the primary drive gear.

ICM UNIT

Removal/Installation

The ICM unit (**Figure 20**) unit is mounted on the right side of the battery box.

1. Remove the seat and left side cover (**Figure Fourteen**).
2. Disconnect the ICM unit electrical connectors as follows:
   a. 6-pin black connector (A, **Figure 21**).
   b. 4-pin white connector (B, **Figure 21**).
   c. Single connector (green/orange wire).
3. Remove the ICM unit (**Figure 20**) from its rubber mount.
4. Install the ICM unit by reversing these steps.

IGNITION COIL

Testing

There are 2 ignition coils: one fires the plugs for the front cylinder and the other fires the plugs for the rear cylinder.

The ignition coil is a transformer which develops the high voltage required to jump the spark plug gap. The only maintenance required is that of keeping the electrical connections clean and tight and occasionally making sure the coil is mounted securely.

If the condition of the coil is doubtful, you can make several checks to test it.

To make a quick check of the coil, disconnect the high voltage lead from the spark plugs. Remove the spark plugs from the cylinder head. Connect a new spark plug or a spark tester to the high voltage leads and ground the spark plug base or spark tester tool against the cylinder head (**Figure 12**).

WARNING
Do not hold the spark plug cap or spark tester when making a spark test. The high voltage generated by the ignition system could produce serious or fatal shocks.

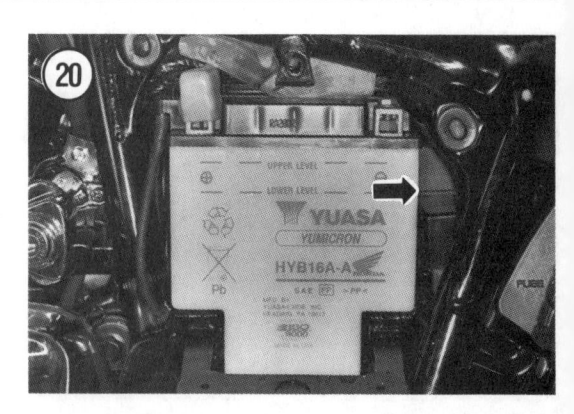

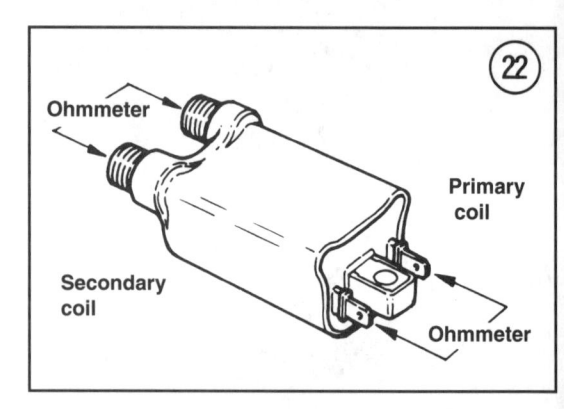

ELECTRICAL SYSTEM

Crank the engine with the starter. If a fat blue spark occurs, the coil is in good condition. If the spark is weak, or if there is no spark, perform the following tests.

Reinstall the spark plugs in the cylinder head.

NOTE
To obtain accurate resistance measurements the coil must be at approximately 20° C (68° F).

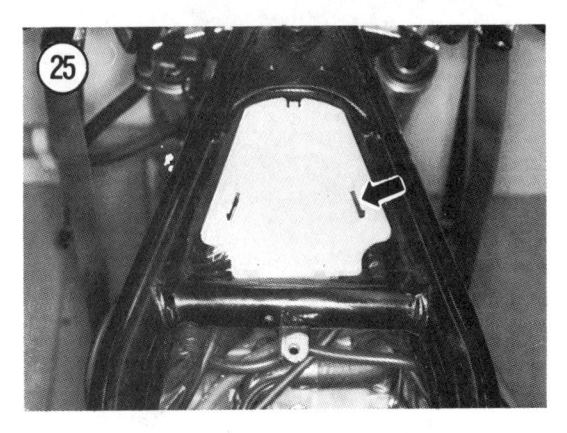

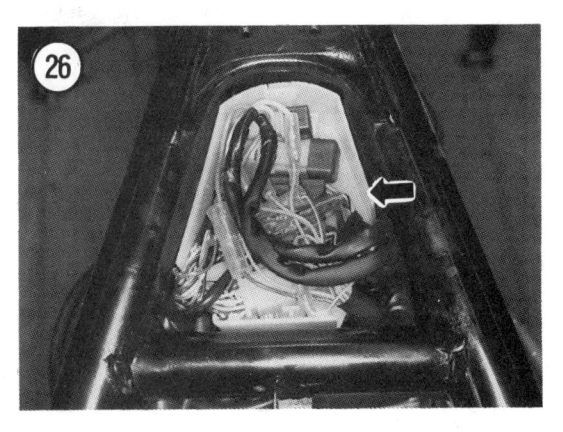

1. Remove the steering side covers (Chapter Fourteen).
2. Disconnect the 2 primary wires (**Figure 13**) from the ignition coil to be checked.
3. Disconnect the 2 spark plug caps (secondary leads) from the spark plugs.
4. Measure the primary coil resistance as follows:
    a. Switch an ohmmeter to R × 1.
    b. Connect the ohmmeter between the 2 primary coil terminals on the coil (**Figure 22**).
    c. Refer to **Table 2** for the correct resistance values.
5. Measure the secondary resistance as follows:
    a. Switch an ohmmeter to R × 1000.
    b. Connect the ohmmeter between the 2 spark plug caps (**Figure 23**) on the same coil. The specified resistance is listed in **Table 2**. If the secondary resistance is incorrect, remove the ignition coil as described in this chapter. Remove the secondary leads from the coil and measure the secondary resistance across the secondary coil terminals (**Figure 22**).
    c. If the coil fails both tests (substeps a and b), the coil is faulty and must be replaced.
    d. If the coil fails the test in substep a but passes the test in substep b, the secondary leads or spark plug caps are damaged. Replace these parts and retest.
6. Repeat for the other ignition coil.
7. Replace the ignition coil if any reading is not within the manufacturer's specifications.
8. Reconnect the ignition coil leads.

Removal/Installation

1. Remove the steering side covers (A, **Figure 24**) as described in Chapter Fourteen.
2. Remove the fuel tank dampers (B, **Figure 24**) from the connector box cover hooks.
3. Remove the connector box cover (**Figure 25**).
4. Disconnect the connectors in the box (**Figure 26**) to remove them from the box.
5. Remove the screws and remove the connector box (**Figure 27**).
6. Remove the turn signal relay (**Figure 28**) from the frame tab.
7. Disconnect the 2 primary wires from each ignition coil.
8. Disconnect all 4 spark plug caps from the spark plugs.

9. Remove the ignition coil mounting bolts from the frame (**Figure 29**). Then remove the bolts connecting the 2 ignition coils together.
10. Carefully pull the secondary wires through the frame, then remove the ignition coils through the frame from the left side.
11. Install the ignition coil by reversing these removal steps. Make sure all electrical connections are tight and free of corrosion.

ELECTRIC STARTING SYSTEM

The starting system consists of the starter motor, starter gears, solenoid and the starter button.

Figure 30 shows an electrical diagram of the starting system.

Table 3 lists starter motor service specifications.

The starter gears and starter clutch are covered in Chapter Five.

CAUTION
Do not operate the starter for more than 5 seconds at a time. Let it cool approximately 10 seconds, then use it again.

Troubleshooting

Refer to Chapter Two.

Starter Removal

1. Remove the left side cover (Chapter Fourteen).
2. Disconnect the negative battery cable from the battery (**Figure 2**).
3. Remove the starter drive gear (Chapter Five).
4. Drain the engine coolant (Chapter Three).
5. Remove the bolts and disconnect the water hose (A, **Figure 31**) from the rear cylinder block.
6. Disconnect the starter motor cable (B, **Figure 31**) from the starter.
7. Remove the bolts and remove the starter motor (C, **Figure 31**) from the crankcase.
8. If necessary, service the starter motor as described in this chapter.

Disassembly

Refer to **Figure 32** for this procedure.

1. Find the alignment marks across the armature housing and both end covers (A, **Figure 33**). If necessary, scribe your own marks.
2. Remove the case bolts (B, **Figure 33**).

NOTE
Record the thickness and alignment of each shim and washer removed during disassembly.

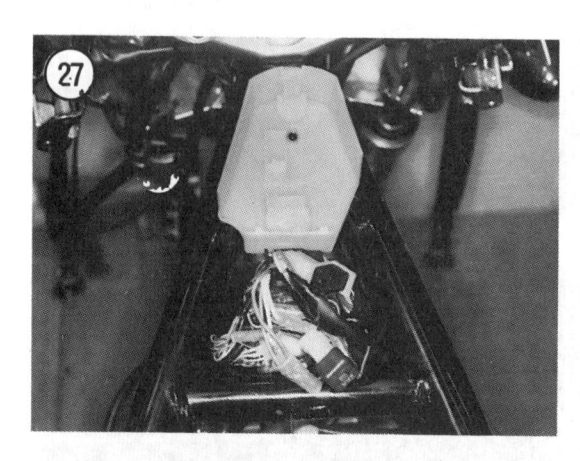

ELECTRICAL SYSTEM

(30) **STARTING SYSTEM (TYPICAL)**

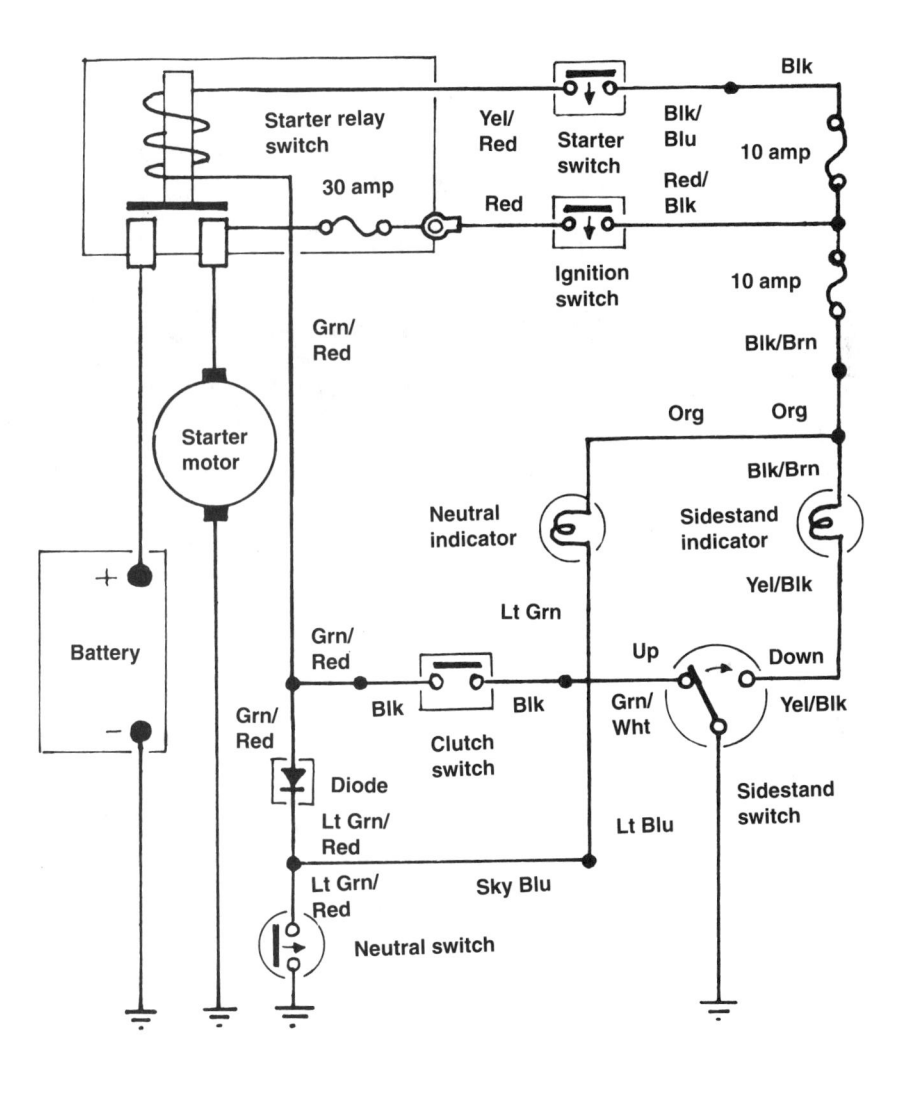

NOTE
The number of shims used in each starter varies. Your starter may use a different number of shims from that shown in **Figure 32**.

3. Remove the front and rear covers (B, **Figure 33**).
4. Remove the lockwasher and shims (**Figure 34**) front the front cover side.
5. Remove the shims from the rear cover side (next to brushes).
6. Remove the armature (**Figure 35**) from the housing.
7. Pull the spring away from each brush and pull the brushes out of their guides.
8. Pull the brush plate (**Figure 36**) off of the armature.
9. Remove the nuts, washers and O-ring (**Figure 37**) securing the cable terminal and brushes to the housing. Then remove the cable terminal assembly (**Figure 38**).
10. Clean all grease, dirt and carbon from the armature, case and end covers.

CAUTION
Do not immerse the wire windings in the case or the armature coil in solvent as the insulation may be damaged. Wipe the windings with a cloth lightly moistened with solvent.

Inspection

If any starter motor component (other than O-rings and brush sets) is excessively worn or dam-

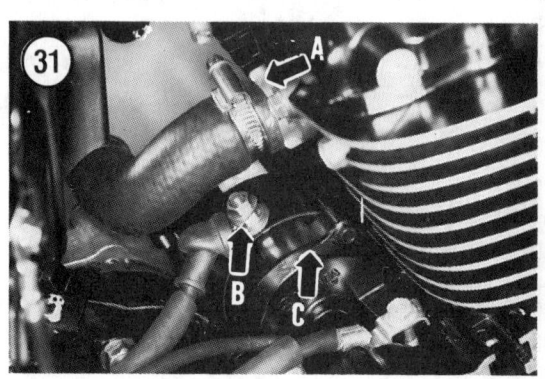

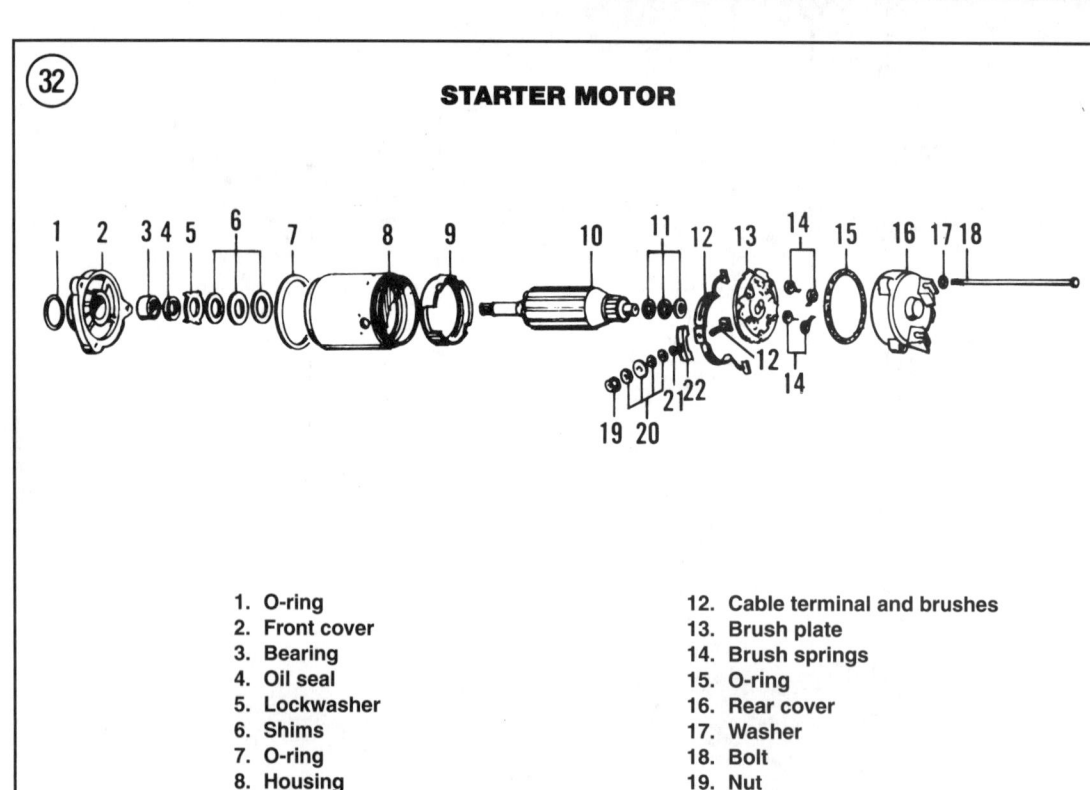

STARTER MOTOR

1. O-ring
2. Front cover
3. Bearing
4. Oil seal
5. Lockwasher
6. Shims
7. O-ring
8. Housing
9. Sleeve
10. Armature
11. Shims
12. Cable terminal and brushes
13. Brush plate
14. Brush springs
15. O-ring
16. Rear cover
17. Washer
18. Bolt
19. Nut
20. Insulated washers
21. Nut
22. Insulator

ELECTRICAL SYSTEM

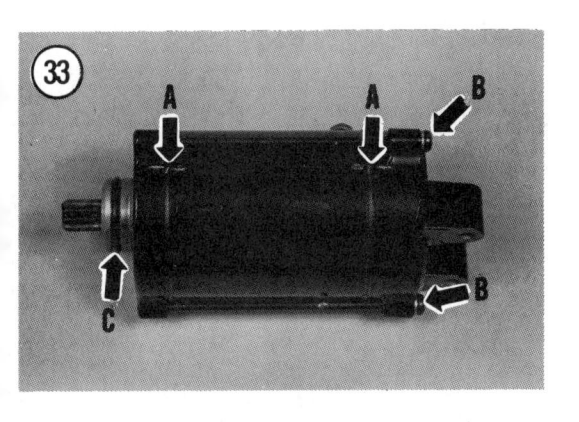

aged, replace the starter motor as an assembly. Individual replacement parts are not available.

1. Measure the length of each brush (**Figure 39**). If the length of any one brush is less than the minimum specification (**Table 3**), replace all 4 brushes as a set.

2. Inspect the brush springs and replace them if weak or damaged. To replace the brush springs, perform the following:

   a. Make a drawing of the brush springs as they are installed on the brush holder, noting the direction in which each spring coil turns.

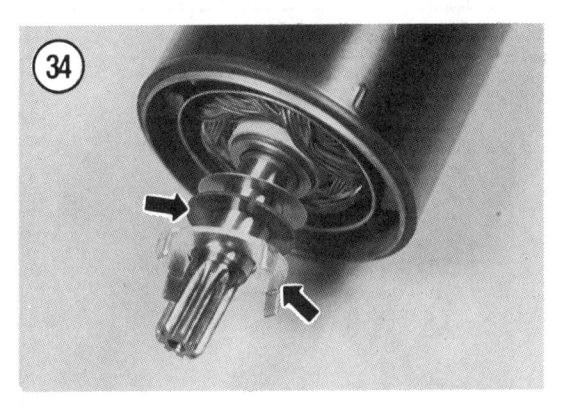

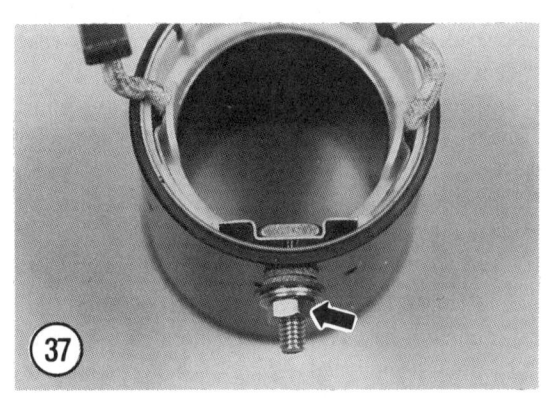

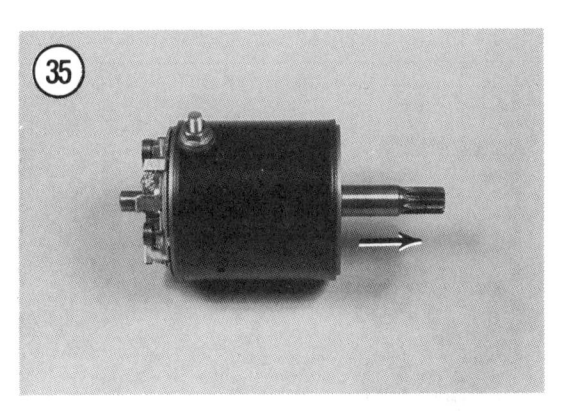

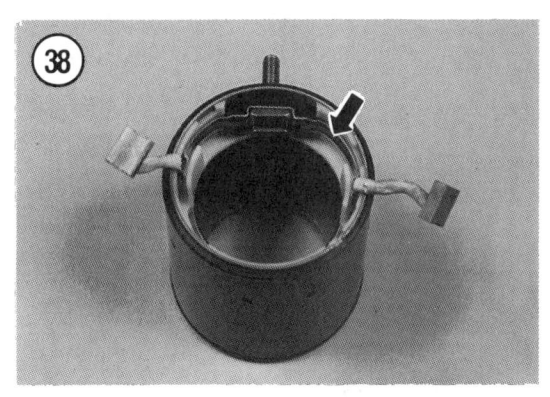

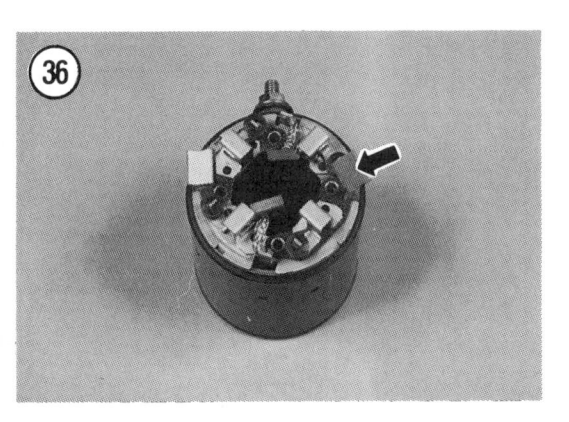

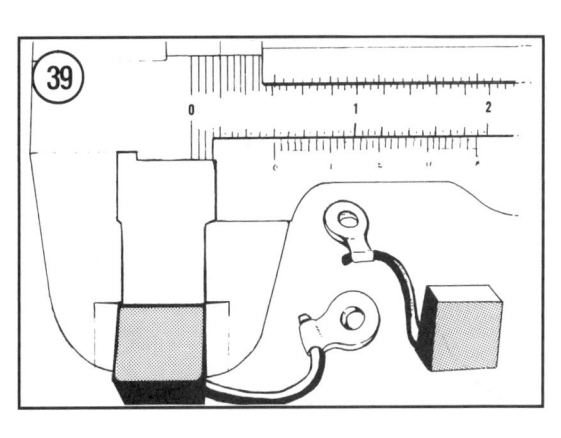

b. Remove and replace both brush springs as a set.

3. Inspect the commutator (**Figure 40**). The mica must below the surface of the copper bars. On a worn commutator, the mica and copper bars are the same level (**Figure 41**). If necessary, have the commutator serviced at a dealership or electrical repair shop.

4. Inspect the commutator copper bars for discoloration. If a pair of bars is discolored, grounded armature coils are indicated.

5. Inspect the armature shaft for wear, scoring or other damage.

6. Inspect the front cover seal and needle bearing.

7. Inspect the rear cover bushing for excessive wear or damage.

8. Inspect the starter housing for cracks or other damage. Then inspect for loose, chipped or damaged magnets.

9. Inspect the O-rings and replace them if worn or damaged.

10. Use an ohmmeter and make the following tests:

   a. Check for continuity between each of the commutator bars (**Figure 42**); there must be continuity (indicated resistance) between pairs of bars.

   b. Check for continuity between the commutator bars and the shaft (**Figure 43**); there must be no continuity (infinite resistance).

NOTE
When performing the following check, install the cable terminal and brush holder onto the starter case.

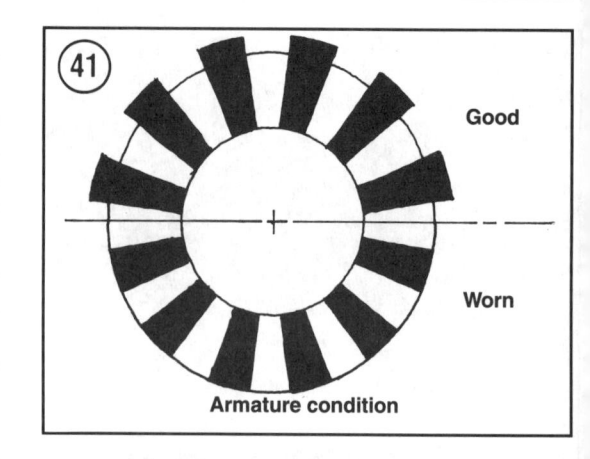

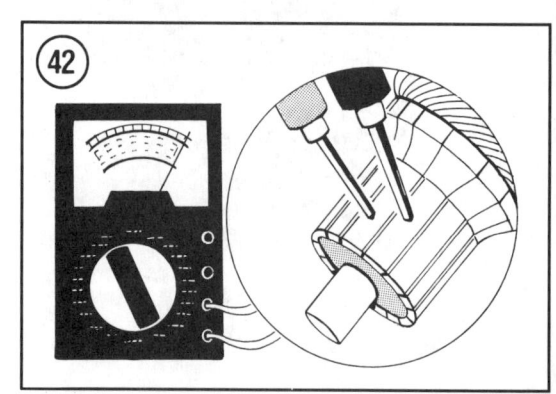

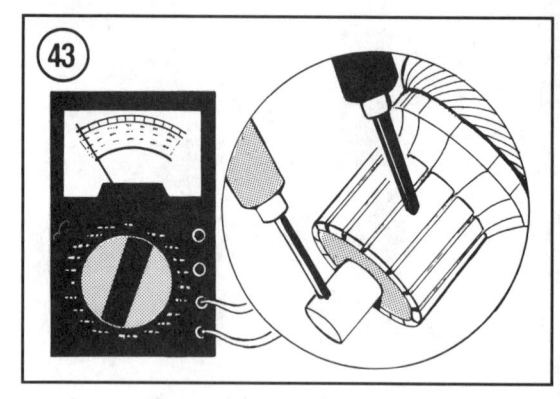

   c. Check for continuity between the cable terminal and starter case (**Figure 44**); there must be no continuity.

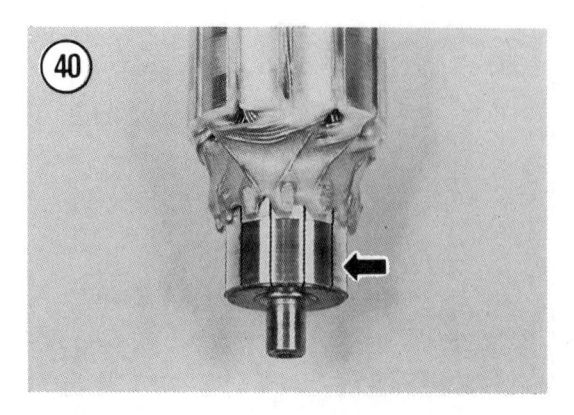

ELECTRICAL SYSTEM

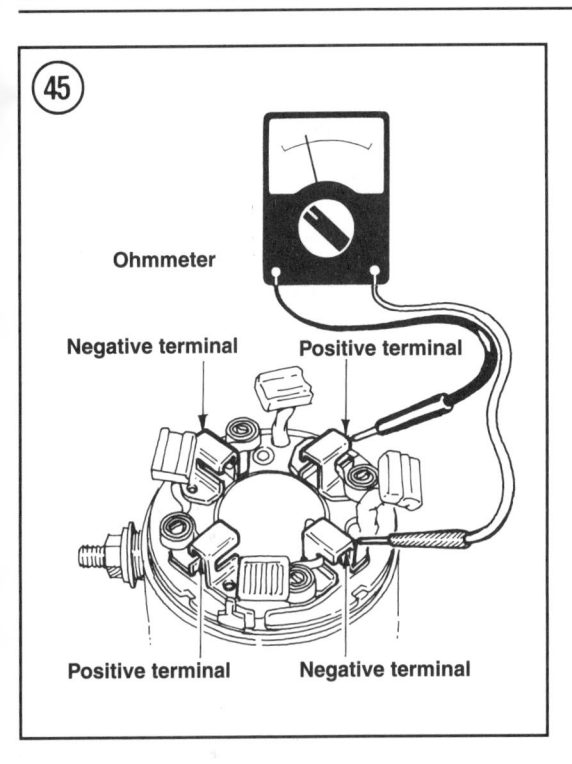

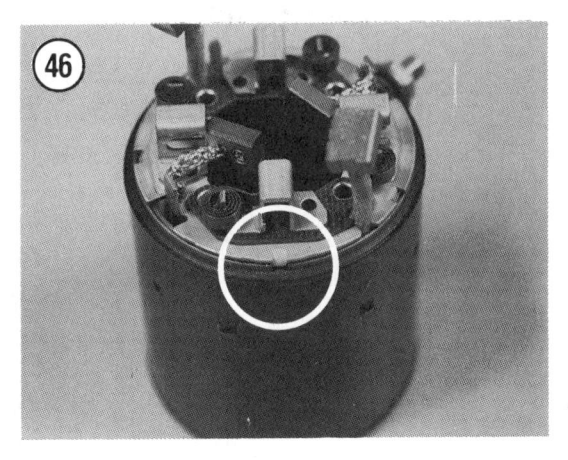

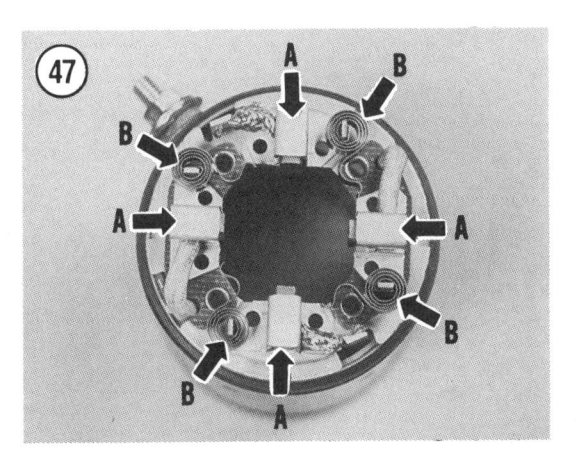

d. Check for continuity between the cable terminal and the brush; there must be continuity.

e. Check for continuity between the positive (+) and negative (−) brush holder terminals (**Figure 45**); there must be no continuity.

f. If the unit fails any one test, replace the starter assembly.

Assembly

1. Install the cable/brush terminal assembly (**Figure 38**).

NOTE
In the next step, reinstall all parts in the same order as noted during removal. This is to properly insulate the brushes from the case.

2. Install the O-ring, washers and nuts (**Figure 37**) securing the brush terminal set to the case.

3. Install the brush holder assembly onto the end of the case. Align the holder locating tab with the case notch (**Figure 46**).

4. Install the brushes into their receptacles (A, **Figure 47**).

5. Install the bush springs (B, **Figure 47**), but do not place them against the brushes at this time.

6. Insert the armature coil assembly (**Figure 35**) in from the rear end of the case. Do not damage the brushes during this step.

7. Bring the end of the springs up and onto the backside of each brush (**Figure 48**).

8. Install the original shims (rear side) onto the armature shaft.

9. Install the O-ring onto the case.

10. Apply a thin coat of grease onto the armature shaft.

11. Align the slot in the rear cover (A, **Figure 49**) with the raised tab on the brush holder (B, **Figure 49**) and install the rear cover.
12. Install the O-ring onto the case (front side).
13. Install the original shims and lockwasher onto the armature shaft (**Figure 34**). The lockwasher tabs must face out (away from starter case).
14. Lubricate the front cover seal lips and bearing with grease.
15. Align the front cover tabs with the lockwasher tabs and install the front cover. Then check that the index marks on the case and front cover align (A, **Figure 33**).
16. Install the starter motor case bolts (B, **Figure 33**) and tighten to the torque specification in **Table 7**.

NOTE
If one or both bolts will not pass through the starter motor, the end covers and/or brush plate are installed incorrectly.

17. Tighten the starter motor terminal nut (19, **Figure 32**) to the torque specification in **Table 7**.

Starter Installation

1. Lubricate the starter motor O-ring (C, **Figure 33**) with engine oil.
2. Install the starter motor (C, **Figure 31**) and seat it into the crankcase.
3. Install and tighten the starter motor mounting bolts securely.
4. Reconnect the starter motor cable to the starter (B, **Figure 31**). Tighten the nut securely.
5. Install a new O-ring into the water hose joint (A, **Figure 31**).
6. Install the washer hose joint onto the cylinder block and secure it with its mounting bolts. Tighten the bolts securely.
7. Install the starter drive gear (Chapter Five).
8. Reconnect the negative battery cable to the battery.
9. Fill and bleed the cooling system (Chapter Three).
10. Install the left side cover.

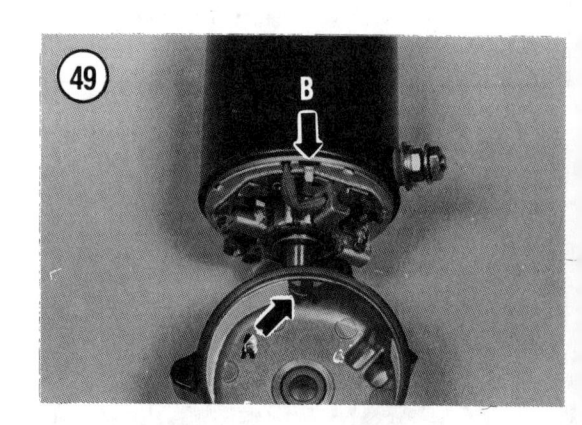

STARTER RELAY SWITCH

The starter relay switch (**Figure 50**) is mounted underneath the seat and to the rear of the air filter housing.

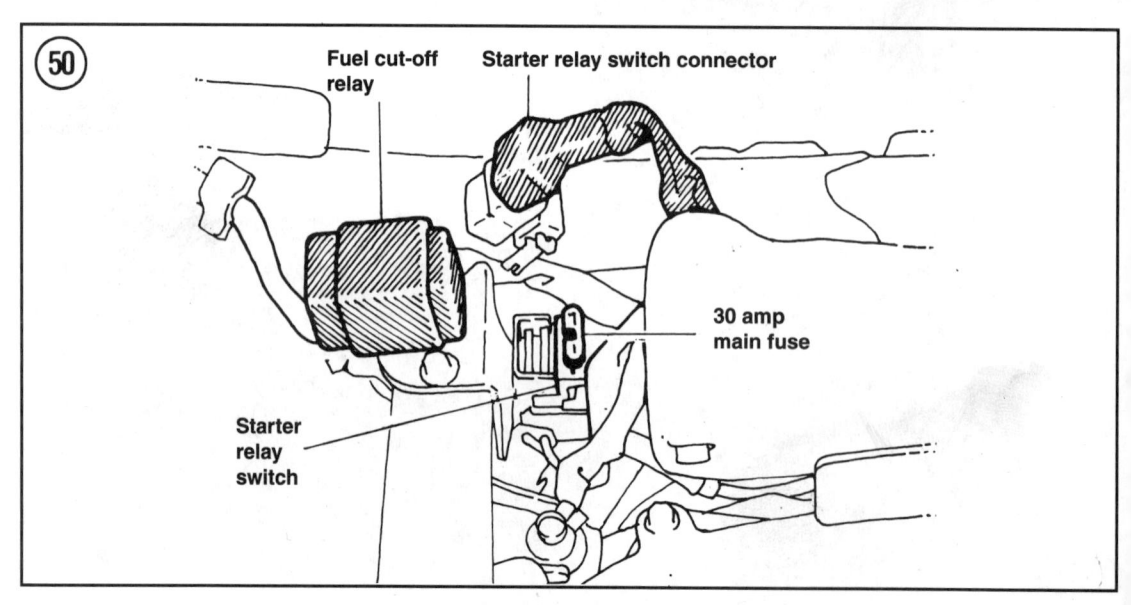

ELECTRICAL SYSTEM

Starter Relay Switch
Testing

1. Remove the seat (Chapter Fourteen).
2. Shift the transmission into NEUTRAL.
3. Turn the ignition switch on and press the starter button. The starter relay is normal if you hear the switch click when the starter button is pressed. If you do not hear a click, continue with Step 4.
4. Test the starter relay switch ground line connection as follows:
   a. Disconnect the starter relay switch electrical connector (**Figure 50**).
   b. Shift the transmission into NEUTRAL.
   c. Using an ohmmeter set on R × 1, check for continuity between the starter relay switch connector green/red wire and a good engine ground.
   d. The ohmmeter must read continuity.
   e. Remove the ohmmeter leads.

   NOTE
   Normally the ohmmeter will read 0 ohms when making a ground test. However, because of the diode placed in the circuit, it is normal for the ohmmeter to show a slight resistance reading.

5. Check for voltage at the starter relay switch as follows:
   a. Reconnect the starter relay switch electrical connector (**Figure 50**).
   b. Shift the transmission into NEUTRAL.
   c. Connect the positive (+) voltmeter lead to the starter relay switch yellow/red wire and the negative (−) voltmeter lead to a good engine ground.
   d. Turn the ignition switch on and press the starter button while reading the voltmeter scale.
   e. The voltmeter must show battery voltage (12 volts).
   f. Turn the ignition switch off and remove the voltmeter leads.
6. Check the starter relay switch operation as follows:
   a. Disconnect the starter relay switch electrical connector (**Figure 50**).
   b. Disconnect the 2 large cable leads from the starter relay switch.
   c. Switch an ohmmeter to the R × 1 scale, then connect its test leads across the 2 large leads on the starter relay switch. The ohmmeter must read infinity.
   d. Connect a fully charged 12 volt battery to the starter relay switch as follows. Connect the positive (+) battery terminal to the yellow/red wire terminal and the negative (−) battery terminal to the green/red wire terminal (**Figure 51**). Now, the ohmmeter must read continuity (low resistance).
   e. Disconnect the battery and ohmmeter leads.
7. Replace the starter relay switch if it failed any part of this test.
8. Reconnect the 2 cable leads and the connector to the starter relay switch.
9. Install the seat (Chapter Fourteen).

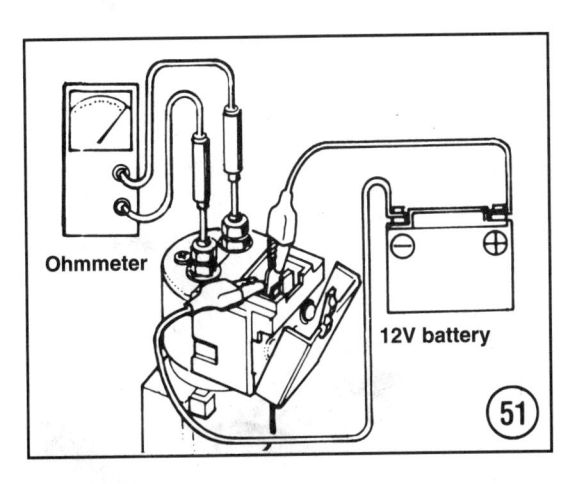

Removal/Installation

1. Remove the seat and left side cover (Chapter Fourteen).
2. Disconnect the negative battery lead from the battery.
3. Disconnect starter relay switch electrical connector (**Figure 50**).
4. Disconnect the 2 large cable leads from the starter relay switch.
5. Remove the starter relay switch from the frame.
6. Install by reversing these removal steps.

CLUTCH DIODE

Testing/Replacement

1. Remove the steering side covers (A, **Figure 24**) as described in Chapter Fourteen.

2. Remove the fuel tank dampers (B, **Figure 24**) from the connector box cover hooks.
3. Remove the connector box cover (**Figure 25**).
4. Disconnect the clutch diode (**Figure 52**) from the wire harness. The clutch diode has 2 wires: green/red and light/green and red.
5. Set an ohmmeter to the R × 1 scale.
6. Check for continuity between the 2 terminals on the diode (**Figure 53**). There must be continuity (in the normal direction) and no continuity (infinite resistance) with the leads reversed. Replace the diode if it fails this test.
7. Reverse Steps 1-3 to install the clutch diode.

LIGHTING SYSTEM

The lighting system consists of a headlight, taillight, turn signals and indicator lights. **Table 4** lists replacement bulbs for these components.

Always use the correct wattage bulb listed in **Table 4**. Using the wrong size bulb will give a dim light or cause the bulb to burn out prematurely.

Headlight Bulb Replacement

1. Remove the 2 outer headlight mounting screws, then lift the headlight and pull it out of its housing (**Figure 54**).

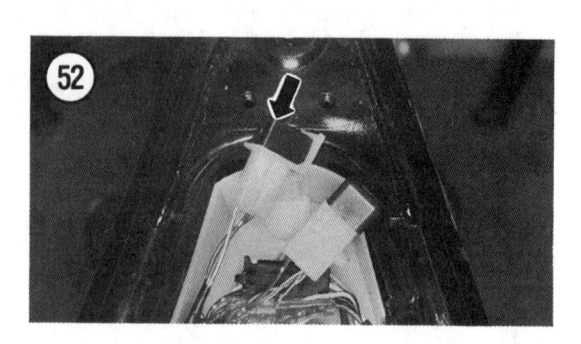

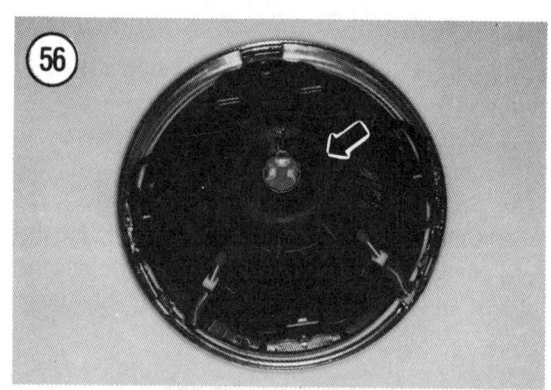

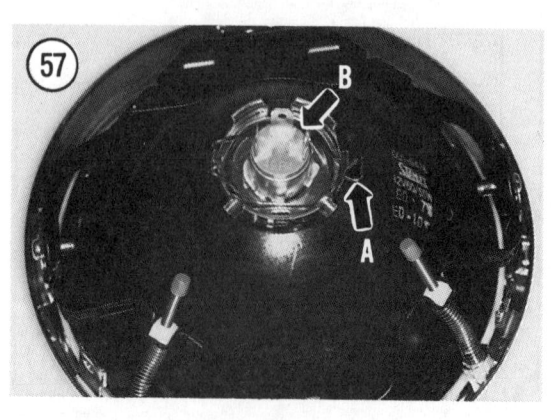

ELECTRICAL SYSTEM

HEADLIGHT ADJUSTMENT

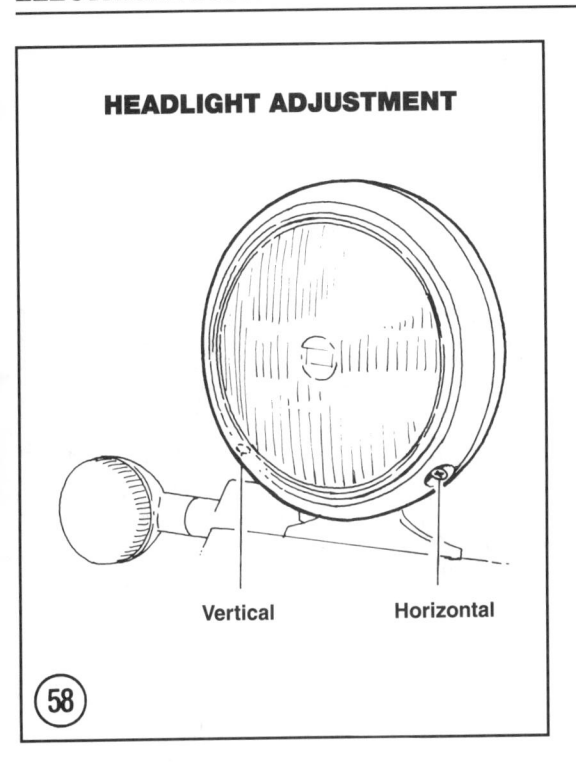

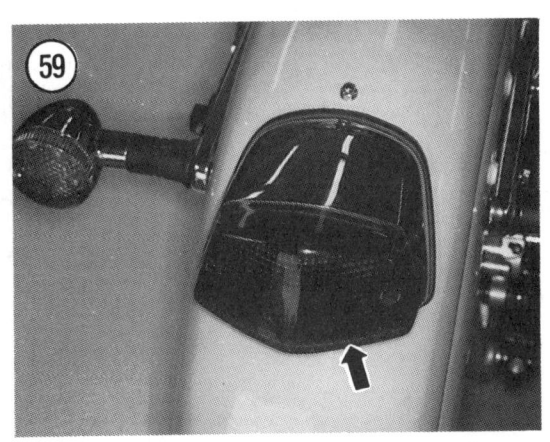

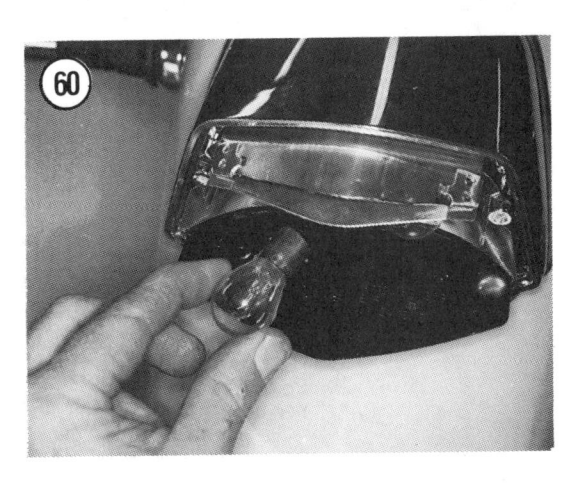

Figure 58: Vertical / Horizontal

2. Disconnect the electrical connector from the bulb (**Figure 54**) and remove the headlight assembly.

CAUTION
*All models use a quartz-halogen bulb (**Figure 55**). Because traces of oil on this type of bulb will reduce the life of the bulb, do not touch the bulb glass with your fingers. Clean any traces of oil or other chemicals from the bulb with a cloth moistened in isopropyl alcohol or lacquer thinner.*

3. Remove the dust cover (**Figure 56**) from around the bulb.
4. Unhook the bulb retainer (A, **Figure 57**) and remove the bulb (B, **Figure 57**).
5. Install the headlight by reversing these removal steps, while noting the following.
6. Align the tabs on the bulb with the notches in the bulb holder and install the bulb.
7. Install the dust cover so its TOP mark is at the top of the housing. Make sure the dust cover fits snugly around the bulb.
8. Hook the tab at the top of the lens with the retainer at the top of the headlight housing, then pivot the lens into the housing and install the 2 mounting screws.
9. Start the engine and check the headlight operation. If necessary, perform the *Headlight Adjustment* in this section.

Headlight Adjustment

Adjust the headlight horizontally and vertically according to the Department of Motor Vehicle regulations in your area.

To adjust the headlight horizontally, turn the screw on the left side of the headlight (**Figure 58**).

To adjust the headlight vertically, turn the screw on the right side of the headlight (**Figure 58**).

Taillight/Brake Light Replacement

1. Remove the screws securing the lens and remove the lens (**Figure 59**).
2. Replace the gasket if damaged.
3. Push the bulb in and turn it counterclockwise to remove it (**Figure 60**).
4. Install the new bulb and lens by reversing these steps. Do not overtighten the screws as the lens may crack.

License Plate Light Replacement

1. Remove the bolts and nuts securing the license plate holder to the rear fender.
2. Disconnect the license light connectors.
3. Working from the back of the license plate holder, remove the nuts securing the license light lens.
4. Push the bulb in and turn it counterclockwise to remove it.
5. Install the new bulb and lens by reversing these steps.

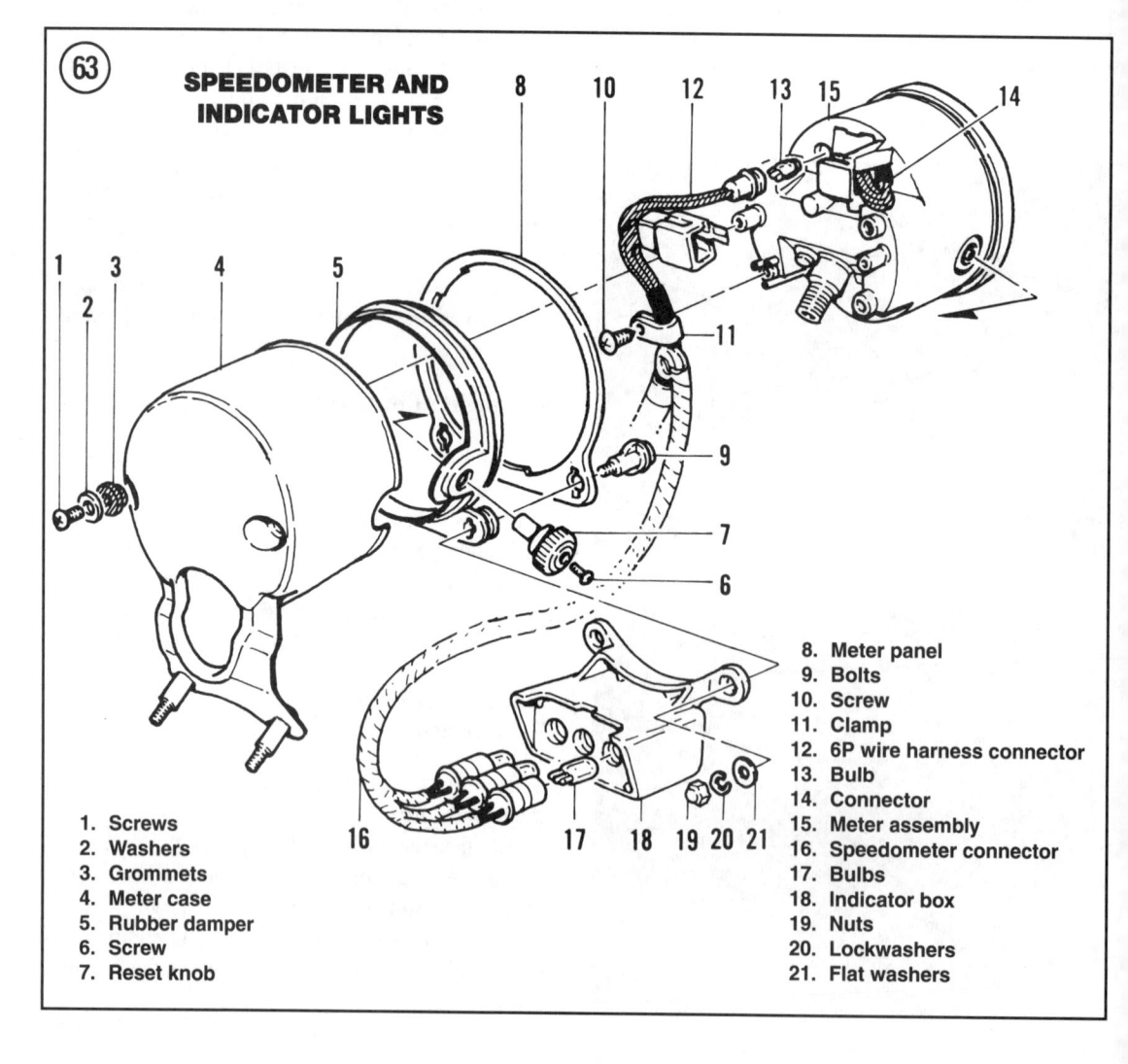

SPEEDOMETER AND INDICATOR LIGHTS

1. Screws
2. Washers
3. Grommets
4. Meter case
5. Rubber damper
6. Screw
7. Reset knob
8. Meter panel
9. Bolts
10. Screw
11. Clamp
12. 6P wire harness connector
13. Bulb
14. Connector
15. Meter assembly
16. Speedometer connector
17. Bulbs
18. Indicator box
19. Nuts
20. Lockwashers
21. Flat washers

ELECTRICAL SYSTEM

Front and Rear Turn Signal Light Replacement

1. Remove the screws securing the lens and remove the lens (**Figure 61**).
2. Replace the gasket if damaged.
3. Push the bulb in and turn it counterclockwise to remove it (**Figure 62**).
4. Install the new bulb and lens by reversing these steps. Do not overtighten the screws as the lens may crack.

Indicator Light Bulb Replacement

Refer to **Figure 63** when performing this procedure.
1. Remove the nuts and washers from the bottom side of the speedometer housing.

CAUTION
The 2 bolts (A, Figure 64) have a single lug that aligns with a groove in each damper. Do not turn the bolts when removing them in Step 2 or they may damage the damper.

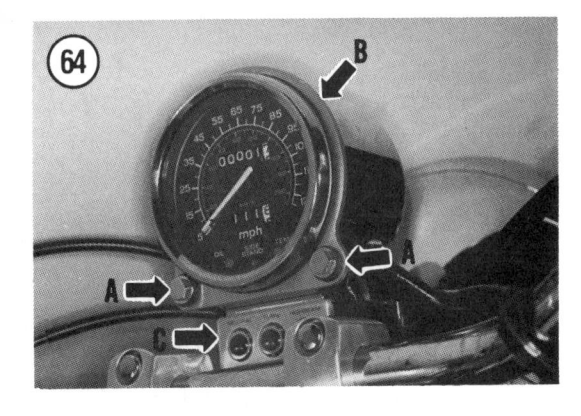

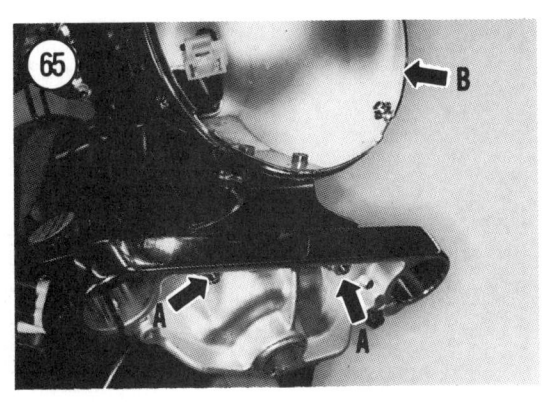

2. Push the 2 bolts (A, **Figure 64**) out of the housing and remove them.
3. Remove the speedometer housing (B, **Figure 64**) and the indicator box (C, **Figure 64**).
4. Pull the indicator box to the right side and out of the speedometer housing.
5. Remove the bulb holder from the indicator box and replace the blown bulb.
6. Reverse these steps to install the indicator box and speedometer housing, while noting the following.
7. When installing the 2 bolts (A, **Figure 64**), align their lugs with the grooves in the meter base dampers.
8. Do not turn the 2 bolts (A, **Figure 64**) to tighten the speedometer housing. Instead, hold the bolts and turn the lower nuts.

Speedometer Bulb Replacement

Refer to **Figure 63** for this procedure.
1. Disconnect the speedometer cable from the speedometer.
2. Remove the 2 screws, washers and grommets from the bottom of the speedometer case.
3. Lift the speedometer and pull the bulb socket out of the speedometer assembly.
4. Replace the bulb.
5. Reverse these steps to install reinstall the speedometer housing and reconnect the speedometer cable.

HEADLIGHT HOUSING

Removal/Installation

1. Remove the headlight as described in this chapter.
2. Remove the housing nuts and bolts (A, **Figure 65**), then remove the housing (B, **Figure 65**).
3. Reverse these steps to install the headlight housing.
4. After installing the headlight, check the headlight adjustment as described in this chapter.

SPEEDOMETER

Removal/Installation

Refer to **Figure 63** for this procedure.
1. Disconnect the speedometer cable from the speedometer.

2. Remove the nuts and washers from the bottom side of the speedometer housing.
3. Remove the 2 bolts (A, **Figure 64**) without turning them.
4. Remove the speedometer housing (B, **Figure 64**) and the indicator box (C, **Figure 64**).
5. Remove the 2 screws, washers and grommets from the bottom of the speedometer meter case.
6. Remove the clamp screw and clamp securing the 6-pin connector to the back of the speedometer assembly.
7. Remove the speedometer assembly.
8. Reverse these removal steps to install the speedometer.
9. Check all meter functions after installation.

SWITCHES

Testing

You can test switches for continuity using an ohmmeter (see Chapter One) or a self-powered test light. Test at the switch connector plug by operating the switch in each of its operating positions and comparing results with its switch continuity diagram (most switches). For example, **Figure 66** shows the continuity diagram for the horn switch.

When the horn button is pressed, there will be continuity between the white/green and light green terminals. The line joining the two terminals shows continuity (**Figure 66**). An ohmmeter connected between these two terminals will show no resistance or a self-powered test light will light. When the horn button is free, there will be no continuity between the same terminals.

When testing switches, note the following:
   a. Check the fuse as described under *Fuse* in this chapter.
   b. Disconnect the negative battery cable from the battery.

> *CAUTION*
> *Do not attempt to start the engine with the negative battery cable disconnected.*

   c. When you separate two connectors, pull on the connector housings and not the wires.
   d. After finding a defective circuit, check the connectors to make sure they are clean and properly connected. Check all wires going into a connector housing for loose connections or damage.

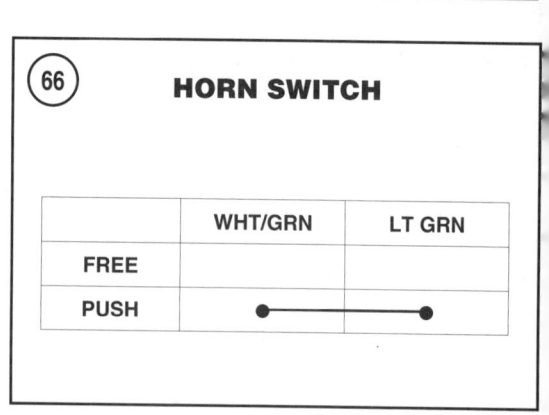

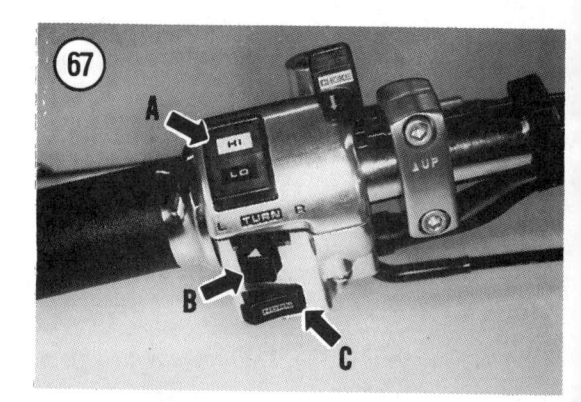

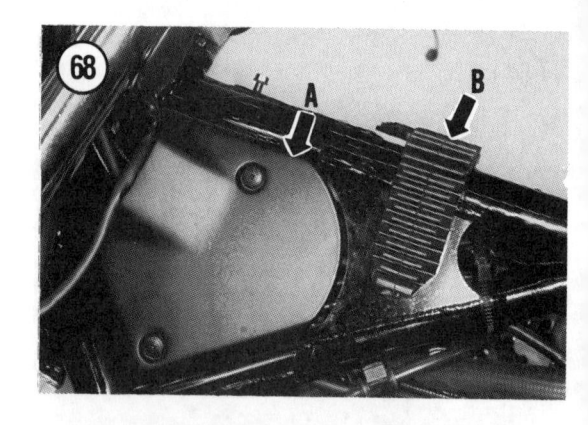

66 HORN SWITCH

	WHT/GRN	LT GRN
FREE		
PUSH	•———————•

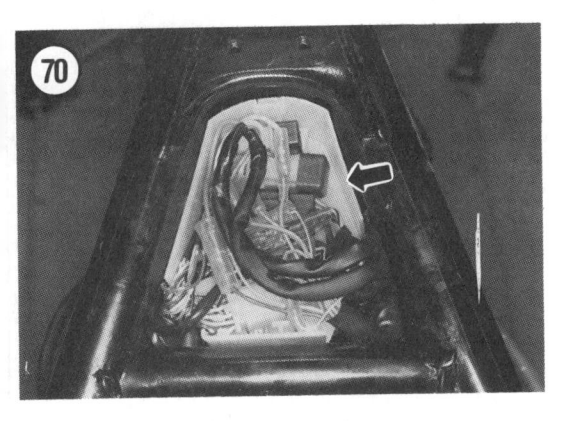

ELECTRICAL SYSTEM

e. When joining 2 connectors, push them until they click or snap into place.

If a switch or button does not perform properly, replace the switch as described in its appropriate section.

Left Handlebar Switch Housing Testing/Replacement

The left handlebar switch housing is equipped with the following switches:

a. Dimmer switch (A, **Figure 67**).
b. Turn signal switch (B, **Figure 67**).
c. Horn switch (C, **Figure 67**).

NOTE
The switches mounted in the left handlebar switch housing are not available separately. If one switch is damaged, you must replace the switch housing assembly.

1. Remove the fuel tank (Chapter Eight).
2. Remove the steering side covers (A, **Figure 68**) as described in Chapter Fourteen.
3. Remove the fuel tank dampers (B, **Figure 68**) from the connector box cover hooks.
4. Remove the connector box cover (**Figure 69**).
5. Disconnect the left handlebar 9-pin white connector and the blue/white single lead connector (**Figure 70**).
6. Referring to *Testing* in this section, use the appropriate continuity diagram to test the switch:

    a. Horn switch (**Figure 66**).
    b. Turn signal switch (**Figure 71**).
    c. Dimmer switch (**Figure 72**).

NOTE
*When testing the dimmer switch low beam circuit, place your meter's test leads between the single lead connector blue/white terminal and the headlight bulb socket white lead (**Figure 73**). Refer to **Headlight Bulb Replacement** in this chapter to remove the headlight lens assembly.*

d. If it is necessary to replace or remove the switch assembly, continue with Step 7.

7. Remove or cut any clamps securing the switch wiring harness to the handlebar. Do not cut the wiring harness.

---

⑦⓪

⑦① TURN SIGNAL SWITCH

	ORG	GRN	LT BLU	BRN/ORG	ORG/WHT	LT BLU/WHT
R		•——	——•	•———	———•	
N				•———	———•———	———•
L		•——	——•		•———	———•

⑦② DIMMER SWITCH

	BLU/WHT	WHT	BLU
LO	•———	———•	
HI	•———————	—————	———•

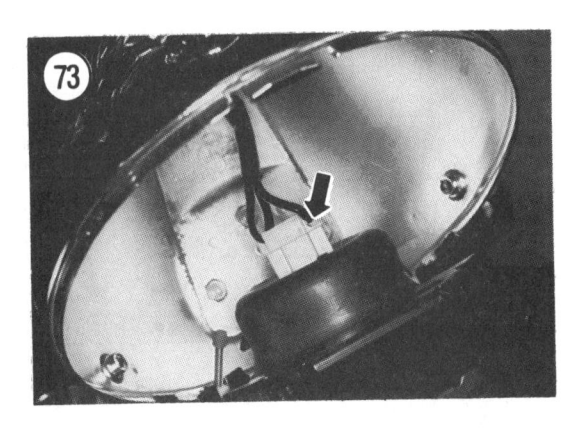

⑦③

CHAPTER NINE

handlebar switch housing
.witch housing (**Figure 67**)
.dlebar.
.ne choke cable (A, **Figure 74**) from
lever.
kemove the wiring harness through the frame, then remove the switch housing from the handlebar.
11. Install the new switch housing, making sure to route the wiring harness along its original path.
12. Mount the left side handlebar switch housing onto the handlebar as follows:
 a. Reconnect the choke cable (A, **Figure 74**) to the choke lever.
 b. Align the switch housing locating pin (B, **Figure 74**) with the hole in the handlebar and close the switch halves around the handlebar. Try to twist the switch; it must not turn.

NOTE
*The front switch housing screw is **shorter** than the rear screw.*

 c. Install the front and rear switch housing screw. Tighten the front screw, then the rear screw. Tighten both screws securely.
13. Reconnect the switch housing electrical connectors (**Figure 70**).
14. Reverse Steps 1-4 to complete installation.
15. Start the engine and check the operation of each switch. Check the choke cable for proper operation. If necessary, adjust the choke cable as described in Chapter Three.

WARNING
Do not ride the motorcycle until each switch is working properly.

Right Handlebar Switch Housing Testing/Replacement

The right handlebar switch housing is equipped with the following switches:
 a. Engine stop switch (A, **Figure 75**).
 b. Starter switch (B, **Figure 75**).

NOTE
The switches mounted in the right handlebar switch housing are not available separately. If one switch is damaged, you must replace the switch housing assembly.

1. Remove the fuel tank (Chapter Eight).

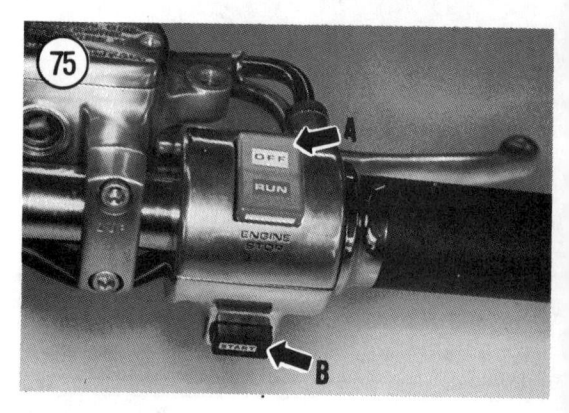

⑦④

⑦⑤

⑦⑥

ENGINE STOP SWITCH

	BLK/BLU	BLK/WHT
OFF		
RUN	•———•	

⑦⑦

STARTER SWITCH

	BLU/WHT	YEL/RED	BLK/RED	BLU/WHT
FREE			•———•	
PUSH	•———•			

ELECTRICAL SYSTEM

2. Remove the steering side covers (A, **Figure 68**) as described in Chapter Fourteen.
3. Remove the fuel tank dampers (B, **Figure 68**) from the connector box cover hooks.
4. Remove the connector box cover (**Figure 69**).
5. Disconnect the right handlebar 9-pin brown connector and the blue/white single lead connector (**Figure 70**).
6. Referring to *Testing* in this section, use the appropriate continuity diagram to test the switch:
   a. Engine stop switch (**Figure 76**).
   b. Starter switch (**Figure 77**).
   c. If it is necessary to replace or remove the switch assembly, continue with Step 7.
7. Remove or cut any clamps securing the switch wiring harness to the handlebar. Do not cut the wiring harness.
8. Disconnect the front brake light switch connectors from the switch (**Figure 78**).
9. Remove the 2 right handlebar switch housing screws and separate the switch housing (**Figure 75**) from around the handlebar and throttle grip.
10. Disconnect the 2 throttle cables from the throttle grip as described under *Throttle Cable Replacement* in Chapter Eight.
11. Remove the wiring harness through the frame, then remove the switch housing from the handlebar.
12. Install the new switch housing, making sure to route the wiring harness along its original path.
13. Install the right side handlebar switch housing as follows:
   a. Reconnect the throttle cables to the throttle grip as described under *Throttle Cable Replacement* in Chapter Eight.
   b. Align the switch housing locating pin (**Figure 79**) with the hole in the handlebar and close the switch halves around the handlebar. Try to twist the switch; it must not turn.

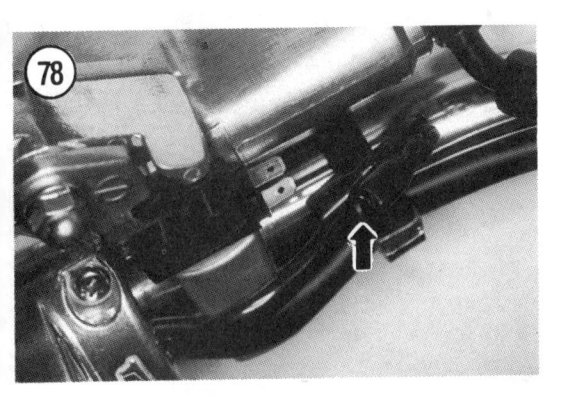

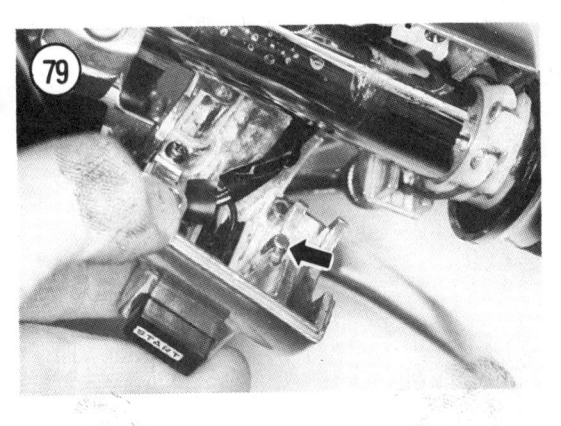

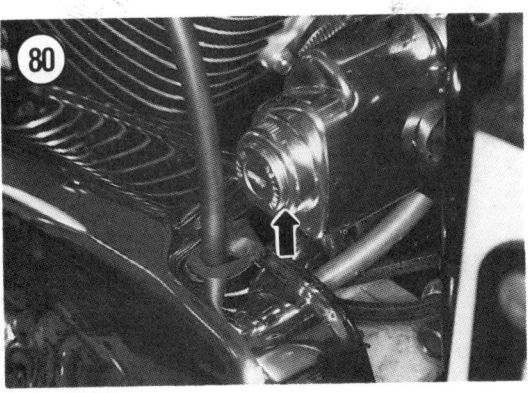

NOTE
*The front switch housing screw is **longer** than the rear screw.*

   c. Install the front and rear switch housing screws and tighten securely.
14. Reconnect the switch housing electrical connectors (**Figure 70**).
15. Check and adjust the throttle cables as described under *Throttle Cable Replacement* in Chapter Eight.
16. Reverse Steps 1-4 to complete installation.
17. Start the engine and check the operation of each switch.

WARNING
Do not ride the motorcycle until each switch and both throttle cables are working properly.

Ignition Switch Testing/Replacement

The ignition switch (**Figure 80**) is mounted on the left side of the bike, next to the battery.

1. Remove the battery holder as described under *Air Filter Housing Removal/Installation* in Chapter Eight.
2. Disconnect the ignition switch 3-pin white connector.
3. Referring to *Testing* in this section, use the continuity diagram in **Figure 81** to test the switch.
4. If the switch fails to operate as described in Step 3, replace it.
5. Remove the ignition switch fasteners and remove the old switch.
6. Reverse these steps to install a new ignition switch.
7. Check the operation of the ignition switch.
8. Install the ignition switch by reversing these removal steps.

IGNITION SWITCH

	RED	RED/BLK	BLU/ORG
ON	•———	———•	———•
OFF			

Clutch Switch Testing/Replacement

The clutch switch (**Figure 82**) is mounted in the clutch lever housing.
1. Disconnect the 2 electrical connectors from the clutch switch.
2. Switch an ohmmeter to the R × 1 scale, then connect the ohmmeter leads across the 2 clutch switch terminals.
3. Read the ohmmeter scale while pulling in, then releasing the clutch lever. There must be continuity with the clutch lever pulled in and no continuity with the lever released. Replace the clutch switch if it fails to operate as described.
4. Remove the clutch switch from the clutch lever housing.
5. Install a new clutch switch by reversing these removal steps.

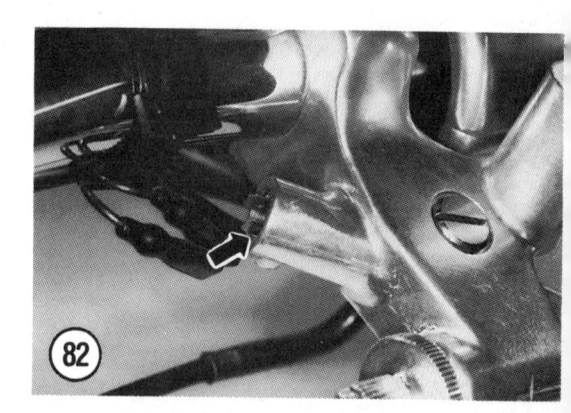

Front Brake Light Switch Testing/Replacement

The front brake switch (**Figure 78**) is mounted on the front master cylinder assembly.
1. Disconnect the 2 electrical connectors from the front brake light switch.
2. Switch an ohmmeter to the R × 1 scale, then connect the ohmmeter leads across the 2 front brake light switch terminals.
3. Read the ohmmeter while pulling in, and then releasing the front brake lever. There must be continuity with the front brake lever pulled in and no

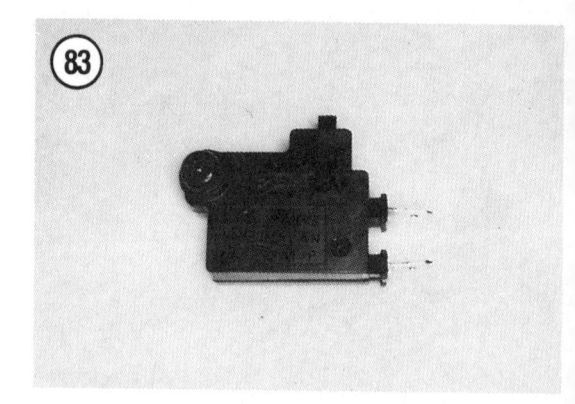

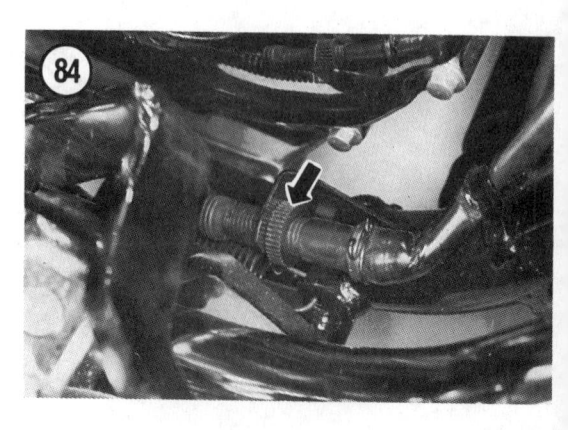

ELECTRICAL SYSTEM

continuity with the lever released. Replace the front brake light switch if it fails to operate as described.

4. Remove the front brake light switch screw and remove the switch (**Figure 83**).

5. Compress the plunger on the new switch and install its shoulder into the hole in the master cylinder. Install and tighten its mounting screw.

6. Reconnect the 2 electrical connectors at the front brake light switch.

7. Turn on the ignition switch and apply the front brake lever. Make sure the brake light operates.

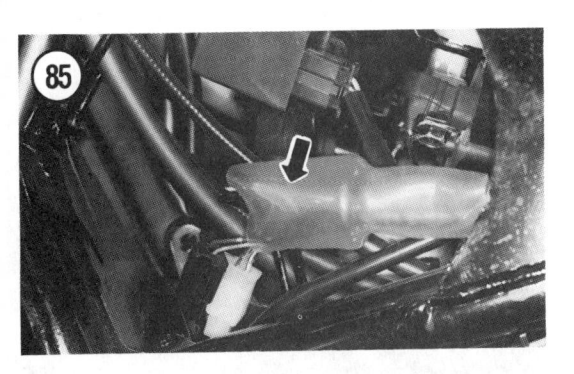

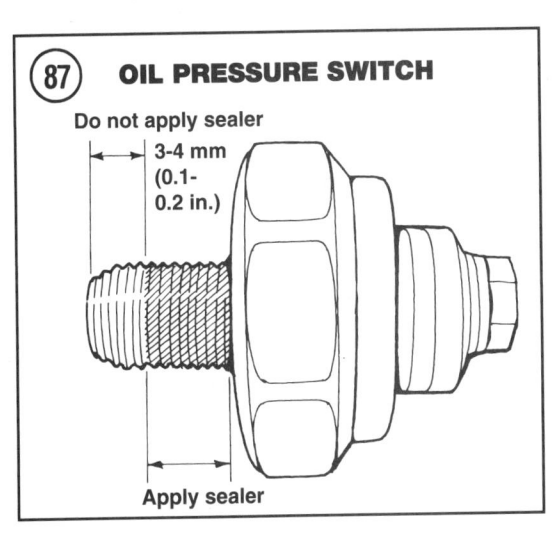

Rear Brake Light Switch Testing/Replacement

The rear brake switch (**Figure 84**) is mounted next to the rear brake pedal.

1. Remove the fuel tank (Chapter Eight).
2. Remove the left side steering cover (A, **Figure 68**).
3. Disconnect the rear brake light switch 2-pin white electrical connector (**Figure 85**).
4. Switch an ohmmeter to the R × 1 scale, then connect the ohmmeter leads across the 2 rear brake light switch terminals.
5. Read the ohmmeter while applying and then releasing the rear brake pedal. There must be continuity with the rear brake pedal applied and no continuity with the pedal released. Replace the rear brake light switch if it fails to operate as described.
6. Remove the rear brake light switch (**Figure 84**) from its mounting bracket and replace it with a new one.
7. Reconnect the rear brake light switch electrical connector.
8. Adjust the rear brake light switch (Chapter Three).
9. Turn on the ignition switch and apply the rear brake pedal. Make sure the brake light operates.

Oil Pressure Switch

The oil pressure switch (**Figure 86**) is mounted underneath the engine, next to the oil filter.

1. Remove the dust cover and disconnect the oil pressure switch wire from the switch.
2. Loosen and remove the oil pressure switch (**Figure 86**).
3. Switch an ohmmeter to the R × 1 scale, then connect the ohmmeter leads across the switch terminal and switch body. The ohmmeter must show continuity. Replace the switch if it does not show continuity.
4. Apply thread sealant to the oil pressure switch threads as shown in **Figure 87**.
5. Install the oil pressure switch and tighten to the torque specification in **Table 7**.
6. Check the engine oil level and add oil if required.
7. Reconnect the oil pressure switch wire to the switch, then install the dust cover.
8. Start the engine and observe the oil pressure indicator light. The light must go out within 1-2 seconds after starting the engine. If not, stop the

engine and check for the cause of the low oil pressure.

Neutral Switch Testing/Replacement

The neutral switch (**Figure 88**) is mounted in the left crankcase half.

1. Remove the fuel tank (Chapter Eight).
2. Remove the left side steering cover (A, **Figure 68**).
3. Disconnect the neutral switch light/green and red electrical connector (**Figure 85**).
4. Switch an ohmmeter to the R × 1 scale. Connect one lead to the neutral switch terminal and the other ohmmeter lead to a good engine ground.
5. Read the ohmmeter scale with the transmission in neutral, and then in gear. Note the following:
   a. The ohmmeter must read continuity (0 ohms) with the transmission in NEUTRAL.
   b. The ohmmeter must read no continuity (infinity) with the transmission in gear.
   c. If the reading is incorrect, replace the neutral switch.
6. To replace the neutral switch:
   a. Remove the left crankcase cover (Chapter Five).
   b. Disconnect the electrical connector from the neutral switch (**Figure 88**).
   c. Install a new neutral switch and washer and tighten to the torque specification in **Table 7**.
   d. Install the left crankcase cover (Chapter Five).
7. Reconnect the neutral switch electrical connector (**Figure 85**).
8. Start the engine and check the neutral switch indicator light operation with the transmission in NEUTRAL and in gear.
9. Reverse Steps 1 and 2 to complete installation.

Sidestand Switch

The sidestand switch (**Figure 89**) is mounted on the sidestand.

1. Remove the battery holder as described under *Air Filter Housing Removal/Installation* in Chapter Eight.

90 SIDESTAND SWITCH

	GRN/WHT	YEL/BLK	GRN
SIDESTAND APPLIED		•————	————•
SIDESTAND RETRACTED		•————	————•

ELECTRICAL SYSTEM

2. Disconnect the sidestand switch 3-pin red connector.

NOTE
Have an assistant support the bike for you while you raise and lower the sidestand during Step 3 and when replacing the switch in Step 4.

3. Referring to *Testing* in this section, use the continuity diagram in **Figure 90** to test the switch with the sidestand applied (down) and retracted (up).

91 SIDESTAND SWITCH

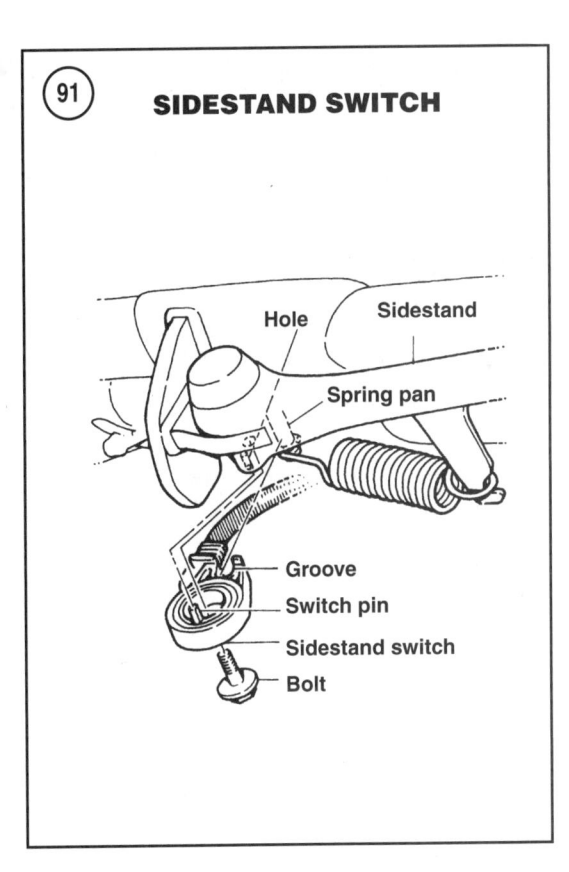

- Hole
- Sidestand
- Spring pan
- Groove
- Switch pin
- Sidestand switch
- Bolt

92

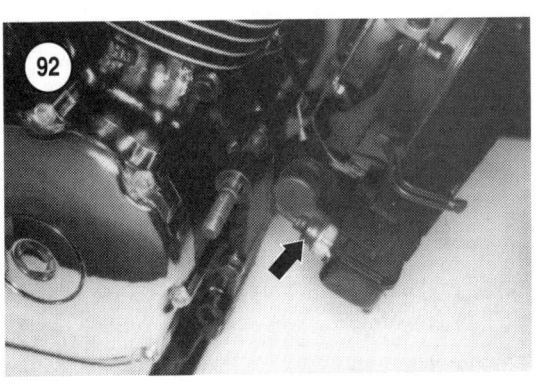

4. If the switch fails to operate as described in Step 3, replace it as follows.
   a. Have an assistant support the bike or mount it on a suitable bike stand.
   b. Release the sidestand switch wiring harness from the frame hooks.
   c. Remove the bolt and sidestand switch (**Figure 91**).
   d. Clean the switch mounting area on the sidestand.
   e. Install the sidestand switch by aligning the switch pin with the sidestand hole and the switch groove with the return spring pin.
   f. Install the sidestand switch mounting bolt and tighten to the torque specification in **Table 7**.
5. Reverse Steps 1 and 2 to reconnect the sidestand switch electrical connector.

Fan Motor Switch
Testing

The fan motor switch (**Figure 92**) is mounted on the bottom lower right side of the radiator (facing engine). It controls the radiator fan according to engine coolant temperature.

When troubleshooting the fan motor switch, make sure the fan motor fuse has not blown. Also clean off any rust or corrosion from the electrical terminals on the fan motor switch. If these items are good, refer to the appropriate fan operating condition listed below:

Fan motor does not stop

1. Turn the ignition switch off and disconnect the fan motor switch connector (**Figure 92**), then turn the ignition switch on again and note the operation of the fan motor.
2. If the fan motor now stops normally, replace the fan motor switch as described in this section.
3. If the fan motor does not stop, check for a short in the wire between the ignition switch and fan switch.

Fan motor does not start

1. Start the engine and warm it to normal operating temperature.
2. Disconnect the connector from the fan motor switch (**Figure 92**).
3. Connect a jumper wire between the fan motor switch connector and ground. Then turn the ignition

switch on and check the fan motor operation. Note the following:

a. If the fan motor runs normally, perform Step 4.
b. If the fan motor does not run normally, go to Step 5.

4. Check the connector at the fan motor switch for a dirty or loose fitting terminal. If the connector is in good condition, replace the fan motor switch and retest.

5. Using a voltmeter, check for voltage between the fan motor switch connector and ground.

6. If there is battery voltage, the fan motor is damaged. Replace the fan motor as described in Chapter Ten.

7. If there is no voltage, check for the following conditions:

a. Damaged fan circuit wiring harness.
b. Blown 10 amp fuse. See *Fuses* in this chapter.
c. Loose, contaminated or damaged ignition switch-to-fuse box electrical connector. Check the connector (blue/orange and red/black wires) leading from the ignition switch to the fuse box. See the wiring diagram at the end of this book.
d. Damaged ignition switch. Test the ignition switch as described in this section.

Fan Motor Switch Replacement

1. Remove the radiator (Chapter Ten).
2. Disconnect the electrical connector (**Figure 93**) from the fan motor switch.
3. Remove the fan motor switch (**Figure 93**) and O-ring.
4. Install a new O-ring onto the fan motor switch.
5. Install the fan motor switch and tighten to the torque specification in **Table 7**.

ELECTRICAL COMPONENTS

This section contains information on electrical components other than switches.

Turn Signal Relay Replacement

1. Remove the left steering side cover (Chapter Fourteen).

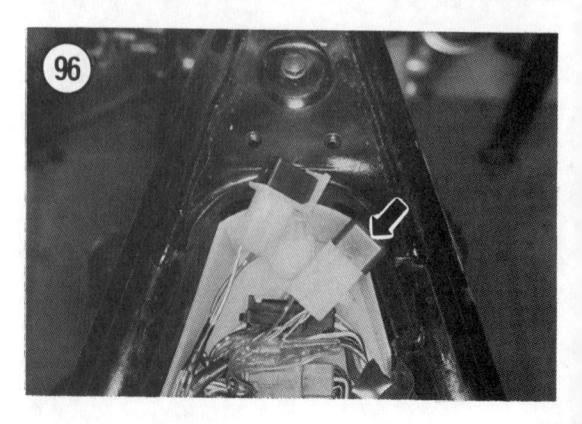

ELECTRICAL SYSTEM

2. Remove the turn signal relay (**Figure 94**) and its rubber mount from the left side of the frame. Disconnect the electrical connector.
3. Remove the rubber mount from the turn signal relay and install it on the new relay.
4. Install by reversing these removal steps.

Sidestand Diode
Testing/Replacement

1. Remove the steering side covers (Chapter Fourteen).
2. Remove the fuel tank dampers from the connector box cover hooks.
3. Remove the connector box cover (**Figure 95**).
4. Disconnect the sidestand diode (**Figure 96**) from the wire harness. The sidestand diode has 3 wires: light green/red, green/white and green/orange.
5. Set an ohmmeter to the R × 1 scale.
6. Check for continuity between the 3 terminals on the diode (**Figure 97**). There must be continuity in the normal direction and no continuity (infinite resistance) with the leads reversed. Replace the diode if it fails this test.
7. Reverse Steps 1-3 to install the sidestand diode.

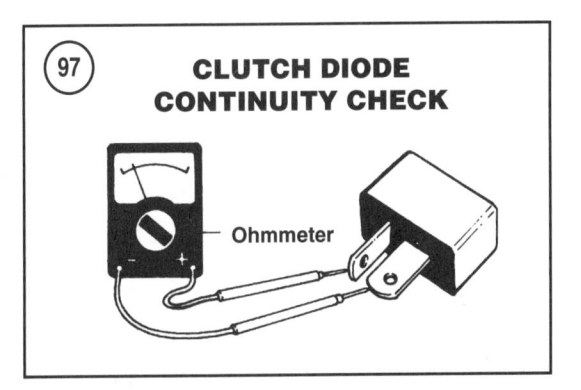

Fuel Pump
System Test

1. Turn the ignition switch to the OFF position.
2. Remove the seat (Chapter Fourteen).
3. Disconnect the electrical connector from the fuel cutoff relay (**Figure 98**).
4. Perform the following voltage test:
   a. Connect the voltmeter positive (+) lead to the fuel cutoff relay connector black terminal; connect the negative (−) lead to a good engine ground. Turn the ignition switch to the ON position and note the voltmeter reading. The correct reading is battery voltage. Turn the ignition switch to the OFF position.
   b. If there is no voltage, check the black wire for an open circuit or a loose connection.
   c. If there is battery voltage, continue with Step 5.
5. Perform the following continuity check:
   a. Switch an ohmmeter to its R × 1 scale.
   b. Connect the ohmmeter between the fuel cutoff relay connector black/blue terminal and to a good engine ground. The correct reading is no continuity (infinity).
   c. If there is continuity, replace the fuel cutoff relay.
   b. If there is no continuity, continue with Step 6.
6. Perform the following voltage test:
   a. Connect a jumper wire between the fuel cutoff relay connector black and black/blue terminals.
   b. Disconnect the fuel pump 2-pin black connector (**Figure 99**).
   c. Connect the voltmeter positive (+) lead to the fuel cutoff relay connector black/blue terminal. Connect the negative (−) lead to the fuel

cutoff relay connector green terminal. Turn the ignition switch to the ON position and note the voltmeter reading. The correct reading is battery voltage. Turn the ignition switch to the OFF position.

d. If there is battery voltage, replace the fuel pump (Chapter Eight).
e. If there is no voltage, check the black/blue and green wires for an open circuit or loose or dirty terminals.

7. Reconnect the fuel cutoff relay electrical connector (**Figure 98**).
8. Reconnect the fuel pump 2-pin black connector (**Figure 99**).
9. Install the seat (Chapter Fourteen).

Fuel Cutoff Relay Replacement

1. Remove the seat (Chapter Fourteen).
2. Disconnect the electrical connector from the fuel cutoff relay (**Figure 98**).
3. Remove the fuel cutoff relay (**Figure 98**) from the frame.
4. Install by reversing these removal steps.

Fuel Pump Flow Test

WARNING
Because gasoline will be flowing into an open container during this procedure, read the fuel system WARNING at the beginning of Chapter Eight before starting this test.

1. Remove the seat and right side cover (Chapter Fourteen).
2. Disconnect the electrical connector from the fuel cutoff relay (**Figure 98**).
3. Connect a jumper wire between the fuel cutoff relay connector black and black/blue terminals.
4. Disconnect the fuel hose from the joint at the fuel pump (**Figure 100**).
5. Place the fuel hose into a graduated beaker (**Figure 100**).
6. Have an assistant turn the ignition switch to the ON position and allow fuel to run out of the fuel hose and into the graduated beaker for 5 seconds, then turn the ignition switch off.
7. Multiply the amount of fuel in the beaker by 12 ($12 \times 5 = 60$ seconds). This will give the fuel pump flow capacity for one minute.

8. See **Table 5** for the correct fuel flow capacity for one minute.
9. If the fuel pump does not flow the specified amount of fuel in one minute, replace the fuel pump as described in Chapter Eight.
10. Pour the fuel from the beaker back into your bike's fuel tank.
11. Reconnect the fuel hose to the joint at the fuel pump. Secure the hose with its clamp.
12. Disconnect the jumper wire, then reconnect the fuel cutoff relay connector to the relay.
13. Install the seat.
14. Start the engine and allow to idle. Inspect the fuel hose for leaks.

WARNING
Repair any fuel leaks before riding the motorcycle.

15. Install the right side cover.

Thermosensor Removal/Installation

The thermosensor (**Figure 101**) is installed in the thermostat housing.
1. Remove the fuel tank (Chapter Eight).
2. Drain the engine coolant (Chapter Three).
3. Disconnect the connector from the thermosensor and remove the thermosensor (**Figure 101**).

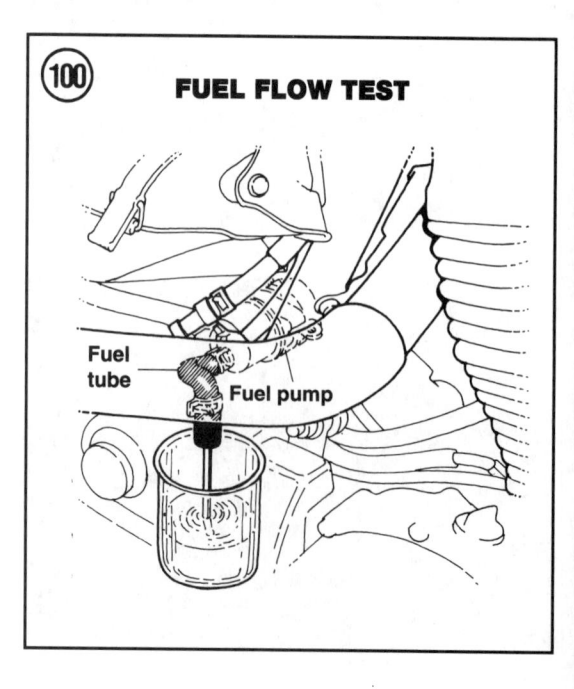

FUEL FLOW TEST

Fuel tube
Fuel pump

ELECTRICAL SYSTEM

THERMOSTAT/THERMOSENSOR

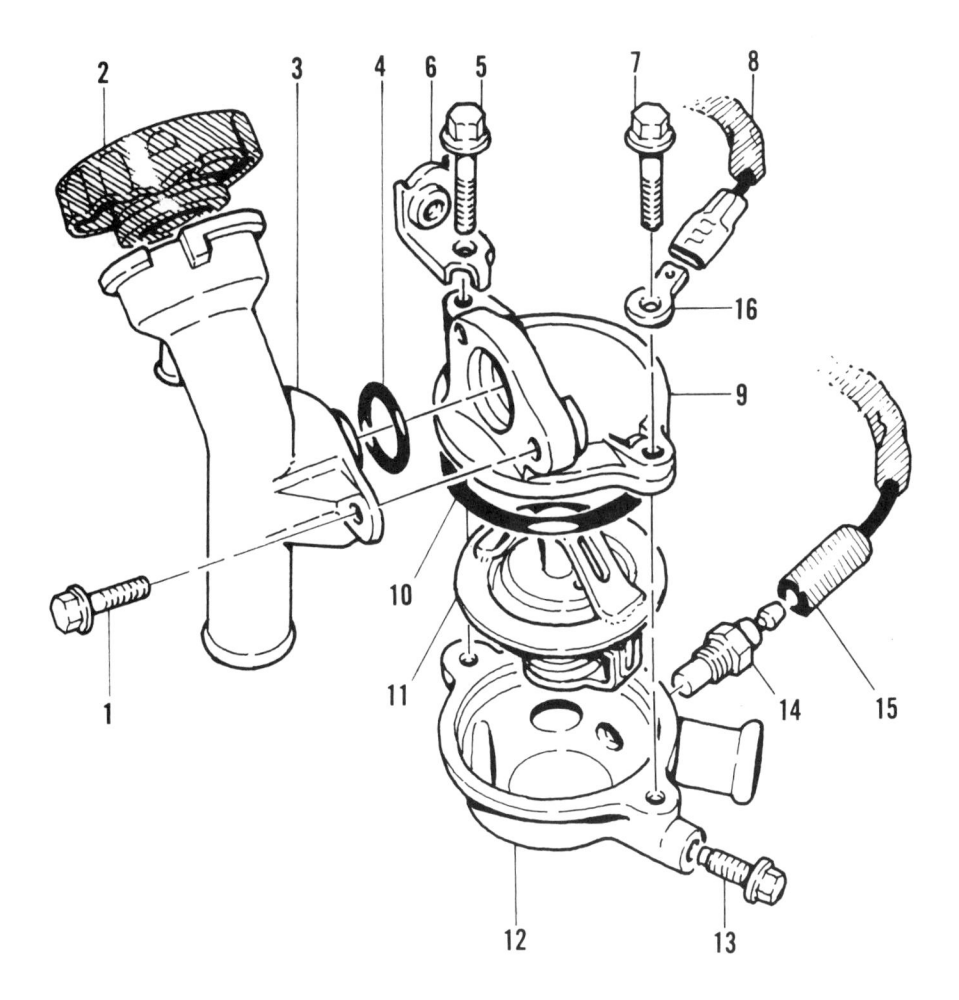

1. Bolt
2. Radiator cap
3. Fill neck
4. O-ring
5. Bolt
6. Bracket
7. Bolt
8. Connector
9. Thermostat housing cover
10. O-ring
11. Thermostat
12. Thermostat housing
13. Bolt
14. Thermosensor
15. Connector

4. If you are going to reinstall the original thermosensor, remove all sealant residue from its threads.
5. Reverse these steps to install the thermosensor while noting the following.
6. Apply sealant to the thermosensor threads. Do not apply sealant to the thermosensor head.
7. Install the thermosensor and tighten to the torque specification in **Table 7**.
8. After starting the engine, check for coolant leaks.

Thermosensor
Testing

The thermosensor (**Figure 101**) is installed in the thermostat housing.

The engine must be cold for this test, preferably not operated for 12 hours.

WARNING
Wear safety glasses or goggles and gloves during this test. Keep all flammable materials away from the burner.

1. Remove the thermosensor as described in this section.
2. Use an ohmmeter with alligator clips on the test lead ends. Attach one of the alligator clips to the electrical connector on the sensor. Attach the other alligator clip to the housing.
3. Suspend the sensor in a small pan filled with coolant (50:50 mixture). The minimum distance from the tip of the sensor to the bottom of the pan must be at least 40 mm (1 1/2 in.).
4. Place a thermometer in the pan of coolant. Do not let the sensor or the thermometer touch the pan as it will give false readings.
5. Heat the coolant and check the resistance at the temperatures listed in **Table 6**.
6. If the sensor readings differ by more than 10 percent at any temperature, replace the thermosensor as described in this section.

Coolant Temperature Indicator Testing

The coolant temperature indicator (**Figure 102**) is mounted inside the speedometer housing. The coolant temperature indicator light comes on when the coolant temperature exceeds a specified temperature.

System test

Refer to **Figure 103** for this procedure.
1. Lower the sidestand and turn the ignition switch ON. The sidestand indicator and oil pressure indicator lights must come on. Note the following:
   a. If the coolant temperature light comes on, refer to the *Coolant Temperature Indicator Test* in this section.
   b. If the sidestand indicator and oil pressure indicator lights do not come on, continue with Step 2.
   c. If the sidestand indicator and oil pressure indicator lights came on, go to Step 4.
2. Remove the speedometer and separate it from its case as described under *Speedometer Removal/Installation* in this chapter.
3. Connect the voltmeter positive (+) lead to the speedometer 6-pin connector orange wire. Connect the negative (−) lead to the green/black wire. Turn the ignition switch on and read the voltage. The correct reading is battery voltage. Note the following:
   a. If the voltmeter does not read battery voltage, check for an open circuit in the orange or black/brown wire between the speedometer 6-pin connector and fuse box. Then check for a loose, dirty or damaged terminal at the speedometer 6-pin connector, fuse box 6-pin connector and the connector box 9-pin black connector.

NOTE
See the wiring schematic for your model (end of book) for a diagram of these connectors.

ELECTRICAL SYSTEM

b. If the voltmeter reading is battery voltage, go to Step 4.

4. Remove the fuel tank (Chapter Eight). Then disconnect the connector from the thermosensor (**Figure 101**). Ground the connector terminal to the thermosensor body with a jumper wire.

5. Turn the ignition switch on and check the coolant temperature indicator light. If the indicator light comes on, the indicator circuit is working correctly. Test the thermosensor as described in this chapter. If the indicator light does not come on, continue with Step 6.

6. Separate the speedometer from its case as described under *Speedometer Removal/Installation* in this chapter.

7. Connect a jumper wire between the speedometer 6-pin connector green/blue wire and a good engine ground. Turn the ignition switch on and check the coolant temperature indicator light.

a. If the indicator light does not come on, the speedometer unit is faulty. Replace the speedometer unit and retest.

b. If the indicator light comes on, check for an open circuit between the speedometer 6-pin connector blue/red wire and the thermosensor. Then check for a loose, dirty or damaged terminal in the speedometer 6-pin connector or in the connector box 9-pin black connector.

8. Reverse the disassembly steps to reconnect the connector(s), install the speedometer unit and install the fuel tank.

9. Check the operation of all indicator lights before riding the bike.

Coolant temperature indicator test

If the coolant temperature indicator light remains on even though the engine is not overheating, perform the following.

103 SPEEDOMETER AND INDICATOR LIGHTS

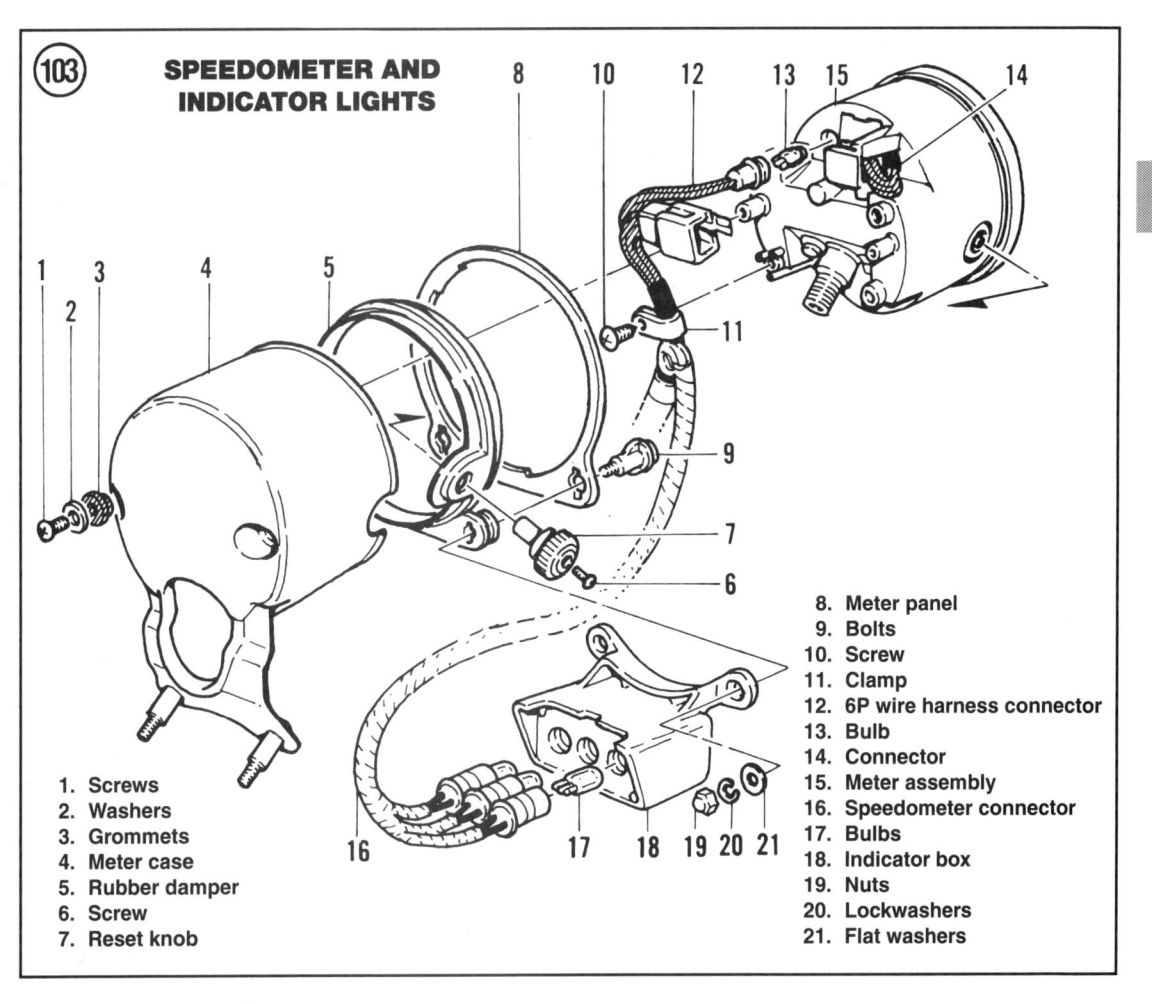

1. Screws
2. Washers
3. Grommets
4. Meter case
5. Rubber damper
6. Screw
7. Reset knob
8. Meter panel
9. Bolts
10. Screw
11. Clamp
12. 6P wire harness connector
13. Bulb
14. Connector
15. Meter assembly
16. Speedometer connector
17. Bulbs
18. Indicator box
19. Nuts
20. Lockwashers
21. Flat washers

CHAPTER NINE

1. Remove the fuel tank (Chapter Eight). Then disconnect the connector from the thermosensor (**Figure 101**).
2. Remove the speedometer and separate it from its case as described under *Speedometer Removal/Installation* in this chapter.
3. Disconnect the speedometer 6-pin connector (**Figure 103**).
4. Switch an ohmmeter to its R × 1 scale. Then connect the ohmmeter between the speedometer connector green/blue terminal (wire harness side) and a good engine ground. Read the ohmmeter scale and note the following:

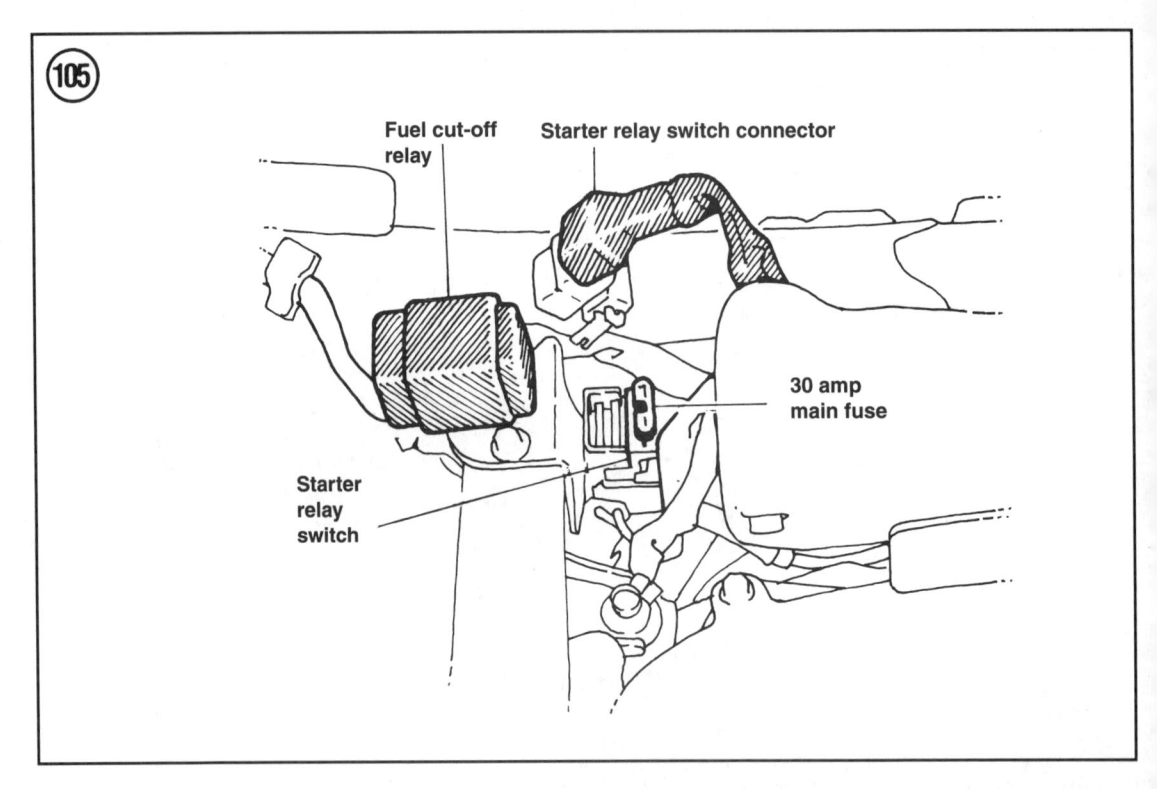

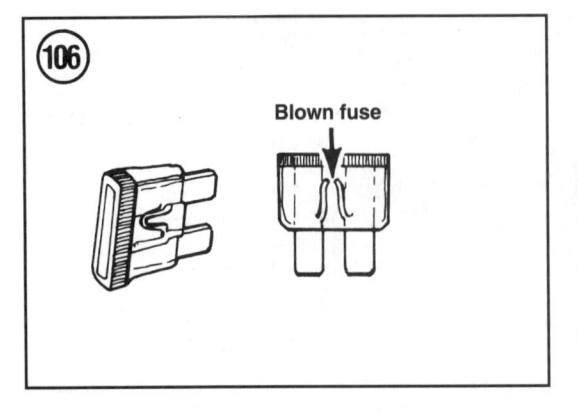

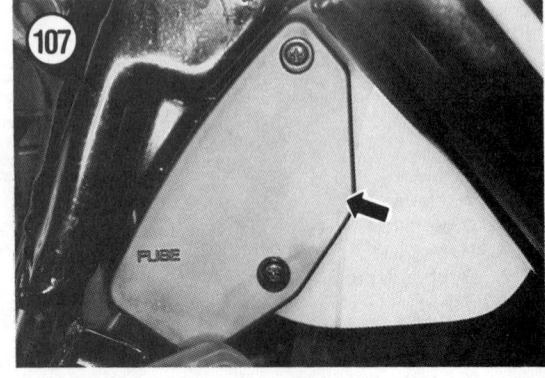

ELECTRICAL SYSTEM

a. If there is no continuity, test the thermosensor as described in this chapter. If the thermosensor is good, the speedometer is faulty and must be replaced.
b. If there is continuity, there is a short circuit in the green/blue wire. Find and repair the short, then retest.

5. Reverse Step 2 to assembly and install the speedometer unit.
6. Reconnect the thermosensor electrical connector.
7. Install the fuel tank (Chapter Eight).

Horn
Removal/Installation

1. Disconnect the electrical connectors from the horn (**Figure 104**).
2. Remove the bolt and washer securing the horn (**Figure 104**) to its mounting bracket and remove the horn.
3. Install by reversing these removal steps. Make sure the electrical connections are tight and free of corrosion.
4. Check the horn operation. If the horn does not work properly, perform the *Horn Testing* procedure in this section.

WARNING
Do not ride the bike until the horn is working properly.

Horn Testing

1. Disconnect the electrical connectors from the horn (**Figure 104**).
2. Connect a 12 volt battery across the horn terminals. The horn must sound loudly.
3. Replace the horn if it does not function as specified.

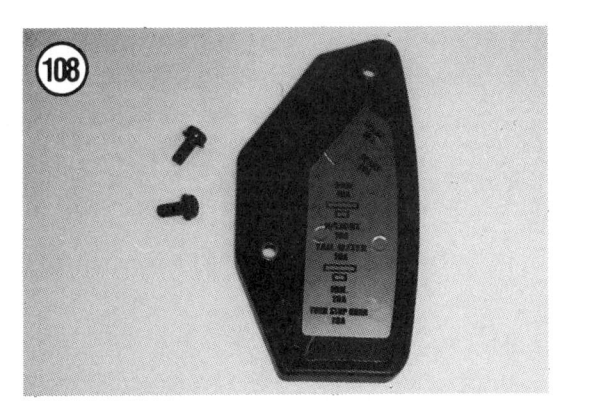

FUSES

If the fuse blows, determine the reason for the failure before replacing the fuse. Usually, the trouble is a short circuit in the wiring. Worn-through insulation may cause this or a short from a disconnected wire to ground.

CAUTION
When replacing a fuse, make sure the ignition switch is in the OFF position. This will lessen the chance of a short circuit.

CAUTION
Never substitute aluminum foil or some other metal object for a fuse. Never use a higher amperage fuse than specified. An overload could cause a fire and complete loss of the motorcycle.

Main Fuse

The 30 amp main fuse is mounted on the starter relay switch (**Figure 105**). The starter relay switch is mounted underneath the seat. To check or replace the main fuse, perform the following.

1. Turn the ignition switch to its OFF position.
2. Remove the seat (Chapter Fourteen).
3. Disconnect the starter relay switch electrical connector (**Figure 105**).
4. Remove and inspect the fuse (**Figure 105**). Replace the fuse if blown (**Figure 106**).

NOTE
A spare 30 amp main fuse is stored in the fuse box (Figure 107).

5. Reconnect the starter relay switch electrical connector (**Figure 105**).
6. Reinstall the seat (Chapter Fourteen).

Fuse Box

The fuse box (**Figure 107**) is mounted on the left side of the bike, next to the battery and behind the left side cover. The fuse rating for each fuse is 10 amps. To identify an individual fuse, use the decal mounted on the back of the fuse box cover (**Figure 108**) and the wiring diagram at the end of this book.

If a fuse in the fuse box blows, perform the following.
1. Turn the ignition switch to its OFF position.
2. Remove the left side cover (Chapter Fourteen).

3. Remove the screws and the fuse box cover (**Figure 107**).
4. Remove and inspect the fuse (**Figure 109**). Replace the fuse if blown (**Figure 106**).

NOTE
A spare 10 amp fuse is stored in the fuse box.

5. Install the fuse box cover.
6. Install the left side cover (Chapter Fourteen).

WIRING DIAGRAMS

Wiring diagrams for all models are located at the end of this book.

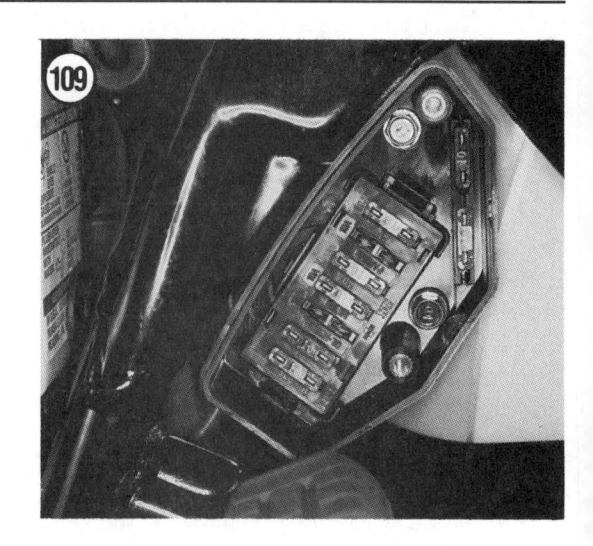

ELECTRICAL SYSTEM

Table 1 ALTERNATOR AND CHARGING SYSTEM SPECIFICATIONS

Stator coil resistance	0.3-0.5 ohms*
Regulator/rectifier regulated voltage	15.5 @ 5,000 rpm
Battery	
Capacity	12 volts, 16 amp hours
Current leakage	1 mA maximum
Charging current	1.6 amps maximum

* Tests must be made at an ambient temperature of 20° C (68° F). Do not test when the engine or component is hot.

Table 2 IGNITION SYSTEM SERVICE SPECIFICATIONS

Ignition coil primary peak voltage	100 volts minimum
Ignition pulse generator peak voltage	0.7 volts minimum
Ignition coil resistance*	
Primary	2.1-2.7 ohms
Secondary with spark plug cap	24-32 k ohms
Secondary without spark plug cap	20-26 k ohms
Ignition pulse generator resistance*	400-500 ohms

* Tests must be made at an ambient temperature of 20° C (68° F). Do not test when the engine or component is hot.

Table 3 STARTER MOTOR SERVICE SPECIFICATIONS

	New mm (in.)	Service limit mm (in.)
Starter clutch housing inside diameter	74.414-74.440 (2.9297-2.9307)	74.50 (2.933)
Starter driven gear outside diameter	57.749-57.768 (2.2735-2.2743)	57.639 (2.2692)
Starter brush length	12.5-13.0 (0.49-0.51)	6.5 (0.26)

Table 4 REPLACEMENT BULBS

Item	Size (all 12 volt)
Headlight (high/low beam)	60/55 w
Tail/brake light	32/3 cp x 2
License plate light	4 cp
Front turn signal/running light	32/3 cp x 2
Rear turn signal light	32 cp
Meter light	3 w
High beam indicator	3.4 w
Turn signal indicator	3.4 w
Neutral indicator	3.4 w

Table 5 FUEL PUMP SPECIFICATIONS

Minimum flow capacity for 1 minute	
1995	650 cc (22.0 U.S. oz. /22.8 Imp. oz)
1996-on	800 cc (27.1 U.S. oz./28.1 Imp. oz.)

Table 6 THERMOSENSOR TEST SPECIFICATIONS

Temperature	80° C	120° C
	(176° F)	(248° F)
Resistance	47-50 ohms	14-18 ohms

Table 7 TIGHTENING TORQUES

	N•m	in.-lb.	ft.-lb.
Fan motor switch	10	88	—
Flywheel bolt	140	—	103
Ignition pulse generator 8 mm clamp bolt (right crankcase bolt)	27	—	20
Neutral switch	12	106	—
Oil pressure switch	12	106	—
Side stand switch bolt	10	88	—
Starter clutch housing bolt	23	—	17
Starter motor assembly bolt	5	44	—
Starter motor terminal nut	7	62	—
Thermosensor	9	80	—

CHAPTER TEN

COOLING SYSTEM

The pressurized cooling system consists of the radiator, water pump, thermostat, electric cooling fan and a coolant reserve tank.

The water pump requires no routine maintenance and is replaced as a complete unit if defective.

It is important to keep the coolant level between the upper and lower level marks on the coolant reserve tank (**Figure 1**). During periodic maintenance, add coolant to the coolant reserve tank, not to the radiator. If the cooling system requires repeated refilling, there is a leak somewhere in the system. Test the cooling system as described in Chapter Three.

CAUTION
Drain and flush the cooling system at least every 2 years. Refill with a mixture of ethylene glycol antifreeze (formulated for aluminum engines) and distilled water. Do not reuse the old coolant as it deteriorates with use. Do not operate the cooling system with only distilled water (even in climates where antifreeze protection is not required). This is important because the engine is all aluminum; it will not rust but it will oxidize and corrode internally. Refer to Chapter Three.

This chapter describes repair and replacement of cooling system components. **Table 1** at the end of this chapter lists all of the cooling system specifications. For routine maintenance of the system, refer to Chapter Three.

The small diameter hoses are very stiff and can be difficult to install. Prior to installing the hoses, apply a small amount of antifreeze to the inside surface of these hoses and they will slide on much easier.

The cooling system must be cool prior to removing any component of the system.

WARNING
*Do not remove the radiator cap (**Figure 2**) when the engine is hot. The coolant is very hot and is under pressure. Severe scalding could result if the coolant contacts your skin.*

Tables 1 and **2** are at the end of the chapter.

COOLING SYSTEM CHECK

Two checks should be made before disassembly if a cooling system fault is suspected.

1. Run the engine until it reaches operating temperature. While the engine is running, a pressure surge should be felt when the upper radiator hose is squeezed.

2. If a substantial coolant loss is noted, a head gasket may be defective. In an extreme case, sufficient coolant can leak into the cylinder to prevent the

engine from cranking with the starter motor. White steam from the muffler(s) might also be observed when the engine is first started. Coolant can also find its way into the engine oil. Remove the dipstick and examine the color of the oil on the dipstick. If the oil has a white, foamy appearance, coolant is present in the oil.

CAUTION
If the engine oil is contaminated with coolant, drain the oil and thoroughly flush the engine to eliminate all traces of antifreeze. Repair the coolant leak and refill the engine with oil as described in Chapter Three.

RADIATOR

Removal/Installation

1. Drain the cooling system (Chapter Three).
2. Remove the steering left side cover (Chapter Fourteen).
3. Disconnect the fan motor switch connector (**Figure 3**).

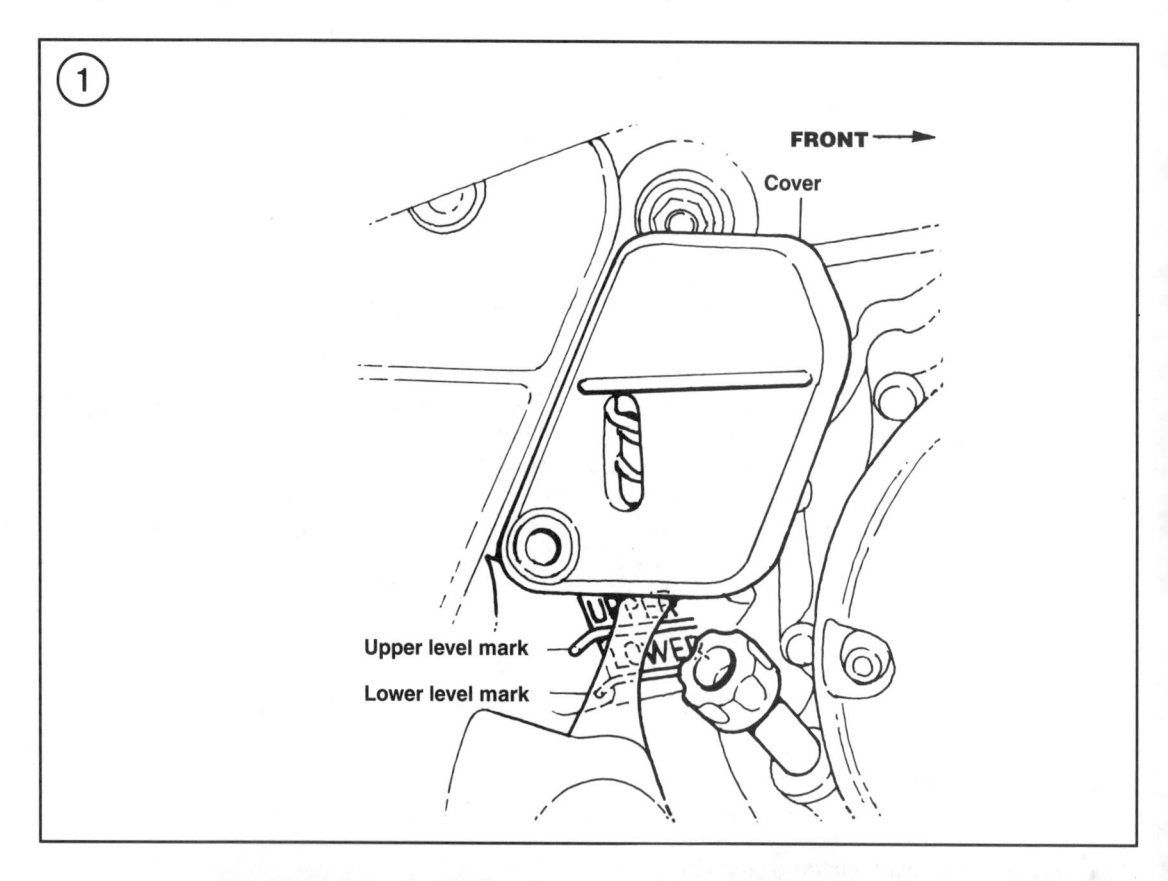

COOLING SYSTEM

4. Remove the radiator grill as follows:

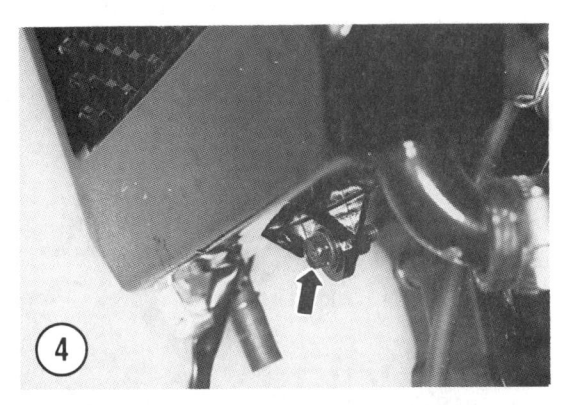

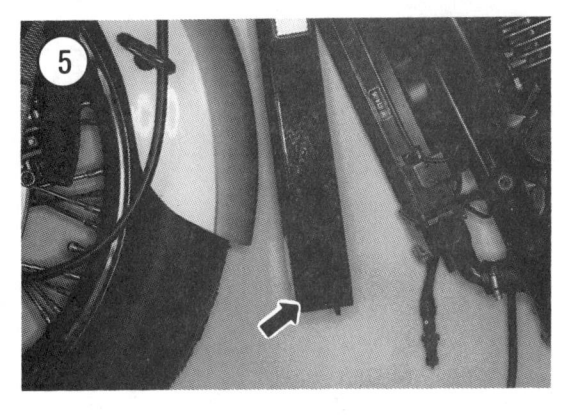

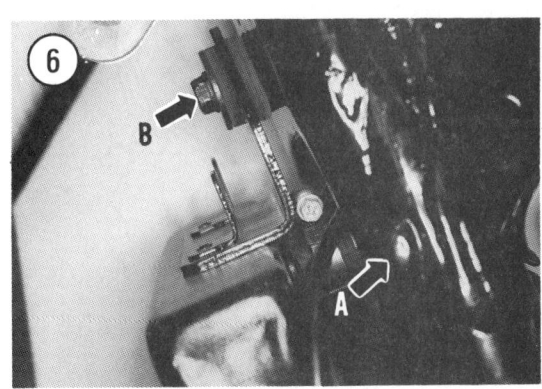

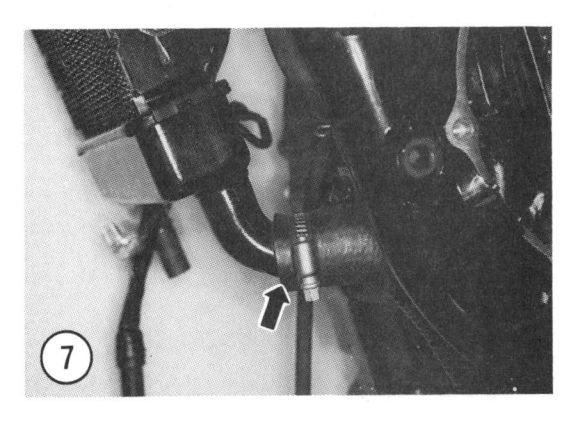

   a. Remove the lower radiator grill mounting bolt (**Figure 4**).

   b. Lift the radiator grill (**Figure 5**) up and disconnect it from the tabs on the radiator, then remove it.

5. Disconnect the upper (A, **Figure 6**) and lower (**Figure 7**) hoses from the radiator.

6. Disconnect the tube, horn and rear brake light switch wires from the clamps on the radiator.

7. Remove the radiator mounting bolt and collar (B, **Figure 6**), then lift the radiator to release it from the frame and remove it. See **Figure 8**.

8. Reverse these steps to install the radiator while noting the following.

9. Replace leaking or damaged radiator hoses.

10. Hook the radiator grill slots over the radiator tabs (**Figure 9**).

11. On California models, route the No. 2 tube (**Figure 10**) between the radiator body and radiator grill. Make sure the hose is not bent.

12. Refill and bleed the cooling system (Chapter Three).

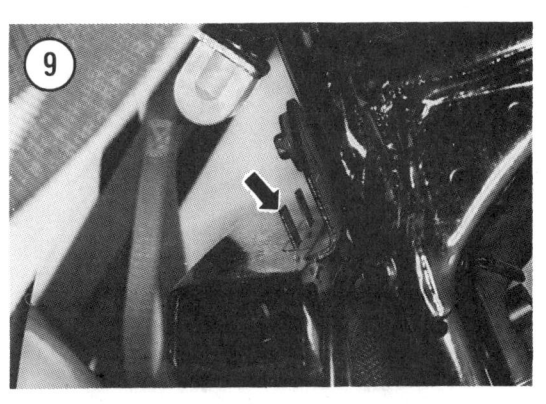

CHAPTER TEN

13. After starting the engine, check the cooling hoses for leaks.

Inspection

1. Flush off the exterior of the radiator with a garden hose on low pressure. Spray the front and back sides to remove all debris. Carefully use a whisk broom or stiff paint brush to remove any stubborn dirt.

CAUTION
Do not press too hard or the cooling fins and tubes may be damaged.

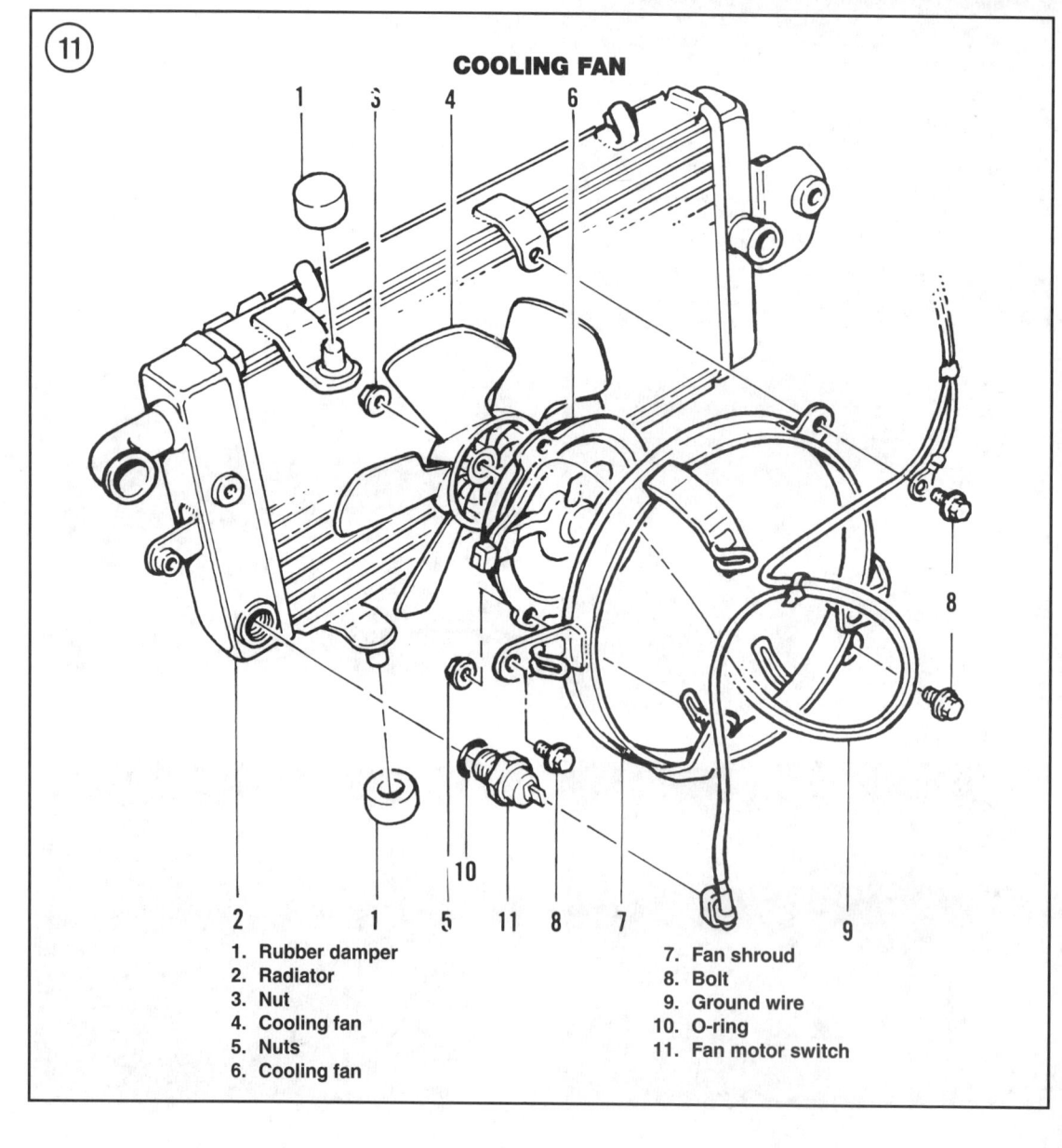

COOLING FAN

1. Rubber damper
2. Radiator
3. Nut
4. Cooling fan
5. Nuts
6. Cooling fan
7. Fan shroud
8. Bolt
9. Ground wire
10. O-ring
11. Fan motor switch

COOLING SYSTEM

2. Carefully straighten out any bent cooling fins with a broad-tipped screwdriver or putty knife.

3. Check for cracks or leakage (usually a moss-green colored residue) at the filler neck, the inlet and outlet hose fittings and the upper and lower tank seams.

4. If the condition of a radiator is doubtful, have it pressure checked as described under *Coolant Change* in Chapter Three. Radiators can be pressure checked while removed or when mounted on the bike.

5. If paint has been worn off in any area of the radiator, repaint with a quality black spray paint. This will help to prolong the radiator life by preventing oxidation. Do not apply too much paint to the cooling fin area as this will reduce the cooling capabilities of the radiator.

6. Make sure the lower mounting bracket rubber grommets are in good condition. Replace if necessary.

7. Inspect the rubber seals on the radiator fill cap. Replace the cap if they are hardened or starting to deteriorate.

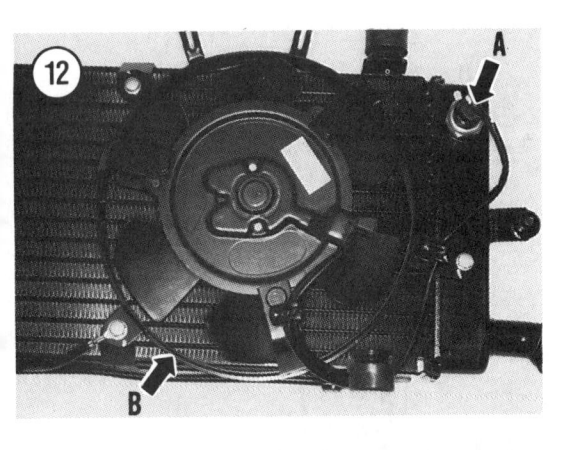

Fan Motor Switch

To test and service the fan motor switch, refer to *Switches* in Chapter Nine.

COOLING FAN

Refer to **Figure 11** when performing the following procedures.

Removal/Installation

1. Remove the radiator as described in this chapter.
2. Disconnect the fan motor switch connector (A, **Figure 12**). Then remove the wire from the clamps on the radiator.
3. Remove the fan mounting bolts and ground wire, then remove the fan (B, **Figure 12**).
4. To separate the fan from the fan motor:

   a. Remove the nut and the cooling fan.

   b. Remove the nuts and the fan motor.
5. Install by reversing these removal steps while noting the following.
6. Install the cooling fan onto the fan motor shaft by aligning the flat surfaces. Install and tighten the fan motor nut securely.
7. Check the wire harness routing.

COOLANT RESERVE TANK

Removal/Installation

1. Remove the right side cover (Chapter Fourteen).
2. Remove the swing arm (Chapter Twelve).
3. Disconnect the hose from the bottom of the coolant reserve tank (**Figure 13**) and drain the coolant from the tank.
4. Remove the 2 coolant reserve tank mounting bolts.
5. Disconnect the filler hose from the coolant reserve tank.
6. Remove the breather tube from the frame clamp.
7. Pull the coolant reserve tank to the rear of the bike and remove it.
8. Flush the reserve tank with clean water. Check the tank for cracks or other damage.
9. Install the coolant reserve tank by reversing these steps.
10. Fill the reserve tank as described under *Coolant Change* in Chapter Three.

THERMOSTAT

Refer to **Figure 14** when servicing the thermostat.

Removal/Installation

1. Drain the cooling system (Chapter Three).
2. Remove the fuel tank (Chapter Eight).
3. Remove the ignition coils (Chapter Nine).
4. Remove the thermostat filler neck bolts.
5. Remove the thermostat housing cover bolts, retainer and ground terminal.
6. Remove the thermostat from the housing.
7. To remove the thermostat housing, perform the following:

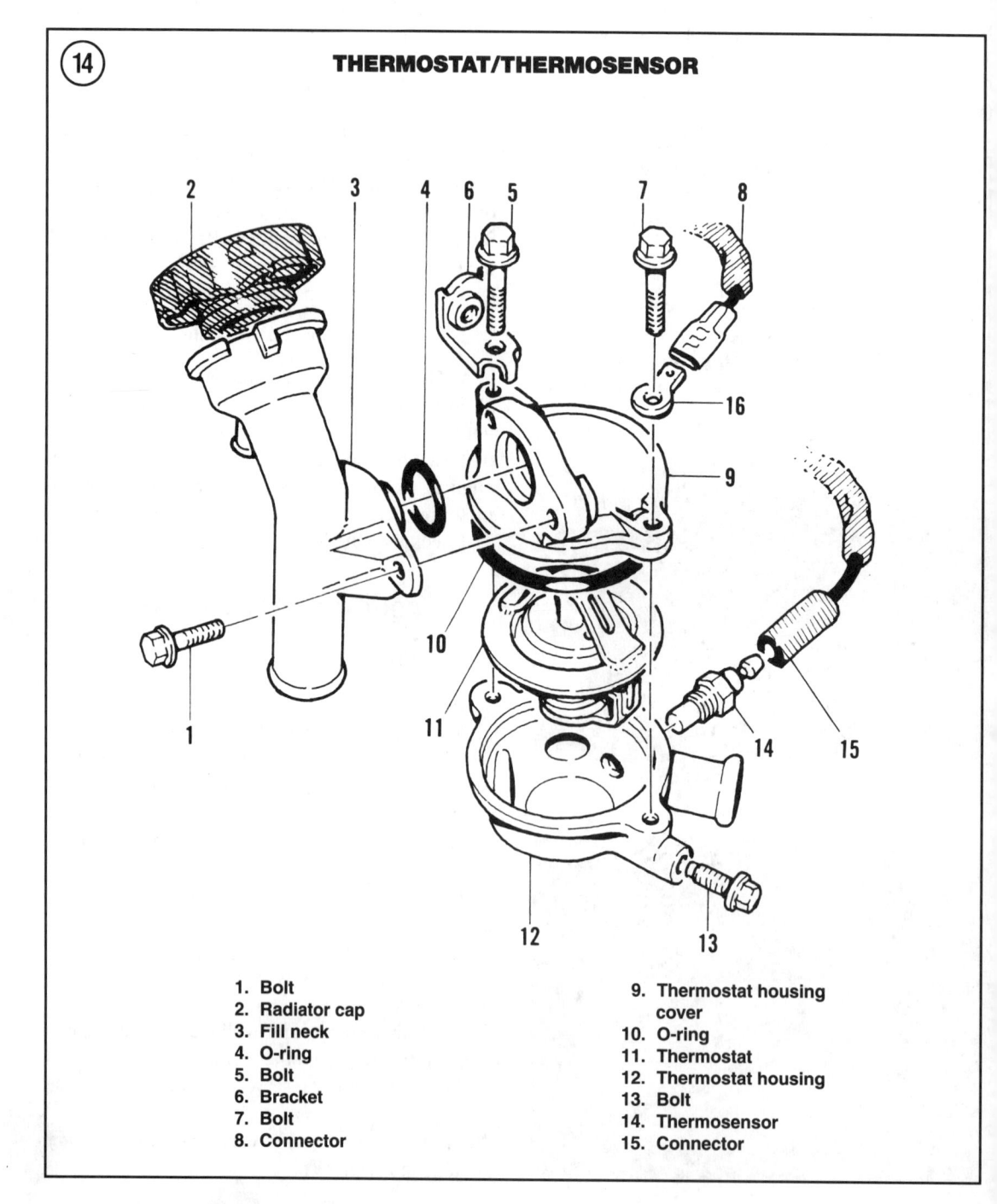

THERMOSTAT/THERMOSENSOR

1. Bolt
2. Radiator cap
3. Fill neck
4. O-ring
5. Bolt
6. Bracket
7. Bolt
8. Connector
9. Thermostat housing cover
10. O-ring
11. Thermostat
12. Thermostat housing
13. Bolt
14. Thermosensor
15. Connector

COOLING SYSTEM

a. Disconnect the electrical connector from the thermosensor.
b. Remove the cooling hoses from the housing.
c. Remove the housing.

8. Install by reversing these removal steps. Note the following.
9. Install new O-rings on the filler neck and thermostat housing cover.
10. Install the thermostat into the housing with its hole facing toward the sealing bolt on the housing (**Figure 14**). Make sure the thermostat outer flange sits flush in the housing and is even with the housing's upper surface.
11. Install the thermostat housing by aligning its cover groove with the notch in the retainer.
12. Install the ground terminal onto the bolt shown in **Figure 14**. Then install the thermostat housing cover bolts and tighten securely.
13. Refill the cooling system with the recommended type and quantity of coolant (Chapter Three).

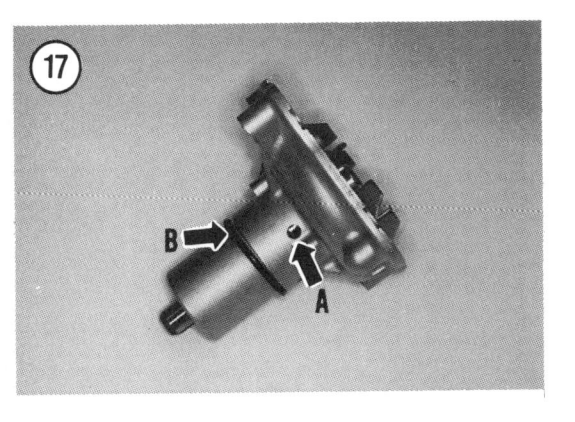

Testing

Test the thermostat to ensure proper operation. Replace the thermostat if it remains open at normal room temperature or stays closed after the specified temperature has been reached during the test procedure.

Support the thermostat in a pan of water (**Figure 15**). The thermostat must not touch the sides or bottom of the pan or a false reading will result. Place a thermometer in the pan of water (use a thermometer that is rated higher than the test temperature). Gradually heat the water and continue to gently stir the water until it reaches 80-84° C (176-183° F). At this temperature, the thermostat valve should start to open. At 95° C (203° F), the minimum valve lift is 8 mm (0.31 in.).

NOTE
Valve operation is sometimes sluggish; it may take 3-5 minutes for the valve to operate properly.

If the valve fails to open at the listed temperatures, or if the valve lift is below minimum at the specified temperature, replace the thermostat. Be sure to replace it with one of the same temperature rating.

WATER PUMP

The water pump (**Figure 16**) is mounted on the bottom, left side of the engine.

The water pump is sold as a complete unit only. If any component is damaged, replace the entire water pump assembly. The 2 water pump O-rings, however, can be replaced separately.

If the coolant level has been dropping, check the vent hole at the bottom of the water pump housing (**Figure 16**). A, **Figure 17** shows the vent hole with the water pump removed for clarity. If coolant leaks

CHAPTER TEN

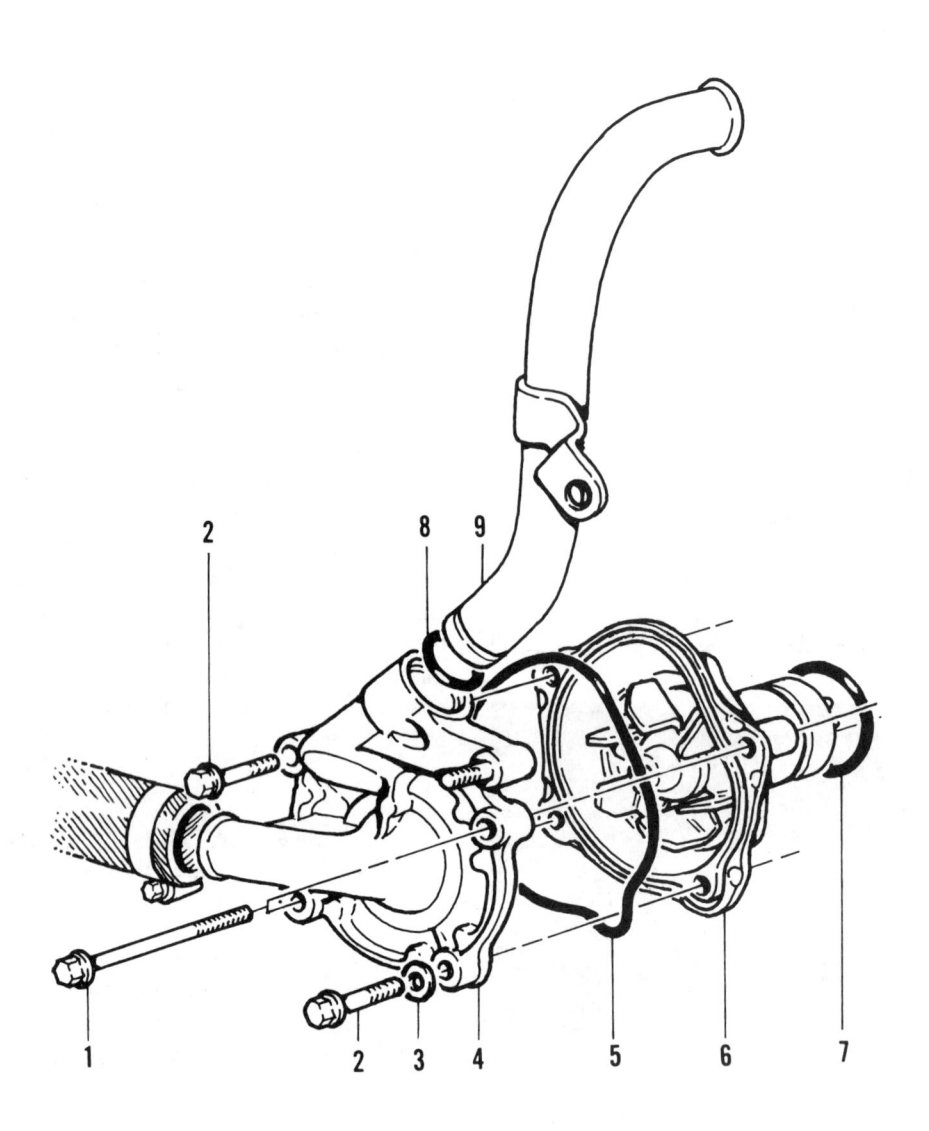

⑱ WATER PUMP

1. Bolt
2. Bolt
3. Washer
4. Cover
5. O-ring
6. Water pump and impeller
7. O-ring
8. O-ring
9. Water pipe

COOLING SYSTEM

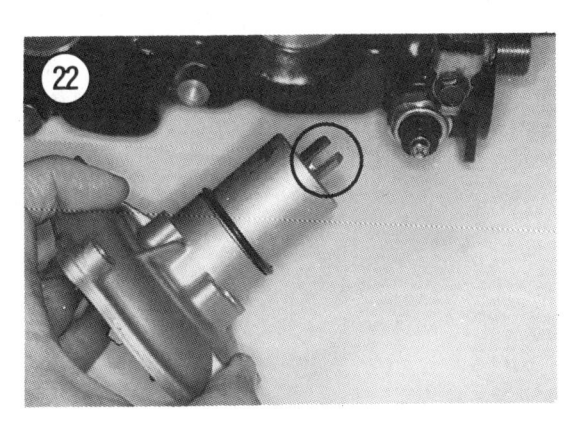

from the hole, the internal water pump seal is leaking; replace the water pump as a unit.

If coolant is not leaking from the vent hole, pressure test the cooling system as described under *Coolant Change* in Chapter Three.

Removal/Installation

Refer to **Figure 18**.
1. Remove the engine from the frame (Chapter Five).
2. Remove the water pipe clamp bolt (A, **Figure 19**).
3. Disconnect the water pipe from the cylinder block hose (**Figure 20**) or remove the hose joint at the cylinder block.
4. Remove the bolts and the water pump cover (B, **Figure 19**).
5. Remove the O-ring (A, **Figure 21**) from the water pump groove.
6. Remove the water pump (B, **Figure 21**) from the crankcase.
7. Inspect the water pump as described in this chapter.
8. Install the water pump by reversing these steps. Note the following.
9. Install a new O-ring (B, **Figure 17**) on the pump body. Lubricate the O-ring with engine oil.
10. When installing the water pump body into the engine, align the water pump rotor shaft slot (**Figure 22**) with the notch in the end of the oil pump shaft (**Figure 23**).
11. Install a new O-ring (A, **Figure 21**) into the water pump housing groove.
12. Tighten the water pump cover mounting bolts to the torque specification in **Table 2**.
13. If you removed the hose joint from the cylinder block (**Figure 20**), install the hose joint with a new O-ring.
14. Install the engine in the frame (Chapter Five).

Inspection

1. Check the impeller blades (**Figure 24**) for corrosion or damage. If the corrosion buildup on the blades is minor, clean the blades. If the corrosion is excessive or if the blades are cracked or broken, replace the water pump assembly.
2. Turn the impeller shaft and check the pump bearing for excessive noise or roughness. If the bearing

operation is rough or abnormal, replace the water pump assembly.

HOSES

Hoses deteriorate with age and should be replaced periodically or whenever they are cracked or leaking. To be safe, replace the hoses every 2 years. The spray of hot coolant from a cracked hose can injure the rider and passenger. Loss of coolant can also cause engine damage.

Whenever any part of the cooling system is removed, inspect the hose(s) and determine if replacement is necessary.

Inspection

1. With the engine cold, check the cooling hoses for brittleness or hardness. A hose in this condition will usually show cracks and must be replaced.
2. With the engine hot, carefully inspect the hoses along their entire length for swollen areas. A swollen hose is defective and eventually will rupture at the swollen area.
3. Check the hose area around the hose clamps. Signs of rust or coolant residue indicate possible leakage points.

Replacement

Perform hose replacement only when the engine is cold.

1. Remove body components as required to access the hose to be replaced. See Chapter Fourteen.
2. Drain the cooling system as described under *Coolant Change* in Chapter Three.
3. Loosen the hose clamps from the hose to be replaced. Slide the clamps along the hose and out of the way.
4. Twist the hose end to break the seal and remove the hose from its connecting joint. If the hose has been on for some time, it may have become fused to the joint. If so, cut the hose parallel to the joint connection. The hose then can be carefully pried free with a screwdriver.

CAUTION
Excessive force applied to the hose during removal could damage the connecting joint.

5. Examine the connecting joint for cracks or other damage. Repair or replace damaged parts as required.
6. Replace worn or damaged hose clamps.
7. Slide the hose clamps over the new hose and install hose to its inlet and outlet connecting joints. Make sure the hose clears all obstructions and is routed properly.

NOTE
If it is difficult to install a hose on a joint, lubricate the inside of the hose with antifreeze.

8. With the hose positioned correctly, position clamps back away from end of hose slightly. Tighten clamps securely, but not so much that the hose is damaged.
9. Refill and bleed cooling system as described under *Coolant Change* in Chapter Three.

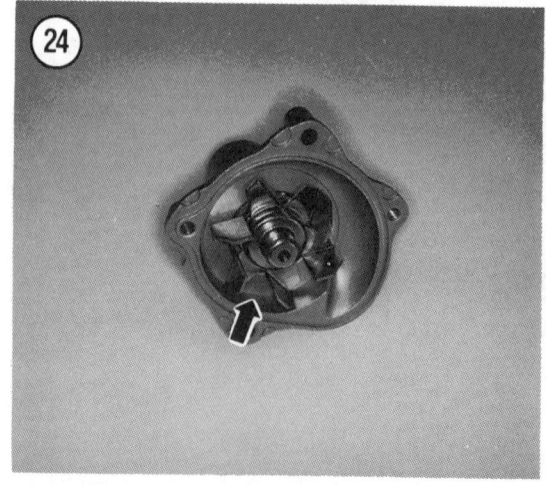

COOLING SYSTEM

Table 1 COOLING SYSTEM TEST SPECIFICATIONS

Radiator cap relief pressure	108-137 kPa (16-20 psi)
Thermostat	
Begins to open	80-84° C (176-183° F)
Fully open	95° C (203° F)
Minimum valve lift	8 mm (0.31 in.)

Table 2 COOLING SYSTEM TIGHTENING TORQUES

	N·m	in.-lb.
Water pump housing bolts	12	106

CHAPTER ELEVEN

FRONT SUSPENSION AND STEERING

This chapter describes repair and maintenance on the front wheel, forks, and steering components.

The following tables list service specifications and tightening torques for the front suspension and steering components. All tables are located at the end of the chapter.

Table 1: Steering and front suspension specifications.

Table 2: Tire inflation pressure.

Table 3: Tightening torques.

FRONT WHEEL

Removal

1. Support the motorcycle on a stand with the front wheel off the ground.

NOTE
Make sure you can safely lift the front of the bike high enough to remove the front wheel with the fender mounted on the bike.

CAUTION
Because the engine drops below the frame, you must support the bike on a stand that contacts the frame rails. Do not apply pressure against the engine or you may damage the crankcase.

2. Remove the speedometer cable screw and pull the cable assembly (**Figure 1**) out of the speedometer gear box.
3. Remove the left and right side bolt caps (**Figure 2**) from the front axle pinch bolts.
4. Loosen the right side axle pinch bolts (A, **Figure 3**), then loosen and remove the axle bolt (B, **Figure 3**). See **Figure 4**.
5. Loosen the left side axle pinch bolts (A, **Figure 5**) and remove the front axle (B, **Figure 5**).
6. Pull the wheel down and roll it forward to remove it from the front fork and the brake caliper.

NOTE
Insert a plastic spacer in the caliper in place of the brake disc. Then, if the brake lever is inadvertently squeezed, the pistons will not be forced out of the caliper.

7. Remove the speedometer gear box (**Figure 6**) from the left side of the wheel.
8. Remove the collar (**Figure 7**) from the right side of the wheel.

FRONT SUSPENSION AND STEERING

9. Inspect the wheel and bearings as described under *Inspection* in this section.

Installation

1. Clean and dry the axle bolt and axle.
2. Clean the axle bearing surfaces in the fork sliders.
3. Apply a light coat of grease to both seal lips (**Figure 8**) in the front wheel.
4. Apply grease to the inside of the speedometer gear box (**Figure 9**).

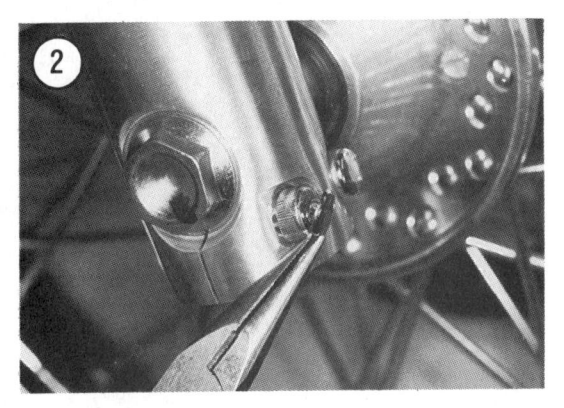

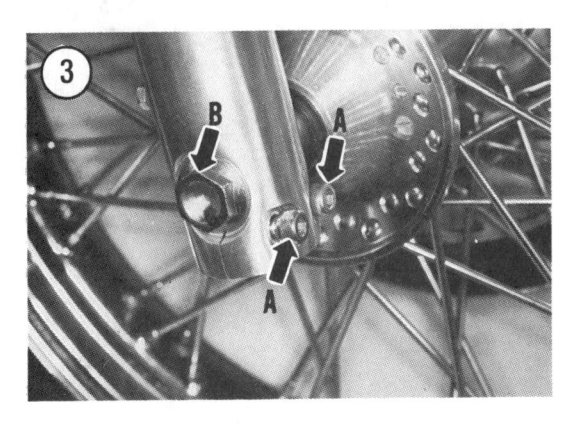

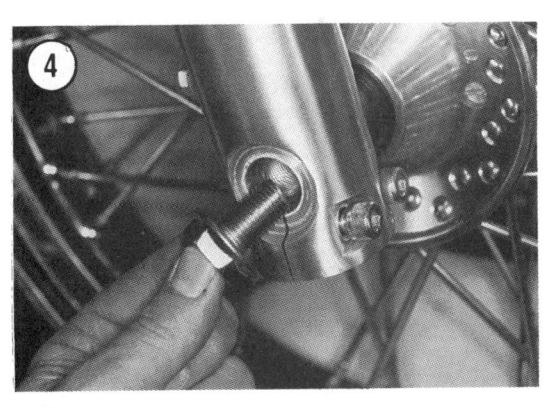

5. Lubricate the axle with grease.
6. Remove the spacer block from between the brake pads.
7. Install the right side collar with its shoulder side (**Figure 10**) facing out. See **Figure 7**.
8. Align the 2 notches in the speedometer gear box (A, **Figure 11**) with the 2 tabs on the speedometer gear retainer (B, **Figure 11**) and install the speedometer gear box into the left side of the wheel. See **Figure 6**.
9. Position the wheel in place with the brake disc between the pads in the caliper. Then lift the wheel and install the front axle (B, **Figure 5**) from the left side.
10. Position the speedometer gear box lug against the back of the stopper on the fork slider. See **Figure 12**.

NOTE
Figure 13 shows the front axle index line called out in Step 11.

11. Push the axle in and align its index line (**Figure 13**) with the fork slider (A, **Figure 14**), then tighten the left side axle pinch bolts (B, **Figure 14**) to the torque specification in **Table 3**.
12. Install the axle bolt (B, **Figure 3**) and tighten to the torque specification in **Table 3**.
13. Tighten the right side axle pinch bolts (A, **Figure 3**) to the torque specification in **Table 3**.
14. Install the bolt caps (**Figure 2**).
15. Align the notch in the speedometer cable with the speedometer gear box arm (**Figure 15**) and install the speedometer gear box. Secure with the mounting screw (**Figure 1**).
16. After the wheel is completely installed, spin it several times. Make sure it rotates freely and that there is no abnormal noise. Then, while the wheel is spinning, apply the front brake as many times as necessary to reposition the brake pads in the caliper.
17. Make sure there is adequate brake disc-to-caliper bracket clearance. If there is insufficient clearance, inspect the brake pads and caliper bracket as described in Chapter Thirteen.

WARNING
Inadequate brake disc-to-caliper bracket clearance can cause brake disc damage while impairing front brake performance.

FRONT SUSPENSION AND STEERING

18. Lower the bike so the front wheel is on the ground, then support the bike with its sidestand.

Inspection

1. Inspect the seals (**Figure 8**) for excessive wear, hardness, cracks or other damage. If necessary, replace the seals as described under *Front Hub* in this chapter.
2. Turn each bearing inner race (**Figure 8**) by hand. The bearing must turn smoothly with no trace of roughness, catching, binding or excessive noise. Some axial play (end play) is normal, but radial play (side play) must be negligible. See **Figure 16**. If one bearing is damaged, replace both bearings as a set. Refer to *Front Hub* in this chapter.
3. Clean the axle, axle bolt and right side collar in solvent to remove all grease and dirt. Make sure all axle contact surfaces are clean prior to installation.

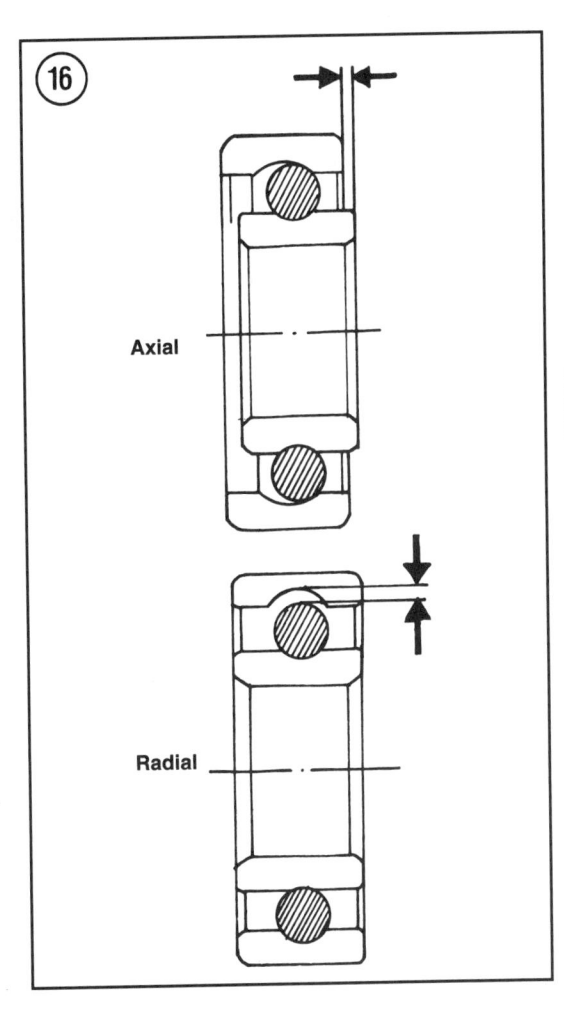

4. Check the front axle runout with a set of V-blocks and dial indicator (**Figure 17**). Replace the axle if its runout exceeds the service limit in **Table 1**.
5. Check the brake disc bolts for tightness. To service the brake disc, refer to Chapter Thirteen.
6. Check wheel runout and spoke tension as described in this chapter.

FRONT HUB

Refer to **Figure 18** when servicing the front hub. Inspect each wheel bearing as follows:

CAUTION
Do not remove the wheel bearings for inspection purposes, as they may be damaged during removal. Remove the wheel bearings only if they must be replaced.

1. Pry the seals out of the hub with a wide-blade screwdriver (**Figure 19**). Support the screwdriver with a rag to prevent damaging the hub or brake disc.
2. Remove the speedometer gear retainer (**Figure 20**) mounted behind the left side seal.
3. Turn each bearing inner race (**Figure 21**) by hand. The bearing must turn smoothly with no trace of roughness, catching, binding or excessive noise. Some axial play (end play) is normal, but radial play (side play) must be negligible; see **Figure 16**.
4. Check the outer bearing seal (**Figure 21**) for damage that would allow dirt to enter the bearing.
5. If one bearing is damaged, replace both bearings as a set.

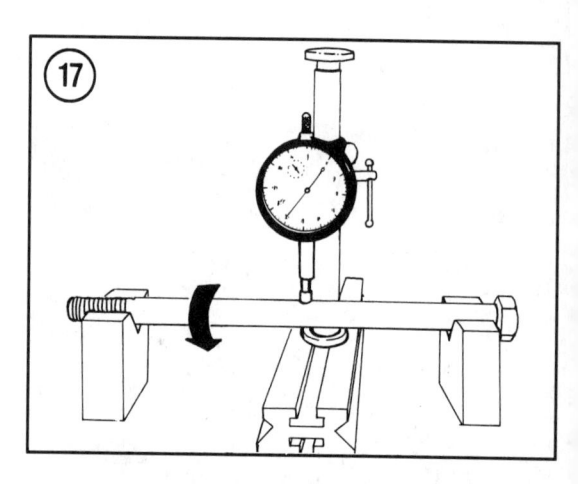

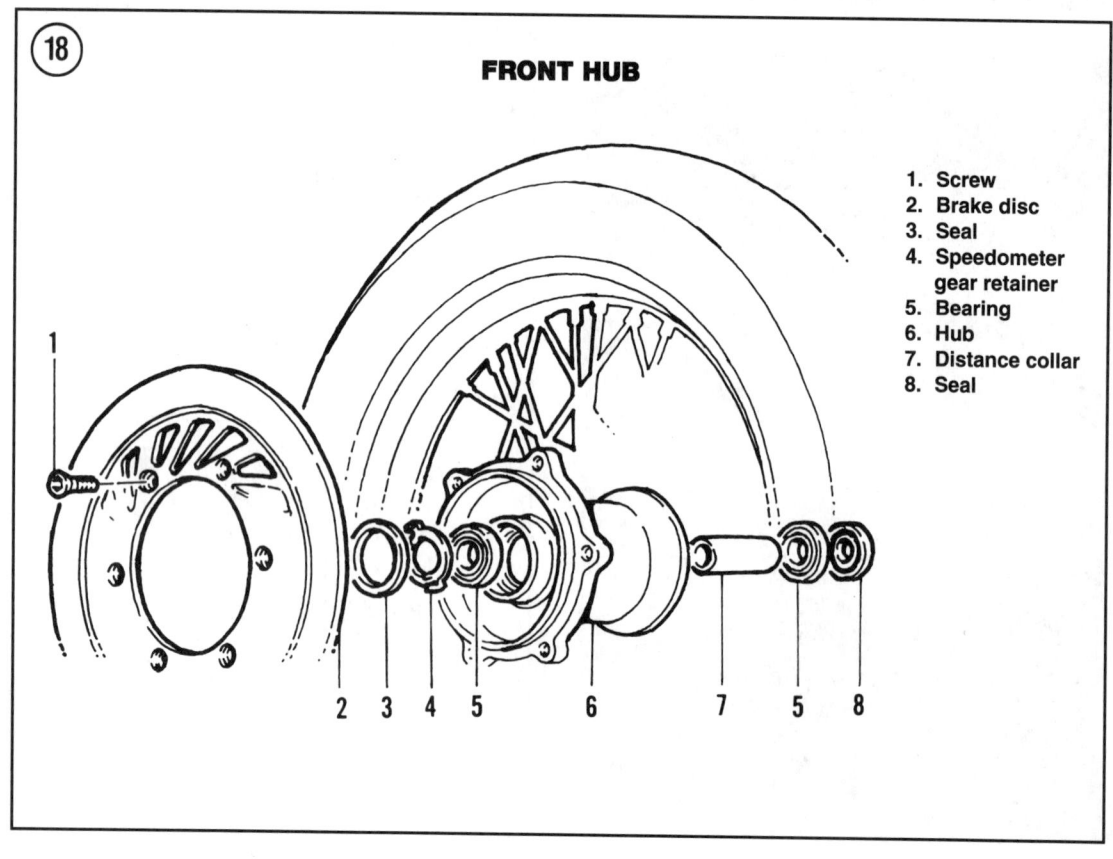

FRONT HUB

1. Screw
2. Brake disc
3. Seal
4. Speedometer gear retainer
5. Bearing
6. Hub
7. Distance collar
8. Seal

FRONT SUSPENSION AND STEERING

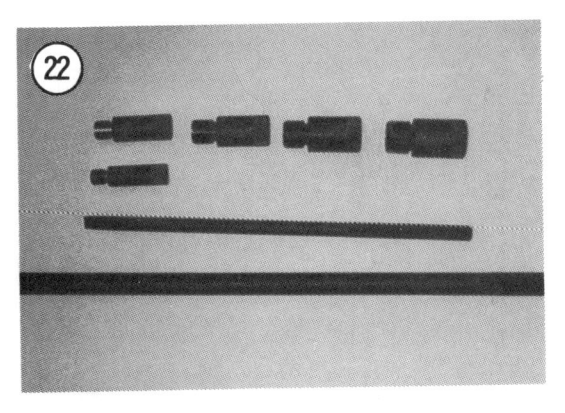

Disassembly

1. Pry the seals out of the hub with a wide-blade screwdriver (**Figure 19**). Support the screwdriver with a rag to prevent damaging the hub or brake disc.
2. Remove the speedometer gear retainer (**Figure 20**) mounted behind the left side seal.

NOTE
Step 3 describes 2 methods of removing the front wheel bearings. Step 3A is recommended by Honda and will require the use of the Kowa Seiki Wheel Bearing Remover set. Step 3B describes how to remove the bearing with a drift and hammer.

3A. To remove the wheel bearings (**Figure 21**) with the Kowa Seiki Wheel Bearing Remover set:

NOTE
*The Kowa Seiki Wheel Bearing Remover set shown in **Figure 22** is available from K & L Supply Co., in Santa Clara, CA. You can order this tool set through your Honda dealership.*

NOTE
Figure 23 shows a cutaway of a typical hub and how the bearing tools mount into the bearing to be removed.

a. Select the correct size remover head tool and insert it into one of the hub bearings (**Figure 24**).
b. From the opposite side of the hub, insert the remover shaft into the slot in the backside of the remover head (**Figure 25**). Then position the hub with the remover head tool resting against a solid surface and strike the remover shaft to force it into the slit in the remover head. This tightens the remover head tool against the bearing's inner race. See **Figure 23**.
c. Position the hub and strike the end of the remover shaft with a hammer (**Figure 25**) to drive the bearing out of the hub. Remove the bearing and tool. Release the remover head from the bearing.
d. Remove the distance collar from the hub.
e. Repeat to remove the opposite bearing.

3B. To remove the wheel bearings without special tools:

a. Using a long drift, tilt the distance collar spacer away from one side of the outer bearing (**Figure 26**).

NOTE
Try not to damage the hub spacer's machined surface when positioning and driving against the long drift. You may have to grind a clearance groove in the drift to enable it to contact the bearing while clearing the spacer.

b. Tap the bearing out of the hub with a hammer, working around the perimeter of the bearing's inner race.
c. Remove the center hub spacer from the hub.
d. Drive out the opposite bearing using a large socket or bearing driver.
e. Inspect the center hub spacer for burrs created during removal. Remove burrs with a file.

4. Clean and dry the hub and distance collar.
5. Discard the bearings and seals.

Assembly

Before installing the new bearings and seals, note the following:
a. The left and right side bearings are identical (same part number).
b. The left and right side seals are different. The left side seal has a larger inside diameter.
c. Install both bearings with their closed side facing out. If the bearings use seals on both sides, install the bearings with their manufacturer's name and size code markings facing out.
d. When grease is called for in the following steps, use a lithium-based multipurpose grease (NLGI#2) or equivalent.

1. Blow any dirt or foreign matter out of the hub before installing the bearings.
2. Pack the open side of each bearing with grease.
3. Place the left side bearing squarely against the bore opening with its closed side facing out. Select

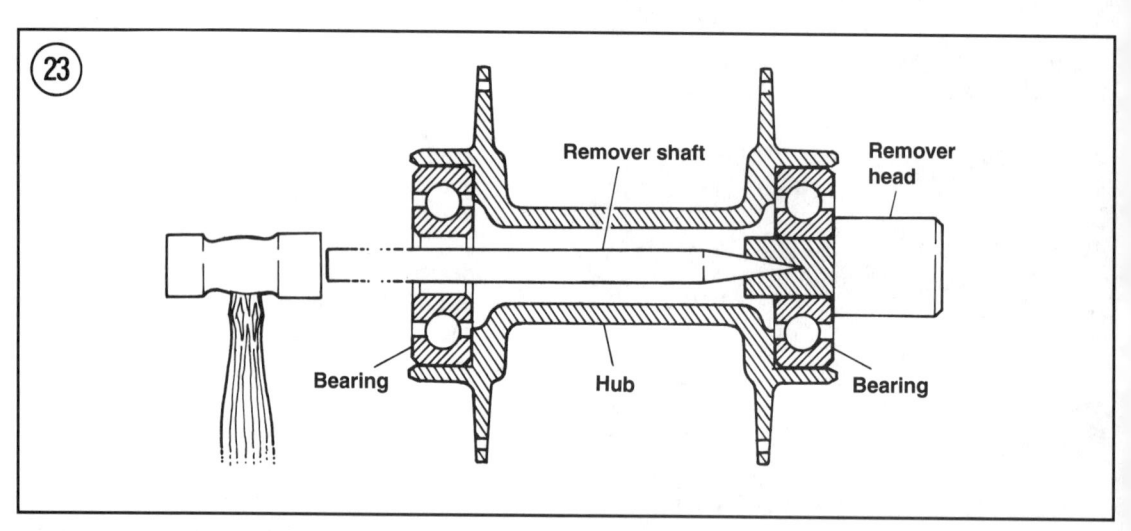

FRONT SUSPENSION AND STEERING

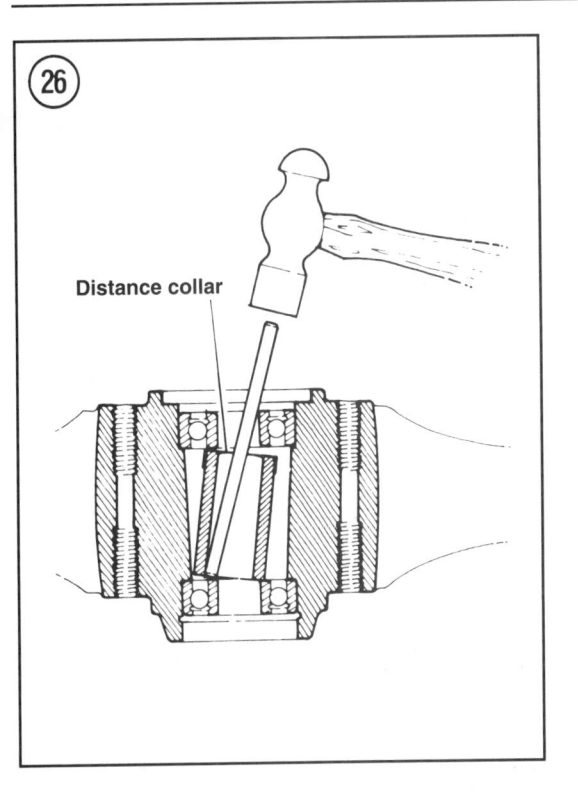

a driver (**Figure 27**) with an outside diameter slightly smaller than the bearing's outside diameter. Then drive the bearing into the bore until it bottoms out (**Figure 28**).

4. Turn the hub over and install the distance collar and center it against the left side bearing's center race.

5. Place the right side bearing squarely against the bore opening with its closed side facing out. Using the same driver as before, drive the bearing partway into the bearing bore. Then stop and check that the distance collar is still centered with the bearing. If not, install the front axle partway through the hub to center the distance collar with the bearing. Then remove the axle and continue installing the bearing until it bottoms out (**Figure 21**).

6. Measure wheel runout as described in this chapter.

NOTE
If the new seals are not prelubricated like the one shown in ***Figure 29****, lubricate them as described in the following steps.*

7. Install the right side seal as follows:

   a. Lubricate the seal lip with grease.

   b. Place the seal in the hub bore with its closed side facing out.

   c. Drive the seal into the bore (**Figure 30**) until its outer surface is flush with the hub, or until it bottoms out. See **Figure 31**.

8. Install the speedometer gear retainer and left side seal as follows:

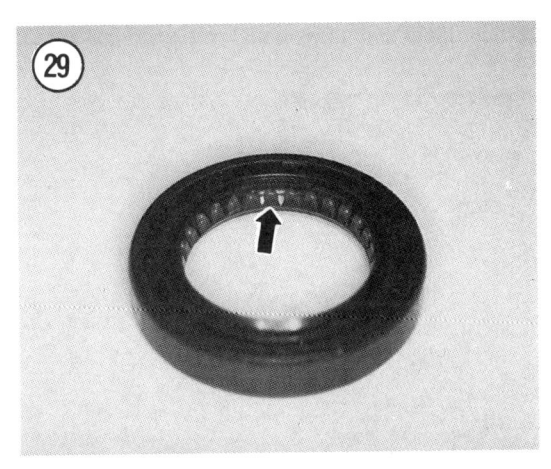

a. Align the outer arms on the speedometer gear retainer with the slots in the hub, and install the retainer. See **Figure 20**.
b. Pack the seal lip with grease.
c. Drive the seal into the bore until it bottoms against the speedometer gear retainer (**Figure 32**).

RIM AND SPOKE SERVICE

The wheel assembly consists of a rim, spokes, nipples and hub (containing the bearings, distance collar and seals).

Loose or improperly tightened spokes can cause hub damage. Periodically inspect the wheel assembly for loose, broken or missing spokes, rim damage and runout. Wheel bearing service is described under *Front Hub* in this chapter.

Rim Inspection and Runout

NOTE
Before checking rim runout, the wheel bearings must be in good condition. If necessary, check the wheel bearings as described in this chapter.

1. Check the rim outer surfaces and inner profile surfaces (**Figure 33**) for cracks, warpage or dents. Check each hub spoke hole (**Figure 34**) for any cracks or other damage. Replace a damaged rim or hub. If there is no visual damage, mount the wheel on a truing stand and measure the wheel's axial and radial runout with a dial indicator at the 2 points shown in **Figure 35**. Wheel runout is the amount of wobble a wheel shows as it rotates. Compare the actual runout with the runout limit listed in **Table 1**.

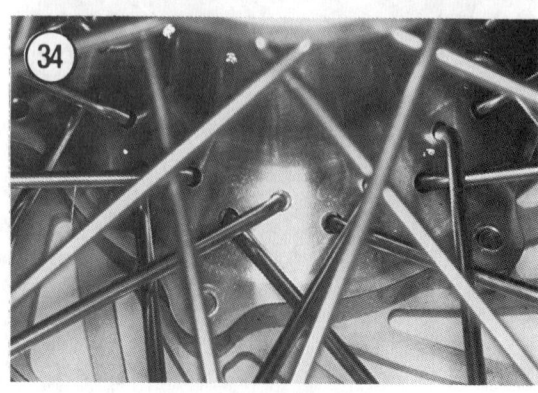

FRONT SUSPENSION AND STEERING

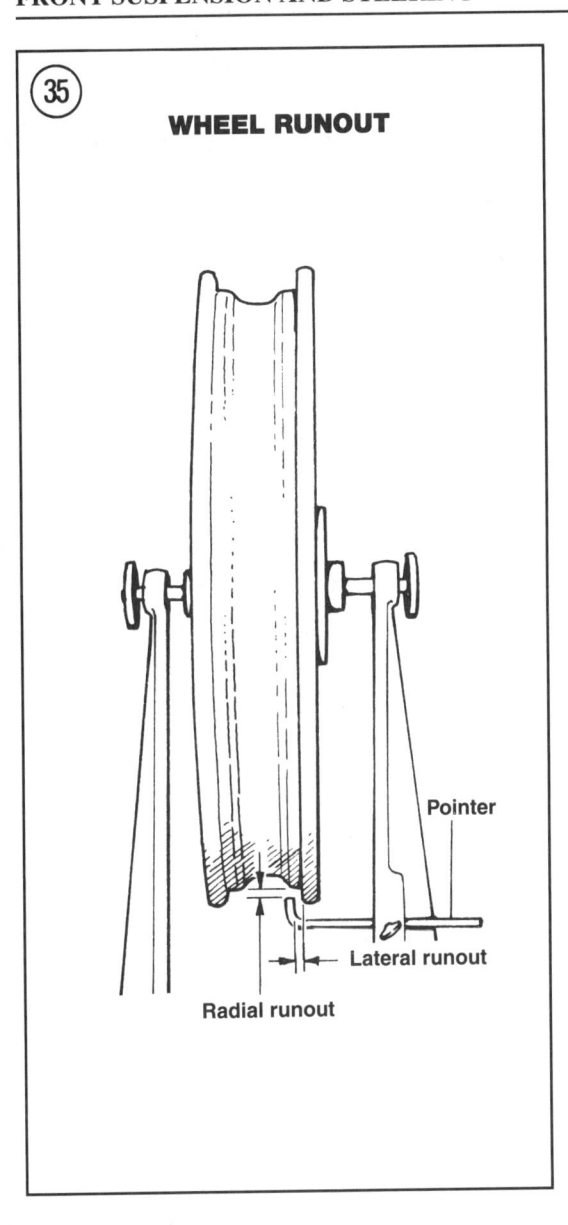

35 WHEEL RUNOUT

Pointer
Lateral runout
Radial runout

36

NOTE
*Use the correct size spoke wrench (**Figure 36**) when checking and tightening the spokes in the following steps. If you are using a torque wrench to tighten the spoke nipples, refer to the spoke nipple torque specification in **Table 3**.*

2. When lacing or truing the wheel, maintain the hub to rim dimensions shown on the following drawings:

   a. **Figure 37** (front wheel).

   b. **Figure 38** (rear wheel).

3. Draw the high point of the rim toward the centerline of the wheel by loosening the spokes in the area of the high point and on the same side as the high point, and tightening the spokes on the side opposite the high point (**Figure 39**).

4. Rotate the wheel and check runout. Continue adjusting until the runout is within specifications. Be patient and thorough, adjusting the position of the rim a little at a time. If you loosen 2 spokes at the high point 1/2 turn, loosen the adjacent spokes 1/4 turn. Tighten the spokes on the opposite side equivalent amounts.

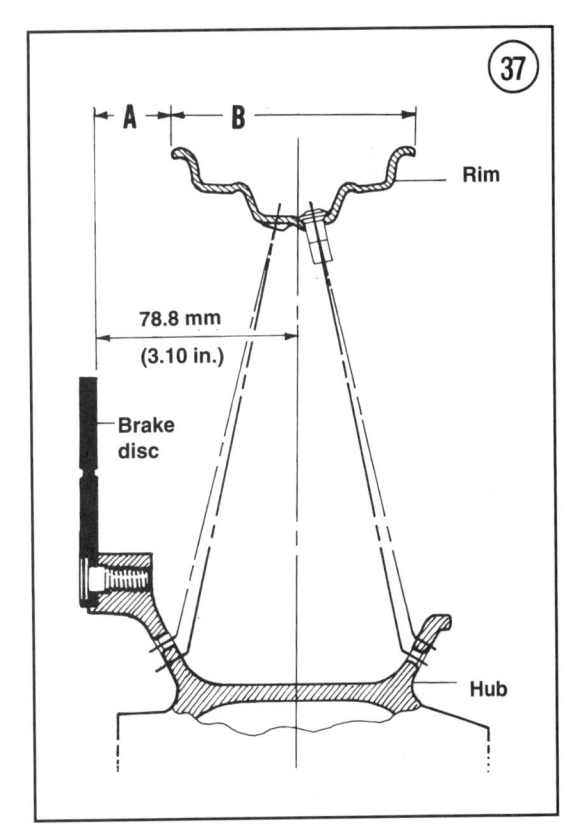

37
A | B
Rim
78.8 mm
(3.10 in.)
Brake disc
Hub

CHAPTER ELEVEN

5. If you cannot properly true the wheel take the wheel to a Honda dealership and have them true the wheel.

TIRE CHANGING

The rims can easily be damaged when changing a tire. Special care must be taken with tire irons when changing a tire to avoid scratches and gouges to the rim surface and to prevent them from puncturing the tube. When removing and installing a tire, use plastic rim protectors to protect the rim from damage. Use tire levers or flat handled tire irons with rounded ends (**Figure 40**).

Removal

1. Remove the wheel as described in this chapter (front) or Chapter Twelve (rear).

CAUTION
To prevent damaging the brake disc, perform the following steps with the brake disc facing down.

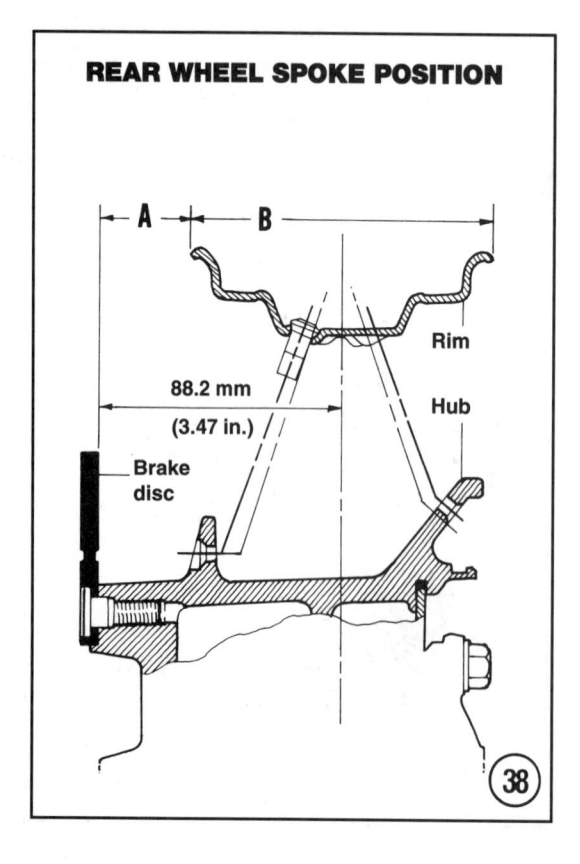

2. If you are going to reinstall the existing tire, mark the valve stem location (**Figure 33**) on the tire so the tire can be installed in the same position for easier balancing.
3. Remove the valve cap and valve core (**Figure 33**) and deflate the tire.
4. Press the entire bead on both sides of the tire into the center of the rim.
5. Lubricate the beads with water.

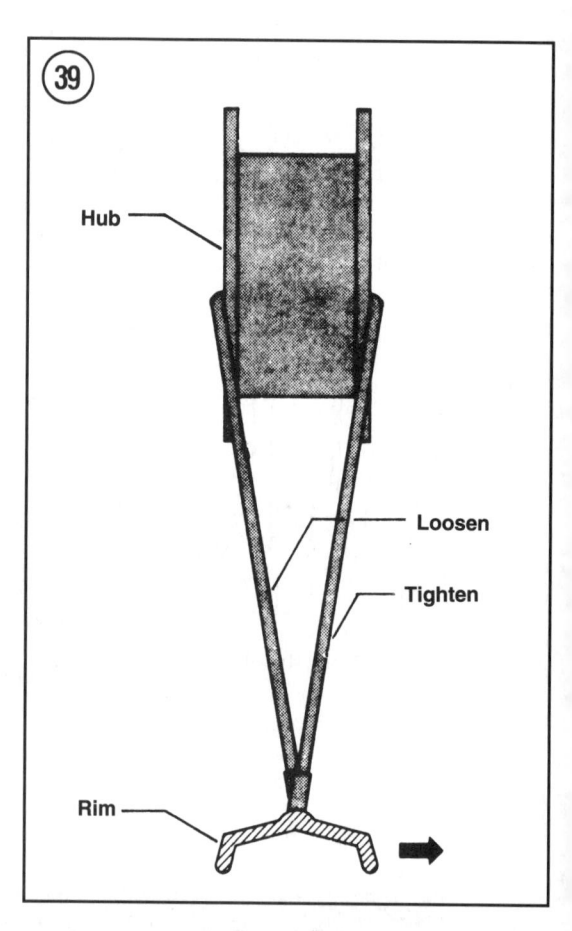

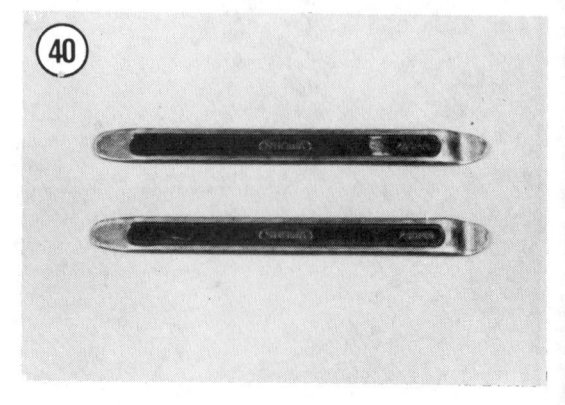

FRONT SUSPENSION AND STEERING

CAUTION
Use rim protectors (Figure 41) between the tire irons and the rim to protect the rim from damage.

6. Insert the first tire iron under the bead next to the valve (**Figure 42**). Force the bead on the opposite side of the tire into the center of the rim and pry the bead over the rim with the tire iron.

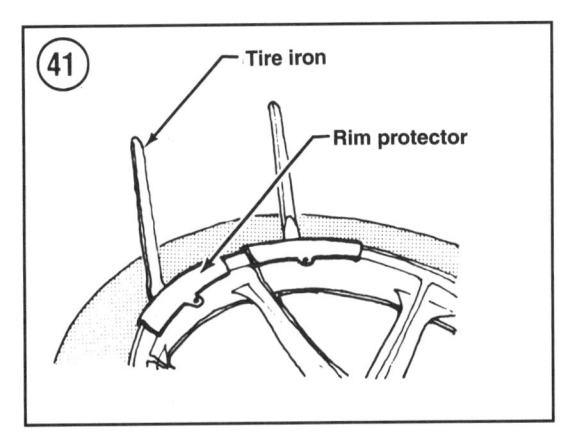

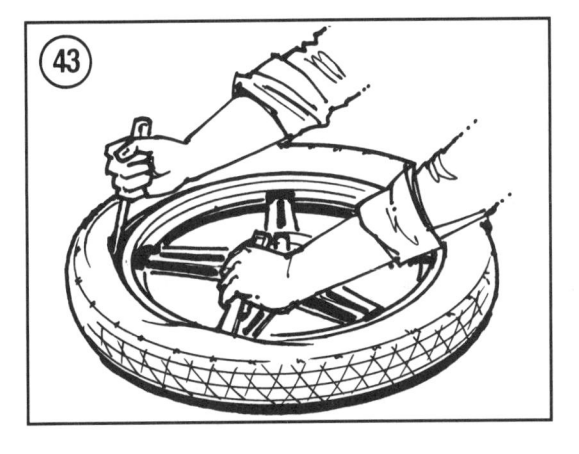

7. Insert a second tire iron (**Figure 43**) next to the first to hold the bead over the rim. Then work around the tire little by little with the first tire iron, prying the bead over the rim. Be careful not to pinch the inner tube with the tire irons. Do not take too big a bite with the second tire iron or you can tear the tire.

8. When the upper bead is off the rim, remove the valve from the hole in the rim and remove the tube from the tire.

NOTE
Step 9 is required only if it is necessary to completely remove the tire from the rim.

9. Stand the tire upright. Insert the tire iron between the second bead and the side of the rim that the first bead was pried over (**Figure 44**). Force the bead on the opposite side into the center of the rim. Pry the second bead off of the rim.

Tire and Rim Inspection

1. Remove and inspect the rubber rim band. Replace if deteriorated or broken.
2. Clean the inner and outer rim surfaces of all dirt, rust, corrosion and rubber residue.
3. Inspect the valve stem hole in the rim. Remove any dirt or corrosion from the hole.

4. Inspect the rim profiles for any cracks or other damage.
5. If you are going to reuse the tube, reinstall the valve core and inflate it to check for any holes.
6. While the tube is inflated, clean it with water.
7. If you are going to reuse the original tire, carefully check the inside and outside of the tire for any damage. Replace the tire if it is damaged.
8. Make sure the spoke ends do not protrude through the nipples into the center of the rim.

Installation

1. Reinstall the rubber rim band. Align the hole in the band with the air valve hole in the rim.
2. Liberally sprinkle the inside tire casing with talcum powder. Talcum powder reduces chafing between the tire and tube and helps to minimize tube damage.
3. When installing the tire onto the rim, make sure that the direction arrow on the tire faces the direction of wheel rotation.
4. If remounting the old tire, align the mark made in Step 2, *Removal* with the valve stem hole in the rim. If a new tire is being installed, align the colored spot near the bead (indicating a lighter point on the tire) with the valve stem hole in the rim (**Figure 45**).
5. Lubricate the bottom tire bead and place the tire against the rim. Using your hands, push as much of the lower bead past the upper rim surface as possible (**Figure 46**). Work around the tire in both directions. If necessary, use a tire iron and a rim protector for the last few inches of bead (**Figure 47**).
6. Turn the tire around the rim, if necessary, to align the index mark or the colored spot with the valve stem hole (**Figure 45**).
7. Install the valve core into the inner tube. Put the tube in the tire and insert the valve stem through the hole in the rim. Inflate just enough to round it out. Too much air will make tire installation difficult, and too little will increase the chances of pinching the tube with the tire irons.
8. Lubricate the upper tire bead and rim with water.
9. Press the upper bead into the rim opposite the valve. Pry the bead into the rim on both sides of the initial point with your hands and work around the rim to the valve. If the tire pulls up on one side, either use a tire iron or one of your knees to hold the tire in place. The last few inches are usually the toughest to install, and it is also where most tubes are pinched. If you can, continue to push the tire into the rim with your hands. Relubricate the bead if necessary. If the tire bead pulls out from under the rim use both of your knees to hold the tire in place. If necessary, use a tire iron and rim protector for the last few inches (**Figure 48**).
10. Wiggle the valve to be sure the tube is not trapped under the bead. Set the valve squarely in its hole before screwing on the valve nut.

NOTE
Make sure the valve stem is not turned sideways in the rim.

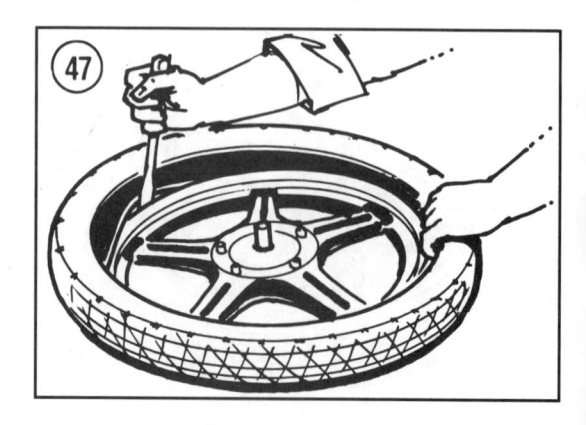

FRONT SUSPENSION AND STEERING

WARNING
In the next step, inflate the tire to approximately 10% over the recommended inflation pressure listed in **Table 2**. *Do not exceed this pressure, as the tire could burst with sufficient force to cause severe injury. Never stand directly over a tire while inflating it.*

11. Check the bead on both sides of the tire for even fit around the rim, then relubricate both sides of the tire. Inflate the tube to seat the tire bead on the rim.

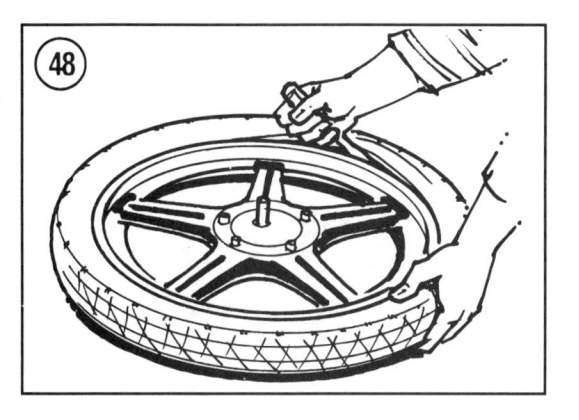

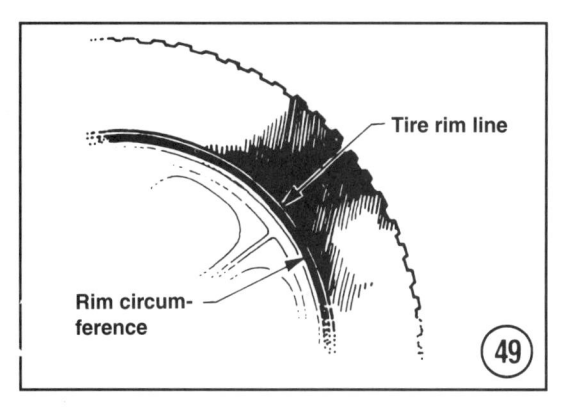

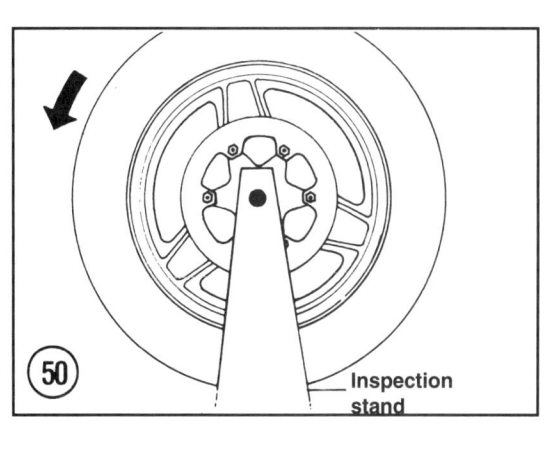

Check to see if the beads are fully seated and that the tire rim lines (**Figure 49**) are the same distance from the rim all the way around the tire. If the beads will not seat, release the air from the tube and then reinflate.

12. Bleed the tire pressure down to the required pressure listed in **Table 2**. Screw on the valve stem nut and tighten it against the rim. Then install the metal air valve cap (**Figure 33**).
13. Balance the wheel as described in this chapter.

WHEEL BALANCE

An unbalanced wheel is unsafe as it will affect the stability and handling performance of the motorcycle. Depending on the degree of unbalance and the speed of the motorcycle, the rider may experience anything from a mild vibration to a violent shimmy which may result in loss of control.

Before you balance a wheel, thoroughly clean the wheel assembly. Then make sure that the wheel bearings are in good condition. The wheel must rotate freely when balancing it. Also check that the balance mark (paint dot on the tire) is aligned with the valve stem (**Figure 45**). If not, break the tire loose from the rim and align it prior to trying to balance the wheel. Refer to *Tire Changing* in this chapter.

NOTE
When balancing the wheel, do so with the brake disc attached. The disc rotates with the wheel and affects the balance.

1. Remove the wheel as described in this chapter or Chapter Twelve.
2. Clean the tire, rim, spokes and hub to remove all dirt and other road residue.
3. Make sure the valve stem nut is tight and that the metal air valve cap is screwed on tightly.
4. Mount the wheel on a wheel balancing stand (**Figure 50**).

NOTE
A wheel balancing stand helps to eliminate friction when the wheel is spun. If you are going to balance the wheel with it mounted on the bike, remove the brake caliper (Chapter Thirteen) and the 2 wheel bearing seals.

5. Remove the balance weight(s) mounted on the wheel (**Figure 51**). If you are only checking wheel balance, leave the weight(s) attached to the wheel.

6. Give the wheel a spin and observe the tire and rim concentricity. If the wheel wobbles, check its runout as described in this chapter. Do not attempt to balance the wheel until its runout is within specification.

7. Apply pressure to the balancing stand spindle to load the wheel bearings (so they will turn) and spin the wheel again. If the bearings turn roughly or with excessive noise, they are worn and must be replaced as described in this chapter or Chapter Twelve.

8. If everything up to this point is good, you are ready to balance the wheel. Spin the wheel and let it coast to a stop. Mark the tire at the highest point. This is the wheel's lightest point.

9. Spin the wheel several more times. If the wheel keeps coming to rest at the same point, it is out of balance. If the wheel stops at a different spot each time, the wheel is balanced.

10. Tape a test weight to the upper, or light side of the wheel.

11. Rotate the wheel 1/4 turn (3 o'clock), release the wheel and observe the following:

   a. If the wheel does not rotate—stays at the 3 o'clock position, the correct balance weight was installed. The wheel is balanced.

   b. If the wheel rotates and the weighted portion goes up, replace the weight with the next heavier size.

   c. If the wheel rotates and the weighted portion goes down, replace the weight with the next lighter size.

   d. Repeat this step until the wheel remains at rest after being rotated 1/4 turn. Rotate the wheel another 1/4 turn, and another 1/4 turn, and another turn to see if the wheel is correctly balanced.

12. Remove the test weight and install the correct size weight.

CAUTION
Do not add more than 60 grams (2.1 oz.) of balance weight to the front wheel or more than 90 grams (3.2 oz.) to the rear wheel. If the balance weight required exceeds this amount, take the wheel to a Honda dealership for inspection and balancing.

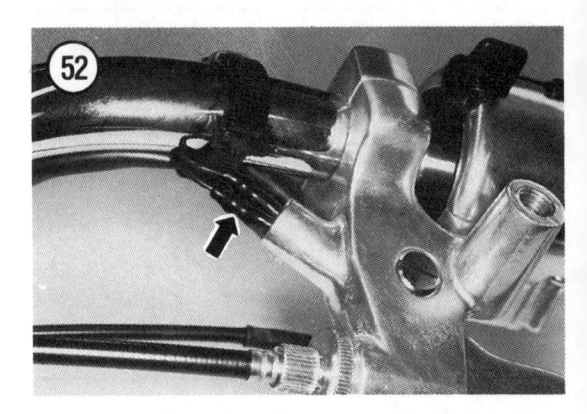

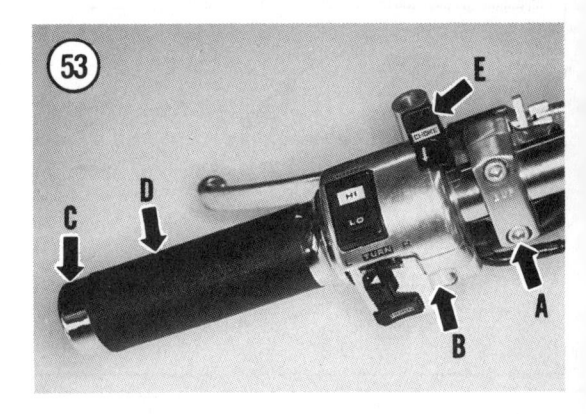

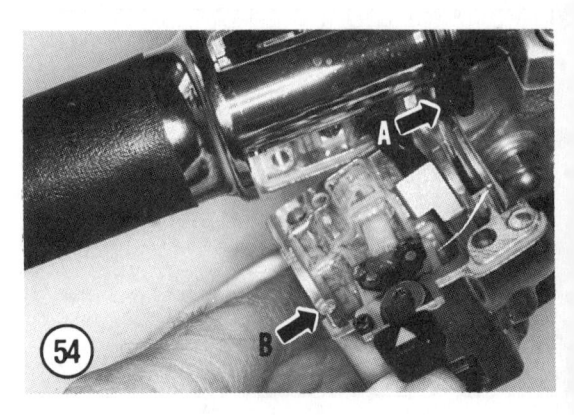

FRONT SUSPENSION AND STEERING

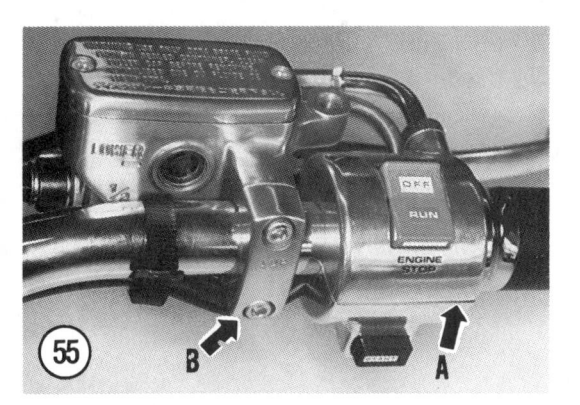

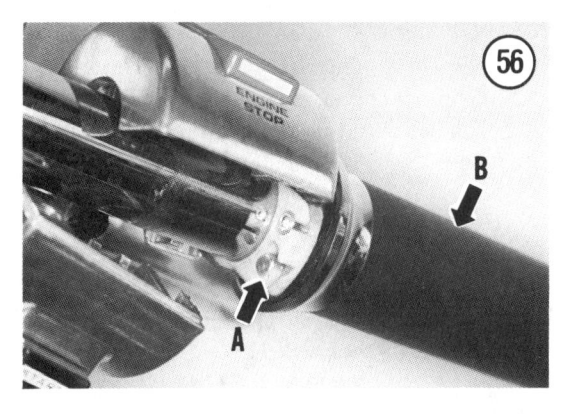

13. Install the wheel as described in this chapter or in Chapter Twelve.

HANDLEBAR

Removal

1. Cover the fuel tank with a thick blanket to protect it from scratches and other damage.
2. Remove the left and right side mirrors.
3. Remove the bands securing the wiring harness to each side of the handlebar.
4. Disconnect the clutch switch electrical connectors from the clutch switch (**Figure 52**).
5. Remove the 2 clutch lever bracket mounting bolts and remove the clutch bracket holder (A, **Figure 53**) and lever bracket.
6. Remove the 2 left handlebar switch housing screws and separate the switch housing (B, **Figure 53**) from around the handlebar.
7. Disconnect the choke cable (A, **Figure 54**) from the choke lever.
8. To remove the left hand grip end cap (C, **Figure 53**) and grip (D, **Figure 53**), perform the following:
   a. Pry the end cap (C, **Figure 53**) off with a screwdriver.
   b. Insert a thin-blade screwdriver between the grip and handlebar and spray electrical contact cleaner in the open gap. Then quickly turn the grip to break the adhesive bond and slide it off the handlebar.
9. Slide the choke lever (E, **Figure 53**) off the handlebar.
10. Remove the 2 right side handlebar switch housing screws and separate the switch housing (A, **Figure 55**) from around the handlebar.
11. Disconnect the 2 throttle cables (A, **Figure 56**) from the throttle grip and slide the throttle grip (B, **Figure 56**) off the handlebar.
12. Disconnect the front brake light switch connectors from the switch (**Figure 57**).

NOTE
After you remove the front master cylinder in the next step, keep it upright so air does not enter the hydraulic system.

13. Remove the 2 front master cylinder holder bolts and remove the holder and front master cylinder (B, **Figure 55**).
14. Remove the handlebar holder bolt caps, bolts and holders (**Figure 58**).

15. Remove the handlebar.

Installation

1. Clean and inspect the handlebar holders and bolts.
2. Install the handlebar (**Figure 58**) as follows:
   a. Place the handlebar onto the lower holders.
   b. Install the upper holders with their punch marks facing forward (**Figure 59**).
   c. Install the handlebar holder mounting bolts and tighten finger-tight.
   d. Align the handlebar's punch mark with the top of the lower handlebar holder (**Figure 59**). Hold the handlebar in this position while tightening the mounting bolts in the next step.
   e. Tighten the front handlebar holder bolts, then the rear bolts to the torque specification in **Table 3**.
   f. Install the bolt caps.
3. Install the right side handlebar switch housing as follows:
   a. Reconnect the 2 throttle cables (A, **Figure 56**) to the throttle grip.
   b. Align the switch housing locating pin (**Figure 60**) with the hole in the handlebar and close the switch halves around the handlebar. Try to twist the switch; it must not turn.

NOTE
*The front switch housing screw is **longer** than the rear screw.*

   c. Install the front and rear switch housing screws and tighten securely.
4. Install the master cylinder as follows:
   a. Clean the handlebar, master cylinder and clamp mating surfaces.
   b. Mount the master cylinder onto the handlebar, then install its clamp (A, **Figure 61**) and both mounting bolts. Install the clamp with its UP mark facing up.
   c. Align the master cylinder and clamp mating halves with the punch mark on the handlebar (B, **Figure 61**). Then tighten the upper master cylinder clamp bolt, then the lower bolt to the torque specification in **Table 3**.
5. Reconnect the front brake light switch connectors to the switch (**Figure 57**).
6. Slide the choke lever (E, **Figure 53**) onto the handlebar.

7. Install a new left side handlebar grip (D, **Figure 53**) as follows:
   a. Clean and dry the left side of the handlebar and inside the grip.

NOTE
When using grip cement in the next step, follow its manufacturer's instructions. Some manufacturers recommend waiting 3-5 minutes after applying the cement to install the grip, and others recommend installing the grip immediately after applying the cement.

   b. Apply Honda Grip Cement, ThreeBond Griplock or an equivalent cement to the handlebar and inside the grip and install the grip.

WARNING
Do not ride the motorcycle until the appropriate amount of drying time has elapsed; otherwise, the grip could move or slide off the handlebar and cause you to lose control. Refer to the drying time

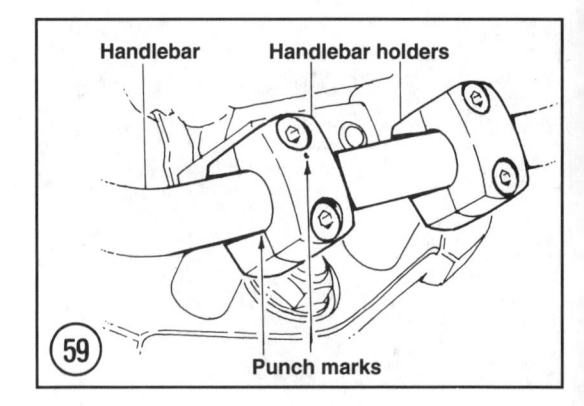

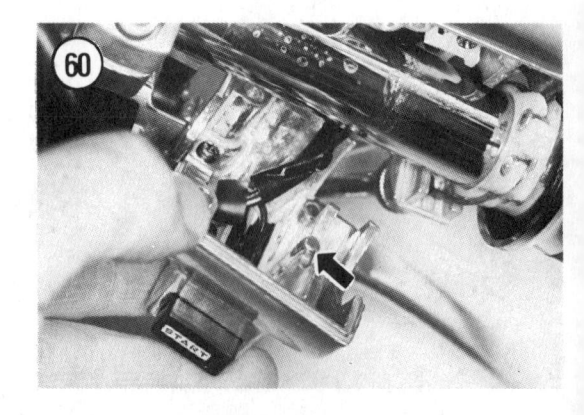

FRONT SUSPENSION AND STEERING

recommendation listed on the cement container or tube.

c. Wipe off any excess cement from outside the grip.
d. Align the tabs on the left hand end cap with the grooves in the handlebar grip and install the cap (C, **Figure 53**).

8. Install the left side handlebar switch housing as follows:
    a. Reconnect the choke cable (A, **Figure 54**) to the choke lever.
    b. Align the switch housing locating pin (B, **Figure 54**) with the hole in the handlebar and close the switch halves around the handlebar. Try to twist the switch; it must not turn.

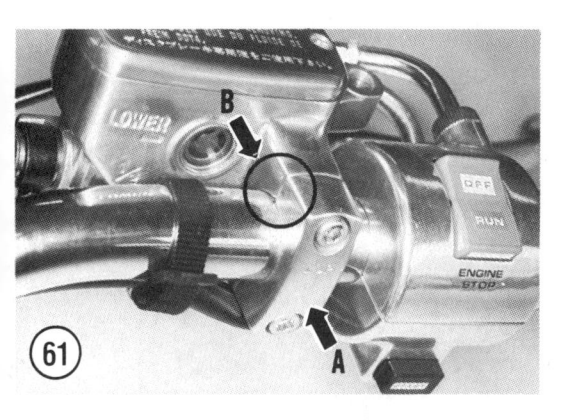

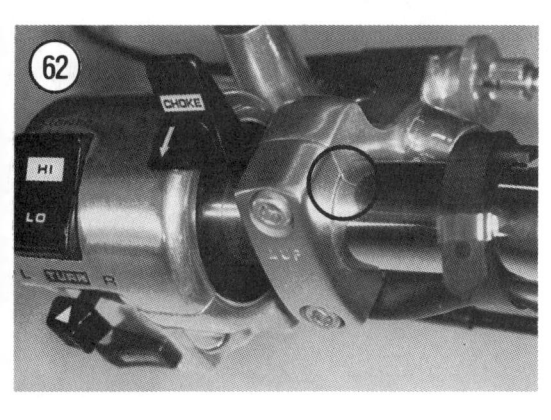

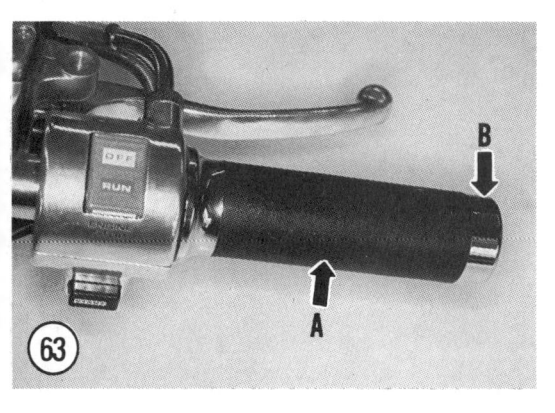

NOTE
*The front switch housing screw is **shorter** than the rear screw.*

   c. Install the front and rear switch housing screw. Tighten the front screw, then the rear screw. Tighten both screws securely.

9. Install the clutch lever bracket as follows:
    a. Clean the handlebar, clutch lever bracket and holder mating surfaces.
    b. Mount the clutch lever bracket onto the handlebar, then install its clamp (A, **Figure 53**) and both mounting bolts. Install the clamp with its UP mark facing up.
    c. Align the end of the clutch lever bracket with the punch mark on the handlebar (**Figure 62**). Then tighten the upper holder bolt first, then the lower bolt. Tighten both bolts securely.
    d. Reconnect the electrical connectors to the clutch switch (**Figure 52**).

10. Install the bands securing the wiring harness to each side of the handlebar.
11. Install and adjust the left and right side mirrors.
12. Start the engine and check the function of each switch.
13. If air entered the front master cylinder brake line, bleed the front brake as described in Chapter Thirteen.

WARNING
Make sure the front brake, clutch and throttle housing and all switches operate correctly before riding the motorcycle.

Right Handlebar Grip End Cap Replacement

1. Hold the throttle grip (A, **Figure 63**) tightly and turn the end cap (B, **Figure 63**) counterclockwise to remove it.
2. To install a new end cap, hold the throttle grip and install the end cap (B, **Figure 63**). Do not overtighten the end cap.

FRONT FORKS

Removal

1. Remove the front wheel as described in this chapter.

NOTE
Insert a plastic spacer in the caliper in place of the disc. Then, if the brake lever is inadvertently squeezed, the pistons will not be forced out of the caliper.

2. Remove the brake caliper as follows:
   a. Remove the brake hose clamp (A, **Figure 64**) from the left side of the fender.
   b. Remove the 2 brake caliper mounting bolts (B, **Figure 64**) and remove the brake caliper from the left fork tube. Support the caliper with a piece of heavy wire.
3. If you are going to disassemble the front fork(s), loosen, but do not remove, the Allen bolt (**Figure 65**) at the bottom of the slider.
4. Remove the fender mounting bolts (**Figure 66**) at the first fork tube you are going to remove.
5. Remove the bolt, collar, stopper plate and the turn signal light assembly from the fork tube.
6. Remove the bolt caps from the upper and lower fork tube pinch bolts.
7. Loosen the upper fork tube pinch bolt (**Figure 67**).
8. If you are going to disassemble the front fork(s), loosen, but do not remove, the fork cap (**Figure 68**).
9. Loosen the lower fork tube pinch bolt (**Figure 69**), then twist the fork tube slightly and remove it from the upper fork bridge and steering stem.
10. Remove the remaining front fender mounting bolts and remove the front fender.
11. Repeat these steps to remove the opposite fork tube.
12. Clean the fork tubes, upper fork bridge and steering stem clamping surfaces.
13. Remove, clean and inspect the fork tube pinch bolts. Replace damaged bolts.

Installation

1. Install the fork tube through the steering stem and turn signal light assembly, then align its top edge with the upper fork bridge surface as shown in **Figure 70**.

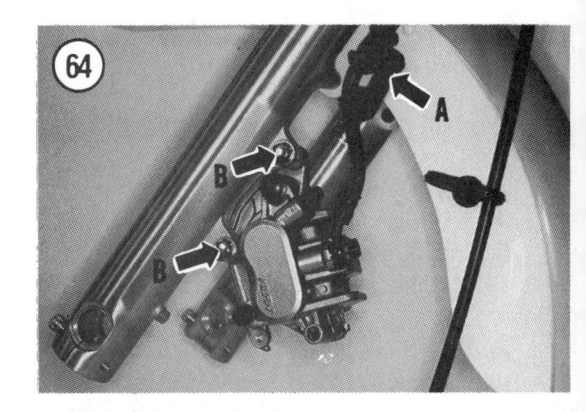

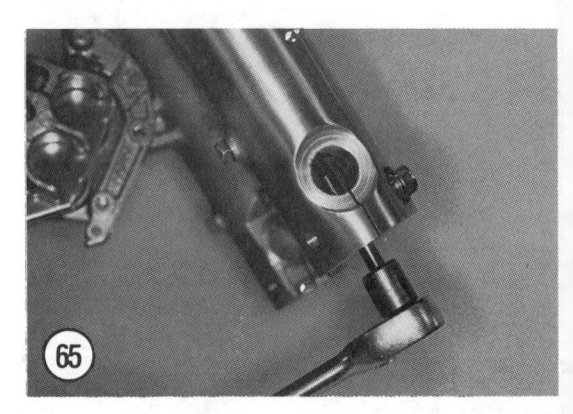

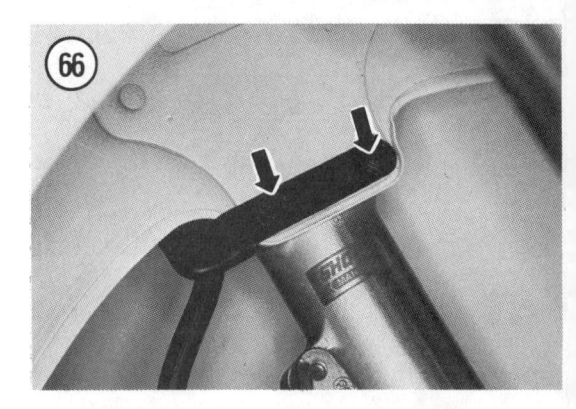

FRONT SUSPENSION AND STEERING 347

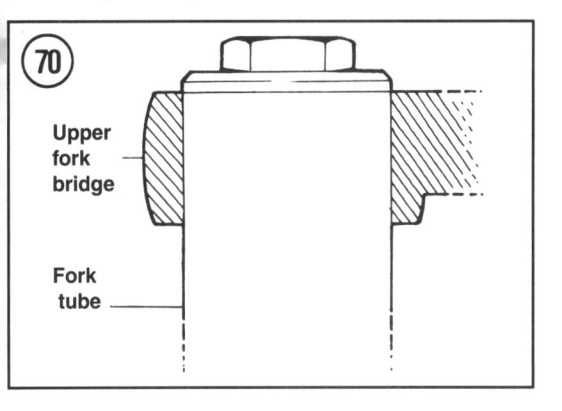

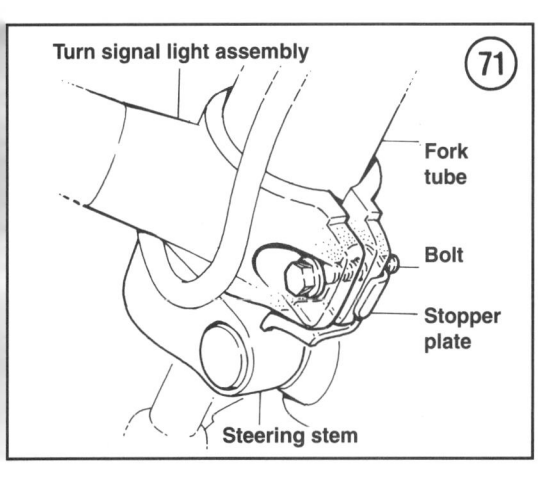

2. Tighten the lower fork tube pinch bolt (**Figure 69**) to the torque specification in **Table 3**.

3. If the fork cap (**Figure 68**) is loose, tighten it to the torque specification in **Table 3**.

4. Tighten the upper fork tube pinch bolt (**Figure 67**) to the torque specification in **Table 3**.

5. Install the bolt caps into the pinch bolts.

6. Rotate the turn signal light assembly around the fork tube and position it with the stopper plate, collar and bolt (**Figure 71**). Tighten the front turn signal stopper plate bolt to the torque specification in **Table 3**.

7. Install the front fender with the hose clamp stay (**Figure 66**) and cable guide installed on the left side. Tighten the fender bolts securely. Route the speedometer cable through the cable guide.

8. Install the brake caliper and secure it to the fork tube with new mounting bolts (B, **Figure 64**). Tighten the brake caliper mounting bolts to the torque specification in **Table 3**.

9. Install the front brake hose clamp bolt (**Figure 72**) and tighten to the torque specification in **Table 3**.

10. Install the front wheel as described in this chapter. Then turn the front wheel and squeeze the front brake lever to reposition the pistons and brake pads in the caliper. If the brake lever feels spongy, bleed the front brake (Chapter Thirteen).

11. With both wheels on the ground, apply the front brake and compress the fork up and down several times to check fork operation.

Disassembly

Refer to **Figure 73** during the disassembly and reassembly procedures.

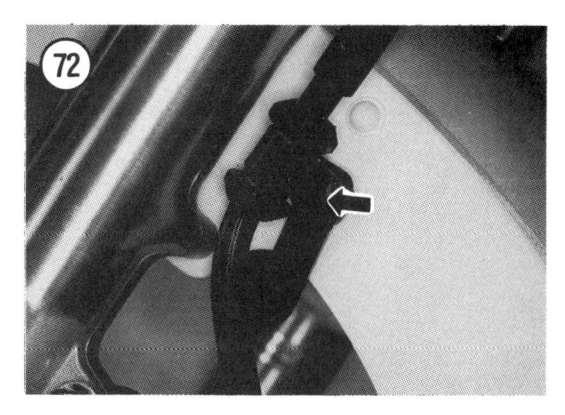

348

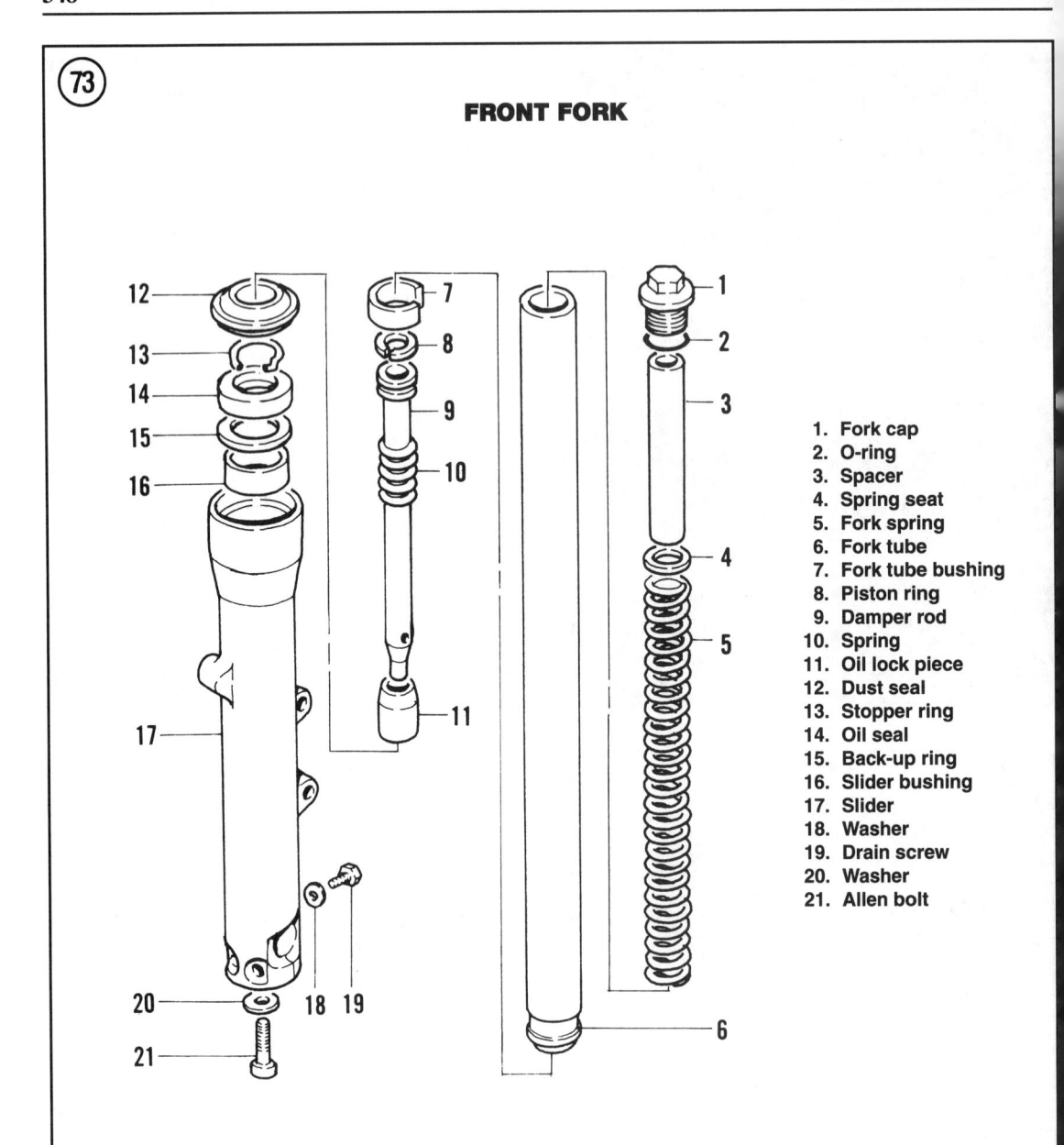

CHAPTER ELEVEN

FRONT FORK

⑦③

1. Fork cap
2. O-ring
3. Spacer
4. Spring seat
5. Fork spring
6. Fork tube
7. Fork tube bushing
8. Piston ring
9. Damper rod
10. Spring
11. Oil lock piece
12. Dust seal
13. Stopper ring
14. Oil seal
15. Back-up ring
16. Slider bushing
17. Slider
18. Washer
19. Drain screw
20. Washer
21. Allen bolt

FRONT SUSPENSION AND STEERING

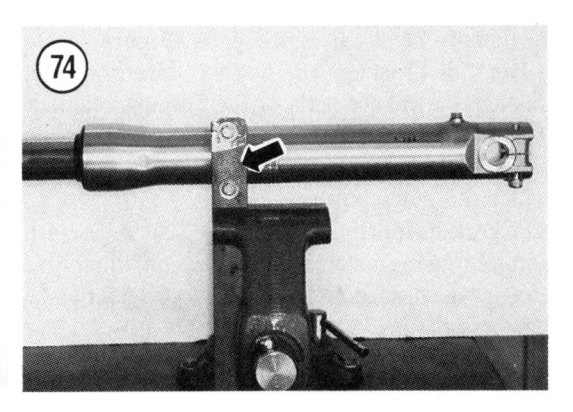

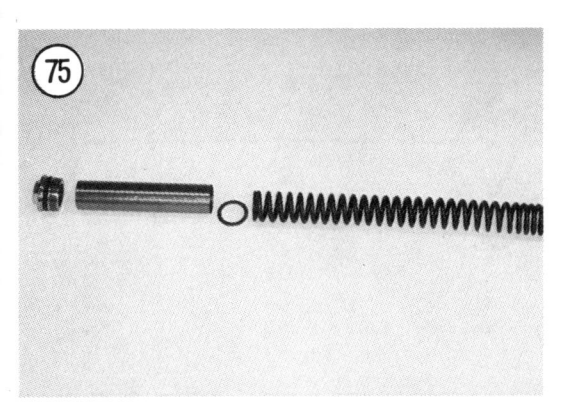

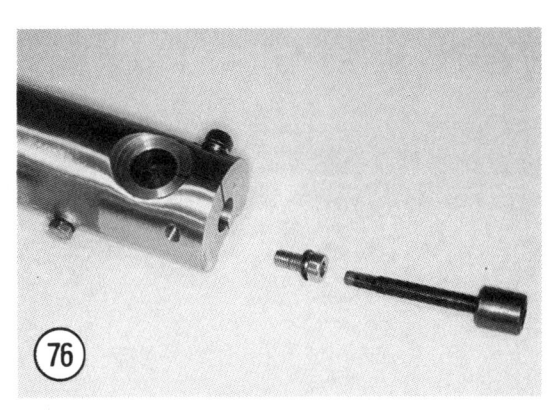

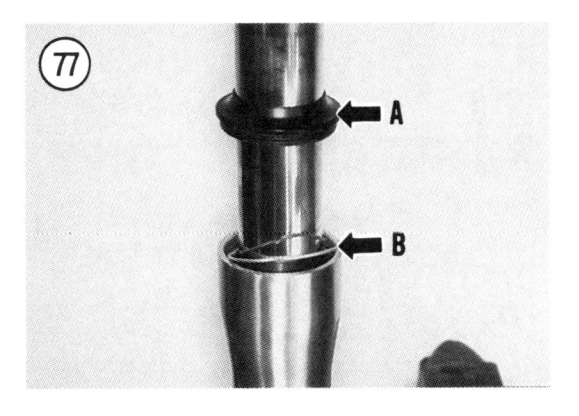

1. To prevent scratching the fork tube assembly when servicing it in the following steps, make a holder out of a piece of flat metal (**Figure 74**), then mount the holder into a vise.

CAUTION
The fork cap is under spring pressure. Remove the fork cap carefully in Step 2.

2. Remove the fork cap, spacer, spring seat and fork spring (**Figure 75**) from the fork tube.
3. Turn the fork assembly upside down and drain the fork oil into a drain pan. Pump the fork several times by hand to expel the remaining oil.
4. Secure the fork as shown in **Figure 74**.
5. Remove the Allen bolt and gasket (**Figure 76**) from the bottom of the slider. If you did not loosen the Allen bolt during the fork removal procedure, temporarily install the fork spring, spring seat, spacer and fork cap to apply pressure against the damper rod, then remove the Allen bolt and washer.
6. Pry the dust seal (A, **Figure 77**) out of the slider.
7. Remove the stopper ring (B, **Figure 77**) from the groove in the slider.
8. Hold the fork tube and slowly move the slider up and down. The slider must move smoothly. If there is any noticeable binding or roughness, check the fork tube for dents or other damage.
9. There is an interference fit between the slider and fork tube bushings. To separate the fork tube and slider, hold the fork tube and pull hard on the slider using quick in and out strokes (**Figure 78**). This action withdraws the bushing, backup ring and seal from the fork tube. See **Figure 79**.
10. Remove the fork tube from the slider.
11. Remove the oil lock piece from the end of the damper rod, then remove the damper rod and spring from the fork tube.
12. Remove the following parts from the slider:

   a. Dust seal (A, **Figure 79**).
   b. Stopper ring (B, **Figure 79**).
   c. Oil seal (C, **Figure 79**).
   d. Backup ring (D, **Figure 79**).
   e. Slider bushing (E, **Figure 79**).

NOTE
*Do not remove the fork tube bushing (A, **Figure 80**) unless it is necessary to replace it. Fork tube bushing replacement is described under **Inspection**.*

13. Inspect the fork assembly as described under *Inspection* in this chapter.

Inspection

NOTE
*Handle the fork bushings (**Figure 80**) carefully when cleaning them in Step 1. Harsh cleaning can damage them by removing some of their coating material.*

1. Initially clean all of the parts (**Figure 81**) in solvent, first making sure that the solvent will not damage the rubber parts or the bushing coatings. Then clean with soap and water and rinse with plain water. Dry with compressed air. Clean the bushings with a soft nylon brush.

2. Check the fork tube (A, **Figure 82**) for nicks, rust, chrome flaking or creasing; these conditions will damage the dust and oil seals. Replace the fork tube if necessary.

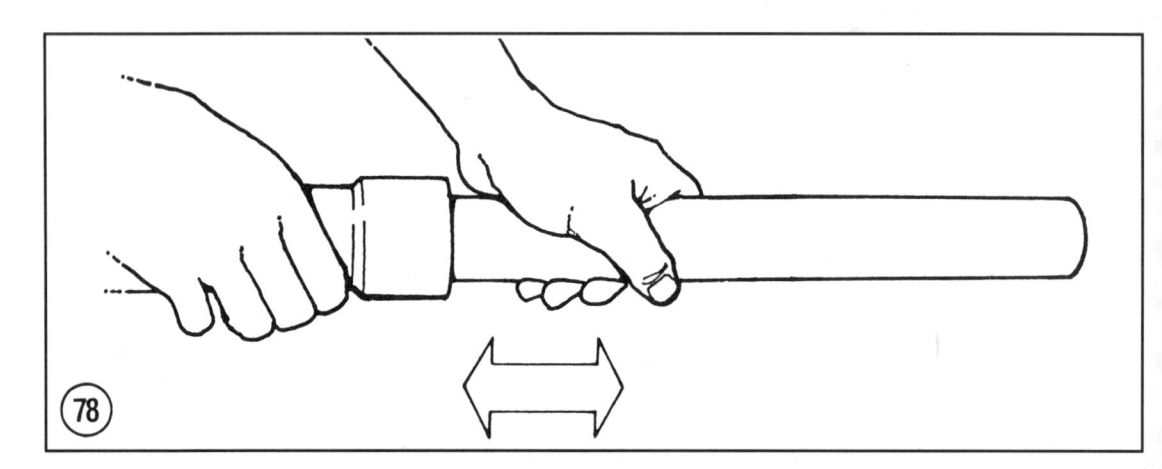

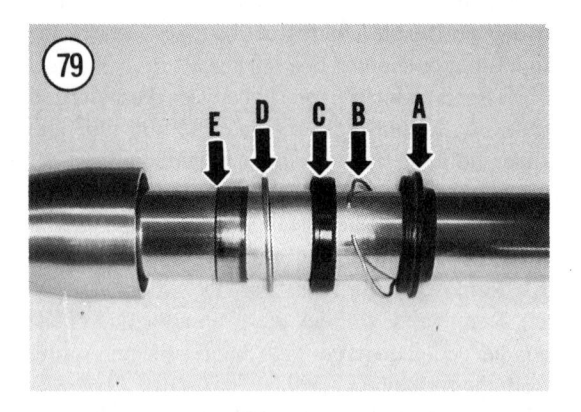

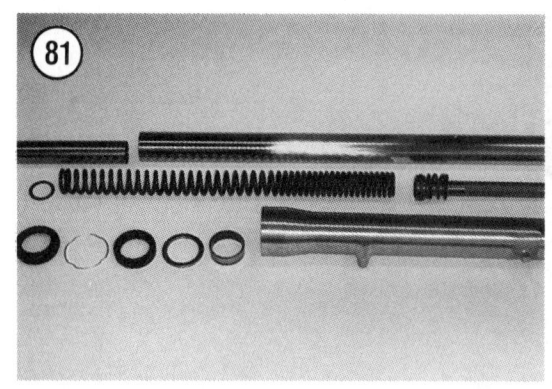

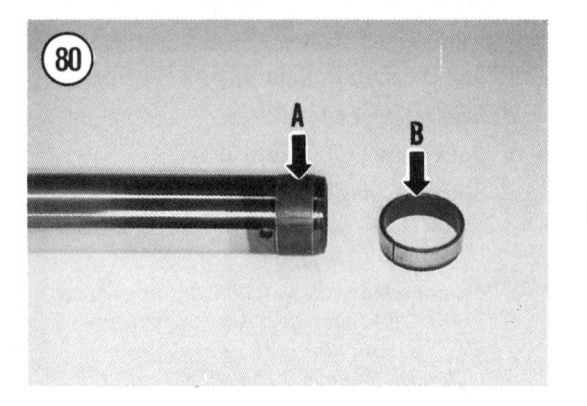

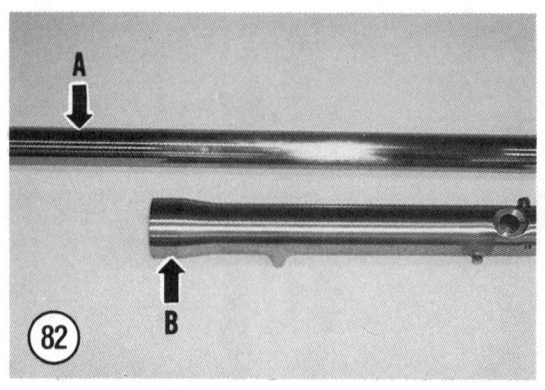

FRONT SUSPENSION AND STEERING

3. Check the fork tube runout with a set of V-blocks and dial indicator. Replace the fork tube if its runout exceeds the service limit in **Table 1**.
4. Check the slider (B, **Figure 82**) for dents or exterior damage. Check the stopper ring groove for cracks or other damage. Check the oil seal bore for dents other damage. Replace the slider if necessary.
5. Check the damper rod assembly (**Figure 83**) for:
   a. Bent, cracked or otherwise damaged damper rod.
   b. Excessively worn spring.
   c. Damaged oil lock piece.
   d. Excessively worn or damaged piston ring (**Figure 84**).

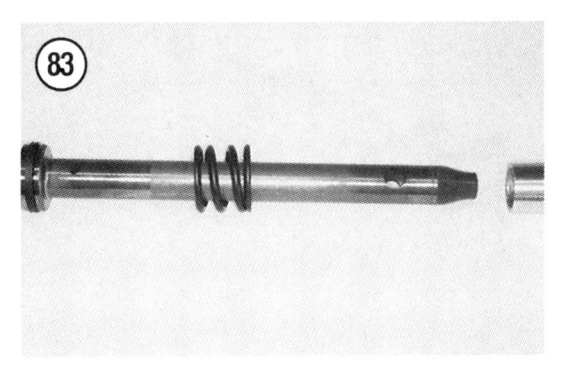

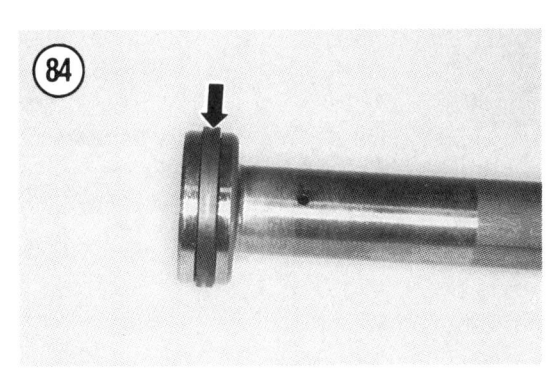

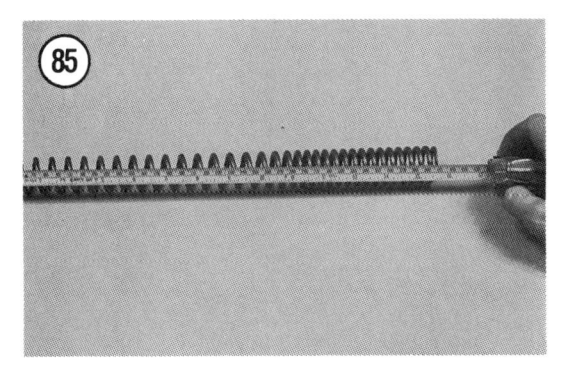

6. Measure the fork spring free length as shown in **Figure 85**. Replace the spring if it is sagged to the service limit in **Table 1**.
7. Inspect the fork tube (A, **Figure 80**) and slider (B, **Figure 80**) bushings. If the Teflon coating is worn so the copper base material is showing on approximately 3/4 of the bushing's total surface (**Figure 86**), replace the bushing.
8. To replace the fork tube bushing, open the bushing slot with a screwdriver (**Figure 87**) and slide the bushing off the fork tube. Lubricate the new bushing with fork oil, then open its slot slightly and slide it onto the fork tube groove.
9. Inspect the backup ring and replace it if there is any distortion at the points indicated in **Figure 86**.
10. Inspect the fork cap O-ring (**Figure 88**) and replace if it is leaking or damaged.
11. Inspect the spacer and spring seat (**Figure 88**) and replace if they are damaged.

Assembly

When fork oil is called for in the following steps, use the fork oil type, or a suitable equivalent, called out in **Table 1**.
1. If removed, install the fork tube bushing (A, **Figure 80**) onto the fork tube groove.
2. Coat all internal parts with fork oil before installation.

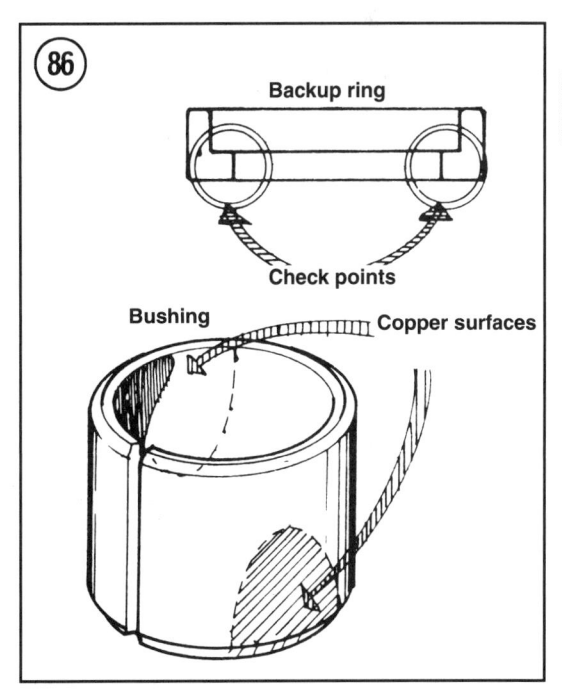

3. Install the rebound spring (**Figure 89**) onto the damper rod.
4. Slide the damper rod and rebound spring through the top of the fork tube (**Figure 90**).
5. Install the oil lock piece onto the end of the damper rod (**Figure 91**).
6. Install the fork tube into the slider (**Figure 92**) and bottom it out.
7. Mount the slider into a vise (**Figure 74**).
8. Temporarily install the fork spring, spring seat, spacer and fork cap.
9. Install a new washer onto the Allen bolt (**Figure 76**).
10. Apply a medium strength threadlocking compound onto the threads of the Allen bolt. Then install the bolt into the damper and tighten it (**Figure 93**) to the torque specification in **Table 3**.
11. Remove the fork cap, spacer, spring seat and fork spring.

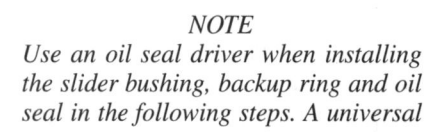

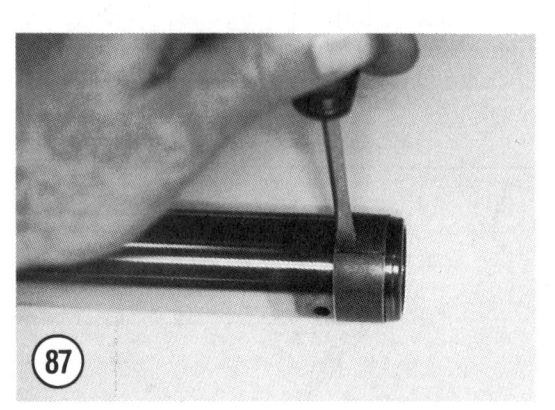

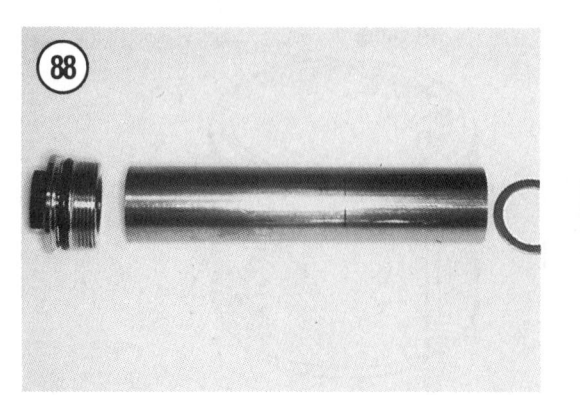

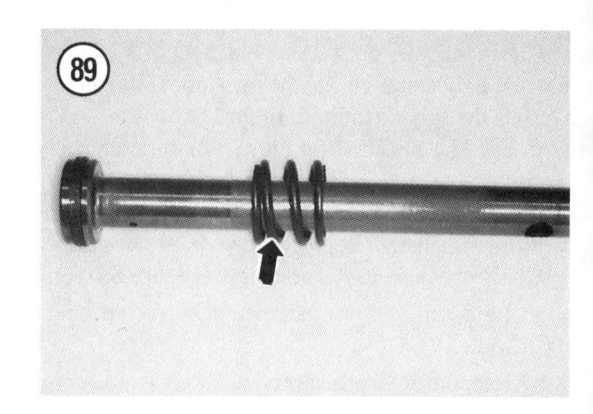

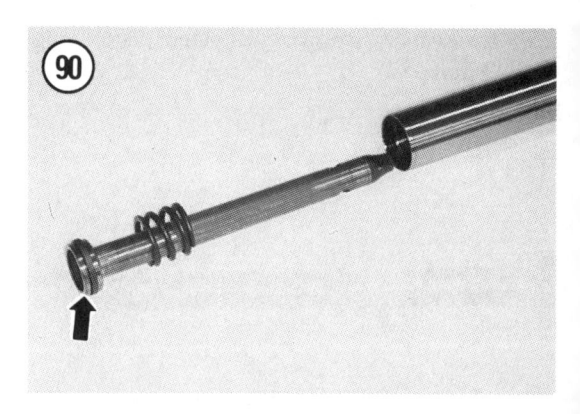

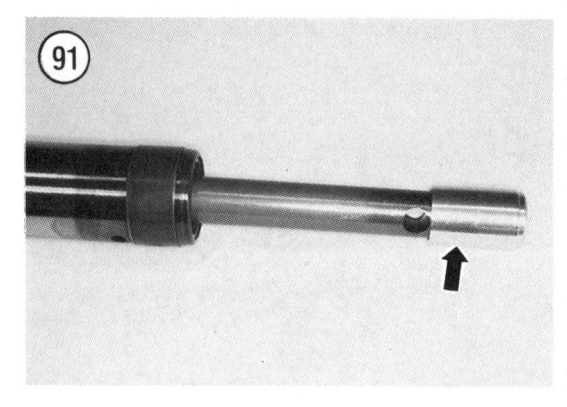

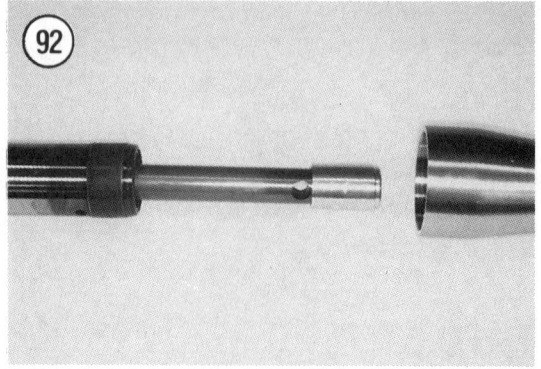

NOTE
Use an oil seal driver when installing the slider bushing, backup ring and oil seal in the following steps. A universal

FRONT SUSPENSION AND STEERING 353

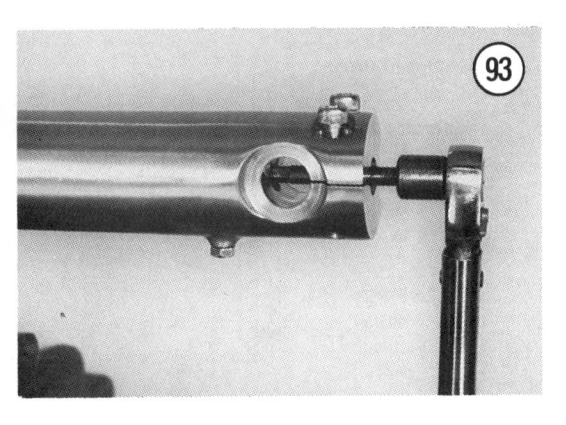

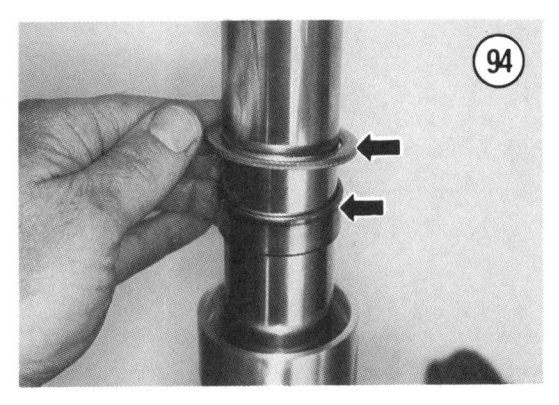

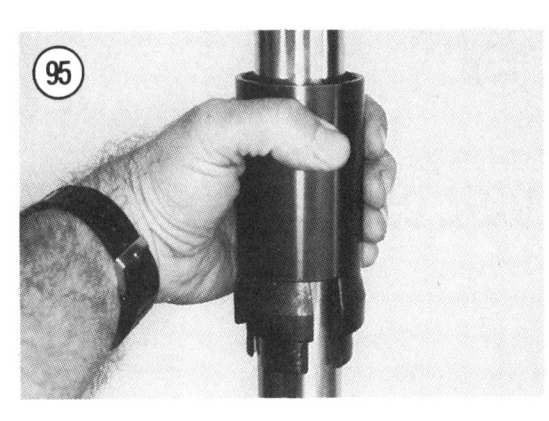

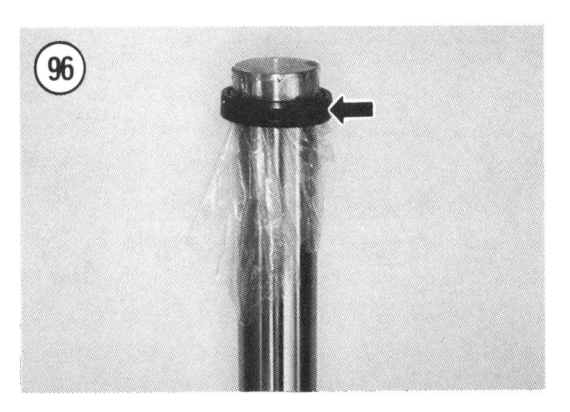

type oil seal driver is shown in the following photographs.

12. To install the slider bushing and backup ring, perform the following:
    a. Slide the slider bushing and backup ring (**Figure 94**) down the fork tube until they stop at the top of the slider.
    b. Drive the slider bushing with the backup ring on top of it (**Figure 95**) into the slider until the slider bushing bottoms out.
13. To install the oil seal, perform the following:
    a. Place a plastic bag over the top of the fork tube and lubricate it with fork oil.

NOTE
The plastic bag prevents the fork tube from tearing the oil seal and dust seal when installing them in the following steps.

   b. Lubricate the lips of the new oil seal with fork oil.
   c. Slide the oil seal (**Figure 96**) over the fork tube with its manufacturer's name and size code numbers facing up.
   d. Drive the seal into the slider with the same tool (**Figure 95**) used during Step 12. Continue to drive the oil seal into the slider until the groove in the slider is visible above the top surface of the oil seal.

14. Install the stopper ring (**Figure 97**) over the fork tube and seat it into the groove in the slider. See **Figure 98**.
15. Lubricate the lip of the new dust seal with fork oil, then slide it over the fork tube with its closed side facing up (**Figure 99**) and seat it into the slider. See **Figure 100**.

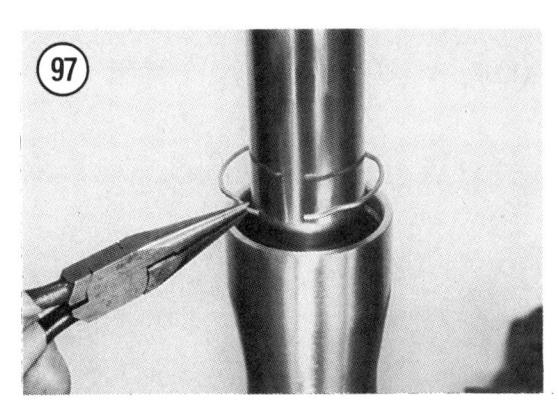

16. Compress the fork tube and pour the specified amount and type of fork oil (**Table 3**) into the fork tube.

17. Check and adjust the fork oil level as follows:

   a. Hold the slider and pump the fork tube several times to remove any air trapped in the slider.

   b. Compress the fork tube to bottom it out completely.

   c. With fork tube facing straight up (90°) set the fork oil level (**Figure 101**) to the dimension

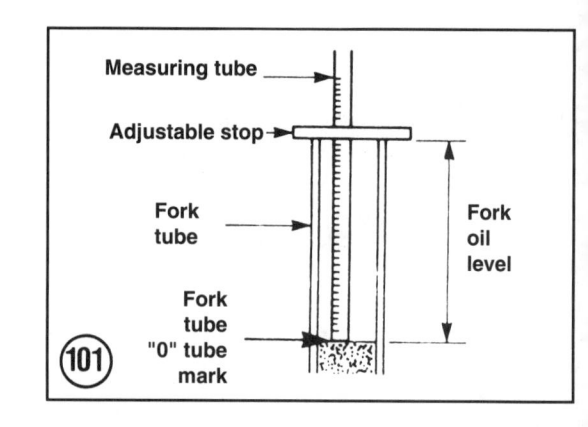

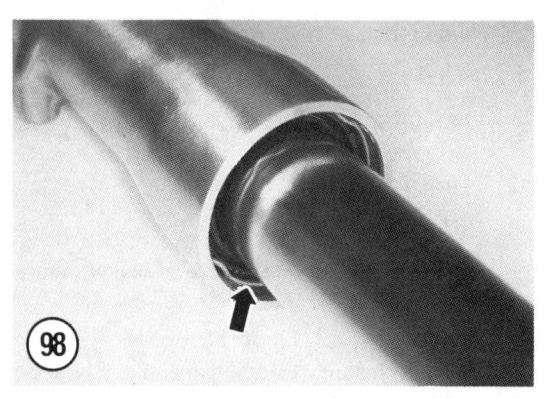

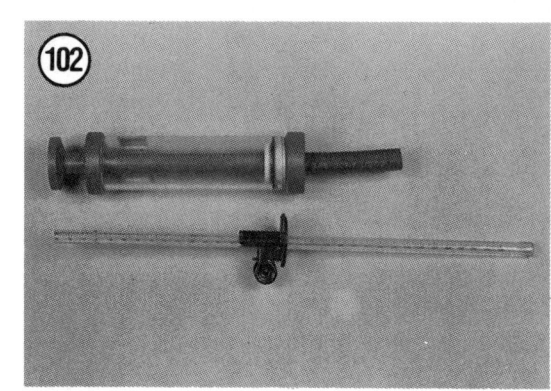

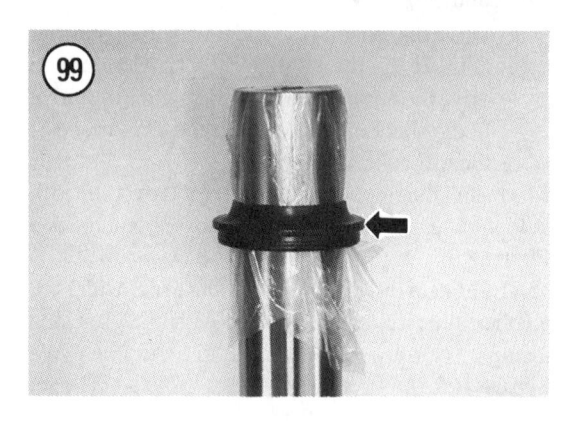

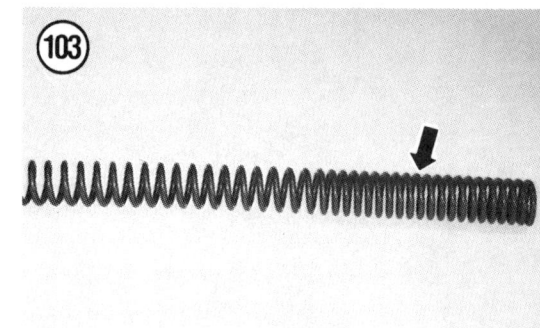

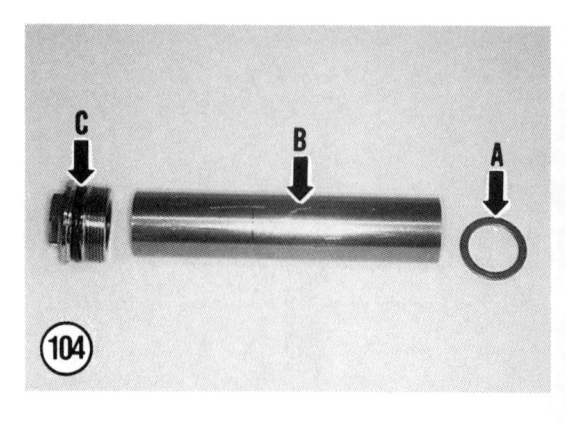

FRONT SUSPENSION AND STEERING

listed in **Table 1**. Use an oil level gauge to set the fork oil level. See **Figure 102**, typical.

18. Pull the fork tube all the way up, then install the fork spring with its tighter wound coils (**Figure 103**) facing down.

19. Lubricate fork cap O-ring and threads with fork oil.

20. Install the spring seat (A, **Figure 104**), spacer (B, **Figure 104**) and fork cap (A, **Figure 104**). Tighten the fork cap as tight as you can. Then, after you install the fork tube back onto the motorcycle, tighten the fork cap to the torque specification in **Table 3**. See *Front Fork Installation* in this chapter.

STEERING HEAD

The steering head (**Figure 105**) on these models uses retainer-type steel bearings at the top and bottom pivot positions.

Disassembly

1. Remove the front wheel as described in this chapter.
2. Remove the front fender.
3. Remove the headlight (Chapter Nine).
4. Remove the speedometer assembly (Chapter Nine).

105 STEERING STEM

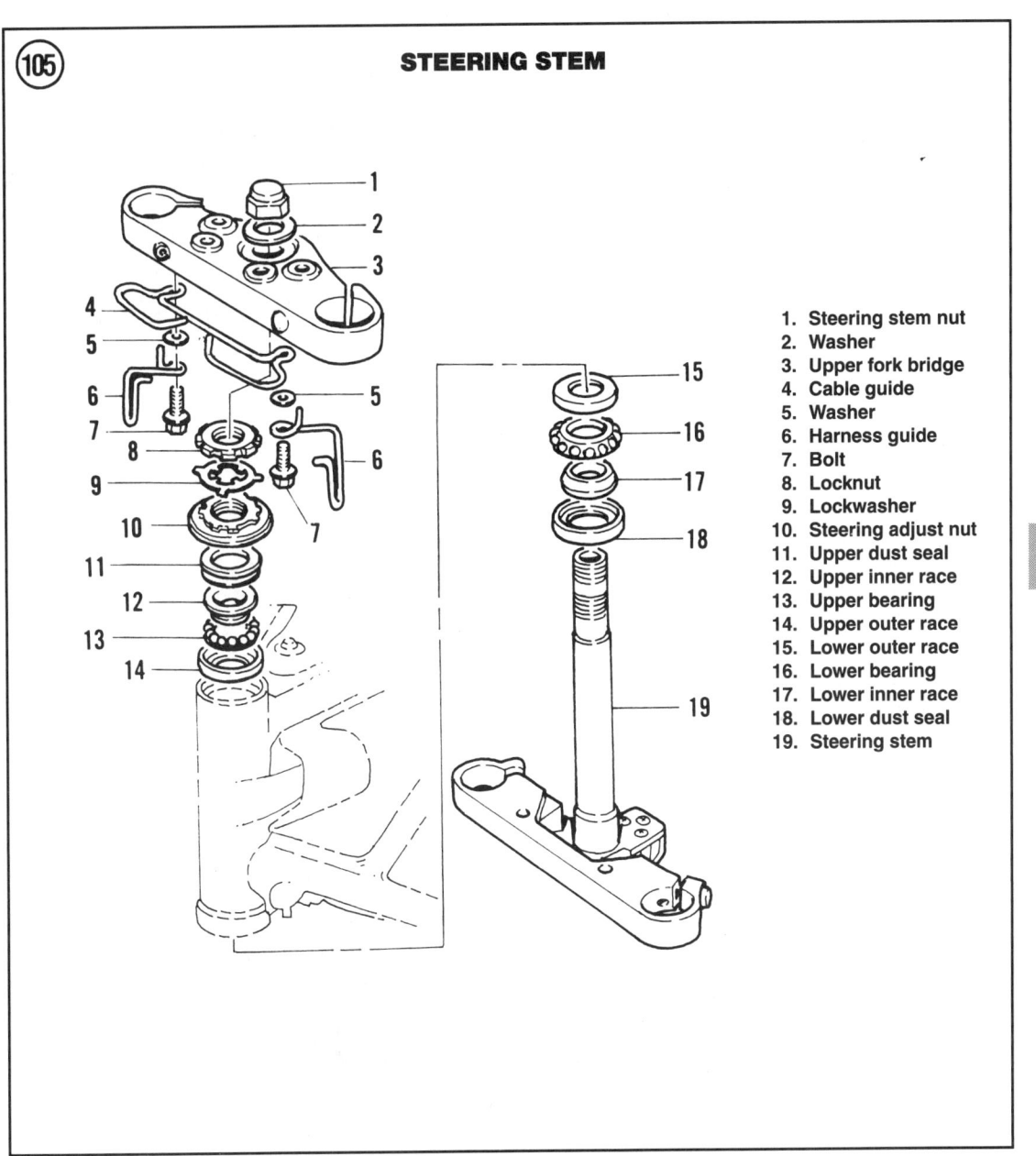

1. Steering stem nut
2. Washer
3. Upper fork bridge
4. Cable guide
5. Washer
6. Harness guide
7. Bolt
8. Locknut
9. Lockwasher
10. Steering adjust nut
11. Upper dust seal
12. Upper inner race
13. Upper bearing
14. Upper outer race
15. Lower outer race
16. Lower bearing
17. Lower inner race
18. Lower dust seal
19. Steering stem

5. Remove the handlebar as described in this chapter.
6. Remove the front forks as described in this chapter.
7. Remove the brake hose clamp from the steering stem.
8. Loosen and remove the steering stem nut (A, **Figure 106**) and flat washer (**Figure 107**).
9. Remove the upper fork bridge (B, **Figure 106**).
10. Pry back the lockwasher tabs from the locknut (**Figure 108**), then remove the locknut and lockwasher. See **Figure 109**.

NOTE
Hold onto the steering stem before removing the steering adjust nut in the next step.

11. Loosen and remove the steering adjust nut (**Figure 110**) and upper dust seal and the steering stem.
12. Remove the upper inner race and the upper bearing (**Figure 111**).
13. Remove the lower bearing (**Figure 112**) from the steering stem.

NOTE
*The lower inner race (A, **Figure 113**) is a press fit on the steering stem. Do not*

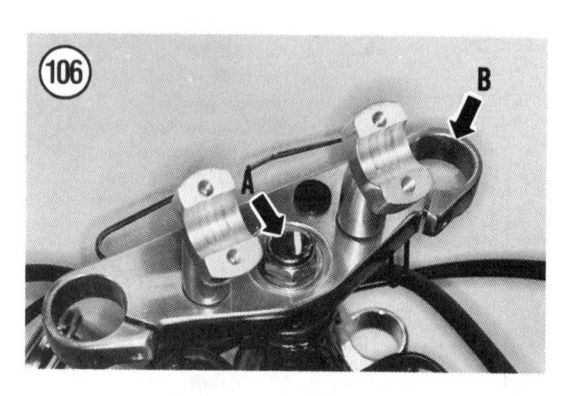

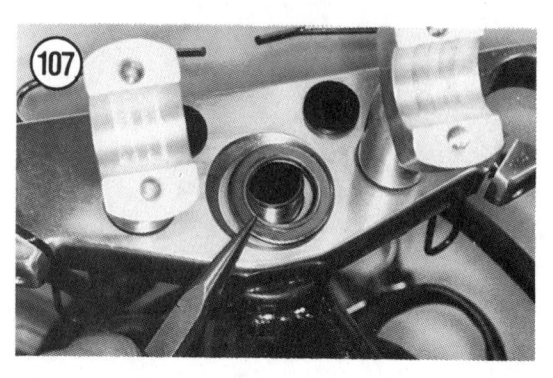

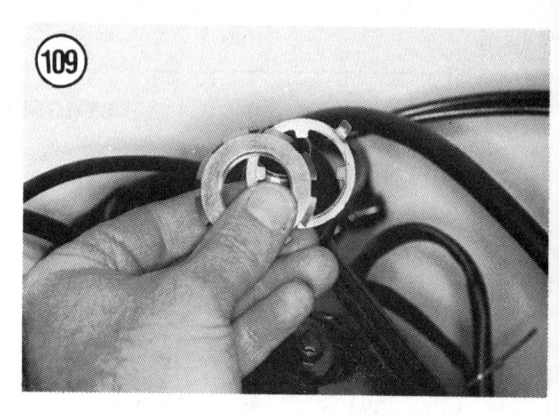

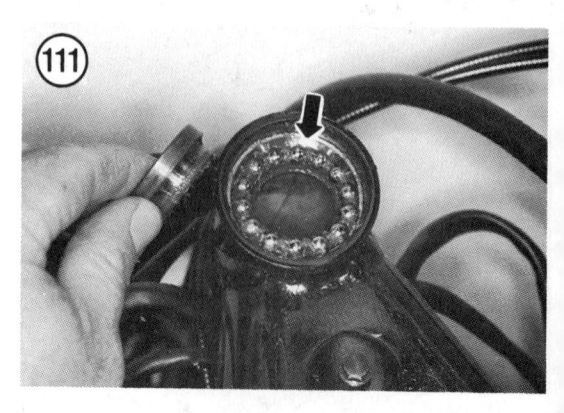

FRONT SUSPENSION AND STEERING

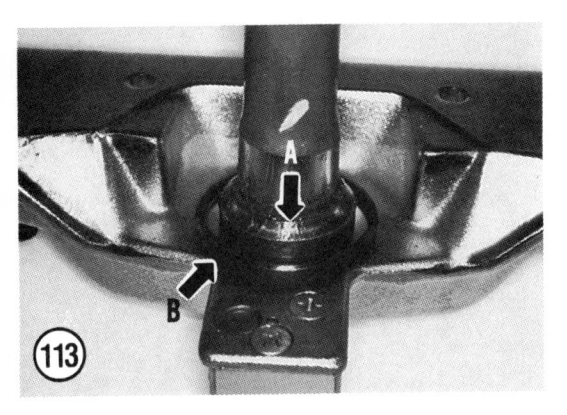

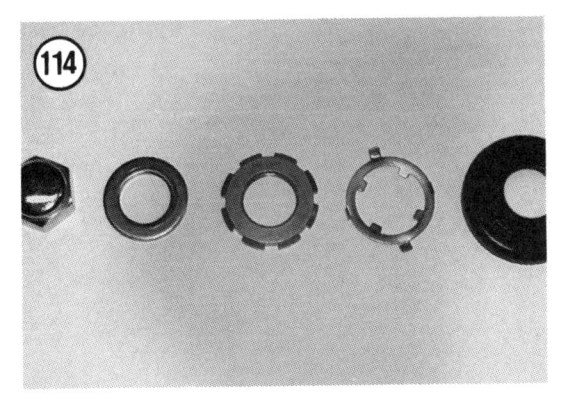

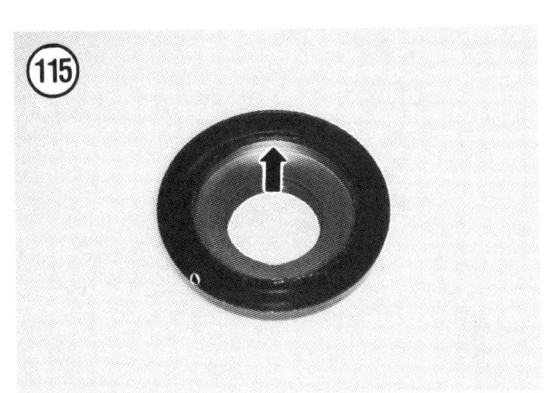

remove the lower inner race unless you are going to replace the lower bearing assembly.

Inspection

1. Clean all of the parts in solvent and dry thoroughly.
2. Check the frame for cracks and fractures. Refer repair to a qualified frame shop or welding service.
3. Inspect the steering stem nut, locknuts and washer (**Figure 114**) and replace if damaged. Discard the lockwasher as a new one must be installed during reassembly.
4. Inspect the upper dust seal (installed in the steering adjust nut) and replace if worn or damaged. See **Figure 115**.
5. Check the steering stem (**Figure 116**) for:
   a. Cracked or bent stem.
   b. Damaged lower bridge.
   c. Damaged threads.
6. Check the upper fork bridge (**Figure 117**) for cracks or other damage. Replace if necessary.
7. Inspect the bearing assemblies as follows:

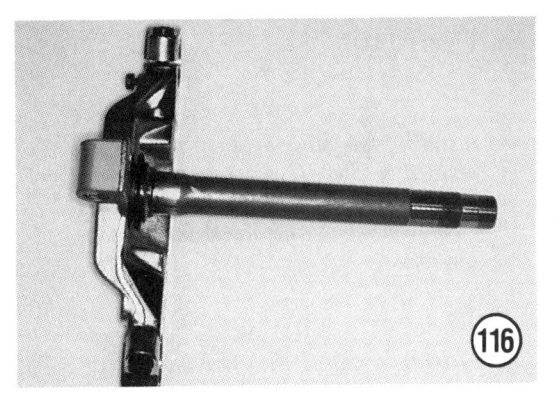

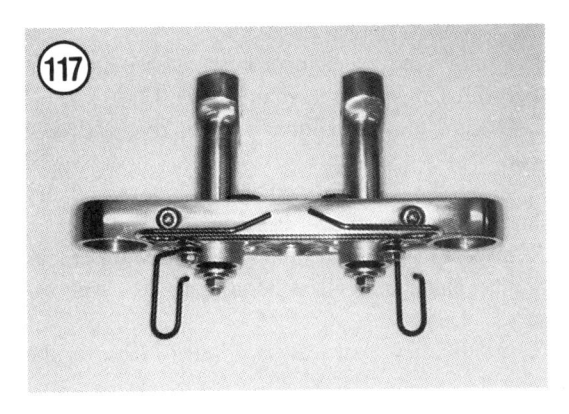

a. Inspect the upper and lower inner bearing race (A, **Figure 113** and A, **Figure 118**) for excessive wear, cracks or other damage. To replace the lower inner bearing race, refer to *Lower Inner Bearing Race Replacement* in this chapter.
b. Inspect the upper (B, **Figure 118**) and lower (C, **Figure 118**) bearings for pitting, excessive wear or retainer damage.
c. Inspect the upper (**Figure 119**) and lower (**Figure 120**) outer bearing races for pitting, cracks or discoloration that indicate excessive wear or damage.
d. Replace the upper and lower bearing assemblies at the same time. To replace the outer bearing races, refer to *Outer Bearing Race Replacement* in this chapter.

8. When reusing bearings, clean them thoroughly with a bearing degreaser and dry thoroughly. Repack each bearing with 3 g (0.11 oz.) of grease.

Lower Inner Bearing Race Replacement

Perform the following steps to replace the lower inner bearing race (A, **Figure 113**).

1. Thread the steering stem nut onto the steering stem (**Figure 121**).

NOTE
Installing the steering stem nut as described in Step 1 will help to prevent damage to the steering stem threads when you remove the lower inner bearing race.

WARNING
Striking a chisel with a hammer can cause flying chips. Wear safety glasses in Step 2 to prevent eye injury.

2. Remove the lower inner bearing race and dust seal with a chisel as shown in **Figure 122**.
3. Discard the lower inner bearing race and dust seal.
4. Clean the steering stem with solvent and dry thoroughly.
5. Inspect the steering stem race surface for cracks or other damage. Replace the steering stem if necessary.
6. Install a new dust seal (B, **Figure 113**) over the steering stem.

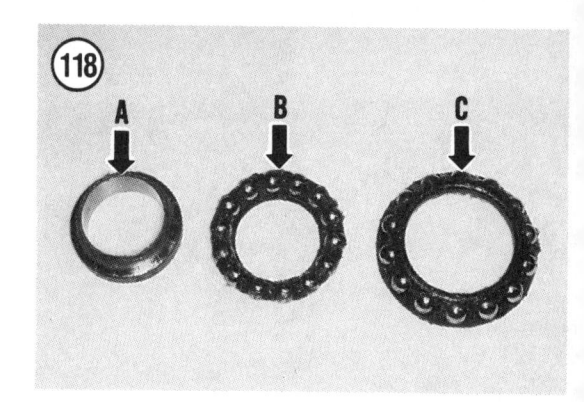

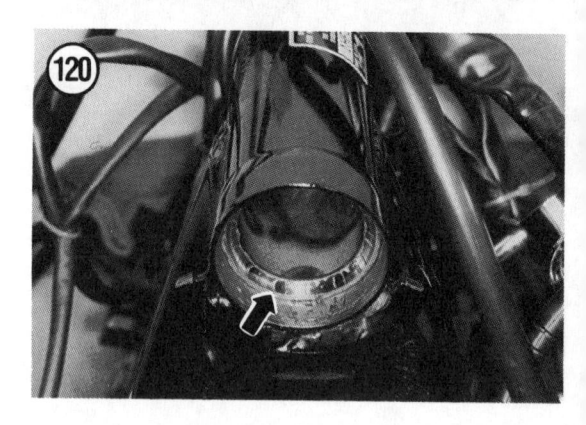

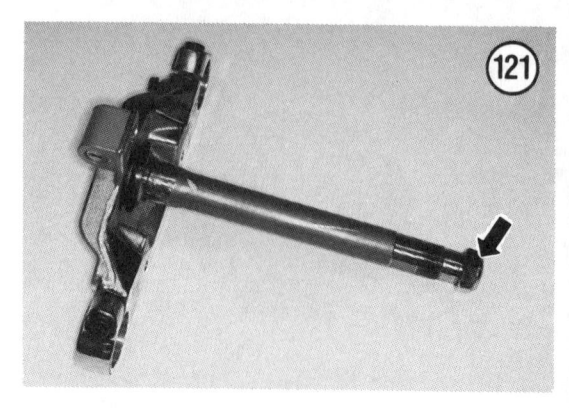

FRONT SUSPENSION AND STEERING

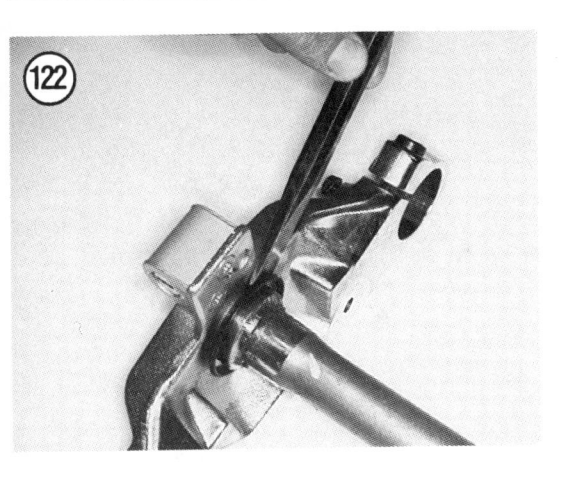

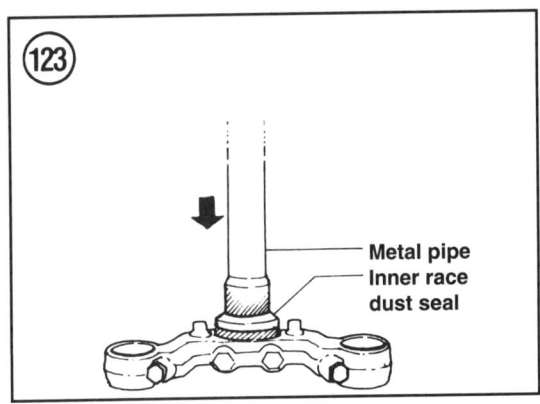

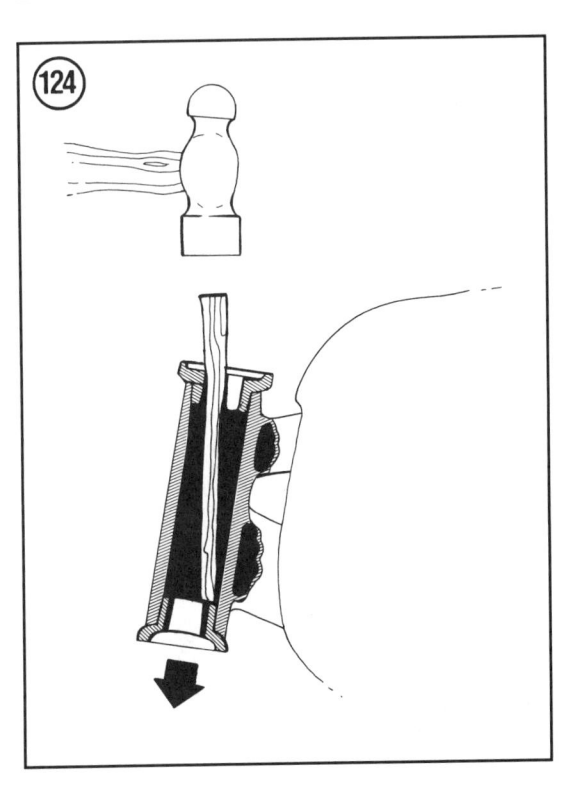

7. Slide the new lower inner bearing race—bearing surface facing up—onto the steering stem until it stops.
8. Install the steering stem in a press. Then install a bearing driver (**Figure 123**) over the steering stem and seat it against the inner bearing race inside shoulder. Do not allow the bearing driver to contact the bearing race surface.
9. Press the bearing onto the steering stem until it bottoms out (A, **Figure 113**).

Outer Bearing Race Replacement

Do not remove the upper (**Figure 119**) and lower (**Figure 120**) outer bearing races unless they are going to be replaced. If you replace a bearing race, you must replace the complete bearing assembly (bearing, retainer, inner and outer race).

1. Insert an aluminum drift into the frame tube (**Figure 124**) and carefully drive the race out from the inside. Strike at different spots around the race to prevent it from binding in the frame bore. Repeat for the other race.
2. Clean the race bore and check for cracks or other damage.
3. Place the new race squarely into the bore opening with its tapered side facing out.
4. Drive the new race into the steering head (**Figure 125**) until it bottoms out.
5. Repeat for the other race.
6. Lubricate the upper and lower bearing races with grease.

Steering Stem Assembly and Steering Adjustment

Refer to **Figure 105** when assembling the steering stem assembly.

1. Make sure the upper (**Figure 119**) and lower (**Figure 120**) bearing races are properly seated in the frame's steering head.
2. Apply 3 g (0.11 oz.) of grease to each steering bearing.
3. Install the lower steering bearing (**Figure 126**) onto the lower inner bearing race.
4. Lubricate the upper dust seal lip (**Figure 127**) with grease.
5. Install the steering stem into the steering head and hold it in place.
6. Install the upper bearing and seat it into its outer race (**Figure 128**).

7. Install the inner race (**Figure 129**) and seat it into the bearing (**Figure 130**).
8. Install the upper dust seal (**Figure 131**).
9. Install the steering adjust nut (**Figure 132**) finger-tight.
10. Tighten the steering adjust nut (**Figure 132**) as follows:

   a. Use a spanner wrench and torque wrench (**Figure 133**) to seat the bearings in the following steps.

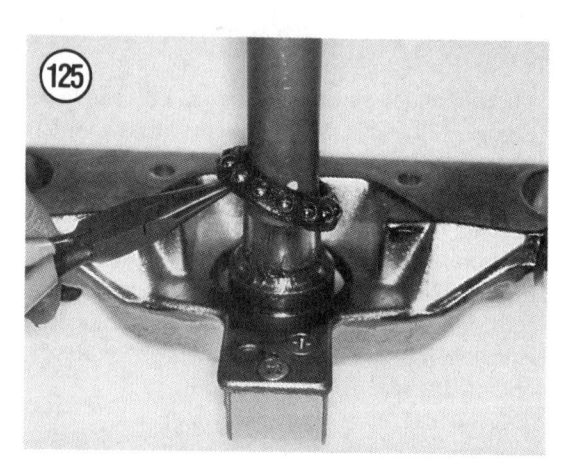

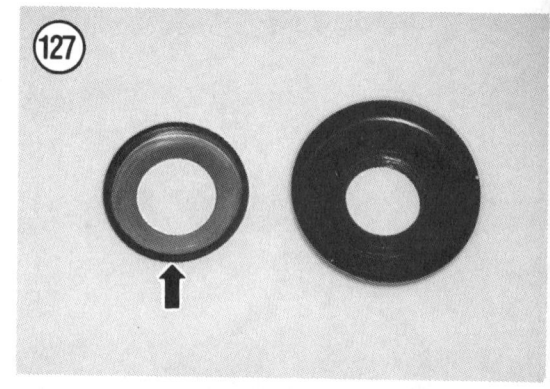

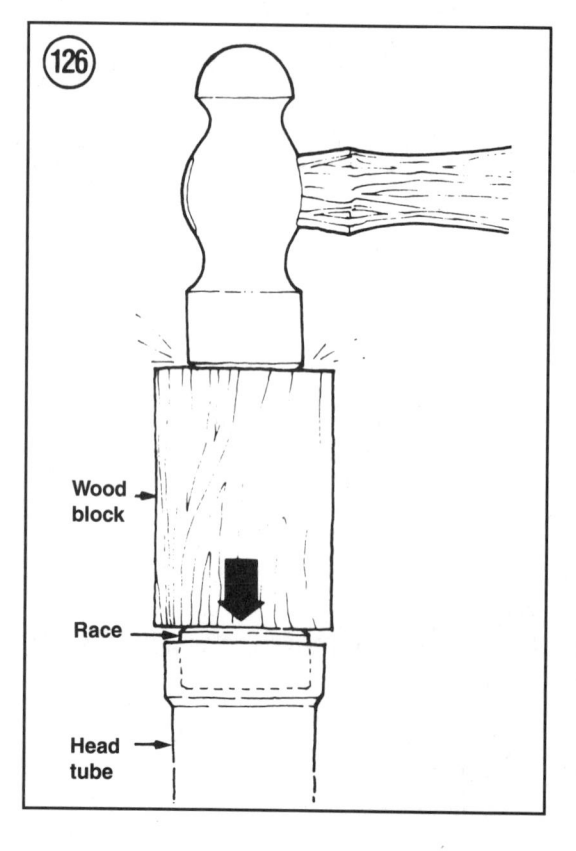

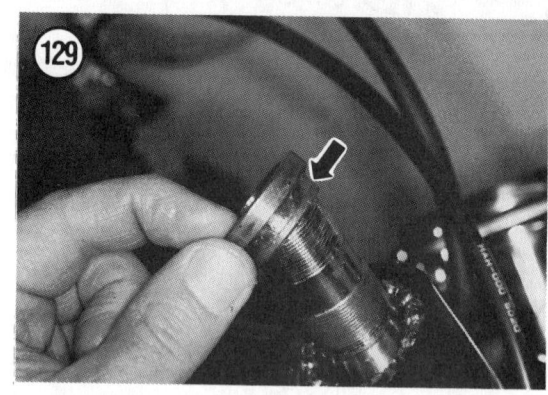

FRONT SUSPENSION AND STEERING

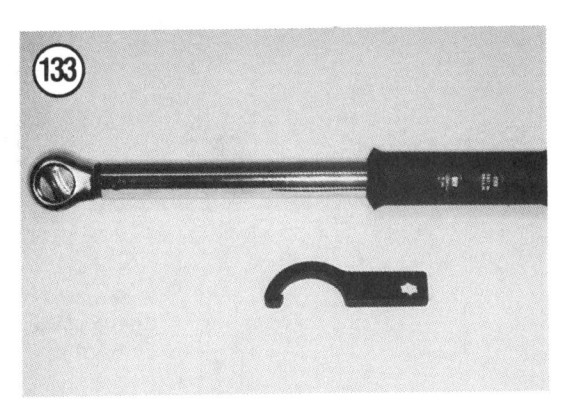

b. Tighten the steering adjust nut (**Figure 132**) to 21 N•m (15 ft.-lb.).

c. Loosen the steering adjust nut, then retighten it to the same torque specification.

d. Turn the steering stem from lock to lock 4 or 5 times, then retighten the steering adjust nut to the same torque specification.

e. Repeat substep d several times to seat the steering bearings.

f. Check bearing play by turning the steering stem from lock to lock. The steering stem must pivot smoothly with no binding or roughness.

11. Align the bent tabs on a new lockwasher with the grooves in the steering adjust nut and install the lockwasher (**Figure 134**).

12. Install and tighten the locknut as follows:

a. Install the locknut (**Figure 135**) and tighten finger-tight.

b. Hold the steering adjust nut (to keep it from turning) and tighten the locknut approximately 1/4 turn (90°) to align its grooves with the outer lockwasher tabs.

c. Bend the outer lockwasher tabs (**Figure 136**) into the locknut grooves.

13. Install the upper fork bridge, washer and steering stem nut. Tighten the nut finger-tight.

14. Temporarily install and tighten both fork tubes to align the steering stem with the upper fork bridge.

15. Tighten the steering stem nut (**Figure 137**) to the torque specification in **Table 3**.

16. Turn the steering stem from lock to lock. Make sure it moves smoothly with no trace of binding or roughness.

17. Remove the front fork tubes.

18. Secure the brake hose clamp onto the steering stem.
19. Install the handlebar as described in this chapter.
20. Install the speedometer assembly (Chapter Nine).
21. Install the headlight (Chapter Nine).
22. Install the front fender and front forks as described in this chapter.
23. Install the front wheel as described in this chapter.
24. Perform the *Steering Bearing Preload Check* in this chapter.
25. Check the choke, clutch and throttle cables for proper operation. If necessary, adjust each cable as described in Chapter Three.
26. Make sure the front brake works properly.

WARNING
Do not ride the motorcycle until all of the cables and front brake work properly.

STEERING BEARING PRELOAD CHECK

A spring scale will be required for this procedure.
1. Support the bike with the front wheel off the ground.
2. Attach a spring scale onto one of the fork tubes between the top fork bridge and steering stem. See **Figure 138**.
3. Center the front wheel. Then pull the spring scale and note the scale reading when the steering stem just starts to turn. The correct steering preload adjustment is 0.9-1.3 kg (2.0-2.0 lb.). If any other reading is obtained, readjust the steering adjust nut as described under *Steering Stem Assembly and Steering Adjustment* in this chapter.
4. Remove the spring scale from the fork tube.
5. Lower the bike so both wheels are on the ground. Support the bike with its sidestand.

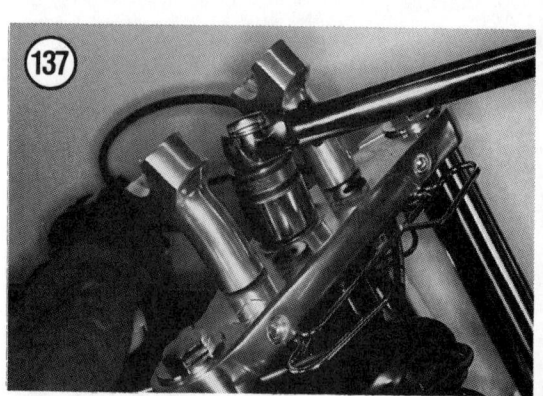

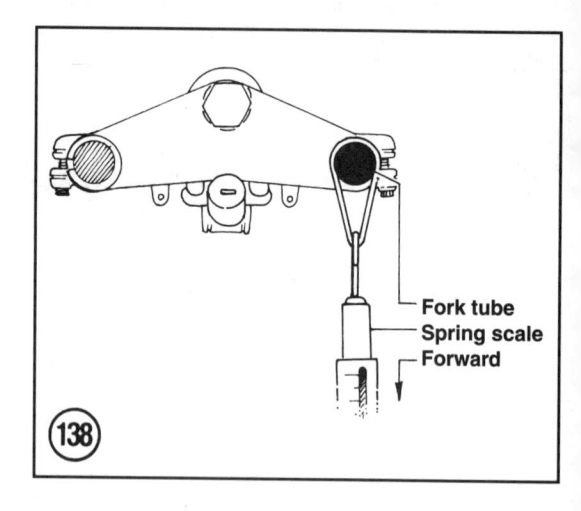

FRONT SUSPENSION AND STEERING

Table 1 STEERING AND FRONT SUSPENSION SPECIFICATIONS

Front axle runout limit	0.20 mm (0.008 in.)
Front fork oil	
Oil capacity	
1995-1998	482 cc (16.3 U.S. oz./16.9 Imp. oz.)
1999	495 cc (16.7 U.S. oz./17.4 Imp. oz.)
Oil type	10 wt. fork oil
Oil level	
1995-1998	151 mm (5.9 in.)
1999	139 mm (5.6 in.)
Front fork spring free length	
Standard	
1995-1997	449.4 mm (17.69 in.)
1998	469.9 mm (18.50 in.)
1999	447.9 mm (17.63 in.)
Service limit	
1995-1997	440.4 mm (17.34 in.)
1998	460.5 mm (18.13 in.)
1999	438.9 mm (17.28 in.)
Front fork tube runout	
Service limit	0.20 mm (0.008 in.)
Front wheel rim runout limit	
Axial	2.0 mm (0.08 in.)
Radial	2.0 mm (0.08 in.)
Front wheel travel	124 mm (4.9 in.)
Steering	
Caster angle	32 degrees 15 minutes
Trail length	155 mm (6.1 in.)
Steering bearing preload	0.9-1.3 kg (2.0-2.9 lb.)
Tires	
Size	
Front	120/90-18 65H
Rear	170/80-15M/C 77H
Type	
Front	Dunlop K177F
Rear	Dunlop K555
Wheel balance weight (maximum)	60 g (2.1 oz.)

Table 2 TIRE INFLATION PRESSURE*

	psi	kPa
Up to 200 lbs. (90 kg) load		
Front		
1995-1996	33	225
1997-1999	29	200
Rear	33	225
Up to maximum weight capacity		
Front	33	225
Rear	41	280

* The tire inflation pressures listed here are for factory equipped tires. Aftermarket tires may require different inflation pressure; refer to tire manufacturer's specifications.

Table 3 TIGHTENING TORQUES

	N•m	in.-lb.	ft.-lb.
Fork cap	23	–	17
Fork tube Allen bolt	22	–	16
Fork tube drain bolt	8	71	–
Fork tube pinch bolts			
Upper	11	97	–
Lower	50	–	36
Front axle bolt	60	–	43
Front axle pinch bolts	22	–	16
Front brake caliper mounting bolts	31	–	22
Front brake hose clamp bolt	12	106	–
Front turn signal stopper plate bolt	9	80	–
Handlebar holder bolts	30	–	22
Spoke nipples	4.3	38	–
Steering adjust nut	21	–	15
Steering stem nut	105	–	77
Valve stem nut	2.8	25	–
Master cylinder clamp bolts	12	106	–

CHAPTER TWELVE

REAR SUSPENSION

This chapter contains repair and replacement procedures for the rear wheel, hub, rear suspension and shaft components. Refer to Chapter Eleven for changing and wheel balancing procedures.

Rear suspension specifications are listed in **Table 1** and **Table 2**. **Table 1** and **Table 2** are located at the end of this chapter.

REAR WHEEL

Removal

1. Support the bike on a stand with the rear wheel off the ground.

NOTE
If you cannot lift the rear wheel far enough to remove it with the rear fender mounted on the bike, remove the rear fender as described in Chapter Fourteen.

2. Loosen and remove the rear axle nut (**Figure 1**).
3. Loosen the rear caliper stopper pin bolt (A, **Figure 2**) completely.
4. Loosen the rear axle pinch bolt (B, **Figure 2**) completely.
5. Pull the rear caliper stopper pin bolt out until it contacts the exhaust pipe (**Figure 3**).
6. Remove the axle (**Figure 4**) and its thrust washer (**Figure 5**).
7. Lift the brake caliper and its holder off the brake disc (**Figure 6**) and support it with a wire hook.
8. Remove the right side collar (**Figure 7**).

9. Move the wheel toward the right to separate it from the final gearcase (**Figure 8**), then remove it from between the swing arm.

10. Insert a plastic spacer block in the caliper between the brake pads.

NOTE
The spacer block installed in Step 10 will prevent the piston from being forced out of its cylinder if the brake pedal is operated. If the piston is forced out too far, you will have to disassemble the caliper to reseat the piston.

Inspection

1. Inspect the right side seal (**Figure 9**) for excessive wear, hardness, cracks or other damage. If necessary, replace seal as described under *Rear Hub* in this chapter.

2. Turn each bearing inner race (**Figure 9**). Each bearing must turn without excessive noise. Some axial play (end play) is normal, but radial play (side play) must be negligible. See **Figure 10**. Replace both wheel bearings as a set. Refer to *Rear Hub* in this chapter.

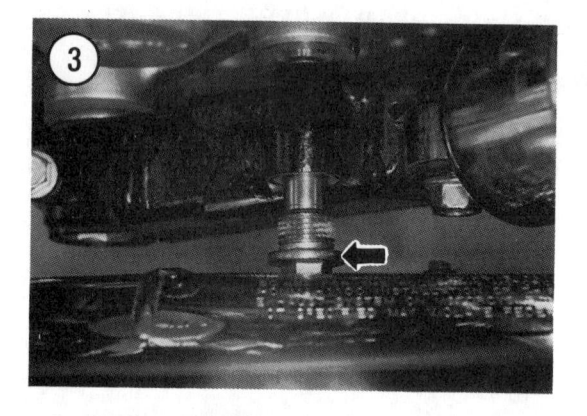

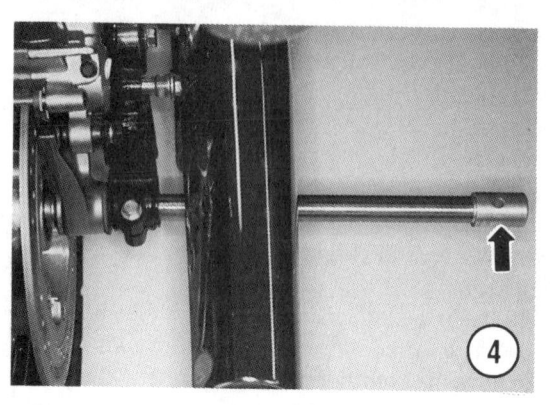

REAR SUSPENSION

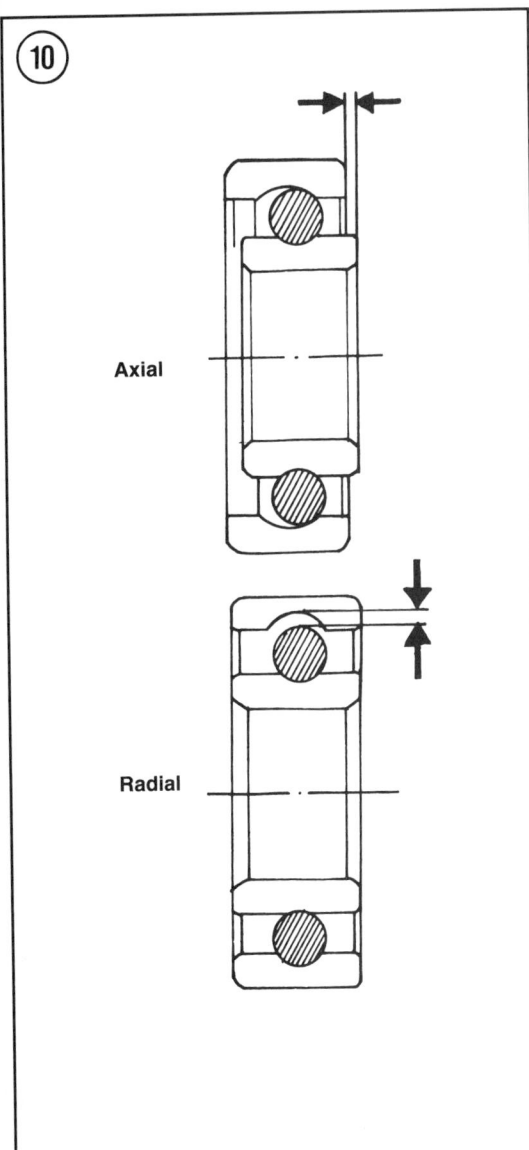

3. Clean the axle, collar and nut in solvent to remove all old grease and dirt. Make sure all axle contact surfaces are clean prior to installation. If these surfaces are corroded or dirty, the axle may be difficult to remove later on.
4. Check the rear axle runout with a set of V-blocks and dial indicator (**Figure 11**). Replace the axle if its runout exceeds the service limit in **Table 1**.
5. Check the brake disc bolts for tightness. To service the brake disc, refer to Chapter Thirteen.
6. Check wheel runout and spoke tension as described in Chapter Eleven.
7. To service the final gear flange assembly, refer to *Rear Hub* in this chapter.

Installation

1. Lubricate the rear axle and the right side seal lip (**Figure 9**) with grease.
2. Loosen the final gearcase mounting nuts (**Figure 12**).

NOTE
Loosening the final gearcase mounting nuts helps ease axle installation while

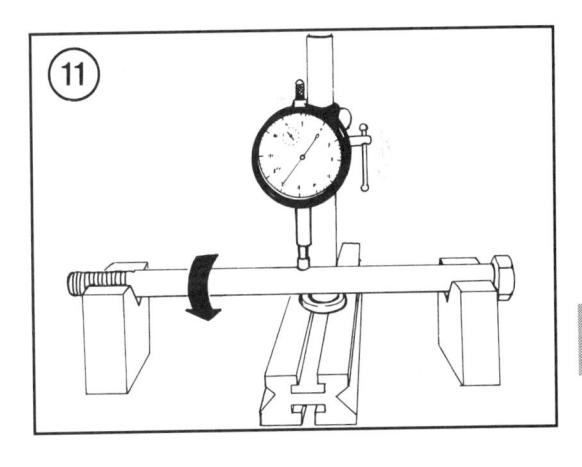

368

CHAPTER TWELVE

ensuring correct final gearcase spline alignment.

3. Check that the final gear flange (**Figure 13**) and final gearcase (**Figure 14**) splines are coated with grease. If not, lubricate them with molybdenum disulfide paste. If the splines are dry, lubricate them as follows:

   a. Apply 1-2 g (0.04-0.07 oz) of molybdenum disulfide paste to the final gearcase O-ring guide and driven flange splines (**Figure 13**).

   b. Apply 5 g (0.18 oz) of molybdenum disulfide paste to the final gear flange splines and O-ring (**Figure 14**).

4. Install the right side collar—shoulder side facing out—into the seal (**Figure 15**).
5. Remove the spacer block from between the brake pads.
6. Slide the wheel between the swing arm, then lift it and engage the final gear splines (**Figure 8**).
7. Remove the wire hook from the rear brake caliper bracket. Then install the rear brake caliper bracket so the brake pads slide over the brake disc and the bottom of the caliper bracket fits between the collar and swing arm. See **Figure 16**.
8. Install the thrust washer between the swing arm and rear brake caliper bracket (**Figure 5**), then install the rear axle (**Figure 4**). Make sure the washer did not fall out.

CAUTION
Tighten the rear axle nut before tightening the rear axle pinch bolt to prevent axle misalignment.

9. Install the rear axle nut (**Figure 1**) and hold the axle with a 17 mm hex socket and breaker bar. Then tighten the rear axle nut (**Figure 1**) to the torque specification in **Table 2**.
10. Tighten the final gearcase mounting nuts (**Figure 12**) to the torque specification in **Table 2**.
11. Tighten the rear axle pinch bolt (B, **Figure 2**) to the torque specification in **Table 2**.
12. Install a rear caliper stopper pin bolt (A, **Figure 2**) through the caliper bracket, then tighten to the torque specification in **Table 2**.
13. After the wheel is completely installed, rotate it several times while applying the rear brake to reposition the rear brake pads and to make sure the wheel rotates freely.

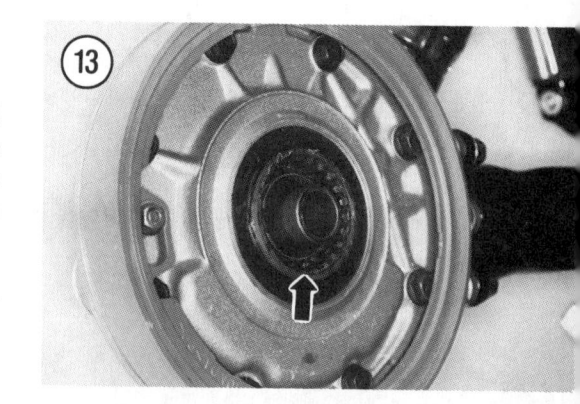

REAR SUSPENSION

14. Remove the stand from the bike and lower the rear wheel onto the ground. Support the bike with its sidestand.

REAR HUB

This section describes complete service to the rear hub and final gear flange assembly.

Refer to **Figure 17** when servicing the rear hub.

Disassembly

1. Pry the dust seal from the right side of the wheel (**Figure 18**).

2. Pull the final gear flange assembly up and out of the hub, then remove the thrust washer (**Figure 19**).

NOTE
Do not attempt to disassemble the final gear flange assembly.

3. Remove the damper holder plate bolts (**Figure 20**).

4. Turn the damper holder plate to align its arrow mark between any 2 projection tabs on the hub (**Figure 21**), then remove the damper holder plate.

5. Remove the O-ring (A, **Figure 22**) from the groove in the hub.

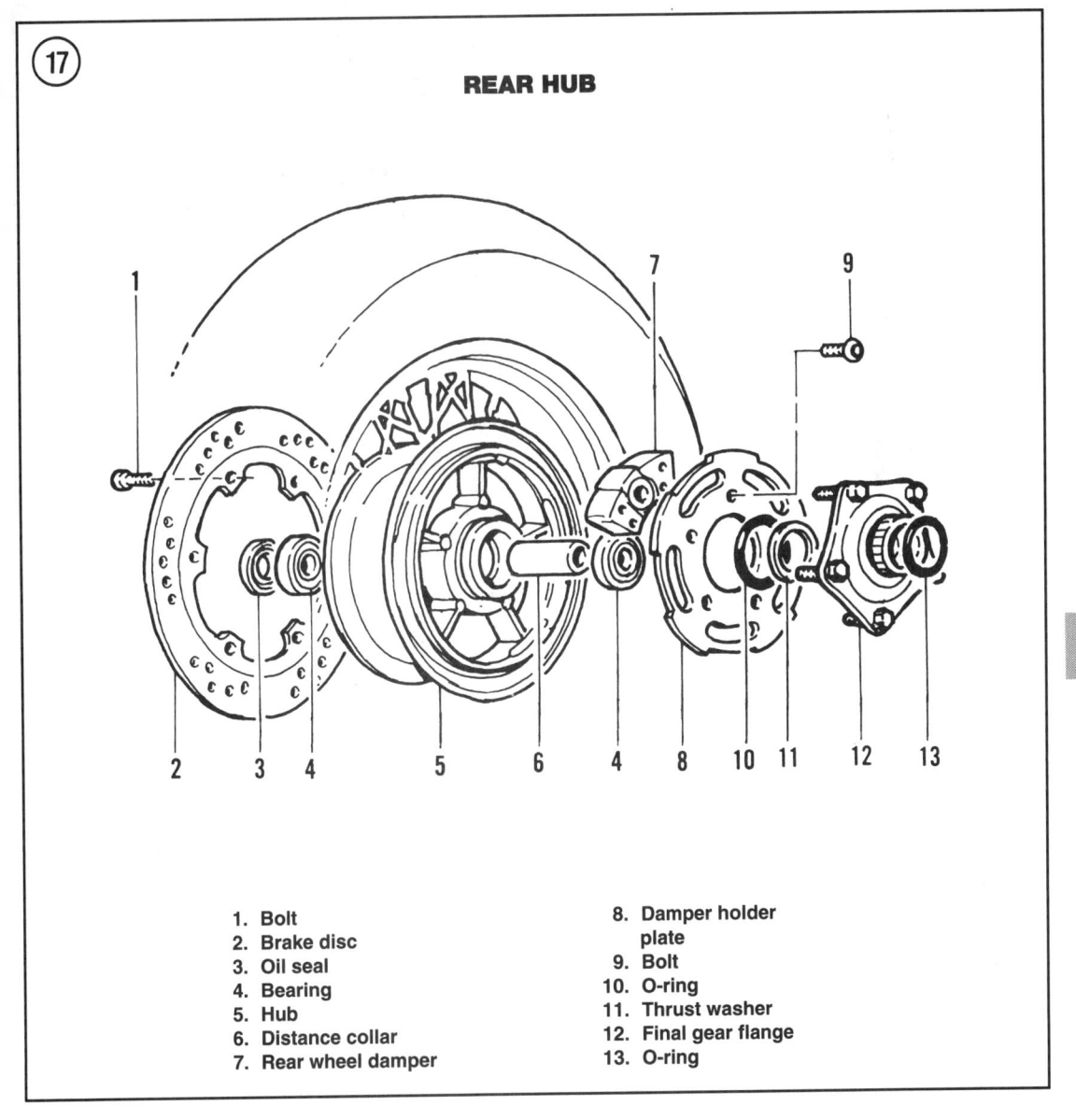

REAR HUB

1. Bolt
2. Brake disc
3. Oil seal
4. Bearing
5. Hub
6. Distance collar
7. Rear wheel damper
8. Damper holder plate
9. Bolt
10. O-ring
11. Thrust washer
12. Final gear flange
13. O-ring

6. If necessary, remove the rear wheel dampers (**Figure 23**) from in the hub.

CAUTION
Do not remove the wheel bearings for inspection purposes as they may be damaged during their removal. Remove the wheel bearings only if they are to be replaced.

Inspection

1. Inspect the wheel bearings as follows:
   a. Turn each bearing inner race (B, **Figure 22**) by hand. The bearing must turn smoothly with no trace of roughness, catching, binding or excessive noise. Some axial play (end play) is normal, but radial play (side play) must be negligible; see **Figure 10**.
   b. Check the outer bearing seal (B, **Figure 22**) for damage that would allow dirt to enter the bearing.
   c. If one bearing is damaged, you must replace both bearings as a set.
   d. If necessary, replace the wheel bearings as described in this section.
2. Inspect the rear wheel dampers (**Figure 23**) for deterioration, cracks or other damage. Replace the rear wheel dampers as a set.
3. Replace the final gear flange assembly O-ring (A, **Figure 24**) if excessively worn or damaged.

NOTE
*Do not disassemble the final gear flange (**Figure 24**) when inspecting it in the following steps. If any part (other than the O-ring) is worn or damaged, replace the final gear flange as an assembly. Replacement parts are not available from Honda.*

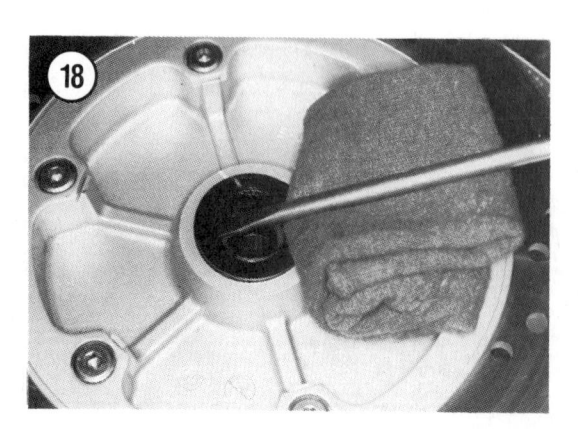

REAR SUSPENSION

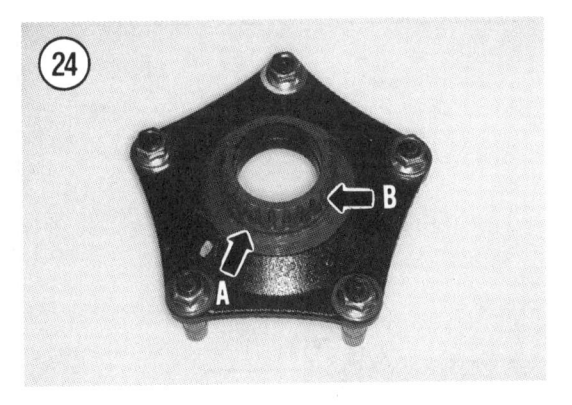

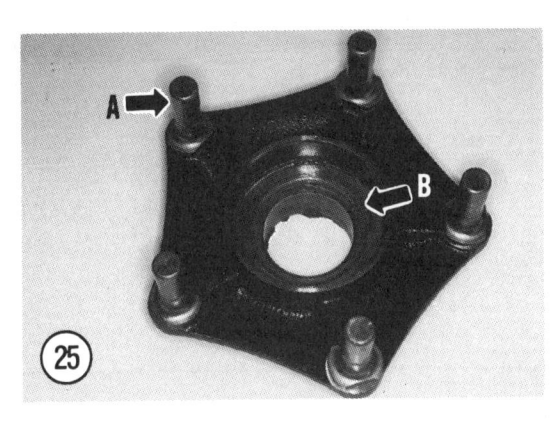

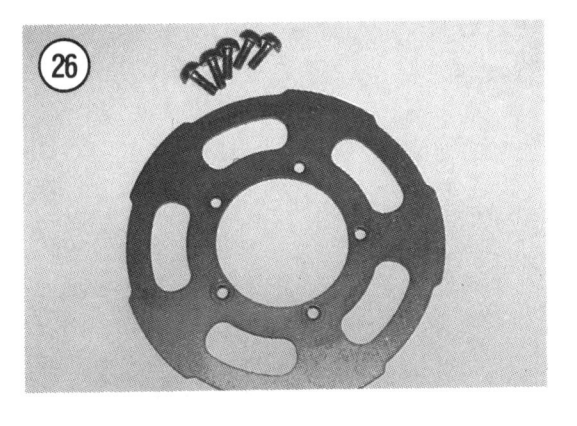

4. Inspect the final gear flange splines (B, **Figure 24**) for excessive wear or damage. If these splines are damaged, check the final gear splines (**Figure 13**) for the same type of damage.
5. Inspect the final gear flange mounting arms (A, **Figure 25**) for cracks or other damage. If these arms are damaged, check the mating holes in the hub for damage.
6. Inspect the final gear flange bore (B, **Figure 25**) for excessive wear, cracks or other damage.
7. Inspect the damper holder plate (**Figure 26**) for cracks, warpage or other damage. Replace the plate if necessary.
8. Discard the damper holder plate mounting bolts (**Figure 26**), as new bolts must be installed during reassembly.

Wheel Bearing Removal

1. Remove the seal and final gear flange as described under *Disassembly* in this section.

> *NOTE*
> *Step 2 describes two methods of removing the rear wheel bearings. Step 2A is recommended by Honda and will require the use of the Kowa Seiki Wheel Bearing Remover set. Step 2B describes how to remove the bearings with a drift and hammer.*

2A. To remove the wheel bearings (**Figure 17**) with the Kowa Seiki Wheel Bearing Remover set:

> *NOTE*
> *The Kowa Seiki Wheel Bearing Remover set shown in **Figure 27** is available from K & L Supply Co., in Santa Clara, CA. You can order this tool set through your Honda dealership.*

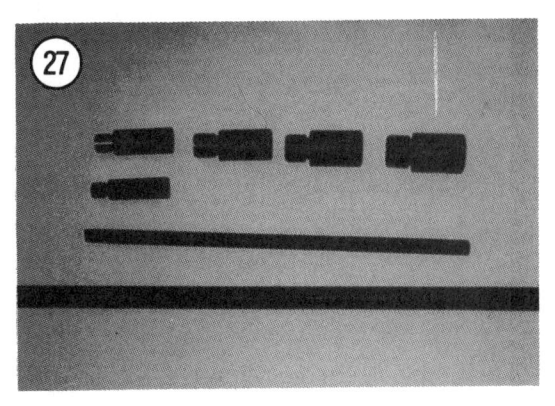

CHAPTER TWELVE

NOTE
Figure 28 *shows a cutaway of a typical hub and how the bearing tools mount into the bearing to be removed.*

a. Select the correct size remover head tool and insert it into one of the wheel bearings (**Figure 29**).

b. From the opposite side of the hub, insert the remover shaft into the slot in the backside of the remover head (**Figure 30**). Then position the hub with the remover head tool resting against a solid surface and strike the remover shaft to force it into the slit in the remover head. See **Figure 28**.

c. Position the hub and strike the end of the remover shaft with a hammer (**Figure 30**) and drive the bearing out of the hub. Remove the bearing and tool. Release the remover head from the bearing.

d. Remove the distance collar from the hub.

e. Repeat to remove the opposite bearing.

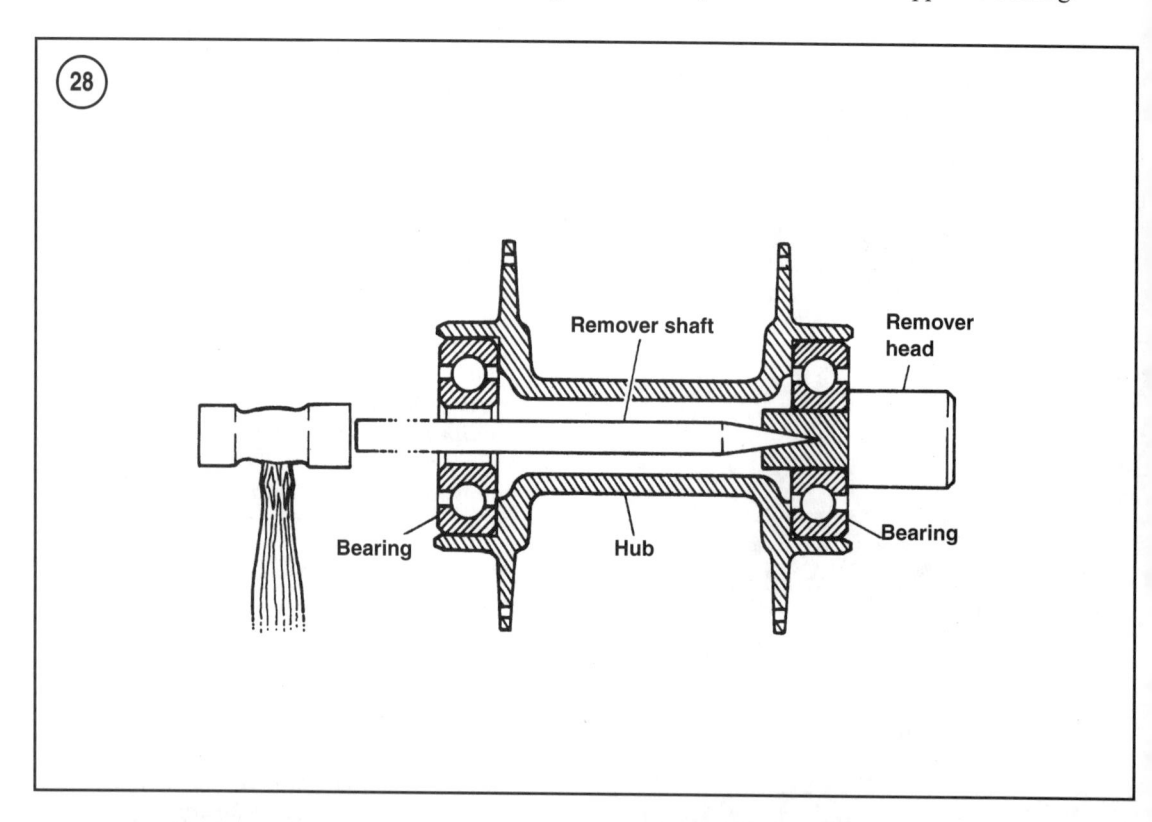

REAR SUSPENSION

2B. To remove the wheel bearings without special tools:

   a. Using a long drift, tilt the center hub spacer away from one side of the right side bearing (**Figure 31**).

> *NOTE*
> *You may have to grind a clearance groove in the drift to enable it to contact the bearing while clearing the spacer.*

   b. Tap the bearing out of the hub with a hammer, working around the perimeter of the bearing's inner race.

   c. Remove the distance collar from the hub.

   d. Remove the opposite bearing with a bearing driver.

   e. Inspect the distance collar and hub bore for burrs created during removal. Remove burrs with a file.

3. Clean and dry the hub and distance collar.

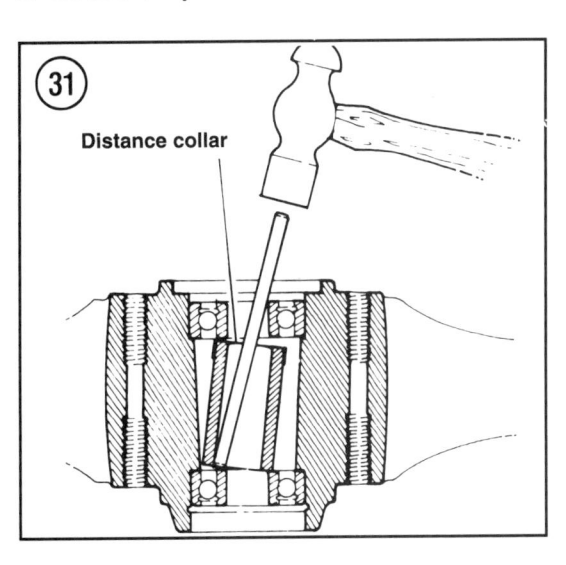

4. Discard the bearings and seal.

Wheel Bearing Installation

Before installing the new bearings and oil seal, note the following:

   a. The left and right side bearings are different. The critical dimensions are as follows: left side bearing ($20 \times 47 \times 20.6$ mm); right side bearing ($20 \times 47 \times 14$ mm).

   b. Install each bearing with its manufacturer's number and code markings facing out.

   c. When grease is called for in the following steps, use a lithium-based multipurpose grease (NLGI#2) or equivalent.

> *WARNING*
> *Do not install bearings that were previously removed from the hub.*

1. Blow any dirt or foreign matter out of the hub before installing the bearings.

2. If the bearing has an open side, pack it with grease. Double sealed bearings do not require lubrication.

3. Place the right side bearing squarely against the bore opening. Select a driver with an outside diameter just a little smaller than the bearing's outside diameter. Then drive the bearing into the bore until it bottoms out. See **Figure 32**.

4. Turn the wheel over and install the distance collar. Center it against the right side bearing's center race.

5. Place the left side bearing squarely against the bore opening. Using the same driver as before, drive the bearing partway into the bearing bore. Then stop and check that the distance collar is still centered in the hub. If not, slide the rear axle through the hub to center the spacer with the bearing. Then remove the axle and continue installing the bearing until it bottoms out. See B, **Figure 23**.

Assembly

1. If removed, install the wheel bearings and distance collar as described in this section.

2. Lubricate the right side seal lip with grease.

3. Place the right side seal squarely against the bore opening with its closed side facing out. Then drive the seal (**Figure 33**) in the bore until it is flush with or slightly below the upper hub surface. See **Figure 34**.

4. Install the rear wheel dampers (**Figure 23**) with their OUTSIDE mark facing out.

NOTE
Always replace the rear wheel dampers as a set.

5. Pack the O-ring groove in the hub (A, **Figure 22**) with molybdenum disulfide paste.

6. Lubricate the O-ring with molybdenum disulfide paste and install it into the groove in the hub (A, **Figure 22**).

7. Install the damper holder plate (**Figure 26**) as follows:
   a. Install the damper holder plate with its OUTSIDE mark facing out.
   b. Align the damper holder plate arrow between any 2 projection tabs on the hub (**Figure 21**), then install the plate onto the hub.
   c. Turn the damper holder plate clockwise until the bolt holes in the plate align with the holes in the hub. See **Figure 35**.
   d. Install 5 new damper holder plate bolts (**Figure 20**) and tighten to the torque specification in **Table 2**.

8. Lubricate and install the final gear flange assembly as follows:
   a. Apply 3 g (0.11 oz) of molybdenum disulfide paste onto the wheel hub and thrust washer mating surfaces (**Figure 36**).
   b. Install the thrust washer (**Figure 36**) onto the wheel hub surface.
   c. Lubricate the final gear flange inside bore surfaces (**Figure 25**) with molybdenum disulfide paste.
   d. Install the final gear flange assembly studs into the holes in the hub. See A, **Figure 37**.
   e. Pack the O-ring groove in the final gear flange (B, **Figure 37**) and its O-ring with molybdenum disulfide paste.
   f. Install the O-ring into its groove (B, **Figure 37**).

9. Before installing the rear wheel, check the brake disc for any grease or moly paste. If necessary, clean the brake disc with a commercial brake cleaner.

TIRE CHANGING AND TIRE REPAIRS

Refer to Chapter Eleven.

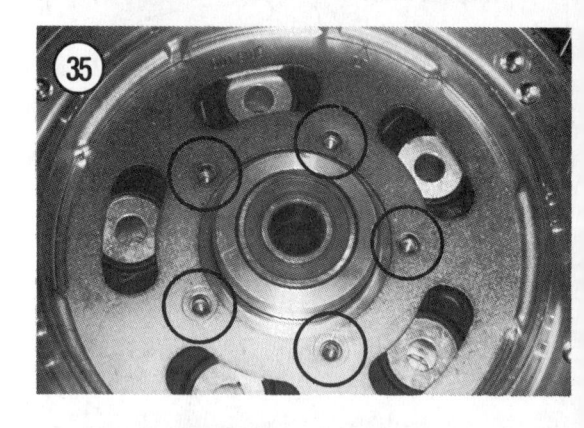

REAR SUSPENSION

RIM AND SPOKE SERVICE

Refer to *Rim and Spoke Service* in Chapter Eleven for complete service.

SHOCK ABSORBER

The shock absorbers are spring-loaded and hydraulically-damped. Each shock has 5 adjustment positions for different riding and load conditions.

The shocks are sealed and cannot be disassembled or rebuilt. Service is limited to replacing the shock mount dampers.

Adjustment

Each shock absorber can be adjusted to any of 5 spring preload settings. The softest setting is No. 1 and the stiffest setting is No. 5. The standard factory setting is No. 2. Adjust the shock absorbers to best suit different load and riding conditions.

1. Remove the tool kit from your bike and assemble the spanner wrench and its extension bar.

CAUTION
Always adjust the shock absorber in single increment numbers. For example, if the shock is in position No. 2 and you want to go to position No. 5, turn the adjuster to the No., 3, No. 4 and then to position No. 5. Do not turn the adjuster directly from the No. 2 to the No. 5 position without stopping at the other adjustment numbers or you can damage the shock absorber.

2. Using the pin spanner, adjust the shock absorber to the desired adjustment position (**Figure 38**).

WARNING
Both shock absorbers must be adjusted to the same position. If they are set to different settings, it will result in an

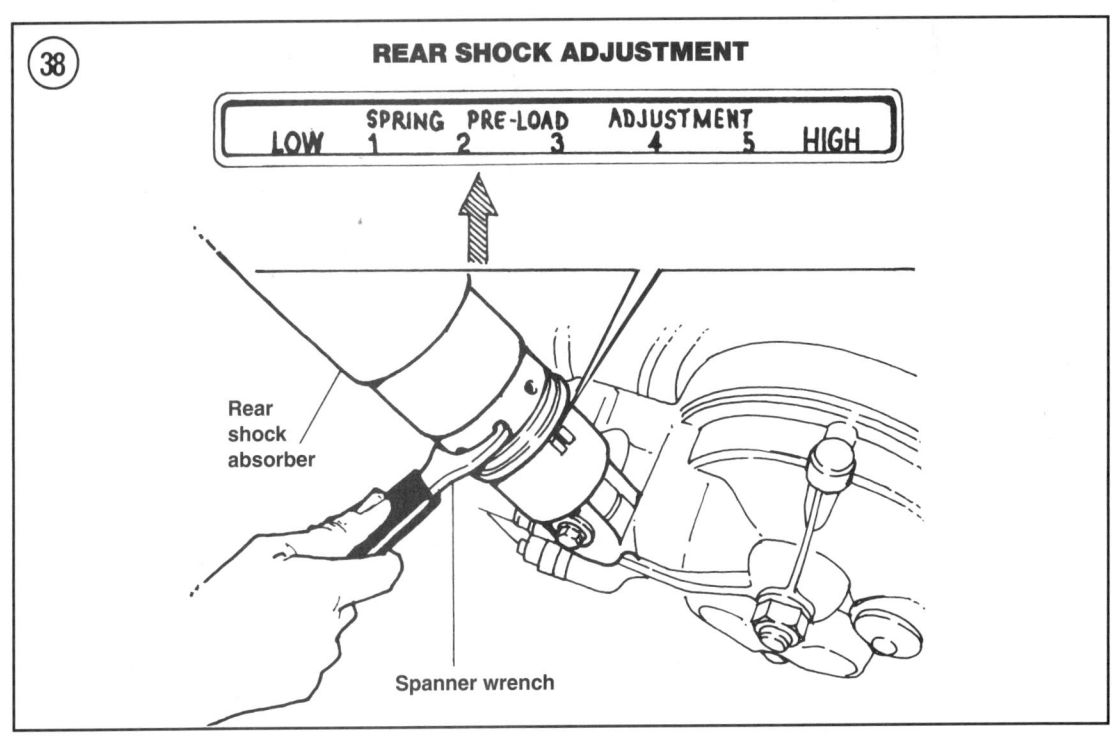

unsafe riding condition that could lead to an accident.

Shock Absorber Removal/Installation

1. Support the bike on a workstand so that the rear wheel clears the ground.
2. Remove the seat (Chapter Fourteen).
3. Before removing the right side shock absorber, loosen all of the muffler fasteners to provide clearance for removing the lower shock mounting bolt (**Figure 39**). Refer to Chapter Fourteen.

NOTE
*The left and right side shock absorbers (**Figure 40**) are different. Identify the shock absorbers before removing them in the following steps.*

4. Remove the upper and lower shock mounting bolts (**Figure 41**) and remove the shock absorber.
5. Inspect the shock absorber as described in this section.
6. Install the shock absorber with its adjustment decal facing toward the back of the bike.
7. Install and tighten the mounting bolts (**Figure 41**) to the torque specification in **Table 2**.
8. After installing the right side shock absorber, tighten the muffler fasteners as described in Chapter Fourteen.
9. Install the seat (Chapter Fourteen).

Shock Inspection

1. Inspect the shock absorber (**Figure 42**) for oil leaks or other damage. Replace the shock absorber if it is leaking.
2. Inspect the upper and lower shock dampers (**Figure 42**) for severe wear, age deterioration or other damage. Replace the shock dampers with a press. The left and right lower shock bushings are different (**Figure 40**); identify the bushings before removing them.

FINAL GEARCASE AND DRIVE SHAFT

Refer to **Figure 43** when servicing the final gearcase and drive shaft in this section.

Removal

1. Drain the final gear oil (Chapter Three).

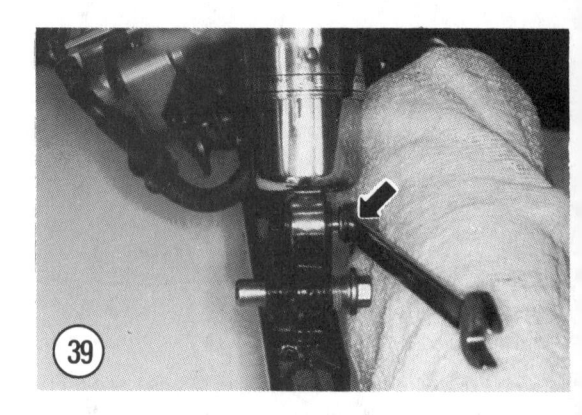

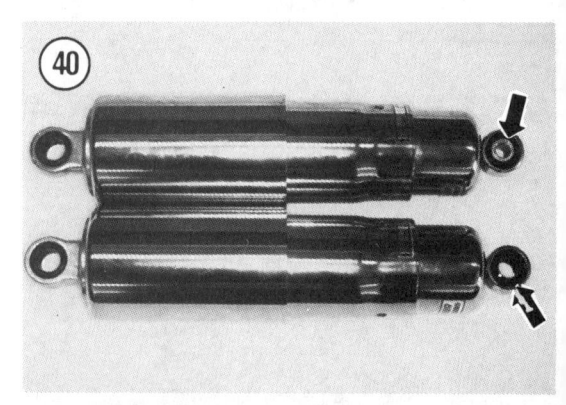

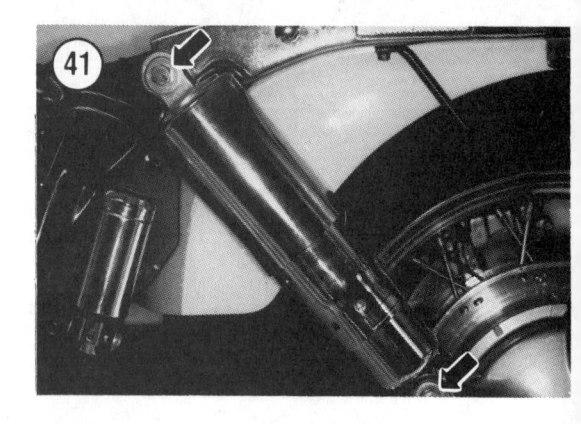

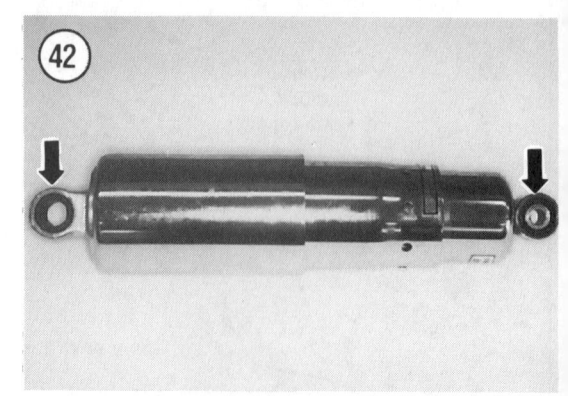

REAR SUSPENSION

2. Remove the rear wheel as described in this chapter.
3. Remove the left side shock absorber mounting bolts and remove the shock absorber.
4. Remove the nuts (A, **Figure 44**) securing the final gearcase to the swing arm.
5. Pull the final gearcase (B, **Figure 44**) back and remove it and the drive shaft from the swing arm. See **Figure 45**.
6. To remove the drive shaft, hold onto the final gearcase, then turn and pull the drive shaft out (**Figure 46**).
7. Remove the spring (A, **Figure 47**), stopper ring (B, **Figure 47**) and seal (C, **Figure 47**) from the drive shaft. Discard the stopper ring and seal as new ones must be installed during installation.

Inspection

Disassembly and assembly of the final gearcase (**Figure 48**) requires a considerable number of special Honda tools. The price of these tools exceeds the cost of most repairs on the final gearcase performed

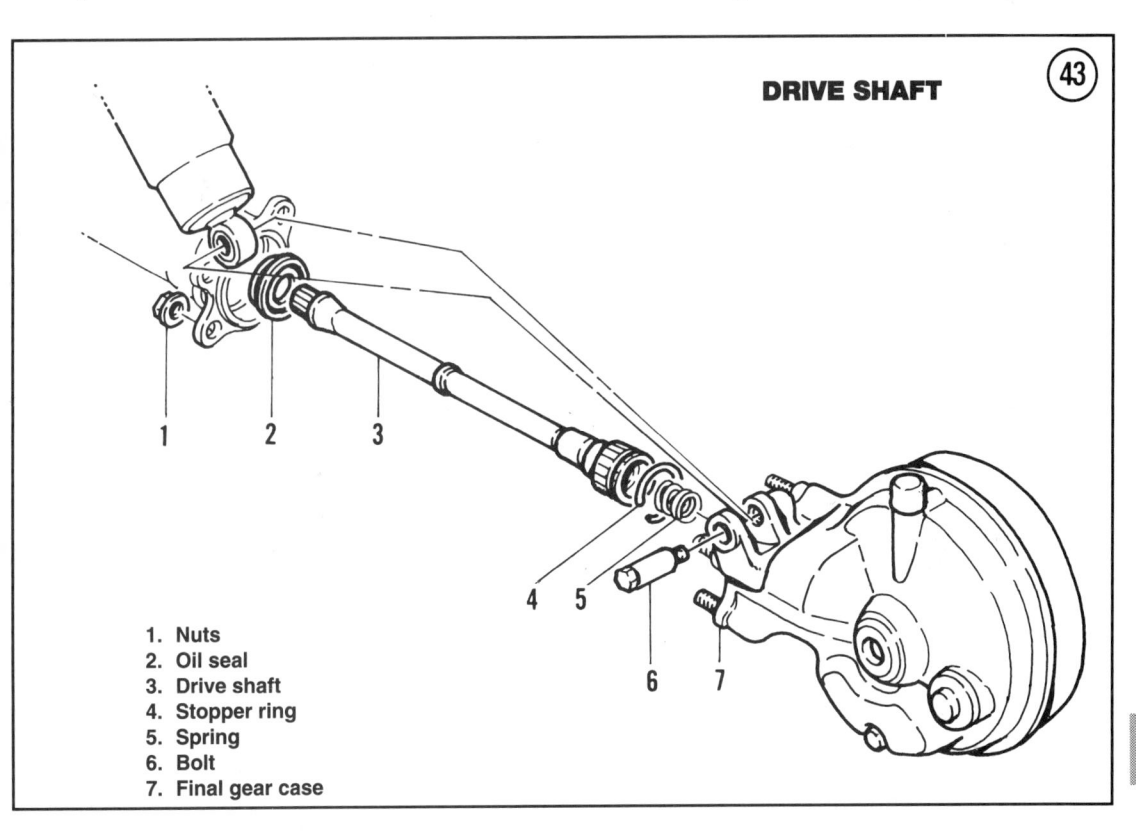

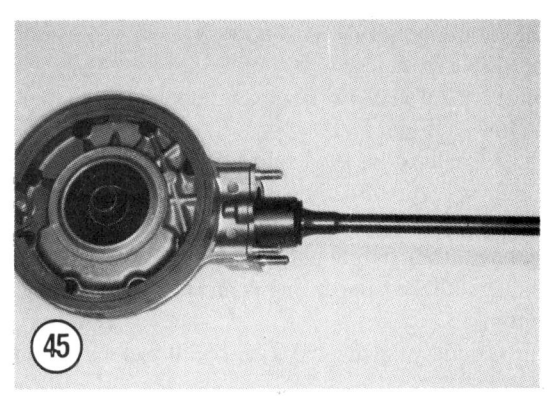

DRIVE SHAFT (43)

1. Nuts
2. Oil seal
3. Drive shaft
4. Stopper ring
5. Spring
6. Bolt
7. Final gear case

(44)

(45)

at a Honda dealership. Refer final gear service to a Honda dealership.
1. Clean and dry the drive shaft and spring.
2. Check the drive shaft (**Figure 49**) for damage and fatigue.
3. Inspect the front and rear splines (**Figure 49**). If they are worn or damaged, replace the drive shaft. If these splines are damaged, also inspect the splines in the universal joint and the final gearcase.

NOTE
To inspect and service the universal joint, remove the swing arm as described in this chapter.

4. Replace the spring (A, **Figure 47**) if cracked or damaged in any way.
5. Remove the distance collar (**Figure 50**) and inspect it for cracks or excessive wear. Install the distance collar—machined end first (**Figure 50**)—into the final gearcase.
6. Check the 4 final gearcase studs (A, **Figure 51**) for looseness or damage. If you must tighten or replace a stud, note the following:
   a. To tighten a loose stud, first remove it from the final gearcase. Then remove all thread sealer residue from the stud and case threads.
   b. Apply a medium strength threadlocking compound onto the threads of the stud and install the stud to the dimension shown in **Figure 52**.

Installation

Use molybdenum disulfide grease when grease is called for in the following steps.
1. Install a new stopper ring (B, **Figure 47**) into the drive shaft groove.
2. Pack the lips of a new seal with grease. Then install the seal (C, **Figure 47**) so its closed side faces away from the stopper ring.
3. Install the spring (A, **Figure 47**) into the end of the drive shaft.
4. Pack 2 g (0.08 oz) of grease into the pinion joint spline (B, **Figure 51**).
5. Align the drive shaft splines with the pinion joint splines (**Figure 46**), then install the drive shaft until its stopper ring seats into the pinion joint spline groove. Then lightly pull back on the drive shaft to make sure the stopper ring is properly seated in the groove.
6. Carefully tap the seal (**Figure 53**) into the pinion joint.

7. Pack 1 g (0.04 oz) of grease into the drive shaft splines.
8. Insert the drive shaft through the swing arm and engage it with the universal joint splines. Push the gearcase (B, **Figure 44**) studs through the holes in the swing arm.
9. Install the nuts (A, **Figure 44**) and tighten finger-tight.

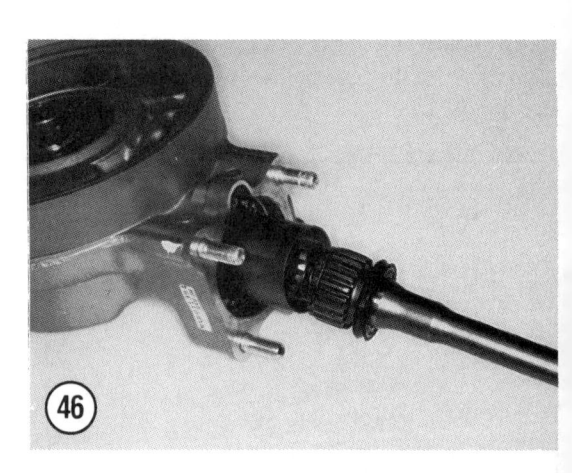

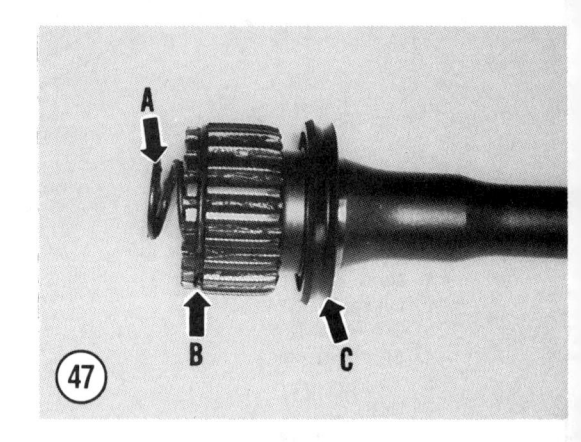

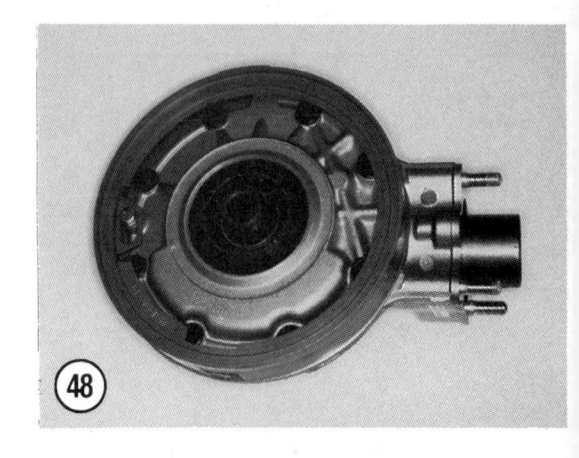

REAR SUSPENSION

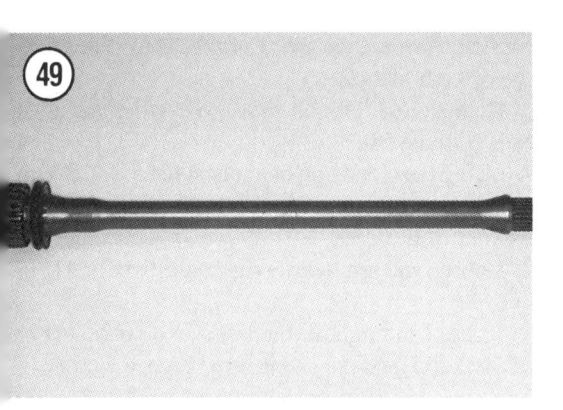

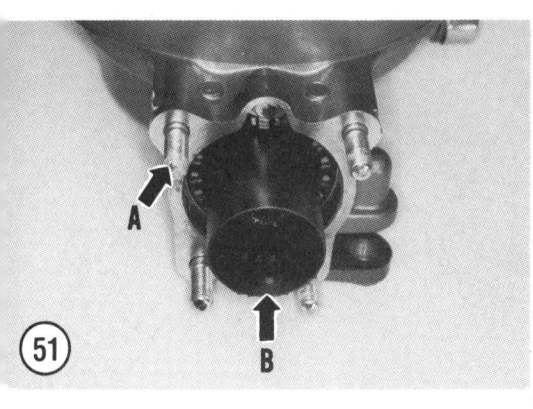

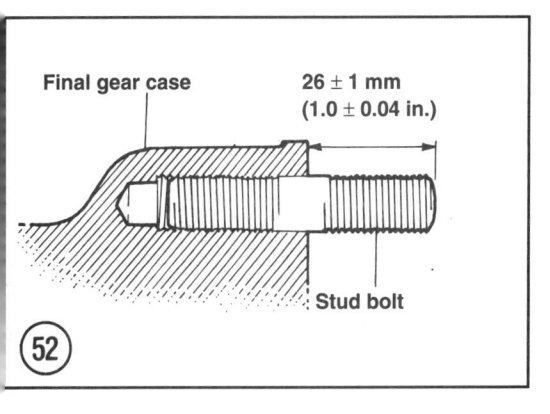

NOTE
*Do not tighten the final gearcase mounting nuts (A, **Figure 44**) until after you install the rear wheel and tighten the rear axle. This sequence is described under **Rear Wheel Installation** in this chapter.*

10. Install the rear wheel as described in this chapter.
11. Install the left side shock absorber as described in this chapter.
12. Refill the final gearcase with oil as described in Chapter Three.

REAR SWING ARM

This section describes complete service for the rear swing arm. Refer to **Figure 54** when servicing the swing arm in the following steps.

Service Note

Along with your normal hand tools, you need the following 2 tools to remove and install the swing arm:

   a. Honda pivot adjust wrench (part No. KS-HBA-08-469). See A, **Figure 55**.
   b. 17 mm socket bit. See B, **Figure 55**.

Removal

1. Remove the rear wheel as described in this chapter.
2. Remove the rear shock absorbers as described in this chapter.
3. Remove the final gearcase as described in this chapter.
4. Remove the front and rear (**Figure 56**) brake clamps from the rear swing arm.

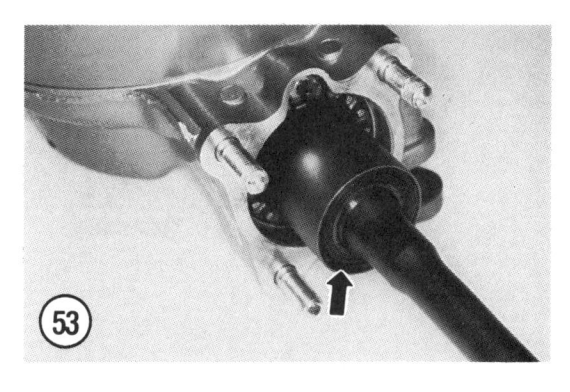

NOTE
Have an assistant steady the bike when performing Step 5.

5. Grasp the rear end of the swing arm (**Figure 57**) and try to move it from side to side in a horizontal arc. There must be no noticeable side play. Then grasp the rear of the swing arm once again and pivot it up and down through its full travel. The swing arm must pivot smoothly with no roughness or binding. If play is evident and the pivot bolts are tightened correctly, inspect the swing arm bearings for excessive wear or damage.

6. Remove the left and right side swing arm pivot caps (**Figure 58**).
7. Using the Honda pivot adjust wrench (A, **Figure 55**), loosen and remove the right side pivot bolt locknut (**Figure 59**).
8. Loosen and remove the right side pivot bolt (**Figure 60**).
9. Loosen and remove the left side pivot bolt (**Figure 61**) and then the swing arm (**Figure 57**).

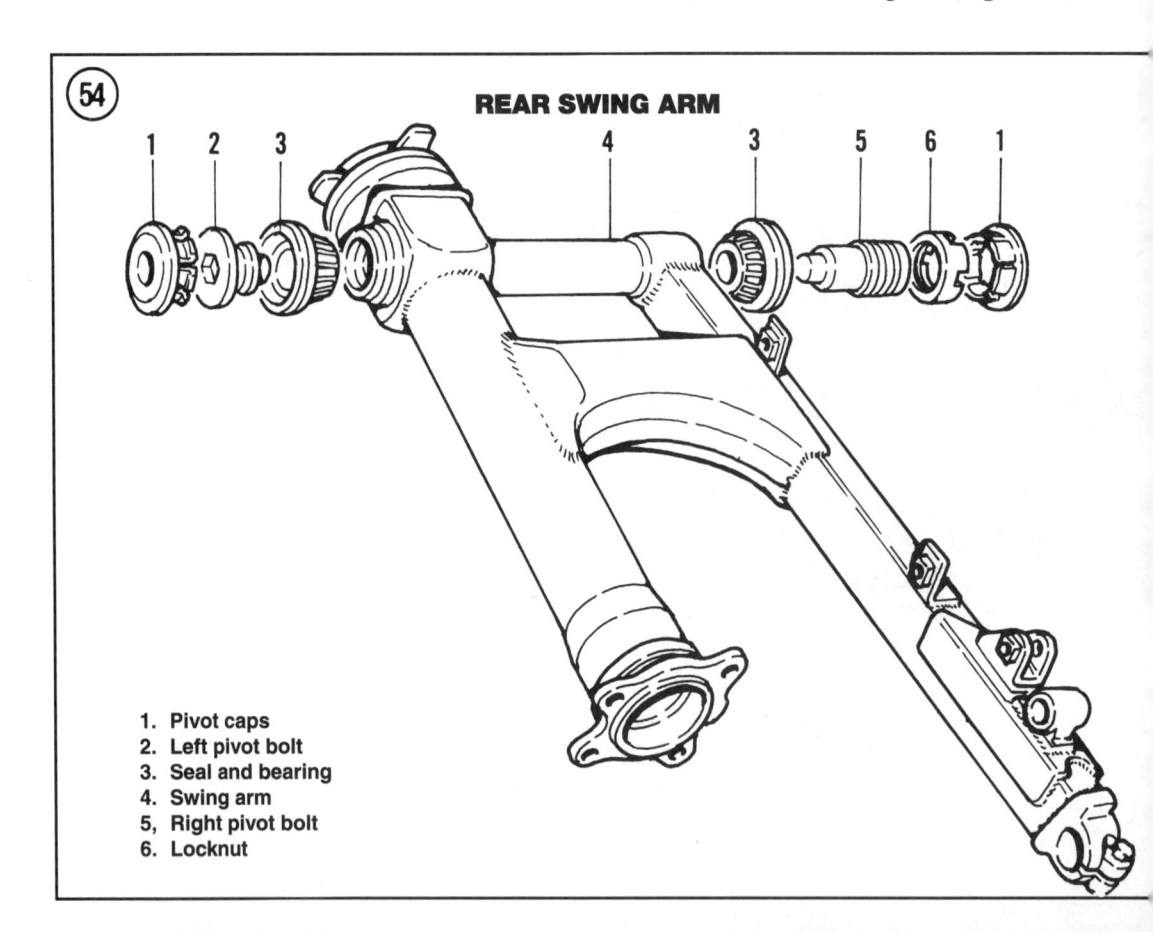

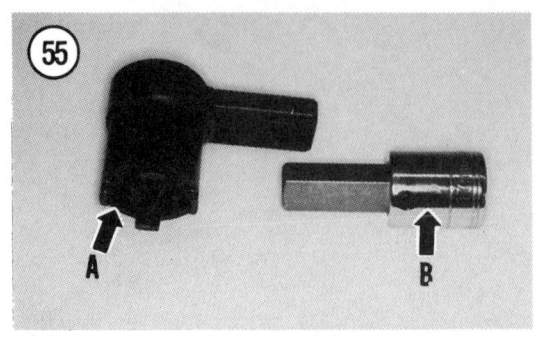

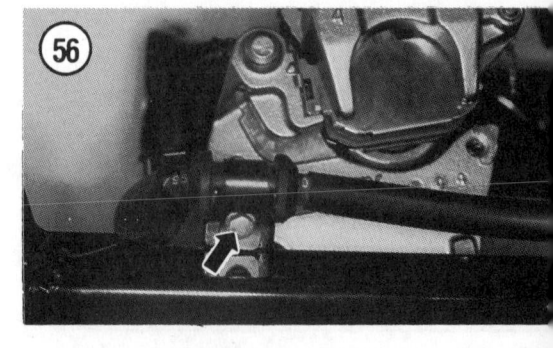

54

REAR SWING ARM

1. Pivot caps
2. Left pivot bolt
3. Seal and bearing
4. Swing arm
5, Right pivot bolt
6. Locknut

REAR SUSPENSION

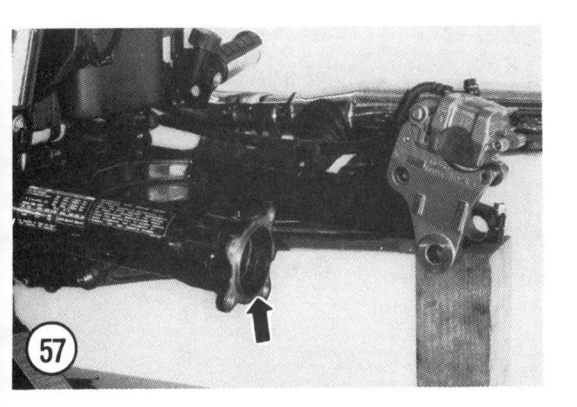

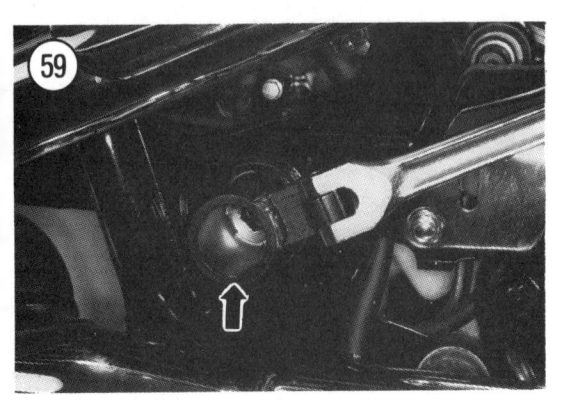

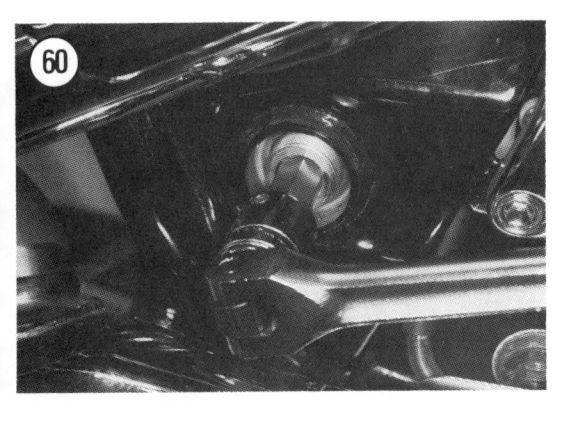

10. Remove the universal joint (**Figure 62**) from the swing arm.
11. Remove the rear brake caliper bracket stopper pin bolt from the swing arm.

NOTE
If the bearings are going to be reused, they must be installed in their original positions. Identify each bearing to avoid mixing them up during reassembly.

12. Remove the left and right side bearings and dust seals (**Figure 63**) from the swing arm.

Swing Arm Inspection

1. Clean and dry the swing arm and its components.
2. Inspect the welded sections on the swing arm (**Figure 64**) for cracks or other damage.
3. Replace the bearing dust seals (**Figure 65**) if worn or damaged.
4. Inspect each bearing (**Figure 66**) and its race (A, **Figure 67**) for wear, pitting or other damage. If necessary, replace the bearings and races as described under *Bearing Replacement* in this section.
5. Make sure each grease retainer plate (B, **Figure 67**) fits tightly in its swing arm bore.

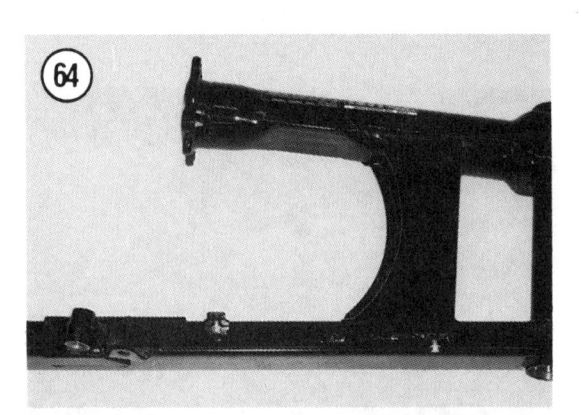

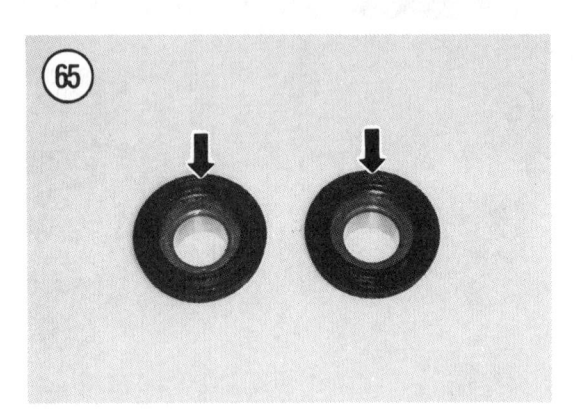

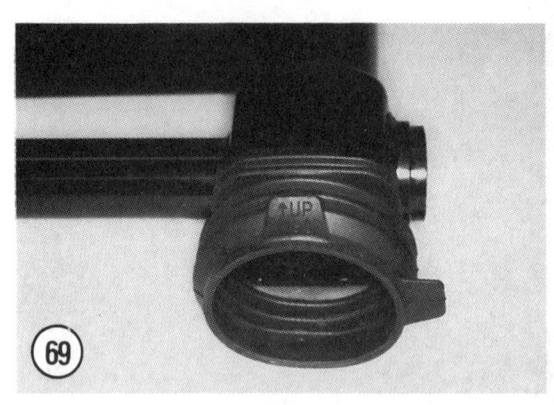

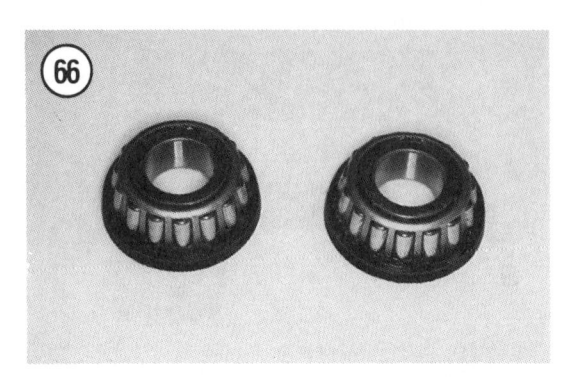

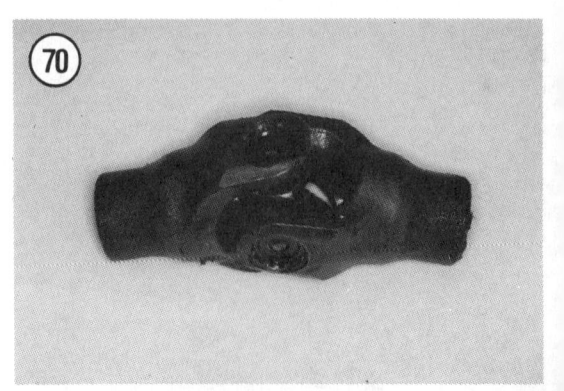

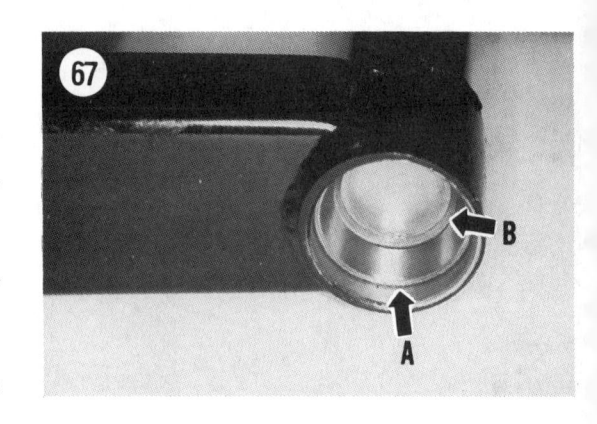

REAR SUSPENSION

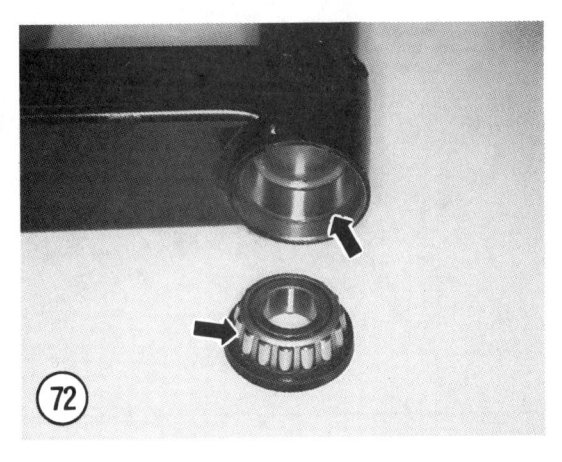

6. Inspect the pivot bolts (**Figure 68**) for excessive wear, thread damage or corrosion. Make sure the machined end on each pivot bolt is smooth. Replace if necessary.
7. Replace the boot (**Figure 69**) if damaged.

Universal Joint Inspection

1. Check that the universal joint (**Figure 70**) pivots smoothly.
2. Inspect both universal joint spline ends of damage. If these splines are damaged, inspect the final drive case and engine output shaft splines for damage.

Bearing Replacement

You must replace the left (**Figure 71**) and right (**Figure 72**) side bearings and races at the same time.
Refer to **Figure 73**.
1. Drill a suitable-size hole through one of the grease retainer plates (**Figure 74**).
2. Insert a drift through this hole (**Figure 75**) and drive out the opposite bearing race and grease retainer plate. See **Figure 76**.
3. Repeat Step 2 to remove the opposite bearing race and grease retainer.

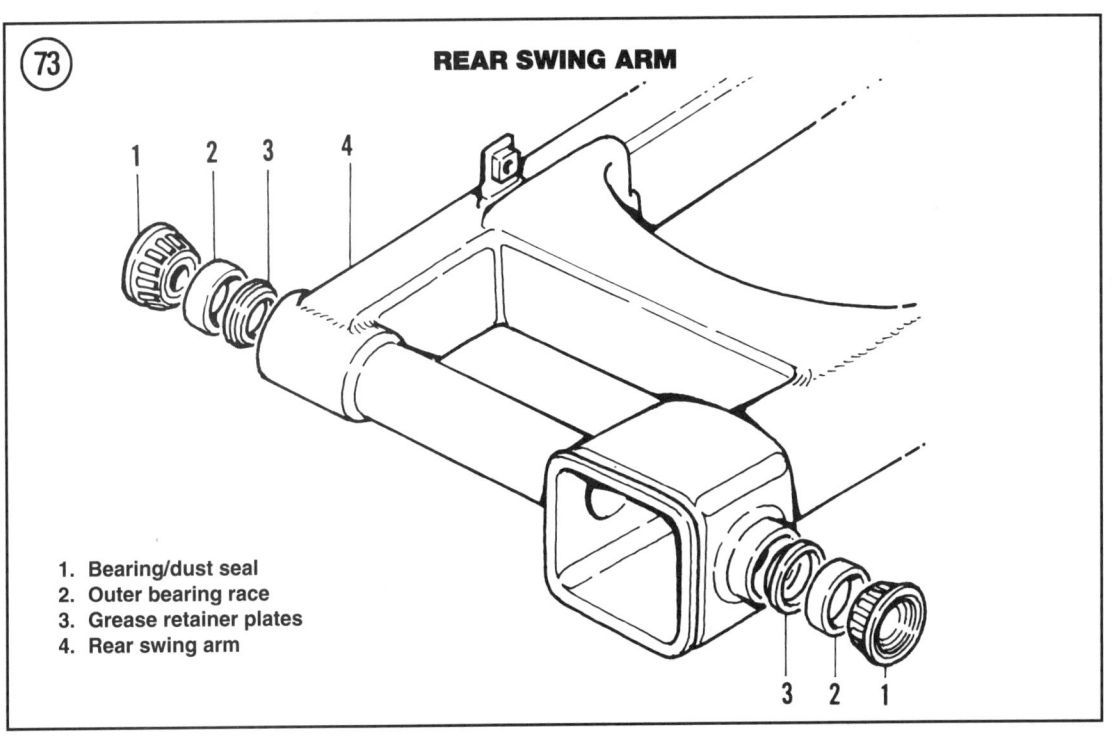

⑦

⑫

㊆ **REAR SWING ARM**

1. Bearing/dust seal
2. Outer bearing race
3. Grease retainer plates
4. Rear swing arm

4. Drive a new grease retainer and bearing race (**Figure 77**) into each side of the swing arm.
5. Lubricate each bearing race with grease.

Installation

1. Remove the left crankcase rear cover as described in Chapter Five.
2. Install the boot onto the swing arm with its UP mark facing up (**Figure 69**).
3. Lubricate the bearing races and bearings (**Figure 71** and **Figure 72**) with grease.
4. Install the left (**Figure 78**) and right (**Figure 79**) side bearings and dust seals into the swing arm.
5. Install a new rear brake caliper stopper pin bolt (**Figure 80**) into the swing arm.
6. Install the universal joint partway into the swing arm (**Figure 81**).
7. Remove the drive shaft (**Figure 82**) from the final gearcase as described in this chapter. Then insert the drive shaft through the swing arm (**Figure 83**) and engage it with the universal joint.
8. Lubricate the output driven gear shaft splines (**Figure 84**) with molybdenum disulfide paste.

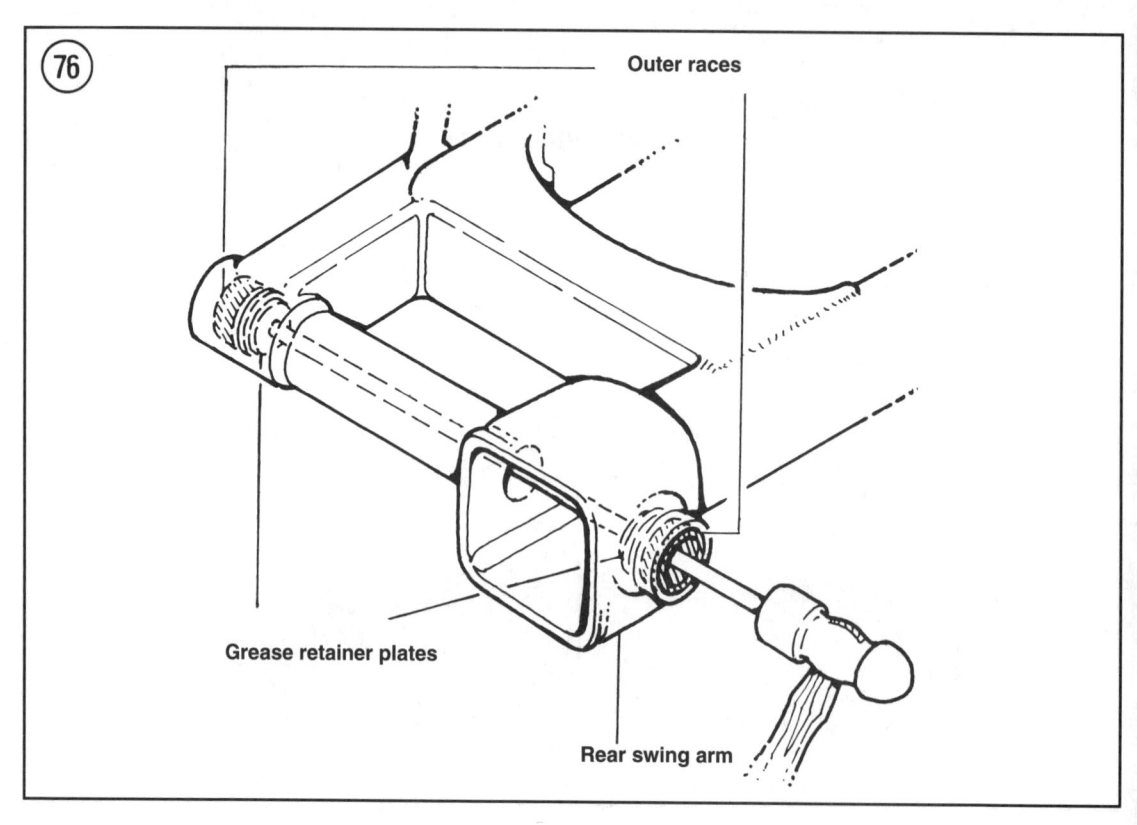

REAR SUSPENSION

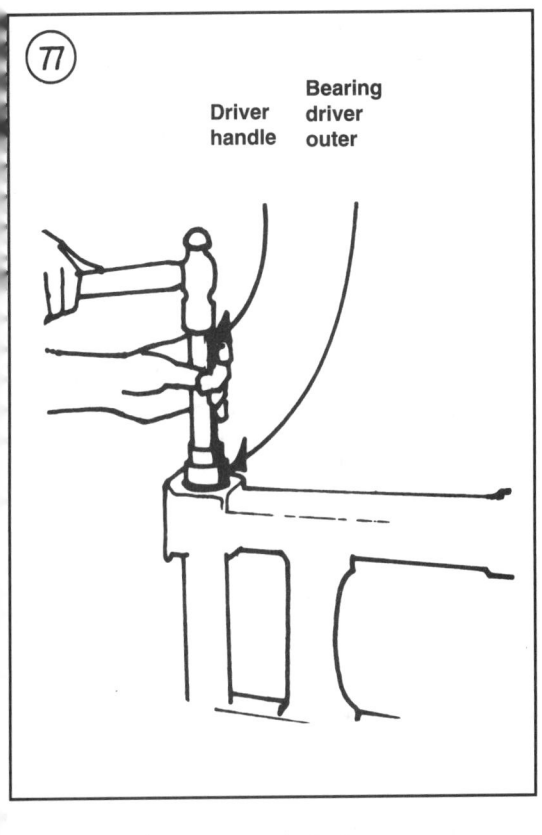

9. Install the swing arm into the frame, while noting the following:

   a. Install the left side swing arm pivot flange into the frame hole, then install the left side pivot bolt (**Figure 61**).

   b. Turn the drive shaft to engage the universal joint with the engine output shaft splines. Then remove the drive shaft.

   c. Install the right side swing arm pivot bolt (**Figure 60**).

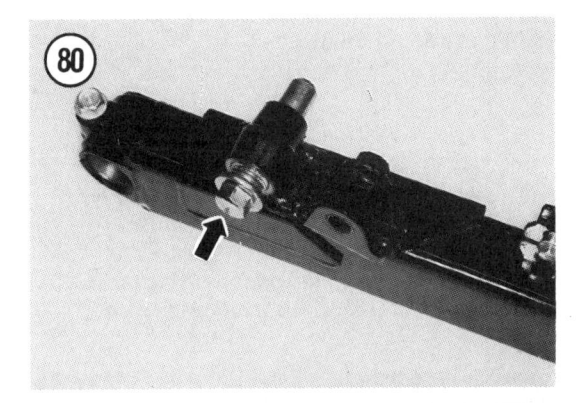

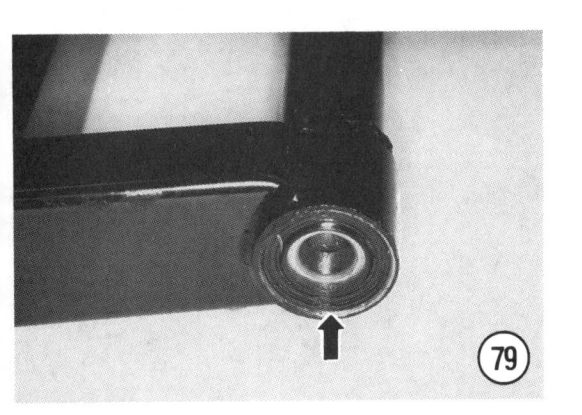

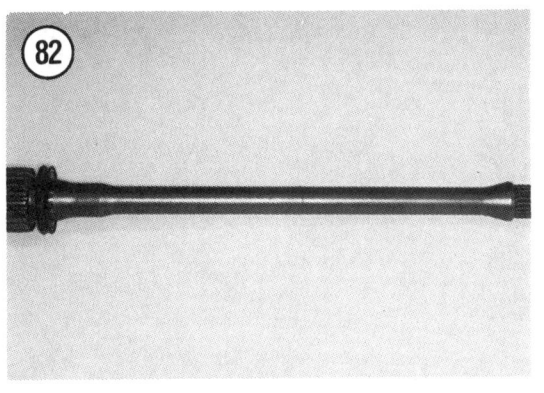

10. Install the boot over the output gear case on the engine.

11. Tighten the left side pivot bolt (**Figure 61**) to the torque specification in **Table 2**.

12. Tighten the right side pivot bolt (**Figure 60**) to the torque specification in **Table 2**.

13. Pivot the swing arm up and down several times to help seat the pivot bearings.

14. Retighten the right side pivot bolt (**Figure 60**) to the torque specification in **Table 2**.

15. Install the right side pivot bolt locknut (**Figure 85**) and tighten it with the Honda pivot adjust wrench (A, **Figure 55**) as follows:

NOTE
Because the Honda pivot adjust wrench effectively lengthens the torque wrench, the torque value set on the torque wrench will not be the same amount of torque applied to the fastener. Before using a horizontal adapter you must recalculate the torque reading. To recalculate the torque reading, use the information supplied with your torque wrench..

  a. Hold the right side pivot bolt with a 17 mm socket (A, **Figure 86**).
  b. Tighten the right side pivot bolt locknut with the Honda pivot adjust wrench and a torque wrench as specified in **Table 2**.

16. Install the left and right side swing arm pivot caps.

17. Install the front and rear brake hose clamps onto the swing arm and secure them with new bolts. Tighten the brake hose clamp bolts to the torque specification in **Table 2**.

18. Install the left crankcase cover (Chapter Five).

19. Install the drive shaft and final gear case as described in this chapter.

20. Install the rear shock absorbers as described in this chapter.

21. Check that the battery breather tube and air filter drain tubes are connected to the frame clamp.

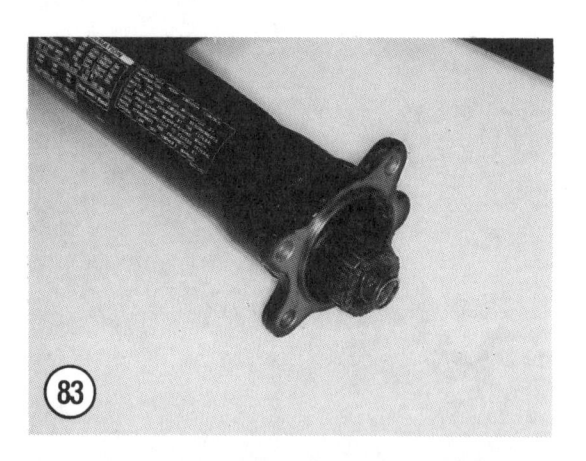

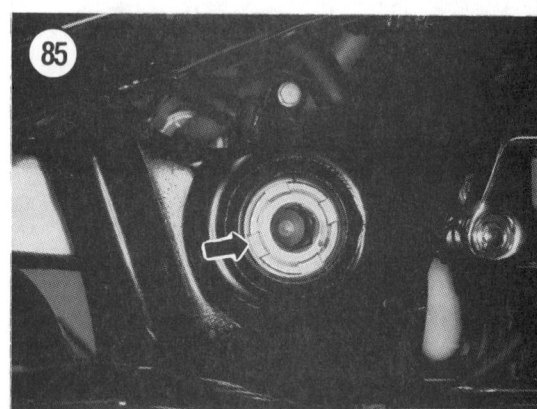

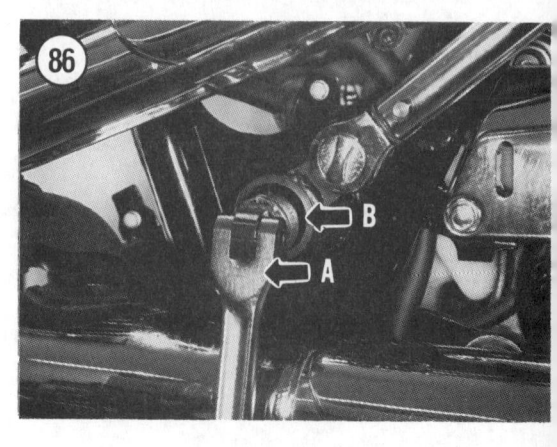

REAR SUSPENSION

Table 1 REAR SUSPENSION SPECIFICATIONS

Axle runout	0.20 mm (0.008 in.)
Rear wheel runout	
Axial	2.0 mm (0.08 in.)
Radial	2.0 mm (0.08 in.)
Rear wheel travel	100 mm (3.9 in.)
Shock absorber	
Standard adjustment position	No. 2
Wheel balance weight (maximum)	60 g (2.1 oz.)

Table 2 REAR SUSPENSION TIGHTENING TORQUES

	N•m	in.-lb.	ft.-lb.
Brake hose clamp bolts (at swing arm)	12	106	—
Damper holder plate bolt	20	—	14
Final gear case mounting nuts	65	—	47
Rear axle nut	90	—	66
Rear axle pinch bolt	27	—	20
Rear brake hose clamp bolt	12	106	—
Shock absorber			
Upper mounting bolt	27	—	20
Lower mounting bolt			
Left side	23	—	17
Right side	35	—	25
Spoke nipples	4.3	38	—
Swing arm right side pivot bolt locknut	115	—	85
Swing arm pivot bolts			
Left side	105	—	77
Right side	18	—	13
Valve stem nut	2.8	—	—

CHAPTER THIRTEEN

BRAKES

This chapter describes service procedures for the front and rear disc brakes.

Tables 1-4 (end of chapter) list front and rear brake specifications and tightening torques.

BRAKE FLUID SELECTION

Use DOT 4 brake fluid in the front and rear brakes.

PREVENTING BRAKE FLUID DAMAGE

Brake fluid will damage most surfaces that it comes in contact with. To prevent brake fluid damage when working on your Honda, note the following:
1. Before you perform any procedure in which there is the possibility of brake fluid contacting your motorcycle, cover the area in which you will be working with a large piece of plastic. It only take a few drops of brake fluid to damage an expensive chromed or painted part.
2. Before handling brake fluid or working on the brake system, fill a bucket with soap and water and keep it close to the bike as you work on it. If you do spill brake fluid on your bike, clean the area with the soapy water and a soft cloth.

DISC BRAKE

The front and rear disc brakes are actuated by hydraulic fluid and controlled by a hand or foot lever on the master cylinder. As the brake pads wear, the brake fluid level drops in the reservoir and automatically compensates for brake lining wear.

When working on the brake system, the work area and all tools must be absolutely clean. Any tiny particles of foreign matter and grit in the caliper assembly or master cylinder can damage the components.

Consider the following when servicing the disc brakes.
1. Do not allow disc brake fluid to contact any plastic parts or painted surfaces as damage will result.
2. Always keep the master cylinder reservoir and spare cans of brake fluid closed to prevent dust or moisture from entering. This would result in brake fluid contamination and brake failure.
3. Use disc brake fluid to wash and lubricate parts. Never clean any internal brake components with solvent or any other petroleum base cleaner.
4. Whenever you loosen any brake hose banjo bolt or brake line nut, the brake system is considered opened. You must bleed the system to remove air

BRAKES

FRONT BRAKE PADS

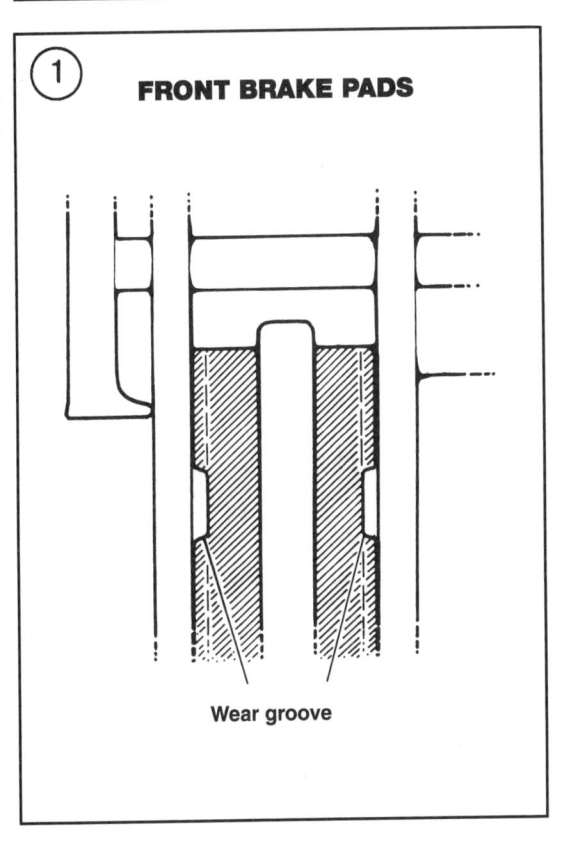

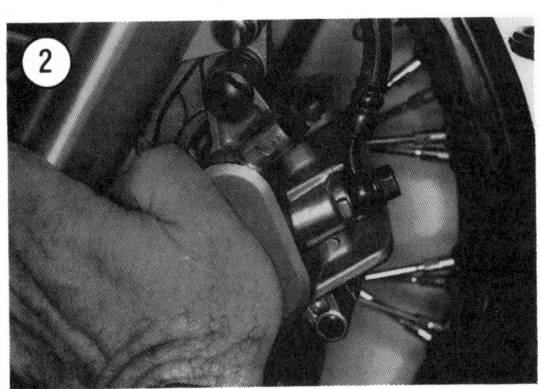

Wear groove

bubbles. Also, if the brake feels spongy, this usually means there is air in the system. To bleed the brakes, refer to *Brake Bleeding* in this chapter

CAUTION
Do not reuse brake fluid. Contaminated brake fluid can cause brake failure. Dispose of brake fluid according to local EPA regulations.

FRONT CALIPER

Front Brake Pad Replacement

Honda does not list an interval for replacing the front brake pads. Pad wear depends greatly on riding habits and conditions. Replace the brake pads if the pad wear indicator is worn to the edge of the brake disc (**Figure 1**).

To maintain even brake pressure on the front disc, replace both brake pads at the same time.

1. Read the information listed under *Disc Brake* in this chapter.

CAUTION
Do not allow the master cylinder reservoir to overflow when performing Step 2. Brake fluid will damage most surfaces it contacts.

2. Hold the caliper body (from the outside) and push it toward its brake disc (**Figure 2**). This will push the pistons into the caliper to make room for the new brake pads.
3. Remove the pad pin bolt plug (**Figure 3**).
4. Remove the pad pin bolt (**Figure 4**).
5. Remove the outer (A, **Figure 5**) and inner (B, **Figure 5**) brake pads.

NOTE
*Note the shim installed on the inner brake pad (**Figure 6**).*

6. Replace the pad spring (**Figure 7**) if it is damaged.
7. Inspect the brake pads (**Figure 8**) for uneven wear, damage or grease contamination. Replace both brake pads as a set.
8. Clean and inspect the pad pin plug and pin (**Figure 9**). Replace if they are damaged.

NOTE
If you detect brake fluid leaking from around the pistons, overhaul the brake caliper as described in this chapter.

9. Check the brake disc for wear as described in this chapter.
10. If removed, install the pad spring (**Figure 7**) onto the caliper body.

NOTE
***Figure 10** shows the pad spring installed into the caliper body with the caliper removed for clarity.*

11. Install the pad shim (**Figure 6**) onto the back of the inner brake pad.

WARNING
Do not use grease to hold the pad shim in place. Heat will thin the grease and cause it to run onto the brake pads and disc.

NOTE
The friction material on both brake pads must face against the brake disc.

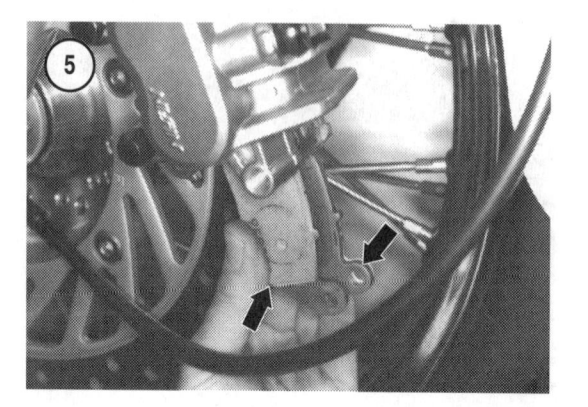

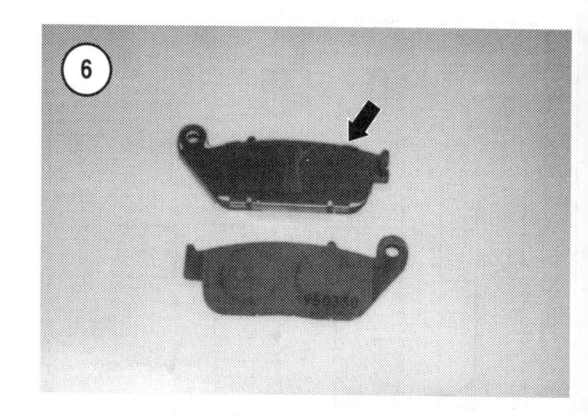

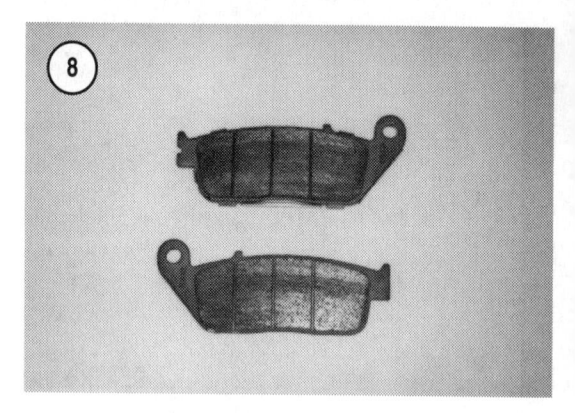

BRAKES

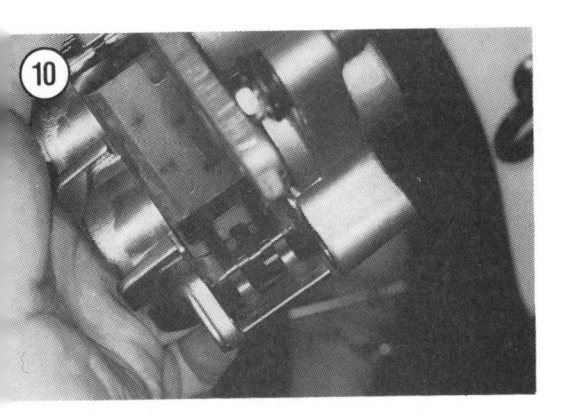

NOTE
After installing the brake pads in the following steps, make sure their ends rest on the pad spring.

12. Install the outer brake pad (**Figure 11**) into the caliper and hold it in place.
13. Install the pad pin through the outer brake pad (**Figure 4**).
14. Install the inner brake pad and its shim into the caliper (**Figure 12**), then install the pad pin through it. See **Figure 13**.
15. Tighten the pad pin (**Figure 4**) to the torque specification in **Table 3**.
16. Tighten the pad pin plug (**Figure 3**) to the torque specification in **Table 3**.
17. Operate the brake lever a few times to seat the pads against the disc, then check the brake fluid level in the reservoir. If necessary, add new DOT 4 brake fluid (Chapter Three).

WARNING
Do not ride the motorcycle until you are sure that the front brake is operating correctly with full hydraulic advantage. If necessary, bleed the front brake as described in this chapter.

Brake Caliper Removal/Installation (Caliper Will Not Be Disassembled)

To remove the caliper without disassembling it, perform this procedure. To disassemble the caliper, refer to *Caliper Removal/Piston Removal* in this chapter.

1. Drain the brake fluid from the front master cylinder as described under *Brake Fluid Draining* in this chapter.
2A. To remove the caliper, perform the following:
   a. Remove brake hose banjo bolt (A, **Figure 14**) and both washers at the caliper. Seal the hose so brake fluid cannot leak out.
   b. Remove the bolts (B, **Figure 14**) that hold the brake caliper to the fork slider. Then lift the caliper off the brake disc.
2B. To remove the brake caliper without disconnecting the brake hose, perform the following:
   a. Remove the bolts (B, **Figure 14**) that hold the brake caliper to the fork slider. Then lift the caliper off the brake disc.

b. Insert a spacer block between the brake pads.

NOTE
The spacer block will prevent the pistons from being forced out of the caliper if someone applies the front brake lever while the brake caliper is removed from the brake disc.

c. Support the caliper with a wire hook.

3. Install the caliper by reversing these steps, while noting the following.

4A. If you removed the caliper from the motorcycle, perform the following:
   a. Check that the brake pads are not contaminated with brake fluid. If they are, replace the brake pads as described in this chapter.
   b. Carefully install the caliper assembly over the brake disc. Be careful not to damage the leading edge of the pads during installation.
   c. Install the 2 brake caliper mounting bolts (B, **Figure 14**) and tighten to the torque specification in **Table 3**.
   d. Place a washer (**Figure 15**) on each side of the brake hose. Then thread the banjo bolt (A, **Figure 14**) into the caliper. Tighten the brake hose banjo bolt (A, **Figure 14**) to the torque specification in **Table 3**.

CAUTION
*After you tighten the banjo bolt, make sure the brake hose seats against the caliper as shown in **Figure 16**.*

   e. Refill the master cylinder and bleed the front brake as described in this chapter.

4B. If you did not remove the caliper from the motorcycle, perform the following:
   a. Remove the spacer block from between the brake pads.
   b. Install the caliper over the brake disc. Be careful not to damage the leading edge of the pads during installation.
   c. Install the 2 brake caliper mounting bolts (B, **Figure 14**). Then tighten the bolts to the torque specification in **Table 3**.
   d. Operate the brake lever to seat the pads against the brake disc.

WARNING
Do not ride the motorcycle until the front brake operates with full hydraulic

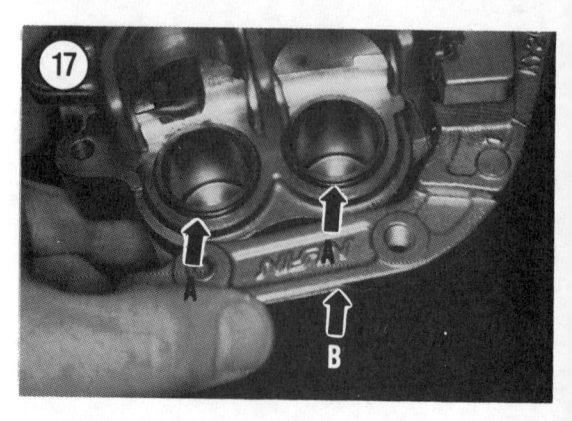

BRAKES

advantage. If necessary, bleed the front brake as described in this chapter.

Caliper Removal/Piston Removal (Caliper Will Be Disassembled)

Force is required to remove the pistons from the caliper. This procedure describes how to remove the pistons with the caliper still connected to the front brake system. If there is no hydraulic pressure in the system, remove the pistons as described under *Disassembly* in this section.

1. Remove the brake pads as described in this chapter.
2. Wrap a large cloth around the brake caliper.
3. Hold the caliper so your hand and fingers are placed away from both pistons.
4. Operate the front brake lever to force the pistons (A, **Figure 17**) as far out of the caliper as possible.

NOTE
If one or both pistons do not come out, you must remove them with compressed air. Refer to Disassembly in this section.

5. Remove the caliper banjo bolt (A, **Figure 14**) and both washers. Seal the brake hose to prevent brake fluid from leaking.
6. Take the caliper to a workbench for disassembly.

Disassembly

Refer to **Figure 18** for this procedure.

1. Remove the brake caliper as described in this chapter.

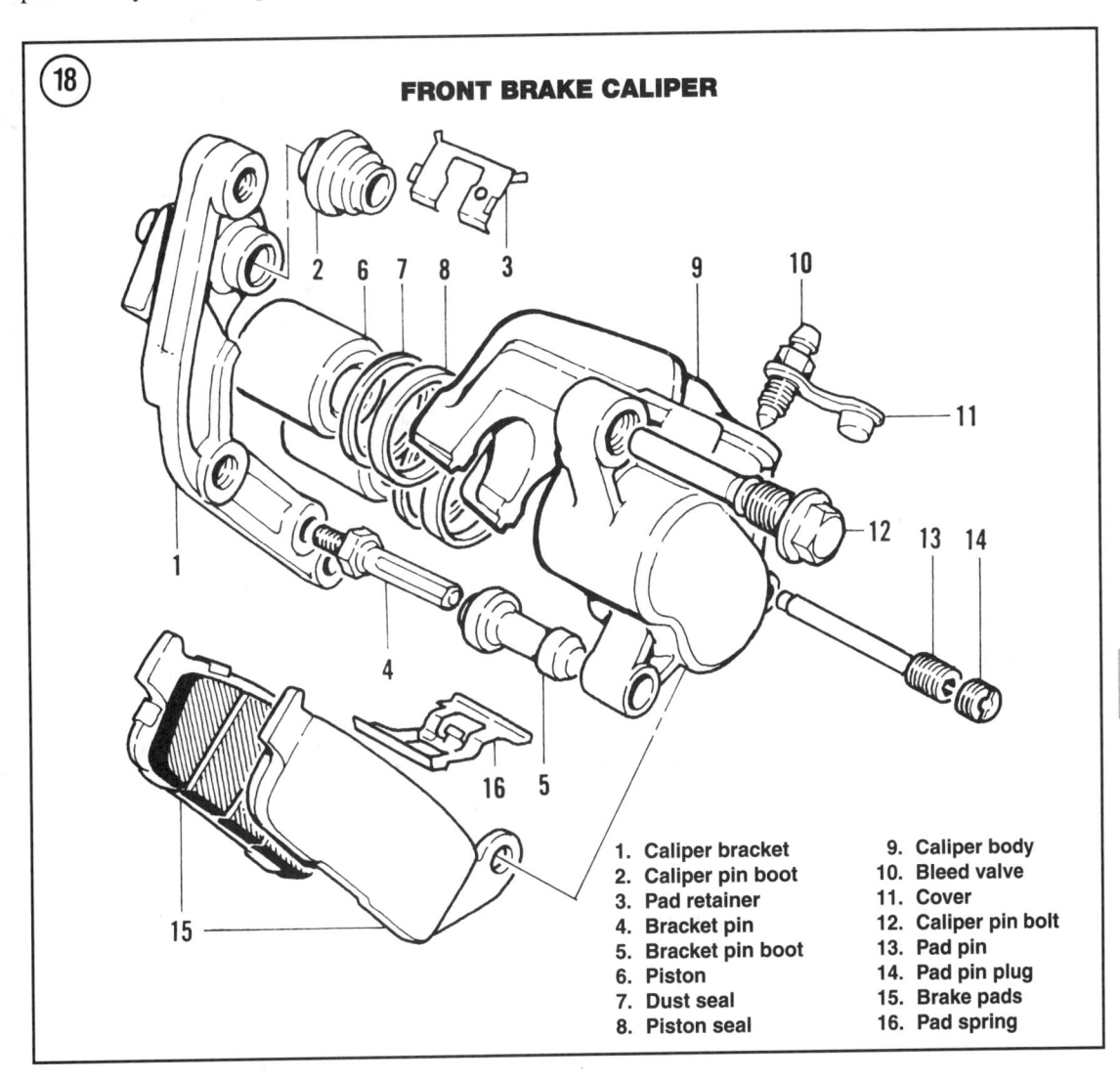

FRONT BRAKE CALIPER

1. Caliper bracket
2. Caliper pin boot
3. Pad retainer
4. Bracket pin
5. Bracket pin boot
6. Piston
7. Dust seal
8. Piston seal
9. Caliper body
10. Bleed valve
11. Cover
12. Caliper pin bolt
13. Pad pin
14. Pad pin plug
15. Brake pads
16. Pad spring

2. Slide the caliper bracket (B, **Figure 17**) out of the caliper.

WARNING
Compressed air forces the pistons out of the caliper under considerable force. Do not cushion the pistons with your fingers, as injury will result.

3. Cushion the caliper pistons with a shop rag, making sure to keep your hand away from the pistons. Then apply compressed air through the brake line port (**Figure 19**) and remove the pistons (**Figure 20**).

If only one piston is forced out, block its bore opening with a piece of thick rubber (old inner tube) or a rubber ball, then apply compressed air through the caliper again (**Figure 19**), making sure to keep your hand away from the piston.

4. Remove the dust and piston (**Figure 21**) seals from the cylinder bore grooves.
5. Remove the bleed valve and its cover from the caliper.
6. Remove the bracket pin boot from the caliper housing.

Inspection

1. Clean and dry the caliper housing and the other metal parts (**Figure 22**) with a commercially available brake cleaner.
2. Discard the dust and piston seals.
3. Check each cylinder bore (A, **Figure 23**) for deep scratches or other wear marks. Do not hone the cylinder bores.
4. Measure each cylinder bore diameter (**Figure 24**) and check against the dimension in **Table 1**. Replace the caliper if any one bore diameter exceeds the service limit.
5. Inspect the pistons for excessive wear, cracks or other damage.
6. Measure each piston outside diameter (**Figure 25**) and check against the dimension in **Table 1**. Replace the piston if its diameter is less than the service limit.
7. Clean the bleed valve with compressed air. Check the valve threads for damage. Replace the dust cap if missing or damaged.
8. Clean the banjo bolt with compressed air. Replace worn or damaged washers.
9. Service the support bracket assembly as follows:

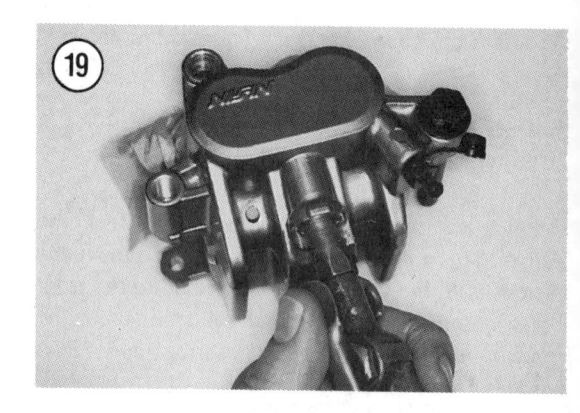

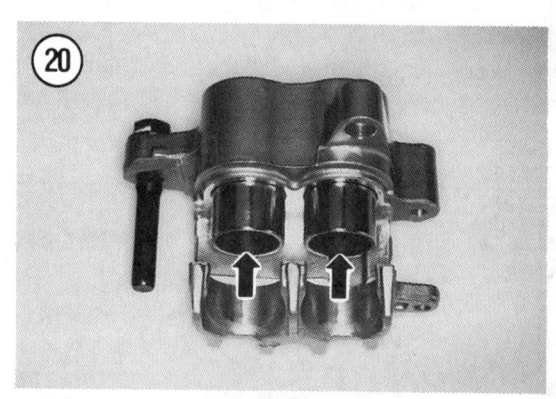

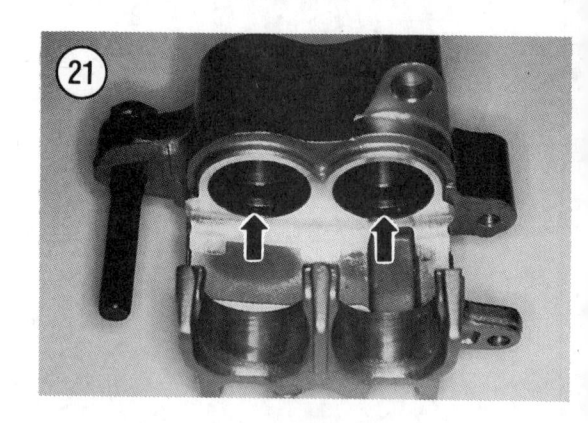

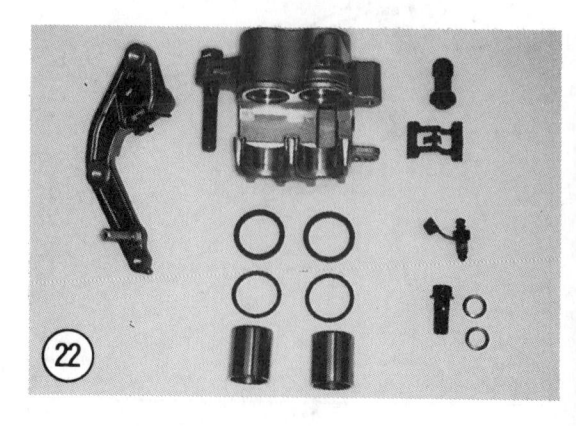

BRAKES

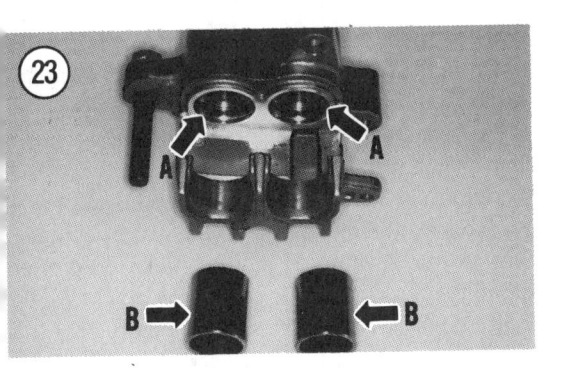

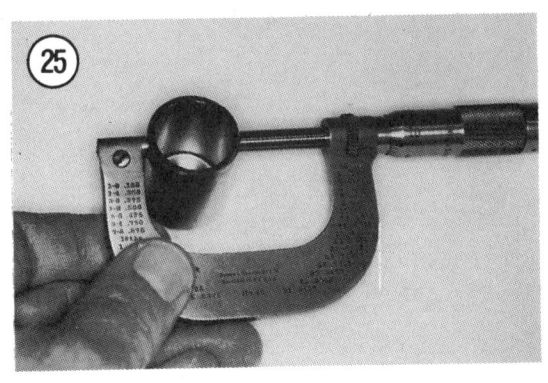

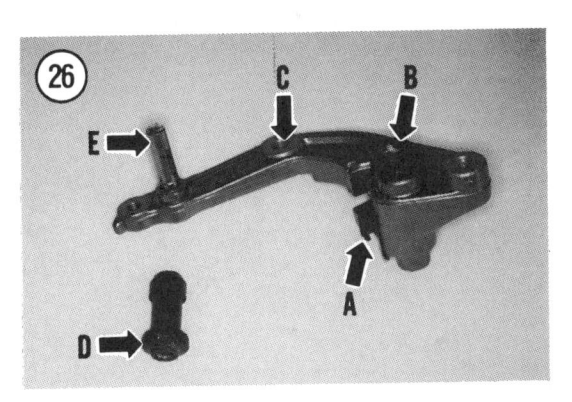

395

a. Remove and inspect the pad retainer (A, **Figure 26**). Replace if damaged.
b. Remove the caliper pin boot (B, **Figure 26**) from the caliper bracket.
c. Inspect the support bracket (C, **Figure 26**) for excessive wear or damage.
d. Inspect both rubber boots (B and D, **Figure 26**) for holes, hardness or other damage. Replace if necessary.
e. Inspect the caliper bracket pin bolt (E, **Figure 26**) for steps, excessive wear or damage. To replace the bolt, go to Step 11.

10. Inspect the caliper pin bolt (A, **Figure 27**) for steps, excessive wear or damage. If necessary, replace the bolt as described in Step 11.

11. To replace the caliper bracket pin bolt (E, **Figure 26**) or the caliper pin bolt (A, **Figure 27**), perform the following:

a. Remove the old bolt and discard it.
b. Remove all thread sealer from the caliper bracket or caliper hole threads.
c. Apply a medium strength threadlocking compound onto the threads of the new bolt.
d. Tighten the bolt to the torque specification in **Table 3**. Note that the tightening torques for the caliper bracket and caliper pin bolts are different.

Assembly

Use new DOT 4 brake fluid when lubricating the parts in the following steps.

1. Install the bleed valve (B, **Figure 27**) and its cover into the caliper. Tighten hand-tight.
2. Soak the new piston and dust seals in brake fluid for approximately 5 minutes.

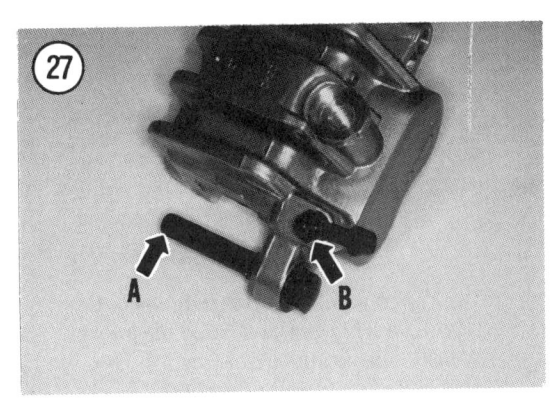

3. Lubricate the pistons and cylinder bores with brake fluid.
4. Install a new piston seal (A, **Figure 28**) into each cylinder bore rear groove.
5. Install a new dust seal (B, **Figure 28**) into each cylinder bore front groove.

NOTE
*Make sure each seal fits squarely into its respective cylinder bore groove (**Figure 21**).*

6. Install each piston into its respective caliper bore with its open side facing out (**Figure 20**). Install both pistons until they bottom out.
7. Install the bracket pin boot into the caliper housing (**Figure 29**).
8. Assemble and install the caliper bracket as follows:
   a. Install the caliper pin boot (A, **Figure 30**) into the caliper bracket.
   b. Hook the pad retainer onto the caliper bracket (B, **Figure 30**).
   c. Lubricate the caliper pin bolt (A, **Figure 27**) and the bracket pin (E, **Figure 26**) with silicone grease.
   d. Slide the caliper bracket (B, **Figure 17**) into the caliper. Then hold the caliper and slide the caliper bracket back and forth. It must move with no sign of binding or roughness.
9. Install the brake caliper assembly and brake pads as described in this chapter.

FRONT MASTER CYLINDER

Read the information listed under *Disc Brake* in this chapter before servicing the front master cylinder.

Refer to **Figure 31** when servicing the front master cylinder in this section.

Removal/Installation

1. Support the bike on its sidestand.
2. Cover the area under the master cylinder and over the fuel tank to prevent spilled brake fluid from damaging any component that it might contact.

CAUTION
Wipe up any spilled brake fluid immediately as it will stain or destroy the finish of most plastic and metal surfaces. Use soapy water and rinse thoroughly.

3. Remove the right side mirror.
4. Drain the front master cylinder as described under *Brake Fluid Draining* in this chapter.
5. Disconnect the connectors from the front brake light switch (**Figure 32**).
6. Remove the banjo bolt (A, **Figure 33**) and washers securing the brake hose to the master cylinder. Seal the brake hose to prevent brake fluid from dripping out.
7. Remove the bolts and clamp (B, **Figure 33**) holding the master cylinder to the handlebar and remove the master cylinder.

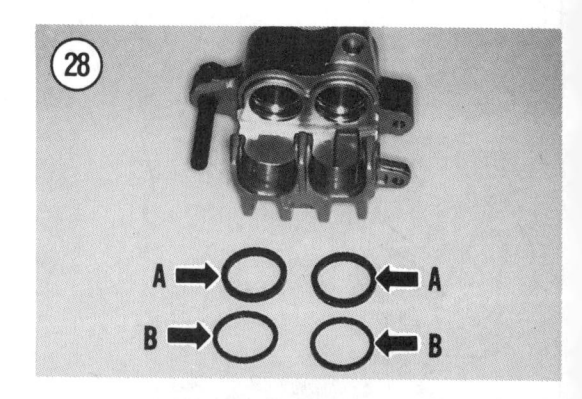

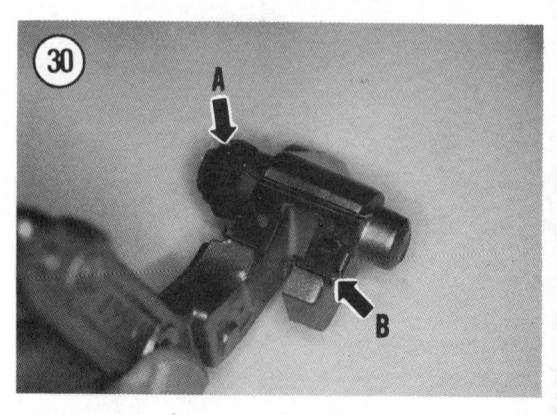

BRAKES

8. If necessary, service the master cylinder as described in this chapter.
9. Clean the handlebar, master cylinder and clamp mating surfaces.
10. Mount the master cylinder onto the handlebar, then install its clamp (B, **Figure 33**) and both mounting bolts. Install the clamp with its UP mark facing up.
11. Align the master cylinder and clamp mating halves with the punch mark on the handlebar (C, **Figure 33**). Then tighten the upper master cylinder clamp bolt, then the lower bolt to the torque specification in **Table 3**.
12. Secure the brake hose to the master cylinder with the banjo bolt and 2 washers—install a washer on each side of the brake hose (**Figure 34**). Position the brake hose arm against the master cylinder bracket as shown in **Figure 35**, then tighten the banjo bolt to the torque specification in **Table 3**.
13. Bleed the front brake as described under *Brake Bleeding* in this chapter.
14. After bleeding the brake and before riding the bike, turn the ignition switch on and make sure the rear brake light comes on when you operate the front brake lever. If not, check the front brake light switch and connectors.

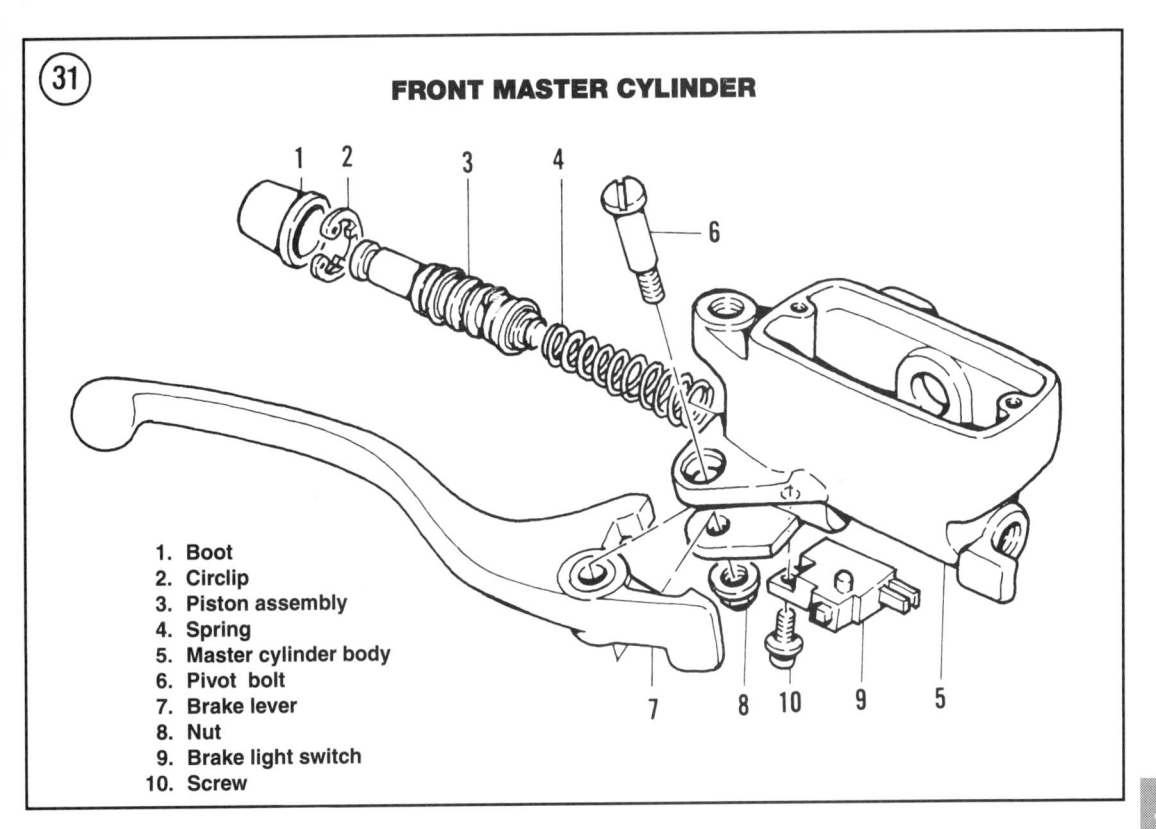

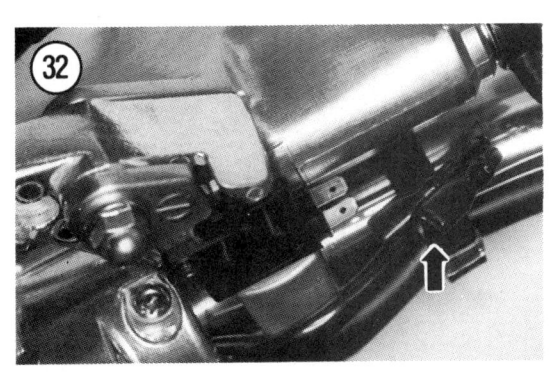

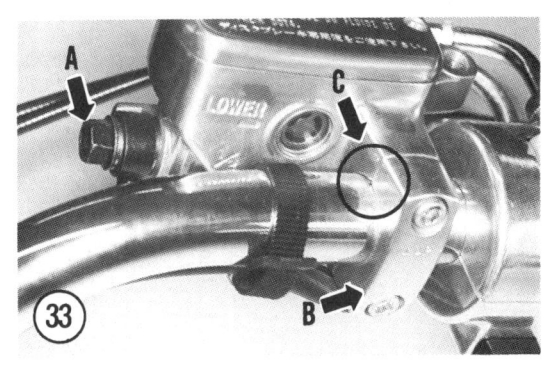

FRONT MASTER CYLINDER

1. Boot
2. Circlip
3. Piston assembly
4. Spring
5. Master cylinder body
6. Pivot bolt
7. Brake lever
8. Nut
9. Brake light switch
10. Screw

WARNING
Do not ride the motorcycle until the front brake and brake light work properly.

Disassembly

1. Remove the master cylinder (**Figure 36**) as described in this chapter.
2. Remove screw and the front brake light switch (A, **Figure 37**).
3. Remove the nut, pivot bolt and the front brake lever (B, **Figure 37**).
4. Remove the master cylinder cover, float and diaphragm.
5. Remove the dust cover from the groove in the end of the piston (A, **Figure 38**).

NOTE
If brake fluid is leaking from the piston bore, the piston cups are worn or damaged. Replace the piston assembly.

NOTE
*To hold the master cylinder when you remove and install the piston circlip, thread a bolt and nut into the master cylinder and secure the nut and bolt in a vise (**Figure 39**).*

6. Compress the piston and remove the circlip (A, **Figure 40**) from the groove in the master cylinder.
7. Remove the piston assembly (B, **Figure 40**) from the master cylinder bore.

Inspection

1. Clean and dry the master cylinder housing, cover and the other metal parts (except the piston assembly) (**Figure 41**) with a commercially available

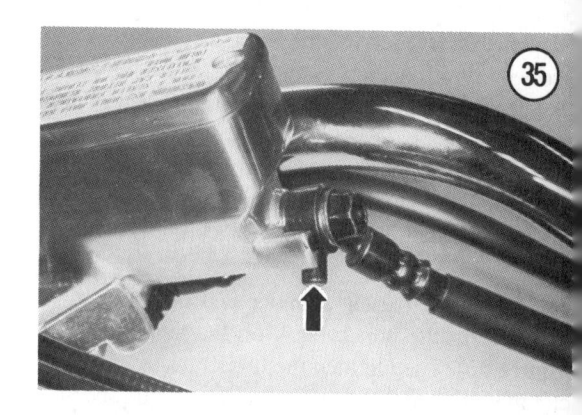

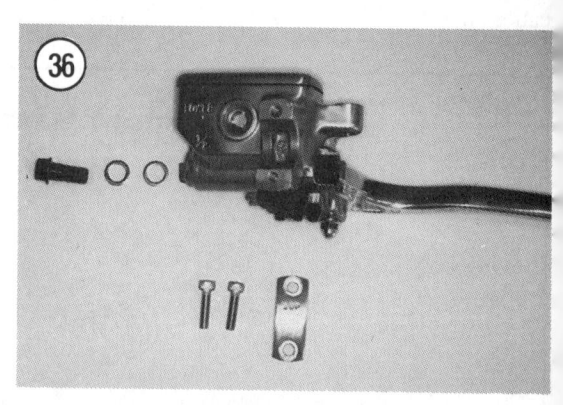

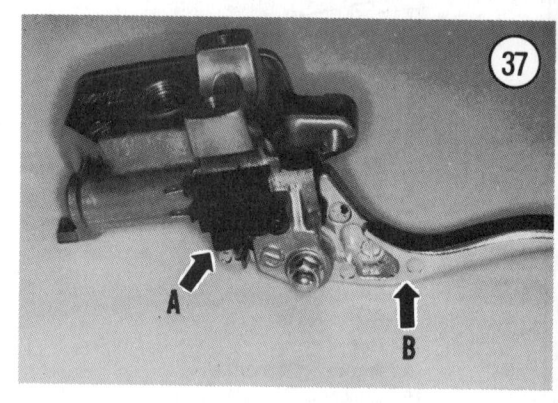

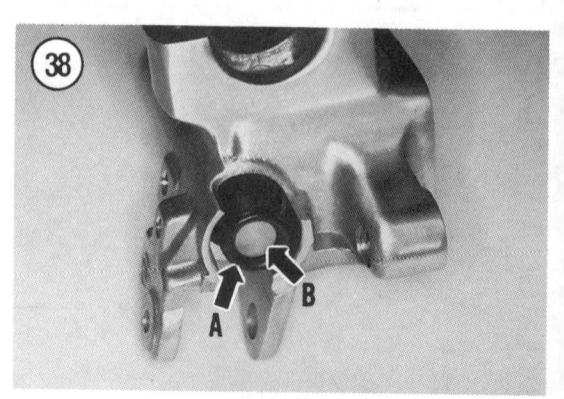

BRAKES

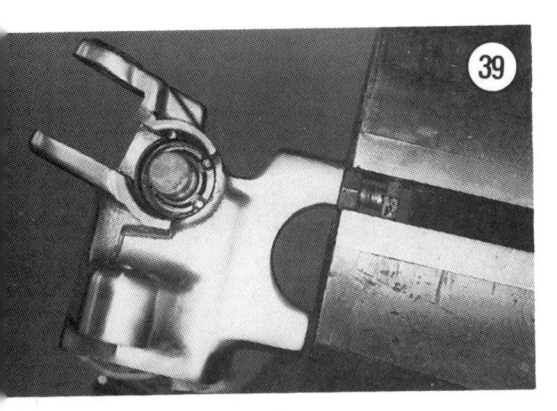

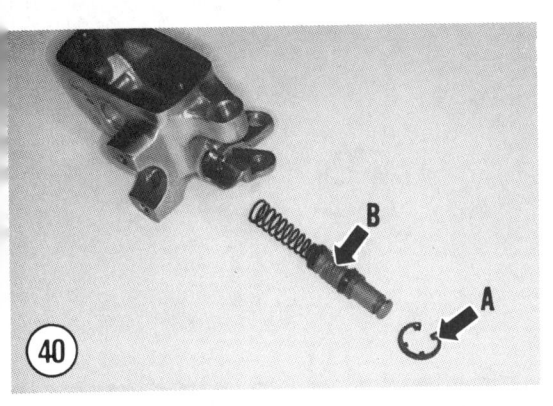

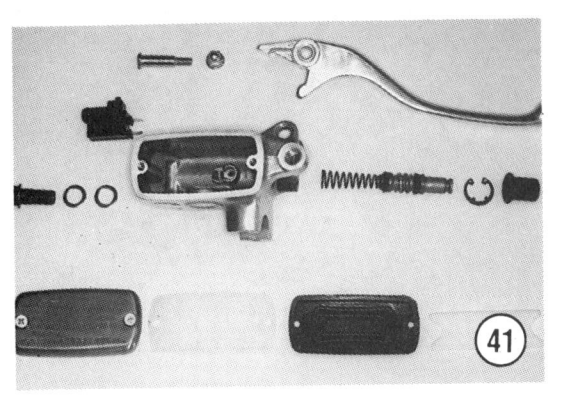

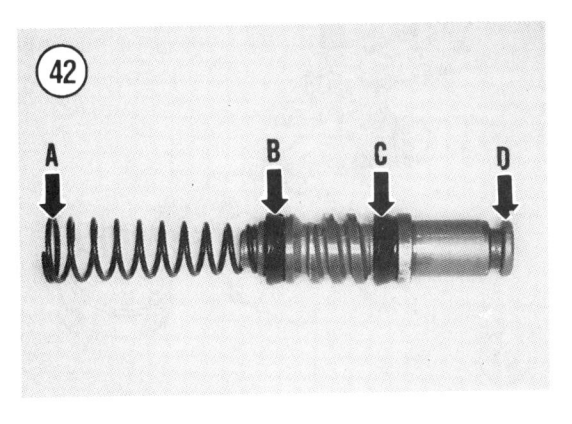

brake cleaner. Clean the piston assembly and the other non-metal parts with DOT 4 brake fluid. Place all of the cleaned parts on a lint-free cloth for inspection and reassembly.

2. **Figure 42** identifies the piston assembly:
   a. Spring.
   b. Primary cup.
   c. Secondary cup.
   d. Piston.

CAUTION
Do not remove the primary and secondary cups from the piston assembly for cleaning or inspection purposes.

3. Check the piston assembly (**Figure 42**) for the following defects:
   a. Broken, distorted or collapsed piston return spring (A, **Figure 42**).
   b. Worn, cracked, damaged or swollen primary (B, **Figure 42**) and secondary cups (C, **Figure 42**).
   c. Scratched, scored or damaged piston (D, **Figure 42**).
   d. Corroded, weak or damaged circlip (A, **Figure 40**).
   e. Worn or damaged dust cover (A, **Figure 38**).

If any of these parts are worn or damaged, replace the piston assembly.

4. Measure the piston outside diameter (**Figure 43**) and check against the dimension in **Table 1**. Replace the piston assembly if the piston outside diameter is less than the service limit.

5. To assemble a new piston assembly (**Figure 44**), perform the following:
   a. When you replace the piston, you must install the new primary (A, **Figure 45**) and secondary cups (B, **Figure 45**) onto the piston.

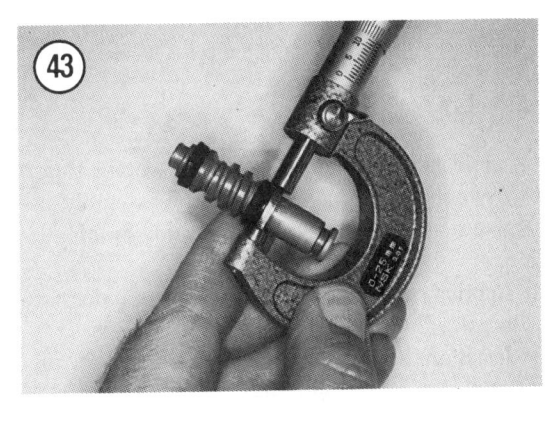

b. Use the original piston assembly (**Figure 42**) as a reference when installing the new cups onto the piston.

c. Before installing the new piston cups, soak them in brake fluid for approximately 5-10 minutes. This will soften them and ease installation. Clean the new piston in brake fluid.

NOTE
In substep d, install each piston cup with its closed side facing toward the front of the piston. The primary cup (A, Figure 45) has a smaller inside diameter than the secondary cup (B, Figure 45).

d. Install the primary (A, **Figure 45**), and then the secondary (B, **Figure 45**) cups onto the piston. See **Figure 42**.

6. Inspect the master cylinder bore (**Figure 46**). Replace the master cylinder if its bore is corroded, cracked or damaged in any way. Do not hone the master cylinder bore to remove scratches or other damage.

7. Measure the master cylinder bore diameter (**Figure 47**) and check against the dimension in **Table 1**. Replace the master cylinder if its diameter exceeds the service limit.

8. Check for plugged supply and relief ports in the master cylinder. Clean with compressed air.

9. Check the brake lever and pivot bolt (**Figure 48**) for the following defects:

   a. Cracked brake lever.

   b. Worn brake lever bushing.

   c. Worn or damaged pivot bolt.

   d. Damaged nut.

10. Check the reservoir cover, float and diaphragm for damage. Check the diaphragm for cracks or deterioration. Replace damaged parts as required.

Assembly

Lubricate the parts with new DOT 4 brake fluid.
1. If you are installing a new piston assembly, assemble it as described under *Inspection* in this section.
2. Lubricate the piston assembly and cylinder bore with brake fluid.
3. Install the spring—small end first—onto the piston as shown in A, **Figure 42**.

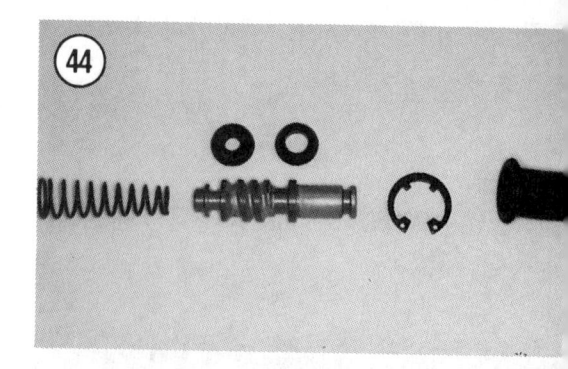

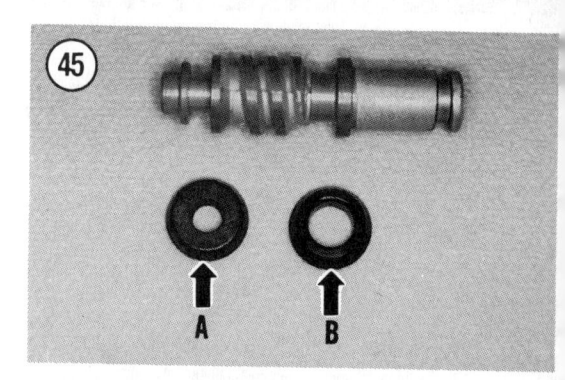

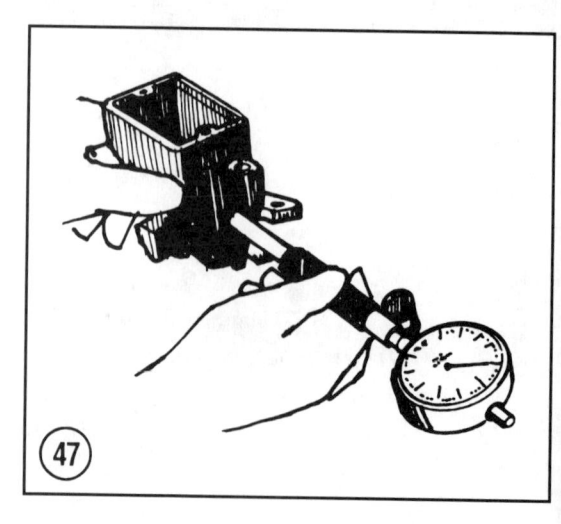

BRAKES

CAUTION
Do not allow the piston cups to tear or turn inside out when installing the piston into the master cylinder bore. Both cups are larger than the bore. To ease installation, lubricate the cups and piston with brake fluid.

4. Insert the piston assembly—spring end first—into the master cylinder bore (A, **Figure 40**).

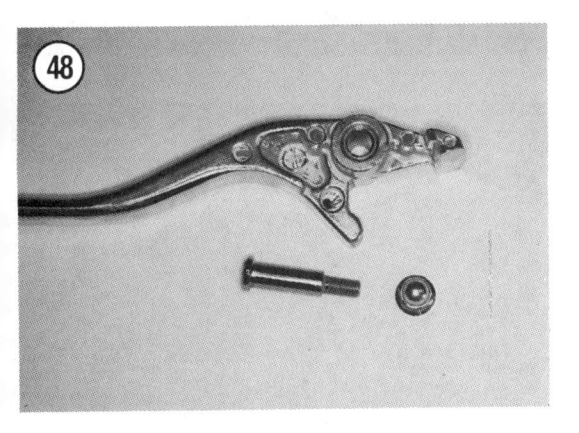

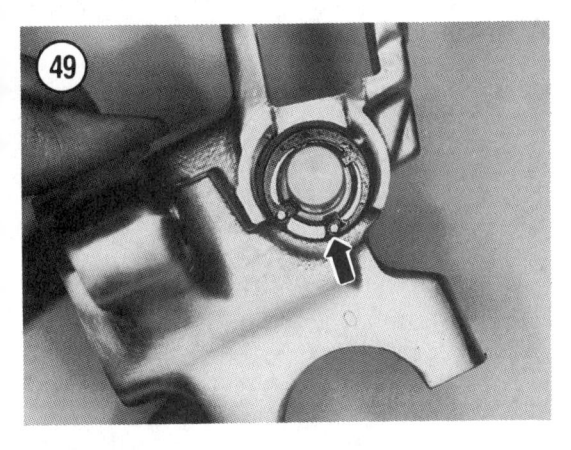

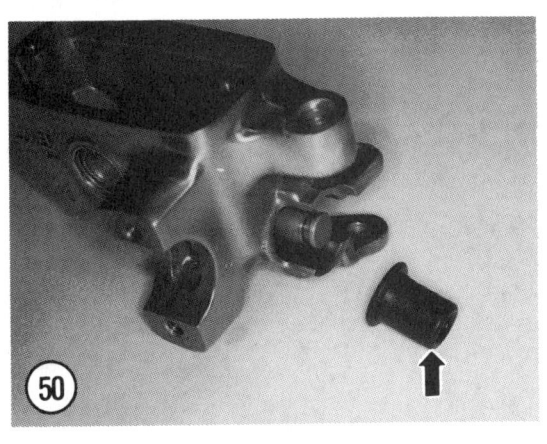

NOTE
*Before installing the circlip, mount the master cylinder in a vise (**Figure 39**) as described under Disassembly.*

5. Compress the piston assembly and install the circlip (A, **Figure 40**).

CAUTION
*The circlip (**Figure 49**) must seat in the master cylinder groove completely. Push and release the piston a few times to make sure it moves smoothly and that the circlip does not pop out.*

6. Slide the dust cover—shoulder side first (**Figure 50**)—over the piston. Seat the outer dust cover lip into the groove in the end of the piston (A, **Figure 38**).
7. Lubricate the piston contact surface (B, **Figure 38**) with silicone grease.
8. Install the brake lever assembly (**Figure 48**) as follows:
   a. Lubricate the pivot bolt with silicone grease.
   b. Install the brake lever (B, **Figure 37**).
   c. Install and tighten brake lever pivot bolt to the torque specification in **Table 3**. Check that the brake lever moves freely with no binding or roughness.
   d. Install and tighten the brake lever pivot nut to the torque specification in **Table 3**. Check that the brake lever moves freely with no binding or roughness.
9. Install the master cylinder diaphragm, float and cover.
10. Install the front brake light switch (A, **Figure 37**) and secure it with its mounting screw.
11. Install the master cylinder (**Figure 36**) as described in this chapter.

REAR CALIPER

Rear Brake Pad Replacement

Honda does not list an interval for replacing the rear brake pads. Pad wear depends greatly on riding habits and conditions. Replace the brake pads if either pad wear indicator is worn to the edge of the brake disc (**Figure 51**).

To maintain even brake pressure on the rear disc, replace both brake pads at the same time.

1. Read the information listed under *Disc Brake* in this chapter.

CAUTION
Do not allow the master cylinder reservoir to overflow when performing Step 2. Brake fluid will damage most surfaces it contacts.

2. Take hold of the caliper body (from the outside) and push it toward its brake disc (**Figure 52**). This will push the piston into the caliper to make room for the new brake pads.
3. Remove the pad pin bolt plug (A, **Figure 53**).
4. Loosen the pad pin bolt (B, **Figure 53**).
5. Remove the caliper bracket bolt (**Figure 54**), then pivot the caliper up.
6. Remove the pad pin bolt (A, **Figure 55**), then remove the outer (B, **Figure 55**) and inner (C, **Figure 55**) brake pads.

NOTE
Note the shim installed on the backside of each brake pad (Figure 56).

NOTE
***Figure 57** shows the pad spring with the caliper removed for clarity.*

7. Replace the pad spring (**Figure 57**) if it is damaged.

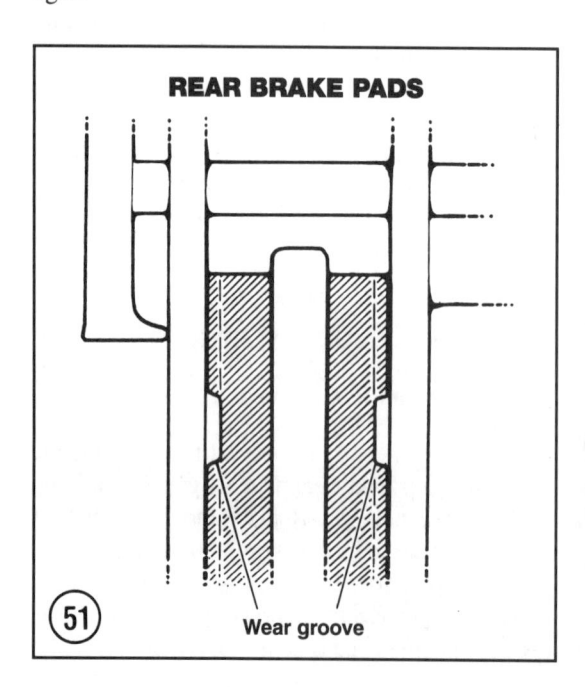

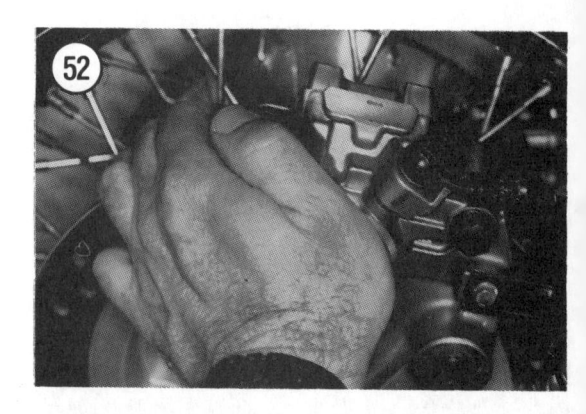

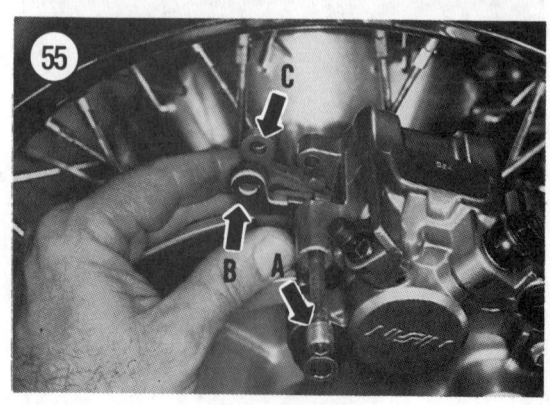

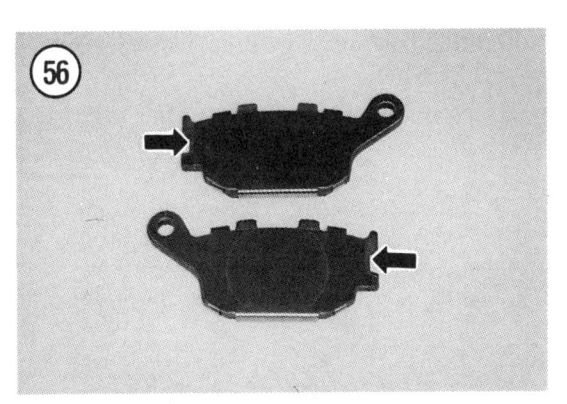

BRAKES

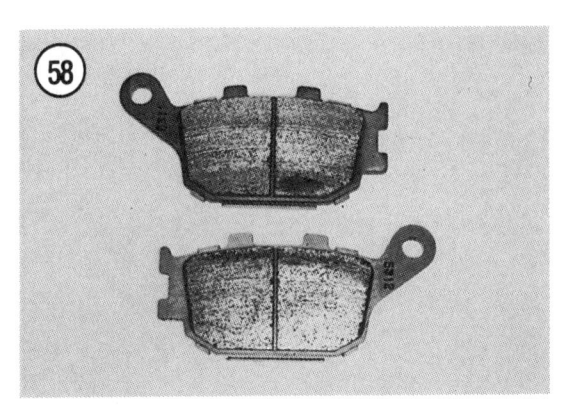

8. Inspect the brake pads (**Figure 58**) for uneven wear, damage or grease contamination. Replace both brake pads as a set.

9. Clean and inspect the pad pin plug, pin and caliper bracket bolt (**Figure 59**). Replace severely worn or damaged parts.

NOTE
If brake fluid is leaking from around the piston, overhaul the brake caliper as described in this chapter.

10. Check the brake disc for wear as described in this chapter.

11. If removed, install the pad spring (**Figure 57**) onto the caliper body.

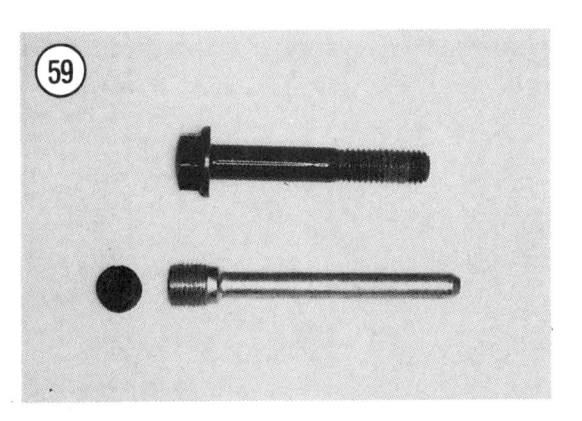

NOTE
Figure 57 *shows the pad spring with the caliper removed for clarity.*

12. Install a pad shim onto the backside of each brake pad (**Figure 56**).

WARNING
Do not use grease to hold the pad shims in place. Heat will thin the grease and cause it to run onto the brake pads and disc.

NOTE
The friction material on both brake pads must face against the brake disc.

NOTE
*After installing the brake pads in the following steps, make sure their ends rest on the pad retainer (****Figure 60****) on the caliper bracket.*

13. Install the outer (A, **Figure 61**) and inner (B, **Figure 61**) brake pads into the caliper and hold them in place.
14. Push both brake pads against the pad spring, then install the pad pin through the caliper and both brake pads (**Figure 62**).
15. Lower the brake caliper over the brake disc, while at the same time checking that the ends of each brake pad rest on the pad retainer (**Figure 60**) on the caliper bracket.
16. Install and tighten the caliper bracket bolt (A, **Figure 55**) to the torque specification in **Table 4**.
17. Tighten the pad pin (B, **Figure 53**) to the torque specification in **Table 4**.
18. Tighten the pad pin plug (A, **Figure 53**) to the torque specification in **Table 4**.
19. Depress and release the rear brake pedal a few times to seat the pads against the disc, then check the brake fluid level in the reservoir. If necessary, add fresh brake fluid (Chapter Three).

WARNING
Do not ride the motorcycle until you are sure that the rear brake is operating correctly with full hydraulic advantage. If necessary, bleed the rear brake as described in this chapter.

Brake Caliper
Removal/Installation
(Caliper Will Not Be Disassembled)

To remove the caliper without disassembling it, perform this procedure. To disassemble the caliper, refer to *Caliper Removal/Piston Removal* in this section.
1. Drain the brake fluid from the rear master cylinder as described under *Brake Fluid Draining* in this chapter.
2A. To remove the caliper, perform the following:
   a. Remove the brake hose banjo bolt (A, **Figure 63**) and both washers at the caliper. Seal the hose so that brake fluid cannot leak out.
   b. Remove the bolt (B, **Figure 63**) that holds the brake caliper bracket. Lift the caliper away from the brake disc, then slide it off of the caliper bracket to remove it. See **Figure 64**.
2B. To remove the brake caliper without disconnecting the brake hose, perform the following:
   a. Remove the bolt (B, **Figure 63**) that holds the brake caliper to the caliper bracket. Lift the caliper away from the brake disc, then slide it off of the caliper bracket to remove it. See A, **Figure 64**.
   b. Insert a spacer block between the brake pads.

NOTE
The spacer block will prevent the piston from being forced out of the caliper if the rear brake lever is applied while the brake caliper is removed from the brake disc.

   c. Support the caliper with a wire hook.

BRAKES

3. Remove and inspect the pad retainer (**Figure 65**). Replace if corroded, worn or damaged.
4. Install the caliper by reversing these steps, while noting the following.
5. Hook the pad retainer (A, **Figure 65**) onto the caliper bracket so that it sits flush against the bracket.
6A. If you removed the caliper from the motorcycle, perform the following:

  a. Make sure the brake pads are not contaminated with brake fluid. If the pads are contaminated, replace the brake pads as described in this chapter.
  b. Lubricate the caliper pin bolt (B, **Figure 64**) with silicone grease.
  c. Slide the caliper pin bolt (B, **Figure 64**) into the caliper bracket pin boot (C, **Figure 64**), then pivot the caliper assembly over the brake disc. Be careful not to damage the leading edge of the pads during installation.
  d. Install and tighten the caliper bracket bolt (B, **Figure 63**) to the torque specification in **Table 4**.
  e. Place a washer (**Figure 66**) on each side of the brake hose, then center the brake hose between the 2 arms on the caliper (A, **Figure 63**). Thread the banjo bolt (A, **Figure 63**) into the caliper and tighten to the torque specification in **Table 4**.
  f. Refill the master cylinder and bleed the rear brake as described in this chapter.

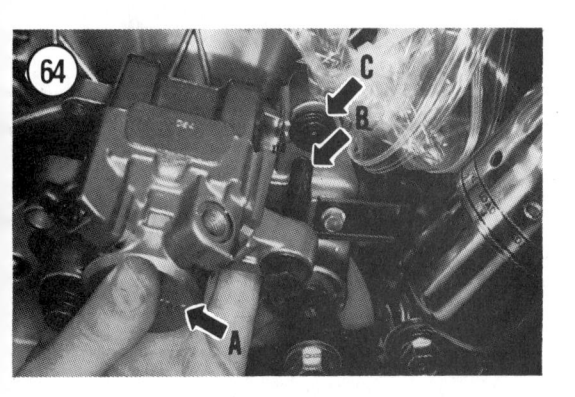

6B. If you did not remove the caliper from the motorcycle, perform the following:

  a. Remove the spacer block from between the brake pads.
  b. Lubricate the caliper pin bolt (B, **Figure 64**) with silicone grease.
  c. Slide the caliper pin bolt (B, **Figure 64**) into the caliper bracket pin boot (C, **Figure 64**), then pivot the caliper assembly over the brake disc. Be careful not to damage the leading edge of the pads during installation.
  d. Install and tighten the caliper bracket bolt (B, **Figure 63**) to the torque specification in **Table 4**.
  e. Depress the rear brake pedal to seat the pads against the brake disc.

WARNING
Do not ride the motorcycle until the rear brake operates with full hydraulic advantage. If necessary, bleed the rear brake as described in this chapter.

Caliper Removal/Piston Removal (Caliper Will Be Disassembled)

Force is required to remove the piston from the caliper. This procedure describes how to remove the piston with the caliper connected to the rear brake system. If there is no hydraulic pressure in the system, remove the piston as described under *Disassembly* in this section.

1. Remove the brake pads as described in this chapter.

2. Wrap a large cloth around the brake caliper.
3. Hold the caliper so that your hand and fingers are placed away from the piston.
4. Operate the rear brake lever and force the piston as far out of the caliper as possible. If the piston moved out far enough to be removed by hand, leave it in place until you remove the caliper. This will help to prevent a large amount of brake fluid from leaking out of the caliper.

NOTE
If the piston did not come out, remove it with compressed air as described under Disassembly in this section.

5. Remove the caliper banjo bolt and both washers (**Figure 66**). Seal the brake hose to prevent brake fluid from leaking out.
6. Take the caliper to a workbench for disassembly.

Disassembly

Refer to **Figure 67** for this procedure.
1. Remove the brake caliper as described in this chapter.

WARNING
Compressed air forces the piston out of the caliper under considerable force. Do not cushion the piston with your fingers, as injury will result.

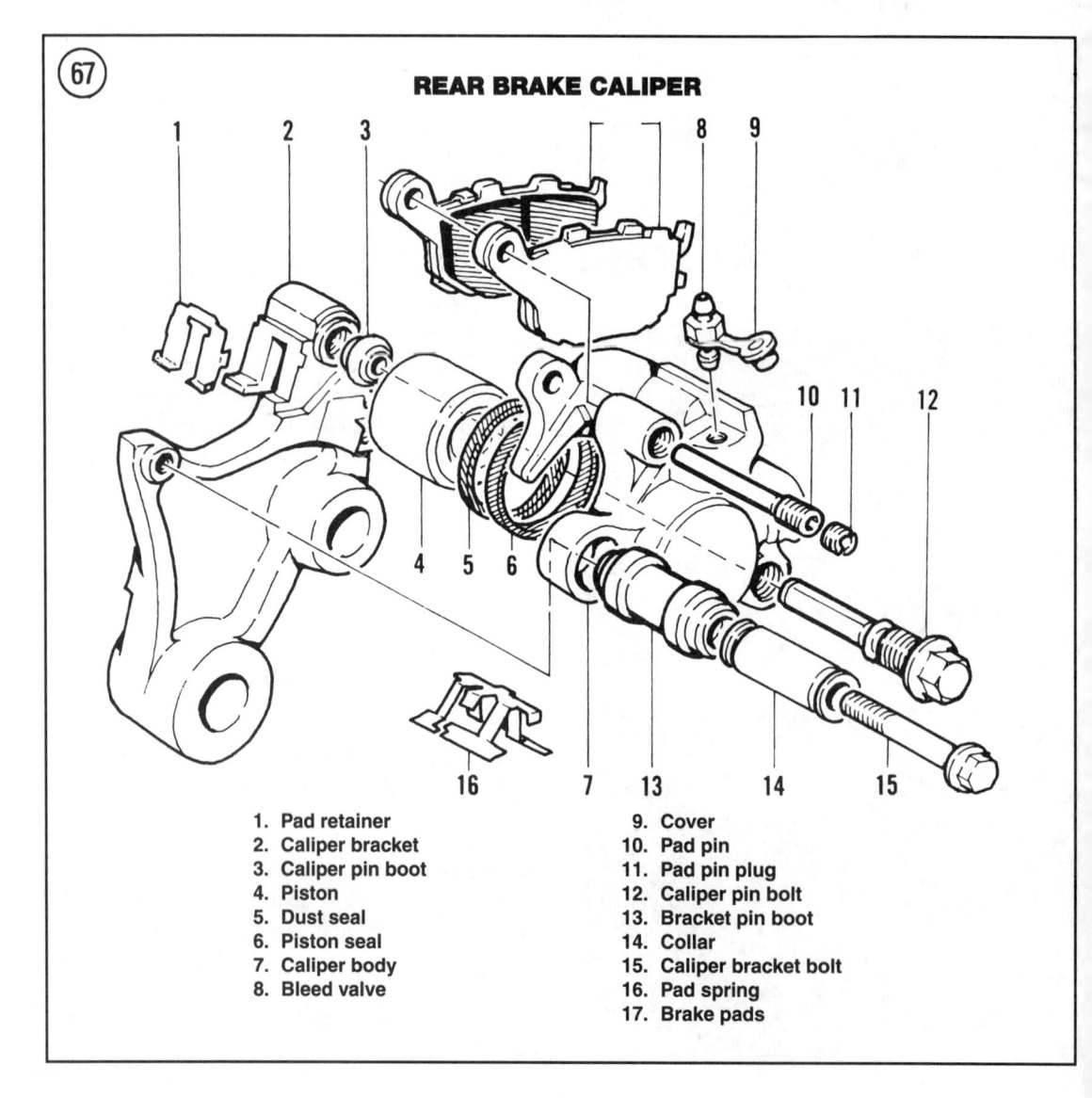

REAR BRAKE CALIPER

1. Pad retainer
2. Caliper bracket
3. Caliper pin boot
4. Piston
5. Dust seal
6. Piston seal
7. Caliper body
8. Bleed valve
9. Cover
10. Pad pin
11. Pad pin plug
12. Caliper pin bolt
13. Bracket pin boot
14. Collar
15. Caliper bracket bolt
16. Pad spring
17. Brake pads

BRAKES

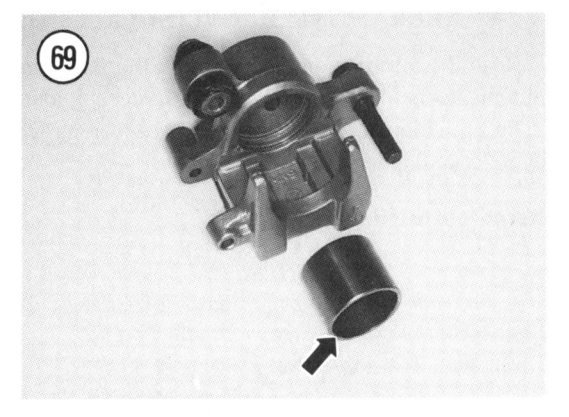

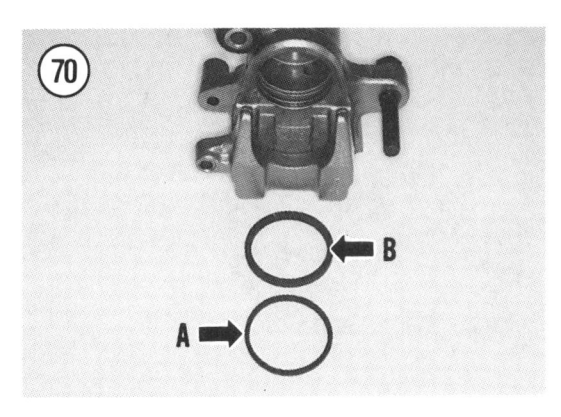

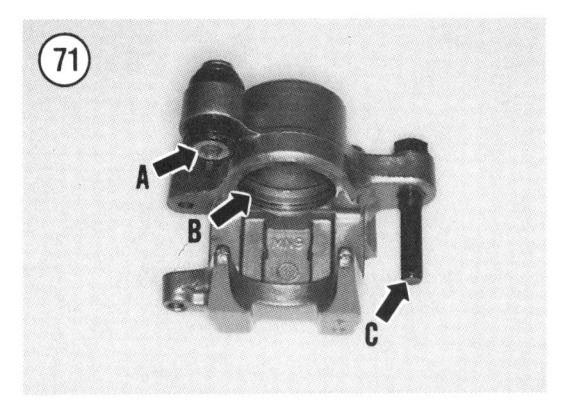

2. Cushion the caliper piston with a shop rag, making sure to keep your hand away from the piston area. Then apply compressed air through the brake line port (**Figure 68**) and remove the piston (**Figure 69**).
3. Remove the dust (A, **Figure 70**) and piston (B, **Figure 70**) seals from the cylinder bore grooves.
4. Remove the bleed valve and its cover from the caliper.
5. Remove the collar and bracket pin boot (A, **Figure 71**) from the caliper housing.

Inspection

1. Clean and dry the caliper housing and the other metal parts (**Figure 72**) with a commercially available brake cleaner.
2. Discard the dust and piston seals.
3. Check the cylinder bore (B, **Figure 71**) for deep scratches or other wear marks. Do not hone the cylinder bore.
4. Measure the cylinder bore diameter (**Figure 73**) and check against the dimension in **Table 2**. Replace the caliper if its diameter exceeds the service limit.
5. Inspect the piston for excessive wear, cracks or other damage.
6. Measure the piston outside diameter (**Figure 74**) and check against the dimension in **Table 2**. Replace the piston if its diameter is less than the service limit.

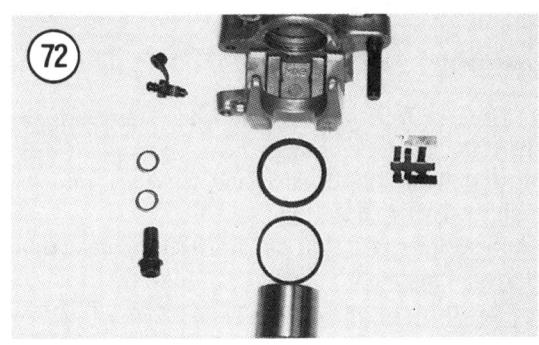

7. Clean the bleed valve with compressed air. Check the valve threads for damage. Replace the dust cap if missing or damaged.
8. Clean the banjo bolt with compressed air. Replace worn or damaged washers.
9. Service the support bracket assembly as follows:
   a. Remove and inspect the pad retainer (A, **Figure 65**). Replace if damaged.
   b. Remove the caliper pin boot (B, **Figure 65**) from the caliper bracket.
   c. Inspect the support bracket for severe wear or damage.
   d. Inspect both rubber boots (B, **Figure 65** and A, **Figure 71**) for holes, hardness or other damage. Replace if necessary.
   e. Inspect the collar (A, **Figure 63**) and replace if worn or damaged.
10. Inspect the caliper pin bolt (C, **Figure 63**) for steps, excessive wear or damage. If necessary, replace the bolt as described in Step 11.
11. To replace the caliper pin bolt (C, **Figure 63**), perform the following:
   a. Remove the old bolt and discard it.
   b. Remove all thread sealer residue from the caliper hole threads.
   c. Apply a medium strength threadlocking compound onto the threads of the new bolt.
   d. Install and tighten the caliper pin bolt to the torque specification in **Table 4**.

Assembly

Use new DOT 4 brake fluid when lubricating the parts in the following steps.
1. Install the bleed valve and its cover into the caliper. Tighten hand-tight.
2. Soak the new piston and dust seals in brake fluid for approximately 5 minutes.
3. Lubricate the piston and cylinder bore with brake fluid.
4. Install a new piston seal (B, **Figure 70**) into the rear cylinder bore groove.
5. Install a new dust seal (A, **Figure 70**) into the front cylinder bore groove.

NOTE
Check that each seal fits squarely into its respective cylinder bore groove.

6. Install the piston into the caliper bore with its open side facing out (**Figure 75**). Push the piston in until it bottoms out.

7. Install the bracket pin boot and collar (A, **Figure 71**) into the caliper housing.
8. Assemble the caliper bracket as follows:
   a. Install the caliper pin boot (B, **Figure 65**) into the caliper bracket.
   b. Hook the pad retainer onto the caliper bracket (A, **Figure 65**).
   c. Lubricate the inside of each boot and the pin bolts with silicone grease.
9. Install the brake caliper assembly and brake pads as described in this chapter.

REAR MASTER CYLINDER

Read the information listed under *Disc Brake* in this chapter before servicing the rear master cylinder.
Refer to **Figure 76** when servicing the rear master cylinder in this section.

Removal/Installation

NOTE
You can remove the rear master cylinder with the exhaust system mounted on the bike. However, this procedure shows rear master cylinder removal with the exhaust system removed for clarity.

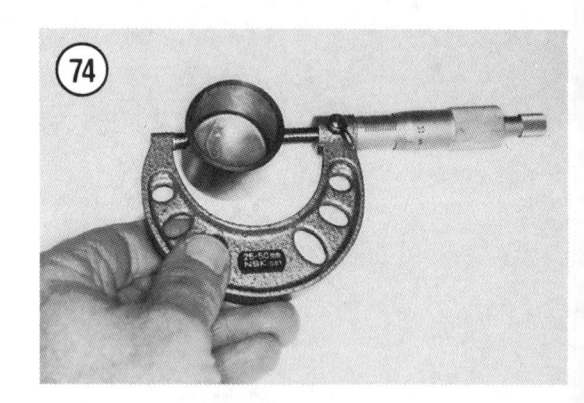

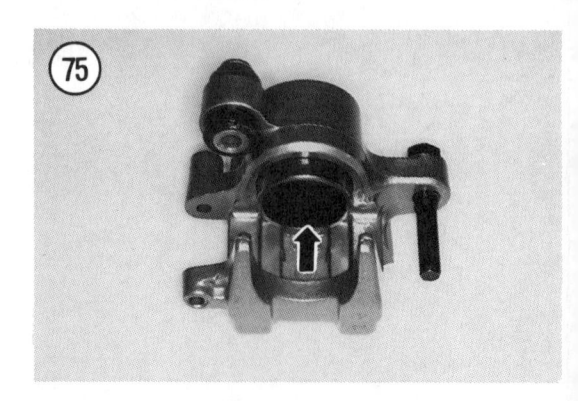

BRAKES

1. Park the motorcycle on level ground. Block the front wheels so the motorcycle cannot roll in either direction.

CAUTION
Wipe up any spilled brake fluid immediately as it will stain or destroy the finish of most plastic and metal surfaces. Use soapy water and rinse thoroughly.

2. If the exhaust system is mounted on the bike, cover it with a plastic drop cloth to prevent spilled brake fluid from damaging it.

3. Drain the brake fluid from the rear master cylinder as described under *Brake Fluid Draining* in this chapter.

4. Remove the master cylinder mounting bolts (A, **Figure 77**) and the protector plate (B, **Figure 77**).

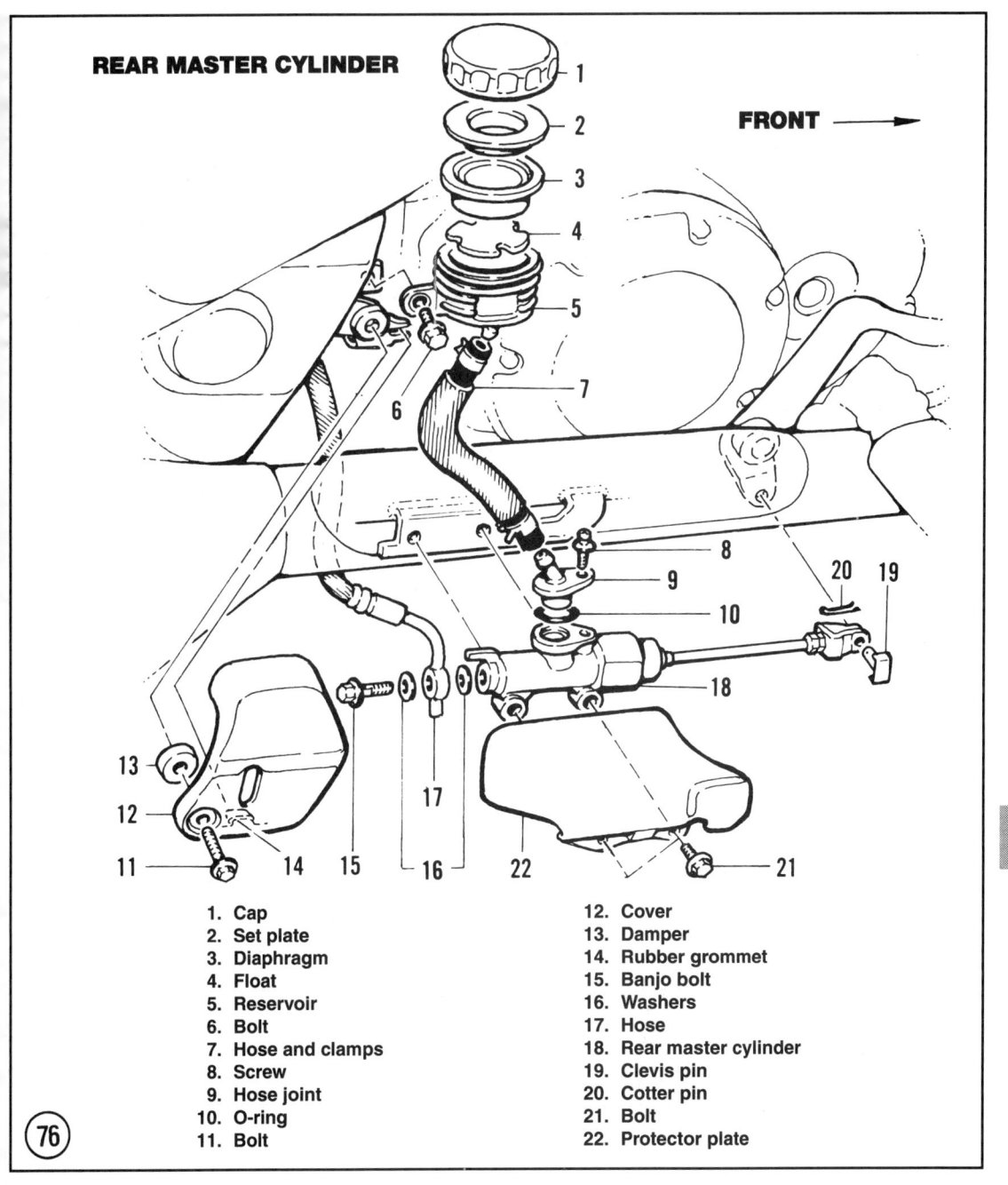

76 — REAR MASTER CYLINDER

1. Cap
2. Set plate
3. Diaphragm
4. Float
5. Reservoir
6. Bolt
7. Hose and clamps
8. Screw
9. Hose joint
10. O-ring
11. Bolt
12. Cover
13. Damper
14. Rubber grommet
15. Banjo bolt
16. Washers
17. Hose
18. Rear master cylinder
19. Clevis pin
20. Cotter pin
21. Bolt
22. Protector plate

5. Remove the circlip (**Figure 78**) and washer and slide the rear brake pedal off of its pivot shaft.
6. Remove the cotter pin (**Figure 79**) and clevis pin (**Figure 80**). Discard the cotter pin.
7. Remove the banjo bolt (A, **Figure 81**) and both washers. Seal the brake hose to prevent brake fluid from dripping out.
8. Remove the hose joint screw and separate the hose joint (B, **Figure 81**) from the master cylinder.
9. Remove and discard the hose joint O-ring (**Figure 82**).
10. If necessary, service the master cylinder as described in this chapter.
11. Lubricate a new hose joint O-ring with DOT 4 brake fluid and install it in the master cylinder (**Figure 82**).
12. Connect the hose joint (B, **Figure 81**) to the master cylinder and secure it with its mounting screw.
13. Reconnect the pushrod to the brake pedal with the clevis pin (**Figure 80**) and a new cotter pin (**Figure 79**). Spread the cotter pin arms over to lock it.
14. Lubricate the brake pedal pivot shaft with grease and install the brake pedal. Then install the washer and circlip (**Figure 78**). Reconnect the brake pedal spring(s).

NOTE
Make sure the clevis pin fits flush against the pushrod clevis as shown in Figure 83.

15. Align the master cylinder with the frame, then install the protector plate (B, **Figure 77**) and the 2 master cylinder mounting bolts (A, **Figure 77**). Tighten the bolts to the torque specification in **Table 4**.

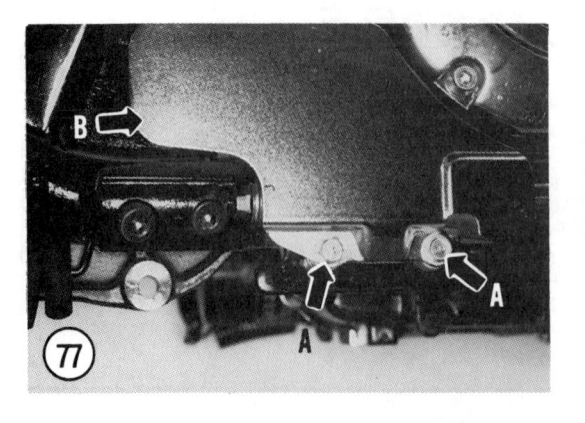

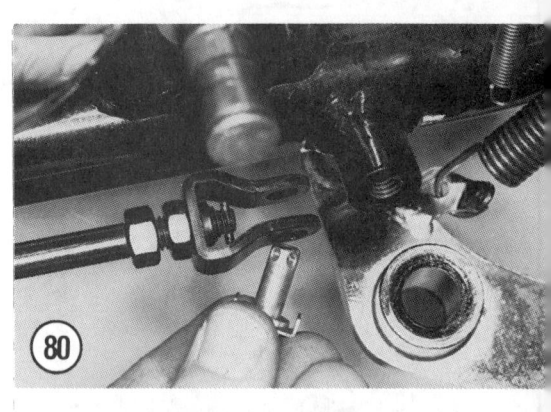

BRAKES

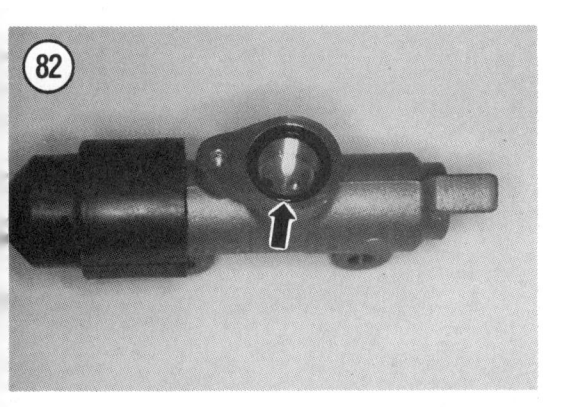

16. Secure the brake hose to the master cylinder with the banjo bolt (A, **Figure 81**) and 2 washers. Install a washer on each side of the brake hose Position the brake hose against the master cylinder projection. Tighten the banjo bolt to the torque specification in **Table 4**.
17. Refill the master cylinder with brake fluid and bleed the brake as described in this chapter.
18. Adjust the rear brake pedal height as described in Chapter Three.
19. Turn the ignition switch on and make sure the rear brake light comes on when the rear brake pedal is depressed.

WARNING
Do not ride the motorcycle until the rear brake and brake light work properly.

Disassembly

Refer to **Figure 84**.
1. Slide the dust cover (A, **Figure 85**) off the master cylinder.
2. Slide the boot (B, **Figure 85**) out of the master cylinder.

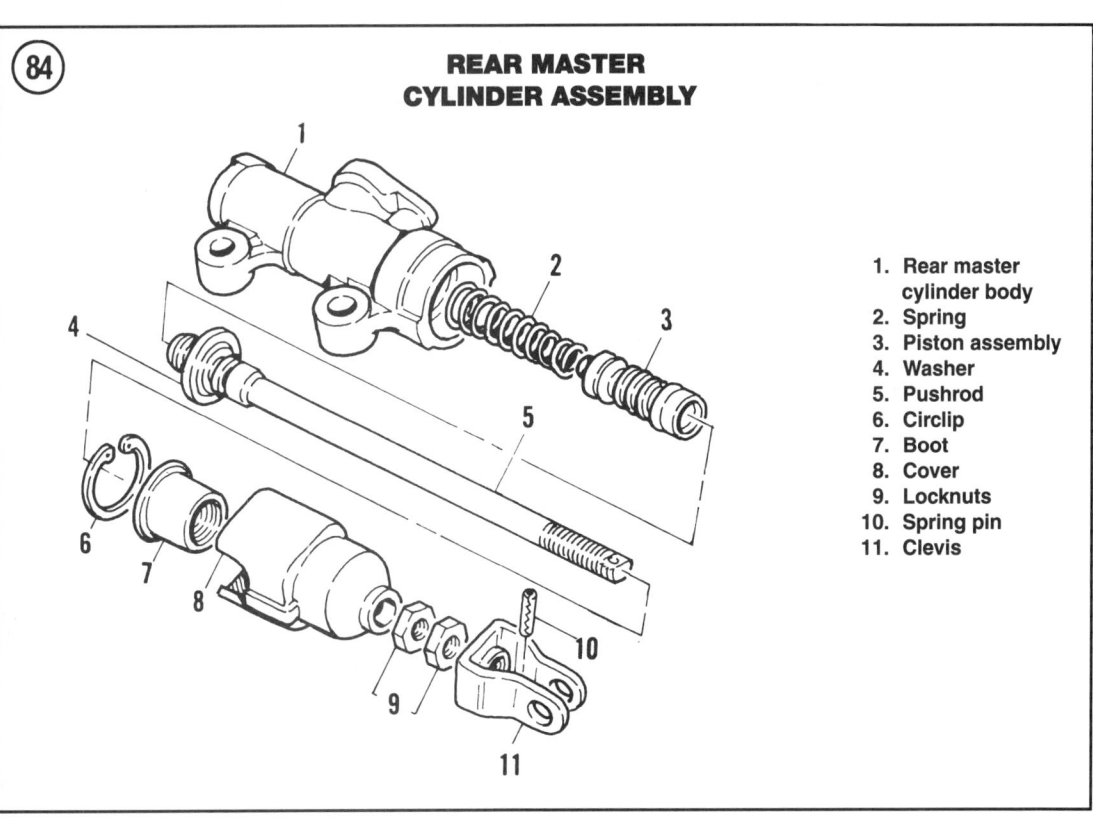

REAR MASTER CYLINDER ASSEMBLY

1. Rear master cylinder body
2. Spring
3. Piston assembly
4. Washer
5. Pushrod
6. Circlip
7. Boot
8. Cover
9. Locknuts
10. Spring pin
11. Clevis

CHAPTER THIRTEEN

NOTE
If brake fluid is leaking from the front of the piston bore, the piston cups are worn or damaged. Replace the piston assembly.

NOTE
*To hold the master cylinder when you remove and install the piston circlip, thread a bolt and nut into the master cylinder. Then tighten the nut against the master cylinder and clamp the bolt and nut in a vise as shown in **Figure 86**.*

3. Compress the piston and remove the circlip from the groove in the master cylinder, then remove the pushrod assembly (**Figure 87**).
4. Remove the piston assembly (**Figure 88**).

Inspection

1. Clean and dry the master cylinder housing, cover and the other metal parts (except the piston assembly) (**Figure 89**) with a commercially available brake cleaner. Clean the piston assembly and the other non-metal parts with DOT 4 brake fluid. Place all of the cleaned parts on a lint-free cloth for inspection and reassembly.
2. **Figure 90** identifies the piston assembly:
   a. Spring.
   b. Primary cup.
   c. Secondary cup.
   d. Piston.

CAUTION
Do not remove the primary and secondary cups from the piston assembly for cleaning or inspection purposes.

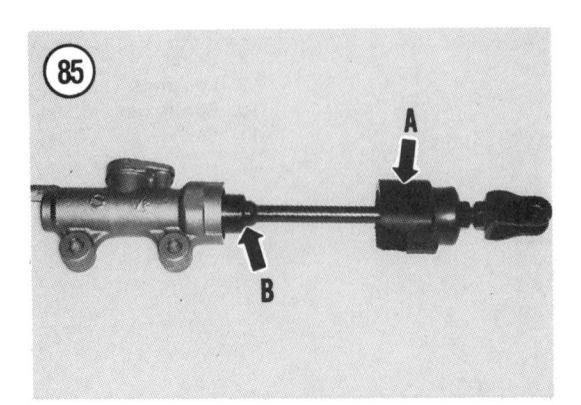

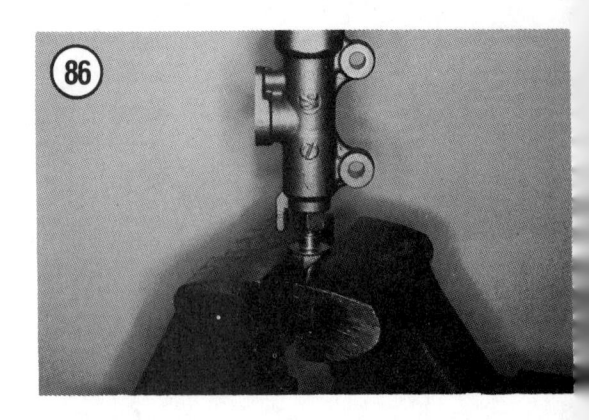

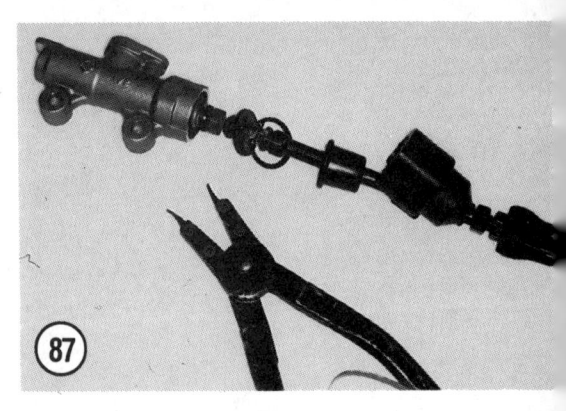

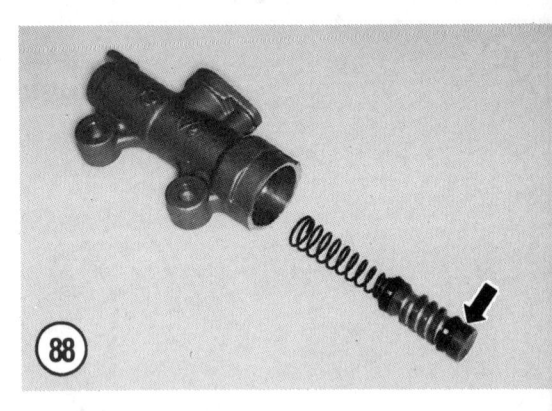

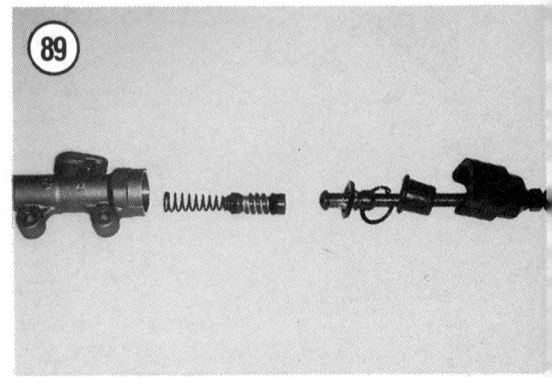

BRAKES

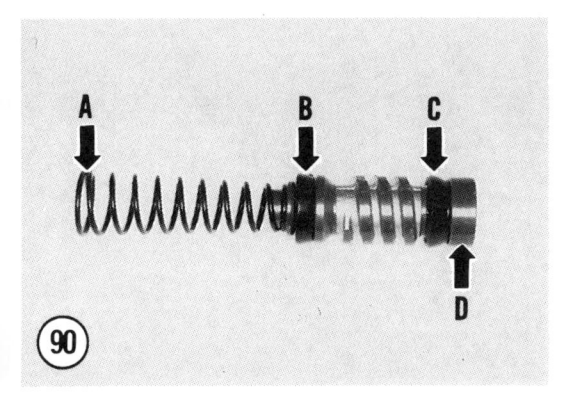

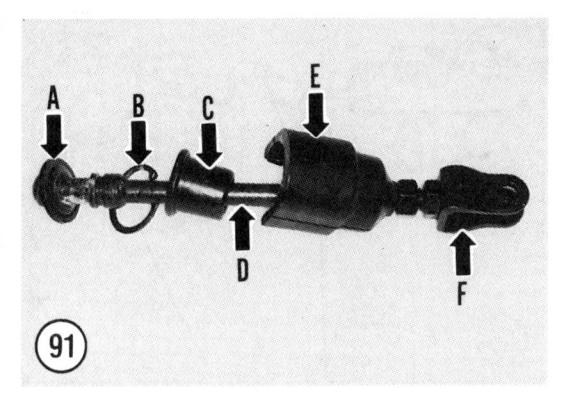

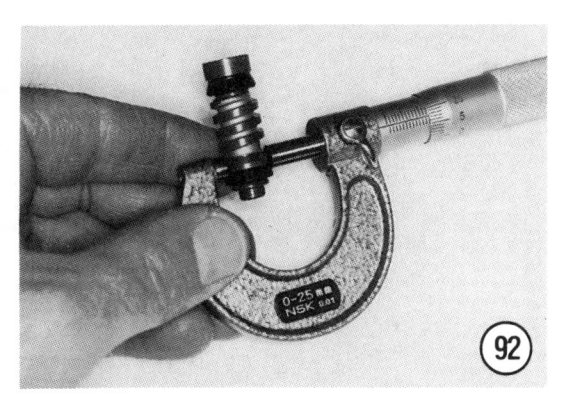

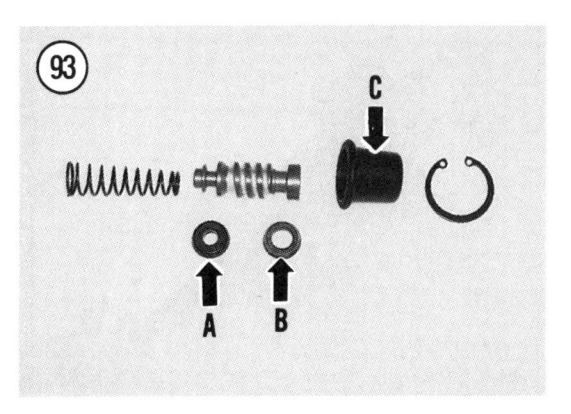

3. Check the piston assembly (**Figure 90**) for the following defects:
    a. Broken, distorted or collapsed piston return spring (A, **Figure 90**).
    b. Worn, cracked, damaged or swollen primary (B, **Figure 90**) and secondary cups (C, **Figure 90**).
    c. Scratched, scored or damaged piston (D, **Figure 90**).
    d. Corroded or damaged washer (A, **Figure 91**).
    e. Corroded, weak or damaged circlip (B, **Figure 91**).

If any of these parts are worn or damaged, replace the piston assembly.

4. Measure the piston outside diameter (**Figure 92**) and check against the dimension in **Table 2**. Replace the piston assembly if the piston outside diameter is less than the service limit.

5. To assemble a new piston assembly (**Figure 93**), perform the following:
    a. When you replace the piston, you must install the new primary (A, **Figure 93**) and secondary cups (B, **Figure 93**) onto the new piston.
    b. Use the original piston assembly (**Figure 90**) as a reference when installing the new cups onto the piston.
    c. Before installing the new piston cups, soak them in brake fluid for approximately 5-10 minutes. This will soften them and ease installation. Clean the new piston in brake fluid.

NOTE
In substep d, install each piston cup with its closed side facing toward the front of the piston. The primary cup (A, Figure 93) has a smaller inside diameter than the secondary cup (B, Figure 93).

    d. Install the primary (A, **Figure 93**), and then the secondary (B, **Figure 93**) cups onto the piston. See **Figure 90**.
    e. To install the new boot (C, **Figure 93**) onto the pushrod, loosen the 2 pushrod locknuts and remove the clevis (F, **Figure 91**). Remove the dust cover (E, **Figure 91**) and replace the boot (C, **Figure 91**). Then reverse to install the removed parts.

NOTE
Adjust the pushrod length after reassembling the master cylinder.

6. Check the pushrod assembly (**Figure 91**) for the following defects:
   a. Deteriorated or damaged boot (C, **Figure 91**).
   b. Corroded or damaged pushrod (D, **Figure 91**).
   c. Deteriorated or damaged dust cover (E, **Figure 91**).
   d. Bent or damaged clevis (F, **Figure 91**).

   Replace any worn or damaged parts.

7. Inspect the master cylinder bore (**Figure 94**). Replace the master cylinder if its bore is corroded, cracked or damaged in any way. Do not hone the master cylinder bore to remove scratches or other damage.

8. Measure the master cylinder bore diameter (**Figure 95**) and check against the dimension in **Table 2**. Replace the master cylinder if its bore diameter exceeds the service limit.

9. Check for plugged supply and relief ports in the master cylinder. Clean with compressed air.

Assembly

Lubricate the parts with new DOT 4 brake fluid.

1. If you are installing a new piston assembly, assemble it as described under *Inspection* in this section.
2. Lubricate the piston assembly and cylinder bore with brake fluid.
3. Install the spring—small end first—onto the piston as shown in A, **Figure 90**.

> *CAUTION*
> *Do not allow the piston cups to tear or turn inside out when installing the piston into the master cylinder bore. Both cups are larger than the bore. To ease installation, lubricate the cups and piston with brake fluid.*

4. Insert the piston assembly—spring end first—into the master cylinder bore (**Figure 88**).
5. Lubricate the end of the pushrod that contacts the piston with silicone grease.

> *NOTE*
> *Before installing the circlip, mount the master cylinder in a vise (**Figure 84**) as described under **Disassembly**.*

6. Install the pushrod into the master cylinder bore and seat it against the piston

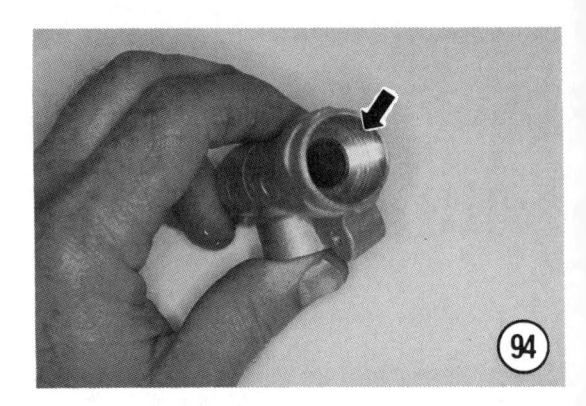

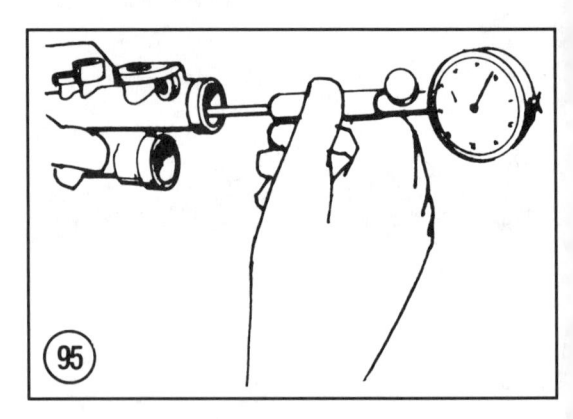

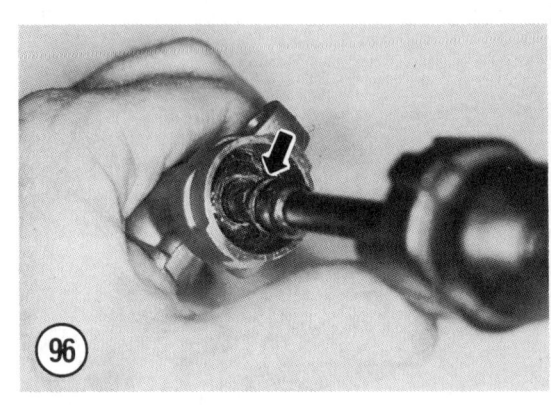

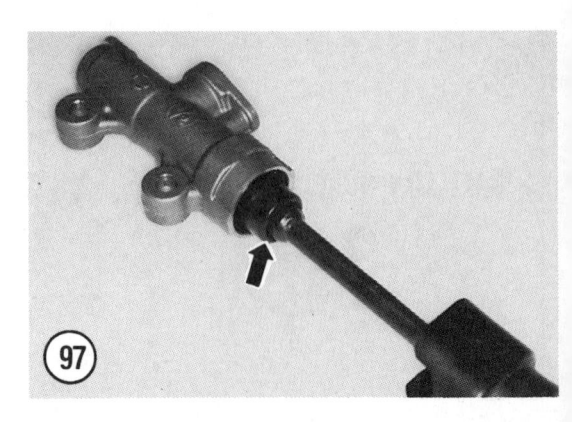

BRAKES

CAUTION
*The circlip (**Figure 96**) must seat in the master cylinder groove completely. Push and release the piston a few times to make sure it moves smoothly and that the circlip does not pop out.*

7. Push the pushrod to compress the piston assembly and install the washer below the circlip groove, then install the circlip (**Figure 96**) into the master cylinder groove.

8. Apply silicone grease into the boot groove in the pushrod. Then slide the boot (**Figure 97**) down the pushrod and seat it against the washer. Seat the outer end of the boot into the pushrod groove.

9. Align the dust cover slots with the master cylinder mounting boss and slide it onto the master cylinder (**Figure 98**).

10. Measure the pushrod length from the center of the front master cylinder mounting bolt hole to the center of the hole in the clevis (**Figure 99**). The correct length is 169 mm (6.7 in.). To adjust, loosen the pushrod locknuts (A, **Figure 100**) and turn the clevis (B, **Figure 100**). Tighten the locknuts and remeasure the push rod length distance.

11. Install the master cylinder as described in this chapter.

REAR MASTER CYLINDER RESERVOIR

Refer to **Figure 101**.

Removal/Installation

1. Park the motorcycle on level ground. Block the front wheels so the motorcycle cannot roll in either direction.

CAUTION
Wipe up any spilled brake fluid immediately as it will stain or destroy the finish of most plastic and metal surfaces. Use soapy water and rinse thoroughly.

2. If the exhaust system is mounted on the bike, cover it with a plastic drop cloth to prevent spilled brake fluid from damaging it.

3. Drain the brake fluid from the rear master cylinder as described under *Brake Fluid Draining* in this chapter.

4. Remove the bolt and the reservoir cover.

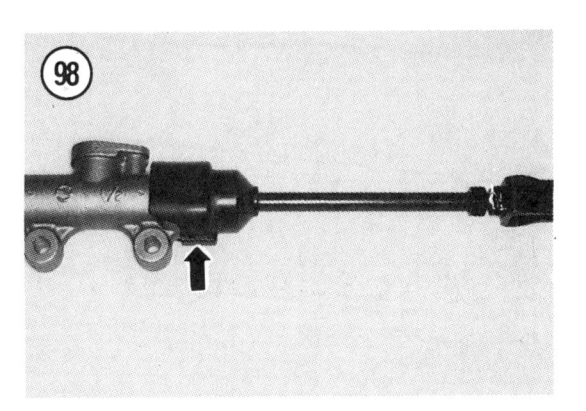

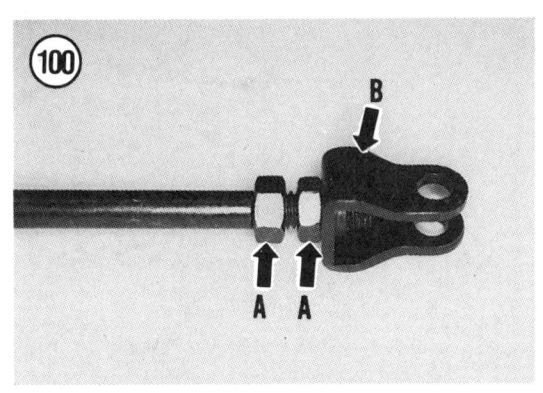

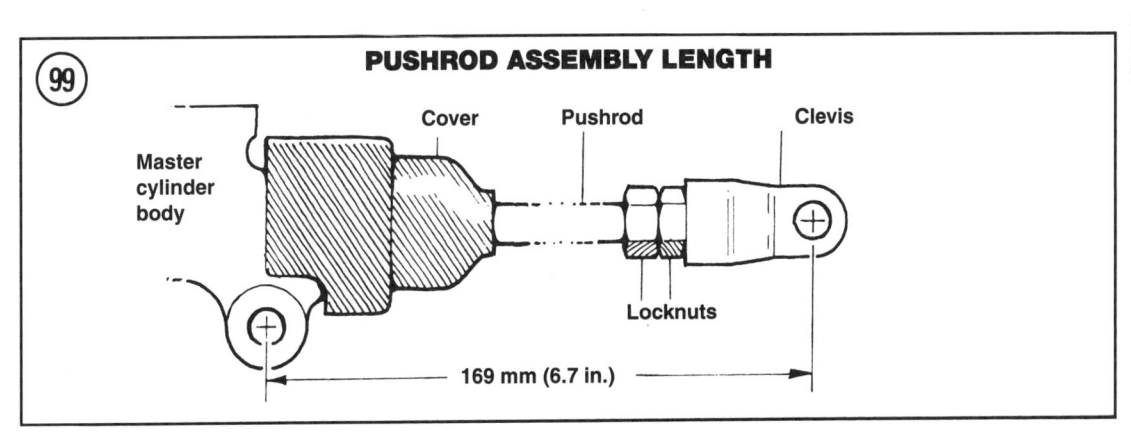

CHAPTER THIRTEEN

NOTE
Don't lose the rubber grommet installed on the reservoir cover tab.

5. Remove the reservoir mounting bolt (**Figure 102**).

6. Disconnect the reservoir hose from the reservoir, then remove the reservoir.

7. Cover the exposed reservoir hose end to prevent contamination or brake fluid from leaking out.

8. Reverse these steps to install the master cylinder reservoir, while noting the following.

9. Tighten the master cylinder reservoir mounting bolt to the torque specification in **Table 4**.

10. If removed, install the rubber grommet onto the reservoir cover tab.

11. Align the reservoir cover rubber grommet with the frame cutout and install the reservoir cover.

12. Tighten the reservoir cover mounting bolt to the torque specification in **Table 4**.

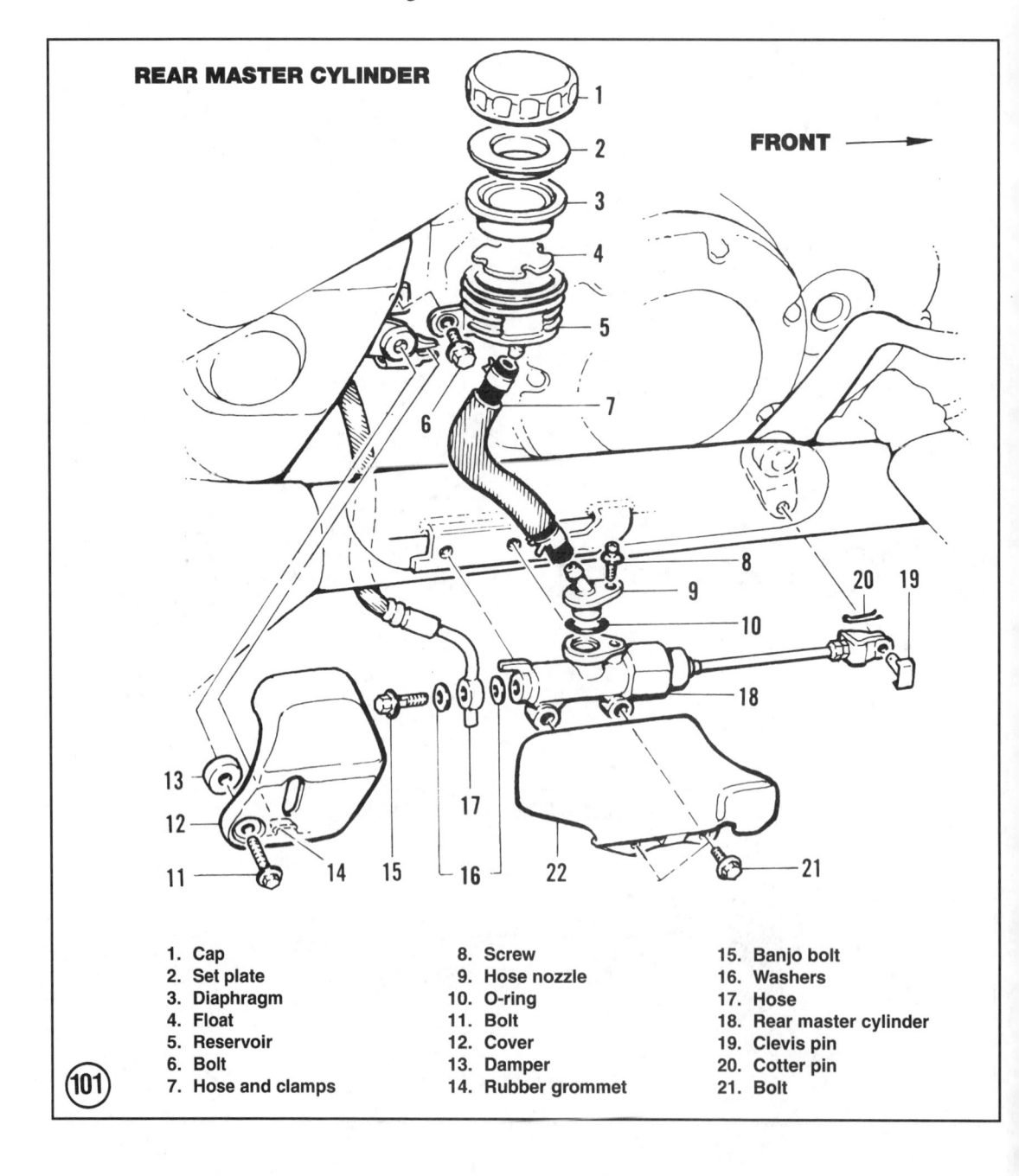

REAR MASTER CYLINDER

1. Cap
2. Set plate
3. Diaphragm
4. Float
5. Reservoir
6. Bolt
7. Hose and clamps
8. Screw
9. Hose nozzle
10. O-ring
11. Bolt
12. Cover
13. Damper
14. Rubber grommet
15. Banjo bolt
16. Washers
17. Hose
18. Rear master cylinder
19. Clevis pin
20. Cotter pin
21. Bolt

101

BRAKES

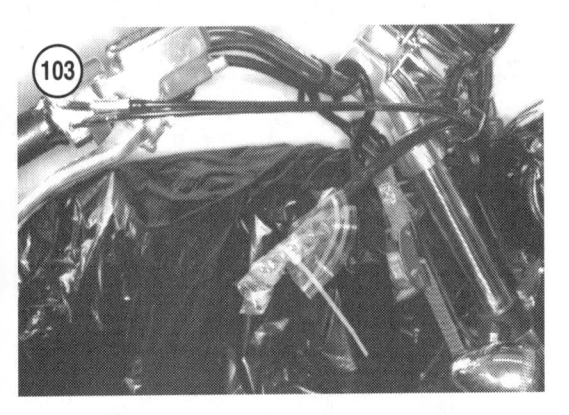

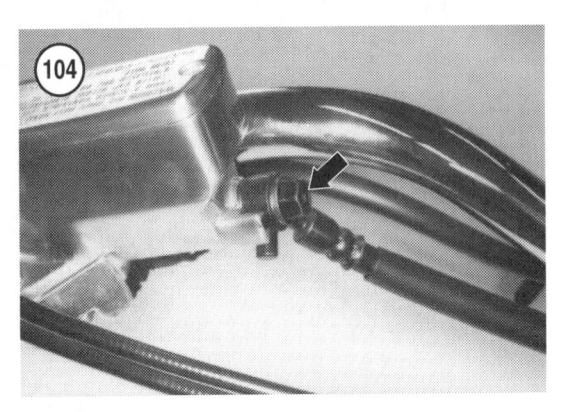

13. Refill the brake system and bleed the rear brake as described in this chapter. Check the reservoir and reservoir hose for leaks.

WARNING
Do not ride the motorcycle until the rear brake is working properly.

BRAKE HOSE REPLACEMENT

Replace the brake hoses if they show signs of wear or damage, or if they have bulges or signs of chafing. As a precaution, replace the brake hoses every 4 years, even if they look good. Check the brake hoses at the brake inspection intervals listed in Chapter Three.

To replace a brake hose or line, perform the following:

1. Drain the brake system (front or back) as described under *Brake Fluid Draining* in this chapter.
2. Use a plastic drop cloth to cover areas (**Figure 103**) that could be damaged by spilled brake fluid. See *Preventing Brake Fluid Damage* in this chapter.
3. When removing a brake hose, note the following:
   a. Note the routing of the brake hose on a piece of paper.
   b. Remove any bolts or brackets securing the front brake hose to the frame, front fork (front hose) or swing arm (rear hose).
   c. For the front brake hose, remove the upper (**Figure 104**) and lower (A, **Figure 105**) banjo bolts and washers.
   d. For the rear brake hose, remove the front (**Figure 106**) and rear (A, **Figure 107**) banjo bolts and seal washers.
4. Install new seal washers (**Figure 108**) during installation.
5. Replace the banjo bolt(s) if damaged.

6. Reverse these steps to install the new brake hose, while noting the following.

7. Install a seal washer on each side of the brake hose. See **Figure 109**, typical.

8. Referring to your removal notes, route the brake hose along its original path.

9. Position the end of each brake hose as follows:

   a. On the front master cylinder, position the brake hose arm against the master cylinder bracket as shown in **Figure 104**.
   b. On the front brake caliper, position the brake hose so that its rests against the caliper as shown in A, **Figure 105**.
   c. On the rear master cylinder, position the brake hose arm against the master cylinder bracket as shown in **Figure 106**.
   d. On the rear brake caliper, center the brake hose between the 2 arms on the caliper as shown in A, **Figure 107**.

10. Tighten the banjo bolts to the torque specification in **Table 3** or **Table 4**.

11. Refill the master cylinder and bleed the brake(s) as described in this chapter.

WARNING
Do not ride the motorcycle until you are sure that the front and rear brakes operate correctly with full hydraulic advantage, and that both brake light switches work properly.

BRAKE DISC

The front brake disc is mounted on the front hub (**Figure 110**). The rear brake disc is mounted on the rear hub (**Figure 111**).

Inspection

You can inspect the brake disc with it mounted on the motorcycle. Small marks on the disc are not important, but deep scratches or other marks may reduce braking effectiveness and increase brake pad wear. If these grooves are evident, and the brake pads are wearing rapidly, replace the brake disc.

Table 1 and **Table 2** list service specifications for the front and rear brake discs. When servicing the brake discs, do not recondition (grind) the discs to compensate for warpage. The discs are thin and grinding will only reduce their thickness, causing them to warp quite rapidly. A warped disc will cause the brake pads to drag and overheat the disc.

1. Support the vehicle with the wheel (front or rear) off the ground.

2. Measure the thickness around the disc at several locations with a micrometer (**Figure 112**). Replace the disc if its thickness at any point is less than the service limit dimension specified in **Table 1** or **Table 2**.

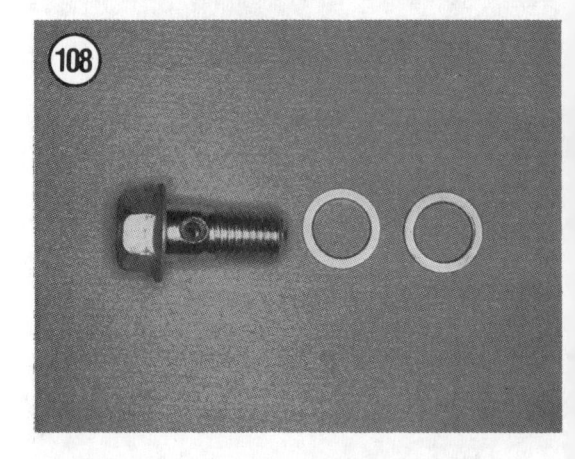

BRAKES

NOTE
Before checking the disc runout, the brake disc bolts must be tight and the wheel bearings must be in good condition; otherwise, the measurements will be inaccurate.

3. Install a dial indicator and position its stem against the brake disc. Then zero the dial gauge. Slowly turn the wheel and measure runout. If the runout exceeds the service limit in **Table 1** or **Table 2**, replace the brake disc.
4. Clean the disc of any rust or corrosion and wipe clean with lacquer thinner. Never use an oil-based solvent that may leave an oil residue on the disc.
5. Repeat these steps for the other brake disc.

Removal/Installation

1A. To remove the front brake disc:
   a. Remove the front wheel (Chapter Eleven).
   b. Remove the bolts securing the disc to the wheel and remove the disc (**Figure 110**).
1B. To remove the rear brake disc:
   a. Remove the rear wheel (Chapter Twelve).
   b. Remove the bolts securing the disc to the wheel and remove the disc (**Figure 111**).
2. Reverse these steps to install the brake disc, while noting the following.
3. Install new brake disc bolts.
4. Clean the disc of any rust or corrosion and wipe clean with lacquer thinner. Never use an oil-based solvent that may leave an oil residue on the disc.
5. Tighten the brake disc bolts to the torque specification in **Table 3** or **Table 4**.

REAR BRAKE PEDAL

The rear brake pedal is an important safety device and must be kept in good working order.

Removal/Installation

Refer to **Figure 113** when servicing the rear brake pedal.
1. Remove the exhaust assembly (Chapter Fourteen).
2. Remove the 2 bolts and the right-side footpeg assembly.
3. Disconnect the brake pedal return spring (A, **Figure 114**) from the brake pedal.
4. Disconnect the rear brake light switch spring (B, **Figure 114**) from the brake pedal.
5. Remove the cotter pin and clevis pin and disconnect the brake rod clevis from the brake pedal. Discard the cotter pin.
6. Remove the circlip and washer and slide the rear brake pedal off of its pivot shaft.
7. Remove the dust seals from the brake pedal.

CHAPTER THIRTEEN

REAR BRAKE PEDAL

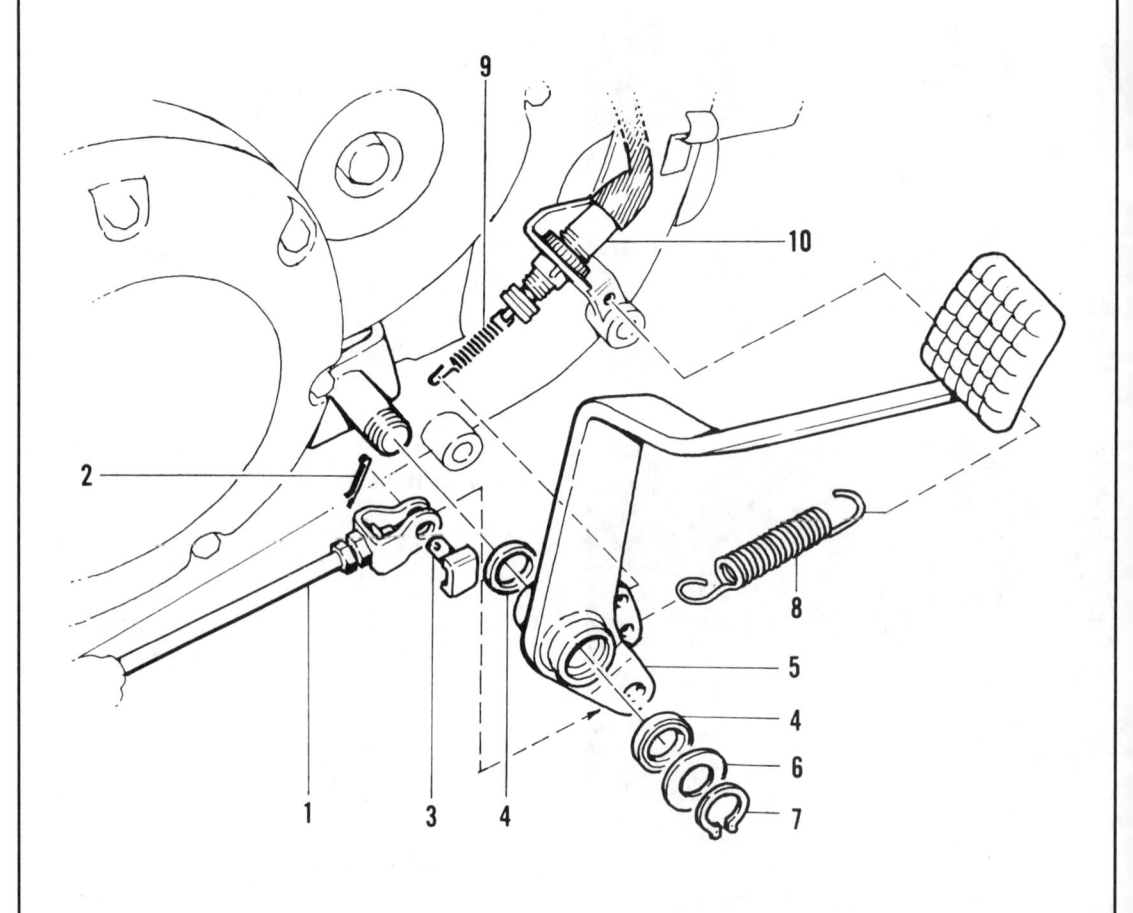

1. Master cylinder pushrod
2. Cotter pin
3. Clevis pin
4. Dust seals
5. Brake pedal
6. Washer
7. Circlip
8. Brake pedal return spring
9. Brake switch return spring
10. Brake switch

BRAKES

8. Clean and dry the brake pedal and its pivot shaft (on frame).
9. Inspect the dust seals and replace if leaking or damaged.
10. Lubricate the dust seal lips with grease and install them onto the brake pedal.
11. Lubricate the pivot shaft (on frame) with grease.
12. Install the brake pedal onto the pivot shaft (on frame).
13. Install the washer and circlip.

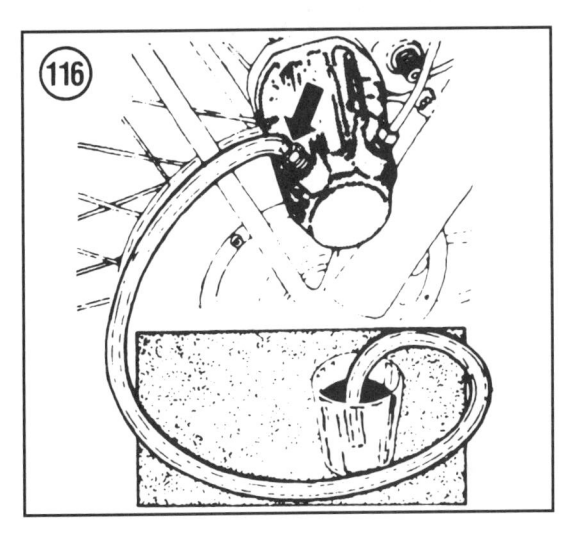

14. Reconnect the brake rod clevis onto the brake pedal with the clevis and a new cotter pin. Spread the cotter pin arms to lock it.

NOTE
Make sure the clevis pin fits flush against the pushrod clevis as shown in **Figure 115**.

15. Reconnect the brake pedal return spring (A, **Figure 114**) to the brake pedal.
16. Reconnect the rear brake light switch spring (B, **Figure 114**) to the brake pedal.
17. Install the right-side footpeg assembly and its 2 mounting bolts. Tighten the bolts to the torque specification in **Table 3** or **Table 4**.
18. Turn the ignition switch on and depress the rear brake pedal to make sure the brake light comes on.
19. Install the exhaust system (Chapter Four).

WARNING
Do not ride the motorcycle until the rear brake, brake pedal and brake light work properly.

BRAKE FLUID DRAINING

1. Connect a hose to the bleed screw (B, **Figure 105** or B, **Figure 107**) on the brake caliper. Insert the other end of the hose into a container. See **Figure, 116** typical.
2. Place a thick rag on the exhaust pipe underneath the rear brake pedal.

NOTE
Because the brake pedal will travel farther down as hydraulic pressure is released from the system, the rag used in Step 2 will prevent the pedal from scratching the exhaust pipe.

3. Open the bleed valve with a wrench (**Figure 116**) and operate the brake lever (front) or brake pedal (rear) to force brake fluid from the master cylinder reservoir. Close the bleed screw and remove the hose. Discard the brake fluid.

BRAKE BLEEDING

Bleeding the brakes removes air from the brake system. Air in the brake system will increase lever or pedal travel while causing it to feel spongy and less responsive. Under severe conditions, it can cause complete loss of the brake.

The brakes can be bled manually or with the use of a vacuum pump. Both methods are described in this section.

When adding brake fluid during the bleeding process, use the DOT 4 approved brake fluid. Do not reuse brake fluid drained from the system or use a silicone based brake fluid. Brake fluid is very harmful to most surfaces, so wipe up any spills immediately with soap and water.

NOTE
When bleeding the brakes, check the fluid level in the master cylinder frequently. If the reservoir runs dry, air will enter the system and you must start over.

Manual bleeding

This procedure describes how to bleed the brake system with an empty bottle, length of clear hose that fits tightly onto the caliper bleed screw, and an 8 mm wrench (**Figure 116**).

1. Make sure all of the brake system banjo bolts are tight.
2. Flip off the dust cap from the brake bleeder valve.
3. Connect the clear hose to the bleeder valve on the caliper (**Figure 116**). Place the other end of the hose into a clean container. Fill the container with enough new brake fluid to keep the end submerged. Loop the hose higher than the bleeder valve to prevent air from being drawn into the caliper during bleeding (**Figure 116**).

CAUTION
Cover all parts which could become contaminated by the accidental spilling of brake fluid. Wash any spilled brake fluid from any surface immediately, as it will destroy the finish. Use soapy water and rinse completely.

4. Clean the top of the front master cylinder or the rear reservoir cap of all dirt and foreign matter. Remove the cap and diaphragm. Fill the reservoir to about 10 mm (3/8 in.) from the top. Insert the diaphragm to prevent the entry of dirt and moisture.
5. Apply the brake lever or brake pedal, then open the bleeder valve. This will force air and brake fluid from the brake system. Close the bleeder valve before the brake lever or pedal reaches its maximum limit or before brake fluid stops flowing from the bleeder screw. Do not release the brake lever or pedal while the bleeder valve is open.

NOTE
As the brake fluid enters the system, the level will drop in the master cylinder reservoir. Maintain the level at 10 mm (3/8 in.) from the top of the reservoir to prevent air from being drawn into the system.

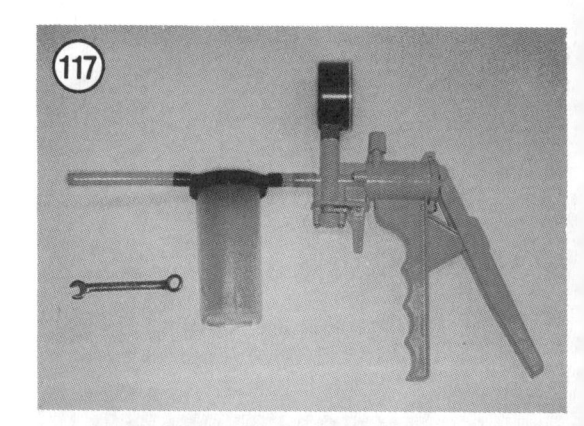

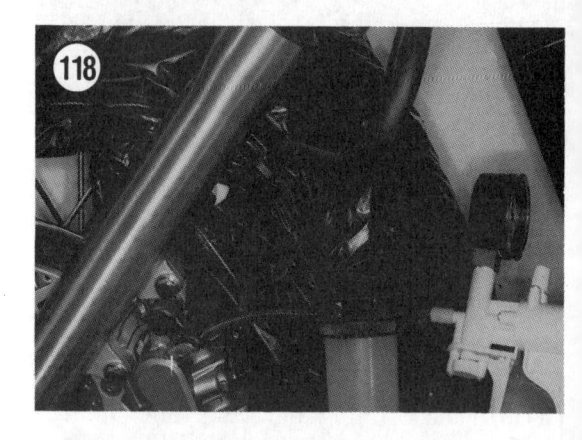

BRAKES

6. Repeat Step 5 until the brake fluid exiting the system is clear, with no air bubbles. If the system is difficult to bleed, lightly tap the master cylinder and caliper housing with a mallet to release air bubbles trapped in the system.
7. The system is bled when the brake lever or pedal feels firm, and there are no air bubbles exiting the system. Then make sure the bleeder screw is tight and remove the bleed hose. If the lever or pedal feels spongy, air is still trapped in the system and you must continue the bleeding procedure.
8. If necessary, add brake fluid to correct the level in the master cylinder reservoir. It must be above the level line.

WARNING
Before riding the bike, make sure both brakes are working properly.

Pressure bleeding

This procedure describes how to bleed the brake system with a Mityvac vacuum pump (**Figure 117**).
1. Make sure all of the brake system banjo bolts are tight.
2. Flip off the dust cap from the brake bleeder valve.

CAUTION
Cover all parts which could become contaminated by the accidental spilling of brake fluid. Wash any spilled brake fluid from any surface immediately, as it will destroy the finish. Use soapy water and rinse completely.

3. Clean the top of the front master cylinder or the rear reservoir cap of all dirt and foreign matter. Remove the cap and diaphragm. Fill the reservoir to about 10 mm (3/8 in.) from the top. Insert the diaphragm to prevent the entry of dirt and moisture.
4. Assemble the vacuum tool by following its manufacturer's instructions.
5. Attach the vacuum pump hose onto the bleeder valve (**Figure 118**).

NOTE
When using the Mityvac in the following steps, the brake fluid level in the master cylinder will drop quite rapidly. This is especially true for the rear reservoir because it does not hold as much brake fluid as the front reservoir. Stop often and check the brake fluid level. Maintain the level at 10 mm (3.8 in.) from the top of the reservoir to prevent air from being drawn into the system.

6. Pump the Mityvac handle a few times to create a vacuum, then open the bleeder valve with a wrench (**Figure 119**). Doing so draws air and brake fluid from the system. Close the bleeder valve before the brake fluid stops flowing from the bleeder or before the master cylinder reservoir runs empty. If your Mityvac is equipped with a vacuum gauge, close the bleeder valve before the vacuum reading on the gauge reaches 0 HG vacuum.
7. Repeat Step 6 until the brake fluid exiting the system is clear, with no air bubbles. If the system is difficult to bleed, lightly tap the master cylinder and caliper housing with a mallet to release air bubbles trapped in the system.
8. The system is bled when the brake lever or pedal feels firm, and there are no air bubbles exiting the system. Then make sure the bleeder screw is tight and remove the hose. If the lever or pedal feels spongy, air is still trapped in the system and you must continue the bleeding procedure.
9. If necessary, add fluid to correct the level in the master cylinder reservoir. It must be above the level line.

WARNING
Before riding the bike, make sure both brakes are working properly.

Table 1 FRONT BRAKE SERVICE SPECIFICATIONS

	New mm (in.)	Service limit mm (in.)
Brake caliper cylinder bore diameter	27.000-27.050 (1.0630-1.0650)	27.06 (1.065)
Brake caliper piston outside diameter	26.935-26.968 (1.0604-1.0617)	26.91 (1.059)
Brake disc runout	—	0.30 (0.012)
Brake disc thickness	5.8-6.2 (0.23-0.24)	5.0 (0.20)
Master cylinder bore diameter	12.700-12.743 (0.5000-0.5017)	12.75 (0.502)
Master cylinder piston diameter	12.657-12.684 (0.4983-0.4994)	12.64 (0.498)

Table 2 REAR BRAKE SERVICE SPECIFICATIONS

	New mm (in.)	Service limit mm (in.)
Brake caliper cylinder bore diameter	38.180-38.320 (1.5031-1.5051)	38.24 (1.506)
Brake caliper piston diameter	38.115-38.148 (1.5006-1.5019)	38.09 (1.500)
Brake disc runout	—	0.30 (0.012)
Brake disc thickness	5.8-6.2 (0.23-0.24)	5.0 (0.20)
Master cylinder bore diameter	12.700-12.743 (0.5000-0.5017)	12.75 (0.502)
Master cylinder piston diameter	12.657-12.684 (0.4983-0.4994)	12.64 (0.498)

Table 3 FRONT BRAKE TIGHTENING TORQUES

	N•m	in.-lb.	ft.-lb.
Brake hose banjo bolt	35	—	25
Brake light switch screw	1.2	10	0.9
Caliper bleed valve	5.5	49	4.0
Caliper bracket pin bolt	13	115	9
Caliper mounting bolt	31	—	33
Caliper pin bolt	23	—	17
Front right-side footpeg	27	—	20
Master cylinder clamp bolt	12	106	9
Pad pin	18	—	13
Pad pin plug	2.5	22	1.8
Front brake lever			
Pivot bolt	1	8.8	—
Nut	6	53	—
Brake disc mounting bolts*	43	—	31

* Install new bolts during reassembly.

BRAKES

Table 4 REAR BRAKE TIGHTENING TORQUES

	N·m	in.-lb.	ft.-lb.
Brake hose banjo bolt	35	—	25
Caliper bleed valve	5.5	49	—
Caliper bracket bolt	23	—	17
Caliper pin bolt	28	—	20
Caliper stopper pin bolt	70	—	51
Front right-side footpeg	27	—	20
Master cylinder hose joint screw	1.5	13	—
Master cylinder mounting bolt	12	106	—
Master cylinder pushrod locknut	18	—	13
Master cylinder reservoir cover mounting bolt	0.9	8	—
Master cylinder reservoir mounting bolt	12	106	—
Pad pin	18	—	13
Pad pin plug	0.25	—	—
Brake disc mounting bolts	43	—	31

CHAPTER FOURTEEN

BODY AND EXHAUST SYSTEM

This chapter contains removal and installation procedures for the seat, side covers, fenders and exhaust system. Torque specifications are listed in **Table 1** (end of chapter).

SEAT

Refer to **Figure 1** when servicing the seat in this section.

Removal/Installation

1. Remove the 3 mounting bolts and remove the seat.
2. To separate the front and rear seats, perform the following:
    a. Remove the bracket nuts and remove the bracket (**Figure 2**).
    b. Separate the seats.
3. Reverse these steps to install the seat. Note the following.
4. If you separated the front and rear seats, attach them with the bracket and the bracket nuts. Tighten the nuts securely.
5. Check that the 4 rubber dampers are mounted on the bottom of the seat.

CAUTION
If one or more of the rubber dampers are missing from the bottom of the seat, the seat will sit lower on the frame and block the air filter housing intake port.

6. Install the seat by inserting its front hook into the raised lip on the frame member (**Figure 1**).
7. Install and tighten the seat mounting bolts securely.

SIDE COVERS

Left Side Cover
Removal/Installation

1. Carefully pull the side cover bosses out of the frame dampers and remove the side cover (**Figure 3**).

NOTE
*The emission control decals are mounted onto the back of the left side cover (**Figure 4**).*

2. Replace any missing or damaged frame dampers (**Figure 5**).
3. Install by reversing these steps. Check that the side cover is secure on the frame.

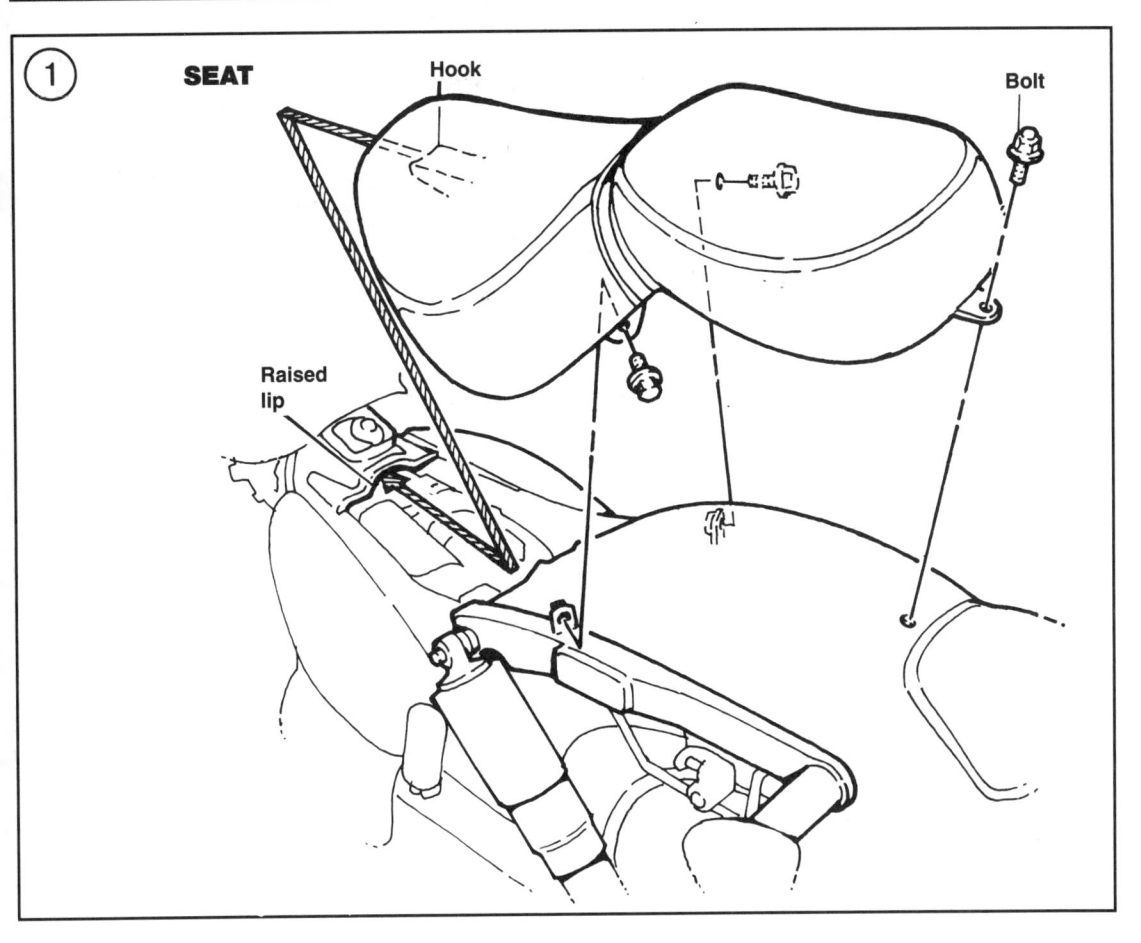

BODY AND EXHAUST SYSTEM 427

① **SEAT**

Hook, Bolt, Raised lip

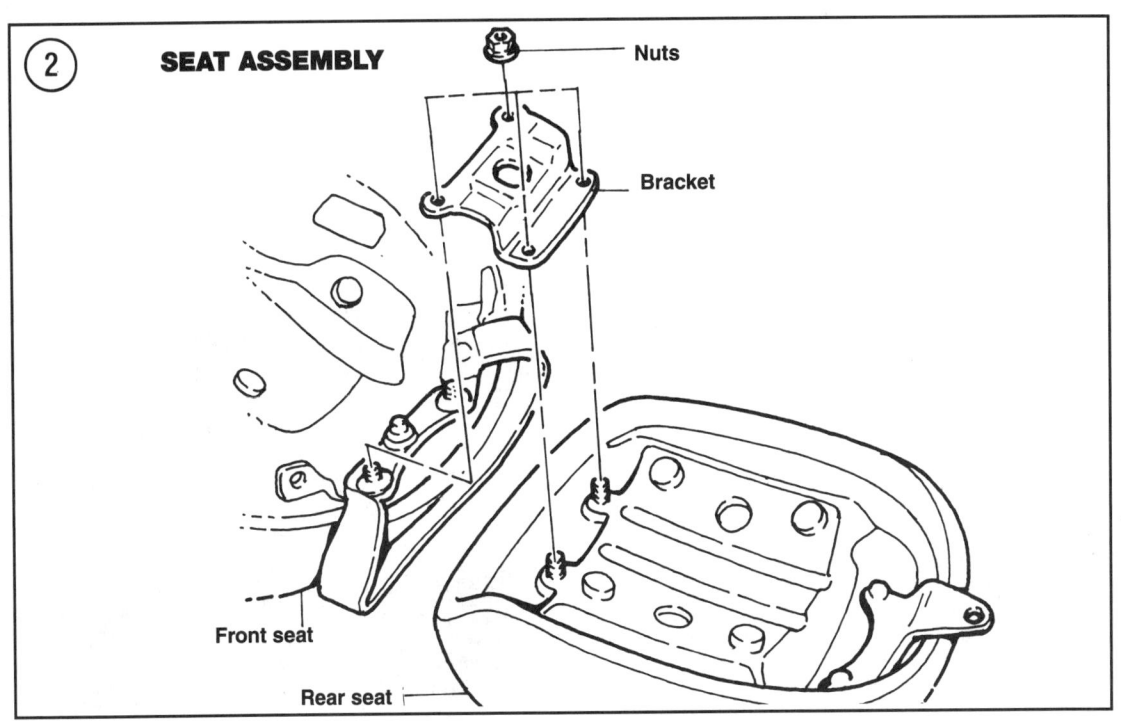

② **SEAT ASSEMBLY**

Nuts, Bracket, Front seat, Rear seat

CHAPTER FOURTEEN

③ **LEFTSIDE COVER**

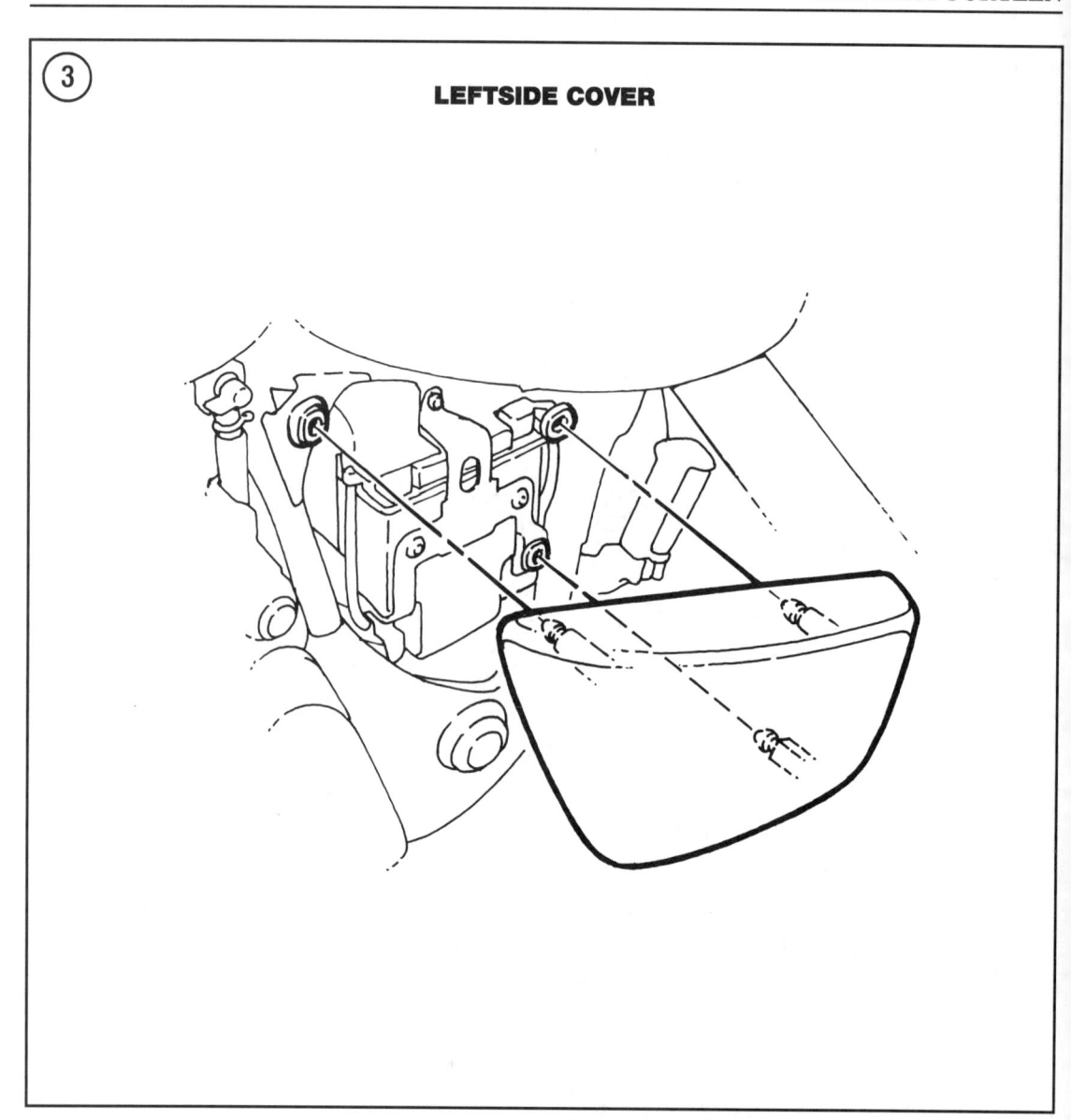

④

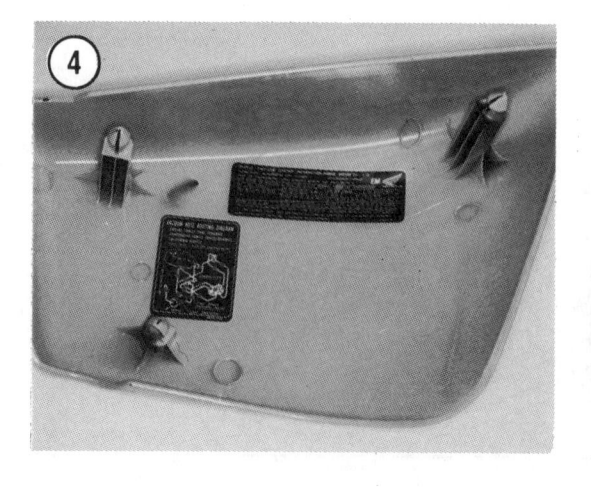

⑤

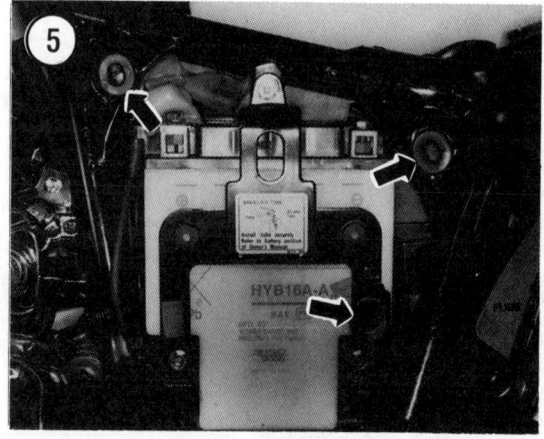

BODY AND EXHAUST SYSTEM

Right Side Cover
Removal/Installation

1. Insert the ignition key into the cover lock and turn the key 90° clockwise (**Figure 6**).
2. Pull the right side cover back and disconnect it from its frame damper and remove it from the bike.
3. Replace any missing or damaged frame dampers.
4. Inspect the lock (**Figure 7**) for damage.
5. Install the right side into position on the frame and align the lock arm with the frame hole. Then push the cover into place so that its bosses fit into the frame dampers.
6. Hold the lock, then turn the key 90° counterclockwise. Remove the ignition key from the lock.
7. Check that the side cover is secure on the frame.

FRONT FENDER

Removal/Installation

1. Remove the front wheel (Chapter Eleven).
2. Remove the speedometer cable from its guide (A, **Figure 8**) and position it away from the front fender.
3. Remove the front brake hose bracket bolt (B, **Figure 8**) at the front fender.

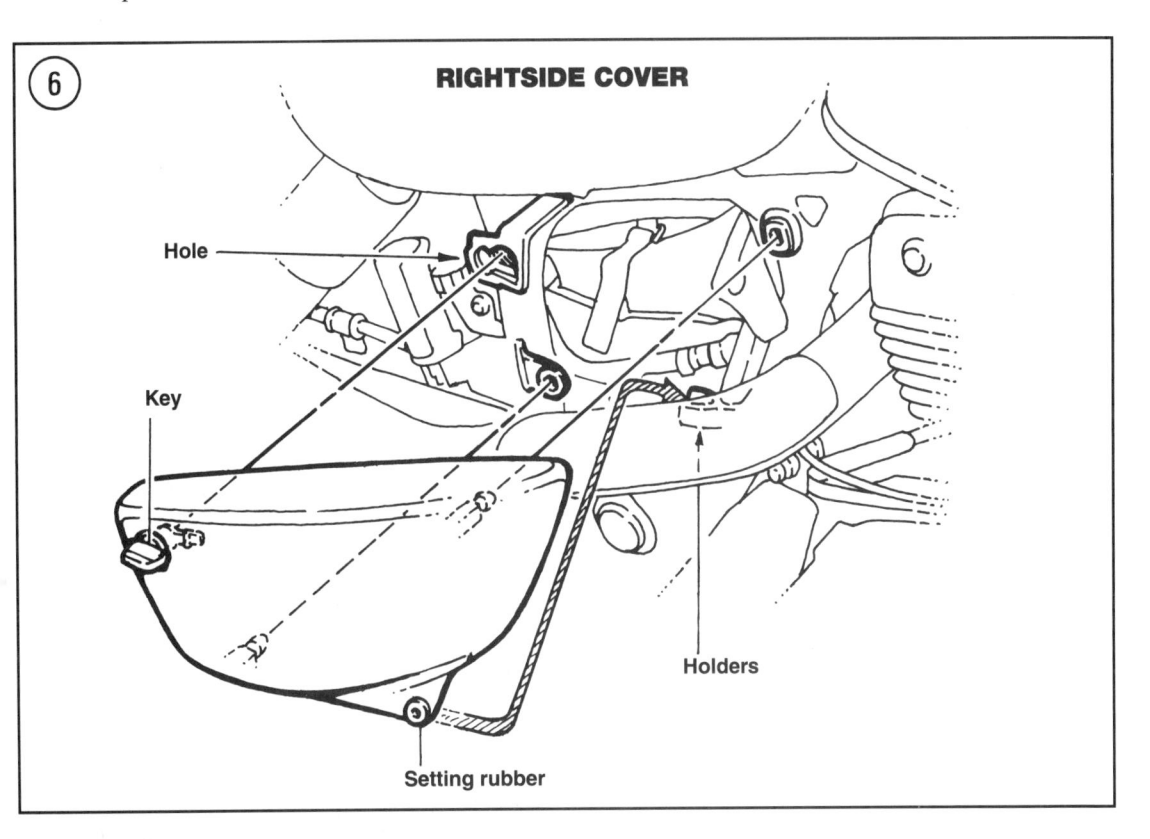

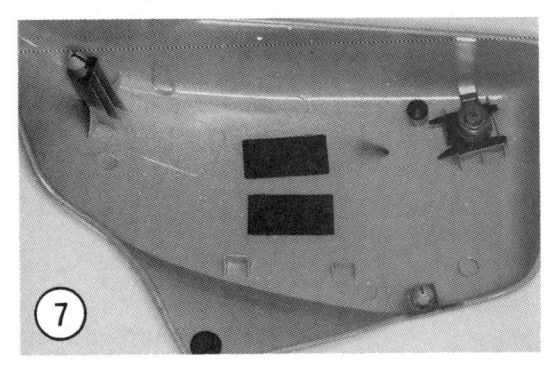

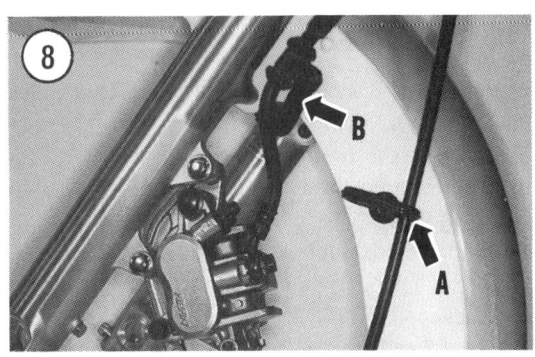

4. Remove the front fender mounting bolts (**Figure 9**) and remove the front fender. See **Figure 10**.

5. Reverse these steps to install the front fender. Note the following.

6. Install the front fender with the hose clamp stay (**Figure 8**) and cable guide installed on the left side. Tighten the fender bolts securely. Route the speedometer cable through the cable guide (A, **Figure 8**).

7. Check the front brake operation before riding the bike.

WARNING
Do not ride the bike until the brakes are working properly.

REAR FENDER

Refer to **Figure 11** when servicing the rear fender in this section.

Removal/Installation

1. Remove the seat as described in this chapter.
2. Disconnect the taillight and brake light connectors.
3. Disconnect the fuse box 2-pin white connector (**Figure 12**) from the fender stay—push the connector tab toward the connector wires, then slide the connector off of the fender tab.
4. Remove the left and right side bolts and washers (A and B, **Figure 13**) securing the rear fender to the fender stay.

NOTE
The rear part of the fender is heavy because of the taillight assembly. When you release the rear fender in Step 5, do not let the back of the fender assembly fall down and rub against the frame and fender stays.

5. Carefully remove the rear fender (**Figure 14**) from between the fender stays and remove it from the bike.
6. Reverse these steps to install the rear fender, plus the following.
7. Lubricate the 10 mm bolts and washers (A, **Figure 13**) seating surfaces and threads with oil prior to installing them.
8. Tighten the 10 mm (A, **Figure 13**) and 8 mm (B, **Figure 13**) fender mounting bolts to the torque specification in **Table 1**.
9. Check the rear lights for proper operation.

REAR FENDER STAY

Refer to **Figure 15** when servicing the rear fender stay this section.

Removal/Installation

1. Remove the seat as described in this chapter.
2. If you are going to remove both rear fender stays, remove the rear fender as described in this chapter.
3. Remove the rear shock absorber (A, **Figure 15**) from the side you are working on. See Chapter Twelve.
4. Disconnect the turn signal electrical connectors.
5. If you did not remove the rear fender, perform the following:

   a. Remove the two 8 mm bolts and washers (B, **Figure 13**).

   b. Remove the 10 mm bolt and washer (A, **Figure 13**).

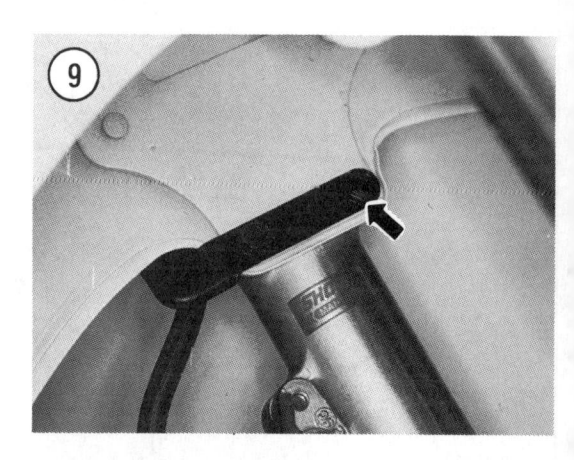

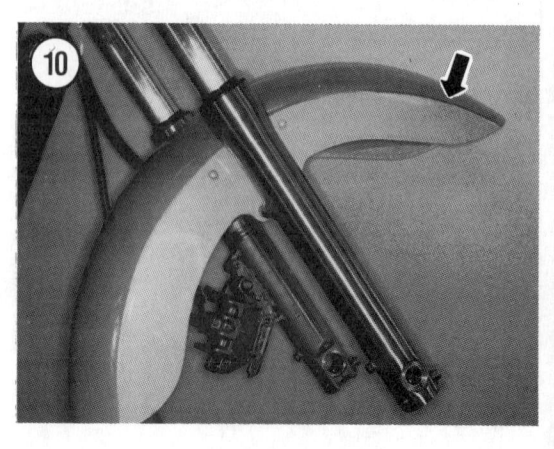

BODY AND EXHAUST SYSTEM

6. Remove the rear shock absorber upper 14 mm pivot bolt (A, **Figure 15**), then remove the rear fender stay (B, **Figure 15**).

7. Reverse these steps to install the rear fender stay, while noting the following.

8. Lubricate the shock absorber 14 mm pivot bolt and the 10 mm bolt threads and seating surfaces with oil prior to installation.

9. Tighten the rear shock absorber upper 14 mm pivot bolt to the torque specification in **Table 1**.

⑪ **REAR FENDER**

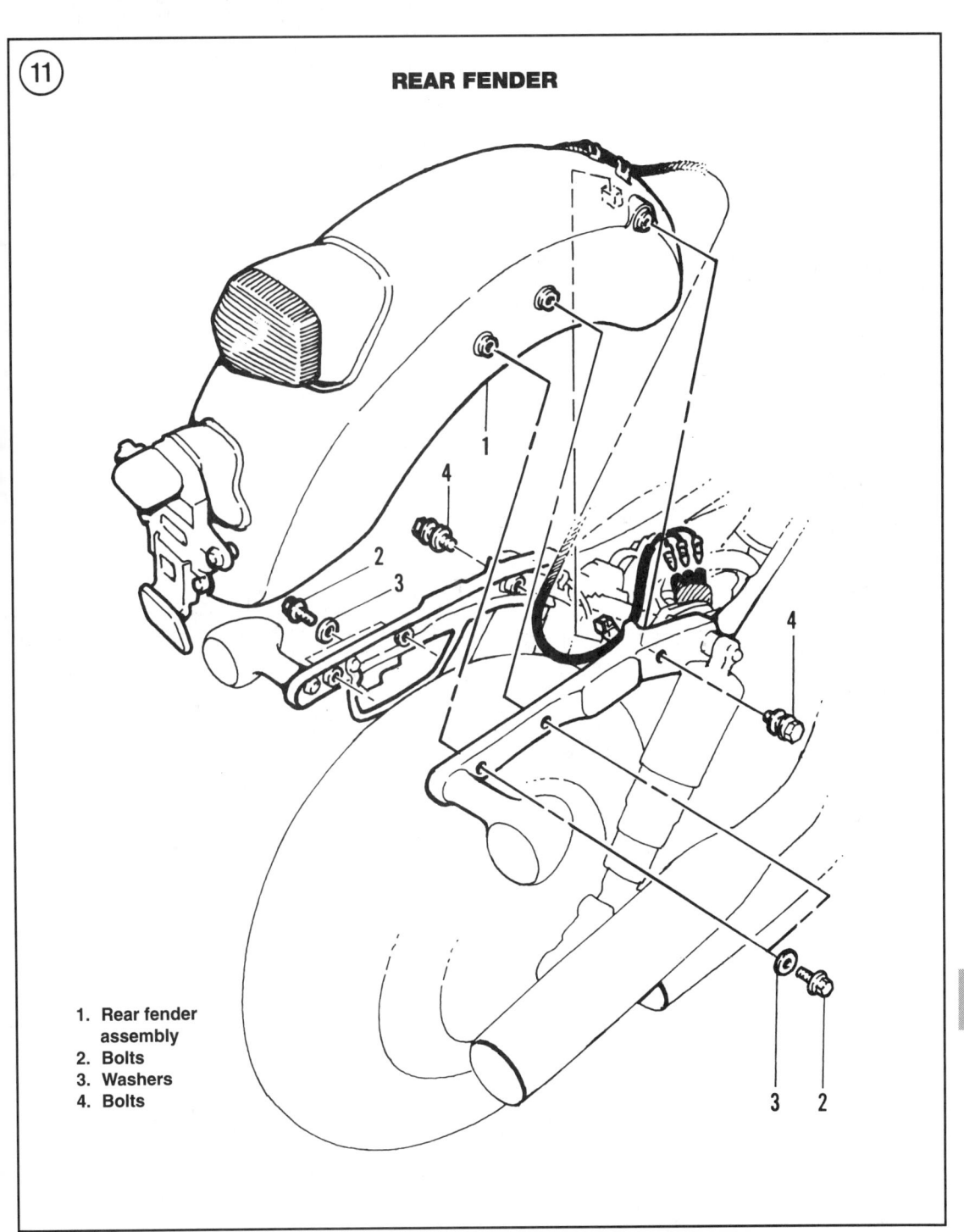

1. Rear fender assembly
2. Bolts
3. Washers
4. Bolts

10. Tighten the 8 mm and 10 mm rear fender bolts to the torque specification in **Table 1**.
11. Check the rear lights for proper operation.

STEERING SIDE COVERS

Removal/Installation

1. Remove the fuel tank (Chapter Eight).

NOTE
*The trim clips removed in Step 2 consist of an inner screw and outer holder (**Figure 16**).*

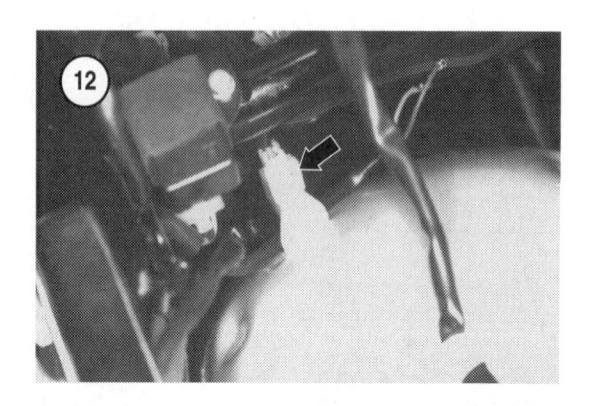

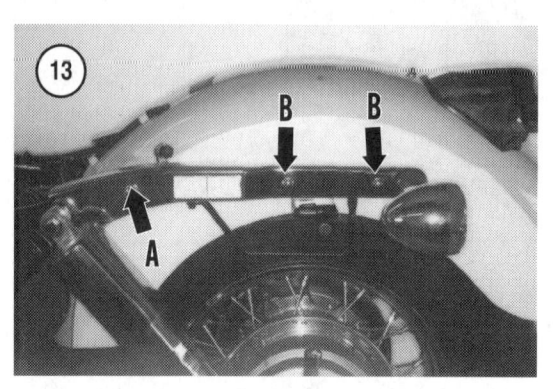

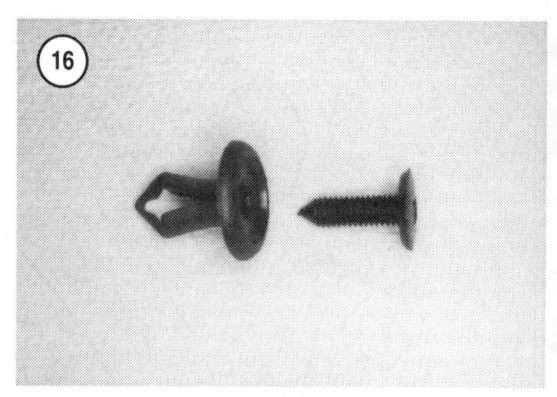

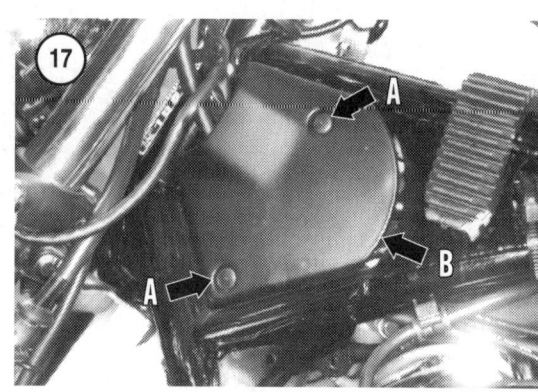

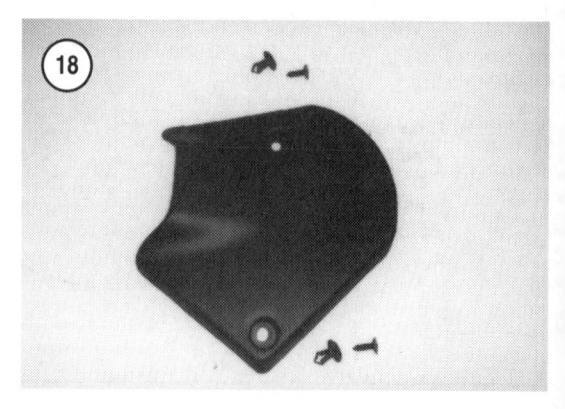

BODY AND EXHAUST SYSTEM

2. Remove the trim clips (A, **Figure 17**) and remove the steering side cover (B, **Figure 17**).

3. Inspect the side cover (**Figure 18**) and replace if damaged.

4. Replace the trim clips if severely worn or damaged.

5. Reverse these steps to install the steering side cover(s) while noting the following.

6. When installing the outer holders, make sure they fit into the frame holes before installing and tightening the inner screws.

EXHAUST SYSTEM

Refer to **Figure 19** when servicing the exhaust system in this section

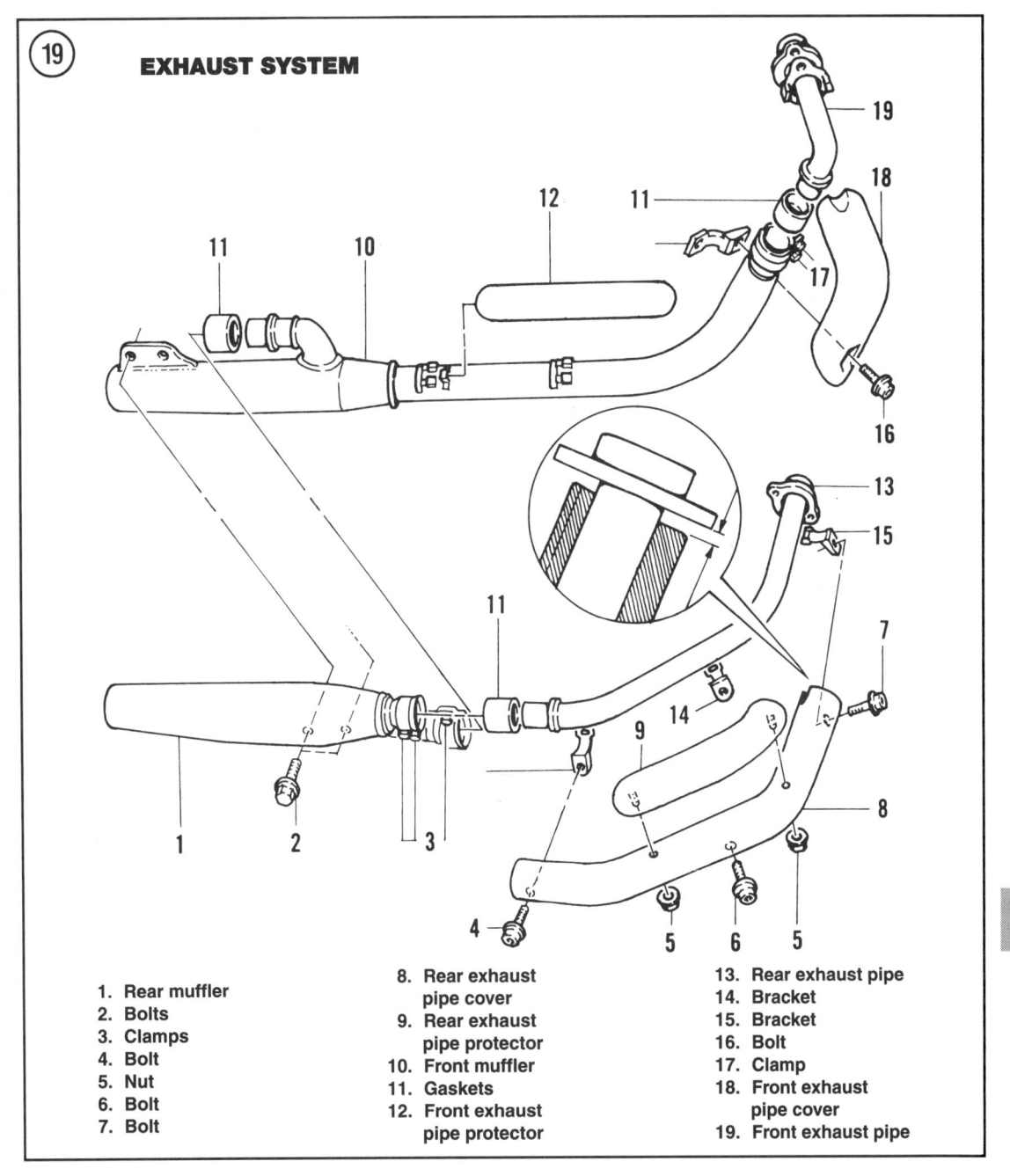

19 EXHAUST SYSTEM

1. Rear muffler
2. Bolts
3. Clamps
4. Bolt
5. Nut
6. Bolt
7. Bolt
8. Rear exhaust pipe cover
9. Rear exhaust pipe protector
10. Front muffler
11. Gaskets
12. Front exhaust pipe protector
13. Rear exhaust pipe
14. Bracket
15. Bracket
16. Bolt
17. Clamp
18. Front exhaust pipe cover
19. Front exhaust pipe

Front Exhaust Pipe Cover and Protector Removal/Installation

The front exhaust pipe cover and protector can be removed with the exhaust pipe assembly installed on the bike.

1. To remove the front exhaust pipe cover, remove the cover bolts and clamp, then remove the cover.
2. To remove the front exhaust pipe protector:
   a. Drive the front exhaust pipe protector toward the front of the bike with a plastic hammer until its lock tab breaks (**Figure 20**) and frees the protector from the exhaust pipe.
   b. Remove the front exhaust pipe protector and discard it as a new one must be installed.
3. Hook a new front exhaust pipe protector onto the exhaust pipe.
4. To install the front exhaust pipe cover:
   a. If removed, install the exhaust system as described in this chapter.

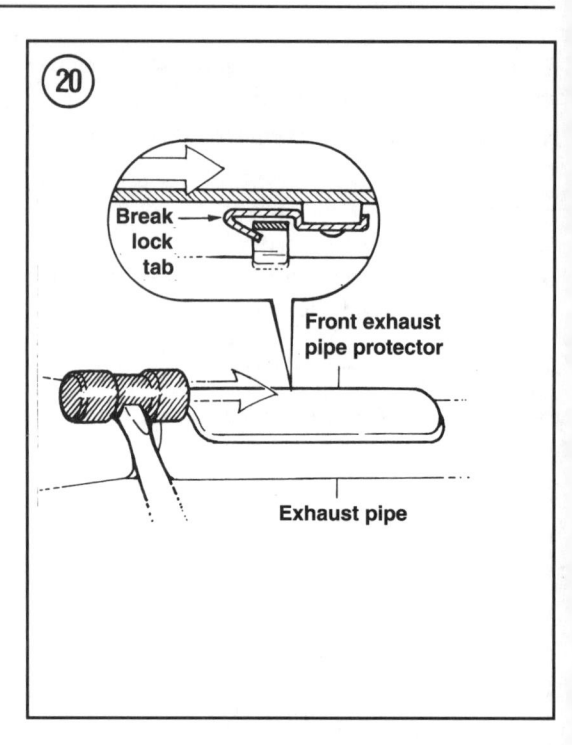

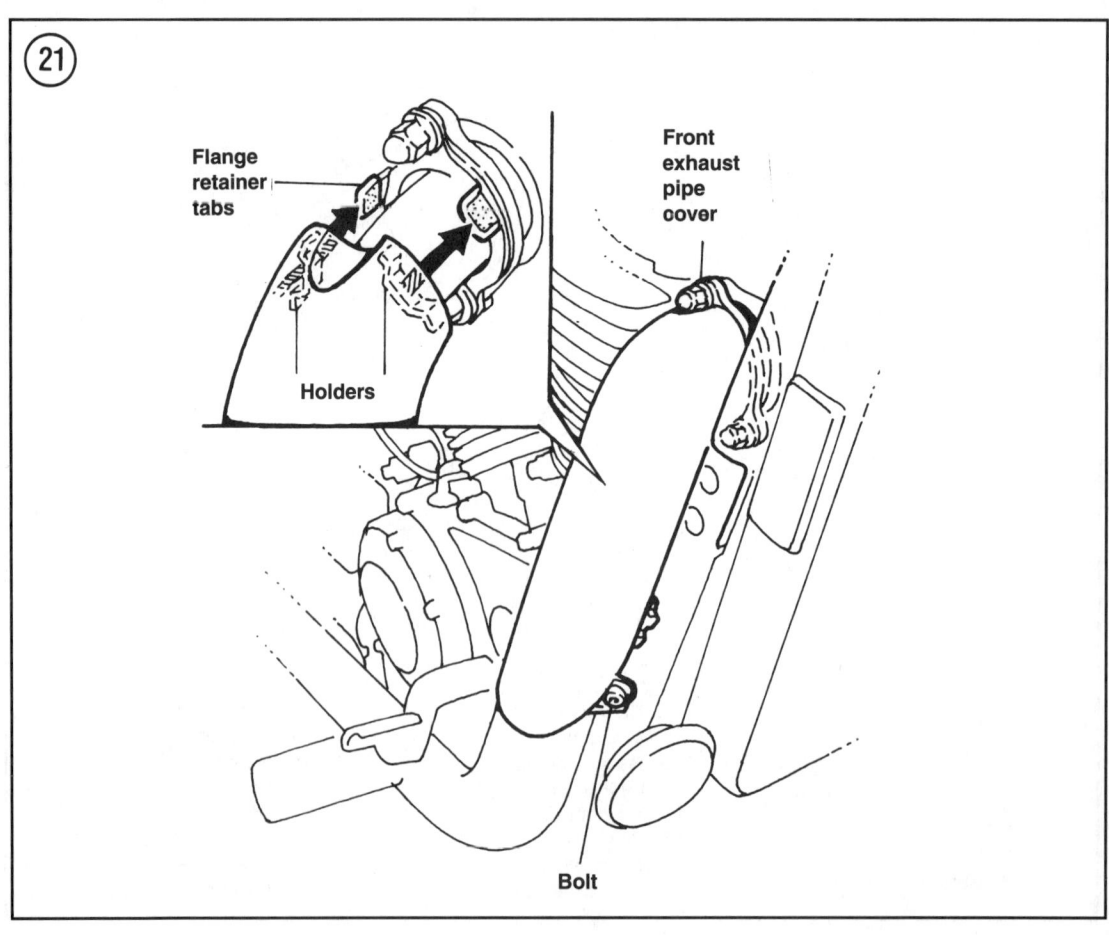

BODY AND EXHAUST SYSTEM

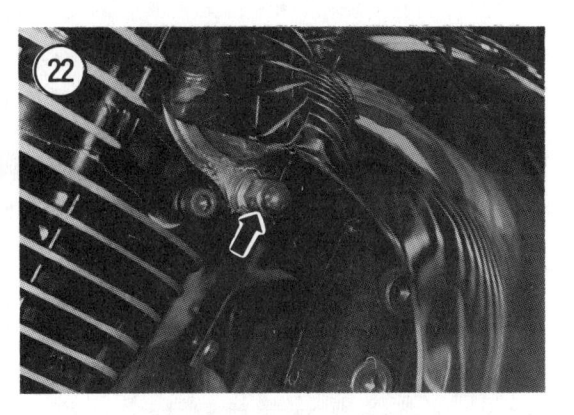

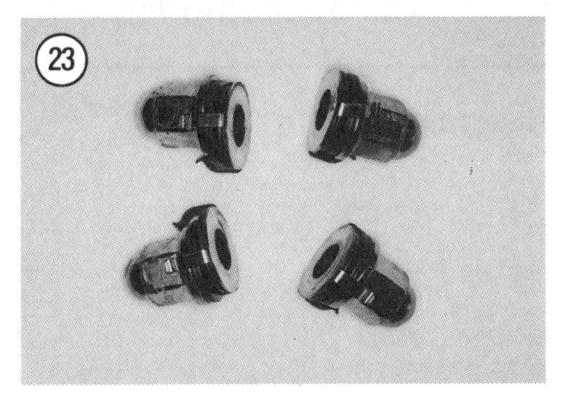

435

b. Install the cover over the exhaust pipe, then align its holders with the flange retainer tabs (**Figure 21**).

c. Install the lower bolt through the exhaust pipe cover and thread it into the cover band.

d. Tighten the front exhaust pipe cover bolt to the torque specification in **Table 1**.

Exhaust System
Removal

This procedure describes removal of the complete exhaust pipe assembly.

1. If the muffler is going to be removed later, loosen the muffler joint and band bolts.
2. Loosen, then remove the 2 exhaust pipe joint nuts (**Figure 22**) at each cylinder head. Remove each nut with its retainer and 4 spring washers (**Figure 23**).
3. Loosen, then remove the 3 lower exhaust pipe mounting bolts and nuts (**Figure 24**).
4. Remove the exhaust pipe and mufflers as an assembly.
5. Remove and discard the gasket (**Figure 25**) from each exhaust port.

Exhaust System
Installation

Exhaust pipe assembly was not disassembled

1. If the exhaust pipe joint nuts (**Figure 23**) were disassembled, assemble them in the order shown in **Figure 26**. Then set the nuts aside until installation.

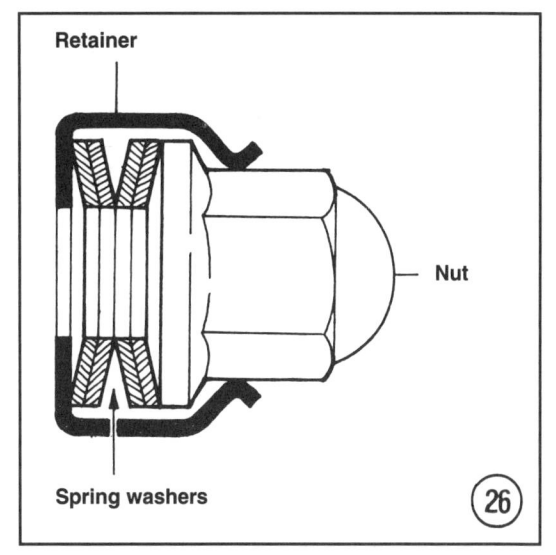

2. Install a new gasket in each exhaust port (**Figure 25**).

3. Lift the exhaust pipe assembly and install the 2 exhaust pipes into their respective cylinder heads.

4. Install each exhaust pipe flange with its UP mark (**Figure 27**) facing up.

5. Install the exhaust pipe joint nuts (**Figure 22**) finger-tight.

6. Install the 3 lower exhaust pipe mounting bolts and nuts (**Figure 24**) finger-tight.

7. Tighten the exhaust pipe joint nuts (3 and 4, **Figure 28**) in 2-3 steps to the torque specification in **Table 1**.

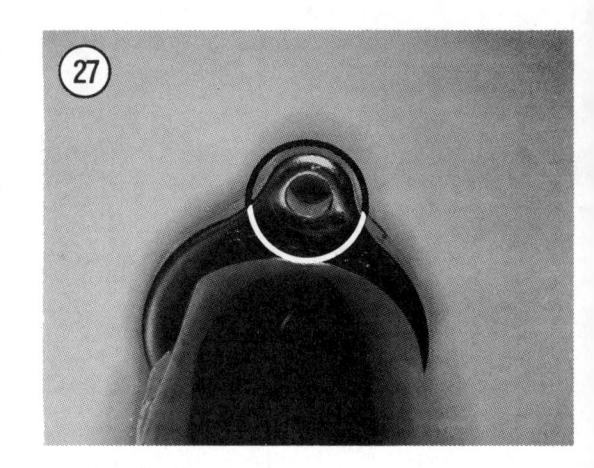

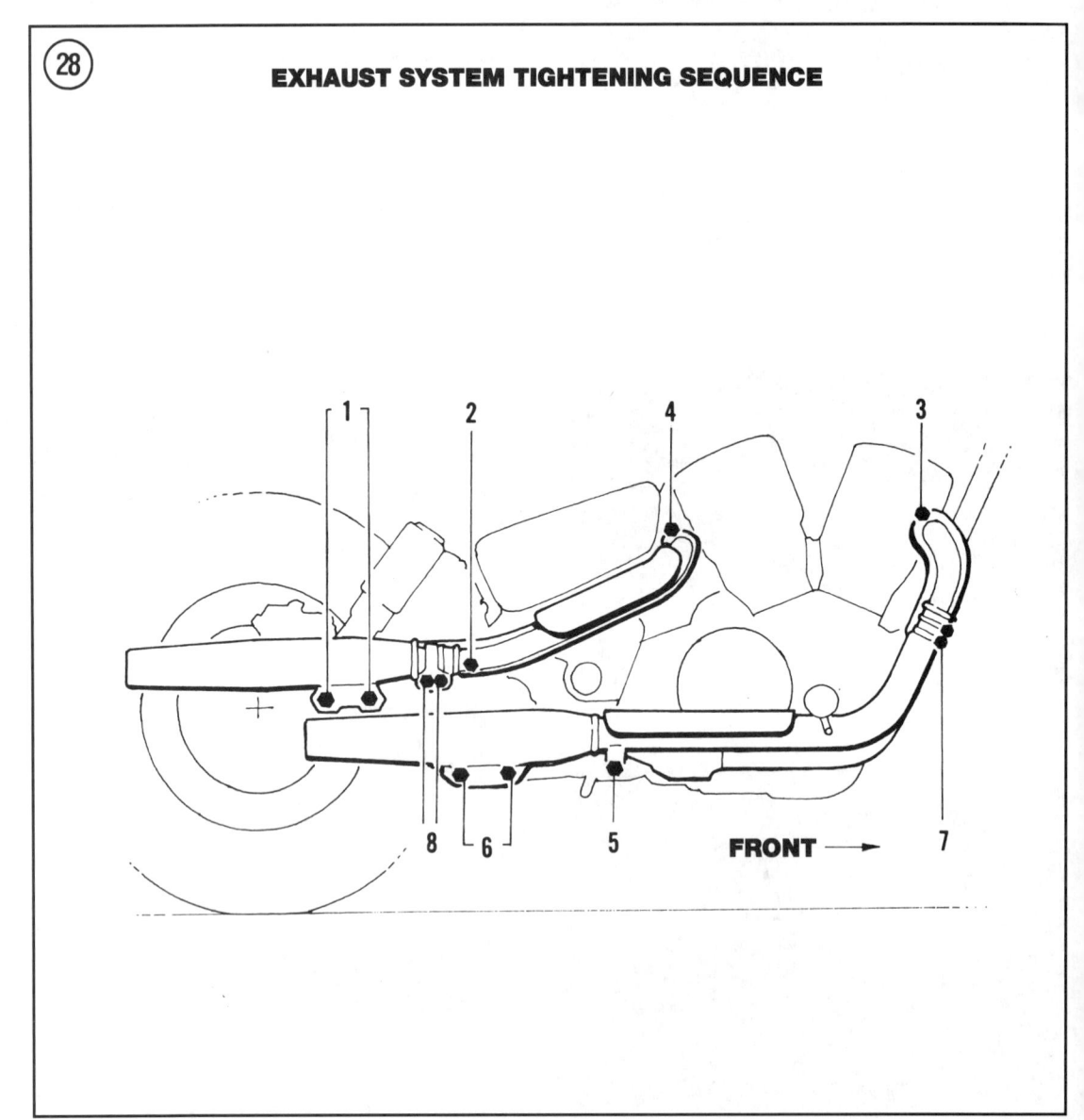

EXHAUST SYSTEM TIGHTENING SEQUENCE

BODY AND EXHAUST SYSTEM

8. Tighten the lower mounting bolt (5, **Figure 28**) to the torque specification in **Table 1**.
9. Tighten the 2 lower mounting bolts (6, **Figure 28**) to the torque specification in **Table 1**.
10. Start the engine and check for exhaust leaks.

Exhaust pipe assembly was disassembled

1. Assemble the exhaust pipe assembly as shown in **Figure 19**. Note the following:
   a. Tighten the muffler joint bolt (1, **Figure 28**) to the torque specification in **Table 1**.
   b. Tighten the muffler band bolt (2, **Figure 28**) to the torque specification in **Table 1**.
   c. When installing the rear exhaust pipe cover, leave a distance of 5 mm (0.2 in.) between the cover and the exhaust pipe flange as shown in **Figure 19**.
2. Temporarily tighten the exhaust pipe band bolts (7 and 8, **Figure 28**).
3. If the exhaust pipe joint nuts (**Figure 23**) were disassembled, assemble them in the order shown in **Figure 26**. Then set the nuts aside until installation.
4. Install a new gasket in each exhaust port (**Figure 25**).
5. Lift the exhaust pipe assembly and install the 2 exhaust pipes into their respective cylinder heads.
6. Install each exhaust pipe flange with its UP mark (**Figure 27**) facing up.
7. Install the exhaust pipe joint nuts (**Figure 22**) finger-tight.
8. Install the 3 lower exhaust pipe mounting bolts and nuts (**Figure 24**) finger-tight.
9. Tighten the exhaust pipe joint nuts (3 and 4, **Figure 28**) in 2-3 steps to the torque specification in **Table 1**.
10. Tighten the lower mounting bolt (5, **Figure 28**) to the torque specification in **Table 1**.
11. Tighten the 2 lower mounting bolts (6, **Figure 28**) to the torque specification in **Table 1**.
12. Tighten the exhaust pipe band bolts (7 and 8) to the torque specification in **Table 1**.
13. Start the engine and check for exhaust leaks.

Table 1 TIGHTENING TORQUES

	N·m	in.-lb.	ft.-lb.
Exhaust pipe joint nuts	23	—	17
Front and rear muffler joint bolts	35	—	25
Front exhaust pipe cover bolts	9	80	—
Front footpeg bracket bolts	27	—	20
Front muffler mounting bolt	35	—	25
Muffler and exhaust pipe band bolts	20	—	14
Rear fender bolts			
8 mm	27	—	20
10 mm	65	—	47
Rear shock absorber upper 14 mm pivot bolt (@ fender stay)	110	—	81
Lower exhaust pipe mounting bolts	35	—	25

INDEX

A

Air filter housing.................... 242-245
Alternator 278-279

B

Ball bearing replacement 30-35
Battery............................. 71-75
Body and exhaust system
   exhaust system....................... 433
   fender
      front......................... 429-430
      rear.............................. 430
         fender stay 430-432
   seat.................................. 426
   side covers...................... 426-429
      steering........................ 432-433
Brakes
   hose replacement.................. 417-418
   bleeding............................. 421
   disc.............................. 418-419
   fluid draining....................... 421
   fluid selection 388
   caliper
      front......................... 389-396
      rear.......................... 401-408
   master cylinder
      front......................... 396-401
      rear.......................... 408-415
         reservoir..................... 415-417
   preventing brake fluid damage 388
   problems 65-66
   rear pedal........................ 419-421

C

Camshafts 117-126
Carburetor
   adjustment...................... 260-263
   troubleshooting 63-64
   operation 245-246
   service 246-260
Charging system
   electrical system 274-278
   troubleshooting 56-57
Choke cable replacement 264-265
Clutch 204-210
   cable replacement 225
   diode 293-294
   external shift mechanism 215-219
   lifter arm 168-170
   outer............................ 210-213
Cooling system
   coolant reserve tank.................. 321
   cooling fan.......................... 321
   cooling system check 317
   hoses 326
   radiator 318-321
   thermostat 322-323
   water pump 323-326
Crankcase breather system, U.S. only 269
Crankcase and crankshaft............. 179-190
Crankcase cover
   and stator coil, left................. 171-173
   rear cover, left................... 167-168
   right................................ 210
Crankshaft........................ 190-192
Cylinder 140-141
   head............................ 126-130
   head cover and rocker arms.......... 104-113
   stud replacement 153-157

D

Disc brake........................ 388-389

E

Electrical components................ 306-313
Electrical system...................... 274
   charging system.................. 274-278

INDEX

Electrical system (continued)
   components 306-313
   fuses........................... 313-314
   headlight housing 297
   ICM unit 284
   ignition coil 284
   ignition pulse generator............ 282-284
   ignition system 279-282
   lighting system 294-297
   speedometer..................... 297-298
   starter relay switch................ 292-293
   starting system................... 286-292
   switches........................ 298-306
   wiring diagrams................... 442-445
Engine
   bottom end
      break-in 201
      connecting rods 192-196
      crankcase 179-190
      crankshaft..................... 190-192
      flywheel (rotor) 173-176
      installation 164-167
      removal 161-164
      servicing in frame 157
      starter drive gear and
         torque limiter 170-171
      starter driven gear and
         starter clutch 176-179
      subframe 157-161
   top end
      camshaft...................... 117-129
      cylinders...................... 140-141
      head 126-130
         cover and rocker arms 104-113
         stud replacement 153-157
      hydraulic tappets 113-117
      oil jet 153
      piston and piston rings........... 144-153
      service notes 104
      valves and valve components 130-140
Excessive vibration 64
Evaporative emission control system
   California only 269
Exhaust system 433
External shift mechanism 215-219

F

Fasteners 6-9

Final gearcase and drive shaft.......... 376-379
Flywheel (rotor) 173-176
Fuel and emission control systems
   air filter housing 242-245
   carburetor
      adjustment..................... 260-263
      operation 245-246
      service 246-260
   choke cable replacement........... 264-265
   crankcase breather system, U.S. only 269
   evaporative emission control system
      California models only 269
   fuel filter 265
   fuel pump 265-266
   fuel system identification 242
   fuel tank....................... 266-269
Fuses 313-314

G

Gearshift linkage..................... 51-52

H

Handlebar 343-346
Headlight housing...................... 297
Hoses.............................. 326

I

Ignition system 279-282
   troubleshooting.................... 57-61
ICM unit 284
Ignition coil......................... 284
Ignition pulse generator 282-284
Internal shift mechanism............. 238-242

L

Lighting system 294-297
Lubricants 9-10
Lubrication, maintenance and tune-up
   battery 71-75
   engine tune-up....................... 93
   lubrication, periodic 76-81
   maintenance, periodic 81-93

INDEX

Lubrication, maintenance and tune-up (continued)
   new battery installation 75
   routine inspection 66-68
   service intervals..................... 68-69
   tires and wheels..................... 70-71

M

Manual organization 1-2
Mechanic's tips 28-30

O

Oil jet............................... 153
Oil pump 219-225
Operating requirements................. 40-41
Output gear assembly 196-201

P

Piston and piston rings 144-153

R

Radiator......................... 318-321
Routine inspection 66-68

S

Safety first............................ 2-3
Sealant, cements and cleaners........... 10-12
Seals 35
Seat 426
Serial numbers......................... 5
Service hints 3-5
Service notes......................... 104
Servicing engine in frame................ 157
Shock absorber 375-376
Side covers 426-429
Speedometer 297-298
Starter drive gear and torque limiter..... 170-171
Starter driven gear and starter clutch 176-179
Starter relay switch 292-293
Steering bearing preload check............ 362
Steering head...................... 355-362

Steering side covers 432-433
Subframe......................... 157-161
Supplies, expendable 12
Suspension and steering, front
   forks........................... 346-355
   handlebar...................... 343-346
   hub............................ 332-336
   rim and spoke service 336-338
   steering head 355-362
   steering bearing preload check 362
   tire changing 338-341
   wheel.......................... 328-332
      balance...................... 341-343
Suspension, rear
   final gearcase and drive shaft 376-379
   hub............................ 369-374
   rim and spoke service 375
   shock absorber................... 375-376
   swing arm 379
   tire changing and tire repairs......... 374-375
   wheel............................. 365
Switches 298-306

T

Thermostat 322-323
Throttle cable replacement 263-264
Tire changing 338-341
Tire changing and tire repairs.......... 374-375
Tools
   basic hand 12-16
   precision measuring 16-26
   special 27-28
Torque specifications 5-6
Transmission 52
   identification 227
   inspection 235-238
   internal shift mechanism............ 238-242
   overhaul...................... 227-235
   troubleshooting 227
Troubleshooting
   brake problems 65-66
   carburetor 63-64
   charging system................... 56-57
   clutch........................... 50-51
   electrical 52-53
   engine
      leakdown test................... 49-50
      lubrication 48-49

INDEX

Troubleshooting (continued)
   engine (continued)
      noises 47-48
      gearshift linkage 51-52
      hydraulic tappets 49
      ignition system 57-61
      operating requirements 40-41
      starting difficulties.................. 43-45
      test equipment 53-54
      transmission......................... 227

V

Valves and valve components 130-140

W

Water pump....................... 323-326
Wheels............................. 69-71
Wheel balance..................... 341-343
Wiring diagrams 442-445

WIRING DIAGRAMS

1995-1999 HONDA VT1100C2 SHADOW ACE

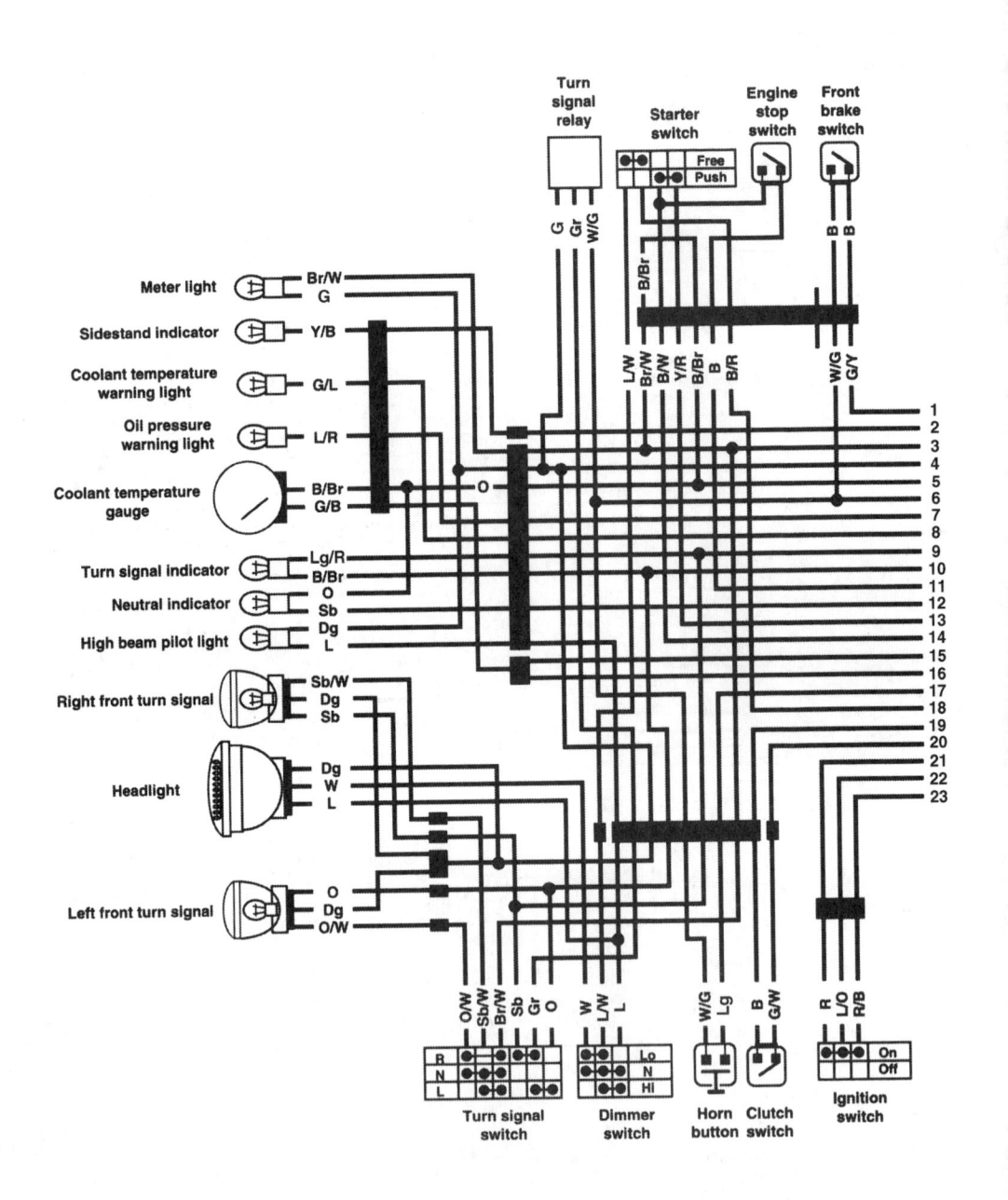

WIRING DIAGRAMS

1995-1999 HONDA VT1100C2 SHADOW ACE (continued)

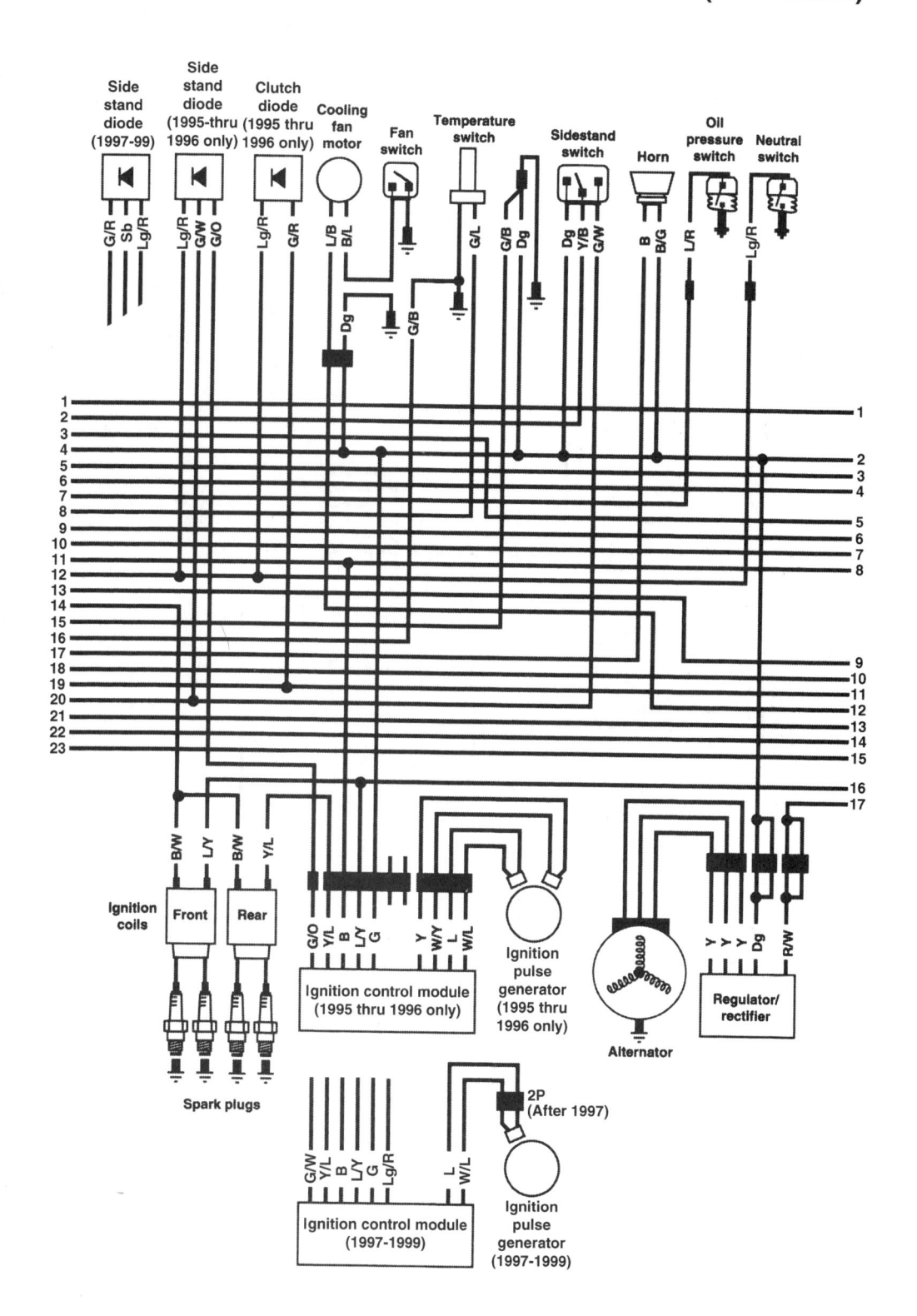

WIRING DIAGRAMS

1995-1999 HONDA VT1100C2 SHADOW ACE (continued)

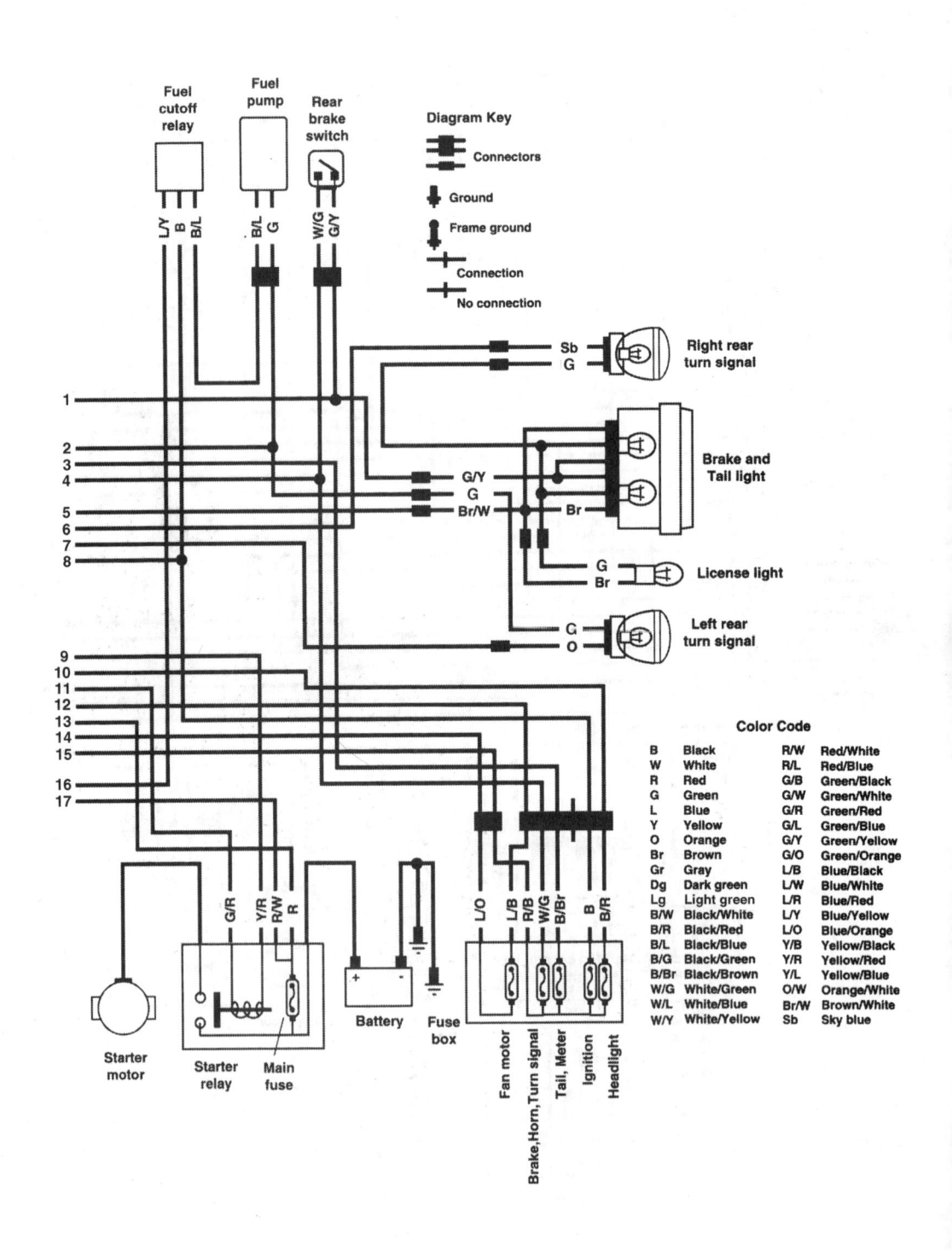